CORE TAX ANNUALS

Inheritance T…

CORE TAX ANNUALS

Inheritance Tax 2018/19

Mark McLaughlin CTA (Fellow) ATT (Fellow) TEP

Iris Wünschmann-Lyall MA (Cantab) TEP

and

Chris Erwood CTA ATT TEP

Series General Editor: Mark McLaughlin CTA (Fellow) ATT (Fellow) TEP

Bloomsbury Professional

LONDON • DUBLIN • EDINBURGH • NEW YORK • NEW DELHI • SYDNEY

Bloomsbury Professional
Bloomsbury Publishing Plc
41–43 Boltro Road, Haywards Heath, RH16 1BJ, UK

BLOOMSBURY and the Diana logo are trademarks of Bloomsbury Publishing Plc

British Library Cataloguing-in-Publication Data

A catalogue record for this book is available from the British Library.

ISBN: 978-1-52650-554-5

Typeset by Evolution Design & Digital Ltd (Kent)

Printed and bound by CPI Group (UK) Ltd, Croydon, CR0 4YY

To find out more about our authors and books visit www.bloomsburyprofessional.com. Here you will find extracts, author information, details of forthcoming events and the option to sign up for our newsletters

Preface

Welcome to the *Inheritance Tax Annual 2018/19*. It is the thirteenth year of this title in the Core Tax Annuals series, published by Bloomsbury Professional.

It seemed strange not to have experienced a Spring Budget in 2018, unlike in recent years. However, the lack of tax notices and yet another Finance Bill early in 2018 undoubtedly provided some welcome respite for many tax practitioners straining under the weight of legislation introduced in quick succession in *Finance Act 2017, Finance (No 2) Act 2017* and *Finance Act 2018* respectively, not to mention secondary legislation, tax cases and other new developments.

Keeping up-to-date with significant tax changes is a difficult task. There have probably been fewer recent changes to inheritance tax (IHT) than some of the other taxes and duties, but there always seems to be something happening on the IHT front.

Since the *Inheritance Tax Annual 2017/18* was published, two very significant IHT provisions have become law. The first of them changed the 'deemed' domicile rules for IHT purposes from 6 April 2017. The second was designed to ensure that, from 6 April 2017, rights and interests in certain types of property are not excluded property to the extent that its value is attributable to a UK residential property interest. The *Inheritance Tax Annual 2018/19* includes some new and updated content on these important changes.

In addition, the *Inheritance Tax Annual 2018/19* features significant developments since the previous edition of this book, including case law and changes affecting HMRC administration and practice.

Aside from a hard copy of the *Inheritance Tax Annual*, subscribers to Bloomsbury Professional online continue to benefit from regular online updates to this book and other titles in the Core Tax Annuals series. I hope this is useful in terms of keeping readers more up-to-date in this constantly changing tax world.

The *Inheritance Tax Annual 2018/19* (and the Core Tax Annuals generally) is intended to focus on day-to-day tax issues that are most frequently encountered, rather than on subjects that are probably peripheral to the majority of readers. The intention also remains to provide short, concise paragraphs written in plain English, punctuated by plenty of worked examples. The annuals also feature 'signposts' at the start of chapters which are designed to assist readers in finding the material they need more quickly and efficiently. Key commentary in the chapters is highlighted under the heading 'Focus', to help readers identify and remember important points. In addition, the many examples in the Core Tax Annuals are shown in shaded boxes, to give them greater prominence.

As always, it has been a pleasure to work with my two co-authors on the IHT Annual, Iris Wünschmann-Lyall and Chris Erwood. Their names will be familiar to many practitioners involved in trust and estate work. Both are very experienced and talented experts in their field, as well as being thoroughly nice people.

I would like to thank Paul Crick for all his help and support in the publication of this title, and to everyone else at Bloomsbury Professional who has been involved in the Core Tax Annuals, and the *Inheritance Tax Annual* in particular.

Last but not least, thanks to you, the reader, for picking up and reading this book. I hope that you find it a useful source of reference. Constructive comments and suggestions for enhancing the *Inheritance Tax Annual* or Core Tax Annuals generally are always welcome.

Whilst every care has been taken to ensure that the contents of this work are complete and accurate, no responsibility for loss occasioned by any person acting or refraining from action as a result of any statement in it can be accepted by the authors or the publishers.

Mark McLaughlin
Manchester, August 2018

Contents

Preface	*v*
Table of examples	*xiii*
Table of statutes	*xxi*
Table of statutory instruments and other guidance	*xxxiii*
Table of cases	*xxxvii*
List of abbreviations	*xlv*
Chapter 1 Inheritance tax: introduction	**1**
Signposts	1
Background	2
Who is liable?	2
What is chargeable to IHT?	3
Cumulation and the IHT threshold	3
Rates of IHT	4
Transfers of value	6
Potentially exempt transfers	7
Chargeable lifetime transfers	7
IHT on death	8
Excluded property	8
Exemptions—summary	15
Taper relief: outline	20
Quick succession relief: outline	21
Double taxation relief	22
Close companies	23
Chapter 2 Domicile	**27**
Signposts	27
Background	27
Domicile under general law	28
'Elective' and 'deemed' domicile for IHT purposes	32
Chapter 3 Transferable nil rate bands	**43**
Signposts	43
Background	44
Outline of the rules	46
Calculating the unused nil rate band	46
Transfer claims	50

Clawback of nil rate band	53
Deaths before 25 July 1986	60
Practical issues	62
Planning issues	65
Other issues	73
Residence nil rate band	75
Chapter 4 Lifetime transfers	**79**
Signposts	79
Introduction	79
Exempt lifetime transfers	80
Potentially exempt transfers	82
Chargeable lifetime transfers	89
Valuing lifetime transfers	92
Gifts with reservation	94
Associated operations	94
Property added to multiple trusts on the same day	96
Calculating IHT	97
Reporting chargeable lifetime transfers	100
Chapter 5 IHT on death	**103**
Signposts	103
Introduction	104
Estate on death	106
Liabilities	111
Rules for amount or value of liability	114
Asset valuations: outline	119
Related property: introduction	120
Calculating IHT on the death estate	121
Chargeable and exempt estate	126
IHT compliance	138
Chapter 6 Valuation of assets	**141**
Signposts	141
General	141
Related property	147
Particular assets	151
Chapter 7 Gifts with reservation of benefit	**169**
Signposts	169
Introduction	169
Scope and effect of the GWR rules	171
Exceptions and exclusions from charge	189
GWR and double IHT relief	197
GWR and 'shearing' arrangements	198

Chapter 8 Compliance **199**
Signposts 199
Liability and incidence of tax 199
Accounts and returns 200
Excepted estates 218
Particular compliance points 223
Payment of IHT 224
Disclosure of Tax Avoidance Schemes (DOTAS) 228
Penalties 230
Time limits for HMRC assessments 245
Record keeping 245
Determinations and appeals 246

Chapter 9 Trusts: interest in possession **253**
Signposts 253
IHT treatment 253
IPDI 258
Disposal of a qualifying interest in possession 262
Termination of interest in possession 264
Reversionary and purchased interests 269
Transitional provisions, 2006–2008 273
Excluded property trusts 278
Insurance policy trusts 284

Chapter 10 Relevant property trusts **291**
Signposts 291
Types of discretionary or relevant property trusts 292
The relevant property IHT regime 306
Transfers into trust: the entry charge 307
The proportionate or 'exit' charge during the first ten years 315
The periodic or 'ten-year' charge 332
The impact of APR and BPR 352
The special charge under section 70 356

Chapter 11 Exemptions and excluded property **363**
Signposts 363
Introduction 363
Lifetime exemptions 366
Dispositions which are not transfers of value 370
General exemptions 373
Death exemption 379
Excluded property 381

Chapter 12 Reliefs – General **389**
Signposts 389
Introduction 389

Taper relief 390
Quick succession relief 393
Related property relief 395
Transfers within seven years before death 397
Post-death reliefs 402
Double taxation relief 406
Double charges relief 408
Woodlands relief 409
Heritage property 411

Chapter 13 Business property relief and agricultural property relief 415
Signposts 415
Scope of business property relief 415
Conditions 426
Valuation, excepted assets 437
Scope of agricultural property relief 441
Conditions for APR 450
Loss of BPR and APR 458

Chapter 14 Lifetime planning 463
Signposts 463
Use all the reliefs 463
Individual Savings Accounts (ISAs), Inherited ISAs, Lifetime ISAs, Flexible ISAs and Innovative Finance ISAs 469
Shares listed on the Alternative Investment Market (AIM) and other tax efficient investments 471
Outright gifts 472
Disabled persons trusts 477
Protected gifts without trusts 484
Traditional protected gifts 486

Chapter 15 Wills and estate planning 491
Signposts 491
EU Succession Regulation No 650/2012 492
The nil rate band 493
The residence nil rate band 499
Deferral of tax using spouse relief 500
BPR, APR and woodlands relief 506
Exempt gifts on death 512
Policy trusts 516
Post-death variations 517

Chapter 16 The family home and residence nil rate band 525
Signposts 525
The family home 526

Ownership	536
Lifetime planning	538
Will planning	546
Residence nil rate band	561
Downsizing and the residence nil rate band	574
Chapter 17 Pre-owned assets	**581**
Signposts	581
Introduction	582
The pre-owned assets charge on land	583
The pre-owned assets charge on chattels	586
Pre-owned assets charge on intangible property comprised in settlor-interested settlements	588
Scope of the pre-owned assets legislation	589
Calculation of tax charge in relation to land	590
Calculation of tax charge in relation to chattels	591
Calculation of tax charge in relation to intangible property	593
Valuation problems	594
Excluded transactions	595
Exemptions	596
'Opting out' of the pre-owned assets charge	601
Remedial action in relation to existing arrangements	602
Index	*607*

Table of examples

[All references are to paragraph number]

Chapter 1 Inheritance tax: introduction
Example 1.1—Lifetime transfers 1.8
Example 1.2—Foreign settled property 1.14
Example 1.3—Offshore company and UK residential property 1.18

Chapter 2 Domicile
Example 2.1— 'Deemed' domicile: the 'three-year rule 2.9
Example 2.2—'Deemed' domicile: in two minds 2.9
Example 2.3—'Deemed' domicile: the '15 out of 20' rule 2.10
Example 2.4—'Deemed' domicile: transitional rule 2.10
Example 2.5—'Deemed' domicile: the '17 out of 20' rule 2.12
Example 2.6—'Deemed' domicile: the 'formerly domiciled resident' 2.13

Chapter 3 Transferable nil rate bands
Example 3.1—Practical effect of a nil rate band transfer 3.6
Example 3.2—Maximum claim 3.7
Example 3.3—Lifetime transfers and the death estate 3.10
Example 3.4—Heritage property 3.12
Example 3.5—Practical effect of a clawback 3.13
Example 3.6—Pension funds and the clawback 3.14
Example 3.7—Elderly testatrix 3.20
Example 3.8—Record of use of the nil rate band for IHT purposes 3.21
Example 3.9—Appointment from nil rate band trust 3.28
Example 3.10—Nil rate band discretionary trust: too late for action 3.30
Example 3.11—Discretionary will trust: estate planning updated 3.30
Example 3.12—Multiple nil rate bands: the effect of marrying 3.32
Example 3.13—'Doubling up' BPR 3.33

Chapter 4 Lifetime transfers
Example 4.1—Death within seven years of a PET 4.15
Example 4.2—Cumulation of chargeable lifetime transfers 4.16
Example 4.3—Chargeable lifetime transfers: position on death 4.17
Example 4.4—Associated operations 4.23

Example 4.5—Cumulation of lifetime gifts 4.27

Chapter 5 IHT on death
Example 5.1—Effect of *FA 1986, s 103* 5.10
Example 5.2—Free estate and settled property 5.23
Example 5.3—*Section 39A* pitfall 5.30
Example 5.4—Simple grossing (no lifetime gifts) 5.33
Example 5.5—Simple grossing (lifetime gifts below nil rate band) 5.34
Example 5.6—Simple grossing (lifetime gifts above nil rate band) 5.35
Example 5.7—Double grossing 5.37
Example 5.8—'*Ratcliffe*' will clause 5.41

Chapter 6 Valuation of assets
Example 6.1—Loss in value of estate 6.4
Example 6.2—Estate assets 6.5
Example 6.3—Related property (land) 6.7
Example 6.4—Related property (shares) 6.9
Example 6.5—Valuation of quoted investments: 'quarter-up' method 6.16

Chapter 7 Gifts with reservation of benefit
Example 7.1—GWR: sales at undervalue 7.6
Example 7.2—'Caught' by GWR rules (1) 7.7
Example 7.3—'Caught' by GWR rules (2) 7.8
Example 7.4—GWR exception: deed of variation 7.32
Example 7.5—GWR exception: excluded property 7.33

Chapter 8 Compliance
Example 8.1—Gift of a share in a flat 8.6
Example 8.2—Excepted transfers: generous grandfather 8.6
Example 8.3—Death affecting prior transactions 8.9
Example 8.4—Accounting for a gift (and illustration of some rules) 8.10
Example 8.5—Checking lifetime gifts 8.11
Example 8.6—Penalties: a difficult estate to administer 8.38
Example 8.7—Penalties: too casual an approach to compliance 8.40
Example 8.8—Late filing of return 8.46
Example 8.9—Progress of a dispute with HMRC (I) 8.56
Example 8.10—Progress of a dispute with HMRC (II) 8.64
Example 8.11—Progress of a dispute with HMRC (III) 8.66

Chapter 9 Trusts: interest in possession
Example 9.1—Half share of a house in a trust 9.1
Example 9.2—House in a nil rate trust 9.9
Example 9.3—IPDI by default 9.9
Example 9.4—Pilot trust 9.9

Example 9.5—'Old' interests in possession: coming of age 9.10
Example 9.6—'Old' interests in possession: protected heiress 9.10
Example 9.7—'Old' interests in possession: long-delayed enjoyment of the fund 9.10
Example 9.8—Using the TSI facility but still controlling the capital 9.10
Example 9.9—Partition of a life interest fund 9.11
Example 9.10—TSI: making the beneficiary wait for the capital 9.27
Example 9.11—No TSI: spinning out the fund 9.27
Example 9.12—Continuing interest: sharing out the fund 9.27
Example 9.13—Simple creation of a TSI 9.27
Example 9.14—Availability of spouse relief 9.27
Example 9.15—Trusts for bereaved minors: 'wait and see how they turn out' 9.31
Example 9.16—Excluded property trust: benefiting from the rule years later 9.34
Example 9.17—Disclaimed interest: trigger of relevant property trust regime 9.35
Example 9.18—Pre-22 March 2006: side-stepping the relevant property trust regime 9.35
Example 9.19—Effect on an excluded property trust 9.35

Chapter 10 Relevant property trusts
Example 10.1—Tax charges on setting up a trust 10.4
Example 10.2—The test of a BMT 10.6
Example 10.3—Further tests of a BMT 10.6
Example 10.4—Wording to create a BMT or 18-to-25 trust 10.6
Example 10.5—Reallocation of capital share 10.9
Example 10.6—18-to-25 trust: simple release 10.11
Example 10.7—18-to-25 trust: net release 10.11
Example 10.8—18-to-25 trust: fall in value of the fund 10.11
Example 10.9—Grandchildren's trust: the notional transfer 10.14
Example 10.10—Life interest trust: lifetime transfer failing to comply with new rules 10.15
Example 10.11—Transfer into trust: small family trust 10.17
Example 10.12—Migration of a trust to relevant property regime 10.17
Example 10.13—Simple gross gift 10.17
Example 10.14—Net gift following previous chargeable transfer 10.18
Example 10.15—Death within three years of a small chargeable transfer 10.19
Example 10.16—Death within three years of a large chargeable transfer 10.20
Example 10.17—Review of earlier tax charge and re-computation at death rates 10.21
Example 10.18—A&M trust: no 'election' by the trustees 10.24
Example 10.19—Transitional provisions: action by the trustees 10.25

Example 10.20—Hypothetical transfer: simplest version 10.28
Example 10.21— Hypothetical transfer: related settlement and business property 10.29
Example 10.22— Hypothetical transfer: allowance for tax debt 10.30
Example 10.23— Hypothetical transfer: mixed (but not exempt) settlement 10.31
Example 10.24—Trust migrating to the relevant property regime under the new rules 10.31
Example 10.25— Hypothetical transfer: death same day as settlement 10.32
Example 10.26— Hypothetical transfer: death same-day as settlement 10.33
Example 10.27— Hypothetical transfer: exempt share of the trust 10.34
Example 10.28— Hypothetical transfer: extra funds for a while 10.35
Example 10.29—Failed PET coming to light 10.35
Example 10.30— The 'effective rate' for distribution made 30 November 2018 10.36
Example 10.31—(Continued from the previous scenarios)—in each case, with the exception of Dennis's trust, there is a distribution of £50,000 cash on 30 November 2018 before the first ten year charge 10.37
Example 10.32—Reporting the charge 10.38
Example 10.33—Form of computation of the hypothetical transfer required to calculate the ten-year charge occurring on or after 18 November 2015 10.44
Example 10.34—Computation of the hypothetical transfer (for ten-year charge purposes) 10.45
Example 10.35—Computation of the hypothetical transfer (ten-year charge) (for ten-year charge purposes) before 18 November 2015 10.46
Example 10.36—Computation of the hypothetical transfer (ten-year charge) (for ten-year charge purposes) post 17 November 2015 10.47
Example 10.37—Computation of the hypothetical transfer (ten-year charge) (for ten-year charge purposes) post 17 November 2015 10.48
Example 10.38—Computation of the hypothetical transfer (ten-year charge) (for ten-year charge purposes) pre 18 November 2015 10.48
Example 10.39—Comparison of position of non-relevant property exclusion post *F(No 2)A 2015* 10.48
Example 10.40—Calculating the aggregate transfer: previous transfers 10.53
Example 10.41—Calculating the aggregate transfer: addition to a trust 10.53
Example 10.42—The effective rate 10.56

Example 10.43—Tax charge 10.57
Example 10.44—Tax charge where funds have been added to the trust 10.57
Example 10.45—Ten-year charge where there has been a distribution 10.57
Example 10.46—Release of farmland 10.62
Example 10.47—Distribution of cash 10.62
Example 10.49—Letters of wishes 10.71

Chapter 11 Exemptions and excluded property
Example 11.1—Annual exemptions and PETs 11.7
Example 11.2—Disposition for family 11.12
Example 11.3—Annual exemption and business property relief 11.13
Example 11.4—HMRC's Inheritance Tax Manual, at IHTM14143 11.14
Example 11.5—Spouse exemption and domicile 11.17
Example 11.6—Settlement of excluded property 11.30
Example 11.7—Reversionary interest (I) 11.40
Example 11.8—Reversionary interest (II) 11.40
Example 11.9—Reversionary interest (III) 11.40

Chapter 12 Reliefs — General
Example 12.1—Taper relief on PETs made within seven years of death 12.3
Example 12.2—Taper relief on chargeable lifetime transfers made within seven years of death 12.3
Example 12.3—QSR in action 12.5
Example 12.4—Related property relief (I) 12.7
Example 12.5—Related property relief (II) 12.7
Example 12.6—Fall in value of property and shares 12.12
Example 12.7—Sale of shares by PRs 12.16
Example 12.8—Sale of land interests by PRs 12.18
Example 12.9—Loss of relief claim and discount on joint ownership 12.18
Example 12.10—Sale of timber following woodlands relief claim 12.25

Chapter 13 Business property relief and agricultural property relief
Example 13.1—Frustrated appropriation or variation 13.3
Example 13.2—Diversified investments 13.4
Example 13.3—Order of gifts: getting it wrong 13.7
Example 13.4—Replacement property: business angel 13.9
Example 13.5—Period of ownership: capital changes 13.9
Example 13.6—Net value of business 13.21
Example 13.7—Loss of APR on farmhouse 13.26
Example 13.8—Period of occupation: deathbed purchase 13.37

Example 13.9—Period of occupation: small let farm 13.38
Example 13.10—Successions: keeping it in the family 13.39
Example 13.11—Replacements: trading up 13.41
Example 13.12—ESC F17 in action 13.45
Example 13.13—Agricultural value: farmhouse in East Norfolk 13.46
Example 13.14—Agricultural value: farmhouse in Dedham Vale 13.46
Example 13.15—Clawback of BPR 13.50
Example 13.16—BPR: gift of minority holding 13.51
Example 13.17—A&M trust: partial BPR clawback 13.52

Chapter 14 Lifetime planning
Example 14.1—Case study (I): background 14.1
Example 14.2—Case study (II): existing wills etc 14.1
Example 14.3—Case study (III): marriage and downsizing 14.1
Example 14.4—Case study (IV): gifts and wills 14.1
Example 14.5—Case study (V): the tax effect of lifetime planning 14.1
Example 14.6—Case study (VI): incidental benefits for the family 14.1
Example 14.7—Child trust funds, junior ISAs and NISAs: generous but forgetful grandfather 14.2
Example 14.8—BPR: recycling business property into investments 14.6
Example 14.9—Failed PET: a gift that should not have been made 14.10

Chapter 15 Wills and estate planning
Example 15.1—UK national with holiday home in France 15.2
Example 15.2—Spouse relief: post-war nuclear family 15.14
Example 15.3—Life interest for spouse: William's life 15.15
Example 15.4—Termination of interest: failure to revise a will 15.18
Example 15.5—Life interests for grandchildren: by-passing the next generation 15.22
Example 15.6—APR and spouse exemption (I): simple farming situation15.23
Example 15.7—APR and spouse exemption (II): wastage of exemption and the scope for 'double dipping' 15.23
Example 15.8—Woodlands relief: ownership of wood 15.25
Example 15.9—Woodlands relief: no deferral of taxable event 15.26
Example 15.10—BPR and *s 39A*: a will that should be varied 15.27
Example 15.11—Case study: will-drafting traps 15.29
Example 15.12—Gifts to charity: non-exempt charitable gifts 15.33
Example 15.13—Gifts to charity: calculation of reduced rate 15.33
Example 15.14—Minor beneficiaries: no need for an application to the court 15.41
Example 15.15—Minor beneficiaries: avoiding an application to the court 15.41
Example 15.16—Deed of variation: trying it on 15.44

Chapter 16 The family home and the residence nil rate band

Example 16.1—'IOU scheme' 16.10
Example 16.2—Joint tenancy: notice of severance 16.12
Example 16.3—Joint occupation: gift to family member 16.20
Example 16.4—Gift of house and change in circumstances: infirmity of donor 16.24
Example 16.5—Tapered residence nil rate band 16.59
Example 16.6—Interest in home passing to a direct descendant 16.61
Example 16.7—Effective IHT threshold of £1 million 16.67
Example 16.8—Downsizing to a less expensive residence 16.75
Example 16.9—No residential interest at death 16.76

Chapter 17 Pre-owned assets

Example 17.1—No POAT charge: father moves in with donee son 17.6
Example 17.2—POAT and IHT: sale at an undervalue 17.6
Example 17.3—Link with property broken 17.6
Example 17.4—Contribution condition: funding of residence 17.6
Example 17.5—Contribution condition: change of circumstances 17.6
Example 17.6—Exemption from charge: retained painting 17.11
Example 17.7—Possession of chattels: costly storage arrangements 17.11
Example 17.8—Contribution condition: shared campervan 17.11
Example 17.9—Cash gift: no trace of the money 17.13
Example 17.10—Calculation of POAT on land: moving in with daughter 17.14
Example 17.11—Calculation of POAT on chattels: gift and leaseback 17.15
Example 17.12—Calculation of POAT on intangibles 17.16
Example 17.13—Equity release: daughter moves in 17.18
Example 17.14—Excluded transaction: gift of cash 17.18
Example 17.15—POAT exemption: illness intervening 17.22
Example 17.16—Not UK resident 17.23
Example 17.17—Not UK domiciled 17.23
Example 17.18—*De minimis* exemption: over the limit 17.26
Example 17.19—Property subject to the 'Ingram' scheme 17.29

Table of statutes

[All references are to paragraph numbers]

A

Administration of Estates Act 1925 ... 5.1, 8.34
 s 46 ... 5.1
  (2A) ... 5.1
 47 ... 5.1
 Sch 1A ... 5.1

B

Banking Act 1987 ... 11.36
Blank Bonds and Trusts Act 1696 ... 6.21

C

Civil Partnership Act 2004 ... 1.20, 11.17
 Sch 4
  para 7–12 ... 5.1
Constitutional Reform and Governance Act 2010
 s 41, 42 ... 2.2

D

Data Protection Act 1998 ... 10.3
Diplomatic Privileges Act 1964
 s 2(1) ... 11.38
Domicile and Matrimonial Proceedings Act 1973 ... 2.5

E

Enduring Powers of Attorney Act 1985
 s 3(5) ... 8.40
Equitable Life (Payments) Act 2010 ... 5.5

F

Family Provision Act 1966
 s 1 ... 5.1
Finance Act 1894 ... 1.1
Finance Act 1930
 s 40(2) ... 12.30, 15.38
Finance Act 1975 ... 1.1, 13.43
Finance Act 1982
 s 96 ... 11.36
Finance Act 1986 ... 1.1
 s 102 ... 4.12, 4.22, 6.15, 6.21, 6.31, 7.1, 7.5, 7.11, 7.15, 14.22, 14.24, 15.18, 16.10, 16.63
  (1) ... 7.5, 16.32
   (a) ... 7.4, 7.5

Finance Act 1986 – *contd*
 s 102(1)(b) ... 7.4, 7.5, 7.6, 7.28, 16.7, 16.19
  (3) ... 5.3, 6.5, 7.7, 7.11, 7.13, 7.14, 7.19, 16.65
  (4) ... 4.13, 4.22, 7.1, 7.11, 7.14, 7.36, 16.63
  (5) ... 7.2, 7.13, 7.15, 7.25
   (d)–(i) ... 17.22
  (5A) ... 7.9, 7.15, 7.26, 9.6, 16.9
  (5B), (5C) ... 7.9, 7.15, 7.26
 102A ... 4.22, 7.1, 7.11, 7.12, 7.13, 7.14, 7.15, 16.7, 16.8, 17.22
  (2) ... 7.12, 7.22
  (3) ... 7.12, 7.13, 16.7
  (4)(a), (b) ... 7.12
  (5) ... 7.12, 7.13, 16.7, 16.8
 102B ... 4.22, 7.1, 7.11, 7.14, 7.15, 16.22, 17.22
  (1) ... 16.20
  (3)(a), (b) ... 7.14, 16.21
  (4) ... 7.14, 16.21, 16.22, 16.23, 17.18, 17.22
 102C ... 4.22, 7.1, 7.11, 7.15
  (2) ... 7.15
  (3) ... 7.15, 7.31, 16.25, 17.22
  (6) ... 7.14
  (7) ... 7.11
 102ZA ... 6.31, 7.19, 7.20, 9.7, 9.9, 15.16, 15.17, 15.18, 16.9, 16.32
  (1)(b)(ii) ... 9.25
  (2) ... 4.12, 7.19, 15.17
 103 ... 3.30, 5.18, 12.23, 14.11, 15.4, 15.5, 16.10, 16.49, 16.53
  (1) ... 15.6
   (a) ... 16.48
  (4) ... 5.10
  (5) ... 4.13
 103(7) ... 5.11
 104 ... 6.31, 7.8, 7.38
  (1)(c) ... 5.11
 106 ... 7.23

Finance Act 1986 – *contd*
s 107(4), (5) 8.2
122(1) 7.23
Sch 19
para 46 .... 4.8
Sch 20 .... 4.22, 7.1, 7.15, 9.7
para 1(1) 7.20
2 .... 7.16, 7.17
(2)(b) 7.17
(4)–(7) 7.17
3 .... 7.16, 7.17
4 .... 7.16, 7.17
4A 7.19
(5) 7.20
5 .... 7.20
(1) 7.18, 7.20
(2)–(5) 7.20
6(1)(a) 7.2, 7.29, 16.19
(b) 7.15, 7.30, 7.31, 16.25, 17.22
(c) 7.5
7 .... 7.22
8(1A)(a), (b) 7.23
(2)(a), (b) 7.23
(3) 7.23
(b) 7.23
(5) 7.23
Finance Act 1998 .... 12.30
Finance Act 1999 .... 7.11, 7.14
Finance Act 2002 .... 9.23, 11.18
Finance Act 2003 .... 7.9, 10.1
Pt 3 (ss 24–41) 16.2
s 43(1) 16.52
55(2) 16.1
185 .... 9.6
Sch 4
para 1 .... 16.52
Sch 4A 16.1
Sch 6ZA 16.2
Finance Act 2004 .... 10.1, 17.2, 17.8
s 84 .... 7.3, 17.1
Pt 4 (ss 149–284) 3.14
Sch 15 .... 17.1, 17.16
para 1 .... 17.9, 17.12
3 .... 17.4
(1) 17.3
(2) 7.13, 16.7, 16.53, 17.5, 17.18
(3) 16.53, 17.6
(4) 16.7
4 .... 17.14
(1) 7.30
6 .... 17.7
(2) 17.9
(3) 17.10
7 .... 17.15

Finance Act 2004 – *contd*
Sch 15 – *contd*
para 7(1) 7.30, 17.15
8 .... 17.12, 17.16
9 .... 17.16
10 .... 17.18
(1)(a) 16.17
(c) 16.9
(2)(a) 16.53
(c) 17.13, 17.18
(d) 16.18
11 .... 17.19
(1) 9.15, 17.20
(2) 9.15
(5) 7.3, 7.14, 17.21, 17.22
(a) 16.8, 17.6, 17.11
(c) 16.10, 16.23
(d) 7.30, 16.25, 17.22
(6), (7) 16.9, 16.11
(9) 9.15
(11)–(13) 9.15
12 .... 17.19, 17.23
13 .... 17.19, 17.25
15 .... 17.17
21 .... 7.3, 17.27
22 .... 17.27
23 .... 17.27
(3) 17.27
Sch 29 .... 9.40
para 13(c) 9.40
15(1)(c) 9.40
Finance Act 2005 .... 11.17
s 23–45 .... 14.19
Sch 1A 14.17
para 2–7 .... 14.17
Finance Act 2006 .... 7.9, 7.19, 7.36, 8.1, 8.4, 8.16, 8.25, 8.29, 9.1, 9.9, 9.10, 9.12, 9.15, 9.16, 9.24, 9.31, 9.36, 9.37, 9.38, 9.40, 9.42, 10.1, 10.4, 10.5, 10.12, 10.17, 10.22, 10.24, 10.26, 10.27, 10.31, 10.32, 10.48, 10.64, 10.70, 11.16, 11.4, 12.5, 13.6, 13.52, 14.1, 14.3, 14.6, 14.10, 14.12, 14.14, 14.15, 14.22, 14.26, 14.28, 14.29, 14.31, 14.32, 15.15, 15.21, 15.22, 15.23, 15.52, 16.42, 16.44
s 80 .... 9.15, 9.35
(1) 9.35
(4) 9.35
(b) 9.35
89 .... 9.19
156 .... 9.7

Finance Act 2006 – *contd*
Sch 20 .... 9.19
para 3 .... 10.12, 10.25
(3) 10.25
13 .... 9.20
14, 15 .... 9.12
16 .... 9.16
Finance Act 2007 .... 4.25, 8.48, 9.40, 17.27
Sch 24 .... 3.17, 8.38, 8.39, 8.40
para 1 .... 3.17
(1) 8.38
1A 3.17, 8.38
4–4AA 3.17
4C 8.40
6–6AB 3.17
6 .... 8.40
9 .... 8.42
(3) 8.44
10 .... 8.42
(3), (4) 8.44
11 .... 8.42, 8.45
12 .... 8.42, 8.45
14 .... 8.50
18(3) 8.51
Finance Act 2008 .... 3.1, 3.3, 3.5, 3.14, 3.15, 3.17, 3.19, 3.20, 3.24, 8.38, 8.40, 8.42, 8.45, 9.32, 10.1, 10.71, 11.17, 15.6, 15.7, 15.8, 15.19, 16.28
s 10 .... 15.3
24 .... 9.34
25 .... 9.34
67 .... 3.17
91 .... 9.40
Pt 7 (ss 113–139) 8.3
s 113 .... 8.3, 8.55
115–117 .... 8.3
140 .... 9.8
Sch 4 .... 15.3
para 10(2)–(5) 3.20
11 .... 3.20
Sch 7 .... 9.34
Sch 18 .... 3.17
Sch 28 .... 9.40
Sch 36 .... 8.3, 8.55
Sch 37 .... 8.3, 8.55
Sch 39 .... 8.3
Sch 40 .... 3.17, 8.3, 8.39
Finance Act 2009 .... 10.48, 12.24
s 96 .... 8.3, 8.55
99 .... 8.54
101 .... 8.49
(1) 8.49
105 .... 8.52, 8.53
106 .... 8.38, 8.52
Finance Act 2009 – *contd*
s 107 .... 8.38
Sch 48 .... 8.3, 8.55
Sch 51 .... 8.54
Sch 50 .... 8.51
Sch 53 .... 8.49
para 7(7), (8) 8.2
9 .... 8.2
Sch 55 .... 8.53
paras 6–6AB 3.17
Sch 56 .... 8.52
Finance Act 2010 .... 9.12, 9.18, 9.25, 11.19, 13.15
s 8 .... 3.1, 4.25, 4.26
(3) 3.27
52 .... 9.24, 10.15
53 .... 9.22, 9.25, 9.26, 9.32, 10.15, 11.6
(2)(a) 9.25
(8) 9.25
Sch 6 .... 1.20
Sch 10 .... 4.17
Finance Act 2011 .... 3.14, 5.24, 10.16
Finance Act 2012 .... 1.4, 1.7, 1.13, 3.27, 4.26, 7.36, 9.26, 15.33, 16.1
Sch 14
para 1 .... 1.20, 4.3
Sch 38 .... 3.18
Finance Act 2013 .... 1.6, 1.8, 1.12, 1.13, 1.20, 2.2, 2.6, 2.14, 3.2, 5.5, 5.13, 5.17, 11.17, 11.36, 13.21, 14.11, 14.12, 14.18, 14.28, 15.44, 16.1, 15.7
s 99(4) 16.2
133 .... 1.18
177 .... 11.17
216 .... 14.17
Sch 6
para 5 .... 5.13
Schs 33–35 .... 16.2
Sch 44 .... 14.17
Finance Act 2014 .... 1.4, 1.12, 1.20, 4.3, 4.19, 4.25, 4.26, 5.13, 5.14, 8.3, 8.28, 8.37, 9.35, 10.26, 10.57, 11.26, 11.36, 14.12, 14.14, 16.2, 16.15
s 110 .... 16.2
Finance (No 2) Act 2014 .... 9.35
Finance Act 2015 .... 1.8, 1.13, 1.18, 3.17, 5.5, 8.1, 8.37, 8.41, 10.43, 10.46, 11.26, 11.27, 14.28, 16.2
s 75 .... 11.26
120 .... 3.17

Finance Act 2015 – *contd*
s 120(2) 3.17
Sch 8 .... 16.2
Sch 21 .... 3.17
Finance (No 2) Act 2015 .... 1.3, 3.28, 4.26, 8.2, 10.26, 10.29, 10.31, 10.32, 10.39, 10.40, 10.48, 10.59, 15.6, 15.13, 15.50, 16.70
s 10 .... 3.27
236 .... 11.32
Finance Act 2016 .... 1.13, 3.48, 4.4, 5.5, 5.25, 14.4, 15.13, 15.38, 16.63, 16.64, 16.69, 16.70, 16.77
Sch 22 .... 3.17
Finance Bill 2016 .... 1.18, 2.7, 2.10, 2.13
Finance Act 2017 .... 1.2, 11.20, 14.4
Finance (No 2) Act 2017 .... 1.2, 1.13, 1.15, 2.9, 2.13, 2.14, 3.17, 5.5, 7.37, 8.41. 9.33, 10.59, 11.6, 11.17, 16.3
s 30(10), (11) 2.9, 2.10
s 30(12) 2.10, 2.14
Finance Act 2018 .... 16.2
Financial Services and Markets Act 2000
s 236 .... 11.32
243 .... 11.32
Freedom of information Act 2000 .... 7.40

G

Gambling Act 2005 .... 5.10

H

Housing Act 1996 .... 11.21
Housing Associations Act 1985 .... 11.21

I

Income and Corporation Taxes Act 1988
s 615 .... 9.40
(3) 1.20, 5.5, 9.40
Sch 9 .... 11.24
Income Tax Act 2007
s 403 .... 8.49
497 .... 10.58
720–730 .... 17.16
991 .... 5.5
1005 .... 13.4
Income Tax (Earnings and Pensions) Act 2003
s 181 .... 17.15
Sch 2 .... 11.24
Income Tax (Trading and Other Income) Act 2005
s 369(1) 15.11

Income Tax (Trading and Other Income) Act 2005 – *contd*
s 423 .... 4.5
461 .... 17.16
Pt 5 Ch 5 (ss 619–648) 13.3
s 624 .... 14.21, 17.16
625 .... 17.12
(1) 17.12
629 .... 14.2, 14.21
694A 14.4
703(1) 11.33
717 .... 4.5
727 .... 17.29
Inheritance Tax Act 1984 .... 8.56, 17.27
s 1 .... 1.1
2 .... 1.11
(1) 1.3, 1.27, 4.1, 4.16
(4) 14.10
3 .... 10.2
(1) 1.9, 1.11, 4.7, 4.23, 6.4
(2) 1.9, 1.14, 4.19, 7.36, 11.6, 11.29
(3) 9.40
(4) 5.3
3A 1.10, 4.11, 4.15, 9.25, 10.2, 11.2
(1) 4.7, 4.8
(1A) 4.7, 4.8, 7.19
(c)(iii) 4.8
(2) 4.13
(3), (3A) 4.8
(4) 7.27, 16.18
(5) 4.1, 4.5
(6) 4.10, 4.14
(6A) 4.8, 4.10, 4.12, 9.25
(7) 4.10
4 .... 10.26, 15.48, 16.58
(1) 1.3, 1.12, 5.1, 5.2, 5.23, 5.25
(2) 5.7
5(1) 1.14, 6.5, 11.6, 11.29
(a)(i), (ii) 9.25
(b) 1.14, 11.37
(1A) 4.14, 9.24
(1B) 4.8, 4.14, 5.2, 5.25, 9.25, 9.26, 11.6, 16.64
(2) 6.5, 6.21, 7.26
(3) 4.19
(5) 1.12, 4.19, 5.9, 5.12, 16.57
6 .... 11.6, 11.28, 11.30
(1) 1.2, 1.13, 1.15, 1.18, 5.5, 7.33, 9.33, 11.40

Inheritance Tax Act 1984 – *contd*
s 6(1A) ... 1.18, 5.5, 11.32
(1B) ... 1.13, 11.27
(1BA) ... 1.13, 11.27
(2) ... 1.13, 1.18, 2.14, 11.31
(3) ... 1.13, 2.14, 11.33
(4) ... 11.34
(5) ... 1.2
7 ... 1.4, 4.25, 4.26, 5.23, 12.1
(1) ... 14.10
(2) ... 1.6
(4) ... 1.21, 10.19, 10.20, 12.2
(5) ... 1.22, 12.3
8 ... 1.4, 3.27
8A ... 1.5, 3.1, 3.5, 3.20, 5.24, 11.17, 16.29
(1) ... 3.6
(2) ... 3.6, 3.12
(3) ... 3.6, 3.7, 3.8, 3.9, 3.10
(4) ... 3.6, 3.12
(5) ... 5.6
(6)(a), (b) ... 3.7
8B ... 1.5, 3.1, 3.5, 3.8, 5.24, 16.29
(1)(b) ... 3.8
(2) ... 3.9
(3) ... 3.8
(a), (b) ... 3.8
(4) ... 3.9
8C ... 1.5, 3.1, 3.5, 3.6, 3.30, 5.24, 16.29
(1) ... 3.11
(2), (3) ... 3.12
(4), (5) ... 3.13
8D–M ... 3.4, 15.13
8D ... 3.4, 3.42, 16.1, 16.56
(2) ... 16.58
(3) ... 16.58, 16.61
(5) ... 16.57, 16.58, 16.59
(5)(b) ... 5.25
8E ... 3.4, 3.42, 5.25, 16.1, 16.56
(2) (5) ... 16.61
(6) ... 16.61, 16.71
(7) ... 16.61, 16.71
8F ... 3.4, 3.42, 5.25, 16.1, 16.56, 16.62, 16.74
8FA ... 16.71, 16.75
(8), (9) ... 16.71
8FB ... 16.72, 16.76
(7) ... 16.72, 16.75
(8) ... 16.72

Inheritance Tax Act 1984 – *contd*
s 8FC ... 16.73
8FD ... 16.74
(3)–(6) ... 16.74
8FE ... 16.71, 16.72, 16.75
(3) ... 16.75, 16.76
(3)–(5) ... 16.76
(4)–(6), (9) ... 16.75
(10) ... 16.76
8G ... 3.4, 3.42, 5.25, 16.1, 16.56
(2),(3) ... 16.66
(4),(5) ... 16.67
8H ... 3.4, 3.42, 5.25, 16.1, 16.56, 16.63
(4A) ... 16.64, 16.71
(4B) ... 16.63, 16.64, 16.71
(4C) ... 16.63, 16.64, 16.71
(4D) ... 16.63, 16.71
(4E) ... 16.71
(4F) ... 16.71
(5) ... 16.63
(6) ... 16.63
8HA ... 16.64, 16.71
(3) (6) ... 16.64
... 3.4, 3.42, 5.25, 16.1, 16.56
8J ... 3.4, 3.42, 5.25, 16.1, 16.56, 16.65
(4)–(6) ... 7.7, 16.65
(4) ... 7.7, 16.65
(4)(a) ... 16.31
(5) ... 16.32
8K ... 3.4, 3.42, 5.25, 16.1, 16.56, 16.65
8L ... 3.4, 3.42, 3.45, 5.25, 16.1, 16.56, 16.68
(1) (3) ... 16.71
(1) (7) ... 16.68
8M ... 3.4, 3.42, 3.46, 5.25, 16.1, 16.56, 16.69
(2A)–(2F) ... 16.69
(2B)–(2E) ... 16.61
(2G) ... 16.69, 16.72
((2H) ... 16.69
(3), (5)–(7) ... 16.69
10–17 ... 1.20
10 ... 1.9, 1.20, 4.8, 4.14, 4.4, 5.3, 9.11, 9.22, 9.23, 9.25, 11.25, 16.17, 16.18
11 ... 1.9, 1.20, 4.4, 5.3, 9.11, 10.3, 11.12, 16.17, 17.18
(3) ... 11.12, 16.18
(6)(b) ... 11.12

Inheritance Tax Act 1984 – *contd*
s 12 .... 1.9, 4.4, 5.3, 10.3
(2ZA) 9.40
13 .... 5.3, 10.3, 11.12
14, 15 .... 1.9, 4.4, 5.3
16 .... 5.3, 10.10
17 .... 5.3, 15.48
(a) 15.48
18 .... 1.20, 3.2, 3.28, 4.3, 4.29, 7.9, 7.25, 7.26, 8.11, 11.4, 11.16, 15.44, 15.50, 14.33, 16.28, 16.31, 16.44
(2) 1.20, 2.5, 2.6, 11.17
(2A) 2.5, 2.6
(3) 11.16
19 .... 1.20, 4.3, 6.12, 8.11, 11.2, 14.28, 17.18
(1) 11.7
(3)(b) 10.17
(3A) 4.15
(5) 5.4, 7.1, 7.27
20 .... 1.20, 4.3, 7.1, 7.25, 8.11, 11.2, 11.8, 14.28, 17.18
(3) 5.4
21 .... 1.20, 4.3, 4.15, 4.29, 6.12, 8.9, 8.10, 8.11, 8.12, 8.18, 8.40, 9.28, 10.16, 10.50, 11.2, 11.9, 11.10, 14.1, 14.2, 14.8, 14.20, 14.28, 15.39, 16.16
(1)(b) 8.13
(2) 4.5, 6.14, 11.10
(3), (4) 4.5
(5) 5.4, 7.1, 7.27
22 .... 1.20, 4.3, 7.25, 8.11, 11.2, 11.11
(4) 11.11
(6) 5.4
23 .... 1.20, 4.3, 5.5, 7.25, 8.11, 11.4, 11.18, 11.19
(1) 15.33
(2) 11.19, 15.33
(4) 11.19
(6) 11.18
24 .... 1.20, 4.3, 5.20, 7.25, 11.4, 11.20
24A 1.20, 4.3, 5.20, 7.25, 11.4, 11.21
25 .... 1.20, 4.3, 5.20, 7.25, 11.4, 11.22
(3) 1.20
26 .... 1.20
27 .... 1.20, 4.3, 7.25, 11.4, 15.34

Inheritance Tax Act 1984 – *contd*
s 27(1A) 1.20
28 .... 1.20, 4.3, 7.25, 11.4, 11.24
(1)(b) 11.24
(2) 11.25
28A 1.20, 4.3, 7.25, 11.25
29A 5.4
30 .... 2.3, 3.12, 11.4, 11.23, 12.1, 12.27, 12.30
(3BA) 15.38
31 .... 2.3, 11.4, 11.23, 12.27, 15.34
32 .... 2.3, 3.11, 3.12, 3.46, 11.4, 11.23, 12.27, 16.69
32A 3.11, 3.46, 16.69
33 .... 2.3, 11.4, 11.23
(5) 15.34
34 .... 2.3, 11.4, 11.23
35 .... 2.3, 11.4, 11.23
35A 11.23
36 .... 5.28
37 .... 5.28, 5.29
38 .... 5.28, 5.36
(6) 5.29
39 .... 5.28
39A 14.1, 15.27, 15.28
(2) 5.30
(4) 5.30
(6) 3.33
40 .... 5.28, 5.32
41 .... 5.28, 5.38
(a) 5.39
(b) 5.39, 5.40
42 .... 5.28
(1) 5.29
(2) 5.29, 5.39
43 .... 8.16
(1)(a) 9.5
(2) 16.26, 16.45
(a) 16.26
(b) 8.16
(3) 9.32, 16.26, 16.34
(4) 6.30
46 .... 6.30
(5) 10.21
s 46A 9.36, 9.37, 14.28
s 46B 9.37
(1) 10.21
47 .... 6.30
47A 9.23
48 .... 11.40, 17.23
(1) 1.13, 9.32, 11.39
(a) 11.40
(3) 1.13, 1.15, 2.13, 5.5, 7.35, 7.36, 9.33, 10.59, 11.30, 11.40

Inheritance Tax Act 1984 – *contd*
s 48(3)(a) 1.18, 2.13, 7.35
(3A) 1.13, 1.18, 5.5, 7.35
(3B) 1.13, 5.5, 7.35, 7.36, 9.26, 9.34, 11.40
(3C) 7.35, 7.36
(3D) 1.13, 4.14, 5.5, 7.36
(3E) 1.13, 2.13, 5.5, 7.35
(4) 1.18, 2.14, 11.31
49 .... 9.1
(1) 5.2, 6.10, 6.29, 9.10, 14.14, 16.64
(1A) 4.8, 5.2, 6.29, 9.10, 9.25
(1B) 5.2
(2) 6.29
49A 4.29, 5.2, 9.9, 14.16, 15.19, 15.22, 16.31
(1)(d) 8.7
49B 4.29, 5.2, 8.7
49C 4.29, 8.7, 9.27
49D 4.29, 8.7, 9.27, 14.26
49E 4.29, 8.7, 9.29, 14.26
51(1) 9.11
(1A) 4.12, 9.25, 10.22
(1B) 4.12, 10.22
(2) 9.11
52 .... 4.8, 4.10, 4.12, 4.14, 9.11, 9.12, 9.13, 9.15, 9.20, 9.25, 9.27, 10.23
(1) 1.3, 10.23, 15.51
(2) 10.23
(2A) 9.25, 10.23
(3A) 9.25
53 .... 9.12, 9.14
(1A) 4.12, 10.23
(2A) 9.27
(4) 9.15
(5), (6) 9.13, 9.14
(7), (8) 9.13
54 .... 9.14
(2B) 9.21
(4) 5.7
54A 9.16
54B 9.16
55A 9.23
57 .... 1.20, 14.1
(3) 8.7
(4) 9.17
57A(1A) 9.25
58(1) 1.18, 11.24
(d) 9.40

Inheritance Tax Act 1984 – *contd*
s 58(1)(f) 1.18, 10.41
59 .... 7.59, 10.26
62 .... 10.29
(2) 10.26, 10.34
(3)–(4) 10.26
62A 4.25
62B 4.25
62C 4.25, 10.26
(3)(a), (b) 4.25
63 .... 10.12
64 .... 4.25, 10.27, 10.38, 10.59, 15.50
(1B) 2.13
(2) 11.37
65 .... 10.12, 10.27
(1) 10.12
(4) 3.28, 10.12, 10.26
(7) 1.18
(7B) 2.13
(8) 1.18
66 .... 4.25, 4.26, 10.27,10.38, 10.59
(3) 10.59
(4) 10.40, 10.58
(5)(a) 10.51
67 .... 10.27, 10.38, 10.59
(1) 10.50
(2) 10.50
(a), (b) 10.59
(3) 10.53
(b) 10.58
(4)(b) 10.53
(5) 10.53
68 .... 4.25, 10.27
(1) 3.38, 10.26
(2) 10.37
(3) 10.37
(b) 10.37
(4) 10.26, 10.28
(5) 10.30
(6) 10.26, 10.28, 10.40
69 .... 4.25, 10.27
(2)(b) 10.12
(4) 10.12
70 .... 10.6, 10.66, 10.74, 10.67, 10.68, 10.69, 10.70
(7) 10.6, 8.74, 10.67
71 .... 4.7, 4.8, 10.5, 10.9
(1)(a) 4.7, 10.16
(1A) 10.25
(1B) 10.17
71A 4.12, 4.29, 5.2, 8.7, 9.12, 9.20, 9.31,9.38, 10.5, 10.9, 10.17, 10.22, 10.70, 15.22, 16.64, 16.65

Inheritance Tax Act 1984 – *contd*
s 71A(4)(a) 10.6
71B 10.70
71C 8.7, 9.31
71D 4.12, 9.12, 9.20, 9.31, 9.38, 10.5, 10.19, 10.22, 16.65
(1)–(5) 10.19
(7) 10.8
71E 10.10, 10.70
71F 10.27, 10.70
(5) 10.31
71G(1)(b) 10.70
74A–74C 1.13, 4.14, 5.5, 7.36
79 .... 15.50
80 .... 9.32, 9.35, 10.26
(1) 10.17
(2) 9.35
81A 4.8, 4.9, 9.24, 11.40
(1), (2) 9.24
82 .... 2.13, 11.30
86 .... 1.20, 4.3
(1) 11.24
(3) 11.24
89 .... 4.8, 4.29, 12.13, 14.10, 14.13, 14.16
(1)(d) 14.16
89A 4.8, 4.29, 14.14, 14.15, 14.16
89B 4.29, 5.2, 14.16
(1)(a) 4.8
(b) 4.8
(c) 4.8, 14.14, 14.16, 14.18
(d) 4.8, 14.14, 14.16
91 .... 6.5
92 .... 5.8
94 .... 1.11, 1.27, 4.16, 8.4
(1) 4.8
(2) 1.27
(4) 1.28
(5) 1.28, 4.21
95 .... 4.16
96 .... 4.16
97 .... 4.16
98 .... 1.11, 1.28, 1.29
(1) 4.21, 5.19
(3) 4.8, 4.21
100(1A) 9.25
101(1A) 9.25
102(3) 5.3
(4) 4.13
103 .... 13.7

Inheritance Tax Act 1984 – *contd*
s 103(3) 13.1
(4) 5.10
105 .... 13.1, 13.51
(1)(a) 13.1
(b) 13.5
(bb) 13.4
(cc) 13.5, 13.51
(d) 10.61, 13.6
(e) 13.6
(1ZA) 13.4
(3) 13.1, 13.3, 13.10, 13.12, 13.13, 13.14, 13.15, 13.23
(4) 13.23
(b) 13.3, 13.16
106 .... 7.23, 13.5, 13.9
(1)(a) 13.7
107 .... 13.5, 13.9, 13.12
(1)(a) 13.9
(4) 13.9
108, 109 .... 13.5
110 .... 13.7, 13.21
(b) 5.13
111 .... 13.23
112 .... 13.9, 13.22, 13.23
(2)(b) 13.23
(4) 13.23
(6) 13.22, 13.23
113 .... 13.50
113A 10.64, 13.50, 14.6
(1) 13.52
(3A)(a) 13.51
(b) 13.50, 13.51
115 .... 13.26
(2) 12.24, 13.28
(3) 13.46, 13.48
116 .... 13.29
117 .... 13.25, 13.26, 13.37, 13.38, 15.24
117A 13.40
117B 13.41
118 .... 13.40, 13.41
(3) 13.41
120 .... 15.23, 15.24
(1)(a) 13.39
122 .... 10.61
(1) 7.23
(b) 10.61
124 .... 13.50
124A 10.64, 13.50
(1) 13.52
125 .... 5.6, 12.1, 16.63
(1) 12.24
126 .... 3.11, 12.1
127 .... 12.1, 15.25

Inheritance Tax Act 1984 – *contd*
s 128 .... 12.1
129 .... 12.1
130 .... 12.1
(2) 12.25
131 .... 4.18, 12.1, 12.8
132 .... 4.18, 12.1, 12.11
133–140 .... 4.18, 12.1
141 .... 5.7, 5.26, 6.30, 12.1, 12.4
(1)(a), (b) 1.23
(2) 1.23, 5.26
(3) 12.5
142 .... 3.30, 7.32, 13.3, 15.31, 15.40, 15.41, 15.42, 15.43, 15.44, 15.45, 15.46, 15.48, 15.49, 16.27, 16.47, 16.65
(1) 12.13
(b) 15.45
(2) 15.47
(2A) 15.45
(3) 15.43, 15.44
143 .... 3.37, 10.71, 15.49
144 .... 3.28, 3.30, 9.9, 10.6, 10.26, 10.71, 15.13, 15.49, 15.50, 15.52, 15.53, 16.36, 16.42, 16.65
(1) 15.50, 15.52
(a) 15.50
(b) 3.28
(1A) 15.52
(2) 15.52
(4) 15.53
147 .... 8.2
(4) 8.2
(10) 3.13
151A 3.5, 3.14, 5.24
151B 3.5, 3.14, 3.15, 5.24
151BA 3.5
(5)–(7) 3.14
(8)–(12) 3.15
151C 3.5, 3.14, 5.24
151D 3.5, 3.14
151E 3.5, 3.14
152 .... 1.20, 5.5
153 .... 5.5, 11.35
153A 1.20, 3.5, 11.5, 9.27
153ZA 1.13, 11.28
154 .... 1.9, 1.20, 5.5, 11.5, 11.26, 11.27
155 .... 5.5
(1) 11.34
155A ....
157 .... 1.13, 1.20, 4.19, 5.5, 5.13, 5.14, 11.5, 11.36, 16.15

Inheritance Tax Act 1984 – *contd*
s 158 .... 1.25, 1.26, 5.27, 12.20
(6) 1.25, 2.14
159 .... 1.26, 5.27, 12.20, 12.22
(2)–(5) 1.26
(7) 1.26
160 .... 4.19, 5.19, 6.1 6.2, 6.5, 6.8, 6.13, 6.15, 6.16, 6.18, 6.27, 6.33, 8.14, 8.23, 13.42, 17.17
161 .... 5.20, 6.6, 12.1, 12.6, 12.10
(1) 6.8
(2) 6.6
(3) 6.7, 6.8
(4) 6.8, 6.9
(5) 6.9
162(1) 5.12, 5.13
(2), (3) 5.13, 16.61
(4) 4.19, 5.13, 5.17, 14.11
(5) 5.13, 14.11
162A 5.9, 5.13, 14.11, 16.15, 16.16
162B 5.9, 5.13, 5.17, 14.11, 16.15, 16.16
162C 5.9, 5.14
163 .... 6.1
166 .... 6.32
167 .... 15.39
(1) 6.12
(2)(a), (b) 6.12
(3), (4) 6.12
168 .... 6.18
171 .... 1.12, 5.19
(1), (2) 5.19
172 .... 1.12, 5.16
173 .... 5.17
174(1) 5.9
175 .... 5.17
175A 1.12, 5.9, 5.13, 5.15, 14.11, 15.12, 16.13
(7) 5.14
176 .... 5.20, 6.10, 12.6
(2) 6.10
(3) 6.10, 12.6
(5) 5.20, 12.7
177 .... 13.43
178 .... 12.1, 12.14
179 .... 12.14
180 .... 12.14
(1) 12.15
181–189 .... 12.14
190 .... 12.1, 12.17

Inheritance Tax Act 1984 – *contd*
s 191 .... 12.17
(2), (3) 12.17
192 .... 12.17
193 .... 12.17
194 .... 12.17
195 .... 12.17
196 .... 12.17
197 .... 12.17
197A 12.17
198 .... 12.17
199(1) 8.26
200(1) 9.42
(a), (b) 5.23
201 .... 9.42
(1)(b) 9.42
202 .... 1.27, 1.28, 4.16, 8.4
(2) 1.28
203(1) 5.13
204 .... 8.27
208 .... 8.27
211 .... 8.34
(1)–(3) 5.29
216 .... 8.38, 15.6
(3A) 8.15
(6)(a) 8.46
(c) 4.29
217 .... 8.38, 8.48
218 .... 8.2, 8.46
219 .... 8.55
219A 8.55, 15.44
220 .... 8.55
221 .... 2.2
222 .... 8.57
223 .... 8.64
227 .... 8.49
(1C) 8.29
228 .... 8.29, 8.30
229 .... 8.49
233(1)(b) 8.2, 8.49
234(2) 8.31
237(1) 8.33
(3C) 8.33
239 .... 3.5, 3.16
(4)(aa) 3.16
241 .... 12.7
242 .... 3.5
245(2) 8.46
(7) 8.46
245A 8.46
247 .... 8.44
(1) 3.18
(2) 3.18
(4) 3.18, 8.47
248(1) 8.48
254, 255 .... 8.55

Inheritance Tax Act 1984 – *contd*
s 256 .... 3.17, 8.38, 8.55
257–261 .... 8.55
262 .... 5.17
263 .... 4.5, 6.14
(2) 6.14
266(3) 4.28
267 .... 2.2, 2.8, 9.34, 11.17, 12.21, 17.23
(1) 2.9, 2.9, 2.14, 12.19
(a) 2.9
(aa) 2.13, 7.33
(b) 1.15, 2.10, 9.34
(2) 1.25, 2.14
(3) 2.14
267A 11.17, 13.3
267ZA 2.6
(2)–(4) 2.7
(5) 1.25
(6) 1.15, 1.25
(8) 1.7, 2.8, 2.14
s 267ZB 2.14
(4)(a) 2.7
(10) 2.7
268 .... 4.5, 4.23, 6.14, 7.17
(1)–(3) 4.24
268A 11.17
269(2) 6.6
271A 5.5
272 .... 2.13, 4.23, 3.5
274 .... 6.19
Sch 1 .... 1.4, 3.27, 4.26, 5.23
Sch 1A 1.2, 1.7, 1.13, 1.18, 3.24, 5.24
Sch 2 .... 3.13
Sch 3 .... 1.20, 4.3, 11.22, 11.23
Sch 4 .... 1.20, 4.35, 5.5
Sch 5A 1.13
Sch 6
para 2 .... 3.35
4(2) 12.3
Sch A1 .... 1.2, 1.13, 1.17, 1.18, 5.5, 7.37, 16.3
para 1–5 .... 1.18
5(2)(b) 1.13
6–7 .... 1.18
Inheritance and Trustees' Powers Act 2014 .... 5.1, 15.20

L

Law of Property Act 1925
s 30 .... 6.28

Law of Property Act 1925 – *contd*
s 36(2) 16.13
149(3) 7.13
184 .... 3.26, 5.7
Law Reform (Succession) Act 1995 .. 8.38
Limited Liability Partnerships Act 2000 .... 13.3

M

Marriage (Same Sex Couples) Act 2013 .... 11.17
Mental Health Act 1983 .... 14.17
Mental Capacity Act 2005 .... 8.11
s 12 .... 8.10

P

Perpetuities and Accumulations Act 2009 .... 10.3

T

Taxation of Chargeable Gains Act 1992
s 2(4) 14.10
2B–2F 16.2
4(3A) 16.2
62 .... 14.25
(1) 7.1
(6) 15.47
71 .... 10.5
72 .... 9.15, 14.14
(1)(b) 9.15
73 .... 9.15
77 .... 10.1, 14.21, 17.16
86 .... 17.16
87 .... 9.33
89 .... 14.10, 14.13
91 .... 9.33
97(5) 9.33
126 .... 13.9
165 .... 10.1, 14.6, 14.8
169B 10.1, 14.8
222 .... 16.19

Taxation of Chargeable Gains Act 1992 – *contd*
s 222(8A)–(8D) 16.63
222C 16.2
223(1) 16.2
225 .... 9.15, 16.32, 16.39, 16.41
260 .... 10.1, 10.4, 10.12, 10.24
(2)(a) 10.12
(da) 10.6
272 .... 6.16
(5) 6.17
274 .... 3.19, 6.19, 6.34, 8.55
Sch B1, paras 1(6), 2, 4 .... 1.19
Sch 4ZZA 16.2
Taxes Management Act 1970
s 12ZA–12ZN 16.2
s 49A 8.63
s 49C 8.63
s 49E 8.63
Tribunals, Courts and Enforcement Act 2007 .... 8.58
Trustee Act 1925
s 31 .... 8.16, 9.10, 9.27, 10.16, 10.24, 13.52, 14.10, 15.20, 15.22
32 .... 8.16, 10.6, 10.8, 15.20
49 .... 13.52
Trusts of Land and Appointment of Trustees Act 1996 .... 16.38
s 12 .... 16.38, 16.39
13 .... 16.38, 16.39
(7) 16.38, 16.39
14 .... 6.28
22 .... 16.39
(1) 16.39

W

Welfare Reform Act 2013 .... 14.17

Table of statutory instruments and other guidance

[*All references are to paragraph numbers*]

A

Annual Tax on Enveloped Dwellings (Indexation of Annual Chargeable Amounts) Order 2017, SI 2017/1246 .... 16.2

C

Charge to Income Tax by Reference to Enjoyment of Property Previously Owned Regulations 2005, SI 2005/724 .... 7.3, 16.11, 17.17, 17.24
- reg 3 .... 17.15
- 4 .... 17.29
- 5 .... 14.11, 16.17, 17.24
- 6 .... 7.3, 5.39

D

Double Taxation Relief (Estate Duty) (France) Order 1963, SI 1963/1319 .... 12.21
Double Taxation Relief (Estate Duty) (India) Order 1956, SI 1956/998 .... 12.21
Double Taxation Relief (Estate Duty) (Italy) Order 1968, SI 1968/304. .... 12.21
Double Taxation Relief (Ireland) Order 1978, SI 1978/1107 .... 12.21
Double Taxation Relief (Pakistan) Order 1975, SI 1957/1522 .... 12.21
Double Taxation Relief (South Africa) Order 1979, SI 1979/576 .... 12.21
Double Taxation Relief (Switzerland) Order 1957, SI 1957/426 .... 12.21
Double Taxation Relief (Taxes on Estates of Deceased Persons and Inheritances and on Gifts) (Netherlands) Order 1980, SI 1980/706 .... 12.21
Double Taxation Relief (Taxes on Estates of Deceased Persons and Inheritances and on Gifts) (Netherlands) Order 1996, SI 1996/730 .... 12.21
Double Taxation Relief (Taxes on Estates of Deceased Persons and Inheritances and on Gifts) (Sweden) Order 1981, SI 1981/840 .... 12.21
Double Taxation Relief (Taxes on Estates of Deceased Persons and Inheritances and on Gifts) (Sweden) Order 1989 1989/986. .... 12.21
Double Taxation Relief (Taxes on Estates of Deceased Persons and Inheritances) (Switzerland) Order 1994, SI 1994/3214 .... 12.21
Double Taxation Relief (USA) Order 1979, SI 1979/1454 .... 12.21

E

Enactment of Extra-Statutory Concessions Order 2009, SI 2009/730
- art 13 .... 11.37
- 14 .... 1.13

Extra-Statutory Concessions
- ESC F1 .... 5.16
- F7 .... 11.37
- F12 .... 11.12
- F17 .... 13.45
- F19 .... 1.13, 11.27
- F20 .... 1.13, 10.5, 11.28

F

Family Provision (Intestate Succession) Order 2009, SI 2009/135 .... 5.1
Finance Act 2008, Schedule 40 (Appointed Day, Transitional Provisions and Consequential Amendments) Order 2009, SI 2009/571 .... 3.18, 8.38
Finance Act 2009, Section 96 and Schedule 48 (Appointed Day, Savings and Consequential Amendments) Order 2009, SI 2009/3054 .... 8.3
Finance Act 2010, Schedule 6, Part 2 (Commencement) Order 2012, SI 2012/736 .... 1.20

Finance Act 2012, Schedule 38 (Tax Agents: Dishonest Conduct) (Appointed Day and Savings) Order 2013, SI 2013/279 .... 3.18
Finance Act 2015, Schedule 20 (Appointed Days) Order 2016, SI 2016/456
reg 3(2)(a) 3.17

H

Housing (Northern Ireland) Order 1981, SI 1981/156 (NI 3) 11.21

I

Individual Savings Account (Amendment No 2) Regulations 2015, SI 2015/869 .... 14.4
Inheritance and Trustees' Powers Act 2014 (Commencement) Order 2014, SI 2014/2039 .... 5.1
Inheritance Tax Avoidance Schemes (Prescribed Description of Arrangements) Regulations 2011, SI 2011/170 .... 8.37
Inheritance Tax Avoidance Schemes (Prescribed Descriptions of Arrangements) Regulations 2017, 2017/1172 .... 8.37, 14.34
Inheritance Tax (Delivery of Accounts) (Excepted Estates) (Amendment) Regulations 2006, SI 2006/2141 .... 8.17
Inheritance Tax (Delivery of Accounts) (Excepted Estates) (Amendment) Regulations 2011, SI 2011/214 .... 8.11, 8.17, 8.20, 11.10
Inheritance Tax (Delivery of Accounts) (Excepted Estates) Regulations 2004, SI 2004/2543 .... 8.17, 8.19
reg 4(6) 8.18
Inheritance Tax (Delivery of Accounts) (Excepted Settlements) Regulations 2008, SI 2008/606 .. 8.4, 8.8
reg 4 .... 10.38
Inheritance Tax (Delivery of Accounts) (Excepted Transfers and Excepted Terminations) Regulations 2008, SI 2008/605 .. 8.4, 8.6, 8.7, 8.9
reg 4 .... 4.29
(5) 8.8
5 .... 4.29
Inheritance Tax (Double Charges Relief) Regulations 1987, SI 1987/1130 .... 4.22, 6.31, 7.2, 7.8, 7.38, 12.1, 12.23
reg 5 .... 7.38
(3) 7.8
(a) 7.38
(b) 7.38
(4) 7.39
6 .... 5.11
(a), (b) 5.11
9 .... 5.11, 7.39
Schedule 5.11
Inheritance Tax (Double Charges Relief) Regulations 2005, SI 2005/3441 .... 7.39, 12.1, 17.28
reg 3 .... 16.11

M

Market Value of Shares, Securities and Strips Regulations 2015, SI 2015/616
reg 2 .... 6.16
3 .... 6.16

O

Offshore Asset Moves Penalty (Specified Territories) Regulations 2015, SI 2015/866 .... 8.41

R

Revenue and Customs Briefs
Brief 71/07 .... 6.8
23/08 .... 6.15
65/08 .... 14.29
21/09 .... 6.15, 14.29
18/11 .... 11.25
26/11 .... 5.5
22/13 .... 6.15

S

Special Commissioners (Jurisdiction and Procedure) Regulations 1994, SI 1994/1811
reg 21 .... 8.65
Statements of Practice
SP 10/79 .... 9.5, 9.6, 15.29, 16.34, 16.40, 16.42
12/80 .... 13.50
8/86 .... 10.37, 8.57
7/87 .... 5.16
E4 .... 4.5, 6.14
E7 .... 10.6
E13 .... 11.18

T

Taxation of Equitable Life (Payments) Order 2011, SI 2011/1502
art 5(1)(a) 5.5
Taxes (Definition of Charity) (Relevant Territories) Regulations 2010, SI 2010/1904 .... 1.20
Taxes (Definition of Charity) (Relevant Territories) (Amendment) Regulations 2014, SI 2014/1807 1.20
Tribunal Procedure (First-tier Tribunal) (Tax Chamber) Rules 2009, SI 2009/273 .... 8.65
r 10 .... 8.65

Table of cases

[All references are to paragraph number]

A

ACC Green v HMRC [2015] UKFTT 0236, TC 13.1, 13.15
Abacus Trust Co (Isle of Man) Ltd v NSPCC; sub nom Abacus Trust Co (Isle of Man) Ltd v National Society for the Prevention of Cruelty to Children [2001] STC 1344, [2002] BTC 178, [2001] WTLR 953, (2000-01) 3 ITELR 846, [2001] STI 1225, (2001) 98(35) LSG 37, Ch D 14.10
Allnutt v Wilding; sub nom Strain (Deceased), Re; Allnutt v Allnutt [2007] EWCA Civ 412, [2007] BTC 8003, [2007] WTLR 941, (2006-07) 9 ITELR 806, CA 14.10
Antrobus (No 2), Re [2005] Lands Tribunal DET/47/2004 ..... 8.56, 13.25, 13.34, 13.47
Antrobus, Re. See Lloyds TSB v IRC.
Application to Vary the Undertakings of A, Re; Application to vary the undertakings of B, Re [2005] STC (SCD) 103, [2005] WTLR 1, [2004] STI 2502, (2004) 148 SJLB 1432, Sp Comm 12.30
Arkwright (Williams Personal Representative) v IC; sub nom IRC v Arkwright [2004] EWHC 1720 (Ch), [2005] 1 WLR 1411, [2004] STC 1323, [2005] RVR 266, 76 TC 788, [2004] BTC 8082, [2004] WTLR 855, [2004] STI 1724, (2004) 101(31) LSG 26, Ch D 6.8
Arnander (Executors of McKenna Deceased) v HMRC [2006] STC (SCD) 800, [2007] WTLR 51, [2006] STI 2460 ..... 13.27, 13.28, 13.33
Association Belge des Consommateurs Test-Achats ASBL v Conseil des Ministres (C-236/09) [2012] 1 WLR 1933, [2012] All ER (EC) 441, [2011] 2 CMLR 38, [2011] CEC 1107, [2011] Eq LR 409, [2011] Lloyd's Rep IR 296, [2011] Pens LR 145, (2011) 161 NLJ 363, ECJ 6.15
Atkinson (Inspector of Taxes) v Dancer; Mannion (Inspector of Taxes) v Johnston [1988] STC 758, 61 TC 598, [1988] BTC 364, (1988) 85(17) LSG 50, Ch D 13.7
Atkinson v HMRC; sub nom HMRC v Atkinson [2011] UKUT 506 (TCC), [2012] STC 289, [2011] BTC 1917, [2012] WTLR 197, [2012] STI 277, UT 13.7

B

Baird's Executors v IRC [1991] 1 EGLR 201, 1991 SLT (Lands Tr) 9, Lands Tr (Scot) . 13.43
Barclays Bank Trust Co v IRC [1998] STC (SCD) 125 ..... 13.23
Barclays Wealth Trustees (Jersey) Ltd and another v HMRC [2017] EWCA Civ 1512 ..... 1.14, 11.30
Barlow Clowes International Ltd (in liquidation) and others v Henwood. See Henwood v Barlow Clowes International Ltd (In Liquidation)
Barnes v Phillips [2015] EWCA Civ 1056 ..... 6.5
Barty-King v Ministry of Defence [1979] 2 All ER 80, [1979] STC 218, QBD 11.26
Beckman v IRC [2000] STC (SCD) 59, [2003] WTLR 773, [2000] STI 162, Sp Comm. 13.2
Bedford (Duke) (Deceased), Re; sub nom Russell v Bedford [1960] 1 WLR 1331, [1960] 3 All ER 756, (1960) 39 ATC 340, [1960] TR 327, (1960) 104 SJ 1058, Ch D 15.37
Benham's Will Trusts, Re; sub nom Lockhart v Harker [1995] STC 210, [1995] STI 186, Ch D 5.40, 5.42, 8.1, 15.29
Bennett v IRC [1995] STC 54, [1995] STI 13, Ch D 8.13, 11.9, 14.1
Best v HMRC [2014] UKFTT 77 (TC), [2014] WTLR 409, TCt 13.1, 13.11, 13.15
Bhatt v Bhatt and [2009] EWHC 734, [2009] All ER (D) 58 (Apr) 15.4
Blackwell v Blackwell; sub nom Blackwell, Re [1929] AC 318, 67 ALR 336, HL 9.5
Blades v Isaac [2016] EWHC 601 (Ch), [2016] WTLR 589, Ch D 10.3

Bower v HMRC; sub nom HMRC v Bower; Bower (Deceased), Re [2008] EWHC 3105 (Ch), [2009] STC 510, [2009] STI 188, Ch D 6.15, 14.29
Bowring v HMRC [2015] UKUT 550 ..... 9.33
Brander (Representative of Earl of Balfour deceased) v HMRC [2010] UKUT 300 (TCC), [2010] STC 2666, 80 TC 163, [2010] BTC 1656, [2010] WTLR 1545, [2010] STI 2427, UT 13.12
Brown's Executors v IRC [1996] STC (SCD) 277, Sp Comm 13.2, 13.6
Buccleuch v IRC. See Duke of Buccleuch v IRC
Bull v Bull [1955] 1 QB 234, [1955] 2 WLR 78, [1955] 1 All ER 253, (1955) 99 SJ 60, CA 16.37
Bullard v Bullard and Anther [2017] EWHC 3 ..... 12.13, 14.10
Burden v United Kingdom (13378/05) [2008] STC 1305, [2008] 2 FLR 787, [2008] 2 FCR 244, (2008) 47 EHRR 38, 24 BHRC 709, [2008] BTC 8099, 10 ITL Rep 772, [2008] WTLR 1129, [2008] Fam Law 628, [2008] 18 EG 126 (CS), (2008) 158 NLJ 672, ECHR 3.3, 11.17, 16.29
Burkinyoung v IRC [1995] STC (SCD) 29, Sp Comm 13.11
Buzzoni and Others v HMRC [2013] EWCA Civ 1684, [2014] BTC 1, [2014] WTLR 421, CA 7.5, 7.14, 16.7

C

CVC/Opportunity Equity Partners Ltd v Demarco Almeida [2002] UKPC 16, [2002] BCC 684, [2002] 2 BCLC 108, PC (CI) 13.20
Cairns v HMRC; sub nom HMRC v Cairns [2009] UKFTT 67 (TC), [2009] STC (SCD) 479, [2009] WTLR 793, [2009] STI 1801, Sp Comm 6.2, 8.3, 8.15
Cancer Research Campaign v Ernest Brown & Co [1997] STC 1425, [1998] PNLR 592, Ch D 15.30, 15.31, 15.32
Caton's Administrators v Couch. *See* Couch (Inspector of Taxes) v Administrators of the Estate of Caton
Chadda & Ors v Revenue & Customs [2014] UKFTT 1061 (TC) 16.13
Chadwick v HMRC; sub nom. The Smokery House, Mill Lane, Broom, Alcester, Warwickshire B50 4HR [2010] UKUT 82 (LC), [2010] RVR 300, [2010] WTLR 961, UT 6.2
Charkham (Deceased) v IRC [2000] RVR 7, Lands Tr 6.24
Chick v Stamp Duties Commissioner [1958] AC 435, [1958] 3 WLR 93, [1958] 2 All ER 623, (1958) 37 ATC 250, (1958) 102 SJ 488, PC (Aust) 7.29
Clark v HMRC [2005] STC (SCD) 823, [2005] WTLR 1465, [2005] STI 1758n Comm 13.1
Cleaver (Deceased), Re; sub nom Cleaver v Insley [1981] 1 WLR 939, [1981] 2 All ER 1018, (1981) 125 SJ 445, Ch D 9.5
Clore (Deceased) (No 2), Re; sub nom Official Solicitor v Clore [1984] STC 609, Ch D 2.4
Cole (A Bankrupt), Re; sub nom ex p Trustee v Cole [1964] Ch 175, [1963] 3 WLR 621 [1963] 3 All ER 433, (1963) 107 SJ 664, CA 7.4
Corbally-Stourton v HMRC [2008] STC (SCD) 907, Sp Comm 8.3
Couch (Inspector of Taxes) v Administrators of the Estate of Caton; sub nom: Administrators of the Estate of Caton v Couch (Inspector of Taxes); Caton's Administrators v Couch (Inspector of Taxes) [1997] STC 970, 70 TC 10, [1997] BTC 360, (1997) 94(30) LSG 29, CA (Civ Div); affirming [1996] STC 201, Ch D; reversing [1995] STC (SCD) 34, Sp Comm 13.19
Courthope, Re (1928) 7 ATC 538 ..... 13.20
Curnock v IRC [2003] STC (SCD) 283, [2003] WTLR 955, [2003] STI 1052, Sp Comm 14.8
Customs and Excise Comrs v Lord Fisher; sub nom Lord Fisher DSC v Customs and Excise Comrs [1981] 2 All ER 147, [1981] STC 238, QBD 13.14
Cyganik v Agulian; sub nom Agulian v Cyganik [2006] EWCA Civ 129, [2006] 1 FCR 406, [2006] WTLR 565, (2005-06) 8 ITELR 762, CA 2.4

D

Daniel v HMRC [2014] UKFTT 173 (TC) 9.34

Davies v HMRC [2009] UKFTT 138 (TC), [2009] WTLR 1151, [2009] STI 2095, FTT (Tax) 9.5
Denekamp v Pearce (Inspector of Taxes) [1998] STC 1120, 71 TC 213, [1998] BTC 413, Ch D 13.20
Dixon v IRC [2002] STC (SCD) 53, [2002] WTLR 175, [2002] STI 43, Sp Comm 13.29
Duke of Buccleuch v IRC; sub nom Duke Devonshire's Trustees v IRC [1967] 1 AC 506, [1967] 2 WLR 207, [1967] 1 All ER 129, [1967] RVR 25, [1967] RVR 42, (1966) 45 ATC 472, [1966] TR 393, (1967) 111 SJ 18, HL 6.5, 13.42

E

Ellesmere (Earl) v IRC [1918] 2 KB 735, KBD 13.42
Executors of D Golding Deceased v HMRC [2011] UKFTT 352 (TC) 13.1, 13.25, 13.35
Executors of Marquess of Hertford v IRC. *See* Ninth Marquess of Hertford (executors of Eighth Marquess of Hertford) v IRC
Executors of Mrs Mary Dugan-Chapman v HMRC (2008) SpC 666 ..... 13.9
Executors of Patch deceased [2007] SpC 600 ..... 9.1, 7.11, 15.51

F

Farmer v IRC [1999] STC (SCD) 321, Sp Comm 13.12
Faulkner v IRC [2001] STC (SCD) 112, [2001] WTLR 1295, [2001] STI 943, Sp Comm 9.5, 16.45
Fetherstonaugh (formerly Finch) v IRC; sub nom Finch v IRC [1985] Ch 1, [1984] 3 WLR 212, [1984] STC 261, (1984) 81 LSG 1443, (1984) 128 SJ 302, CA 13.6
Foote Estate, Re, 2009 ABQB 654 ..... 2.4
Frankland v IRC [1997] STC 1450, [1997] BTC 8045, CA 3.28, 9.9, 10.26, 15.50
Freedman v Freedman [2015] EWHC 1457 (Ch), [2015] WTLR 1187, [2015] STI 1735, [2015] 2 P & CR DG19, Ch D 12.13
Fryer v HMRC [2010] UKFTT 87 (TC), FTT (Tax) 9.40
Fuld (Deceased) (No 3), In the Estate of [1968] P 675, [1966] 2 WLR 717, [1965] 3 All ER 776, (1966) 110 SJ 133 ..... 2.4
Furness v IRC [1999] STC (SCD) 232, Sp Comm 13.11
Furse (Deceased), Re [1980] 3 All ER 838, [1980] STC 596, [1980] TR 275, Ch D 2.4
Futter v Futter; Futter (No) Life Interest Settlement, Re [2010] EWHC 449 (Ch), [2010] Pens LR 145, [2010] WTLR 609, [2010] STI 1442, Ch D 14.10

G

Gartside v Inland Revenue Comrs; sub nom Gartside's Will Trusts, Re [1968] AC 553, [1968] 2 WLR 277, [1968] 1 All ER 121, (1967) 46 ATC 323, [1967] TR 309, (1967) 111 SJ 982, HL 9.5
Gilbert (t/a United Foods) v HMRC [2011] UKFTT 705, TC 13.7
Gray v IRC; sub nom Executors of Lady Fox v IRC; Lady Fox's Executors v IRC [1994] STC 360, [1994] 38 EG 156, [1994] RVR 129, [1994] STI 208, [1994] EG 32 (CS), [1994] NPC 15, CA 6.5, 13.42, 13.44
Gulliver v HMRC [2017] UKFTT 222, TC 2.4, 9.34

H

HMRC v Atkinson [2011] UKUT B26 (TCC) 13.30, 13.38
HMRC v Bower. *See* Bower v HMRC
HMRC v Khawaja [2008] EWHC 1687 (Ch), [2009] 1 WLR 398, [2009] Bus LR 134, [2008] STC 2880, [2008] STI 1748, (2008) 158 NLJ 1076, Ch D 8.3
Hall (Hall's Executors) v IRC [1997] STC (SCD) 126 ..... 13.11
Halsall v Champion Consulting Ltd [2017] EWHC 1079 (QB); [2017] B.T.C. 19 QBD. 16.5
Hanson v HMRC [2012] UKFTT 95 (TC), [2012] SFTD 705, [2012] WTLR 597, [2012] STI 1388, TC 13.28, 13.38
Hardcastle v IRC [2000] STC (SCD) 532, [2001] WTLR 91, [2000] STI 1520, Sp Comm 13.2
Harding (executors of Loveday) v IRC [1997] STC (SCD) 321 ..... 15.49

Harrold v IRC [1996] STC (SCD) 195, [1996] EG 70 (CS), Sp Comm 13.30, 13.38
Hastings-Bass (Deceased), Re; sub nom Hastings-Bass Trustees v IRC [1975] Ch 25, [1974] 2 WLR 904, [1974] 2 All ER 193, [1974] STC 211, [1974] TR 87, (1974) 118 SJ 422, CA 12.13, 14.10
Hatton v HMRC [2010] UKUT 195 (LC), [2011] RVR 63, UT 6.2
Hawkings-Byass v Sassen (Inspector of Taxes) [1996] STC (SCD) 319, Sp Comm 13.20
Henwood v Barlow Clowes International Ltd (In Liquidation) [2008] EWCA Civ 577, [2008] BPIR 778, [2008] NPC 61, CA 2.3
Hertford (Marquess), Executors of v IRC [2004] SpC 00444 .... 13.23
Higginson's Executors v IRC [2002] STC (SCD) 483 .... 13.32, 13.46, 15.23
Holland v IRC [2003] STC (SCD) 43, [2003] WTLR 207, [2003] STI 62, (2003) 147 SJLB 267, Sp Comm 3.3, 11.17
Holliday v Musa [2010] EWCA Civ 335, [2010] 2 FLR 702, [2010] 3 FCR 280, [2010] WTLR 839, [2010] Fam Law 702, CA 2.4
Holmes v McMullan; sub nom Ratcliffe (Deceased), Re [1999] STC 262, [1999] BTC 8017, (1999) 96(11) LSG 70, Ch D 5.40, 5.41, 8.1
Hood v HMRC [2016] UKFTT 59 (TC) 7.5, 7.13, 16.7
Hood v HMRC [2017] UKUT 276 (TCC), [2017] STI 1773 .... 7.5, 7.13, 16.7
Howarth's Executors v IRC [1997] STC (SCD) 162 .... 8.32
Hurlingham Estates Ltd v Wilde & Partners [1997] 1 Lloyd's Rep 525, [1997] STC 627, [1997] BTC 240, (1997) 147 NLJ 453, Ch D 16.4
Hutchings v HMRC [2015] UKFTT 9 (TC), [2015] WTLR 1359, [2015] STI 1260 .... 8.40

I

IRC v Bullock [1976] 1 WLR 1178, [1976] 3 All ER 353, [1976] STC 409, 51 TC 522, [1975] TR 179, (1976) 120 SJ.591, CA 2.4
IRC v Crossman [1937] AC 26, [1936] 1 All ER 762, 15 ATC 94, 105 LJKB 450, 80 Sol Jo 485, 154 LT 570, 52 TLR 415, HL 13.18
IRC v Eversden; sub nom IRC v Greenstock's Executors; Essex (Somerset's Executors) v IRC [2003] EWCA Civ 668, [2003] STC 822, 75 TC 340, [2003] BTC 8028, [2003] WTLR 893, [2003] STI 989, (2003) 100(27) LSG 38, (2003) 147 SJLB 594, CA; affirming [2002] EWHC 1360 (Ch), [2002] STC 1109, [2002] BTC 8035, [2002] WTLR 1013, [2002] STI 1008, (2002) 99(36) LSG 40, [2002] NPC 96, Ch D 7.9, 7.26. 9.6, 16.9, 17.1
IRC v George; sub nom Stedman's Executors v IRC; George v IRC [2003] EWCA Civ 1763, [2004] STC 147, 75 TC 735, [2004] BTC 8003, [2004] WTLR 75, [2003] STI 2276, (2004) 101(3) LSG 34, CA 13.11, 13.14, 13.15
IRC v Lloyds Private Banking Ltd [1998] STC 559, [1999] 1 FLR 147, [1998] 2 FCR 41, [1998] BTC 8020, [1999] Fam Law 309, (1998) 95(19) LSG 23, (1998) 142 SJLB 164, Ch D 9.2, 16.26, 16.45
IRC v Mallender. *See* Mallender v IRC
Ingram v IRC [1998] UKHL 47, [2001] AC 293, [1999] 1 All ER 297, [1999] 2 WLR 90, (1999) STC 37, HL 7.11, 7.12, 16.8, 17.1

J

J v U; U v J (No 2) (Domicile) [2017] EWHC 449 (Fam) 2.2
Jones v IRC [1997] STC 358, [1997] BTC 8003, [1997] EG 21 (CS), [1997] NPC 26, Ch D 12.17
John Carlisle Allen (TC5100) 13.25
Jones v Kernott [2011] UKSC 53, [2012] 1 AC 776, [2011] 3 WLR 1121, [2012] 1 All ER 1265, [2012] 1 FLR 45, [2011] 3 FCR 495, [2011] BPIR 1653, [2012] HLR 14, [2012] WTLR 125, 14 ITELR 491, [2011] Fam Law 1338, [2011] 46 EG 104 (CS), (2011) 155(43) SJLB 35, [2011] NPC 116, [2012] 1 P & CR DG9, SC 6.5
Judge (Walden's Personal Representative) v HMRC [2005] STC (SCD) 863, [2005] WTLR 1311, (2006-07) 9 ITELR 21, [2005] STI 1800, Sp Comm 9.3, 9.4, 9.6, 9.9, 15.29, 16.34, 16.35, 16.36, 16.40, 16.46

Jump v Listor [2016] EWHC 2160 .... 5.8

K

Kernott v Jones. *See* Jones v Kernott
Kennedy v Kennedy [2014] EWCA 4129, Ch 14.10

L

Lau v HMRC [2009] SpC 740 .... 15.45
Lillingston (Deceased), Re; Sub Nom Pembery v Pembery [1952] 2 All ER 184, [1952] 1 TLR 1622, [1952] WN 338, (1952) 96 SJ 462. Ch D 7.4
Lidher v Revenue and Customs [2017] UKFTT 153 (TC) 6.21
Lloyds TSB Bank Plc (Personal Representative of Antrobus (Deceased)) v IRC [2002] STC (SCD) 468, [2002] WTLR 1435, [2002] STI 1398, (2002) 146 SJLB 249m Sp Comm 249 .... 13.33, 13.47, 15.23
Lloyds TSB Private Banking Plc (Personal Representative of Antrobus (Deceased)) v Twiddy [2006] 1 EGLR 157, [2006] RVR 138, [2005] WTLR 1535, Lands Tr 6.55, 13.46,13.47
Loring v Woodland Trust [2014] EWCA Civ 1314 .... 3.40
Loring v Woodland Trust [2013] EWHC 4400 (Ch), [2014] 2 All ER 836, [2014] BTC 26, [2014] WTLR 593, Ch D 3.40, 15.5
Lyon's Personal Representatives v HMRC [2007] STC (SCD) 675, [2007] WTLR 1257, [2007] STI 1816, Sp Comm 7.18

M

Mallender v IRC; sub nom IRC v Mallender [2001] STC 514, [2001] BTC 8013, [2001] WTLR 459, [2001] STI 548, [2001] NPC 62, Ch D 13.2
Mannion (Inspector of Taxes) v Johnston. *See* Atkinson (Inspector of Taxes) v Dancer
Marjorie Ross (dec'd) v HMRC [2017] UKFTT 507, TC 13.1, 13.15
Marquess of Linlithgow v HMRC [2010] CSIH 19, [2010] STI 1278, 2010 GWD 11-206, IH (Ex Div) 8.4,14.8
Marr v Collie [2017] UKPC 17, [2017] 3 WLR 1507, [2017] 2 FLR 674, [2018] 1 P & CR 5, 20 ITELR 602, PC (Bah) 6.5
Martin v IRC [1995] STC (SCD) 5, Sp Comm 13.11
Matthews v HMRC [2012] UKFTT 658 (TC), [2013] WTLR 93, [2013] STI 299, TC 6.21, 7.26, 14.10
Maureen Vigne (dec'd) v HMRC [2017] UKFTT 13.14
McArthur's Executors v HMRC; sub nom McArthur (Deceased), Re [2008] STC (SCD) 1100, [2008] WTLR 1185, Sp Comm 13.18
McCall v RCC [2009] NICA 12, [2008] STC (SCD) 752, [2008] WTLR 865, [2008] STI 1256, Sp Comm 8.56, 13.1, 13.14, 13.15, 13.25, 13.28
McDowall's Executors v IRC [2004] STC (SCD) 22, [2004] WTLR 221, [2004] STI 146, Sp Comm 11.10
McGregor (Inspector of Taxes) v Adcock [1977] 1 WLR 864, [1977] 3 All ER 65, [1977] STC 206, (1977) 242 EG 289, 51 TC 692, [1977] TR 23, Ch D 13.7
McKelvey v HMRC; sub nom McKelvey Deceased), Re [2008] STC (SCD) 944, [2008] WTLR 1407, [2008] STI 1752, (2008) SPC 694, Sp Comm 4.4, 11.12, 16.18
Mehjoo v Harben Barker (A Firm) [2014] EWCA Civ 358, [2014] STC 1470, [2014] BTC 17, [2014] STI 1627, CA 16.9
Melville v IRC [2001] EWCA Civ 1247, [2002] 1 WLR 407, [2001] STC 1271, 74 TC 372, [2001] BTC 8039, [2001] WTLR 887, (2001-02) 4 ITELR 231, [2001] STI 1106, (2001) 98(37) LSG 39, [2001] NPC 132, CA 8.23
Mettoy Pension Trustees Ltd v Evans [1990] 1 WLR 1587, [1991] 2 All ER 513, Ch D. 12.13

N

Nadin v IRC [1997] STC (SCD) 107 .... 8.12

Nelson Dance Family Settlement Trustees v HMRC; sub nom HMRC v Nelson Dance Family Settlement Trustees [2009] EWHC 71 (Ch), [2009] BTC 8003, [2009] STI 260, [2009] NPC 11, Ch D 13.1, 11.2, 13.7, 13.14, 13.24
Ninth Marquess of Hertford (executors of Eighth Marquess of Hertford) v IRC [2005] STC (SCD) 177, [2005] WTLR 85, [2004] STI 2546, Sp Comm 13.20

O

Oakes v Commissioner of Stamp Duties of New South Wales [1954] AC 57, [1953] 3 WLR 1127, [1953] 2 All ER 1563, 47 R & IT 141, (1953) 32 ATC 476, [1953] TR 453, (1953) 97 SJ 874, PC (Aus) 7.21
Ogden v Trustees of the RHS Griffiths 2003 Settlement [2008] EWHC 118 (Ch), [2009] 2 WLR 394, [2008] 2 All ER 655, [2008] STC 776, [2009] BTC 8027, [2008] WTLR 685, [2008] STI 250, Ch D 12.13, 12.8
O'Kelly v Davies [2014] EWCA Civ 1606 .... 4.6
O'Neill & O'Neill's Executors v CIR, SpC [1998] SSCD 110 .... 6.21
Oxley v Hiscock; sub nom Hiscock v Oxley [2004] EWCA Civ 546, [2005] Fam 211, [2004] 3 WLR 715, [2004] 3 All ER 703, [2004] 2 FLR 669, [2004] 2 FCR 295, [2004] WTLR 709, (2003-04) 6 ITELR 1091, [2004] Fam Law 569, [2004] 20 EG 166 (CS), (2004) 101(21) LSG 35, (2004) 148 SJLB 571, [2004] NPC 70, [2004] 2 P & CR DG14, CA 6.5

P

Palliser v HMRC [2018] UKUT 71, LC 6.27
Pankhania v Chandegra [2012] EWCA Civ 1438, [2013] 1 P & CR 16, [2013] WTLR 101, [2012] 47 EG 127 (CS), [2013] 1 P & CR DG5, CA 6.5
Pawson (Deceased) v HMRC [2012] UKFTT 51 (TC), [2012] WTLR 665, TC 13.1, 13.11, 13.14, 13.15
Pearson v IRC; sub nom Pilkington Trustees v IRC [1981] AC 753, [1980] 2 WLR 872, [1980] 2 All ER 479, [1980] STC 318, [1980] TR 177, (1980) 124 SJ 377, HL 9.5
Pepper (Inspector of Taxes) v Daffurn [1993] STC 466, [1993] 41 EG 184, 66 TC 68, [1993] EG 122 (CS), (1993) 90(32) LSG 40, Ch D 13.7
Phillips v Burrows (Inspector of Taxes) (Set Aside) [2000] STC (SCD) 112, [2000] STI 168, Sp Comm 8.65
Phillips v HMRC [2006] STC (SCD) 639, [2006] WTLR 1281, [2006] STI 2094, Sp Comm 13.13
Phizackerley v HMRC [2007] STC (SCD) 328, [2007] WTLR 745, [2007] STI 559, (2007) SpC 591, Sp Comm 3.30, 4.4, 5.10, 14. 29, 15.4, 15.5, 15.6, 15.7 16.49
Phoenix Office Supplies Ltd v Larvin; Phoenix Office Supplies Ltd, Re [2002] EWCA Civ 1740, [2003] BCC 11, [2003] 1 BCLC 76, (2003) 100(5) LSG 29, CA 13.20
Pitt v Holt; Futter v Futter [2013] UKSC 26, [2013] 2 WLR 1200, [2013] STC 1148, [2013] Pens LR 195, [2013] BTC 126, 15 ITELR 976, [2013] STI 1805, SC............... 12.13, 14.10
Powell v IRC [1997] STC (SCD) 181 .... 13.11
Price v HMRC; sub nom Price (Deceased), Re [2010] UKFTT 474 (TC), [2011] SFTD 52, [2011] WTLR 161, [2011] STI 310, FTT (Tax)........................... 6.8, 6.24
Prosser v IRC DET/1/2000 .... 6.27, 8.22, 8.40, 6.41

R

R v IRC, ex p Bishopp; sub nom IRC v Pricewaterhouse Coopers; IRC v Ernst & Young; R v IRC, ex p Allan [1999] STC 531, (1999) 11 Admin LR 575, 72 TC 322, [1999] BTC 158, [1999] COD 354, (1999) 149 NLJ 682, [1999] NPC 50, QBD.... 13.3
R (on the application of Davies) v HMRC [2011] UKSC 47, [2011] 1 WLR 2625, [2012] 1 All ER 1048, [2011] STC 2249, [2011] BTC 610, [2012] WTLR 215, [2011] STI 2847, (2011) 155(40) SJLB 31, [2011] NPC 107, SC 9.34
RBC Trustees and Others v Stubbs & Others [2017] EWHC 180.............................. 12.13, 14.10

RSPCA v Sharp [2010] EWCA Civ 1474, [2011] 1 WLR 980, [2011] PTSR 942, [2011] STC 553, [2011] WTLR 311, 13 ITELR 701, [2011] STI 253, (2011) 155(1) SJLB 30, CA; reversing [2010] EWHC 268 (Ch), [2010] STC 975, [2010] WTLR 855, [2010] STI 1519, (2010) 154(9) SJLB 30, Ch D 3.38, 5.42, 15.30
Ramsay (W T) Ltd v IRC [1982] AC 300, [1981] 1 All ER 865, [1981] 2 WLR 449, 125 Sol Jo 220, [1981] STC 174, 54 TC 101, [1982] TR 123, HL........ 16.10
Ratcliffe, Re, Holmes v McMullan. *See* Holmes v McMullan; sub nom Ratcliffe (Deceased), Re
Robertson v IRC (No 1) [2002] STC (SCD) 182, [2002] WTLR 885, [2002] STI 766, Sp Comm........ 8.15, 8.40
Robertson v IRC (No 2) [2002] STC (SCD) 242, [2002] WTLR 907, [2002] STI 899, Sp Comm........ 8.15, 8.40, 8.65
Rose (Deceased), Re; sub nom Rose v IRC [1952] Ch 499, [1952] 1 All ER 1217, [1952] 1 TLR 1577, (1952) 31 ATC 138, [1952] TR 175, CA........ 14.8
Rosser v IRC [2003] STC (SCD) 311, [2003] WTLR 1057, [2003] STI 1152, Sp Comm........ 13.30, 13.34, 14.9
Routier & Anor v Revenue & Customs [2017] EWCA Civ 1584........ 1.20, 11.19
Royal Society for the Prevention of Cruelty to Animals v Sharp [2010] EWHC 268 (Ch), Ch D, [2010] STC 975, [2010] WTLR 855........ 13.29
Russell v IRC [1988] 1 WLR 834, [1988] 2 All ER 405, [1988] STC 195, (1988) 132 SJ 659, Ch D........ 15.43, 13.46
Rysaffe Trustee Co (CI) Ltd v IRC; sub nom Rysaffe Trustee Co (CI) Ltd v HMRC; HMRC v Rysaffe Trustee Co (CI) Ltd [2003] EWCA Civ 356, [2003] STC 536, [2003] BTC 8021, [2003] WTLR 481, (2002-03) 5 ITELR 706, [2003] STI 452, (2003) 100(22) LSG 31, (2003) 147 SJLB 388, [2003] NPC 39, CA........ 4.25, 7.17, 10.47, 10.62, 10.61

S

St Barbe Green v IRC; sub nom Green v IRC [2005] EWHC 14 (Ch), [2005] 1 WLR 1772, [2005] STC 288, [2005] BPIR 1218, [2005] BTC 8003, [2005] WTLR 75, [2005] STI 106, (2005) 102(7) LSG 26, [2005] NPC 6, Ch D... 5.9
Salinger and Kirby v HMRC [2016] UKFTT 677........ 11.39
Sansom v Peay (Inspector of Taxes) [1976] 1 WLR 1073, [1976] 3 All ER 375, [1976] STC 494, 52 TC 1, [1976] TR 205, (1976) 120 SJ 571, Ch D......1 6.41
Scott, Re, Scott v Scott [1916] 2 Ch 268, 85 LJ Ch 528, 60 Sol Jo 478, 114 LT 1114..... 15.37
Scott v HMRC [2015] UKFTT 266 (TC), [2015] WTLR 1461, [2015] STI 2635........ 7.4
Sieff v Fox; sub nom Bedford Estates, Re [2005] EWHC 1312 (Ch), [2005] 1 WLR 3811, [2005] 3 All ER 693, [2005] BTC 452, [2005] WTLR 891, (2005-06) 8 ITELR 93, [2005] NPC 80, Ch D........ 12.13, 14.10
Sillars v IRC [2004] STC (SCD) 180, [2004] WTLR 591, [2004] STI 900, (2004) 148 SJLB 536, [2004] SSCD 180, Sp Comm........ 6.21, 14.10
Smallwood v HMRC; sub nom Trevor Smallwood Trust, Re; HMRC v Smallwood [2010] EWCA Civ 778, [2010] STC 2045, [2010] BTC 637, 12 ITL Rep 1002, [2010] WTLR 1771, [2010] STI 2174, (2010) 154(27) SJLB 30, CA; reversing [2009] EWHC 777 (Ch), [2009] STC 1222, [2009] BTC 135, 11 ITL Rep 943, [2009] WTLR 669, [2009] STI 1092, (2009) 106(17) LSG 15 .... 9.34
Smith v HMRC [2007] EWHC 2304 (Ch), [2008] STC 1649, 78 TC 819, [2007] BTC 8010, [2008] WTLR 147, [2007] STI 2560, (2007) 157 NLJ 1506, Ch D........ 4.5, 6.14, 9.30, 14.22, 14.24, 14.3029
Smith v HMRC [2008] SpC 680........ 8.3
Smith v HMRC [2009] SpC 742........ 5.23, 9.5
Snowden (Deceased), Re [1979] Ch 528, [1979] 2 WLR 654, [1979] 2 All ER 172, (1979) 123 SJ 323, Ch D........ 9.5
Sokoya v HMRC [2008] EWHC 2132 (Ch), [2008] STC 3332, [2008] BTC 635, [2008] STI 1641, Ch D........ 8.3

Stack v Dowden; sub nom Dowden v Stack [2007] UKHL 17, [2007] 2 AC 432, [2007] 2 WLR 831, [2007] 2 All ER 929, [2007] 1 FLR 1858, [2007] 2 FCR 280, [2007] BPIR 913, [2008] 2 P & CR 4, [2007] WTLR 1053, (2006-07) 9 ITELR 815, [2007] Fam Law 593, [2007] 18 EG 153 (CS), (2007) 157 NLJ 634, (2007) 151 SJLB 575, [2007] NPC 47, [2007] 2 P & CR DG11, HL ... 6.5
Starke (Brown's Executors) v IRC [1996] 1 All ER 622, [1995] 1 WLR 1439, 139 Sol Jo LB 128, [1995] STC 689, [1996] 1 EGLR 157, [1996] 16 EG 115, [1995] 23 LS Gaz R 32, CA ... 13.30
Stedman's Executors v IRC. *See* IRC v George.
Stevenson (Inspector of Taxes) v Wishart [1987] 1 WLR 1204, [1987] 2 All ER 428, [1987] STC 266, [1987] 1 FTLR 69, 59 TC 740, (1987) 84 LSG 1575, (1987) 131 SJ 744, CA ... 8.12
Stoneham, Re; Sub Nom Stoneham v Stoneham [1919] 1 Ch 149, Ch D ... 7.4
Swain Mason v Mills & Reeve; sub nom Mason v Mills & Reeve [2012] EWCA Civ 498, [2012] STI 1511, CA ... 13.50

T

Taylor & Another v RCC [2008] SSCD 1159 (SpC 704) ... 6.21, 8.24
Thomas v Lord Advocate; sub nom Thomas v IRC, 1953 SC 151, 1953 SLT 119, 46 R & IT 484, (1953) 32 ATC 18, [1953] TR 19, IH (2 Div) ... 8.4
Trustees of the Zetland Settlement v HMRC [2013] UKFTT 284 (TC), [2013] WTLR 1065, [2013] STI 2424, TC ... 13.1, 13.11

U

Udny v Udny (1866-69) LR 1 Sc 441, (1869) 7 M (HL) 89, HL ... 2.2

V

Vaughan-Jones v Vaughan-Jones [2015] EWHC 1086 (Ch), [2015] WTLR 1287, [2015] STI 1883, Ch D ... 12.13
Vinton v Fladgate Fielder (A Firm) [2010] EWHC 904 (Ch), Ch D ... 13.9

W

Wade v Baylis [2010] EWCA Civ 257, CA (Civ Div) ... 6.5
Watkins v HMRC [2011] UKFTT 745 (TC), [2012] WTLR 677, [2012] STI 38, TC ... 6.15, 14.3029
Wells (Personal Representative of Glowacki (Deceased)) v HMRC [2008] STC (SCD) 188, [2007] WTLR 1863, [2007] STI 2232, Sp Comm ... 8.65, 15.48
Weston v IRC [2000] STC 1064, [2000] BTC 8041, [2001] WTLR 1217, [2000] STI 1635, (2001) 98(2) LSG 41, [2000] NPC 126, Ch D ... 13.11
White v Jones [1995] 2 AC 207, [1995] 2 WLR 187, [1995] 1 All ER 691, [1995] 3 FCR 51, (1995) 145 NLJ 251, (1995) 139 SJLB 83, [1995] NPC 31, HL ... 15.5
Whitlock v Moree [2017] UKPC 44, 20 ITELR 658, PC (Bah) ... 6.21
Wight v IRC (1982) 264 EG 935, [1984] RVR 163, Lands Tr ... 6.24
Williams v HMRC [2005] STC (SCD) 782, [2005] WTLR 1421, [2005] STI 1682, Spc Comm ... 13.26, 13.36
Williams v Hensman [1861] 70 ER 862 ... 16.13
Winans v Attorney General (No 1) [1904] AC 287, HL ... 2.2
Wolff v Wolff [2004] EWHC 2110 (Ch), [2004] STC 1633, [2009] BTC 8017, [2004] WTLR 1349, [2004] STI 2068, [2004] NPC 135, Ch D ... 15.4
Woodhall v IRC [2000] STC (SCD) 558, [2001] WTLR 475, [2000] STI 1653, Sp Comm ... 9.5, 16.45
Wrottesley, Lord v HMRC [2015] UKUT 637 (TCC) ... 2.2

List of abbreviations

A&M	accumulation and maintenance trust
AIM	alternative investment market
APR	agricultural property relief
APS	additional permitted subscription
ATED	annual tax on enveloped dwellings
BMT	bereaved minor trust
BPR	business property relief
CA	Court of Appeal
CGT	capital gains tax
CIOT	Chartered Institute of Taxation
CLT	capital lifetime transfer
CTT	capital transfer tax
EOT	employee-ownership trust
EPA	enduring power of attorney
FA	Finance Act
FIFO	first in, first out
F(No 2)A 2015	Finance (No 2) Act 2015
FSMA 2000	Financial Services and Markets Act 2000
GAAR	General anti-abuse rule
GWR	gifts with reservation
HMRC	Her Majesty's Revenue and Customs
ICTA 1988	Income and Corporation Taxes Act 1988
IHT	inheritance tax
IHTA 1984	Inheritance Tax Act 1984
IHTM	Inheritance Tax Manual
IPDI	immediate post-death interest
IRA	Inland Revenue Affidavit
IRC	Inland Revenue Commissioners
ITA 2007	Income Tax Act 2007
ITEPA 2003	Income Tax (Earnings and Pensions) Act 2003
ITTOIA 2005	Income Tax (Trading and Other Income) Act 2005
LISA	Lifetime ISA
LPA	lasting power of attorney
LPA 1925	Law of Property Act 1925
MCA 2005	Mental Capacity Act 2005
NNP	non-natural person
PET	potentially exempt transfer
POAT	pre-owned asset tax
QNUP	qualifying non-UK pension scheme
QSR	quick succession relief

Reg	Regulation
RNRB	residence nil rate band
s	section
Sch	Schedule
SDLT	stamp duty land tax
SI	Statutory Instrument
SP	HMRC Statement of Practice
SRT	statutory residence test
SSCBA	Social Security Contributions and Benefits Act 1992
STEP	Society of Trusts and Estates Practitioners
TA 1925	Taxes Act 1925
TCGA 1992	Taxation of Chargeable Gains Act 1992
TLATA 1996	Trusts of Land and Appointment of Trustees Act 1996
TNRB	transferable nil rate band
TSI	transitional serial interest

Chapter 1

Inheritance tax: introduction

SIGNPOSTS

- **Scope** – Inheritance tax (IHT) broadly applies to lifetime chargeable transfers, the value of an individual's death estate, and certain chargeable events relating to settled property. In broad terms, liability to IHT depends on a person's domicile, and on the situs of property (see **1.1**).
- **Who is liable to IHT?** – Domicile is an important factor in the determination of a person's liability to IHT. A person's domicile is a matter of general law. However, 'deemed' and 'elective' domicile in the UK may apply for IHT purposes in certain circumstances, notwithstanding the person's non-UK domicile under general law (see **1.2**).
- **Calculation and rates** – IHT is a cumulative tax (at rates of 20% or 40%), based on lifetime chargeable transfers within the previous seven years, and on the value of an individual's estate on death, subject to the IHT threshold ('nil rate band'). A reduction in the IHT 'death rate' from 40% to 36% may apply in certain circumstances where charitable legacies are involved (see **1.3–1.8**).
- **Transfers of value** – These may be potentially exempt transfers (PETs), or immediately chargeable transfers. However, transfers of certain property ('excluded property') are outside the scope of IHT (see **1.9–1.14**).
- **Non-UK domicile and UK residential property** – UK residential property interests owned directly or indirectly by non-UK domiciliaries are generally not excluded property for IHT purposes, from 6 April 2017. The 'non-excluded overseas property' provisions (introduced in *Finance (No 2) Act 2017*) are aimed at blocking what HMRC has described as 'enveloping' (ie holding property indirectly through offshore structures) (see **1.15–1.19**).
- **Reliefs and exemptions** – Certain transfers of value are exempt. IHT on chargeable transfers may be subject to relief in certain circumstances (eg taper relief, quick succession relief, double tax relief) (see **1.20–1.26**).

- **Close companies** – IHT charges can arise on transfers of value by close companies, and on certain changes in their capital (see **1.27–1.29**).

BACKGROUND

1.1 Inheritance tax (IHT) replaced the previous regime of capital transfer tax (CTT) in *Finance Act 1986*, with effect from 18 March 1986. CTT in turn replaced estate duty, which was originally introduced in *Finance Act 1894* and applied to deaths occurring up to and including 12 March 1975, prior to its abolition in *Finance Act 1975*.

The IHT regime continued the basic framework and administrative provisions of CTT, whilst following the estate duty principle of only charging tax on lifetime gifts made within seven years of the donor's death. The primary IHT legislation is contained in the *Inheritance Tax Act 1984* (*IHTA 1984*), as amended and supplemented by subsequent Finance Acts, etc.

IHT is a tax on chargeable transfers (*IHTA 1984, s 1*). It applies to chargeable transfers made by an individual during lifetime, and to the value of his estate on death, subject to various exemptions, exclusions and reliefs. IHT also applies to certain chargeable events relating to settled property.

This chapter provides a brief introduction to the IHT system, the main principles of which are expanded upon in subsequent chapters.

WHO IS LIABLE?

1.2 Individuals domiciled in the UK are liable to IHT on chargeable worldwide property. Non-UK domiciled individuals are also liable to IHT, but generally on chargeable UK property (*IHTA 1984, s 6(1)*).

However, legislation was introduced (in *Finance (No 2) Act 2017*) in relation to 'non-excluded overseas property' of non-UK domiciliaries broadly to ensure that, from 6 April 2017, the value of interests in UK residential property owned directly or indirectly by non-UK domiciliaries (eg through an interest in a close company or partnership) are not excluded from the scope of IHT (*IHTA 1984, s 6(5), Sch A1*), with a view to blocking what HMRC describes as 'enveloping' (ie holding property indirectly through offshore structures); see **1.15–1.19** below.

A person's domicile status is a matter of private international law. However, in addition to the general law concerning domicile, there are also 'elective domicile' and 'deemed domicile' provisions in the IHT legislation. For commentary on domicile under general law, and for IHT purposes, see **Chapter 2**.

WHAT IS CHARGEABLE TO IHT?

1.3 IHT is a direct tax on transfers of capital (eg lifetime gifts) made on or after 18 March 1986. It is broadly a cumulative tax charge on the following:

- the value transferred by a chargeable transfer made by an individual during his lifetime within the preceding seven-year period (ie broadly the loss to the donor), and on the value of his estate on death. A 'chargeable transfer' is any 'transfer of value' (see below) made by an individual, other than an exempt transfer (*IHTA 1984, s 2(1)*); and
- certain events relating to settlements (eg gifts to a discretionary trust).

The IHT charge on death (and in respect of certain settled property) is brought into charge by deeming a transfer of value to have been made immediately before death, equal to the value of the person's estate (and the value of the settled property, if appropriate) (*IHTA 1984, ss 4(1), 52(1)*). The IHT legislation specifically precludes certain property from charge (see below).

CUMULATION AND THE IHT THRESHOLD

1.4 Chargeable transfers within the seven-year period ending with the date of the latest chargeable transfer are cumulated, for the purposes of determining the IHT rate (*IHTA 1984, s 7*). Where chargeable lifetime transfers and the individual's death estate do not exceed the IHT threshold (or 'nil rate band', as it is more commonly known) there is no IHT liability.

The nil rate band can normally be expected to increase annually by reference to an indexation factor. The increase in the indexation factor in September in each year is applied to the rates of chargeable transfers made on or after 6 April in the following year (*IHTA 1984, s 8*). However, Parliament may determine the nil rate band otherwise than by reference to the indexation factor, and in some previous Finance Acts have done so.

Historically, the indexation factor was the retail prices index (RPI). Legislation to move the default indexation factor for direct taxes, including IHT, from the RPI to the consumer price index (CPI) was included in *FA 2012*, which amended *s 8* with effect for chargeable transfers from 6 April 2015. However, automatic indexation of the nil rate band using the CPI is subject to override if Parliament determines that a different amount should apply.

The IHT nil rate band was initially frozen at £325,000 up to and including 2014/15. The nil rate band was further frozen (in *Finance Act 2014*) at £325,000 for tax years up to and including 2017/18. Subsequently, the indexation of the nil rate band in *IHTA 1984, s 8* was disapplied again (in *Finance (No 2) Act 2015*), such that the nil rate band is to remain at £325,000 for the tax years 2018/19, 2019/20 and 2020/21.

The nil rate band for the current and recent tax years is as follows (*Sch 1*):

Table 1.1—The 'nil rate band'

Transfer of value	*Threshold*
	£
2009/10 to 2020/21	325,000
2008/09	312,000
2007/08	300,000

1.5 In addition to the IHT threshold or nil rate band above, the transferable nil rate band provisions (*IHTA 1984, ss 8A–8*C) broadly allow claims for the unused nil rate band of a deceased spouse or civil partner to be transferred to a surviving spouse or civil partner (who dies on or after 9 October 2007). The survivor's nil rate band can be increased by up to 100%, or one additional nil rate band.

Extra nil rate band is also available from 6 April 2017 where a residence is passed on death to a direct descendant (see **16.55**). This 'residence nil rate band' is £100,000 in 2017/18, rising to £125,000 in 2018/19, £150,000 in 2019/20, and £175,000 in 2020/21.

RATES OF IHT

Lifetime

1.6 Chargeable lifetime transfers are charged at half of the rate on death (*IHTA 1984, s 7(2)*). The 'death rate' of IHT for 2018/19 is 40%, and, therefore, chargeable lifetime transfers above the nil rate band are charged at 20%.

Death

1.7 Transfers made within seven years of death are charged at the rate on death, subject to taper relief for transfers made between three and seven years from death.

However, a lower IHT rate of 36% applies to a deceased person's estate in certain circumstances involving charitable legacies (*IHTA 1984, Sch 1A*). This reduced rate broadly applies where 10% or more of a deceased's net estate (after deducting liabilities, exemptions, reliefs and the nil rate band) is left to charity or a registered club. In such cases, the normal 40% rate is reduced to 36%. The relevant legislation was introduced in *FA 2012*. The lower rate of IHT potentially has effect for deaths on or after 6 April 2012.

An 'Inheritance Tax reduced rate calculator' is included on the HMRC website (www.hmrc.gov.uk/tools/iht-reduced-rate/calculator.htm). In addition, HMRC's technical guidance on the reduced rate for charitable gifts (at IHTM45000 and following) includes an example of the wording of a clause that can be included in a will, which HMRC accept will ensure that a specific legacy to charity will always meet the 10% test (see IHTM45008).

Grossing-up

1.8 IHT is based on the loss in value of the donor's estate as the result of a chargeable transfer. If the donor also pays the IHT on a gift, that payment results in a further loss to his estate. The tax must, therefore, be taken into account in the transfer of value. The gift (net of IHT) must be 'grossed-up' to determine the actual chargeable transfer.

Example 1.1—Lifetime transfers

Mr A transfers £129,000 to a discretionary trust on 1 May 2018, £219,000 on 31 December 2018 and a further £35,000 on 1 February 2019. He bears the tax and he has made no other chargeable transfers.

His IHT position is as follows:

	£	£	£
Gift on 1 May 2018		129,000	
Deduct annual exemption			
– 2018/19	3,000		
– 2017/18	3,000	6,000	
		123,000	
Covered by nil rate band of £325,000			
Gift on 31 December 2018		219,000	
(Note: Annual exemption already used for 2018/19)			
Cumulative net transfers		£342,000	
Tax thereon:			
£0–£325,000		0	
£325,001–£342,000 (£17,000 × ¼)		4,250	
Tax on gift		£4,250	

Gift on 1 February 2019

	Gross	Tax	Net
Cumulative totals	346,250	4,250	342,000
Add Latest net transfer of £35,000	43,750	8,750	35,000
	£390,000	£13,000	£377,000
Tax on £377,000			
£0–£325,000		Nil	
£325,001–£377,000 (£52,000 × ¼)		13,000	
		13,000	
Deduct tax on previous transfers		4,250	
Tax on latest gift		£8,750	

TRANSFERS OF VALUE

1.9 A transfer of value is a disposition by a person resulting in the value of his estate immediately after the disposition being less than it would be but for the disposition. The amount by which his estate is reduced is the measure of the transfer of value (*IHTA 1984, s 3(1)*). This is sometimes referred to as the 'loss to the donor' principle.

However, the transfer of 'excluded property' (see below) does not count for the above purposes (*IHTA 1984, s 3(2)*; see **1.14**).

Focus

Some 'dispositions' (eg gifts or transfers) are not treated as transfers of value, where certain conditions are satisfied (*IHTA 1984, ss 10–17*). These include:

- gifts without gratuitous intent (*IHTA 1984, s 10*);
- transfers for family maintenance (*IHTA 1984, s 11*);
- dispositions which are allowable for income tax or corporation tax purposes (*IHTA 1984, s 12*); and
- waivers of remuneration and dividends (*IHTA 1984, ss 14, 15*).

For further commentary on dispositions that are not transfers of value, see **11.12** and following.

POTENTIALLY EXEMPT TRANSFERS

1.10 Most types of gifts made during lifetime are potentially exempt transfers (PETs). A PET is broadly a lifetime transfer of value that satisfies the following conditions (*IHTA 1984, s 3A*):

- it is made by an individual on or after 18 March 1986;
- the transfer would otherwise be a chargeable transfer;
- for transfers of value before 22 March 2006, if it is either a gift to another individual or a gift into an accumulation and maintenance trust or a disabled person's trust;
- for transfers of value from 22 March 2006, if the transfer of value is made to another individual, a disabled person's trust or a 'bereaved minor's' trust on the ending of an 'immediate post-death interest' (see **Chapter 9**), ie lifetime gifts into the vast majority of trusts do not qualify as PETs from that date.

A PET made more than seven years before death becomes an exempt transfer. Conversely, a PET becomes a chargeable transfer if made within seven years of death.

CHARGEABLE LIFETIME TRANSFERS

1.11 A lifetime transfer is broadly a disposition (eg a gift) made by a person resulting in a reduction in the value of the person's estate (*IHTA 1984, s 3(1)*). A chargeable transfer is a transfer of value by an individual, other than an exempt transfer (*IHTA 1984, s 2*).

As mentioned, most lifetime transfers are PETs, which are assumed will prove to be exempt when made, and which only become chargeable if the transferor dies within seven years of making them. A lifetime transfer that does not qualify as a PET will, therefore, generally be immediately chargeable to IHT. For example:

- transfers to a company;
- gifts to a discretionary trust; or
- lifetime gifts to an interest in possession settlement (which is not a disabled person's interest) created since 22 March 2006.

Other transfers of value prevented from being PETs include transfers by a close company, and deemed dispositions on the alteration of share rights or capital of close companies (*IHTA 1984, ss 94, 98*).

With regard to lifetime transfers in general, see **Chapter 4**.

IHT ON DEATH

1.12 IHT is charged on the deceased's estate as if, immediately before his death, he had made a transfer of value. The value transferred is deemed to equal the value of his estate immediately before death (*IHTA 1984, s 4(1)*).

The estate for IHT purposes includes the value of all property to which the deceased was beneficially entitled, certain interests in possession in settled property (see **Chapter 9**) and any gifts with reservation of benefit (see **Chapter 7**), but not excluded property (see **1.13** below).

Changes in the value of the estate caused by the death may be taken into account (*IHTA 1984, s 171*). HMRC guidance (at IHTM04046) cites various examples, including a life assurance policy maturing on death on the footing that it will often pay out a greater sum than the open market value of the policy immediately before the death.

Liabilities of the deceased may generally be deducted if imposed under a legal obligation, or if incurred for valuable consideration (*IHTA 1984, s 5(5)*), together with reasonable funeral expenses (*IHTA 1984, s 172*). However, certain restrictions on deductions for liabilities (introduced in *FA 2013* and *FA 2014*) include provisions in relation to the repayment of liabilities after a person's death (*IHTA 1984, s 175A*), where this occurs on or after 17 July 2013 (ie the date on which *FA 2013* received Royal Assent). Provisions applicable to liabilities relating to certain 'relievable property' apply to liabilities incurred on or after 6 April 2013 (see **5.13**).

The amount of IHT chargeable on the death estate is subject to any IHT reliefs and/or exemptions to which the deceased's estate may be entitled (eg business or agricultural property relief, or the spouse or civil partner exemption), and depends on the total chargeable lifetime transfers and potentially exempt transfers made within the seven years before death.

With regard to IHT on death generally, see **Chapter 5**.

EXCLUDED PROPERTY

1.13 Some types of property are outside the scope of IHT. Such property is known as 'excluded property', and includes the following:

- Property situated abroad (and investments in an authorised unit trust or open ended investment company) if the beneficial owner is a non-UK domiciled individual (*s 6(1), (1A)*). However, an exception (introduced in *Finance (No 2) Act 2017*) applies to 'non-excluded overseas property', which broadly extends the scope of IHT (from 6 April 2017) for non-UK domiciled individuals to residential property interests in the UK where they are held through offshore structures (*IHTA 1984, Sch A1*; see below).

- Settled property situated outside the UK, if the settlor was non-UK domiciled when the settlement was made (*IHTA 1984, s 48(3)*).

  However, if a UK-domiciled person acquires an interest in possession in the settled property (from 5 December 2005) for valuable consideration, that interest is not excluded property (*IHTA 1984, s 48(3B)*). In addition, the excluded property and settled property provisions were amended (by anti-avoidance legislation in *FA 2012*) with effect for arrangements entered into on or after 20 June 2012, to close certain schemes involving the acquisition by UK-domiciled individuals of interests in excluded property trusts (*IHTA 1984, ss 48(3D), 74A–74C*).

  Furthermore, following a reform of the taxation of non-UK domiciled individuals (in *Finance (No 2) Act 2017*), where the settlor was non-UK domiciled when the settlement was made, the property is not excluded property (under *IHTA 1984, s 48(3) or (3A)*) at any time in a tax year if the settlor is a 'formerly domiciled resident' (see **2.13**) for that tax year (*IHTA 1984, s 48(3E)*).

- Settled property (situated abroad or not) consisting of investments in an authorised unit trust or open ended investment company, if the settlor was non-UK domiciled when the settlement was made (*IHTA 1984, s 48(3A)*). However, if a UK-domiciled person acquires an interest in possession in settled property from 5 December 2005 for valuable consideration, that interest is not excluded property (*IHTA 1984, s 48(3B)*). See also the exception for formerly domiciled resident settlors in the previous bullet point.

- A 'reversionary interest' (ie a future interest under a settlement), subject to certain anti-avoidance provisions (eg if the interest has previously been acquired for valuable consideration; see *IHTA 1984, s 48(1)*).

- Certain government securities owned by persons not ordinarily resident (and in certain cases, not domiciled) in the UK (*s 6(2)*) (although as to ordinary residence, see **2.9**).

- National Savings certificates, war savings certificates, premium savings bonds or deposits with the National Savings Bank or a trustee savings bank, or a 'certified SAYE savings arrangement' (as defined) of persons domiciled in the Channel Islands or the Isle of Man (*IHTA 1984, s 6(3)*).

However, as to the first two bullet points above, see **1.15–1.19** below on legislation bringing UK residential property interests held directly or indirectly by non-UK domiciled persons into charge for IHT purposes, even where the property is owned through an offshore structure such as an offshore company or partnership.

There is also an exclusion from the death estate in respect of foreign (ie non-sterling) currency bank accounts of a person who was not domiciled or resident in the UK immediately prior to death (*IHTA 1984, s 157*). However, this exclusion is subject to an exception (following legislation introduced in *Finance (No 2) Act 2017*) broadly for disposals and repayments in respect of 'non-excluded overseas property' held in a qualifying foreign currency account within *IHTA 1984, s 157*, for a two year period (*IHTA 1984, Sch A1, para 5(2)(b)*; see **1.15–1.19** below). Note that there was an additional condition for the exclusion as to ordinary residence in the UK, but this requirement was removed by *FA 2013* for deaths on or after 6 April 2013.

In addition, certain other types of property are left out of account for IHT purposes:

- decorations (eg medals) and other awards, which have never been the subject of a disposition for consideration in money or money's worth. When originally enacted (in *IHTA 1984, s 6(1B)*), this statutory exclusion applied specifically to decorations or awards for valour or gallant conduct. (Note – this provision replaced ESC F19 with effect in relation to transfers etc occurring from 6 April 2009 (*SI 2009/730, art 14*).)

  Excluded property status was extended (in *FA 2015*) to various categories of 'relevant decoration or award' (see *IHTA 1984, s 6(1BA)*), with effect in relation to transfers of value made (or treated as made) from 3 December 2014. These broadly include decorations awarded by the Crown or another country or territory outside the UK to the armed forces, an 'emergency responder' (as defined in *IHTA 1984, s 153A*: see **1.20**) and individuals in recognition of their achievements and service in public life; and

- certain compensation etc for World War II claims.

  Legislation in *IHTA 1984, s 153ZA* and *Sch 5A* (introduced in *Finance Act 2016*) replaced previous concessionary treatment (under ESC F20 'Late compensation for World War II claims'), in respect of qualifying payments of compensation and ex-gratia payments for World War II claims. The legislation also extended the scope of the concession to include one-off compensation payments of €2,500 made under the 'Child Survivor Fund', and allows the Treasury to add any further schemes by way of regulations. The legislation operates as a relief rather than an exemption, as the IHT on the amount of the qualifying compensation or ex-gratia payment is allowed as a credit against the IHT arising on the chargeable value of the recipient's estate.

  ESC F20 has effect until 1 January 2015. The relevant legislation introduced in *Finance Act 2016* is backdated to deaths occurring on or after 1 January 2015.

Settled property

1.14 The excluded property legislation generally refers to the settlor's domicile when the settlement was made.

HMRC take the view that, in the case of added property, a further settlement is made when that property is transferred. If the settlor was domiciled in the UK at that point, the property will not be excluded property. HMRC's Inheritance Tax Manual gives the following example (IHTM04272):

Example 1.2—Foreign settled property

S, when domiciled abroad, creates a settlement of Spanish realty. Later he acquires a UK domicile and then adds some Australian property to the settlement.

The Spanish property is excluded property because of S's overseas domicile when he settled that property. However, the Australian property is not excluded property as S had a UK domicile when he added that property to the settlement.

If settled property leaves an excluded property settlement, but that property (or property derived therefrom) is later reintroduced into the settlement at a time when the settlor had become UK domiciled, the original property (or other property representing it) is nevertheless capable of retaining its excluded property status (*Barclays Wealth Trustees (Jersey) Ltd and another v HM Revenue and Customs* [2017] EWCA Civ 1512).

IHT is not charged on lifetime transfers of excluded property. Nor does excluded property form part of a person's estate on death; the same applies to a foreign-owned work of art situated in the UK only for the purposes of public display, cleaning and/or restoration (*IHTA 1984, s 3(2)*; *IHTA 1984, s 5(1)(b)*).

However, excluded property is taken into account when measuring the loss in value of a person's estate if there is a transfer of non-excluded property. This is implicit from the wording of *IHTA 1984, s 3(2)*, which provides that no account is taken of dispositions of excluded property (but not otherwise) and *IHTA 1984, s 5(1)*, which provides that a person's estate on death (but not at other times) does not include excluded property.

Non-UK domicile and UK residential property interests

1.15 As indicated at **1.2** above, non-UK domiciled individuals are liable to IHT on chargeable UK property. Thus if the individual dies owning UK assets directly, their estate is liable to IHT at 40% on the value of those assets (subject to reliefs, exemptions and the nil rate band, if available).

By contrast, property beneficially owned by a non-UK domiciled individual which is situated outside the UK is normally 'excluded property' for IHT purposes. Such property is generally taken outside the ambit of an IHT charge (*IHTA 1984, s 6(1)*).

Owning assets indirectly through an overseas company whose shares are situated abroad has been a popular strategy for non-UK domiciliaries, on the basis that the shares in the non-UK company are excluded property. If a UK asset such as an industrial unit (which is not excluded property) is held by the overseas company, its value would generally be taken outside the scope of IHT.

In addition, property comprised in a settlement and situated outside the UK will generally be excluded property for IHT purposes if the settlor was domiciled outside the UK when the settlement was made (*IHTA 1984, s 48(3)*) (see **1.13**). Thus a non-UK domiciled individual with assets abroad who is considering becoming domiciled in the UK, or is about to become 'deemed' domiciled in the UK under *IHTA 1984, s 267,* would often consider settling those assets before becoming UK domiciled, so that they could remain outside the scope of IHT.

Furthermore, if the non-UK domiciled settlor has UK assets such as commercial property, consideration could be given to the trust owning the shares of an offshore company (which, as mentioned above, are generally excluded property if situated outside the UK), with the investment company owning the UK assets. The settled property would then be the foreign company shares, not the UK assets.

However, as noted at **1.13** and **2.13**, as a result of legislation introduced in *Finance (No 2) Act 2017* even if the settlor of a settlement was not domiciled in the UK when the settlement was made, the property is not excluded property within *IHTA 1984, s 48(3)* or *(3A)* at any time in a tax year if the settlor is a 'formerly domiciled resident' for that tax year.

1.16

> **Focus**
>
> In the case of residential property, the prospect of increased stamp taxes, the annual tax on enveloped dwellings (ATED) and ATED-related capital gains tax (CGT) charges made property ownership by a 'non-natural person' potentially unattractive for other tax purposes (see **Chapter 16**).

Furthermore, as indicated at **1.13,** an exception to excluded property status (introduced in *Finance (No 2) Act 2017*) generally applies to UK residential property interests effectively owned by non-UK domiciliaries (regardless of their residence status for tax purposes), with effect from 6 April 2017. This change is aimed at blocking what HMRC has described as 'enveloping' (ie holding property indirectly through offshore structures).

1.17 The broad effect of the above provision (in *IHTA 1984, Sch A1*) is to restrict the excluded property provisions for IHT purposes, so that rights or interests in a close company, or interests in a partnership, are generally not excluded property if and to the extent that the value of the right or interest is directly or indirectly attributable to a UK residential property interest. There is also an exception from excluded property in relation to a 'relevant loan' (see **1.18**).

However, the IHT position for non-UK domiciliaries and excluded property trusts remains unchanged in relation to the value of UK assets other than UK residential property interests, as well as in respect of non-UK assets.

The IHT charge on UK residential property interests

1.18 As indicated at **1.16**, the restrictions in excluded property status in relation to overseas property with value attributable to UK residential property (*IHTA 1984, Sch A1*) are aimed at ensuring that (from 6 April 2017) rights and interests in certain types of property are not excluded property of a non-UK domiciled individual (within *IHTA 1984, s 6(1)*), or excluded property of an offshore settlement (within *IHTA 1984, s 48(3)(a)*), to the extent that the value of the right or interest is directly or indirectly attributable to a UK residential property interest.

The types of property potentially affected by this measure include rights or interests as a participator in a close company (as defined), if and to the extent that the value of the right or interest is attributable to the UK residential property interest. The same broadly applies to an interest in a partnership.

Example 1.3—Offshore company and UK residential property

Henrik (who was not resident or domiciled in the UK) died on 31 March 2018. He owned all the share capital of an offshore close company (Henco). The company's shares have an open market value of £2 million, which is attributable to a UK residential property (£1.2 million) and a property in Spain (£800,000). The shares passed on death to his son Frederik.

The shares in Henco are excluded property to the extent that their value is attributable to the Spanish property. However, the value of the shares attributable to the company's UK residential property is not excluded property (within *IHTA 1984, s 6(1)*), and therefore forms part of Henrik's estate for IHT purposes.

However, an interest in a close company or partnership is disregarded for these purposes if the value of that interest is less than 5% of the total value of all interests in the close company or partnership, although a connected person's interest in the close company or partnership should be included in valuing the person's interest (*IHTA 1984, Sch A1, para 2*).

A further category of affected property is loans (*IHTA 1984, Sch A1, para 3*). This broadly includes any rights of a creditor in respect of a 'relevant loan', as well as security, collateral or guarantees up to the value of such a loan.

A loan is a 'relevant loan' for these purposes if used directly or indirectly for certain specified purposes, including the acquisition of a UK residential property interest by an individual, partnership or settlement trustees. The same applies to loans used to finance the acquisition of an interest in a close company or partnership, and also where a loan is directly or indirectly used by a close company or partnership for the acquisition of a UK residential property interest. References to the acquisition of a UK residential property interest for these purposes includes the maintenance or enhancement of the value of that interest (*IHTA 1984, Sch A1, para 4*).

There are also provisions (*IHTA 1984, Sch A1, para 5*) concerning certain disposals and repayments in respect of property within the above categories (ie consideration for the disposal of an interest in a close company or partnership, or of a relevant loan, or any money or money's worth paid for a creditor's rights in respect of a relevant loan, or property directly or indirectly representing consideration for the disposal of an interest in a close company or partnership or a relevant loan, or paid for a creditor's interest in a relevant loan).

Where those provisions apply, such property is not excluded property (within *IHTA 1984, ss 6(1), (1A), (2)* or *48(3)(a), (3A)* or *(4)*) for a two year period beginning with the date of disposal or payment. If that property is held within a qualifying foreign currency bank account (within *IHTA 1984, s 157*), the property falls to be taken into account for a two year period in determining the value of a person's estate on death (ie *IHTA 1984, s 157* does not apply to it for that period).

The above restrictions on overseas property with value attributable to UK residential property include a targeted anti-avoidance rule (*IHTA 1984, Sch A1, para 6*), which disregards arrangements entered into with a main purpose of securing a tax advantage by avoiding or minimising the effect of the restrictions in determining whether (or to what extent) non-UK property is excluded property.

Furthermore, the terms of a double tax arrangement between the UK and another territory explicitly does not prevent an IHT liability under the above provisions on a chargeable transfer if, under the law of the non-UK territory, no tax similar to IHT is charged thereon, or is charged at an effective rate of 0% (*IHTA 1984, Sch A1, para 7*). As to double taxation relief generally, see **1.24–1.26**.

1.19 A 'UK residential property interest' for the purposes of the above IHT provisions is an interest in UK land to the extent that it consists of or includes a dwelling, or if it subsists under a contract for an off-plan purchase (*IHTA 1984, Sch A1, para 8(1)*).

The scope of CGT was extended (by *FA 2015*) to include gains on the disposal of UK residential property interests by non-UK resident persons (or by individuals in the overseas part of a split year) from 6 April 2015 (see **16.2**).

The terms 'interest in UK land', 'dwelling' and 'contract for an off-plan purchase' have the same meaning for IHT purposes as provided for CGT purposes by *TCGA 1992, Sch B1, paras 2, 4* and *1(6)* respectively.

> **Focus**
>
> In many cases, the offshore close company, etc may own other assets in addition to UK residential property, such as foreign land, or UK commercial (non-residential) property. However, the above IHT provisions are specifically aimed at the value directly or indirectly attributable to rights and interests in UK residential property.

In practice, this extension of IHT in relation to UK residential property interests potentially increases complexity and compliance burdens (eg in relation to valuations, and also reporting requirements to HMRC).

Some non-UK domiciliaries and trustees may wish to 'de-envelope' UK residential property from offshore structures as a result of the proposed IHT changes, and into a simpler structure (outside the scope of the ATED and ATED-related CGT regimes). However, no specific de-enveloping provisions are intended by the government at the time of writing.

EXEMPTIONS—SUMMARY

1.20 The following types of property are exempt and, therefore, outside the IHT charge:

- **Transfers between spouses or civil partners** (*IHTA 1984, s 18*)

  There is a complete exemption for all transfers (ie lifetime and on death) between UK-domiciled spouses.

  However, where the transferor spouse is UK domiciled but the transferee spouse is foreign domiciled, the exemption is restricted to a *cumulative* total of the prevailing nil rate band (£325,000 for 2018/19) (*IHTA 1984, s 18(2)*).

  If the non-domiciled transferee spouse subsequently becomes UK domiciled, unfortunately any preceding transfers to them are still considered to be subject to the above restriction. Furthermore, in HMRC's view if an individual has been married to or in civil partnership with more than one person, the restriction applies to the cumulative total of all transfers to all spouses or civil partners (IHTM11033). Following the *Civil Partnership Act 2004*, same-sex couples who enter into a civil relationship are given parity of tax treatment with married couples. A gift to a non-UK domiciled spouse that is within the gift with reservation rules may not be protected by spouse relief and may eventually prove to be chargeable.

The above upper limit was increased to the prevailing nil rate band at the time of the transfer, with effect in relation to transfers of value made on or after 6 April 2013 (previously £55,000, for transfers between 9 March 1982 and 5 April 2013), following changes introduced in *FA 2013*. However, there are provisions for an election to allow non-UK domiciled spouses to be treated as domiciled in the UK for IHT purposes, so that the inter-spouse exemption is unlimited (but electing spouses are then generally subject to IHT on their worldwide estates).

The broad effect is that, if no election is made to be treated as UK domiciled, the overseas assets of the non-UK domiciled spouse generally continue to be excluded property for IHT purposes, but transfers from their spouse or civil partner would be subject to the 'capped' exempt limit. By contrast, the effect of making an election to HMRC will broadly be to avoid a possible IHT charge on the first death, but as mentioned the worldwide estate of the surviving spouse generally becomes liable to IHT on the second death.

The election must be made in writing, but there is no prescribed form for making it. However, HMRC guidance states that the election should be made to WMBC Assets Risk Team (Elections), Inheritance Tax, HM Revenue and Customs, BX9 1HT, and must include the following information (IHTM13043):

- full name and address of the person making the election (or for whom the personal representatives are making an election);
- date of birth, and (if appropriate) date of death;
- full name of their spouse or civil partner who is domiciled in the UK; and
- date from which the election is to take effect.

The election is irrevocable, and continues to apply while the electing individual remains resident in the UK. However, an election ceases to have effect if the electing person is later resident outside the UK for more than four full consecutive tax years (*IHTA 1984, s 267ZB(10)*). Thus overseas assets may cease to be liable to IHT once more, subject to the person not being actually or deemed domiciled in the UK at that point.

- **Annual exemption** (*IHTA 1984, s 19*)

  Lifetime transfers of value up to £3,000 per tax year are completely exempt from IHT. Any unused part of the exemption may be carried forward for one tax year only, and deducted after the annual exemption has been fully used in that later year (IHTM14144). If the value of the gift or transfer exceeds the annual exemption, the excess will either be a potentially exempt transfer or an immediately chargeable transfer.

- **Small gifts to same person** (*IHTA 1984, s 20*)

  Lifetime gifts in a tax year with a total value not exceeding £250 to any one person are exempt from IHT. If the total value of gifts to that person exceeds £250 in the tax year, the exemption is completely lost (eg it cannot be set against part of a larger gift). The gifts must be outright. For example, they cannot be gifts of premiums on a life policy that has been written in trust (although the exemption for normal expenditure out of income in *IHTA 1984, s 21* might apply (see below)).

- **Normal expenditure out of income** (*IHTA 1984, s 21*)

  The exemption applies to lifetime gifts which:

  (a) form part of the normal expenditure of the person making it;

  (b) were made out of income (taking one year with another); and

  (c) left the donor with sufficient income to maintain their normal standard of living.

  Unlike other lifetime exemptions (eg the annual exemption), the normal expenditure out of income exemption is not subject to an upper maximum, ie it is only restricted to the extent of the donor's gifts that satisfy the above conditions. Evidence is crucial to support claims to this relief.

- **Gifts in consideration of marriage or civil partnership** (*IHTA 1984, ss 22, 57*)

  Marriage gifts are exempt within certain limits. The amount of the exemption depends on the donor's relationship to the bride, groom or civil partner. Gifts of up to £5,000 by a parent of a party to a marriage or civil partnership are exempt. In the case of gifts by a grandparent or remoter ancestor, or by one party to the marriage or civil partnership to the other, the exemption limit is £2,500. For marriage gifts made by any other person, the upper limit is £1,000. These exemptions apply per marriage.

  The gifts must be made on or shortly before the marriage or civil partnership in HMRC's view, and must become fully effective on the event taking place (IHTM14191). Gifts in excess of the above exempt limits are chargeable to IHT, but only to the extent of the excess.

- **Gifts to charities or registered clubs** (*IHTA 1984, s 23*)

  Gifts to charities or registered clubs are exempt from IHT, if certain conditions are satisfied. For periods prior to changes included in *Finance Act 2010*, it was necessary for a charity to be established in the UK.

However, a statutory definition of 'charity' was introduced (in *FA 2010, Sch 6*), which includes a four-stage test to determine if an organisation is eligible for UK charity tax reliefs. This includes a jurisdiction condition, which broadly allows the organisation to be located in the UK or an EU member state or specified country, of which Iceland and Norway are included (*SI 2010/1904*), and Liechtenstein was subsequently added from 31 July 2014 (*SI 2014/1807*). The *Finance Act 2010* changes apply for IHT purposes from 1 April 2012 (*The Finance Act 2010, Schedule 6, Part 2 (Commencement) Order, SI 2012/736*) (Note – for HMRC guidance as to transfers before that date, see IHTM11112). The IHT charity exemption is relevant to outright gifts to charity or to certain charitable trusts, and applies to lifetime gifts or transfers on death with no upper limit.

In *Routier and another v Revenue and Customs* [2016] EWCA Civ 938, a charitable gift to a trust was held not to be eligible for the charity exemption, on the grounds that the trust was established under and governed by Jersey law. The Court of Appeal considered that the phrase 'held on trust for charitable purposes only' (in *IHTA 1984, s 23(6)*) carries the implicit requirement that the trust must be governed by UK law and subject to the jurisdiction of the UK courts. On a subsequent appeal ([2017] EWCA Civ 1584), the Court of Appeal concluded that the restriction did not violate the EU law principle of freedom of movement of capital so as not to be enforceable in relation to the legacy to the Jersey trust.

It should be noted that the four-stage test mentioned above includes a 'management condition', which in turn includes a 'fit and proper person' test. This could deprive some organisations of their charitable status. There is no statutory definition of a 'fit and proper' person, although a helpsheet (and fit and proper person declaration) is available on the gov.uk website (www.gov.uk/government/publications/charity-tax-relief-model-declaration).

- **Gifts to political parties** (*IHTA 1984, s 24*)

  Transfers of value to qualifying political parties are exempt transfers for IHT purposes without limit. A political party qualifies for the exemption if at the last general election preceding the transfer two members of the party were elected to the House of Commons, or alternatively if one member of that party was elected and not less than 150,000 votes were given to candidates who were members of that party.

  The government announced in Autumn Statement 2016 its intention to legislate in a future Finance Bill to expand the IHT exemption for donations to political parties to include donations made to qualifying political parties in the devolved legislatures and parties that have acquired representatives through by-elections.

- **Gifts to housing associations** (*IHTA 1984, s 24A*)

  Gifts of UK land to a registered housing association or registered social landlord are exempt without upper limit. For the purposes of the exemption, 'land' includes any buildings that are attached to that land (IHTM11211).

- **Gifts for national purposes** (*IHTA 1984, s 25, Sch 3*)

  An unlimited exemption applies to qualifying transfers of value to those bodies designated in *IHTA 1984, Sch 3*. Gifts to the nation (within *FA 2012, Sch 14, para 1*) are also exempt (*IHTA 1984, s 25(3)*).

- **Gifts for public benefit** (*IHTA 1984, s 26*) (repealed)

  Gifts within certain specified categories to bodies not established for profit were exempt from IHT if the Board so directed. This exemption was repealed for gifts made from 17 March 1998.

- **Maintenance funds for historic buildings, etc** (*IHTA 1984, s 27, Sch 4*)

  Transfers of value (during lifetime or on death) into settlement for the maintenance, repair or preservation of historic buildings and assets of outstanding scenic, historic or scientific interest, etc are exempt subject to certain conditions, where HMRC so direct (under *IHTA 1984, Sch 4*). The exemption must be claimed within two years after the date of the transfer concerned, or within such longer period as HMRC may allow (*IHTA 1984, s 27(1A)*).

- **Employee trusts** (*IHTA 1984, ss 28, 28A*)

  Transfers, by an individual, of shares or securities in a company to 'trusts for the benefit of employees' of the company (within *IHTA 1984, s 86*) are exempt from IHT, if certain conditions are satisfied (*IHTA 1984, s 28)*.

  Furthermore, legislation concerning companies owned by 'employee-ownership trusts' (introduced in *FA 2014*) provides that a transfer of shares in a company by an individual to a trust is exempt from IHT, broadly if the company meets a 'trading requirement' as defined, the trust meets an 'all-employee benefit requirement', and the trust does not meet a 'controlling interest' requirement immediately before the start of the tax year of transfer but does so at the end of that tax year (*IHTA 1984, s 28A*).

- **Other exemptions**

  – Annuities payable on a person's death under a registered pension scheme, a qualifying non-UK pension scheme or to a 'section 615 scheme' (ie a superannuation fund within *ICTA 1988, s 615(3)*) or, prior to 6 April 2006, either a retirement annuity contract or a personal pension scheme to a spouse, civil partner, dependant or nominee, where under the terms of the scheme a capital sum might at the deceased's option have become payable instead to his personal representatives (*IHTA 1984, s 152*).

– 'Killed in war', etc exemption (ie broadly property of a member of the armed services (or certain associated services) passing on death caused by injury or disease received or aggravated whilst on active service (*IHTA 1984, s 154*)). This exemption was extended in *FA 2015*, broadly to include circumstances where armed service personnel die while responding to an emergency, or where their death is hastened by injury or illness resulting from that emergency.

  In addition, provisions introduced in *FA 2015* extended IHT exemption in relation to an 'emergency responder' (ie broadly emergency services personnel and humanitarian aid workers) who die from an injury sustained, accident occurring or illness contracted in the line of duty, or whose death is hastened by illness aggravated when responding to emergency circumstances (*IHTA 1984, s 153A*). A further IHT exemption applies in relation to police constables and armed service personnel who die from an injury sustained or illness contracted as a result of being attacked due to their status, or from an illness aggravated in such circumstances (*IHTA 1984, s 155A*). These extended exemptions, which include any additional IHT on death for chargeable lifetime transfers and potentially exempt transfers, have effect in relation to deaths occurring from 19 March 2014.

– Foreign currency bank accounts held on the death of an individual not resident or domiciled in the UK immediately before death (*s 157*) (see **1.13**). A further condition as to ordinary residence in the UK applies where the person died before 6 April 2013.

Aside from the above exemptions, it should be noted that certain dispositions do not represent transfers of value for IHT purposes (*IHTA 1984, ss 10–17*), such as dispositions not intended to confer gratuitous benefit (*s 10*) and dispositions for the maintenance of family (*IHTA 1984, s 11*); see **11.12**.

TAPER RELIEF: OUTLINE

1.21 IHT on all lifetime transfers (chargeable lifetime transfers and PETs) made within seven years before death is subject to a potential reduction for taper relief, if the lifetime transfer was made more than three years before death. Note that the relief reduces the IHT that would otherwise be payable on a transfer, not the value of the transfer itself.

Tax on chargeable lifetime transfers is calculated at lifetime rates. If the transferor dies within seven years the tax is recomputed at full death rates, subject to taper relief where the death is more than three years after the gift. However, taper relief cannot reduce the tax payable below that originally charged.

In addition, IHT at full death rates is calculated at the time of death on any PETs made within seven years prior to death, subject to the availability of taper relief. The value of the transfer stays the same for taper relief purposes, but the full rate(s) of IHT charged are reduced to a percentage of those rates on the following scale (*IHTA 1984, s 7(4)*):

Table 1.2—Taper relief rates

Transfer:	3–4 years before death: rate reduced to:	80%
	4–5 years before death:	60%
	5–6 years before death:	40%
	6–7 years before death:	20%

1.22 However, if IHT on a chargeable lifetime transfer is recalculated on death with taper relief and produces a lower tax figure than the tax originally calculated at lifetime rates, the original figure stands (*IHTA 1984, s 7(5)*); in other words, no IHT repayments result from the application of taper relief.

For further commentary on taper relief, see **12.2–12.3**.

QUICK SUCCESSION RELIEF: OUTLINE

1.23 Quick succession relief (QSR) is available on the death of an individual whose estate has increased in value as the result of a chargeable transfer (ie during lifetime or a transfer on death) made within five years before his death (*IHTA 1984, s 141(1)(a)*).

QSR is also available in relation to the lifetime termination of an interest in possession in settled property (*s 141(1)(b)*), where certain conditions are satisfied (in *IHTA 1984, s 141(2)*).

If QSR applies, the tax charge on the later transfer is calculated in the normal way. The relief is then given by reducing the IHT on death by a percentage of the tax attributable to the net increase (see below) in the deceased's estate from the original transfer. It is not necessary for the asset in question to be retained.

The percentage varies according to the length of time between the dates of transfer and death, as follows:

Table 1.3—Quick succession relief

Period between transfer and death	*Relief percentage*
One year or less	100%
1–2 years	80%
2–3 years	60%
3–4 years	40%
4–5 years	20%

The earlier transfer can, for example, be a failed PET on which IHT becomes payable. The same rates of quick succession relief apply to successive IHT charges within five years on trust property with an interest in possession.

Note one practical point in calculating QSR; the reference above to 'the net increase'. Suppose that, on an earlier death, the tax on the transfer was actually paid by the residue of the estate. Gifts of UK assets will be 'free of tax', in the sense that tax is borne by residue, unless the will provides for the contrary. In such a case, what the beneficiary gets is the full value of the gift, so his estate is increased by the full amount, and on death soon after the full amount features in the calculation of QSR (IHTM22072).

By contrast, suppose that the will on the earlier death had put the burden of tax on the gift itself: in that case what the beneficiary inherits is effectively less, and QSR on the later death is reduced accordingly (see example at IHTM22073).

For further commentary on QSR, see **12.4–12.5**.

DOUBLE TAXATION RELIEF

1.24 Where IHT is chargeable in the UK and tax of a similar nature (or which is chargeable by reference to death or lifetime gifts) is charged in another territory on the same property, double taxation relief may be available.

Treaty relief

1.25 Relief is given if the UK has a double taxation agreement with the overseas territory containing provisions to eliminate the double taxation chargeable by reference to death or lifetime gifts (*IHTA 1984, s 158*).

A person can be deemed domiciled in the UK for IHT purposes even though he is domiciled elsewhere under private international law (see **2.8–2.13**). That person may also be domiciled elsewhere under the domestic law of another state. The 'deemed domicile' IHT rule does not apply in all cases, such as where certain pre-CTT double taxation agreements are still in force (ie by virtue of *IHTA 1984, s 158(6);* see *IHTA 1984, s 267(2)*). Those agreements contain their own rules for domicile and for resolving the issue where both countries claim domicile.

As indicated at **2.9**, HMRC accept that domicile issues exclude deemed domicile when considering the double tax agreements with France, Italy, India and Pakistan, although if domicile under common law is in those countries, the deemed domicile rules can apply to chargeable *lifetime* transfers (IHTM13024).

However, the terms of double tax agreements will not prevent a person from being liable to IHT under the provisions outlined at **1.18** dealing with non-excluded overseas property (ie overseas property with value attributable to UK residential property) where no similar tax is charged on a transfer of value under the law of a territory outside the UK, or where tax is charged there (otherwise than by virtue of a relief or exemption) at an effective rate of 0%.

It should also be noted that an election to treat a non-UK spouse as domiciled in the UK (see **1.20, 2.6**) does not apply for certain purposes, including when considering a person's domicile in connection with double taxation agreements with France, Italy, India or Pakistan (*IHTA 1984, s 267ZA(5), (6)*; see IHTM13047).

The double taxation conventions between the UK and other countries in force for IHT purposes (under *IHTA 1984, s 158*) are listed in HMRC's Inheritance Tax Manual (at IHTM27161), and also on the gov.uk website (www.gov.uk/inheritance-tax-double-taxation-relief#11).

Unilateral relief

1.26 Where relief is not provided under a double tax agreement, credit is available against UK tax for tax suffered in an overseas territory, on the same property (*IHTA 1984, s 159*). Unilateral relief may also be claimed if it provides greater relief than by applying treaty relief (*IHTA 1984, s 159(7)*).

If the property is situated in the overseas territory and not in the UK, credit is available on the whole amount of overseas tax (*IHTA 1984, s 159(2)*). However, if the overseas tax exceeds the UK tax, the excess is not repayable.

A measure of relief is also available (which is calculated by formula) if the property is situated as follows (*IHTA 1984, s 159(3)*):

- in a third territory; or
- both in the UK and the overseas territory (ie due to different laws on the situs of assets in the UK and that territory).

Relief similarly applies if tax is imposed in two or more overseas territories if the property is situated as follows (*IHTA 1984, s 159(4)*):

- neither in the UK nor those territories; or
- both in the UK and in each of those territories.

If relief under *IHTA 1984, s 159(2)* or treaty relief under *IHTA 1984, s 158* (see **1.25**) is due as well as under *IHTA 1984, s 159(3)*, the credit allowed under *s 159(3)* is calculated on the basis that the IHT paid (in the formula in *s 159(3)*) is the net amount of IHT after allowing the credit under *s 158* or *s 159(2)* (*IHTA 1984, s 159(5)*).

CLOSE COMPANIES

Transfers of value

1.27 Anti-avoidance provisions apply to transfers of value (eg sales at undervalue) by close companies. Only individuals can make a chargeable transfer for IHT purposes (*IHTA 1984, s 2(1)*). However, if a close company makes a transfer of value, the transfer is generally apportioned between the participators in that company (*IHTA 1984, s 94*). Each participator is deemed to have made an immediately chargeable transfer of value (ie not a PET) equal to the amount so apportioned. The company is primarily liable to pay any IHT liability arising (*IHTA 1984, s 202*).

However, if the participator's estate increases as a result of the transfer, that increase may be deducted from the amount so apportioned. The balance reflects the net decrease in value of the person's estate. Therefore, a transfer of value to a participator with a 100% interest in the close company should not normally result in an overall decrease in the value of his estate.

> **Focus**
>
> A transfer of value is not apportioned to participators in the following circumstances (*s 94(2)*):
>
> - if the amount is liable to income tax or corporation tax (or would be taken into account but for exemption in respect of UK company distributions) in the recipient's hands (eg as employment income or dividend income of the individual); or
> - the participator is not domiciled in the UK, and the relevant asset is situated abroad.

1.28 If the participator has less than 5% of the transfer apportioned to him, tax on the transfer is not added to his cumulative total of transfers for IHT purposes (*IHTA 1984, s 94(4)*), and no IHT liability attaches to that person in respect of the transfer if the IHT remains unpaid after it ought to have been paid; the liability in that case remains with the company (*IHTA 1984, s 202*; see IHTM30124).

The tax is calculated by reference to the participator's IHT position at that time, although as indicated a person to whom 5% or less of the value transferred is apportioned cannot be held liable to pay the IHT if the company is in default (*IHTA 1984, s 202(2)*). The annual IHT exemption may be deducted (if not already used elsewhere) from the value of any amount apportioned (*IHTA 1984, s 94(5)*).

Alterations of capital

1.29 The IHT anti-avoidance rules for close companies also include provisions relating to alterations in unquoted share capital, loan capital or rights attaching to its unquoted shares or debentures.

Participators to whom those provisions apply are broadly treated as having made a disposition for IHT purposes, which is not a PET (*IHTA 1984, s 98*).

HMRC guidance on the provisions (at IHTM14855) includes two examples, the first involving two new classes of shares being created and issued to one of the company's three existing shareholders, and the second illustrating the issue of shares to two new shareholders, which vary the proportions in which the company's share capital are held by the two original shareholders.

Chapter 2

Domicile

SIGNPOSTS

- **Scope** – A person's domicile status is an important issue for inheritance tax (IHT) purposes. Domicile is generally a primary factor in determining the scope of a person's liability to IHT (together with the situs of property) (see **2.1**).
- **Domicile under general law** – Domicile is a matter of private international law. There are three different types of such domicile: domicile of origin; domicile of dependence; and domicile of choice (see **2.2–2.5**).
- **'Elective' domicile for IHT purposes** – An election facility is available for non-UK domiciled individuals with a UK-domiciled spouse or civil partner to elect in writing to HMRC to be treated as UK domiciled for IHT purposes, notwithstanding the individual's non-UK domicile under general law (see **2.6–2.7**).
- **'Deemed' domicile for IHT purposes** – A person can be deemed to be domiciled in the UK for IHT purposes in certain circumstances, even though he is domiciled elsewhere under general law. The government introduced reforms to the taxation of non-UK domiciled individuals in *Finance (No 2) Act 2017* from 6 April 2017, subject to transitional rules. The effects of these reforms include bringing forward the point at which an individual can be treated as 'deemed' domiciled in the UK to 15 out of 20 tax years of residence in the UK. The provisions also treat 'formerly domiciled resident' persons as UK domiciled for IHT purposes for the relevant tax year if they were born in the UK with a domicile of origin in the UK, are resident in the UK for that tax year, and were UK resident for at least one of the previous two tax years. (see **2.8–2.14**).

BACKGROUND

2.1 A person's domicile status is an important issue for IHT purposes. For example, the IHT legislation does not generally tax a transfer where neither the transferor nor the property transferred has a sufficient connection with the UK. The factors normally used to determine whether a sufficient connection exists are the domicile of the transferor and the place where the property is situated.

As to the general scope of liability to IHT for individuals who are domiciled in the UK, and for non-UK domiciled individuals, see **1.2**.

DOMICILE UNDER GENERAL LAW

2.2 As a general rule, an individual is domiciled in the country (or state) considered to be his permanent home (eg see *Winans v Attorney General* [1904] AC 287).

There are three different types of domicile: domicile of origin; domicile of dependence; and domicile of choice. It should be noted that both a domicile of origin and a domicile of dependence are acquired by operation of law rather than by choice. There is no statutory definition of domicile for UK tax purposes. Domicile is a matter of private international law. The task of determining an individual's domicile can be a difficult forensic exercise (for example, see *J v U; U v J (No.2) (Domicile)* [2017] EWHC 449 (Fam)).

In addition to the general law concerning domicile, there is also a 'deemed domicile' rule for IHT purposes (*IHTA 1984, s 267*). Domicile is to be distinguished from residence, but residence can be a factor when determining domicile, especially deemed domicile, so knowledge of the rules on residence is important.

Historically, it did not help taxpayers (or tax practitioners) that very little statutory guidance on residence existed. This resulted in extensive case law. The uncertainty over residence status also often resulted in reliance being placed on non-statutory HMRC guidance such as in HMRC6 ('Residence, domicile and the remittance basis'), which replaced booklet IR20. HMRC have also stated that guidance on domicile in the Residence, Domicile and Remittance Basis manual should enable most trust settlors to decide for themselves whether or not they are UK domiciled, where appropriate. HMRC will only consider opening an enquiry where domicile could be an issue, or making a determination of IHT (under *IHTA 1984, s 221*) where there is a 'significant risk of loss of UK tax', although no guidance is given on what amount is considered to be 'significant' in this context (IHTM13034).

It should be noted that a person who is a member of the House of Commons or the House of Lords for any part of a tax year is generally to be treated as resident and domiciled in the UK for IHT (and income tax and capital gains tax) purposes, by virtue of the *Constitutional Reform and Governance Act 2010, ss 41, 42*. 'Ordinary residence' was also a factor, but this status was generally removed for tax purposes (by *FA 2013*) with effect from 2013/14.

A statutory residence test (SRT) was introduced in *FA 2013*, generally with effect for 2013/14 and subsequent tax years. The SRT is intended to enable individuals to determine whether they are resident or non-resident in the UK with certainty. However, the legislation is long and potentially complex, resulting in the publication of lengthy (and non-statutory) HMRC guidance (RDR3: 'Guidance Note: Statutory Residence Test (SRT)'), which is available from the gov.uk website (www.gov.uk/government/publications/rdr3-statutory-residence-test-srt).

The SRT is outside the scope of this publication. Readers are instead referred to the latest edition of *Booth and Schwarz: Residence, Domicile and UK Taxation*, published by Bloomsbury Professional.

The IHT spouse exemption for transfers from a UK-domiciled individual to a non-UK domiciled spouse or civil partner was increased (in *FA 2013*) from £55,000 to the prevailing nil rate band (£325,000 for 2018/19). This is subject to an election facility for the non-UK domiciled spouse or civil partner to be treated as UK domiciled for IHT purposes. The election broadly has the effect of removing the above restriction in the spouse exemption, but bringing the individual's worldwide estate within the scope of IHT. Both measures apply to transfers of value (including on death) on or after 6 April 2013 (see **2.6–2.7**).

HMRC guidance on the common law principles of domicile and its application of those rules in practice is contained in the Residence, Domicile and Remittance Basis Manual at RDRM20000 and following.

Domicile of origin

2.3 A person's domicile of origin is acquired at birth (normally that of the child's father).

HMRC guidance states that a domicile of origin at birth can subsequently be altered only by adoption (RDRM22010). A domicile of origin remains the person's domicile until it is replaced by a domicile of dependence (eg during minority) or a domicile of choice. A domicile of origin can revive when a domicile of choice is lost (see, for example, *Barlow Clowes International Ltd (in liquidation) and others v Henwood* [2008] EWCA 577).

In some cases, it may be necessary to determine a person's domicile of choice (see **2.4**) in order to decide the person's domicile in later years, such as where it is claimed that a domicile of choice has been abandoned and the person's domicile of origin has revived (*Wrottesley v Revenue and Customs* [2015] UKUT 637 (TCC)).

A person's domicile of origin is his father's domicile at the time of his birth unless he was illegitimate or his father died before he was born. In those cases, his domicile of origin will be his mother's domicile. This will often be the country in which he was born, but need not be so.

A domicile of origin will only be displaced if a person acquires a domicile of choice or a domicile of dependence. It will revive if, for example, a domicile of choice is abandoned, unless immediately replaced by a new domicile of choice (*Udny v Udny* (1869) LR 1 Sc&Div 441, HL).

HMRC consider that 'a domicile of origin can be placed into abeyance (that is "temporarily suspended") by the acquisition of a domicile of dependency or a domicile of choice, but it remains in the background to fill any gap that would otherwise arise' (RDRM22100). This is on the basis that an individual must always have one (and only one) domicile.

Domicile of choice

2.4 A domicile of choice is acquired by both physical presence in another country, and the settled intention to voluntarily reside there permanently, or for an unlimited time (*Re Fuld's Estate (No 3)* [1968] P 675). Thus, a domicile of choice will not be acquired if the intention is conditional, or by going to work in another country unless there is a definite intention to remain permanently or indefinitely when the work has ceased.

A domicile of choice can be lost by leaving the country without any definite intention of returning. A new domicile of choice will be acquired if a person moves to another country with the intention of settling there permanently or indefinitely. However, the mere intention to abandon a previous domicile may be insufficient in itself; active steps may be required to acquire a new domicile elsewhere (eg see *Re Foote Estate*, 2009 ABQB 654, a Canadian case reported in *Trusts and Estates Law and Tax Journal*, December 2012).

If a domicile of choice is lost and a new one is not acquired, the person's domicile of origin will revive.

HMRC consider that 'a domicile of choice can only be acquired where the individual is both resident in a territory subject to a distinctive system or "municipal law" … and intends to reside there indefinitely' (RDRM22300). A person seeking to establish that a domicile of origin has been lost and a domicile of choice acquired, or that a domicile of choice has been replaced, must establish the change with very clear proof. HMRC consider that statements of intention by individuals must be considered in the context of all relevant evidence, and states: 'Mere statements are generally less important than actual conduct and may carry little weight if the statement does not correlate with actions taken' (RDRM22320).

Case law has underlined the potential difficulties faced by those wishing to shed a domicile of origin in favour of a domicile of choice; for example, see *Re Clore (No 2)* [1984] STC 609. Subsequently, in *Agulian v Cyganik* [2006] EWCA Civ 129, the Court of Appeal held that an individual born in Cyprus, but who had lived and worked in England for about 43 years between the age of 19 and his death at the age of 63, had not lost his Cypriot domicile of origin and acquired a domicile of choice in England. By contrast, in *Holliday v Musa* [2010] EWCA Civ 335, it was held that an individual (also with a Cypriot domicile of origin) who resided in the UK from 1958 until his death in 2006 had, on the facts, intended to settle permanently in England.

In addition, HMRC consider that the loss of a domicile of choice requires cessation of both residence and intention. An intention subject to a contingency may be insufficient to result in a domicile of choice (*IRC v Bullock* [1976] 1 WLR 1178). On the other hand, in *Furse v IRC* [1980] 3 All ER 838, an individual was born in Rhode Island in 1883 and was a US citizen. He and his wife had a family house in New York and visited it regularly, but they also had a farm in Sussex. It had been bought by his wife in 1924 and the individual lived there until his death in 1963. There was evidence that he was happy and contented in the Sussex farm; the only suggestion that he might ever leave England was if and when he was no longer fit enough to lead an active life on the farm. The court found that he died domiciled in England, as his intention to leave was too vague to form a definite aspiration.

It should be noted that HMRC will not necessarily accept that it is bound by any earlier ruling it has given regarding a person's domicile of choice (*Gulliver v Revenue and Customs* [2017] UKFTT 222 (TC)).

Domicile is essentially a concept of private international law rather than tax law, and a detailed consideration of the principles involved and relevant case law is outside the scope of this book.

Domicile of dependence

2.5 The domicile of a minor initially follows that of the person on whom he is dependent. A domicile of dependence only affects children (under 16, for England, Wales, Scotland and Northern Ireland) and persons of unsound mind. There is a separate statutory basis in Scotland for determining the domicile of any individual under the age of 16; for HMRC guidance, see RDRM22120.

Prior to 1 January 1974, a married woman acquired her husband's domicile on marriage, and her domicile changed with his (ie she acquired a domicile of dependence from her husband). This rule was abolished by the *Domicile and Matrimonial Proceedings Act 1973*. For women who were married before 1 January 1974, their domicile of dependence was effectively reclassified as a domicile of choice on 1 January 1974 (ie capable of being changed by the acquisition or revival of another domicile, in the same way as any other domicile of choice).

However, the above rule has no relevance to women married on or after 1 January 1974, and a woman can therefore have a different domicile than that of her husband.

Care is needed where the domicile of a parent (upon which a child's domicile is dependent) changed from a domicile of origin to a domicile of choice before the child reaches the age of 16. For example, if the child's father had a domicile of origin abroad but subsequently acquired a domicile of choice in the UK when the child was under the age of 16, the child will also become UK domiciled. The child's UK domicile would be retained throughout adulthood, unless replaced by a domicile of choice.

Interestingly, HMRC guidance states (in the context of legitimate children): 'This principle is generally accepted, but it should be noted that it has not been applied in every case' (RDRM22210).

'ELECTIVE' AND 'DEEMED' DOMICILE FOR IHT PURPOSES

Election to be treated as domiciled in the UK

2.6 As intimated at **2.2** above, for transfers between spouses (or civil partners), it is important to know the domicile of both spouses. If the transferor spouse is domiciled in the UK but their spouse is domiciled abroad, the spouse exemption is limited to the prevailing nil rate band (£325,000 for 2018/19). The statutory limit was increased from £55,000 following changes introduced (in *FA 2013*) with effect in relation to transfers of value made on or after 6 April 2013 (*IHTA 1984, s 18(2), (2A)*) (see **1.20**).

Provisions (introduced in *FA 2013*) make available the facility for non-UK domiciled individuals with a UK-domiciled spouse or civil partner to elect in writing to HMRC to be treated as UK domiciled for IHT purposes (*IHTA 1984, ss 267ZA, 267ZB*).

If no election is made to be treated as UK domiciled, the overseas assets of the non-UK domiciled spouse or civil partner generally continue to be excluded property for IHT purposes, but transfers from their spouse or civil partner are subject to the 'capped' spouse exemption limit.

The effect of the election is that transfers from a UK-domiciled spouse (or civil partner) are exempt from IHT without limit. However, the electing spouse's worldwide estate becomes liable to IHT.

2.7 An election may be made if:

- the non-UK domiciled spouse had a UK-domiciled spouse at any time on or after 6 April 2013 and within the seven-year period before the election is made (*IHTA 1984, s 267ZA(3)*) (a 'lifetime election'); or
- the deceased was, at any time from 6 April 2013 and within seven years before death, UK domiciled and the spouse of the person who would

(by virtue of the election) be treated as UK domiciled (*IHTA 1984, s 267ZA(4)*) (a 'death election').

The above provisions effectively allow for a retrospective election following a change of domicile status, in the circumstances outlined. They also allow individuals whose marriage has ended to retrospectively elect to cover the period when they were married to a UK-domiciled person.

Those spouses making a lifetime or death election may choose the date from which it applies, up to a maximum of seven years previously. However, the earliest date that may be specified is 6 April 2013 (*IHTA 1984, s 267ZB(4)(a)*). A lifetime election can be made at any time (but see below), whereas elections following a death must be made within two years of the death, or such longer period as HMRC may allow. The personal representatives of non-domiciled individuals may make death elections on their behalf (*IHTA 1984, s 267ZA(2)*).

An election can only be made on or after 17 July 2013, but as indicated above it can take effect before that date. The lifetime and death elections are irrevocable. However, an election will cease to have effect if the electing person is later resident outside the UK for more than four full consecutive tax years (*IHTA 1984, s 267ZB(10)*).

HMRC guidance on elections for non-UK domiciled spouses and civil partners to be domiciled in the UK is included in the Inheritance Tax Manual (at IHTM13040 and following), including details of how to make an election (IHTM13043).

Note that it is only the domicile of the *transferee* spouse which is relevant in the above context of the exemption limit in *IHTA 1984, s 18(2)*. Thus the limit does not apply if both the transferor and spouse are not domiciled in the UK, or if the transferor is domiciled outside the UK but their spouse is domiciled in the UK.

'Deemed' domicile

2.8

> **Focus**
>
> For IHT purposes, a person can be *deemed* to be domiciled in the UK in certain circumstances, even though he is domiciled elsewhere under general law (*IHTA 1984, s 267*).
>
> See also **2.2** above regarding the deemed domicile status of MPs and members of the House of Lords.
>
> The election for a person to be treated as domiciled in the UK is discussed at **2.6–2.7** above. In determining whether the person making the election

is (or was) domiciled in the UK, the deemed domicile provisions in *IHTA 1984, s 267* are ignored (*IHTA 1984, s 267ZA(8)*).

However, the election does not prevent the deemed domicile provisions applying in the normal way if a person who has elected to be treated as domiciled in the UK becomes deemed domiciled in the UK while the election is in force, by meeting the conditions in *IHTA 1984, s 267* (IHTM13040).

The government reformed the deemed domicile rules for IHT purposes (in *Finance (No 2) Act 2017*), with the aim of restricting non-UK domiciled individuals from being able to claim non-UK domicile status for an indefinite period of time. The changes included the addition of a new deemed domicile test (in *IHTA 1984, s 267*) in relation to a 'formerly domiciled resident' (see **2.13**), and the replacement of another test (ie the 'long term residence' or '17 out of 20' rule; see **2.12**) to reduce the number of years that an individual is resident in the UK before becoming deemed domiciled (see **2.10**).

Separate domicile reforms were also introduced for income tax and capital gains tax purposes.

In relation to times following the introduction of the above changes, two separate and alternative time-based tests potentially apply for determining deemed domicile status for IHT purposes (*IHTA 1984, s 267(1)*); a 'three-year rule' and a long-term residence (or '15 out of 20') rule.

As to a third category of deemed domicile status in relation to a formerly domiciled resident, see **2.13** below.

The 'three-year' rule

2.9 A person is treated as domiciled in the UK if he or she was domiciled in the UK at any time in the three years immediately preceding the time at which the question of his domicile is to be decided.

HMRC's guidance at the time of writing states in the context of the above 'three-year rule' (IHTM13024): 'For the rule to apply the taxpayer must have been domiciled in the UK both on or after 10 December 1974 and at any time within the three *calendar* years before the relevant event (the death or gift)' (emphasis added). However, the legislation refers to the three-year period immediately preceding the 'relevant time' (ie broadly when UK domicile is lost (*IHTA 1984, s 267(1)*).

It is assumed that HMRC's guidance means the third anniversary of the relevant time (and not the alternative interpretation of three calendar years from 1 January to 31 December preceding that date), although the guidance could be clearer.

The 'three-year rule' was retained notwithstanding the changes to deemed domicile introduced in *Finance (No 2) Act 2017.*

Example 2.1—'Deemed' domicile: the 'three-year' rule

Christine is aged 40, and had been resident and domiciled in England all her life. She left the UK on 31 March 2015 and settled in Spain permanently, acquiring a domicile of choice in Spain under general law. She did not subsequently return to the UK.

Christine ceased to be domiciled in the UK for IHT purposes under the 'three-year' rule on 1 April 2018.

However, Christine would also need to consider the '17 out of 20' rule (see **2.12** below), which continues to apply under transitional rules introduced with the domicile reforms mentioned at **2.8** as she was non-UK resident for 2017/18 and subsequently (*F(No 2)A 2017, s 30(10)*).

She would not lose her deemed domicile under the '17 out of 20' rule (see below) until she had been non-resident in the UK for three tax years and the fourth had begun. Her three years of non-residence would be 2015/16, 2016/17 and 2017/18. She would lose her deemed domicile under the latter rule on 6 April 2018 (ie at the start of the 2018/19 tax year).

Care may be needed in some cases, as it may be unclear when an individual has actually abandoned his or her domicile in one territory in favour of another, for the purposes of determining when the three-year period begins and ends.

Example 2.2—'Deemed' domicile: in two minds

Davor, who was born in Croatia, came to live in England at a very early age and established a domicile of choice. Some years later, his lawyers found it difficult to establish whether he had acquired a new domicile of choice in France as soon as he left England in March 2015. The lawyers used a Latin tag for this situation: *sine animo revertendi* (loosely translated as: 'I really haven't yet made up my mind whether or not to return to England').

The lawyers came to the conclusion that Davor had probably retained his domicile of choice in England whilst he made up his mind. On that basis, any delay on his part could postpone the start of the relevant three-year period in *IHTA 1984, s 267(1)(a)*, because he would not lose his domicile in England straight away.

Long-term residence (or '15 out of 20') rule

2.10 As part of the domicile reforms (introduced in *Finance (No 2) Act 2017*) (see **2.8**) the '15 out of 20' long-term residence rule for deemed domicile purposes replaced a '17 out of 20' rule (see **2.12**), thereby potentially bringing more individuals within the scope of IHT.

The '15 out of 20' rule (in *s 267(1)(b)*) generally applies in relation to times after 5 April 2017 (subject to transitional rules; see below). It contains two conditions, both of which must be met. The first condition is that the person was resident in the UK for at least 15 of the 20 tax years immediately preceding the relevant tax year. The second condition is that the person was resident for at least one of the four tax years ending with the relevant tax year.

Both conditions must be met for the person to be deemed domiciled in the UK under the '15 out of 20' rule. Thus, an individual who has been UK resident for at least 15 out of the 20 tax years immediately preceding the relevant tax year, but who was resident in the UK for none of the four tax years ending with the relevant tax year, will not be deemed UK domiciled under *IHTA 1984, s 267(1)(b)*).

Example 2.3—'Deemed' domicile: the '15 out of 20' rule

Nick has a Bulgarian domicile of origin. He came to live in the UK in June 2003, and was resident in the UK for the tax years 2003/04 to 2017/18 inclusive (ie 15 tax years).

Nick becomes deemed domiciled in the UK in 2018/19, even if he leaves the UK and becomes non-UK resident in that tax year.

It should be noted that the first of the above conditions in the '15 out of 20' rule would be satisfied if the person is UK resident for at least 15 of the 20 tax years *immediately preceding* the relevant tax year (see below). The 'relevant tax year' for these purposes is the tax year in which the 'relevant time' falls (ie the time at which the person's domicile status falls to be determined).

By contrast, the '17 out of 20' rule (see **2.12**) refers to UK residence in not less than 17 out of the 20 tax years *ending* with the tax year in which the relevant time falls. Thus there is a difference in the way that years are counted for these purposes. The overall effect of the '15 out of 20' rule is that an individual's deemed UK domicile status can commence significantly sooner than under the '17 out of 20' rule it replaced.

As indicated above, the '15 out of 20' deemed UK domicile rule applies to times after 5 April 2017, subject to certain transitional provisions. Those leaving the UK before 6 April 2017 are not subject to the '15 out of 20 rule' if they were not UK resident for the relevant tax year and for any tax year beginning after 5 April 2017 and preceding the relevant tax year (*F(No 2)A 2017, s 30(10)*).

Example 2.4—'Deemed' domicile: transitional rule

Suppose that Nick (see **Example 2.3**) was resident in the UK for the tax years 2002/03 to 2016/17 inclusive (ie 15 tax years), but left the UK on 31 March 2017 and was non-UK resident in 2017/18.

Nick would normally be deemed domiciled in the UK under the '15 out of 20' rule in 2017/18, even though he had already left the UK. However, as 2017/18 was the first year in which he would otherwise have been deemed domiciled in the UK, the effect of the transitional provisions is that Nick will not become deemed domiciled in the UK for these purposes if he does not resume UK residence.

Nick was not resident in the UK for more than 15 tax years, so he is not caught by the '17 out of 20' rule (see **2.12**).

In addition, the '15 out of 20' rule is not relevant for certain purposes in respect of settled property, including in determining the excluded property status of property which became comprised in the settlement before 6 April 2017 (*F(No 2)A 2017, s 30(11)*).

It should be noted that a non-UK domiciled person (who was not born in the UK with a UK domicile of origin; see below) becomes deemed domiciled in his 16th year after 15 out of 20 years of UK residence, even if he is not resident in the UK in the 16th year, unless he left the UK before 6 April 2017 and remained non-resident thereafter. Consequently, an individual would generally need to leave the UK in the 14th tax year of UK residence to avoid becoming deemed UK domiciled in the 16th tax year.

2.11 The domicile reforms also include a third category of deemed UK domicile for IHT purposes, in relation to a 'formerly domiciled resident' (see **2.13** below).

The 'long-term residence' (or '17 out of 20') rule

2.12 In relation to times prior to the domicile reforms having effect, a '17 out of 20' rule generally needs to be considered instead of the '15 out of 20' rule that replaced it.

The '17 out of 20' rule broadly provides that a person who is not domiciled in the UK under general law is treated as UK domiciled for IHT purposes if he is resident in the UK for 17 out of 20 years of assessment ending with the one in which the relevant time falls. This rule is the most relevant to someone who has come from abroad to live in the UK.

This rule was replaced (in *Finance (No 2) Act 2017*) with the '15 out of 20' rule from 6 April 2017, subject to transitional provisions (see **2.10**).

Example 2.5—'Deemed' domicile: the '17 out of 20' rule

Joseph came to the UK to stay on 1 May 2000. The Inland Revenue (as it then was) treated him as UK resident for the tax year 2000/01 (ie Joseph was resident in the UK for more than 183 days in that tax year). He remained resident in the UK for 2001/02 and all later tax years up to and including 2015/16.

The tax year 2016/17 is the seventeenth tax year. If Joseph had remained resident in the UK during 2016/17, he would have become deemed domiciled in the UK under the above rule. A transfer of foreign situs assets by Joseph would then have been caught for IHT purposes, unless exempt or potentially exempt.

As indicated at **2.10**, the changes to the deemed domicile provisions in *IHTA 1984, s 267* included the replacement of the '17 out of 20' rule with a '15 out of 20' rule, subject to transitional provisions. The revised test is met if the person was UK resident for at least 15 out of 20 tax years immediately preceding the relevant tax year, and for at least one of the four tax years ending with the relevant tax year.

The 'formerly domiciled resident' rule

2.13

Focus

The government's stated intention when the domicile reforms were announced was to make it more difficult for individuals with a domicile of origin in the UK to claim non-UK domicile status if they left the UK and acquired a domicile of choice in another country, but subsequently returned to the UK and maintained that they had retained a foreign domicile of choice.

The reform of the deemed domicile provisions for IHT purposes (introduced in *Finance (No 2) Act 2017*) include an additional category of deemed domicile in the UK, such that a person is treated as domiciled in the UK if he is a 'formerly domiciled resident' for the relevant tax year (*IHTA 1984, s 267(1)(aa)*).

A 'formerly domiciled resident' for a tax year is defined (in *IHTA 1984, s 272*) as a person who was born in the UK, whose domicile of origin was in the UK, who was resident in the UK for that tax year, and who was resident in the UK for at least one of the two tax years immediately preceding that tax year.

In such circumstances, the person would fall to be treated as a deemed UK domiciliary on their return to the UK (subject to the short period of grace mentioned above), irrespective of their domicile status under general law.

In addition, if the settlor of a settlement was not domiciled in the UK when the settlement was made, the property would nevertheless not be excluded property (within *IHTA 1984, s 48(3)* or *(3A)*; see **1.13**) at any time in a tax year if the settlor was a formerly domiciled resident for that tax year (*IHTA 1984, s 48(3E)*).

The IHT regime for certain settled property was amended accordingly as a result of the formerly domiciled resident rule in relation to:

- ten-year anniversary charges for relevant property trusts (*IHTA 1984, ss 64(1B)*);
- exit charges from such trusts (*IHTA 1984, s 65(7B)*);
- initial qualifying interests in possession in favour of the settlor (or spouse or civil partner) which become relevant property trusts; and
- property moving between settlements (*IHTA 1984, s 82*).

It should be noted that the above provision relating to exit charges is a trust protection measure. It broadly provides that an exit charge does not arise solely because of the trust property becoming excluded property (and therefore no longer being relevant property) by virtue of *IHTA 1984, s 48(3E)* ceasing to apply to it, upon the settlor becoming non-UK resident again.

Furthermore, the domicile reforms for IHT purposes amended the definition of 'foreign owned' property (in *IHTA 1984, s 272*) to include settled property where the settlor is not a formerly domiciled resident for the tax year and was domiciled outside the UK when the property was settled.

Example 2.6—'Deemed' domicile: the 'formerly domiciled resident'

James was born in April 1962 in London. His domicile of origin is in the UK. In March 1984, he left the UK to live in Ruritania, and acquired a domicile of choice there. In December 2006, he settled non-UK assets (ie three industrial units situated in Ruritania) on trust. The settled property was excluded property (within *IHTA 1984, s 48(3)(a)*).

In May 2017, James returned to the UK. He became UK resident in the tax year 2017/18 and remained UK resident in subsequent tax years. James therefore became a formerly domiciled resident in 2018/19. The property settled in 2006 therefore ceased to be excluded property. Furthermore, the trust becomes subject to possible IHT charges under the relevant property regime.

Exceptions to deemed domicile

2.14 There are some exceptions to the application of the 'deemed domicile' provisions. The deemed domicile provisions (in *IHTA 1984, s 267(1)*) do not apply in certain circumstances including the following:

- specified government securities in the beneficial ownership of persons not ordinarily resident (and in certain cases not domiciled) in the UK (*IHTA 1984, ss 6(2), 48(4)*);
- certain types of savings by persons domiciled in the Channel Islands or the Isle of Man (*IHTA 1984, s 6(3)*);
- certain pre-CTT double taxation agreements still in force by virtue of *IHTA 1984, s 158(6)*. Those agreements contain their own rules for domicile and for resolving the issue where both countries claim domicile (*IHTA 1984, s 267(2)*);
- for the purposes of deciding whether property settled before 10 December 1974 is excluded property, and for certain other purposes (see *IHTA 1984, s 267(3)*). The deemed domicile changes introduced in *F(No 2)A 2017* (see **2.8**) include the repeal of *IHTA 1984, s 267(3)*, but transitional rules also include a preserving provision in relation to such property (see *F(No 2)A 2017, s 30(12)*).

In addition, as indicated at **2.8** above, the deemed domicile rules are ignored for the purposes of determining whether a spouse or civil partner making an election to be treated as domiciled in the UK (see **1.20**) is or was domiciled in the UK (*IHTA 1984, s 267ZA(8)*). Furthermore, the election provisions (in *IHTA 1984, ss 267ZA, 267ZB*) are ignored for the purposes of determining whether a person is or was domiciled in the UK under the deemed domicile rules (*IHTA 1984, s 267(5)*).

Following legislation introduced in *FA 2013*, the concept of 'ordinary residence' is generally removed for tax purposes. However, the government stated (in its explanatory notes to the *Finance Bill 2013* legislation) that the above IHT provisions in *IHTA 1984, ss 6(2)* and *48(4)* will continue to apply to securities issued on the basis of exemption for persons not ordinarily resident if the beneficial owner acquired them before 6 April 2013. All UK government securities acquired on or after 6 April 2013 will be exempt provided the beneficial owner is resident outside the UK; domicile is relevant only to the issue of 3.5% War Loan (IHTM27241).

With regard to the third bullet point above, HMRC accept that domicile issues exclude deemed domicile when considering the double tax agreements with France, Italy, India and Pakistan. However, if there is a common law domicile in those countries, the deemed domicile rules can apply to chargeable *lifetime* transfers (IHTM13024).

Chapter 3

Transferable nil rate bands

SIGNPOSTS

- **Transfer of unused nil rate band** – The transferable nil rate band (TNRB) provisions broadly allow claims for the unused nil rate band of a deceased spouse or civil partner to be transferred to a surviving spouse or civil partner (who dies on or after 9 October 2007). The survivor's nil rate band can be increased by up to 100%, or one additional nil rate band (see **3.1–3.7**).
- **Claims** – The TNRB must be claimed within a permitted period, although HMRC may allow a longer claim period at its discretion in some cases (see **3.8–3.10**).
- **Reduction or clawback of TNRB** – The TNRB may be reduced or clawed back in certain specific circumstances (eg where a deferred IHT charge arises on woodlands), by reference to the deceased spouse's estate (see **3.11–3.20**).
- **Practical issues** – Records and documents should be kept to support claims for the TNRB on the death of the surviving spouse or civil partner (see **3.21–3.23**).
- **Planning and other issues** – Various considerations may arise in relation to the TNRB, such as whether to use the nil rate band on the first death instead (eg a legacy to a nil rate band discretionary trust); the position of cohabiting couples with TNRBs from previous marriages or civil partnerships; and care fees issues (see **3.24–3.41**).
- **Residence nil rate band** – Extra ('residence') nil rate band is available on death from 6 April 2017 when a home is passed on death to lineal descendants of the deceased. Unused nil rate band is potentially transferable to a spouse or civil partner in a similar way to the transferable nil rate band, subject to a successful claim being made (see **3.42–3.48**).

BACKGROUND

3.1 Estate planning for many married couples and civil partnerships was simplified following changes introduced in *Finance Act 2008*. The transferable nil rate band provisions broadly allow a claim for all or part of an unused nil rate band on the death of a spouse or civil partner to be transferred to a surviving spouse or civil partner (who dies on or after 9 October 2007) (*IHTA 1984, ss 8A–8C*). The rules apply in the same way whether the survivor leaves a will, or dies intestate.

The facility to make claims for the transfer of unused nil rate band remains very useful despite the nil rate band initially remaining frozen at its 2009/10 level of £325,000 for the tax years 2010/11 to 2014/15 inclusive (*FA 2010, s 8*). Furthermore, the effective freezing of the nil rate band at £325,000 was subsequently extended and is to remain at £325,000 until the end of the tax year 2020/21 at the earliest.

3.2 Prior to the introduction of the transferable nil rate band facility, it was generally important to ensure that the estates of spouses or civil partners were sufficient to utilise their available IHT thresholds (or 'nil rate bands') if possible, and that optimum use was made of the nil rate band on the first death. If each spouse or civil partner owned sufficient assets to constitute their nil rate bands, the estates of each individual could be sheltered from IHT up to an amount equal to the nil rate band multiplied by the 40% 'death rate'.

However, as indicated at **1.20**, there is a complete exemption (in *IHTA 1984, s 18*) for transfers between UK-domiciled spouses or civil partners during lifetime and on death. It should be noted that if the transferor spouse or civil partner is UK domiciled but the transferee is non-UK domiciled, the exemption is restricted to a cumulative upper limit. This limit remained unchanged at a relatively modest amount for many years (ie £55,000 up to and including 2012/13), but was increased (in *Finance Act 2013*) to the prevailing nil rate band at the time of the transfer (£325,000 for 2018/19), unless a valid election is made for the transferee spouse or civil partner to be treated as UK domiciled (in which case the upper limit does not apply, but the individual's worldwide estate is then generally liable to IHT in the same way as a UK-domiciled individual).

Thus, if a deceased spouse or civil partner leaves their entire estate to the surviving spouse, then (unless the recipient spouse or civil partner is non-UK domiciled), the legacy will normally be wholly exempt from IHT. However, the estate of the survivor increases accordingly.

3.3 Prior to the *Finance Act 2008* changes, exempt legacies between spouses or civil partners often resulted in an IHT liability on the second death, and a higher IHT liability overall, due to the nil rate band on the first death not being utilised. Therefore IHT planning for married couples or civil partners typically involved ensuring that an amount up to the available nil rate band was left to non-exempt legatees (eg children), or (say) to a family discretionary trust in which the surviving spouse was included among the class of beneficiaries.

This planning was relatively straightforward and simple to implement if each spouse or civil partner owned sufficient 'liquid' assets (eg cash, shares or other investments) to constitute their nil rate bands.

However, lifetime transfers between spouses or civil partners were often necessary to achieve this result on death. In some cases, the only asset of any substantial value would be an interest in the family home. This resulted in relatively complicated (and sometimes artificial) arrangements involving an interest in the family home to constitute the nil rate band, such as 'debt' or 'charge' schemes (see **Chapter 16**).

Transferable nil rate band claims cannot be made by cohabiting couples who are not legally married or civil partners (see *Executor of Holland deceased v IRC* [2003] SpC 350), or by family members who occupy the same property, such as siblings (see *Burden and another v United Kingdom* [2008] All ER (D) 391 (Apr)).

3.4 Whilst nil rate band legacies to chargeable (non-exempt) beneficiaries on the first spouse or civil partner to die are undoubtedly less common or popular than before the introduction of the transferable nil rate band facility, there may be circumstances in which such legacies are necessary or preferred, such as in terms of making provision for family members.

In addition, aside from IHT considerations there may be other reasons why an interest in the home may be left on trust (eg due to concerns about divorce). However, the transferable nil rate band facility has undoubtedly made IHT planning simpler for many spouses or civil partners, compared with the position prior to 9 October 2007.

HMRC's published guidance on the transferable nil rate band provisions is contained in the Inheritance Tax Manual at IHTM43000 onwards, and reference is made to some of this guidance below.

HMRC have also published an 'Inheritance Tax Toolkit' to assist tax agents and advisers in the preparation of IHT account form IHT400 (tinyurl.com/IHT-Toolkit). The toolkit identifies various areas of risk for completing form IHT400. The 'risk' in respect of the transferable nil rate band is 'If full details of any pre-deceased spouse or civil partner have not been obtained the transferable nil rate band may be overlooked or not applied correctly …' The toolkit goes on to suggest various ways to mitigate this risk. See **3.18** below.

Extra (or 'residence') nil rate band is available on death from 6 April 2017 if an interest in the home passes to a lineal descendant (*IHTA 1984, ss 8D–8M*). This residence nil rate band may generally be transferred to a surviving spouse (or civil partner) to the extent that it remains unused on the first death, subject to a successful claim being made.

For commentary on the residence nil rate band see **3.42–3.48** below and **Chapter 16**.

OUTLINE OF THE RULES

3.5 The transferable nil rate band legislation forms *IHTA 1984, ss 8A–8C*, with consequential changes to *IHTA 1984, ss 239, 242* and *272* (Note: *FA 2008* also amended *IHTA 1984, s 151BA*, prior to its repeal in *FA 2011*, with effect for deaths occurring from 6 April 2011).

The provisions broadly allow claims for the transfer of a spouse's or civil partner's unused nil rate band to a surviving spouse or civil partner who dies on or after 9 October 2007. Therefore, if both spouses or civil partners died before 9 October 2007, it is not possible to take advantage of the transferable nil rate band facility.

The amount that can be transferred is based on a percentage of the deceased's nil rate band. That percentage (which cannot exceed 100) represents the nil rate band (or bands, where there was more than one former spouse or civil partner) not used on any previous occasion, taking into account lifetime transfers made within seven years before death, and is applied to the nil rate band in operation on the death of the surviving spouse (*IHTA 1984, s 8A*).

A claim to transfer unused nil rate band must be made by the survivor's personal representatives, within two years from the end of the month in which the survivor dies, or (if later) within three months of the personal representatives first acting as such. However, HMRC may allow a longer period at their discretion. In the absence of a claim by the personal representatives, a late claim may be made by any person liable to IHT on the survivor's death, subject to HMRC's agreement (*IHTA 1984, s 8B*).

There are potentially complicated provisions dealing with the transfer of the nil rate band and the calculation of IHT when certain IHT and capital transfer tax deferred charges (ie on heritage assets and woodlands) are triggered, where the deferred IHT is calculated by reference to the earlier deceased spouse (*IHTA 1984, s 8C*).

There are also rules to determine the amount of nil rate band to be applied in calculating IHT where a dependant who inherits an alternatively secured pension (ASP) fund dies or ceases to be a dependant (see **3.14**). However, following changes introduced in *Finance Act 2011*, the IHT provisions relating to ASP funds (in *IHTA 1984, ss 151A–151E*) do not apply (subject to transitional provisions) with effect for deaths occurring from 6 April 2011.

CALCULATING THE UNUSED NIL RATE BAND

3.6

> **Focus**
>
> - The provisions allowing for the transfer of unused nil rate band between spouses and civil partners broadly apply if someone dies

leaving a surviving spouse or civil partner, and there is some unused nil rate band on the deceased's death (*IHTA 1984, s 8A(1)*).

- It does not matter if the unused nil rate band arises because no assets were owned on death.
- Nor does it matter whether the first spouse or civil partner to die was actually or deemed domiciled in the UK; every person (UK domiciled or not) is potentially entitled to a nil rate band (see HMRC's example at IHTM43042).
- The rules for calculating the unused nil rate band involve a formula approach *(IHTA 1984, s 8A(2))*. However, in essence there is 'unused' nil rate band to the extent that the spouse or civil partner's chargeable estate on the first death was less than their available nil rate band.

On the death of the surviving spouse or civil partner, their available nil rate band is increased by a percentage. The legislation provides a formula for calculating that percentage (*IHTA 1984, s 8A(4)*).

The terminology and formulae used in the legislation for the basic calculation of the transferable nil rate band is reproduced below, but is broadly the amount of the deceased's unused nil rate band, divided by the nil rate band upon the deceased spouse's or civil partner's death.

Unused nil rate band on death (IHTA 1984, s 8A(2)):

M > VT, where:

- M is the maximum amount that could be transferred by a chargeable transfer made on the person's death if it were to be wholly chargeable to tax at the rate of 0%. The residence nil rate band is taken into account in establishing whether there is any unused nil rate band available for transfer to a spouse or civil partner, if appropriate (see **3.44**); and
- VT is the value actually transferred by the chargeable transfer so made (or nil, if applicable).

The percentage increase in the survivor's nil rate band maximum (Note: this is subject to an overriding maximum of 100% (*s 8A(5)*), and to the 'clawback' rules (*IHTA 1984, s 8C*) in respect of heritage property and woodlands relief):

$$\left(\frac{E}{NRBMD}\right) \times 100$$

Where –

- E is the amount by which M is greater than VT in the case of the deceased person; and

- NRBMD is the nil rate band maximum at the time of the deceased person's death.

In HMRC's view, the percentage should be taken to four decimal places, if necessary (IHTM43020).

Example 3.1—Practical effect of a nil rate band transfer

Adam died on 31 March 2018. His chargeable death estate amounted to £145,000, and he had made no lifetime gifts. His wife Bertha died on 1 November 2018 with a chargeable estate of £400,000 and having made no lifetime gifts. They had no children.

Adam's unused nil rate band available on Bertha's death is calculated as follows:

Unused nil rate band (M > VT) (*s 8A(2)*):

£325,000 (M, being the nil rate band maximum for 2017/18) – £145,000 (VT, being the chargeable death estate) = £180,000

Percentage increase

$$\left(\frac{\text{E}}{\text{NRBMD}}\right) \times 100$$

(*s 8A(3), (4)*):

Where E is Adam's unused nil rate band, and NRBMD is the nil rate band on Adam's death:

$$\frac{£180{,}000}{£325{,}000} \times 100 = 55.3846\%$$

On Bertha's death, 55.3846% of unused nil rate band (£325,000 for 2018/19) in respect of Adam can be added to her own:

$$£325{,}000 \times 55.3846\% = £180{,}000$$

The combination of Adam's unused nil rate band (£180,000) and Bertha's nil rate band (£325,000) is sufficient to cover Bertha's chargeable estate of £400,000. No IHT is therefore payable on her death.

3.7 However, the amount of unused nil rate band that can be claimed on the survivor's death is subject to potential restrictions in the following circumstances:

- The estate of the earlier spouse or civil partner to die made a claim to transfer unused nil rate band from a previous deceased spouse or civil partner. The estate of the surviving spouse or civil partner may only claim a maximum of the nil rate band then in force (*IHTA 1984, s 8A(6)(a)*).
- There is also an overriding limit of one additional nil rate band (based on the rate applicable on the survivor's death) if, for example, the surviving spouse was married more than once, and his or her deceased spouses did not use up their nil rate bands on death. The survivor's estate can claim in respect of both previous spouses, but the nil rate band of the survivor's estate can only be increased by 100%, or one additional nil rate band (*IHTA 1984, s 8A(6)(b)*).
- As indicated at **3.5**, the nil rate band of the deceased spouse or civil partner may be subject to adjustment in respect of certain deferred charges (*IHTA 1984, s 8A(3)*) (see **3.11** below).

Example 3.2—Maximum claim

Colin and Delia had been married for many years, until Delia sadly died on 31 January 2005. By her will, Delia left £50,000 to her sister Joanne, with residue to Colin.

Colin subsequently found friendship and love in Elizabeth, and they were married in 2009. Elizabeth died on 1 May 2015, leaving £150,000 to her nieces and nephews, with residue to Colin.

Colin finally passed away on 31 March 2019, leaving a chargeable estate of £800,000 to his siblings.

Delia's unused nil rate band amounted to £213,000, ie £263,000 (the nil rate band maximum for 2004/05), less the chargeable legacy of £50,000. The percentage nil rate band unused was 80.9886%.

Elizabeth's unused nil rate band amounted to £175,000, ie £325,000 (the nil rate band maximum for 2015/16), less chargeable legacies of £150,000. The percentage unused nil rate band was 53.8462%.

On Colin's death, the unused nil rate band percentage from his two marriages amounts to 134.8348% (ie 80.9886% for Delia and 53.8462% for Elizabeth). However, the maximum percentage that can be claimed by Colin's estate is 100%. A claim is therefore made to add 100% of £325,000 (the nil rate band maximum for 2018/19) to Colin's own nil rate band of £325,000. The combined nil rate bands therefore amount to £650,000.

The IHT payable in respect of Colin's estate is as follows:

$$£800,000 - £650,000 = £150,000 \times 40\% = £60,000$$

TRANSFER CLAIMS

3.8 Transfers of unused nil rate band on the death of a spouse or civil partner must be claimed (*IHTA 1984, s 8A(3)*). The rules for such claims are in *IHTA 1984, s 8B*.

> **Focus**
>
> - In practice, the claim is made on Schedule IHT402 ('Claim to transfer unused nil rate band') by the personal representative of the surviving spouse or civil partner within a 'permitted period' (see below).
> - If an excepted estate meets the conditions for a transferable nil rate band claim, the claim can be made by the personal representatives completing form IHT217 ('Claim to transfer unused nil rate band for excepted estates') and submitting it to the Probate Registry (or Sheriff Court in Scotland) along with form IHT205 or form C5 ('Return of estate information') (see IHTM06025).
> - The 'permitted period' is (see *IHTA 1984, s 8B(3)*) two years from the end of the month in which the survivor dies or, if later, three months from the date on which the personal representatives first act as such. If no claim has been made by the personal representatives, a claim can be made by any other person who is liable to IHT on the survivor's death.
> - The legislation permits late claims at HMRC's discretion (*s 8B(3)(b)*).

HMRC may admit claims submitted late due to reasons beyond the claimant's control on a discretionary basis. Possible circumstances may include the following (see IHTM43009):

- if there is a dispute over the estate, which must be resolved before the personal representatives can be identified, and there is subsequently insufficient time (beyond the extended 'permitted period' of three months mentioned above) for the recently identified personal representatives to make a claim;
- unforeseen postal disruptions resulting in the loss or delay of a claim;
- the loss of records supporting a claim due to fire, flood or theft, where the records could not be replaced in time for a claim within the permitted period;
- serious illness of the claimant, if it prevented the claim being dealt with in the permitted period and from that date to the time the claim was made;

- serious illness of a close relative or partner, but only if the situation took up a great deal of the claimant's time and attention during the period from the end of the permitted period to the date the claim was made, and steps had already been taken to have the claim made on time;
- the death of a close relative or partner shortly before the end of the permitted period, where necessary steps had already been taken to make the claim on time;
- the claimant can show that they were not aware (and could not reasonably have been aware) of their entitlement to make a claim.

Schedule IHT402 is available via the gov.uk website (tinyurl.com/IHT-Forms-IHT402), as is form IHT217 in relation to excepted estates (tinyurl.com/IHT-Forms-IHT217).

The nil rate band in force upon the spouse or civil partner's death can generally be found on the gov.uk website (tinyurl.com/IHT-NRB). HMRC's tables list the nil rate band from 16 August 1914 onwards. The nil rate band from that date until 9 April 1946 was £100.

If the personal representatives of the deceased's estate do not make a claim to transfer unused nil rate band (eg if there is no need to take out a grant), any other person liable for tax on the survivor's death (eg the trustees of a settlement, or the donee of a gift) may make a claim, but only when the initial period for claim by the personal representatives (in *IHTA 1984, s 8B(3)(a)*) has passed. In those cases, the claimant should use form IHT216 (IHTM43006), which is available via the gov.uk website (tinyurl.com/IHT-Forms-IHT216).

HMRC's IHT & Trusts Newsletter (August 2008) included the following criticism of claims by agents to transfer unused nil rate bands on behalf of their clients, which is worth noting:

> 'One disappointing feature since the introduction of these new provisions is the very high initial failure rate by agents to provide the supporting details we ask for. The IHT216 claim form lists the documents that we want to see to support the claim for relief, and in only 20 per cent of cases submitted by agents are all the requested documents provided. This is in stark contrast to claims made by unrepresented taxpayers who manage to provide all the documents at the first time of asking.'

3.9 The failure to make a claim on an earlier death could have an unfortunate knock-on effect on the amount of nil rate band that may subsequently be claimed.

However, the legislation provides for some possible relief. For example, when a surviving spouse ('C') dies and C's personal representatives discover that no claim was made on the deceased spouse's ('B') death in respect of an earlier spouse's death ('A'), a claim is allowed in respect of A's death as well as B's death, if the original IHT position of A is unaffected (*s 8B(2)*).

Once a claim is made it can be withdrawn, but no later than one month after the end of the period concerned (*IHTA 1984, s 8B(4)*).

3.10

Focus

- Claims for the transfer of unused IHT nil rate bands between spouses and civil partners apply 'for the purposes of the charge to tax on the death of the survivor' (*s 8A(3)*).
- A transfer could therefore reduce IHT on the survivor's free estate, together with any gifts with reservation of benefit property treated as being included in the estate, and the value of property subject to a qualifying interest in possession.
- It can also reduce the additional tax on a chargeable lifetime transfer, and the tax on a failed PET.

However, surviving spouses or civil partners should not try to claim an extra nil rate band on a chargeable lifetime transfer, such as to a discretionary trust. The deceased's nil rate band is not available in that event, and an unexpected IHT liability could therefore arise.

Of course, should the surviving spouse or civil partner die within seven years, an extra nil rate band may then be available. However, the rules do not provide for the refund of any lifetime IHT paid, in which case the transferred nil rate band effectively provides relief at only 20%, as opposed to 40%.

Example 3.3—Lifetime transfers and the death estate

Ken died in May 2010, leaving his entire estate to his wife Susan. In June 2016, Susan added £200,000 to a discretionary trust for her adult children. She had originally established the trust in July 2011, by settling an investment property worth £200,000. She used her annual exemptions elsewhere each year.

Susan died in September 2018, leaving her estate of £400,000 to her children.

June 2016 – IHT on lifetime transfer to discretionary trust

The value transferred of £200,000, when added to the earlier chargeable transfer of £200,000, exceeded Susan's nil rate band for 2016/17 of £325,000 (note that it is not possible to add Ken's unused nil rate band for this lifetime transfer) by £75,000. The IHT liability is £75,000 × 20% = £15,000.

September 2018 – Susan's death

Susan's estate amounted to £400,000. Her remaining nil rate band, after taking into account the gift of £200,000 in June 2016 (Note: the earlier gift of £200,000 in July 2011 is not taken into account for the purpose of this calculation, as it was made more than seven years previously) is £125,000 (ie £325,000 less £200,000). A claim is made for Ken's unused nil rate band percentage of 100%, giving Susan's estate an additional nil rate band of £325,000.

The total nil rate band of £450,000 is sufficient to cover Susan's death estate, so no IHT is due. However, the lifetime IHT in June 2016 cannot be repaid.

CLAWBACK OF NIL RATE BAND

3.11 It may become necessary to consider the effect on the transferable nil rate band of an IHT charge in respect of heritage assets (*IHTA 1984, ss 32, 32A*) and woodlands (*IHTA 1984, s 126*), where relief was given on an earlier death.

This is because, where property is granted conditional exemption or woodlands relief on the first death, IHT is generally due on the sale proceeds of the property, or its value when the undertaking was breached. As may be imagined, the availability of the nil rate band can affect that tax charge.

IHTA 1984, s 8C takes account of this, by providing rules dealing with the interaction of the nil rate band and the calculation of IHT where a heritage or woodland deferred IHT or capital transfer tax charge applies.

The clawback provisions apply if there was unused nil rate band on the death of a spouse or civil partner, and after the person's death a deferred tax charge arises on heritage assets or woodlands, by reference to the deceased spouse's or civil partner's estate (*IHTA 1984, s 8C(1)*).

Clawback whilst surviving spouse still alive

3.12 If the event triggering the charge happens before the death of the surviving spouse, it becomes necessary to recalculate the available nil rate band. Broadly, the original transferable nil rate band percentage is calculated. A further calculation (under *IHTA 1984, s 8C(2)*) quantifies the nil rate band used by the charge on disposal. The original percentage is then reduced to give the revised percentage of nil rate band available for transfer to the estate of the surviving spouse. To apply the legislation:

- First, find the nil rate band for the first spouse to die (defined as 'NRBMD' in *IHTA 1984, s 8A(4)*).
- Next, find the nil rate band in force at the time of the event triggering the charge (defined by *IHTA 1984, s 8C(2)* as 'NRBME').
- Next, establish 'E': this is the excess of the nil rate band over the chargeable transfer at the first death: effectively the unused nil rate band.
- Finally (for this stage of the computation), calculate 'TA': this is the amount on which the clawback is charged.

Then apply the formula:

$$\left(\frac{\text{E}}{\text{NRBMD}} - \frac{\text{TA}}{\text{NRBME}}\right) \times 100$$

The result represents the percentage of the nil rate band in respect of which a claim may be made.

A worked example is included in the Inheritance Tax Manual (see IHTM43045).

Example 3.4—Heritage property

Edwina owned a painting by a well-known artist, which was the subject of an undertaking (under *IHTA 1984, s 30*) upon her death in January 2017. That undertaking was breached in November 2018 when the general public were no longer allowed reasonable access to the painting, triggering an IHT charge (under *IHTA 1984, s 32*). The painting was worth £200,000.

Edwina had made no chargeable lifetime transfers. In her will, she left £10,000 to her cleaner Mavis, and the residue of her estate (apart from the painting) to her husband Frederick.

Nil rate band, January 2017 (NRBMD):	£325,000
Nil rate band, November 2018 (NRBME):	£325,000
Unused nil rate band, January 2017	
(applying the formula in *IHTA 1984, s 8A(2)* and *(4)*) (E):	£315,000
M = £325,000	
VT = £10,000	
E = (M – VT) = £315,000	

TA: £200,000

Computation: $\left(\dfrac{£315{,}000}{£325{,}000} - \dfrac{£200{,}000}{£325{,}000}\right) \times 100$

(0.9692 – 0.6154) × 100 = 35.3800% of the nil rate band available for transfer to Frederick's estate on his death.

An alternative way of looking at the above outcome is to say that Edwina's estate used up 3.0769% of the nil rate band when she died; on the breach of undertaking, a further 61.5385% of the nil rate band in effect at that time was used up (ie 64.6154% in total), leaving 35.3846% available (rounded down to 35.38% in the above example).

If there is more than one breach of undertaking, or where (for example) there are several woodland clawback charges, the nil rate band that may be transferred is reduced by the proportion of the nil rate band clawed back by all the deferred charges (ie by the aggregate of TA/NRBME in respect of each triggering event (*IHTA 1984, s 8C(3)*)).

Clawback after the second death

3.13 If a deferred charge is triggered after the nil rate band has been transferred (ie after the death of the survivor), *IHTA 1984, s 8C(4)* reduces the nil rate band of the first spouse to die. The mechanics of the adjustment are set out in *IHTA 1984, s 8C(5)*.

The nil rate band of the first to die of the spouses or civil partners is first adjusted by applying *IHTA 1984, Sch 2* (ie the uprating provisions that give the benefit of any reduction in the tax that applies because the nil rate band has been increased over time).

That uprated nil rate band is then potentially both increased and decreased. The increase can apply where the first spouse to die might himself have more than one nil rate band available, perhaps being a widower. The reduction is the amount of any increase in that band by virtue of the nil rate band transfer rules, to the extent that it kept the survivor's estate free of an IHT charge.

A worked example is included in the Inheritance Tax Manual (see IHTM43046).

Example 3.5—Practical effect of a clawback

Jonathan was first married to Katherine, who left her estate to Jonathan when she died in May 2003. Katherine had not used any of her nil rate band.

In January 2009, Jonathan married Lucy.

On Jonathan's death in January 2017, he left Lucy his estate, apart from a cash legacy of £100,000 to his favourite nephew Percy. Jonathan's family's heritage asset was sold for £150,000 by Lucy's executors shortly after her death in October 2018, thereby triggering a clawback charge under *s 32*.

The nil rate band in May 2003 was £255,000. None of it was used by Katherine.

The nil rate band on Jonathan's death in January 2017 was £325,000. The total nil rate band available to his executor is (£325,000 – £100,000 = £225,000 + £325,000) = £550,000.

The nil rate band at Lucy's death in October 2018, and when the heritage asset was sold, is £325,000. The clawback charge is on £150,000. Jonathan's estate now has available an increased nil rate band of (£550,000 – £150,000): £400,000.

Any clawback charge following the death of the survivor (Lucy) under *IHTA 1984, s 8C(5)* would depend upon the extent (if any) to which the nil rate band transferred from Jonathan's estate was required to keep Lucy's estate free of IHT.

[*Note*: If a Scottish law claim to 'legitim' is made after a claim to transfer unused nil rate band following the death of the second parent, HMRC may adjust the claim in respect of the unused nil band accordingly (*IHTA 1984, s 147(10)*; see IHTM43041).]

Unexhausted ASP funds

3.14 As indicated at **3.5** above, the IHT provisions relating to ASP funds (in *IHTA 1984, ss 151A–151E*) ceased to apply following legislation in *FA 2011*, which amended the pension rules (in *FA 2004, Pt 4*) relating to registered pension schemes applying to individuals reaching the age of 75. The changes broadly removed the effective requirement to buy an annuity by the age of 75. From 6 April 2011, IHT generally ceased to apply to drawdown pension funds remaining under a registered pension scheme, including where the individual died after reaching the age of 75.

Although the IHT rules affecting the transferable nil rate band were repealed with effect for deaths occurring from 6 April 2011, they still need to be considered in respect of deaths prior to that date.

The background to the rules is the IHT charge that arises (under *IHTA 1984, s 151B*) on that part of an alternatively secured pension (ASP) fund which has not been used in benefits for the fund member and his dependants. In broad terms, the unexhausted fund is treated as the 'top slice' of the member's estate for IHT purposes. *IHTA 1984, s 151BA(5)* uprates the nil rate band that is to be applied. The provisions were modified in *FA 2008*, by the introduction of *IHTA 1984, s 151BA(6), (7)*.

Once again, a formula first requires the taxpayer to establish certain values:

E (as before) is the unused excess nil rate band available; and

NRBM is the nil rate band in force when the member died.

The formula is:

$$100 - \left(\frac{E}{NRBM}\right) \times 100$$

This produces 'the used up percentage', ie the fraction by which the nil rate band otherwise available to the member is to be reduced.

Example 3.6—Pension funds and the clawback

Martha died in May 2010, when the nil rate band was £325,000. She made no lifetime gifts but left £75,000 to her sister and the rest of her estate, including her pension rights, to her husband Norman. He did not draw the entire pension. He had no dependants. The unexhausted portion of the pension fund, at his death on 2 February 2011, was £150,000.

For Martha's estate:

E = £250,000 (ie £325,000 – £75,000);

NRBM = £325,000; and

The 'used up percentage' is 100 – ((£250,000/£325,000) × 100), ie 100% – 76.9231% = 23.0769%.

This is the part of Martha's nil rate band that has been used.

HMRC's Inheritance Tax Manual states (at IHTM43047): 'The rules were repealed in the Finance Act 2011 for deaths on or after 6 April 2011, so it is very unlikely that you will see an ASP charge and a claim for a transfer of unused nil-rate band in these circumstances. You should seek advice from Technical if you do have a case with a charge under these rules.'

3.15 The position became more complicated following legislation (*IHTA 1984, s 151BA(8)–(12)*) introduced in *Finance Act 2008*, where the pension fund is still not exhausted by the death of the second person benefiting from it.

First, the situation is addressed where there has been an IHT charge on an ASP fund by reference to the first spouse or civil partner to die. This affects the person's nil rate band and restricts the amount available for transfer later: it is 'appropriately reduced' (under *IHTA 1984, s 151BA(9)*) where the chargeable event occurred after the death of the surviving spouse.

If, however, the surviving spouse is still alive when the chargeable event happens, tax is charged when the survivor dies by adjusting the member's transferable nil rate band using a formula (see *IHTA 1984, s 151BA(12)*), which compares the 'adjusted excess' with the 'adjusted nil rate band maximum', expressed as a percentage.

Where the charge arises after both spouses have died, each may have used part of his or her nil rate band, so there may be less available to meet the IHT charge under *IHTA 1984, s 151B* (see *IHTA 1984, s 151BA(9)*), as augmented by the definitions set out in *IHTA 1984, s 151BA(10)*).

Where the charge arises whilst the surviving spouse is still alive, the formula in *IHTA 1984, s 151BA(12)* applies. This restricts the nil rate band available later. AE, the adjusted excess, deducts from the maximum nil rate band the value transferred by chargeable transfers after calculating the taxable amount and after adjusting the nil rate band itself: ANRBM. ANRBM is the nil rate band, adjusted for ASP charges under *IHTA 1984, s 151B*.

IHT clearance certificates

3.16 A 'certificate of discharge' (or clearance certificate) confirms HMRC's satisfaction that all the IHT due in a particular case has been (or will be) paid (*IHTA 1984, s 239*).

Inevitably, there is always a risk that tax charges will be missed. However, the clearance certificate issued by HMRC will not guarantee freedom from IHT charges where the amount of the nil rate band that was transferred must be adjusted, such as by the clawback in respect of heritage property.

IHTA 1984, s 239 is qualified accordingly (with effect from 9 October 2007), so that if too little IHT has been paid because of adjustment to the nil rate band, those persons who are accountable remain liable to pay the balance (*IHTA 1984, s 239(4)(aa)*).

Penalties

3.17 The penalty regime for inaccuracies in tax returns (in *FA 2007, Sch 24*) was extended for IHT purposes (by *FA 2008, Sch 40*) in respect of events and periods from 1 April 2009, where the filing date is 1 April 2010 or later (although if information or a document is produced under *IHTA 1984,* *s 256* ('Regulations about accounts, etc') from 1 April 2009, the tax period must begin on or after that date).

It generally provides for tax-geared penalties of between 0% and 100%, broadly depending on a person's behaviour and the level of disclosure to HMRC.

Note that the penalty regime for offshore tax matters (introduced by *FA 2010, Sch 10*), which provides for significantly higher penalties, did not apply for IHT purposes under the original offshore penalty provisions. However, the offshore penalty regime was extended by *FA 2015* (*s 120, Sch 20*) to include IHT, with effect for transfers of value made on or after 1 April 2016 (*FA 2015, s 120(2)*; *SI 2016/456, art 3(2)(a)*).

Higher penalties than normal can potentially apply to offshore non-compliance ('offshore matters') and 'offshore transfers' in respect of errors in tax returns (*FA 2007, Sch 24, paras 4–4AA*), failure to notify chargeability (for income tax and capital gains tax purposes) (*FA 2008, Sch 41, paras 6–6AB*) and for late filing (*FA 2009, Sch 55, paras 6–6AB*). Further penalty provisions potentially apply in connection with 'offshore asset moves' (*FA 2015, Sch 21*). The penalty provisions relating to offshore matters and offshore transfers were strengthened by amendments introduced in *FA 2016*.

In addition, an asset-based penalty in respect of offshore inaccuracies and failures potentially applies, including for IHT purposes except in relation to a penalty for a failure to notify (*FA 2016, Sch 22*). Furthermore, legislation (in *F(No 2)A 2017, s 67, Sch 18*) broadly includes a requirement to correct certain offshore non-compliance, and provides for enhanced penalties for failing to do so by 30 September 2018.

The circumstances in which a penalty could be imposed potentially includes (for example) an overstated claim for the transfer of unused nil rate band, resulting in an IHT underpayment. Penalties can be imposed on the person making the return, and on another person who deliberately supplies false information resulting in an incorrect return (or who withholds information with the same intention) (*FA 2007, Sch 24, paras 1–1A*).

As to compliance and penalties generally, see **Chapter 8**.

3.18 For periods prior to the introduction of the above penalty regime for inaccuracies for IHT purposes, the relevant penalty rules in respect of the provision of incorrect information are contained in *IHTA 1984, s 247(1), (2)*.

A person liable for the tax who fraudulently or negligently supplies an incorrect account, information or document to HMRC is liable to a penalty (*IHTA 1984, s 247(1)*). The maximum penalty is 100% of the tax potentially lost (ie broadly the difference between the amount of tax correctly payable, and the amount of tax payable based on the incorrect return etc).

Penalties can be calculated in respect of the liability of someone other than the person in default (under *IHTA 1984, s 247(2)*) if incorrect information was supplied in connection with a claim to transfer unused nil rate band. This provision was introduced from 21 July 2008, to apply to an incorrect IHT return delivered in respect of the first death from that date, although *IHTA 1984, s 247(1)* and *(2)* were repealed with effect from 1 April 2009 (*SI 2009/571, art 2*).

The IHT legislation concerning incorrect information provided for a penalty of up to £3,000 where any person (eg an agent) assisted in or induced incorrect returns, information, etc (*IHTA 1984, s 247(4)*). This provision was repealed with effect from 1 April 2013 (by the *Finance Act 2012, Schedule 38 (Tax Agents: Dishonest Conduct) (Appointed Day and Savings) Order 2013, SI 2013/279*), following the introduction of legislation dealing with tax agents who engage in dishonest conduct (*FA 2012, Sch 38*). Those provisions include powers for HMRC to issue agents who are considered to be dishonest with a 'conduct notice', to access the agent's working papers, and to impose a penalty of up to £50,000.

Personal representatives of the surviving spouse or civil partner must be mindful of the potential risk, and exercise due diligence when claiming unused nil rate band from an earlier death.

HMRC's IHT Toolkit includes the following checklist item concerning 'Information gathering': 'Has it been identified whether the deceased had a spouse or civil partner who died before them and if so, have their details been obtained?' The Toolkit defines the transferable nil rate band as an area of risk, if full details of any predeceased spouse or civil partner have not been obtained, and advocates thorough research on their background. The Toolkit also highlights a number of 'common points often overlooked' in connection with claims to transfer unused nil rate band.

The IHT Toolkit is available via the HMRC website: tinyurl.com/IHT-Toolkit.

Valuations

3.19 The 'value ascertained' capital gains tax rule in *TCGA 1992, s 274* ('Value determined for inheritance tax'), under which values ascertained for IHT purposes apply for capital gains tax purposes, was amended in *Finance Act 2008* as a consequence of the introduction of the transferable nil rate band, from 6 April 2008.

The effect is that an asset valuation for the purposes of calculating the amount of transferable nil rate band (as opposed to calculating the amount of any IHT on death) cannot be applied for capital gains tax purposes as well.

DEATHS BEFORE 25 JULY 1986

3.20 IHT was introduced in 1986. However, the transferable nil rate band provisions are adapted in cases where an earlier spouse died before 25 July

1986, and the surviving spouse died on or after 9 October 2007. *Finance Act 2008* modified *IHTA 1984, s 8A* accordingly, so that the rules apply for capital transfer tax purposes where the spouse died between 1 January 1985 and 24 July 1986, or between 13 March 1975 and 31 December 1984, as appropriate (*FA 2008, Sch 4 para 10(2), (3)*).

Similarly, the transferable nil rate band provisions are adapted for estate duty purposes where the spouse died between 16 April 1969 and 12 March 1975, or before 16 April 1969, as appropriate (*FA 2008, Sch 4 para 10(4), (5)*).

Between 22 March 1972 and 12 November 1974, the spouse exemption was limited to £15,000, and it was therefore possible that the estate may have been liable to estate duty. Prior to 22 March 1972 there was no spouse exemption at all. Thus if property was left to a spouse, an estate duty charge could have arisen. If the estate was large enough for duty to be paid, the equivalent of the nil rate band would have been exhausted, so that there would be nothing left to transfer.

Example 3.7—Elderly testatrix

Sarah is now nearly 90. She has savings and investments worth £600,000, and is looked after by her son Thomas in his home. Sarah married Frank in 1960 but he died in November 1971 intestate. Frank's personal estate, which passed to Sarah, was worth £2,500 at a time when the estate duty tax-free band was £12,500.

There was no spouse exemption in November 1971: the relief (limited to £15,000) was not introduced until 22 March 1972. That limitation was lifted from 13 November 1974. Sarah's inheritance therefore used 20% of the then equivalent of the nil rate band, so 80% was unused and is still available for transfer.

Against Sarah's estate of £600,000 her executors may set 180% of the current nil rate band, ie £585,000, leaving £15,000 to suffer an IHT charge at 40% of £6,000 (NB no residence nil rate is assumed to be available in this example).

The 'clawback' provisions dealing with the interaction of the transferable nil rate band and IHT or capital transfer tax charges in respect of heritage relief and woodland relief (see **3.11**) are also adapted accordingly, where the surviving spouse died on or after 9 October 2007 and the earlier spouse died between 13 March 1975 and 24 July 1986 (ie between 1 January 1985 and 24 July 1986, or between 7 April 1976 and 31 December 1984, or between 13 March 1975 and 6 April 1976), so that the clawback rules in *IHTA 1984, s 8C* apply to the appropriate capital transfer tax legislation (*FA 2008, Sch 4 para 11*).

As to ascertaining the nil rate band for earlier years, see **3.8** above.

PRACTICAL ISSUES

Record keeping

3.21 The transferability of unused nil rate band comes at an administrative cost in terms of keeping records and documents. Some discipline will be required on the part of surviving spouses or civil partners and their personal representatives, in terms of obtaining, keeping and maintaining records in respect of the earlier spouse or civil partner to die and their estate.

Practical issues may arise in terms of the valuation of assets and the availability of IHT reliefs. For example, HMRC's present policy seems to be not to check claims for 100% business property relief (BPR) or agricultural property relief (APR) where there is no immediate IHT liability, such as where personal representatives claim relief on an individual's death and no IHT liability would arise on the death regardless of the availability of BPR or APR, due to the deceased's available nil rate band.

However, such an issue will be relevant in determining the unused nil rate band available to the surviving spouse or civil partner. This may result in HMRC testing the availability of BPR or APR following the second death.

Focus

One important self-help procedure is for widows, widowers and surviving civil partners to make and keep a record of the extent to which their late spouses or civil partners had used the nil rate band.

In cases such as Sarah at **Example 3.7**, it may be difficult to produce values many years later.

IHT practitioners should also encourage their clients to keep good records.

A simple form, along the lines of the following, might be placed with the survivor's will. Enterprising practitioners may like to produce a form of 'aide memoire', perhaps embellished with the firm's logo, as a marketing exercise.

Example 3.8—Record of use of the nil rate band for IHT purposes

The following sample record is designed as a fact-finding exercise to establish how much of the nil rate band was used by a former spouse. In it, the terms 'married' and 'widowed' include being a member of a registered civil partnership and still being such a member when the civil partner died.

Part 1: Your relationship to the deceased person(s)

1. Have you been married?
2. If so, how many times?
3. Did your marriage end only on the death of your spouse?
4. If so, state the date your spouse died.
5. If you have been widowed more than once, state the date that each spouse died.

Part 2: Details of transfers and of the nil rate band available

6. If you know it, state the amount of the nil rate band when your spouse died (or when each spouse died).
7. Do you have a copy of the will that your spouse made (if applicable)?
8. Was that will, if any, varied within two years of death? If so, do you have a copy?
9. Did your spouse leave all his or her estate to you?
10. If not, state the value given by your late spouse to others, and specify if any was left exempt (for example, to charity).
11. Did your spouse make gifts to others in the seven years before death?
12. If so, state the amount given and to whom (again noting any gifts that were exempt for any reason).

Documents to support a claim

3.22 In addition to keeping a record of material events, the deceased spouse's or civil partner's personal representatives should provide certain documents in support of their claim to transfer the available unused nil rate band, when submitting form IHT400 on the death of the surviving spouse or civil partner.

Schedule IHT402 'Claim to transfer unused nil rate band' (tinyurl.com/IHT-Forms-IHT402) sets out the photocopied documents which must accompany the claim:

- copy of the grant of representation (Confirmation in Scotland) to the estate of the spouse or civil partner (or, if no grant has been taken out, a copy of the death certificate);
- if the spouse or civil partner left a will, a copy of it;

- if a deed of variation or other similar document was executed to change the people who inherited the estate of the spouse or civil partner, a copy of it.

In addition, the personal representatives of the deceased spouse or civil partner should typically keep the following information in a safe place, or provide it for the survivor to keep in a safe place, to help establish the unused nil rate band available on their death:

- a copy of the HMRC return (form IHT400 or IHT205; in Scotland, forms C1 or C5);
- a copy of the deceased's will (if any);
- a copy of the marriage certificate;
- a copy of any documents (eg a deed of variation) executed after the death of the first spouse or civil partner, that changes who benefits from their estate;
- any valuation(s) of assets that pass under will or intestacy other than to the surviving spouse or civil partner; and/or
- any evidence to support the availability of relief (such as APR or BPR) where the relievable assets pass to someone other than to the surviving spouse or civil partner.

In the case of jointly owned assets, and in certain other cases (eg assets of the deceased's 'estate' interests in possession, lifetime gifts within seven years before death and 'gift with reservation' (GWR) assets), surviving spouses or civil partners (or their personal representatives) will need to obtain whatever relevant information and documentation is available in support of nil rate band claims (eg details of the assets concerned, and any evidence of their values).

3.23 Particularly in cases where the earlier spouse or civil partner died some time ago, there may be gaps in the information and documentation available. The survivor may have been unaware of the importance of keeping them, or documents may have been lost, stolen or accidentally destroyed.

HMRC have previously pointed out that certain documents are obtainable from public records bodies (eg copies of wills, grants of representation or confirmation from the Court Service, or copies of death or marriage (or civil partnership) certificates from the General Register Office (website addresses for which are listed on page 4 of form IHT402)). The documents do not need to be originals, or official copies; certified copies will suffice (HMRC IHT & Trusts Newsletter, April 2008).

In addition, HMRC indicate that provisional claims to transfer any unused nil rate band may be allowed if the personal representatives are having difficulty obtaining all the documents and the time limit for making the claim (see **3.8**) is approaching (IHTM43006).

However, the full details to make a claim may still be incomplete (eg such as assets subject to the GWR rules, as mentioned above). In those circumstances, the survivor's personal representatives will need to complete the claim to the best of their knowledge and ability, attaching whatever documents are available, and explaining to HMRC the reason for any omission.

It will clearly be preferable if personal representatives of the earlier spouse or civil partner can undertake the preparatory work for a possible future claim on the survivor's death, such as by packaging together the required information and documents and passing them to the survivor.

PLANNING ISSUES

Should the nil rate band be used on the first death?

3.24 As mentioned earlier in this chapter, the facility (introduced in *Finance Act 2008*) to allow for claims to transfer the unused nil rate band was backdated to cases where the surviving spouse or civil partner died on or after 9 October 2007.

IHT was once charged on an ascending scale, which encouraged the equalisation of estates between husband and wife. However, since 15 March 1988 the position has been simpler. After the nil rate band (£325,000 for 2018/19) has been used, there is only one single rate of 40% on death (half of that, 20%, for lifetime chargeable transfers), although a lower IHT rate of 36% applies to a deceased person's estate in certain circumstances involving charitable legacies (*IHTA 1984, Sch 1A*).

Thus, as a general rule, there is no advantage for IHT purposes in equalising estates as between husband and wife or civil partners. Following the introduction of the transferable nil rate band facility, it is no longer necessary for the nil rate band to be used on the death of the first spouse or civil partner, due to the possibility of transferring the unused proportion of a nil rate band to the estate of the surviving spouse or civil partner.

The residence nil rate band (from 6 April 2017) is similarly transferable in appropriate circumstances (see **3.42–3.48**).

3.25 The thinking behind utilising the nil rate band on the first death was to leave it to chargeable beneficiaries. However, many testators really wanted the primary benefit to go to the surviving spouse or civil partner, so the trustees of a discretionary nil rate band trust were encouraged to regard the surviving spouse as the primary beneficiary.

The deceased spouse or civil partner would typically leave a sum equivalent to the upper limit of the nil rate band upon a discretionary trust so that the surviving spouse could have the benefit of the fund and at the same time the nil rate band could be utilised and not wasted. Distributions could be made in favour of the surviving spouse in case of need; and if they were of capital any exit charge under the discretionary trust regime in the first ten years would be by reference to the testator's nil rate band.

Much of that thinking was rendered obsolete by the introduction of the transferable nil rate band facility. In most cases, the emphasis is on *not* using the nil rate band on the first death, in the hope that the transferable band will be larger on the second death, when it will really be needed.

However, some individuals may prefer to 'bank' the nil rate band, rather than rely on its availability on the survivor's death. In addition, there are still certain circumstances where consideration should be given to the will containing a nil rate band trust (see **3.28**).

3.26 Particular care should be taken over '28-day' survivorship clauses, especially where the deceased spouse has most of the estate and the surviving spouse has very little. This is because the effect of not passing value to the spouse could be to pass (chargeable) value to the next generation on the first death that exceeded the nil rate band which, had it been channelled through the estate of the (short) surviving spouse, might have benefited from that survivor's unused nil rate band. Do the sums before drafting the will.

In cases where spouses (or civil partners) die at the same time leaving wills, there is a legal presumption (in England and Wales) that the elder died first (*LPA 1925, s 184*). If the terms of the elder's will means that there is unused nil rate band, it is available to be transferred to the estate of the younger.

HMRC guidance points out that different provisions apply in Scotland and Northern Ireland regarding simultaneous deaths, ie both spouses are treated as dying at the same moment, so neither can inherit from the other. Each spouse's estate passes to their heirs, whether by will or under intestacy. If one spouse had any unused nil rate band, it is available to be transferred to the estate of the other in the normal way (IHTM43040).

3.27 If it is appropriate to use the nil rate band, it is worth noting that the threshold can normally be expected to increase annually (*IHTA 1984, s 8*). This increase was historically by reference to the retail prices index (RPI). However, following changes introduced in *FA 2012*, the consumer prices index (CPI) replaced the RPI as the default indexation assumption, albeit that automatic indexation using the CPI will not take effect for IHT purposes until 2021/22 at the earliest (see below). Automatic indexation may be overridden if Parliament so determines.

As mentioned at **3.1**, the nil rate band was initially frozen at £325,000 for the tax years 2011/12 to 2014/15 inclusive (*FA 2010, s 8(3)*). The freezing of the nil rate band at £325,000 was subsequently extended for tax years up to and including 2020/21 (*F(No 2)A 2015, s 10*). In practice, the testator's will is often drafted to ensure that the gift matches the ceiling of the nil rate band when he dies.

The gift in the will should therefore be of an amount equivalent to the upper limit of the IHT nil rate band in force at the time of the testator's death under *IHTA 1984, Sch 1*, as amended in accordance with the indexation provisions of *IHTA 1984, s 8*, if applicable. Such a formula, while most useful for cash gifts, cannot of course operate in the same straightforward way in the case of specific legacies of assets, particularly where business or agricultural reliefs are involved and changes in values may occur.

3.28 For those taxpayers who had previously considered IHT planning in respect of their wills, such as the inclusion of a nil rate band discretionary trust on the first death, there are several arguments for doing nothing at all.

For example, discretionary will trusts are sometimes used in the following cases:

- where there is property qualifying for business or agricultural property relief (ie to 'bank' the relief, in the event of any future reduction or withdrawal of it). Where business or agricultural property relief at 100% is available, the value of the gift on top of the nil rate band is unlimited; relief at 50% effectively doubles the nil rate band, ie the nil rate band (£325,000 for 2018/19) can cover a transfer of £650,000 (although in either case a trust would not really be a 'nil rate band trust' in the normal sense of the term); or
- to shelter property from care fees; or
- for asset protection purposes, such as in the event of a future marriage breakdown; or
- if an asset is likely to appreciate in value faster than the nil rate band; or
- in cases where both individuals have been married before, and up to four nil rate bands are therefore available (see **3.32**).

In some cases, if a discretionary will trust is no longer considered to be desirable, it may be possible to reverse its effects for IHT purposes. This can be achieved during lifetime through a codicil to revoke the nil rate band transfer, or possibly following death by means of a deed of appointment, as illustrated in the example below.

Example 3.9—Appointment from nil rate band trust

Oliver and Patricia, who have been married for many years, made wills in 2007 that incorporate nil rate band discretionary trusts.

There is scope (under *IHTA 1984, s 144*) for the trustees of a discretionary trust to appoint funds or assets to beneficiaries within two years of the death. A distribution from the discretionary trust generally takes effect as if it had been a gift under the terms of the will and not a distribution from the trust. Therefore, there is no need to change the will.

If the will of the *surviving* spouse is drafted in common form, the provision as to the nil rate band will not apply because it has been excluded where the surviving spouse is not married at the date of death. In this scenario, therefore, all that is needed is a deed of appointment by the trustees of the nil rate band set up by the will of the first spouse to die.

Where the testator's death occurred before 10 December 2014, to avoid the difficulty that arose in *Frankland v IRC* [1997] STC 1450 (see **15.50**), the trustees would not normally take any action until three months elapsed from the date of death. On the death of the first to die of husband and wife, the trustees would therefore simply wait three months and appoint the whole of the nil rate band to the surviving spouse. There was no need to wait three months if the effect of the deed of appointment was to create an 'immediate post-death interest' (see **9.9**) – only if the interest created was an absolute one.

However, the '*Frankland* trap' was resolved (in *F(No 2)A 2015*) by a change in legislation (see *IHTA 1984, s 144(1)(b)*, as amended). The provision (in *IHTA 1984, s 65(4)*) that prevents an IHT charge arising in the first three months after a settlement commences (or within a ten-year anniversary) is precluded from applying to appointments out of property settled by will where the testator's death occurs from 10 December 2014. This amendment therefore broadly allows a distribution from the trust made within three months of death in favour of the surviving spouse to be read back into the will, such that the spouse exemption (in *IHTA 1984, s 18*) will generally be available.

3.29 However, family conflict or indolence can delay the application for a grant of probate. Things can get left. If one of the executors is a professional person, he will probably be negligent if he fails to do what is right for the family in terms of IHT. If the executors are all family members and if they miss the various deadlines, they could be worse off than if they had simpler wills.

3.30 The family home, the use of an interest in the family home to constitute the nil rate band, and the residence nil rate band (from 6 April 2017) are discussed in **Chapter 16**.

'Debt' or 'charge' arrangements (see **16.48**) are relatively complicated and difficult for taxpayers to understand. In addition, where there is an *FA 1986, s 103* problem, as illustrated by the *Phizackerley* case (see **16.49**), it can be difficult for professional advisers to explain the schemes to clients. Many people may have been slightly uncomfortable with the complexity of wills containing nil rate band discretionary trusts and they may feel much happier with simple new wills, even though that will involve paying a new fee to have them prepared.

If both spouses or civil partners died before 9 October 2007, it is not possible to make use of the transferable nil rate band provisions. Similarly, if one spouse or civil partner died some time ago, it may be too late to take advantage of those rules.

Example 3.10—Nil rate band discretionary trust: too late for action

Quentin died in 2014, leaving a widow, Rose. Quentin's will included a nil rate band discretionary trust. In this situation, nothing can (or should) be done. By putting in place a nil rate band discretionary trust, Quentin has used his nil rate band.

Due to the time which has elapsed since his death, it is too late to make any changes relying on the 'two-year rule' in *IHTA 1984, s 144*. It is also too late to consider a deed of variation because, to be effective, it also had to be made within two years of death to claim relief under *IHTA 1984, s 142*.

Therefore, the only nil rate band available to Rose in the above example (unless she remarries and survives her second husband!) is the single nil rate band. It would be totally wrong for the family to assume that 'we don't need that silly scheme now' and to appoint all the funds in the discretionary trust to the widow. That would just increase her estate without giving her back her late husband's nil rate band.

If a spouse or civil partner died recently, perhaps with a pre-9 October 2007 will in place, it may be possible in some cases to re-assess earlier estate planning with hindsight.

Example 3.11—Discretionary will trust: estate planning updated

Stanley made a will including a nil rate band discretionary trust for the benefit of his close family, with residue to his wife Tracy. The main asset was their house, worth £700,000, which was held by them as tenants in common in equal shares. Stanley had savings of £200,000. He died on 30 June 2016, having made no chargeable lifetime gifts.

Tracy and her daughter Ursula agreed that Tracy would sell the family home and move to a less expensive property closer to Ursula. The house would now sell for £800,000. Stanley's nil rate band of £325,000 was to be satisfied with his savings of £200,000, plus a further £125,000 from the house sale.

Tracy subsequently realised that she would not need any of the nil rate band, and preferred that, following the house sale, all of the money be released to Ursula. The family met with their adviser in March 2018 to consider whether to take advantage of the transferable nil rate band provisions (which had been introduced after Stanley's will was drafted). They decided that since they were still within two years of Stanley's death, they should effectively rewrite his will so that all Stanley's estate went to Tracy. That way, the whole of Stanley's nil rate band would be available on Tracy's death.

Any assets that were to be transferred to Ursula would not now be from the discretionary trust, but would be treated as a gift by Tracy. If Tracy lived seven years, those gifts would fall out of account. Apart from that, if the will was varied, the sale of the house could be treated as made by Tracy, and the whole of the gain would be tax free. They decided that it would be worthwhile effectively rewriting Stanley's will so that his nil rate band was unused on his death.

Earlier marriages or civil partnerships

3.31 The starting point in a claim to transfer unused nil rate band is that the spouses (or civil partners) were married to each other at the time of the earlier death. It does not matter if, for example, the surviving spouse later remarried (although the surviving spouse's personal representatives can only claim one extra nil rate band) and was subsequently divorced.

If the surviving spouse remarries and dies before their new spouse, the unused nil rate band of the earlier spouse to die from the first marriage may be claimed by the survivor's personal representatives. The surviving spouse from the later marriage may subsequently be able to claim unused nil rate band from the remarried spouse if appropriate, subject to the overriding maximum of 100% of the nil rate band applicable on the last survivor's death.

If an individual has survived more than one marriage or civil partnership, his personal representatives may be able to claim additional nil rate band from more than one estate, subject to the aforementioned maximum. A separate claim form is required in respect of each estate. It is important to remember that unused nil rate band is not available for chargeable lifetime transfers by the survivor, although it may be available when calculating the IHT position in the event of the survivor's death within seven years of making that transfer.

Remarried spouses or civil partners who have already accrued an extra nil rate band from an earlier marriage or civil partnership should consider chargeable legacies (eg to a discretionary trust) in their wills, as opposed to leaving everything to their later spouse. The former course of action could result in three nil rate bands being utilised upon the last surviving spouse's death (ie the nil rate bands of the deceased spouse from the earlier marriage, the remarried spouse and the last surviving spouse). The latter course of action could result in the complete loss of the nil rate band from the earlier marriage.

Cohabiting couples

3.32 In certain circumstances, up to four nil rate bands may be available. This could happen if, for example, a cohabiting couple who had each been married before left their respective estates to chargeable legatees such as adult children (or to the survivor), in order to utilise both their own nil rate band and the transferred nil rate band of their deceased spouse.

However, following marriage their overall IHT position could dramatically worsen.

Example 3.12—Multiple nil rate bands: the effect of marrying

Vera, widowed with one daughter, had inherited from her husband all his estate. Her house was now worth £550,000. She had also accumulated investments worth £300,000.

William was retired. He had also inherited all of his late wife's estate and intended to leave his entire estate worth £680,000 to their son and daughter.

Vera and William decided to set up home together, living in Vera's house and letting out William's house. They consulted a tax adviser about getting married and leaving their estates to each other. Their adviser pointed out that leaving their estates to each other would not only result in the nil rate band of either William or Vera being wasted on the first death, but also the unused nil rate band of the spouse from their first marriage.

Marrying each other may well create a further unused nil rate band on the first of William or Vera to die, but it could not be transferred to the survivor, whose maximum nil rate entitlement had already been reached. The deceased spouse's additional nil rate band entitlement from their first marriage could not be transferred either.

However, if Vera and William did marry in the above example, consideration could be given to including a legacy to chargeable beneficiaries (eg to adult children, or to a discretionary will trust) on the first death, sufficient to use the deceased's nil rate band plus the transferred nil rate band from that person's first marriage.

The residence nil rate band (for deaths from 6 April 2017) will also need to be considered, where appropriate (see **3.42**).

Business or agricultural property

3.33 As discussed elsewhere in this chapter, discretionary trusts are a relatively common feature of wills drafted before the introduction of the transferable nil rate band, as they represented a possible means of using the nil rate band of the first spouse or civil partner to die.

A discretionary will trust may still be a useful vehicle to hold assets that are within the nil rate band, if their value is wholly or partly reduced for IHT purposes by business or agricultural property reliefs. Alternatively, a legacy of assets qualifying for 100% business or agricultural property to non-exempt beneficiaries on the first death should similarly result in the deceased's unused nil rate band being available for later transfer.

The effect of those reliefs is very important. Where relief is at 100% the benefit on top of the nil rate band is unlimited. With relief at 50%, the nil rate band (£325,000 for 2018/19) can cover a transfer of £650,000.

As a general principle, because of this multiplying effect, business and agricultural property should be given to chargeable parties rather than to the surviving spouse, to prevent it being wasted.

Example 3.13—'Doubling up' BPR

Yogi's will left all his family company shares (attracting relief from IHT at 100%) to a discretionary trust for the benefit of his children, and the residue of his estate to his wife Zoe. They had both always taken a keen interest in the family company's business. At the date of Yogi's death, all his shares attracted 100% business property relief (BPR). The shares were worth £800,000.

Zoe received those parts of the estate that did not qualify for any relief, together with substantial cash from insurance policies.

Zoe used some of the cash to buy the shares from the trustees. That gave the trustees far more, in real terms, than the nil rate band, so effectively the children could benefit from more than Yogi could have given in simple cash terms.

If Zoe lives two years from her purchase of the shares, BPR will again be available. Meanwhile, there is control over the children's future inheritance.

In the case of a partially exempt estate (ie because the spouse or civil partner exemption in *s 18* applies) a specific gift should be made of the business or agricultural property itself. It is not sufficient merely to create a specific pecuniary legacy payable out of the business or agricultural property. In the latter situation, relief is denied on the value of the pecuniary legacy and therefore (at least in part) lost (*IHTA 1984, s 39A(6)*). See **5.30**.

Care fees considerations

3.34 Many couples are more concerned about the likely burden of care fees than about IHT. Care fee considerations are outside the scope of this book. However, in very broad terms a discretionary trust, properly run, is expensive (eg compliance procedures such as anti-money laundering rules in the UK have become more detailed and complex) but have been used to shelter from care fees the estate of the first spouse, who is often cared for by the spouse who survives, but who thereafter also needs care.

Alternatively, a simple 'immediate post-death interest' settlement would protect the capital, and might be cheaper to run.

OTHER ISSUES

3.35 The estate duty surviving spouse exemption (*IHTA 1984, Sch 6, para* 2) was unaffected by the introduction of the transferable nil rate band facility. Taxpayers should generally do nothing to disturb that very useful structure, which confers freedom from both IHT and capital gains tax.

3.36 An 'immediate post-death' interest (see **Chapter 9**) in favour of the surviving spouse or civil partner may be a suitable option if, for example, asset protection is a concern. Such a legacy is subject to the spouse or civil partner exemption, resulting in the deceased's unused nil rate band being available on the survivor's death.

3.37 Practitioners should note the effect of *IHTA 1984, s 143* ('Compliance with testator's request') (see **15.49**) and take care to avoid accidental use of the 'first' nil rate band where, for example, the surviving spouse transfers inherited investment assets to family members shortly after the first death.

3.38 As indicated at **3.28** above, a nil rate band relevant property trust may still be considered desirable for various reasons, despite the facility to transfer unused nil rate band. However, some care is required in respect of wills drafted before the introduction of the transferable nil rate band provisions, and also when drafting new wills that incorporate such trusts of the nil rate band.

For example, if the will of a surviving spouse or civil partner leaves a sum 'that is equal to an amount that will not give rise to an IHT charge' on a relevant property trust, in HMRC's view that amount will include nil rate band that has been transferred. The effect when calculating an exit charge before the first ten-year anniversary of the trust is that if the historic value of the fund is greater than the single nil rate band that applies when the property leaves the trust, there will be a positive rate of tax under *IHTA 1984, s 68(1)*, and an IHT liability arises on the exit (IHTM43065).

The inclusion of the transferred nil rate band from the first death with the survivor's own nil rate band legacy could also adversely affect charities, eg if the surviving spouse wished to leave a nil rate band legacy to family members, with the residuary estate after the nil rate band legacy to be left to a charity. Problems can arise if legacies to charities are not carefully worded (see *RSPCA v Sharp and others* [2010] EWCA Civ 1474).

3.39 Potential difficulties can be prevented such as by limiting the nil rate band legacy on the survivor's death by reference to the nil rate band in force at the date of death, rather than by reference to, say, 'such an amount that does not give rise to an IHT charge'.

In HMRC's view, the following wording of legacies will only transfer a single nil rate band (IHTM43065):

- 'To my trustees such sum as I could leave immediately before my death without IHT becoming payable'
- 'I give free of tax to my trustees an amount equal to the upper limit of the nil per cent rate band in the table of rates in Schedule 1'
- 'To my trustees an amount equal to the nil rate band in force at my death'.

3.40 In *Loring v Woodland Trust* [2014] EWCA Civ 1314, the deceased died on 1 September 2011. Her will included the following nil rate band clause, with residue being left to charity:

> 'My trustees shall set aside out of my residuary estate assets or cash of an aggregate value equal to such sum as is at the date of my death the amount of my unused nil rate band for Inheritance Tax and … hold the same for such of the following as shall survive me and in the case of the grandchildren attain 23 and if more than one in equal shares absolutely.'

The net value of the deceased's estate was £680,805. She survived her husband, and her personal representatives claimed her husband's transferable nil rate band in full. The question arose whether the effect of the above clause was to pass £325,000 or £650,000 to the family members under that clause. The residuary legacy to charity was therefore either £355,805 or £30,805.

The High Court ([2013] EWHC 4400 (Ch) concluded that the clause should be construed to mean that the legacy to the family members amounted to £650,000, being the amount of the enhanced nil rate band. The Court of Appeal subsequently considered that the High Court was correct in its interpretation of the above clause. It was held that the implicit purpose of the will was to give as much as possible to the deceased's family without incurring IHT, and to give the rest to charity. The High Court's decision was upheld, and the charity's appeal was dismissed.

The High Court referred to HMRC's guidance at IHTM43065 in its judgment. The clause was considered to be similar to the following specimen clause in HMRC's guidance at IHTM43065, which HMRC state will allow the 'uprated' nil rate band to be transferred:

> 'I give free of tax to my trustees such sum as at my death equals the maximum amount which could be given to them by this Will without inheritance tax becoming payable in respect of my estate'.
>
> The Court of Appeal was referred to a number of specimen clauses drafted by HMRC, together with comments by HMRC on which of those clauses were effective to pass unused nil rate band, and which were not. The HMRC guidance to which the Court was referred was probably IHTM43065. However, the Court of Appeal commented that it did not find the exercise helpful.

The *Woodland Trust* case illustrates the importance of clear drafting in wills, such as in terms of interpreting the extent of legacies by reference to the nil rate band.

3.41 For precedents in cases where the first to die intends to direct some portion of his nil rate band to persons other than his surviving spouse or civil partner, see the latest edition of *Parker's Will Precedents* by Richard Dew and Leon Pickering (Bloomsbury Professional).

RESIDENCE NIL RATE BAND

Background

3.42 Extra (or 'residence') IHT nil rate band is available broadly where a home is passed to a lineal descendant of the deceased on death from 6 April 2017 (*IHTA 1984, ss 8D–8M*).

The maximum amount of the residence nil rate band (or 'residential enhancement') increases in stages, from £100,000 in 2017/18 to £175,000 in 2020/21 (*IHTA 1984, s 8D*).

3.43 However, this extra nil rate band is subject to a tapered withdrawal for estates valued at more than £2 million (for 2018/19).

The rate of withdrawal is broadly £1 for every £2 that the value of the person's estate exceeds the taper threshold.

In calculating IHT on the person's estate, the residence nil rate band is not applied directly to the value of the qualifying residential interest, but to the value of the person's estate on death before applying the standard nil rate band (and any transferred nil rate band), if available (IHTM46003). A possible effect of applying the residence nil rate band before the standard nil rate band is that it could result in unused nil rate band, which may therefore be available for transfer to a surviving spouse or civil partner as described earlier in this chapter.

Transferable residence nil rate band

3.44

> **Focus**
>
> To the extent that there is unused residence nil rate band, a claim is available to transfer the unused element (ie expressed as a percentage) to a surviving spouse or (civil partner).
>
> This brought forward allowance may be claimed on the death of the surviving spouse on or after 6 April 2017.

The circumstances in which residence nil rate band will be unused include where, immediately before death, the estate of the earlier spouse to die did not include a 'qualifying residential interest' as defined. Alternatively, the spouse's estate might include an interest in the home that was not inherited by lineal descendants.

The overriding maximum residence nil rate band available for transfer is 100%, or one additional residence nil rate band. This potential restriction may apply if (for example) a surviving spouse was widowed on more than one occasion, and each earlier spouse's residence nil rate band was wholly or partly unused on death.

On the death of the earlier spouse before 6 April 2017, the amount treated for the above purposes as being available to transfer (and the residential enhancement) is treated as being £100,000, subject to any tapering if the value of the spouse's estate exceeded £2 million (*IHTA 1984, s 8G*). HMRC guidance confirms that for deaths before 6 April 2017, the brought forward amount is 100% of the residential enhancement in force at the later death of a spouse or civil partner, and that the only factor that might reduce this amount is if the earlier estate value was greater than the £2 million taper threshold, in which case the tapering provisions will apply (IHTM46040).

3.45 Unused residence nil rate band must be claimed. The claim is made on form IHT435, which can be downloaded from the gov.uk website (tinyurl.com/HMRC-IHT435), which also includes a form (IHT436) to claim to transfer any unused residence nil rate band (tinyurl.com/HMRC-IHT436).

The claim must be made within certain prescribed time limits, depending on the circumstances. However, there is scope for HMRC to allow a longer claim period at its discretion in some cases (*IHTA 1984, s 8L*; see **16.68**).

3.46 There are potentially complex rules dealing with cases where a residence left to lineal descendants qualifies for conditional exemption, including where the exemption ceases to apply and IHT becomes chargeable (under *IHTA 1984, ss 32* or *32A*), and the effect of conditional exemption on the transfer of residence nil rate band (*IHTA 1984, s 8M*; see **16.69**).

3.47 A combination of transferable nil rate band and unused residence nil rate band results in a maximum effective IHT threshold of £1 million on the surviving spouse's death, although this amount cannot be achieved until 2020/21 at the earliest, when the residence nil rate band increases to £175,000 (ie potentially resulting in a nil rate band of £325,000 and residence nil rate band of £175,000 transferred following the earlier spouse's death, plus the same amounts available on the surviving spouse's death).

3.48 It should be noted that the residence nil rate band may not be available in every instance, such as if the property is held in a discretionary trust (as the residence nil rate band is not available to the trustees), or if an unmarried individual has never owned their own home.

The residence nil rate band provisions were extended (by legislation in *Finance Act 2016*) to allow the allowance to be enhanced, broadly for those who have downsized to a lower value residence, or have ceased to own their home, where other assets of an equivalent value (up to the maximum available residence nil rate band) are left to direct descendants. The downsizing provisions apply for deaths from 6 April 2017 and for downsizing moves or disposals from 8 July 2015.

For detailed commentary on the residence nil rate band, including the transfer of unused residence nil rate band, see **16.55–16.77.**

Chapter 4

Lifetime transfers

SIGNPOSTS

- **Exemptions, etc** – Certain lifetime transfers of value are exempt for IHT purposes, and some dispositions are not treated as transfers of value at all (see **4.1–4.4**).
- **PETs** – Potentially exempt transfers (PETs) are assumed to be exempt when made, and become exempt transfers subject to a seven-year survival period. Most lifetime gifts into trust ceased to qualify as PETs from 22 March 2006. PETs can be actual or 'deemed'. If a PET becomes chargeable, it also affects the individual's cumulative total of chargeable transfers (see **4.5–4.15**).
- **Chargeable lifetime transfers** – These are aggregated over a seven-year period. IHT is charged on a transfer as the highest part of the cumulative total. A lifetime gift is broadly valued based on the reduction in the transferor's estate. A 'gift with reservation' is treated as forming part of the donor's estate on death. There are also anti-avoidance provisions regarding 'associated operations' affecting transfers of value (see **4.16–4.24**).
- **'Pilot' trusts** – Anti-avoidance provisions are targeted at arrangements involving the use of multiple settlements and the addition of assets to those settlements on the same day, subject to certain limited exceptions (see **4.25**).
- **Calculating IHT and reporting chargeable lifetime transfers** – In some cases, it may be necessary to look back at lifetime transfers up to a maximum of 14 years before the date of death. Chargeable lifetime transfers are subject to reporting requirements, unless certain exceptions apply (see **4.26–4.29**).

INTRODUCTION

4.1 IHT is a tax on 'chargeable transfers' (made on or after 18 March 1986) during an individual's lifetime, and on the value of the death estate.

A 'chargeable transfer' is any transfer of value made by an individual, other than an exempt transfer (*IHTA 1984, s 2(1)*).

A 'potentially exempt transfer' (PET) becomes an exempt transfer seven years after the date of the gift. It is assumed that a PET will become an exempt transfer when the gift is made (*IHTA 1984, s 3A(5)*). An outright lifetime gift to another individual (or a trust for disabled persons, or a trust for bereaved minors in certain circumstances; see **1.10**) is a PET, which therefore only becomes chargeable to IHT if the donor dies within seven years of making the gift.

However, transfers to a company and gifts to a relevant property trust (ie discretionary trusts and, from 22 March 2006, most interest in possession trusts) are immediately chargeable lifetime transfers. IHT at the lifetime rate may become due (subject to any reliefs and exemptions) if the total value of those gifts exceeds the IHT threshold or 'nil rate band' (£325,000 for 2018/19).

EXEMPT LIFETIME TRANSFERS

4.2 In addition to PETs made more than seven years before the donor's death, certain lifetime transfers are exempt from IHT.

For further information on IHT exemptions generally, see **1.20** and **Chapter 11**.

4.3 *Lifetime* exemptions are summarised below:

- Gifts between spouses or civil partners (note that the exemption is restricted if the transferor is domiciled in the UK but the transferee is domiciled outside the UK). The exempt transfer limit is the prevailing available nil rate band limit at the time of the transfer (from 6 April 2013; previously, the limit was £55,000 for transfers between 9 March 1982 and 5 April 2013). However, there is an election facility for the non-UK domiciled spouse or civil partner to be treated as UK domiciled for IHT purposes: see **2.6**) (*IHTA 1984, s 18*).
- Annual exemption for gifts not exceeding £3,000 in any tax year. If the total value of gifts in one tax year is less than £3,000, the excess can be carried forward to the next tax year, but no further (*IHTA 1984, s 19*).
- Small gifts in any tax year up to a total of £250 per donee, to as many recipients as the donor wishes (*IHTA 1984, s 20*).
- Normal expenditure out of income is exempt with no upper limit, if certain conditions are satisfied (ie broadly that the gifts are part of the donor's usual expenditure, were made out of income, and left the donor with sufficient income to maintain his normal standard of living (*IHTA 1984, s 21*)).
- Wedding or civil partnership gifts within certain limits (ie £5,000 if the donor is a parent of a party to the marriage or civil partnership, £2,500 if

the donor is a remoter ancestor or is one of the parties to the marriage or civil partnership, or £1,000 for any other donor) (*IHTA 1984, s 22*).

- Gifts to charities or registered clubs (*IHTA 1984, s 23*).
- Gifts to qualifying parliamentary political parties (*IHTA 1984, s 24*).
- Gifts to registered housing associations (*IHTA 1984, s 24A*).
- Gifts for national purposes (eg the National Gallery, National Museums and the National Trust) (*IHTA 1984, s 25, Sch 3*), and qualifying gifts to the nation (within *FA 2012, Sch 14, para 1*).
- Transfers to maintenance funds for historic buildings, where HMRC so direct upon making a claim (*IHTA 1984, s 27, Sch 4*).
- Transfers of shares or securities by an individual to an employee trust (within *IHTA 1984, s 86*) subject to certain conditions (*IHTA 1984, s 28*). In addition (following legislation introduced in *FA 2014*), a transfer of shares in a company by an individual to an 'employee ownership trust' is exempt from IHT broadly if the company meets a 'trading requirement' as defined, the trust meets an 'all-employee benefit requirement' and the trust does not meet a 'controlling interest' requirement immediately before the start of the tax year of transfer but does so at the end of that tax year (*IHTA 1984, s 28A*).
- Transfers of national heritage property may be exempt from IHT where certain conditions are satisfied, ie 'conditionally exempt transfers' (*IHTA 1984, ss 30–35A*).

It should be noted that the IHT exemptions for gifts to charities and qualifying political parties would not currently apply to gifts to campaigning organisations or pressure groups that do not satisfy the criteria for those exemptions. This point received some publicity following donations by individuals to Brexit campaigns, which also highlighted that such donations would not be PETs (see **4.7–4.8**).

4.4

Dispositions that are not transfers of value

Certain actual and deemed 'dispositions' (eg gifts, payments or actions, such as the waiver of salary or dividends) are not treated as transfers of value if certain conditions are satisfied, and are therefore not taken into account for IHT purposes (*IHTA 1984, ss 10–17*) (see **Chapter 11**).

This includes dispositions which are not intended to confer a gratuitous benefit on anyone (*IHTA 1984, s 10*), and payments for the maintenance of certain family members, eg spouse or civil partner, the donor's children (including adopted children and stepchildren) who are under 18 for their education and training, and relatives who are dependent due to old age or infirmity

(*IHTA 1984, s 11*); as to the latter category of disposition, see *R McKelvey (personal representative of D V McKelvey) v HMRC* [2008] SSCD 944 (SpC 694), discussed at **16.18**.

'Maintenance' for the above purposes usually means making periodic payments rather than lump sum provision (see *Phizackerley v HMRC* [2007] WTLR 745).

In addition, following legislation (*IHTA 1984, s 12A*) introduced in *Finance Act 2016*, where a person has failed to exercise their rights to draw designated pension funds from a 'drawdown fund' (including a flexi-access drawdown fund) during the person's lifetime (and as a result has unused funds when they die), this does not give rise to a deemed disposition (under *IHTA 1984, s 3(3)*) as an omission to exercise a right.

POTENTIALLY EXEMPT TRANSFERS

Definition and scope

4.5 A PET is a transfer of value made by an individual (as opposed to a 'person', which has a wider meaning, including a company), which would otherwise be a chargeable transfer. A PET made seven years or more before the transferor's death is exempt; any other PET is a chargeable transfer.

A PET is treated as exempt whilst the donor is alive, and in the seven-year period following the transfer it is assumed that the PET will become exempt (*IHTA 1984, s 3A(5)*).

In the case of a life insurance policy taken out or varied (since 26 March 1974) for the benefit of someone else, if an annuity was also taken out (before, at the same time or after the policy), then unless the taxpayer can show that the purchase of the annuity and the taking out of the policy were not associated operations (within *IHTA 1984, s 268*), a transfer of value of a specified amount is treated as having been made in taking the policy out for someone else, which can qualify as a PET (*IHTA 1984, s 263*; see IHTM20374).

This form of IHT planning (commonly known as 'back-to-back arrangements') is otherwise intended to benefit from the 'normal expenditure out of income' exemption, although an anti-avoidance provision concerning associated operations can deny the exemption (*IHTA 1984, s 21(2)*). HMRC practice is not to treat arrangements as associated operations (and not to disqualify the premiums from being normal expenditure for exemption purposes) if it can be shown that the life policy was issued on 'normal' terms. This means that full evidence of health must have been obtained, and that the terms on which the policy was issued would have been the same even if the annuity had not been bought (*SP E4*).

For back-to-back life policy arrangements involving husband and wife (or civil partners), full medical evidence should be obtained in respect of both parties (*Smith v Revenue and Customs Commissioners* [2008] STC 1649).

In addition, the capital element of a purchased life annuity (within *ITTOIA 2005, s 423*) purchased on or after 13 November 1974, which is exempt for income tax purposes (under *ITTOIA 2005, s 717*), is not regarded as part of the transferor's income for the purposes of the normal expenditure exemption (*IHTA 1984, s 21(3), (4)*).

Transfers before 22 March 2006

4.6 Before 22 March 2006, gifts qualified as PETs if made by an individual to:

- another individual (or to an interest in possession trust for another individual);
- an accumulation and maintenance trust; or
- the trustees of a trust for a disabled person.

Transfers from 22 March 2006

4.7 From 22 March 2006, gifts to an accumulation and maintenance trust (to the extent that such trusts remain in existence) ceased to be PETs, ie they are immediately chargeable transfers (*IHTA 1984, s 3A(1)–(1A)*). Note that it has not been possible to create an accumulation and maintenance settlement under *s 71* since before that date (*IHTA 1984, s 71(1A)*). Gifts to interest in possession trusts are discussed below.

A 'transfer of value' is a disposition made by a person resulting in the value of his estate immediately afterwards being less than it otherwise would be; the difference is the value transferred. The measure of the transfer is, therefore, the reduction in the transferor's estate (*IHTA 1984, s 3(1)*).

A gift to another individual is a PET to the extent that the value transferred becomes comprised in that individual's estate, or to the extent that the transfer results in an increase in his estate (eg the forgiveness of a loan to another individual).

4.8

Focus

- A gift to a disabled person's trust is a PET to the extent that it becomes settled property within *IHTA 1984, s 89* ('Trusts for disabled persons') (*IHTA 1984, s 3A(3), (3A)*).
- A disabled person's interest within *IHTA 1984, s 89A* ('Self-settlement by person expected to fall within the definition of

"disabled person"') is a qualifying interest in possession (ie within *IHTA 1984, s 49(1A)*), so the gift is effectively a non-event for IHT purposes, as it is treated as remaining part of the settlor's estate (*IHTA 1984, s 89B(1)(b)*).

- The same IHT treatment applies to an interest in possession which is self-settled on or after 22 March 2006 by a person with a condition expected to lead to disability, and to which the person is beneficially entitled, where certain conditions are satisfied as to the terms of the settlement and distribution of the settled property (*IHTA 1984, s 89B(1)(d)*).
- An interest in possession to which the disabled person became beneficially entitled on or after 22 March 2006 is also a qualifying interest in possession, where certain conditions are satisfied as to the terms of the settlement and distribution of the settled property (*IHTA 1984, s 89B(1)(c)*).
- A gift to a disabled person's trust by another individual constitutes a PET, within *IHTA 1984, s 3A(1), (1A)* (see IHTM42805).

In addition, a gift into a 'bereaved minor's' trust is a PET if made on the ending of an 'immediate post-death interest' (*IHTA 1984, s 3A(1A)(c)(iii)*) (see **Chapter 9**). Prior to 22 March 2006, a lifetime gift to an accumulation and maintenance trust was also a PET, if it became settled property within *IHTA 1984, s 71* ('Accumulation and maintenance trusts').

Certain transfers of value are specifically prevented from being PETs, including:

- transfers by a close company (*IHTA 1984, s 94(1)*; see IHTM14853);
- the deemed disposition on an alteration in the capital or share rights of close companies (*IHTA 1984, s 98(3)*);
- the release of a life interest between 18 March 1986 and 16 March 1987 (see **4.13** and IHTM04063);
- the gift of a purchased reversionary interest within *IHTA 1984, s 81A* (see **4.9**);
- the lifetime termination of an interest in possession (within *IHTA 1984, s 52*) to which *IHTA 1984, s 5(1B)* applies (ie where a UK-domiciled person became beneficially entitled to the interest following a disposition which was prevented from being a transfer of value by virtue of *IHTA 1984, s 10* ('Dispositions not intended to confer a gratuitous benefit') (*IHTA 1984, s 3A(6A)*) (see **4.14**); and
- a transfer to the extent to which the property transferred consists of woodlands subject to a deferred estate duty charge (*FA 1986, Sch 19, para 46*).

Purchased reversionary interests

4.9 If a reversionary interest (ie a future interest) in relevant property has been purchased for money or money's worth, or is held by the settlor or spouse or civil partner, a deemed disposal arises for IHT purposes when the reversionary interest ends and entitlement to an interest in possession begins. The resulting IHT charge is based on the value of the reversionary interest immediately before it ended. A gift of such a reversionary interest is prevented by legislation from being a PET (*IHTA 1984, s 81A*).

This rule applies to reversionary interests arising from 9 December 2009, but does not affect interests in possession outside the 'relevant property' regime, such as a disabled person's interest.

Deemed PETs

4.10 An exception to the general rule that any occasions of IHT charge where tax is charged as if a transfer of value had been made are excluded from being PETs applies to charges under *IHTA 1984, s 52* ('Charge on termination of an interest in possession') (*IHTA 1984, s 3A(6)–(7)*).

This exception relates to transfers of value from 17 March 1987. The release of a life interest is a PET in the circumstances outlined below.

Before 22 March 2006

4.11 The disposal or release of an individual's beneficial entitlement to an interest in possession in settled property by gift before 22 March 2006 is a PET in the following cases (*IHTA 1984, s 3A*):

- another individual becomes beneficially entitled to the property in question (or to an interest in possession in that property); or
- the property is settled on accumulation and maintenance trusts or trusts for the disabled; or
- the value of another individual's estate is increased.

From 22 March 2006

4.12 An interest in possession created before 22 March 2006 and disposed of or released by gift to someone else from that date is a PET as above; however, there is an exception if the rules for bereaved minors (*IHTA 1984, s 71A*) or 'Age 18-to-25 trusts' (*IHTA 1984, s 71D*) applied to the trust property in which the interest subsisted immediately before that disposal, as no charge under *IHTA 1984, s 52* arises in such cases (*IHTA 1984, ss 51(1B), 53(1A)*).

If an individual has an interest in trust property, which remains comprised in his estate for IHT purposes (eg an immediate post-death interest), if that interest later comes to an end but he continues to enjoy the property thereafter, the rules regarding 'gifts with reservation' (in *FA 1986, s 102*) apply. The individual is treated for the purposes of those anti-avoidance provisions as having made a gift of the interest terminated or given away (*FA 1986*, s *102ZA(2)*).

In the case of an interest created on or after 22 March 2006, a subsequent disposal or release of the life interest by gift is a PET if it is an 'immediate post-death interest', a 'disabled person's interest' or a 'transitional serial interest' (*IHTA 1984, ss 3A(6A), 51(1A)*).

For further information on interests in possession generally, see **Chapter 9**.

4.13 Certain transfers are treated as if they were PETs, ie the lifetime cessation of a benefit in 'gift with reservation' property (*FA 1986,s 102(4)*) (see **4.22**), and the discharge or reduction of a debt subject to abatement (see below).

The release of a life interest between 18 March 1986 and 16 March 1987 cannot be a PET and is, therefore, an immediately chargeable transfer. This is because a transfer of value was originally prevented (by *IHTA 1984, s 3A(2)*) from being a PET if it resulted in settled property becoming comprised in an individual's estate, or in an increase in the value of settled property already comprised in the estate.

A further deemed PET arises on the discharge, or reduction, of a debt subject to abatement under *FA 1986, s 103* ('Treatment of certain debts and incumbrances') on or after 18 March 1986 (*FA 1986, s 103(5)*).

Interests in possession under IHTA 1984, s 5(1B)

4.14 There is an exception from PET treatment in respect of an IHT charge under *IHTA 1984, s 52*, where a UK-domiciled person purchased an interest in possession at arm's length. Such an IHT charge is prevented from being a PET (ie it is immediately chargeable), if the person's beneficial entitlement to the interest arose on or after 9 December 2009 (*IHTA 1984, s 3A(6A)*).

This is a targeted anti-avoidance rule, as the background note to the relevant clause in Finance Bill 2010 explains:

> 'HM Revenue & Customs (HMRC) became aware of arrangements that sought to avoid any IHT charges on assets that are put into a trust. The arrangement was designed to allow individuals who would normally be chargeable to IHT on transfers in to trust to purchase an interest in a trust

that had not been subject to UK IHT charges when property had originally been transferred in to it.'

A disposition which is not intended to confer gratuitous benefit (within *IHTA 1984, s 10*) is not a transfer of value. This could apply to the arm's-length purchase of an interest in possession. A lifetime interest in possession settlement made after 21 March 2006 (other than a disabled person's interest) does not generally form part of the estate of the person beneficially entitled to the interest (*IHTA 1984, s 5(1A)*). Without the above anti-avoidance rule, the arm's-length purchase of such an interest in possession could therefore have resulted in that interest falling outside a person's estate.

However, *IHTA 1984, s 5(1B)* provides that the interest forms part of the estate of a person who was domiciled in the UK upon becoming beneficially entitled to it, if that entitlement arose by virtue of a disposition within *IHTA 1984, s 10*. In addition, the lifetime termination of such an interest is an immediately chargeable transfer, since it is prevented from being a PET, as indicated above.

Further anti-avoidance provisions were introduced in *FA 2012*, which target IHT avoidance schemes involving the acquisition of interests in excluded property trusts (*IHTA 1984, ss 48(3D), 74A–74C*; see **5.5**).

Implications of PETs

4.15 As indicated at **4.1**, it is generally assumed that a PET will become an exempt transfer when made. However, it is necessary to notify HMRC of the transfer if it is relevant to the application of the annual IHT exemption in respect of an immediately chargeable transfer. The same may apply in relation to the normal expenditure out of income exemption (*IHTA 1984, s 21*), where an IHT liability would otherwise arise but for the availability of the exemption. As to the reporting of chargeable lifetime transfers, see **4.29**.

The PET is not cumulated with the immediately chargeable transfer. A PET becomes an exempt transfer if the donor survives seven years after the date of the gift, but is otherwise chargeable to IHT if the donor dies within that seven-year period.

Notwithstanding the assumption that a PET will become an exempt transfer, in HMRC's view the annual exemption (if available) should be allocated against the PET when it is made. This appears to be on the basis that a transfer of value only qualifies as a PET to the extent that it would, apart from *IHTA 1984, s 3A*, be a chargeable transfer (eg if not covered by an exemption) (IHTM04024).

If an individual dies within seven years, the earlier PET becomes chargeable to IHT at the date of that gift. For the purposes of allocating the annual exemption, a chargeable PET is deemed to have been made later than any non-PET made in the same tax year (*IHTA 1984, s 19(3A)*).

However, HMRC practice is to allocate the annual exemption to transfers of value in chronological order, at least initially. For example, if an individual makes a PET (eg a gift to a sibling) earlier in the same tax year than a chargeable lifetime transfer (eg a gift to a discretionary trust), HMRC guidance (at IHTM14143) indicates that the exemption should be applied to the earlier transfer, and that this would be the case irrespective of whether the transfers were PETs or chargeable when made.

If a PET becomes chargeable, IHT is calculated at the death rates applicable at the time of death, subject to any taper relief (see **12.2**). In addition, the transfer is cumulated with the death estate, and will also affect the individual's cumulative total of chargeable transfers (IHTM14513; see **Example 4.1**).

Example 4.1—Death within seven years of a PET

Mr Smith died on 30 April 2018, having made the following lifetime gifts (the estate on death was left to his wife):

		£
1 June 2015	Cash gift to daughter	150,000
6 April 2017	Cash gift to discretionary trust	263,000

Lifetime IHT position of gifts

The IHT position on making the lifetime gifts is that the cash gift to Mr Smith's daughter on 1 June 2015 is a PET, which is not cumulated but uses his annual exemptions of £6,000 (ie £3,000 for 2015/16, plus £3,000 unused exemption brought forward from 2014/15).

The creation of the discretionary trust on 6 April 2017 was an immediately chargeable transfer, but the amount chargeable to IHT of £257,000 (ie £263,000 less £3,000 annual exemptions for 2017/18 and 2016/17) was less than the nil rate band, so no IHT was payable.

IHT position of lifetime gifts on death

(a) On the gift to Mr Smith's daughter:

	£
Gift to daughter	150,000
Less: annual exemption (× 2)	(6,000)
	144,000
Less: nil rate band (2018/19)	(144,000)
	Nil

(b) On creation of the discretionary trust:

	£
Cash gift to trust	263,000
Less: annual exemption (× 2)	(6,000)
	257,000
Less: nil rate band remaining	
(£325,000 – £144,000)	(181,000)
	76,000
IHT @ 40%	£30,400

Taper relief is not in point, as the gift was within three years of Mr Smith's death.

CHARGEABLE LIFETIME TRANSFERS

4.16 A chargeable lifetime transfer is a transfer of value made by an individual, which is not unconditionally or potentially exempt (*IHTA 1984, s 2(1)*). Hence this includes the following:

- transfers into relevant property trusts, such as discretionary trusts, or terminations of pre-22 March 2006 interests in possession in favour of such trusts (and, from 22 March 2006, lifetime gifts into most trusts); and
- transfers by close companies, which can be charged on the shareholders in some cases (*IHTA 1984, ss 94–97, 202*).

In addition, see **4.8** above for transfers of value that are chargeable on the basis that they cannot be treated as PETs.

A chargeable lifetime transfer is aggregated with other such transfers over a seven-year period, following which they fall out of the cumulative total. Business property relief and agricultural property relief may reduce the value of the gift, if the relief conditions are satisfied at the date of transfer (see **Chapter 13**). The rate of IHT is determined by reference to this total. Tax is charged (at half the rate at death) on the transfer as the highest part of the cumulative total, to the extent that it exceeds the nil rate band, after deducting any available reliefs and exemptions.

Where the transferor bears the IHT liability, the tax represents a further loss in the value of his estate, and the transfer must, therefore, be grossed-up to arrive at the overall amount of the chargeable transfer.

Example 4.2—Cumulation of chargeable lifetime transfers

Martin made the following lifetime gifts (after exemptions and reliefs):

			£
1 June 2009	–	Discretionary trust	50,000
6 April 2012	–	Discretionary trust	85,000
31 December 2016	–	Gift to daughter (PET)	100,000
6 April 2018	–	Discretionary trust	340,000

The transfer to the discretionary trust in 2009 was made more than seven years before the transfer in 2018, but the transfer in 2012 is taken into account. The PET in 2016 is ignored when calculating lifetime tax on the chargeable transfer in 2018.

If Martin agrees to pay the tax on his lifetime gifts, his IHT position is as follows:

1 June 2009 – Discretionary trust £50,000

The transfer is covered by the nil rate band.

6 April 2012 – Discretionary trust £85,000

The transfer (although cumulated with the earlier transfer on 1 June 2009) is covered by the nil rate band.

6 April 2018 – Discretionary trust £340,000

The transfer is cumulated with the earlier transfer on 6 April 2012. However, it is not cumulated with the transfer on 1 June 2009 (ie more than seven years ago). Nor is it cumulated with the gift to Martin's daughter on 31 December 2016 (ie a PET when made).

The IHT position is, therefore, as follows:

	£
IHT:	
£240,000 (ie £325,000 – £85,000) × nil	NIL
£100,000 × ¼ (ie grossed-up)	25,000
	£25,000

The gross value of the transfer is £340,000 + £25,000 = £365,000

4.17 Additional IHT becomes chargeable at the 'death rate' (40% for 2018/19) in respect of immediately chargeable lifetime transfers made within seven years from the death of the transferor. The gift is cumulated with immediately chargeable transfers and failed PETs in the preceding seven years (IHTM14573; see **Example 4.3**). The resulting IHT (recalculated at the full death rate) is compared with the lifetime tax paid (if any), for the purposes of calculating any additional liability.

However, if the recomputed figure is lower than the IHT paid at the time of transfer, no additional tax is payable, but the difference is not repaid.

Example 4.3—Chargeable lifetime transfers: position on death

Continuing the above example, suppose that Martin died on 5 October 2018. The additional IHT on death would be as follows (after reliefs and exemptions):

6 April 2012 – Discretionary trust £85,000

The transfer (cumulated with the earlier transfer on 1 June 2009) remains covered by the nil rate band.

31 December 2016 – Gift to daughter £100,000

The 'failed' PET is cumulated with the discretionary trust transfer on 6 April 2012 (but not the gift on 1 June 2009, which falls out of charge). The cumulative total (ie £100,000 + £85,000 = £185,000) is covered by the IHT nil rate band.

6 April 2018 – Discretionary trust £340,000

The transfer is cumulated with the transfers on 6 April 2012 and 31 December 2016. The additional IHT on the gross value of the transfer (ie £365,000) is calculated as follows (Note: the trustees pay the additional IHT liability):

	£
IHT:	
£140,000 (ie £325,000 – £185,000) × nil	NIL
£225,000 × 40% (Note: no taper relief)	90,000
	90,000
Less: IHT paid at lifetime rates	(25,000)
Additional IHT due (paid by the trustees)	£65,000

4.18 The calculation of additional tax on death may be affected by considerations such as the following, which are discussed in subsequent chapters:

- the availability of relief for business and agricultural property (see **Chapter 13**);
- the application of other reliefs (if available). For example, a reduction in additional IHT on death may be claimed (ie by the person liable for the tax) if the value of an asset has fallen between the date of gift and the date of the transferor's death (or an earlier qualifying sale of the gifted property) (*IHTA 1984, ss 131–140* 'Transfers within seven years before death') (see **Chapter 12**); and
- whether the 'gifts with reservation' anti-avoidance rules apply (see **4.22** below and **Chapter 7**).

VALUING LIFETIME TRANSFERS

General

4.19 The general rule is that assets are valued for IHT purposes at the price they might reasonably be expected to fetch if sold in the open market at the time of transfer (*IHTA 1984, s 160*).

The importance of obtaining accurate asset valuations cannot be overstated. HMRC generally take a robust approach to market valuations of property, especially where there might be development potential. HMRC has produced a toolkit to assist tax agents and others when completing the account Form IHT400 (tinyurl.com/IHT-Toolkit). The toolkit identifies particular areas of risk when completing an IHT400, and states: 'Valuations are the biggest single area of risk, accounting for a large part of our compliance checks'.

Inaccurate asset valuations carry the threat of possible interest and penalties, as well as further IHT liabilities. It is therefore advisable to obtain valuations for IHT purposes from at least one suitably qualified professional to help reduce such risks.

However, the value of a lifetime gift is measured by the reduction in value of the transferor's estate as a result of the transfer (but not normally taking into account the value of any excluded property ceasing to form part of the estate (*IHTA 1984, s 3(2)*). The value of the gift will often equal the loss to the estate, but not always. For example, the loss to the estate of a 51% shareholder in a private company who makes a lifetime gift of 2% is greater than the value of the 2% gift; it is the value of the shareholder's loss of control in the company.

Liabilities are taken into account in valuing the estate at the date of transfer, if imposed by law or to the extent of being incurred for consideration in money or money's worth (*IHTA 1984, s 5(3), (5)*).

A liability attaching to a particular asset will generally reduce the value of that asset (*IHTA 1984, s 162(4)*).

However, *FA 2013* introduced restrictions and conditions for deductions in respect of liabilities to be allowable, including rules to determine how liabilities may be deducted in certain circumstances involving excluded property (see **1.13**), 'relievable property' (ie qualifying business or agricultural property (see **Chapter 13**) or property eligible for woodlands relief (see **12.24**)), and also rules concerning the repayment of liabilities after death.

Further legislation (introduced in *FA 2014*) treats funds held in foreign currency accounts in UK banks which are left out of account in determining the value of a person's estate on death for IHT purposes (under *IHTA 1984, s 157*) in a similar way to excluded property for the purposes of the above provisions restricting how liabilities are deducted from the value of the estate for IHT purposes (*IHTA 1984, s 162AA*). The provisions regarding liabilities are outlined at **5.13**.

For commentary on the value of assets generally, see **Chapter 6**.

Valuing PETs

4.20 If property becomes comprised in another individual's estate, or becomes qualifying settled property, the value transferred by a PET is generally calculated by reference to the loss to the transferor's estate. There is no 'grossing-up' because the transferor is not liable for the tax on a PET.

The loss to the transferor's estate will often (but not always) be the same as the increase in value of the transferee's estate. For example, the forgiveness of a loan should result in a loss to the estate and corresponding increase. Conversely, HMRC cite the omission to exercise a right as a circumstance where the 'loss to transferor' principle may not apply (IHTM04066).

Valuing transfers by close companies

4.21 In the case of a close company transfer of value (see **1.27**), IHT is charged as if each individual participator had made a transfer of the amount apportioned to them by reference to their rights and interests in the company immediately before the transfer. The transfer is based on the net amount apportioned to each participator after taking account of any corresponding increase in that participator's estate following the transfer.

The annual exemption explicitly applies to these transfers if not otherwise used elsewhere (*IHTA 1984, s 94(5)*), and the spouse or civil partner exemption is also available to the extent that the estate of the spouse or civil partner of a participator is increased (IHTM04068).

Alterations to a close company's unquoted share or loan capital (eg a subscription for valuable shares at par by an individual), or any rights attaching to its unquoted shares or debentures, are also treated as dispositions made by the participators (*IHTA 1984, s 98(1)*), which are apportioned among the participators in the same way as a transfer by a close company. The disposition is specifically prohibited from being treated as a PET (*IHTA 1984, s 98(3)*).

GIFTS WITH RESERVATION

4.22 The 'gifts with reservation' (GWR) anti-avoidance provisions (*FA 1986, ss 102–102C, Sch 20*) apply to lifetime gifts in certain circumstances. The rules are designed to prevent 'cake and eat it' situations, whereby an individual gifts an asset but continues to have the use or enjoyment of it. As mentioned, most lifetime gifts to individuals are PETs if not otherwise exempt, which only become chargeable if the transferor dies within seven years of the transfer.

Without the GWR rules, if the transferor survived the transfer by seven years, the PET would become an exempt transfer, even though for all practical purposes the transferor may have continued to enjoy the gifted asset until their death.

The effect of the GWR rules is broadly to ensure that the property subject to a GWR is treated as forming part of the donor's death estate. If the benefit is ended during his lifetime, the donor is treated as having made a PET at that time (*FA 1986, s 102(4)*), which becomes a chargeable transfer on death within the following seven years.

However, because the PET is not actual but deemed (ie because there is no actual transfer of value when the GWR ceases) the annual exemption is not available to offset against it. If the property is being taxed as a PET, it is valued on the basis of the loss to the transferor's estate (IHTM04073).

In the absence of provisions to the contrary, IHT could become chargeable on the initial lifetime transfer, and on the value of the relevant asset when the reservation ceased (eg upon death). However, the GWR rules are supplemented by regulations designed to prevent a double tax charge arising (*Inheritance Tax (Double Charges Relief) Regulations, SI 1987/1130*).

For further commentary on the GWR rules, see **Chapter 7**.

ASSOCIATED OPERATIONS

4.23 As mentioned, a transfer of value is any disposition made by a person as a result of which the value of his estate immediately after the disposition is less than it would be but for the disposition; and the amount by which it is less is the value transferred by the transfer (*IHTA 1984, s 3(1)*). A 'disposition' is defined (by *IHTA 1984, s 272*) to include a disposition effected by associated operations.

The 'associated operations' provision is a further anti-avoidance rule, which provides for transactions to be treated as being made (whether directly or indirectly) by way of two or more linked operations (*IHTA 1984, s 268*). Where this rule applies to transfers at different times, the combined effect on the value of the transferor's estate will be taken into account and treated as made at the time of the last transfer. The provision applies to transactions affecting the same property or a series of linked transactions, which need not be effected by the same person.

The following example is taken from HMRC's Inheritance Tax Manual (at IHTM14821):

Example 4.4—Associated operations

Tina has a 100% shareholding in ABC Ltd. At 11 June 2011 it is valued at £100,000.

Tina transfers:

- a 33% holding to Steven on 11 June 2011;
- a 33% holding to Steven on 12 June 2011; and
- a 34% holding to Russell on 13 June 2011.

Following Tina's death in August 2011, the loss to the estate on each transfer is individually valued at:

- £43,000,
- £26,000, and
- £17,000 respectively.

A total of £86,000.

The total of the individual transfers for inheritance tax is only £86,000 but Tina had effectively given away £100,000 worth of assets.

The legislation at *IHTA 1984, s 268* counters this in certain circumstances so that you can look at the overall effect of several events through the concept of 'associated operations'.

4.24 However, case law has effectively restricted the scope of the associated operations rule in certain situations (see **4.25**).

The omission to exercise a right can be an 'operation' treated as an associated operation for these purposes (*IHTA 1984, s 268(1)*). However, the associated operations rule does not apply to associate the grant of a lease for full consideration in money or money's worth with any operation effected more than three years after the grant (*IHTA 1984, s 268(2)*).

The value of a transfer made through associated operations is normally the overall loss to the transferor's estate, measured at the time of the last operation. However, if any of the earlier operations was also a transfer of value by the transferor, the value transferred by the earlier operation(s) (to the extent that the spouse or civil partner exemption is not available) is deducted from the overall amount (*IHTA 1984, s 268(3)*).

PROPERTY ADDED TO MULTIPLE TRUSTS ON THE SAME DAY

4.25 With regard to the creation of settlements, anti-avoidance provisions have been targeted at arrangements involving the use of multiple ('pilot') trusts and the addition of assets to those trusts on the same day.

In a case prior to the introduction of those provisions (*Rysaffe Trustee Co (CI) Ltd v IRC* [2003] STC 536), the Court of Appeal held that as a matter of general law five separate discretionary settlements created on different dates (ie to maximise the availability of nil rate bands) on very similar terms constituted separate settlements for the purposes of the ten-year anniversary charge (under *s 64*). The court rejected HMRC's contention of only a single settlement, existing by associated operations. The settlor had intended separate settlements. Hence each settlement was eligible for its own nil rate band, as each settlement had been created by a 'disposition'.

IHT planning arrangements involving the use of 'pilot' trusts are among those included in 'HMRC's general anti-abuse rule (GAAR) guidance' (see Part D – Examples at tinyurl.com/GAAR-Guidance-D). The guidance states (at D26.5.3): 'The practice was litigated in the case of *Rysaffe Trustee v IRC* [2003] STC 536. HMRC lost the case and having chosen not to change the legislation, must be taken to have accepted the practice'. It concludes: 'The arrangements accord with established practice accepted by HMRC and are accordingly not regarded as abusive.'

However, following a series of HMRC consultations on complexity and fairness issues relating to the IHT rules for trusts, anti-avoidance legislation (*IHTA 1984, ss 62A–62C*) was introduced (in *Finance (No 2) Act 2015*), which is broadly aimed at settlors creating pilot trusts and avoiding IHT through the availability of multiple nil rate bands. The provisions are designed to ensure that where property is added to two or more settlements on the same day (and after the commencement of those settlements) the value of the added property (which can include the value of property settled at the date of commencement, if the settlements are not 'related' by being created by the same settlor on the same day) is generally brought into account in calculating the IHT rate for the purposes of various chargeable events for trusts (ie ten-year charges (under *IHTA 1984, s 66*), exit charges before the first ten-year anniversary (under *IHTA 1984, s 68*) and exit charges between anniversaries (under *IHTA 1984, s 69*)).

There is an exception from the same day additions rules in respect of same day transfers of value of £5,000 or less made during the settlor's lifetime, subject to an 'anti-fragmentation' rule. The same day addition treatment is also subject to certain exceptions (in *IHTA 1984, s 62B*), including additions to 'protected settlements' (see below).

This anti-avoidance measure applies to the above relevant property trust charges arising on or after 18 November 2015 (ie the date on which *Finance (No 2) Act 2015* received Royal Assent).

However, the same day addition provisions do not apply to 'protected settlements' (*IHTA 1984, s 62C*). These are broadly relevant property trusts created before 10 December 2014 (ie the date when draft legislation was initially published), where the settlor has made no additions from that date. Note that whilst there is an exception from the same day additions rule for transfers of value of £5,000 or less (see above), transfers of value of *any* amount by the settlor from 10 December 2014 can result in protection from the same day additions provisions for a protected settlement (under *IHTA 1984, s 62C(3)(a)*) being lost (eg a settlor's payment of trust professional fees)).

Alternatively, a settlement is protected if the settlor's same day addition was effected by a will executed before 10 December 2014, if the will provisions are in substance the same at the settlor's death as they were immediately before that date. However, this exclusion is limited to deaths before 6 April 2017, as it was intended to allow affected individuals an opportunity to change their wills following the introduction of the same day addition provisions (*IHTA 1984, s 62C(3)(b)*).

CALCULATING IHT

4.26 The IHT rates for chargeable lifetime transfers for 2018/19 are shown in **Table 4.1** below (*IHTA 1984, s 7, Sch 1*), and remain unchanged from the previous tax year.

The IHT threshold (or 'nil rate band') was effectively fixed (in *FA 2010, s 8*) at £325,000 for 2010/11 to 2014/15 inclusive.

From 2015/16, the consumer prices index (CPI) becomes the default basis for increasing the nil rate band, as opposed to the retail prices index (RPI) (*IHTA 1984, s 8*). Legislation to this effect was introduced in *FA 2012*. However, the automatic indexation of the nil rate band using the CPI from 2015/16 is subject to override where Parliament considers it appropriate.

Subsequently, legislation (in *FA 2014*) extended the effective freezing of the nil rate band at £325,000 up to and including 2017/18. Furthermore, the indexation of the nil rate band in *IHTA 1984, s 8* was once again disapplied in *Finance (No 2) Act 2015*. Consequently, the nil rate band remains at £325,000 for the tax years 2018/19, 2019/20 and 2020/21.

Extra nil rate band (or 'residence nil rate band') is potentially available when a home is passed on death to direct descendants of the deceased from 6 April 2017, and also in certain circumstances involving 'downsizing' (see **16.55–16.77**).

Table 4.1—Chargeable lifetime transfers on or after 6 April 2018: Tax on gross transfers

Gross taxable transfers £	*Gross Cumulative totals* £	*Rate*
First 325,000	0–325,000	NIL
Above 325,000	20% for each £ over 325,000	

Grossing-up of net lifetime transfers

Net transfers £	*Tax payable thereon* £	
First 325,000	NIL	NIL
Above 325,000	25% (or 1/4) for each £ over 325,000	

No IHT is payable if the chargeable transfers and/or failed PETs do not exceed the IHT threshold. If a transfer has become chargeable because of death, the IHT threshold and rate at the date of death is used to calculate the tax due.

If there has been a change in the IHT rate bands, the new rate bands are used to calculate the tax on a subsequent transfer. The cumulative totals of chargeable transfers may need to be restated where IHT is included, before this calculation can be made.

Chargeable transfers of value are cumulated; the IHT rate will depend on the total value of any such transfers made within the seven-year period ending with the latest transfer. After seven years, these transfers drop out of the cumulative total.

The '14-year backward shadow'

4.27 It may be necessary to look back at transfers made more than seven years before the date of death, up to a maximum of 14 years.

For example, if a PET was made (say) six years and 11 months before death, the period 13 years and 11 months prior to the death will need to be reviewed. However, the only transfers more than seven years before death which need to be considered are immediately chargeable ones.

Example 4.5—Cumulation of lifetime gifts

Mr Jones died on 1 December 2018, having made gifts (after reliefs and exemptions) of £100,000 to his daughter on 5 April 2007, £150,000 to a discretionary trust on 5 April 2010 and £263,000 to his son on 31 December 2016.

The additional IHT liabilities arising on Mr Jones' death are:

5 April 2007 – Gift to daughter £100,000

The gift to Mr Jones' daughter was a PET made more than seven years before death, which, therefore, became exempt. The gift is not cumulated with later gifts.

5 April 2010 – Transfer to discretionary trust £150,000

The gift to the discretionary trust was an immediately chargeable transfer, but no IHT was payable as the gross value was within Mr Jones' available nil rate band (£325,000 for 2009/10). The gift was also made more than seven years before death, and no tax is payable on that event.

31 December 2016 – Gift to son £263,000

The gift to Mr Jones' son was a PET made within seven years of death, which, therefore, becomes chargeable. The gift to the discretionary trust is cumulated, even though made more than seven years before death.

	£
5 April 2010 – Transfer to discretionary trust	150,000
Nil rate band remaining: £325,000 – £150,000 = £175,000	
31 December 2016 – IHT on gift to son:	
£175,000 × nil	NIL
£88,000 × 40%	35,200
	£35,200

Note: No taper relief (ie death within three years of gift).

4.28 Taper relief is applied if appropriate (eg if a PET becomes chargeable, which was made more than three years before the date of death). See **Chapter 12**.

If more than one chargeable transfer is made on the same day and their order affects the transfer values, they are treated as made in the order which results in the lowest value chargeable.

For example, if two chargeable gifts are made on the same day, with tax being paid by the donor on one gift (ie such that 'grossing-up' applies) and by the donee on the other gift, the tax-bearing gift by the donor is treated as having been made first in order to allow grossing-up at a potentially lower rate. This rule applies to lifetime gifts, but not to transfers on death (*IHTA 1984, s 266(3)*).

REPORTING CHARGEABLE LIFETIME TRANSFERS

4.29

> **Focus**
>
> Chargeable lifetime transfers are reportable on an Account for Inheritance Tax (Form IHT100, and supplementary forms), which must be submitted within 12 months from the end of the month of transfer (or three months after the person became liable, if later) (*IHTA 1984, s 216(6)(c)*; see **Chapter 8**).
>
> However, there are exceptions from the requirement to submit an IHT100 account, normally in the circumstances below.

The reporting exceptions mentioned above are as follows:

- gifts or chargeable transfers made by an individual which are wholly exempt (eg gifts to a UK-domiciled spouse within *IHTA 1984, s 18*). HMRC's view is that this general rule is subject to a possible exception in respect of the normal expenditure out of income exemption (*IHTA 1984, s 21*), where an IHT liability would otherwise arise but for the availability of the exemption (IHTM10652);
- gifts or chargeable transfers of value (ie actual, not deemed) made by an individual as follows:
  - *for transfers of cash or quoted shares or securities* – if the value transferred, together with the value of any chargeable transfers made by the transferor in the preceding seven years, does not exceed the IHT threshold (note that if any other assets are included in the transfer, it cannot be excepted under this test); or
  - *for transfers of other assets* – if the value transferred, together with the value of any chargeable transfers made by the transferor in the preceding seven years, does not exceed 80% of the IHT threshold, and the value transferred by the transfer of value giving

rise to the chargeable transfer (excluding business or agricultural property relief) does not exceed that IHT threshold less the value of chargeable transfers in the previous seven years (the *Inheritance Tax (Delivery of Accounts) (Excepted Transfers and Excepted Terminations) Regulations, SI 2008/605, reg 4*).

- 'excepted terminations' of interests in possession in the settled property of a specified trust. A 'specified trust' for these purposes is one in which the person's beneficial entitlement arose before 22 March 2006, or trusts for bereaved minors (within *IHTA 1984, s 71A*), or 'immediate post-death interests' (within *IHTA 1984, s 49A*), or trusts for disabled persons (within *IHTA 1984, ss 89* or *89A*), or a disabled person's interest (within *IHTA 1984, s 89B*) or 'transitional serial interests' (within *ss 49B–49E*). A termination is excepted in any of the following cases:
  - it is wholly covered by an exemption made available by the life tenant and notified to the trustees (eg if no chargeable transfers have been made personally); or
  - the interest related to cash or quoted shares or securities, and the value transferred by the termination, together with the value of any chargeable transfers made by the transferor in the preceding seven years, does not exceed the IHT threshold; or
  - the value transferred by the termination, together with the value of any chargeable transfers made by the transferor in the preceding seven years, does not exceed 80% of the IHT threshold and the value transferred by the termination (excluding business or agricultural property relief) does not exceed that IHT threshold less the value of chargeable transfers in the previous seven years (*SI 2008/605, reg 5*).

Detailed HMRC guidance on excepted transfers and terminations is included in the Inheritance Tax Manual at IHTM06100 to IHTM06113.

For general guidance on the completion of form IHT100, see 'When to use form IHT100' in HMRC Booklet IHT110 ('How to fill in form IHT100'), which is available via the gov.uk website (tinyurl.com/IHT-Forms-IHT110).

As indicated at **4.1** above, a PET is not immediately chargeable, and, therefore, does not need to be reported on form IHT100 when it is made.

Chapter 5

IHT on death

SIGNPOSTS

- **Notional transfer on death** – IHT is charged on the basis that a person makes a notional transfer of value of the whole estate on death. A person's estate potentially consists of the free estate, and certain types of settled property. Gifts with reservation are also taken into account. However, various IHT reliefs, exemptions and exclusions can apply on death, and certain liabilities may be deducted in determining the net estate (see **5.1–5.8**).
- **Deductions** – Liabilities may be taken into account in valuing a person's estate, subject to certain conditions and valuation rules. Reasonable funeral and limited other expenses may also be deducted (see **5.9–5.18**).
- **Valuations** – The general rule is that the value of assets comprised in a person's estate before death is their open market value immediately before death, but there are certain other provisions to consider, such as the 'related property' rules (see **5.19–5.20**).
- **IHT calculation** – Chargeable lifetime transfers and PETs within seven years of death are liable to IHT at death rates, subject to taper relief, if appropriate. The IHT threshold (or 'nil rate band') is taken into account and additionally any residence nil rate band (for deaths from 6 April 2017), including any transferable nil rate band from a previously deceased spouse or civil partner. Quick succession relief and double tax relief may also be deducted in some cases (see **5.21–5.27**).
- **Chargeable and exempt estate** – If the death estate is partly exempt, special provisions apply to determine the extent and impact of IHT liabilities on the non-exempt part, and also how IHT should be borne by the beneficiaries, etc (see **5.28–5.42**).
- **IHT compliance** – HMRC's IHT Toolkit is designed to assist in the completion of account form IHT400 (see **5.43**).

INTRODUCTION

5.1 A person is treated as making a notional transfer of value of the whole estate immediately before his death, and IHT is charged accordingly (*IHTA 1984, s 4(1)*).

The tax charged on the estate broadly depends on the aggregate chargeable lifetime transfers and potentially exempt transfers (PETs) in the seven years preceding death. The estate generally consists of all the property to which the individual was beneficially entitled, less excluded property and liabilities.

The IHT liability will also depend upon the identity of the legatees of the net estate, ie whether the recipient is a 'chargeable person' (eg a son or daughter), or an 'exempt person' (eg a UK-domiciled spouse, or a qualifying charity).

If an individual dies without leaving a will, or if the will is invalid (eg if it is not signed by the testator or testatrix, or was not witnessed as required), the estate is subject to distribution in accordance with the laws of intestacy (see below).

Changes to the distribution of estates on intestacy under the *Administration of Estates Act 1925, s 46* were introduced in the *Inheritance and Trustees' Powers Act 2014* (see below), which entered into force on 1 October 2014 (*Inheritance and Trustees' Powers Act 2014 (Commencement) Order, SI 2014/2039*). For the distribution of estates before and after these changes, see **Table 5.1**.

Table 5.1—The distribution of intestate estates

The distribution of intestate estates is governed by the *Administration of Estates Act 1925, s 46*. The following applies to deaths in England and Wales (see IHTM12111); different provisions apply in Scotland (see IHTM12142) and Northern Ireland (see IHTM12162).

Deaths on or after 1 October 2014

Spouse or civil partner and issue survive:

Spouse or civil partner receives	*Issue receives*
• All personal chattels; • £250,000 absolutely (or the entire interest where this is less); • One half of residue (if any) in trust for the survivor absolutely.	• One half of residue (if any) on statutory trusts.

Spouse or civil partner survives without issue:

Spouse or civil partner receives

The residuary estate in trust for the survivor absolutely.

Deaths before 1 October 2014

Spouse or civil partner and issue survive:

Spouse or civil partner receives	*Issue receives*
• All personal chattels; • £250,000 absolutely (or the entire interest where this is less); • Life interest in one-half of residue (if any).	• One half of residue (if any) on statutory trusts plus the other half of residue on statutory trusts upon the death of the spouse.

Spouse or civil partner survives without issue:

Spouse or civil partner receives	*Residuary estate to*
All personal chattels;	The deceased's parents.
£450,000 absolutely (or entire estate where this is less);	If no parent survives: on trust for the deceased's brothers and sisters of the whole blood and the issue of any such deceased brother or sister.
One half of residue (if any) absolutely.	

Notes

1. For distributions prior to changes introduced in the *Inheritance and Trustees' Powers Act 2014* (see note 2), the above fixed sums of £250,000 and £450,000 apply for deaths on or after 1 February 2009 (*Family Provision Act 1966, s 1*; *The Family Provision (Intestate Succession) Order, SI 2009/135*). Previously, the fixed sums were £125,000 and £200,000 respectively.

   If the intestate dies leaving a surviving spouse or civil partner but no issue, parents, brothers or sisters or their issue, the residuary estate is held in trust for the survivor absolutely.

2. For distributions following the introduction of the *Inheritance and Trustees' Powers Act 2014*, the *Family Provision Act 1966* is repealed with effect from 1 October 2014, and the above fixed sum of £450,000 is no longer required. The fixed sum of £250,000 is determined by the *Administration of Estates Act 1925, Sch 1A*, and is subject to possible future amendment by statutory instrument.

3. The above provisions in favour of the deceased's spouse or civil partner are subject to a 28-day survival period (*Administration of Estates Act 1925, s 46(2A)*).

No spouse or civil partner survives:

Estate held for the following in order given with no class beneficiaries participating unless all those in a prior class have predeceased. Statutory trusts may apply except under (b) and (e) (*Administration of Estates Act 1925, ss 46–47*):

(a) Issue of deceased.

(b) Parents.

(c) Brothers and sisters (or issue).

(d) Half-brothers and half-sisters (or issue).

(e) Grandparents.

(f) Uncles and aunts (or issue).

(g) Half-brothers and half-sisters of deceased's parents (or issue).

(h) The Crown, the Duchy of Lancaster or the Duke of Cornwall.

Note: The *Administration of Estates Act 1925* was extended (by the *Civil Partnership Act 2004, Sch 4, paras 7–12*) to include the remaining surviving civil partner, who effectively acquires the same rights as a spouse in cases of intestacy.

HMRC's Inheritance Tax Manual includes guidance on intestacy as it applies in:

- England and Wales (IHTM12111–IHTM12129);
- Scotland (IHTM12141–IHTM12156); and
- Northern Ireland (IHTM12161–IHTM12179).

ESTATE ON DEATH

General

5.2 A person on death (after 17 March 1986) is treated as having made a transfer of value equal to the value of his estate immediately before death (*IHTA 1984, s 4(1)*). A person's estate consists of the following (as appropriate):

- *free estate* – the aggregate of all property to which the deceased was beneficially entitled, but without taking into account any excluded property; and
- *settled property* – certain settled property in which the deceased was beneficially entitled to an interest in possession (see below).

An interest in possession in settled property to which the deceased originally became beneficially entitled before 22 March 2006 forms part of the estate (*IHTA 1984, s 49(1)*).

In addition, an interest in possession to which the deceased becomes beneficially entitled on or after 22 March 2006 is included in the death estate if it falls within one of the following categories (*IHTA 1984, s 49(1A)*):

- an 'immediate post-death interest' (ie within *IHTA 1984, s 49A*);
- a 'disabled person's interest' (see *IHTA 1984, s 89B*); or
- a 'transitional serial interest' (as defined in *IHTA 1984, s 49B*).

In addition, if an interest in possession is purchased by a UK-domiciled person at arm's length (on or after 9 December 2009), the interest forms part of that person's estate (*IHTA 1984, s 5(1B)*).

However, interests in settled property to which a person became beneficially entitled before 22 March 2006 and to which the rules on trusts for 'bereaved minors' (*IHTA 1984, s 71A*) apply at any time, do not form part of the deceased's estate (*IHTA 1984, s 49(1B)*). See **Chapter 9**.

5.3 Gifts with reservation (GWR) effectively form part of the death estate by being treated as property to which the deceased was beneficially entitled (*FA 1986, s 102(3)*).

The IHT charge on death is a 'deeming' provision, ie it creates a transfer of value. In addition to exemptions which are only intended to apply to lifetime transfers (eg the annual and small gifts exemptions), HMRC do not consider that relief from IHT on death applies under provisions by which certain dispositions are not treated as transfers of value (*IHTA 1984, ss 10–17*), eg dispositions not intended to confer a gratuitous benefit, or for the maintenance of family members (IHTM04042) (see **11.12**). This is on the footing that the rules apply to actual dispositions, and therefore cannot apply to a charge which is based on a deemed transfer (eg on death), unless the legislation specifically applies the provisions to the deemed transfer concerned (IHTM04151).

However, other types of IHT relief are available on the basis that a transfer of value includes a deemed transfer unless specifically excluded by statute (*IHTA 1984, s 3(4)*), such as business and agricultural property relief if the relevant conditions are satisfied (see **Chapter 13**). Various exemptions and exclusions from IHT also apply on death (see **5.4**), and certain liabilities may be deducted in determining the net estate (see **5.9**).

Exemptions and exclusions

5.4 Exemptions from IHT were summarised at **1.20** and are covered in **Chapter 11**. They are generally available on death, unless expressly excluded.

As mentioned at **5.3** above, certain exemptions relate to lifetime transfers only, and cannot therefore be claimed on death. These include the annual exemption (*IHTA 1984, s 19(5)*), the exemptions for small gifts (*IHTA 1984,* *s 20(3)*), normal expenditure out of income (*IHTA 1984, s 21(5)*) and gifts in consideration of marriage (*IHTA 1984, s 22(6)*).

An exemption may be subject to restriction (for deaths after 26 July 1989) if an exempt beneficiary (eg the surviving spouse or civil partner, or a charity) settles any claim against the deceased's estate otherwise than out of the deceased's transfer on death, where the claim is not a deductible liability for IHT purposes (*IHTA 1984, s 29A*).

For example, if the surviving spouse directly settles a claim against the estate by the deceased's mistress, it is treated as a chargeable legacy (and not an allowable estate liability). The spouse exemption is restricted to the net benefit. This restriction removes the advantage of the spouse settling the claim out of her exempt share.

5.5 Some exemptions (eg the spouse or civil partner exemption in *IHTA 1984, s 18*, or the charity exemption in *IHTA 1984, s 23*) are available as a result of death. In addition, certain categories of estate property can be left out of the IHT account on death:

- Cash options under approved pension schemes – where under a registered pension scheme, a 'qualifying non-UK pension scheme' (within *s 271A*) or a '*s 615(3)* scheme' (ie a superannuation fund within *ICTA 1988, s 615(3)*) (or prior to 6 April 2006, either a retirement annuity contract or a personal pension scheme) an annuity becomes payable on a person's death to a spouse, surviving civil partner, dependant or nominee of that person, and a capital sum might at the deceased's option have become payable instead to his personal representatives, the deceased is not to be treated as having been beneficially entitled to that sum, with the result that it escapes liability to IHT (*IHTA 1984, s 152*).
- Overseas pensions – the value of certain pensions payable to the deceased by former colonial governments is not included in the death estate (*IHTA 1984, s 153*).
- Death on active service, etc – no IHT is payable on a person's estate following death arising from a wound, accident or disease sustained or aggravated whilst on active service (or other service of a warlike nature), if certified by the Defence Council or the Secretary of State (*IHTA 1984, s 154*). This exemption extends (following *FA 2015*) broadly to deaths caused or hastened by responding to an emergency.

  Further IHT exemptions (introduced in *FA 2015*) broadly apply in relation to emergency services personnel and humanitarian aid workers who die as a result of responding to an emergency, and police constables and armed service personnel who die as a result of being attacked due to their status (*IHTA 1984, ss 153A, 155A*; see **1.20**).
- Emoluments and tangible moveable property of visiting armed forces members, certain international military headquarters staff and (from

17 July 2012) certain EU civilian staff attached to such headquarters, are excluded property for IHT purposes (*IHTA 1984, s 155*).

- The balances of any qualifying foreign currency accounts are excluded if the deceased was not domiciled and not resident in the UK immediately before his death (*IHTA 1984, s 157*). This exclusion also applies if the deceased was beneficially entitled to an interest in possession in settled property which included the qualifying foreign currency account, unless the settlor was domiciled in the UK when he made the settlement, or if the trustees were domiciled or resident in the UK immediately before the beneficiary's death. In each case, a further condition as to ordinary residence applies if the person died before 6 April 2013 (ie prior to changes introduced in *FA 2013*). See also **1.13** for an exception to the exclusion in *IHTA 1984, s 157* in relation to 'non-excluded overseas property' in certain circumstances. A 'qualifying foreign currency account' means a non-sterling account with a 'bank' (as defined in *ITA 2007, s 991*). The balance on such an account is excluded, whether in credit or debit (IHTM04380).

In addition, legislation in *IHTA 1984, s 153ZA* and *Sch 5A* (introduced in *Finance Act 2016*) broadly provides that IHT on certain qualifying compensation and ex-gratia payments for World War II claims and a one-off payment from the 'Child Survivor Fund' should be allowed as a credit against the IHT arising on the chargeable value of the recipient's estate. The legislation places on a statutory footing and extends Extra Statutory Concession (ESC) F20, which dealt with certain one-off late financial compensation and ex-gratia payments for World War II era claims (see **1.13**).

Offshore (and certain UK) property is excluded property for IHT purposes if the beneficial owner is domiciled outside the UK (*IHTA 1984, s 6(1), (1A)*).

A similar rule applies to settled property, if the settlor was non-UK domiciled when the settlement was made (*IHTA 1984, s 48(3), (3A)*). However, an exception to this excluded property status (introduced in *Finance (No 2) Act 2017*) applies from 6 April 2017 if, at any time in a tax year, the settlor is a 'formerly domiciled resident' for that tax year (*IHTA 1984, s 48(3E)*); see **2.13**.

In addition, if the interest in possession was acquired by a UK-domiciled person (from 5 December 2005) for valuable consideration, that interest is not excluded property (*IHTA 1984, s 48(3B)*).

Furthermore, legislation was introduced (in *Finance (No 2) Act 2017*) with the aim of ensuring that, from 6 April 2017, IHT is payable on the value of UK residential property owned directly or indirectly by non-UK domiciliaries (*IHTA 1984, Sch A1*). The provisions are aimed at blocking what HMRC has described as 'enveloping' (ie holding property indirectly through offshore structures). See **1.18**.

Anti-avoidance provisions (introduced in *FA 2012* with effect from 20 June 2012) are aimed at countering arrangements involving UK-domiciled individuals who acquire an interest in settled excluded property, which would otherwise give rise to a reduction in the individual's estate (*IHTA 1984, ss 48(3D), 74A–74C*). The arrangements covered include situations where a UK corporate settlor has settled assets as part of an avoidance scheme, and to arrangements where individuals retain the interests in settled property they have acquired. If the anti-avoidance provisions apply, the effect is broadly that the property ceases to be excluded property, and an IHT charge arises. For further commentary on excluded property and exempt transfers, see **1.15** and **Chapter 11**.

Secondary legislation (*The Taxation of Equitable Life (Payments) Order 2011, SI 2011/1502*) provides for the tax treatment of payments made under the *Equitable Life (Payments) Act 2010* to investors, and states that where a payment is made to the estate of someone who has died before the payment has been made, it is ignored for IHT purposes (*art 5(1)(a)*). Where personal representatives receive such a payment, there is no need for them to report it to HMRC (by contrast, where the payment is made to someone who is still alive, the money will form part of their estate and be subject to IHT in the normal way when disposed of either during their lifetime or on death; see IHTM10271).

Woodlands relief

5.6 A specific relief is available for transfers of woodlands on death (*IHTA 1984, s 125*), to take account of the fact that trees may take several generations to grow. Where the relief is available, an election may be made to exclude the value of UK trees or underwood (but not the land itself) from the value transferred by the chargeable transfer on the deceased's death. IHT is instead payable when the trees are disposed of (ie by sale or gift), other than to the disposer's spouse or civil partner.

Following a disposal, tax is charged on a subsequent death in the usual way, unless another election is made. In effect, the relief is a deferral of the IHT otherwise due on death.

For further commentary on woodlands relief, see **Chapter 12**. However, if the woodlands form part of a business, business property relief may be available if the conditions for that relief are satisfied; see **Chapter 13**.

Survivorship and the 'commorientes' rule

5.7 The rule as to commorientes (in the *Law of Property Act 1925, s 184*) provides as follows (*Note*: this rule does not extend to Scotland):

> 'In all cases where … two or more persons have died in circumstances rendering it uncertain which of them survived the other or others, such

deaths shall (subject to any order of the court), for all purposes affecting the title to property, be presumed to have occurred in order of seniority, and accordingly the younger shall be deemed to have survived the elder.'

This rule could give rise to double (or multiple) IHT charges on death (subject to 'quick succession relief' (*IHTA 1984, s 141*) if there was a chargeable transfer – see **Chapter 12**).

However, for IHT purposes, where it cannot be known which of two or more persons who have died survived the other or others, they shall be presumed to have died at the same instant. Therefore, the estate of the younger is not swollen if the elder person's estate devolves to the younger person (*IHTA 1984, ss 4(2), 54(4)*).

In some cases, the interaction of the spouse or civil partner exemption for IHT purposes (*IHTA 1984, s 18*) and *LPA 1925, s 184* can result in the estate of an elder spouse or civil partner escaping IHT on simultaneous deaths where property passes from the elder to younger spouse or civil partner. This point is illustrated in HMRC's guidance at IHTM12197 (which also points out that the treatment of simultaneous deaths in Scotland and Northern Ireland is different).

5.8 Double (or multiple) IHT charges may also arise on successive deaths (ie deaths which are not (or are not treated as) simultaneous but follow within a short period of each other, where it is ascertainable which person survived the other, even if only for a relatively short time).

However, if under the terms of the will (or 'otherwise', such as under a settlement), property is held for any person ('Beneficiary A') on condition that he survives another for a specified period of not more than six months, and another beneficiary ('Beneficiary B') becomes entitled to property by reason of the survivorship condition (ie Beneficiary A has not satisfied that condition), the IHT payable is the same as if Beneficiary B had taken the property direct, without the intervention of the survivorship condition. Beneficiary B is therefore deemed to have become entitled from the beginning of the survivorship period (*IHTA 1984, s 92*).

The inclusion of a survivorship clause in the wills of spouses or civil partners should be considered carefully, including the possibility of deaths in commorientes circumstances (see, for example, *Jump & Anor v Lister & Anor* [2016] EWHC 2160 (Ch)).

LIABILITIES

General

5.9 A liability may be taken into account in valuing a person's estate (unless otherwise provided by tax law) if it is legally enforceable and is:

- imposed by law (eg income tax and capital gains tax up to the date of death, and IHT liabilities in respect of chargeable lifetime transfers discharged by the deceased's personal representatives); or
- incurred for a consideration in money or money's worth (*IHTA 1984, s 5(5)*).

For example, if executors claim the deduction of a liability incurred shortly before death, HMRC may be interested to know the whereabouts of the money obtained by the deceased as a result of entering into the liability. If the money cannot be traced and there is no evidence that it has been given away, a deduction may be denied.

A deduction is given in the deceased's estate where certain income tax liabilities arise as a result of death (ie in relation to offshore funds and deeply discounted securities (*IHTA 1984, s 174(1)*).

Mortgages or secured loans can generally be deducted from the property they are charged against (but see below). If the mortgage is for more than the value of the property, the excess can generally be deducted from the deceased's other assets after the mortgage has firstly been deducted from the property against which it has been charged (IHTM28210). However, where a person with liabilities in excess of his assets is tenant for life of a fund, his personal indebtedness cannot offset the value of the trust fund (*St Barbe Green v Inland Revenue Commissioners* [2005] EWHC 14 (Ch)).

There are certain conditions and potential restrictions in respect of the deduction of liabilities such as mortgages, to the extent that the liability was used to acquire, maintain or enhance certain types of property (*IHTA 1984, ss 162A–162C*). In addition, the deduction of liabilities discharged after death is subject to certain requirements (*IHTA 1984, s 175A*) (see **5.13**).

5.10 Following the introduction of the *Gambling Act 2005* from 1 September 2007, deductions for gambling debts are allowed if they can be legally enforced. Prior to 1 September 2007, gambling debts were not an allowable deduction, because the debt could not be legally enforced. This applies to gambling debts in England, Wales and Scotland, but not Northern Ireland (IHTM28130).

Focus

An anti-avoidance rule in *FA 1986, s 103* ('Treatment of certain debts and encumbrances') restricts debts incurred or created by the deceased on or after 18 March 1986 when determining the value of an estate immediately before death, to the extent that:

- the money borrowed originally derived from the deceased; or

- the money was borrowed from a person who had previously received property derived from the deceased (eg an interest in a property is gifted from Miss X to Mr Y. Mr Y retains the property, takes out a loan secured on it and lends the proceeds back to Miss X, who dies more than seven years after the original gift of the property interest).

However, the above restriction does not apply if it can be demonstrated that:

- the original disposition by the deceased was not a transfer of value; and
- it was not part of associated operations (including as set out in *FA 1986, s 103(4)*).

This anti-avoidance rule can affect estate planning (eg 'debt' or 'charge' arrangements), as illustrated in *Phizackerley v HMRC* [2007] STC SCD 328 (see **15.4** and following).

A disallowance of the debt may result in a double IHT charge.

Example 5.1—Effect of *FA 1986, s 103*

On 1 January 2016, Adam gifted cash of £50,000 to Bob. On 6 April 2016, Bob lent £50,000 to Adam. On 1 October 2018, Adam died.

The cash gift from Adam to Bob is a PET which becomes chargeable as the result of Adam's death within seven years.

In addition, Adam's estate includes the £50,000 gifted back to him, but a deduction for the debt of £50,000 is denied under *FA 1986, s 103*, leading to a potential double IHT charge.

5.11 However, relief is given in such circumstances (*FA 1986, s 104(1)(c)*; *Inheritance Tax (Double Charges Relief) Regulations 1987, SI 1987/1130, reg 6*).

The effect is broadly that whichever of the two transfers results in the higher overall IHT liability remains chargeable, and the value transferred by the other is reduced (ie either the debt is disallowed and the gift is correspondingly reduced (*reg 6(3)(a)*), or the gift is taxed and the debt allowed (*reg 6(3)(b)*)).

Examples illustrating the operation of these rules are included as a Schedule to *SI 1987/1130*, although they do not prevail over the regulations themselves (*reg 9*).

No liabilities (eg debts or premiums) in respect of life assurance policies are allowable unless the policy proceeds form part of the estate (*FA 1986, s 103(7)*).

Guarantee debts

5.12 A guarantee debt (ie a promise to pay the debts of a borrower if he is unable to repay those debts) to which the deceased agreed to act as guarantor may be deductible from the death estate if the loan remained outstanding at the time of death. However, before allowing a deduction, HMRC may seek to establish whether consideration was given for the debt (*IHTA 1984, s 5(5)*).

A deduction will generally be available in connection with commercial loan arrangements, but possibly not in family situations (eg where a parent gratuitously agrees to guarantee a child's bank borrowings). In addition, HMRC may consider the financial resources of the borrower at the date of death, as a liability is only taken into account to the extent that reimbursement cannot reasonably be expected (*IHTA 1984, s 162(1)*).

HMRC may regard the giving of the guarantee as a lifetime transfer by the deceased. For example, if the borrower is a 'man of straw' with no financial resources, the outstanding liability will be deductible in full, but the guarantee may be a lifetime transfer up to the full amount of the liability.

Even if there is no outstanding liability at the date of the guarantor's death, HMRC consider that lifetime transfers may nevertheless arise if the guarantee was made within seven years of death and the guarantee was called in and paid within that time, depending on the borrower's financial position when the guarantee was given (IHTM28356–7).

RULES FOR AMOUNT OR VALUE OF LIABILITY

General

5.13 The IHT provisions allowing a deduction for liabilities were amended by *FA 2013* (and also by *FA 2014*; see below).

Those amendments mostly have effect for deaths and chargeable transfers on or after 17 July 2013 (ie the date on which *FA 2013* received Royal Assent), and are therefore retroactive in the sense that they potentially affect liabilities which were already in place. However, the rules on liabilities in respect of 'relievable property' (see below) only apply to liabilities incurred on or after 6 April 2013 (*FA 2013, Sch 36, para 5(2)*).

The above provisions introduced conditions and restrictions in the way that a deduction for liabilities is allowed in certain circumstances (see below).

The general rules for determining the amount or value of liabilities may be summarised as follows:

- A liability for which there is a right to reimbursement is taken into account only to the extent that reimbursement cannot reasonably be expected to be obtained (*IHTA 1984, s 162(1)*).

- If a liability will be discharged after the time at which it is to be taken into account, it must be valued when it is taken into account (ie at its discounted value (*IHTA 1984, s 162(2)*) – but see below regarding *IHTA 1984, s 162(3)*.
- In valuing the transferor's estate immediately after the transfer, his IHT liability is computed as follows (*IHTA 1984, s 162(3)*):
  - (i) without making any allowance for the fact that the tax will not be due immediately; and
  - (ii) as if any tax recovered otherwise than from the transferor (or a person liable for it under *IHTA 1984, s 203(1)*) were paid in discharge of a liability for which the transferor had a right to reimbursement.
- A liability which is an encumbrance on estate property must (as far as possible) be taken to reduce the value of that property (*IHTA 1984, s 162(4)*). However, following the changes introduced in *FA 2013*, this rule applies to the extent that the liability has not been taken into account against 'relievable property' under *IHTA 1984, s 162B* (ie broadly business or agricultural property, or woodlands), if applicable (see below).
- A liability due to a person not resident in the UK which neither falls to be discharged in the UK nor is an encumbrance on UK property must (as far as possible) be taken to reduce the value of property outside the UK (*IHTA 1984, s 162(5)*). However, this rule is subject to the same further condition regarding relievable property mentioned in the previous bullet point (following *FA 2013*).

The provisions introduced by *FA 2013* potentially affect the deduction of liabilities, broadly as follows:

- *Excluded property, etc* – A deduction is not generally taken into account for a liability that has been incurred directly or indirectly to acquire (or maintain or enhance) 'excluded property' (see **Chapter 11**) for IHT purposes. However, where the acquired property is no longer excluded property, or has been disposed of and the proceeds are chargeable assets in the deceased's estate, or where the liability is greater than the value of the excluded property, a deduction may be available to that extent (see *IHTA 1984, s 162A*).
- *Non-residents' bank accounts* – A foreign currency bank account balance (within *IHTA 1984, s 157*) is left out of account on the death of a person who is not domiciled and not resident in the UK. Those funds are not excluded property as such. However, *FA 2014* introduced provisions (for transfers of value made, or treated as made, from 17 July 2014) to treat foreign currency accounts in UK banks in a similar way to excluded property for the purposes of restricting the deduction of liabilities. The

effect is broadly that the liability is disallowed for IHT purposes to the extent that the borrowed money financed the relevant account balance. If the liability exceeds that balance, the excess may be allowed, provided that it has not arisen for the purpose of securing a tax advantage or an increase in the amount of the liability (*IHTA 1984, s 162AA*).

- *Relievable property* – If the liability was incurred directly or indirectly to acquire (or maintain or enhance) 'relievable property', being assets on which an IHT relief (ie business or agricultural property relief, or woodlands relief) is due, the liability reduces the value of those assets. The liability is matched against the assets acquired, and relief is restricted to their net value. Any excess liability is allowable as a deduction against the estate in general, subject to the rule (in *s 175A*) about liabilities on death (see below). However, to the extent that a liability has already been taken into account in arriving at the net value of the business (under *IHTA 1984, s 110(b)*), the provision does not have effect for business property relief purposes (*IHTA 1984, s 162B*).
- *Liabilities on death* – In determining the value of a person's death estate, a deduction for a liability is only allowed to the extent that it is repaid to the creditor out of the deceased's estate or from excluded property owned by the deceased immediately before death (and there are no other IHT provisions that prevent it from being taken into account), unless it is shown that there is a real commercial reason for not repaying the liability, securing a tax advantage is not a main purpose of leaving the liability outstanding, and it is not otherwise prevented from being taken into account (*IHTA 1984, s 175A*).

5.14 There are provisions dealing with the partial repayments of liabilities used to acquire assets including excluded property (or assets which have become excluded property) and relievable assets before an IHT charge arises. Those provisions were also amended accordingly following the introduction of legislation in *FA 2014* concerning liabilities to finance non-UK residents' bank accounts (see above).

In broad terms, in determining the value of an estate on death, any part of a liability which is not attributable to excluded property, relevant account balances or relievable property is treated as having been repaid first. If the partial repayment exceeds that part of the liability, the part of the liability which is attributable to relievable property is treated as having been repaid next, then to any part attributable to relevant account balances, with any remaining liability attributable to excluded property, or assets that have become excluded property, being treated as being repaid last (*IHTA 1984, s 162C(1A)*).

A similar priority rule applies to the partial repayment of a liability otherwise than on death (*IHTA 1984, s 162C(2)*). However, *IHTA 1984, s 157* only applies on death, so any relevant account balance is ignored for the purposes of this order of repayment.

There are also provisions dealing with the partial repayment of liabilities after death, where the liability was used to acquire assets including excluded property, relevant account balances (see above) or relievable property. Any part of the liability which is attributable to excluded property is treated as being repaid first. If the partial repayment exceeds that part of the liability (following *FA 2014*) the part of the liability which is attributable to relevant account balances is treated as being repaid next, followed by relievable property. If the partial repayment was greater than the part of the liability attributable to excluded property, relevant account balances and relievable property, the remainder of the liability can then be deducted against the chargeable estate (see *IHTA 1984, s 175A(7)*).

5.15 The above provisions in *IHTA 1984, s 175A* are anti-avoidance measures to block schemes and arrangements aimed at exploiting the IHT rules on liabilities to reduce the value of an estate. Those arrangements broadly involved obtaining a deduction for a liability and either not repaying the liability after death, or acquiring an asset not chargeable to IHT.

For the purposes of business and agricultural property relief (see **Chapter 13**), in the case of a liability incurred for a non-relievable purpose, securing the debt on qualifying property generally has the effect of reducing the amount on which relief would otherwise be available. Such debts should therefore be secured on non-qualifying property, if possible.

HMRC guidance on liabilities is contained in the Inheritance Tax Manual (at IHTM28000 and following).

Funeral expenses

5.16 In determining the value of a person's estate immediately before his death, deductions can be made as below:

- reasonable funeral expenses (*IHTA 1984, s 172*), including the cost of a tombstone or gravestone (SP 7/87) and reasonable expenditure on flowers (IHTM10372);
- a reasonable amount for mourning for the family. This deduction was originally given by concession (ESC F1). However, in its Technical Note 'Withdrawal of extra statutory concessions' dated 9 December 2009, HMRC stated that this concession would be withdrawn from 9 December 2010, but added: 'We believe that it may not in fact be a concession at all, rather a statement of what HMRC considers reasonable.' HMRC guidance also states (at IHTM10375):

  'ESC F1 which originally allowed the deduction of reasonable mourning expenses was withdrawn on 9 December 2010. This does not alter our practice and any reasonable mourning expense which was previously allowed under ESC F1 should be allowed under IHTA84/S172.'

What is 'reasonable' will depend on the particular circumstances, but relevant factors may include the living standards of the deceased during his lifetime.

A deduction may also be allowed for the reasonable costs of refreshments for mourners (IHTM10377).

Other expenses

5.17 Further principles for determining the deductibility of expenses in certain circumstances are summarised below:

- Costs of administering the UK estate (eg probate fees, estate agent or valuation fees) cannot be deducted for IHT purposes, as they arise after death.
- However, a deduction is allowed for the additional expenses incurred by the deceased's personal representatives in administering or realising property situated abroad. The allowance is deducted from the value of the property, up to a maximum of 5% of the property value (*IHTA 1984, s 173*). HMRC state that 'additional' in this context means the excess of the expenditure over and above which it would have cost to deal with the property in the UK (IHTM27050).
- A deduction is not normally allowable for professional fees in respect of work carried out after the date of death. However, there is an exception for post-death work undertaken in connection with tax repayments included as an asset of the estate. In that case, HMRC may allow a deduction by concession for fees not exceeding 10% of the repayment (IHTM28041).
- Provisions apply to charge IHT in the case of dispositions which are transfers of value made for partial consideration in money or money's worth and the transferor makes a payment or transfers an asset more than one year after the disposition. The effect is that any chargeable part of each payment, or of the asset transfer, is treated as a separate transfer of value at the time it is made (*IHTA 1984, s 262*). If the transferor dies while there are still outstanding liabilities the personal representatives have to complete the remaining payments or asset transfers (*IHTA 1984, s 175*). However, a deduction is only given for the non-gratuitous part of the remaining payments or assets (IHTM14874).

Focus

A liability that represents an encumbrance on property (eg a mortgage) should be deducted from the value of that property as far as possible, but only to the extent that (following the provisions introduced in *FA 2013*) it does not reduce the value of certain 'relievable property' under *IHTA 1984, s 162B* (*IHTA 1984, s 162(4)*).

As intimated at **5.13** above, a debt incurred in respect of non-relievable property should be secured against such property (ie where possible and practical) in preference to property qualifying for, say, 100% business or agricultural property relief.

Debts owed by the deceased

5.18 The IHT account of the estate on death (form IHT400) includes a supplementary form (Schedule IHT419 'Debts owed by the deceased') if the deceased's personal representatives are claiming a reduction in the estate for the following types of debt:

- money spent on the deceased's behalf (eg by a close friend or relative), which is being claimed as a deduction from the estate (eg paying domestic bills);
- loans and liabilities (including loans from close friends and relatives);
- liabilities related to an insurance policy and/or an investment bond (ie where its value is not fully reflected elsewhere in the form IHT400);
- guaranteed debts; and
- gifts to, and loans from, the same person (ie such that a deduction for the debt may be restricted (*FA 1986, s 103*)).

The purpose of the form is to provide HMRC with further information in support of the deductions claimed elsewhere on form IHT400, to establish whether a deduction is due. For example, if a loan was made to the deceased by a friend or family member, was it legally enforceable or made for consideration in money or money's worth? Was an outstanding loan secured on any property? The answers will help to determine the extent of any deduction for the liability. Form IHT419 can be downloaded from the gov.uk website (tinyurl.com/HMRC-IHT419).

ASSET VALUATIONS: OUTLINE

5.19 The asset valuation rule is broadly that the death estate is valued based on a deemed transfer of value immediately before the deceased's death. The value of assets comprised in a person's estate is generally their open market value immediately before death (*IHTA 1984, s 160*).

Changes in estate value caused by death are taken into account when valuing the estate (*IHTA 1984, s 171(1)*). The changes to be taken into account can include the following (see IHTM04046 for further examples):

- an addition to the property in the estate (eg the proceeds from a life policy);
- an increase in the value of any estate property; and
- a decrease in any estate property, other than a decrease resulting from an alteration in the capital or share rights of a close company (*IHTA 1984, s 98(1)*).

However, *IHTA 1984, s 171* does not apply to the termination on the death of any interest or the passing of any interest by survivorship (*IHTA 1984, s 171(2)*). An open market valuation of assets applies instead.

For the purposes of valuing a person's estate, HMRC's approach is that certain items of property may be taken together, even if held under separate titles (and irrespective of whether all the various parts of the estate are chargeable to tax) (IHTM04045). This principle mainly applies to valuations of unquoted shares, interests in land, undivided property interests and 'sets' of assets such as antique chairs.

For further commentary on the valuation of specific types of asset, see **Chapter 6**.

RELATED PROPERTY: INTRODUCTION

5.20 A particular rule deals with the valuation of property in an estate if other property exists which is related to it (*s 161*). It is intended to cover situations such as if a set of assets (eg antique chairs) is divided through an exempt transfer (eg a gift to the spouse), thereby reducing the value of the assets retained. The rule applies to both lifetime transfers and to deemed transfers on death.

'Related property' is broadly property included in the estate of a spouse or civil partner, or in certain cases property belonging to a charity (or held on trust for charitable purposes) or one of the political, national or public bodies to which exempt transfers may be made (in *IHTA 1984, ss 24, 24A* or *25*).

For more detailed commentary on the related property rules, see **Chapter 6**.

Relief is potentially available broadly if related property is sold by a legatee or the deceased's personal representatives to an unconnected person within three years of death for less than the related property valuation on death. If the relief conditions are satisfied, a claim may be made by the deceased's personal representatives to recalculate the tax at death based on the value of the asset concerned, without reference to the related property provisions (*IHTA 1984, s 176*). The relief only applies if the sale price (after adjusting for any change in circumstances) is less than the amount at which the property concerned was originally valued. It does not apply in certain circumstances involving close company shares or securities (see *IHTA 1984, s 176 (5)*).

For more detailed commentary on the relief for sales of related property, see **Chapter 12**.

CALCULATING IHT ON THE DEATH ESTATE

General

5.21 IHT on the death estate is calculated as follows:

Lifetime transfers

5.22 IHT on chargeable lifetime transfers is initially calculated at lifetime rates (see **Chapter 4**). If the transferor dies within seven years, the tax is recomputed at full death rates, subject to taper relief (see **Chapter 12**) where the death is more than three years after the gift. Taper relief cannot reduce the tax payable below that originally charged.

Tax at full death rates is calculated at the time of death on any PETs made within seven years prior to death, subject to the availability of taper relief. As PETs are assumed to be exempt transfers when made, no lifetime IHT would have been paid, and the PET did not enter into the transferor's cumulative total at that time. Upon the transferor's death within seven years of the PET, it becomes a chargeable transfer at the actual date of the gift.

When computing the tax on PETs which become chargeable, any chargeable transfers made within seven years of the PET must be cumulated, even if they were made more than seven years before death. If the PET was made before a chargeable lifetime transfer, the tax on that transfer may need recalculating, and the transferor's cumulative total will need to be revised.

The death estate

5.23 The deceased's estate is taken into account based on a notional transfer of value equal to its value immediately before death (*IHTA 1984, s 4(1)*).

IHT on death is charged according to the thresholds and 'death rate' as shown in **Table 5.2** below (*IHTA 1984, s 7, Sch 1*), which are unchanged from the previous tax year. The IHT threshold may be extended by extra nil rate band (or 'residence' nil rate band) if an interest in the home passes on death to lineal descendants of the deceased from 6 April 2017 (see **5.25**).

A lower IHT rate of 36% may be charged on a deceased person's estate, broadly where 10% or more of the net estate has been left to a charity or a registered club (ie in relation to deaths on or after 6 April 2012) (*IHTA 1984, Sch 1A*).

Table 5.2—Transfers on death after 5 April 2018

Tax on transfers:

Gross taxable transfers £	*Gross cumulative totals* £	*Rate*
First 325,000	0–325,000	NIL
Above 325,000		40% for each £ over 325,000

Grossing-up of specific transfers on death which do not bear their own tax

Net transfers £	*Tax payable thereon* £
First 325,000	NIL
Above 325,000	2/3 for each £ over 325,000

The personal representatives are liable to IHT on the deceased's free estate (*IHTA 1984, s 200(1)(a)*).

If the deceased had an interest in possession in settled property which is deemed to form part of his estate on death (see **5.2**), the settlement trustees are liable to IHT in respect of the trust property (*IHTA 1984, s 200(1)(b)*).

Hence, the IHT calculated must be apportioned between the free estate and the settled property.

Example 5.2—Free estate and settled property

Mr Edwards died on 10 June 2018. His free estate consisted of net chargeable investment assets amounting to £273,000. In addition, he had a life interest in a trust originally created in 2001, which is now worth £640,000. The IHT liability on death is calculated as follows:

	£
Free estate	273,000
Settled property	640,000
Chargeable to IHT	913,000

IHT:

(£913,000 – £325,000) × 40% = £235,200

The IHT is apportioned and payable as follows:

Personal representatives:

$\frac{£273{,}000}{£913{,}000} \times £235{,}200$	70,328
Trustees:	
$\frac{£640{,}000}{£913{,}000} \times £235{,}200$	164,872
	£235,200

Alternatively, an average 'estate rate' of IHT can be calculated and applied to the free estate and settled property, ie £235,200/£913,000 × 100 = 25.76%.

The application of these rules was seen in *Smith and others v HMRC* [2009] SpC 742, where it was found that a settlement existed of money in an account. Whilst the executors were not liable to tax in respect of the fund itself, there was an adjustment to the overall liability that affected the estate in their hands. The case is considered at **9.5**.

Transferable nil rate bands

5.24 The nil rate band of a spouse or civil partner may be wholly or partly unused on their death. Prior to the introduction of the facility to transfer unused nil rate bands, if all the deceased's assets were left to their UK-domiciled surviving spouse, the spouse IHT exemption may have resulted in the loss of the deceased spouse's nil rate band.

However, on the death of the surviving spouse (or civil partner) since 9 October 2007, a claim has been available for the unused proportion of the nil rate band from the earlier death to be added to the survivor's own nil rate band, so that a larger nil rate amount is available against their estate for IHT purposes.

The nil rate band to be transferred is expressed as a percentage (not exceeding 100%, as the limit is one additional nil rate band, even if there was more than one former spouse) of the amount unused from the earlier death. The nil rate band that applies on the death of the surviving spouse is increased by that percentage (*IHTA 1984, s 8A*).

Focus

A claim to transfer unused nil rate band must be made by the survivor's personal representatives, within two years from the end of the month in which the survivor dies or (if later) within three months of the personal representatives first acting as such, although HMRC may allow a longer period at their discretion.

In the absence of a claim by the personal representatives, a late claim may be made by any person liable to IHT on the survivor's death, subject to HMRC's agreement (*IHTA 1984, s 8B*).

There are potentially complicated rules for dealing with the transfer of the nil rate band and the calculation of IHT when certain IHT and capital transfer tax deferred charges (ie on heritage assets and woodlands) are triggered, where the deferred IHT is calculated by reference to the earlier deceased spouse (*IHTA 1984, s 8C*).

For periods prior to the date of changes introduced in *Finance Act 2011*, complex rules also apply to determine the amount of nil rate band available in calculating IHT where a dependant who inherits an alternatively secured pension fund dies or ceases to be a dependant (*IHTA 1984, ss 151A–151C*). However, with effect for deaths from 6 April 2011, IHT does not normally apply to drawdown pension funds remaining under a registered pension scheme, including when the individual dies after reaching the age of 75. The effective requirement to purchase an annuity by that age has been removed, and the complex rules mentioned above have been repealed.

Further information on transferable nil rate bands is available in HMRC's Inheritance Tax Manual (at IHTM43000 and following).

The subject is also discussed in **Chapter 3**.

5.25 Extra nil rate band (or 'residence nil rate band') is available on death from 6 April 2017, where a residence is passed on death to a lineal descendant of the deceased (*IHTA 1984, ss 8D–8M*). The residence nil rate band, if available, is in addition to the IHT threshold (or standard nil rate band).

The residence nil rate band for 2017/18 is £100,000, increasing in stages to £175,000 in 2020/21. However, the residence nil rate band is subject to a taper threshold, which reduces the nil rate band available according to the value of the deceased's estate. This taper threshold is set at £2 million for 2017/18 and subsequent tax years (*IHTA 1984, s 8D(5)(b)*).

If the deceased's estate does not include a qualifying residential interest, or if it does include such an interest but none of it is inherited by lineal descendants, the deceased's residence nil rate band is nil. However, the residence nil rate band that has not been used is available for transfer to a spouse or civil partner

(*IHTA 1984, s 8F*). The transferable amount is expressed as a percentage, which is subject to an overriding maximum of 100%, or one additional residence nil rate band.

The transferable residence nil rate band must be claimed (*IHTA 1984, s 8L*). The claim should generally be made by the deceased's personal representatives within a 'permitted period'. Alternatively, a claim may be made by any other person liable to IHT on the person's death within such later period as HMRC may allow.

The residence nil rate band provisions were extended (in *Finance Act 2016*) to provide for the residence nil rate band to be available in certain circumstances involving downsizing where other assets are passed on death to direct descendants. The provisions apply to downsizing moves or disposals from 8 July 2015, in relation to deaths from 6 April 2017.

For further commentary on the residence nil rate band, see **16.55–16.77**.

Quick succession relief

5.26 Relief for successive charges (or 'Quick succession relief': see **Chapter 12**) applies if the value of the deceased's chargeable estate for IHT purposes was increased by a previous chargeable transfer (either during lifetime or on death) made within five years before his death (*IHTA 1984, s 141*).

Quick succession relief reduces the total IHT chargeable on death by a percentage of the tax attributable to the net increase in the deceased's estate resulting from the previous transfer. The relief percentage depends on the length of time between the two occasions. The relief reduces the tax payable on the death estate. This includes any settled property in which the deceased had a life interest forming part of his estate. If IHT is payable on any part of the deceased's death estate, the relief is due regardless of which part of his estate the tax is chargeable.

The relief is similarly available on lifetime charges in relation to the termination of a qualifying interest in settled property, if certain conditions are satisfied (see *IHTA 1984, s 141(2)*).

If IHT is payable under more than one title (ie personally and as life tenant), the relief is apportioned accordingly (see IHTM22045, at Example 2).

For further commentary on the relief, see **1.23** and **12.4–12.5**.

Double tax relief

5.27 Property situated abroad may be liable to IHT and also to a similar tax imposed by another country or state. Double tax relief is available for all or part of the overseas tax. Relief may be given under the terms of a double tax agreement with another territory (*IHTA 1984, s 158*).

Otherwise, unilateral relief may be given for the tax paid in the overseas territory against the IHT due on the same foreign property, up to the amount of overseas tax paid on those assets (*IHTA 1984, s 159*).

See **Chapter 12**.

CHARGEABLE AND EXEMPT ESTATE

Introduction

5.28 The deceased's estate may be wholly exempt, partly exempt or wholly chargeable to IHT, depending on whether the beneficiaries under a will or intestacy are wholly or partly exempt. If a transfer on death is only partially exempt (eg because the deceased leaves part of his estate to his spouse or to charity), there are provisions (*IHTA 1984, ss 36–42*) to determine the extent and the impact of IHT liabilities on that part of the estate which is not exempt.

The rules can apply to lifetime transfers (eg gifting interests in an asset to exempt and non-exempt beneficiaries), but are more common and of greater relevance in relation to transfers on death.

Terminology

5.29 The value of the estate is divided for IHT purposes into 'specific' and 'residuary' gifts. A 'gift' in this context is the benefit of any disposition or rule of law by which any property becomes the property of any person or applicable for any purpose.

- A *specific gift* is any gift other than a gift of residue or a share of residue (*IHTA 1984, s 42(1)*). Such a gift might include the deceased's residence, company shares or personal effects. Certain liabilities are also treated as specific gifts for these purposes (see *IHTA 1984, s 38(6)*).
- A *residuary gift* is the balance of the estate after all specific gifts have been made.
- A specific gift may '*bear its own tax*', ie IHT comes out of the gift itself so that the beneficiary effectively gets the property less the tax on it, or the IHT attributable to the gift falls upon the beneficiary (*IHTA 1984, ss 42(2), 211(3)*). A specific gift bears its own tax if the deceased's will so states (*s 211(2)*). Otherwise, a specific gift of UK property is 'tax free' (see below), but a specific gift of non-UK property bears its own tax (*IHTA 1984, s 211(1)*). Other property bearing its own tax includes joint property passing by survivorship, nominated property, 'gift with

reservation' property and any other property which does not vest in the deceased's personal representatives (IHTM26126).

- Alternatively, the gift may be '*tax free*' (ie the beneficiary gets the full value of the gift, without reduction for the IHT on the gift, and the IHT is paid out of residue).

The value of a specific gift will normally be a specified sum (eg £50,000 cash) or the market value of a particular asset. However, partial exemption may produce a value of the gift when calculating the IHT due which is different from the specified sum or value of that asset.

If the total value of the specific gifts exceeds the total value of the estate, the specific gifts may need to be reduced so that their total value equals the value of the estate, by a process of 'abatement' (*IHTA 1984, s 37*).

For example, if an individual's estate is worth £400,000 and in his will he gifts £200,000 to charity, £200,000 to his daughter (bearing its own tax) and £400,000 to his wife, abatement will apply. The legacies total £800,000, but the estate is only worth £400,000, so each legacy is reduced by one-half.

Interaction with business and agricultural property relief

5.30 If an estate includes property attracting business property relief (BPR) or agricultural property relief (APR) (see **Chapter 13**), special rules apply for the purposes of valuing specific and residuary gifts if part of the estate is exempt.

If the business or agricultural property is given by a specific gift, its value is reduced by BPR or APR (*IHTA 1984, s 39A(2)*).

However, if any residuary gifts (after 17 March 1986) include business or agricultural assets, any specific gifts of non-business or non-agricultural assets (eg cash gifts to chargeable parties) will be entitled to a due proportion of business or agricultural property relief.

The value of such specific gifts is the 'appropriate proportion' of their value, which is calculated as follows (*IHTA 1984, s 39A(4)*):

Estate (after BPR/APR)	less	Specific gifts of business or agricultural property (net of BPR/APR)
Estate (before BPR/APR)	less	Specific gifts of business or agricultural property (before BPR/APR)

Settled property is excluded from the s 39A calculation (see HMRC examples at IHTM26110 and IHTM26158).

The above rule presents a potential pitfall, as BPR or APR is effectively wasted if given against exempt legacies, possibly resulting in a higher overall IHT liability.

Example 5.3—*Section 39A* pitfall

Richard died on 5 June 2018. His estate of £1,250,000 consists of shares in an unquoted trading company worth £700,000, together with cash and investment assets worth £550,000.

His will leaves cash and some of the other (non-business) assets of £400,000 to his spouse, with the residue to his son and daughter.

The value of Richard's estate (net of BPR) is £550,000. The 'appropriate proportion' (see above) of the spouse's exempt legacy is:

$$£400{,}000 \times \frac{£550{,}000}{£1{,}250{,}000} - £176{,}000$$

The non-exempt residue (ie the chargeable free estate) is £374,000 (ie £550,000 – £176,000). BPR is wasted to the extent that it reduces the legacy to Richard's spouse, which is exempt so that no IHT liability arose in any event (*s 18*).

The loss of BPR (or APR) such as in the above circumstances can be avoided by ensuring that specific gifts of business and agricultural assets which attract 100% relief are made to chargeable parties (possibly in addition to an amount up to the nil rate band if appropriate, although for surviving spouses or civil partners (who have died since 9 October 2007), it may alternatively be possible to transfer unused nil rate band from the first spouse to die).

If the deceased's will does not provide for such specific legacies, it may be possible to vary the dispositions in the will using a deed of variation within two years of the deceased's death, and to include a statement in the deed that it is to apply for IHT purposes (*IHTA 1984, s 142*).

Partly exempt gifts

5.31 The calculation of IHT where gifts are partly chargeable and partly exempt is potentially complex. HMRC's Inheritance Tax Manual (at IHTM26071 onwards) sets out a five-step process for applying the partly exempt transfer rules in the correct order.

Alternatively, a 'grossing up' calculator is available via the gov.uk website (tinyurl.com/40-gross), which will calculate the chargeable estate in most circumstances, if the estate is partially exempt from IHT and there are tax-free legacies. The calculator can be used for legacies at the standard IHT rate of 40%, the reduced IHT rate of 36% (where at least 10% of the estate has been left to charity), and it also takes into account (if applicable) the residence nil rate band (see **16.55**).

The five-step process mentioned is summarised in the table below.

Table 5.3—Partly exempt transfer rules: HMRC's five-step process

Step 1 – Value legacies

Set out the starting values of specific gifts.

Step 2 – Abatement (if applicable)

If the total value of specific gifts exceeds the value of the free estate, consider abatement (see **5.29**).

Step 3 – BPR/APR (if applicable)

The value of specific gifts may need to be reduced if business and/or agricultural property relief has been allowed (*s 39A*).

Step 4 – Grossing-up

The values of any chargeable specific gifts which do not bear their own tax are 'grossed-up' (see **5.32**).

Step 5 – Calculate residue

The total value of specific gifts (exempt and chargeable) is compared with the value of the free estate (after any business and/or agricultural property relief). If the free estate exceeds the specific gifts, the balance is the value of the residue. However, if specific gifts exceed the free estate, there is no residue, and abatement may apply.

Grossing-up

5.32 The process of calculating the chargeable part of the deceased's estate when specific tax-free gifts are made to a chargeable beneficiary and the estate is partly exempt is termed 'grossing-up'. It is therefore important to recognise which gifts bear their own tax and which do not (see **5.29**).

For the purposes of grossing-up, if the deceased's estate on death includes property under different title (eg free estate and settled property), the property chargeable under each title is considered separately and in isolation (*IHTA 1984, s 40*).

Simple grossing

5.33 'Simple' (or 'single') grossing applies only if specific chargeable gifts are all tax free and the residue is wholly exempt. The specific gift is a net transfer, which must be grossed-up.

Example 5.4—Simple grossing (no lifetime gifts)

Daphne died on 6 May 2018. Her free estate is valued at £950,000. In her will, Daphne leaves investment assets worth £450,000 free of tax to her son, and the residue to her husband. She made no lifetime transfers in the seven years preceding her death.

The grossing calculation is as follows:

	£
Chargeable tax-free gift	450,000
IHT on gift:	
(£450,000 – £325,000) × 2/3	83,333
Value of estate (after IHT):	
£950,000 – £83,333	866,667
The net estate is divided:	
Son	450,000
Husband (£500,000 – £83,333)	416,667
	866,667

The above result can be checked by calculating IHT on the grossed-up tax-free gift, ie (£450,000 + £83,333) = £533,333 – £325,000 = £208,333 × 40% = £83,333.

5.34 If lifetime gifts have been made in the previous seven years but their total is less than the IHT nil rate band, the value of those gifts is deducted and the remaining nil rate band is used in the grossing calculation.

Example 5.5—Simple grossing (lifetime gifts below nil rate band)

The facts are as in **Example 5.4** above, except that Daphne made a PET of £150,000 on 24 December 2015. The grossing calculation becomes:

	£
IHT on gift:	
£450,000 – (£325,000 – £150,000) × 2/3	183,333
Value of estate (after IHT):	
£950,000 – £183,333	766,667
The net estate is divided:	
Son	450,000
Husband (£500,000 – £183,333)	316,667
	766,667

(Check: £450,000 + £183,333 IHT = £633,333 – £175,000 nil rate band remaining = £458,333 × 40% = £183,333).

5.35 If lifetime gifts made in the previous seven years exceed the nil rate band, the chargeable specific tax-free gifts are grossed-up by the fraction 5/3.

Example 5.6—Simple grossing (lifetime gifts above nil rate band)

The facts are as in **Example 5.4** above, except that Daphne made a PET of £331,000 on 24 December 2015. The grossing calculation becomes:

	£
£450,000 × 5/3	750,000
IHT on gift:	
£750,000 × 40%	300,000
Value of estate (after IHT):	
£950,000 – £300,000	650,000

The net estate is divided:	
Son	450,000
Husband (£500,000 – £300,000)	200,000
	650,000

Double grossing

5.36 What if the residue is partly exempt and partly chargeable, or there are tax-bearing legacies? Tax-free legacies must be grossed-up using a procedure (in *IHTA 1984, s 38*) commonly referred to as 'double grossing-up'. This procedure is described in HMRC's Inheritance Tax Manual as 'The four stages' (see IHTM26152 onwards), upon which the following summary is based.

Table 5.4—'Double grossing' stages – Summary

Stage 1 – Grossing-up

Gross-up chargeable specific tax-free legacies, as if they were the only chargeable free estate.

Stage 2 – Calculate IHT rate

Using the gross value from Stage 1, calculate the chargeable free estate (ie including any specific chargeable gifts bearing their own tax). Add the value of any exempt specific gifts.

The initial value of the residue is the difference between the resulting total and the overall value of the estate for IHT purposes.

The value of the chargeable part of the residue is then determined (ie the total residue less the exempt residue).

The chargeable free estate for these purposes is the total of the chargeable specific gifts and chargeable residue. Calculate the tax on the chargeable free estate, to arrive at the estate rate.

Stage 3 – Re-gross at estate rate

Gross-up the chargeable specific tax-free gifts by the estate rate found in Stage 2.

Stage 4 – Calculate IHT on chargeable estate

Calculate the chargeable estate (ie the total of all chargeable specific tax-free gifts (Stage 3) and the total value of any chargeable specific gifts bearing their own tax).

Find the total value of all specific gifts (ie including any exempt specific gifts).

Find the value of the residue (ie the value of the estate for IHT purposes, less total specific gifts).

The chargeable residue is the total residue, less the exempt residue.

Calculate the IHT on the chargeable estate (ie the total of the chargeable specific gifts and the chargeable part of residue).

5.37 The following is a comparatively straightforward example of the double grossing procedure for a free estate (ie no settled property, or joint property passing by survivorship) in which there is no business or agricultural property.

Example 5.7—Double grossing

Joe died on 30 April 2018, leaving a free estate of £1,500,000, comprising cash and investments. He made no lifetime gifts and had no other chargeable property such as trust interests.

In his will, Joe left £500,000 to his son tax-free, and the residue equally between his wife (exempt) and daughter (chargeable). The IHT payable on Joe's death and the distribution of his estate is set out below.

Stage 1 – Grossing-up

Gross-up the chargeable specific tax-free legacy (using the available nil rate band):

£325,000 ´ Nil

£175,000 ´ 2/3 = £116,666

The gross value is £500,000 + £116,666 = £616,666

Stage 2 – Calculate IHT rate

Calculate the chargeable free estate, the IHT thereon and the estate rate:

	£
Total free estate	1,500,000
Less: gross specific legacy	(616,666)
Value of residue	883,334
Less: exempt residue (1/2)	(441,667)
Chargeable residue	441,667
Chargeable free estate (£616,666 + £441,667)	1,058,333

IHT thereon:

£325,000 × Nil

£733,333 × 40% = £293,333

The estate rate is:

$$\frac{£293,333}{£1,058,333} \times 100\% = 27.7165\%$$

Stage 3 – Re-gross at estate rate

Gross-up the chargeable specific tax-free gift by the estate rate found in Stage 2:

$$100 \times \frac{£500,000}{100 - 27.7165} = £691,721$$

Stage 4 – Calculate IHT on chargeable estate

Calculate the chargeable estate:

	£
Total free estate	1,500,000
Less: gross specific legacy	(691,721)
Value of residue	808,279
Less: exempt residue (1/2)	(404,140)
Chargeable residue	404,139
Chargeable free estate (£691,721 + £404,139)	1,095,860

Calculate IHT on the chargeable estate:

£325,000 × Nil

£770,860 × 40% = £308,344

Summary

Estate rate:

$$\frac{£308,344}{£1,095,860} \times 100\% = 28.1372\%$$

Tax on gross legacy (£691,721 × 28.1372%) = £194,631

Tax on chargeable residue:

(£404,139 × 28.1372%) = £113,713

Residue:

	£
Total free estate	1,500,000
Less: gross legacy (£500,000 + £194,631)	(694,631)
Value of residue	805,369
Less: exempt residue (1/2)	(402,685)
Chargeable residue	402,684

Division of free estate:

	£
Legacy to son	500,000
Residue to wife	402,685
Residue to daughter (£402,684 – £113,713)	288,971
IHT (£194,631 + £113,713)	308,344
Total estate	£1,500,000

A more complicated example of the 'double grossing' procedures (ie including interaction with BPR (see **5.30**) and settled property) is featured in the Inheritance Tax Manual at IHTM26158.

Allocating the burden of tax

5.38 Having calculated the IHT in double grossing situations involving chargeable and exempt proportions, there are provisions to determine how the tax should be borne by the beneficiaries (*s 41*).

The rules expressly override the terms of the will or other disposition. They provide that no tax falls on any exempt specific gifts (or any exempt part of a specific gift), and that no tax attributable to the value of residue should fall on an exempt share of that residue.

5.39

Focus

The burden of tax can broadly be summarised as follows:

- *Chargeable specific gifts bearing own tax* – the tax is deducted from the gift (*IHTA 1984, s 42(2)*).

- *Exempt specific gifts* – the gift is made without deduction of tax (*IHTA 1984, s 41(a)*).
- *Chargeable specific tax-free gifts* – the gift is made without deduction of tax (Note – HMRC's view is that the tax is paid out of residue, even if it is wholly or partly exempt; see IHTM26203).
- *Residue is dealt with as follows*:
  - the tax on tax-free specific gifts (see above) is deducted from the whole residue;
  - the balance is divided according to the terms of the will or other disposition;
  - the tax on any chargeable part of the residue is borne by that part (*IHTA 1984, s 41(b)*), despite any provisions to the contrary in the will.

HMRC's view is that if the burden of tax attributable to a chargeable specific tax-free gift falls on an exempt share of residue, the tax attributable is calculated by grossing up the value of the specific gift, dividing by the total value transferred by chargeable transfers, and multiplying by the total tax on that chargeable transfer.

Re Benham's Will Trust and Re Ratcliffe

5.40 The interpretation of wills in which the residuary estate is divided between gifts to exempt and chargeable beneficiaries was considered in *Re Benham's Will Trust* [1995] STC 210 and *Re Ratcliffe, Holmes v McMullan* [1999] STC 262.

The question of meaning concerns the proper construction of the following common type of clause in wills:

> 'I give devise and bequeath all my real and personal estate whatsoever and wheresoever not hereby otherwise disposed of unto my Trustees upon trust to sell and convert the same into money with power at their absolute discretion to postpone any such sale and conversion for so long as they shall think fit without being answerable for any loss and after payment thereout of my debts and funeral and testamentary expenses to stand possessed of the residue as to one half part thereof for my children in equal shares absolutely and as to the remainder of my estate upon trust for the following charities …'

Should such a clause be interpreted as meaning that the children should receive their residuary share of the estate subject to IHT, thereby receiving less than the charities?

Prior to *Re Benham* this was widely assumed to be the proper construction. The alternative construction (ie that the IHT should be paid and then the residue split) was disregarded, as it is prohibited (by *IHTA 1984, s 41(b)*) and therefore could not be effected.

Re Benham held that there was a third construction which was not so prohibited (ie that the non-exempt beneficiary's share should be grossed-up so that after his share bore the IHT, he would receive an equal sum to the exempt beneficiary), albeit that this would result in more IHT being payable.

5.41 Subsequently, in *Re Ratcliffe* [1999] STC 262, it was held that on a proper construction of the common will clause, the non-exempt beneficiaries receive their share subject to IHT and without grossing-up.

Thus, in the case of wills drafted in accordance with *Re Ratcliffe*, the proper IHT treatment would be to calculate the residuary estate, deduct the exempt beneficiary's share, and calculate IHT on the balance.

Example 5.8—'*Ratcliffe*' will clause

Alice died on 30 June 2018, leaving an estate comprising cash and investments worth £800,000. She had made no lifetime transfers. In her will (which is drafted in accordance with *Re Ratcliffe*), Alice leaves her estate equally to her husband Albert and her daughter Beatrice.

IHT on Alice's estate is calculated as follows:

	£
Residuary free estate	800,000
Less: exempt residue (1/2)	(400,000)
Chargeable residue	400,000
IHT on chargeable estate:	
£325,000 × Nil	
£75,000 × 40%	30,000
Division of estate:	
Albert	£400,000
Beatrice (£400,000 – £30,000)	£370,000

Construing wills

5.42 HMRC's Inheritance Tax Manual (at IHTM26131) states that grossing-up in accordance with *Re Benham* is 'very rare', but acknowledges (at IHTM26172): 'It is perfectly possible, though unusual, for you to come across wills deliberately drafted to achieve a *Re Benham* result'.

Clearly, it would be better to avoid any doubt by reviewing and clarifying the will, to reduce the possibility that its meaning is given an alternative construction. The type of difficulty which can arise if a will is capable of being construed in different ways was illustrated in *RSCPA v Sharp* [2010] EWCA Civ 1474.

However, in some cases it may be possible to rectify the will following the testator's death by way of a variation (*IHTA 1984, s 142*). It should be noted that (following *FA 2012*) where a variation redirects property to a charity or registered club, the variation is not treated as made by the deceased unless the persons executing the variation show that the 'appropriate person' (ie charity, registered club or trustees) has been notified of it (*IHTA 1984, s 142(3A), (3B)*). This condition applies where the person's death occurs on or after 6 April 2012.

Copies of an exchange of letters between the parties to show that the charity or trustees are aware should be sufficient for these purposes (HMRC Trusts & Estates Newsletter, April 2012).

IHT COMPLIANCE

5.43 For information on IHT compliance in respect of the death estate (eg accounts and returns, payment of IHT), see **Chapter 8**.

HMRC have published an 'Inheritance Tax Toolkit', which is aimed at 'helping and supporting tax agents and advisers for whom Inheritance Tax Accounts do not make up a significant element of their work'. The guidance adds: 'Other agents may still find the toolkit helpful in validating their approach to this work and it may also be of use to anyone, including trustees and personal representatives, in completing form IHT400 Inheritance Tax Account'.

In the context of whether a penalty arises for an error in the IHT400 account, HMRC guidance on the gov.uk website (www.gov.uk/government/collections/tax-agents-toolkits – 'Tax agent toolkits') states: 'HMRC toolkits are designed to help you make sure returns are completed correctly and demonstrate that you and your client have taken reasonable care', and links to HMRC guidance on reasonable care involving agents in its Compliance Handbook manual at CH84540.

The Inheritance Tax Toolkit is available from the gov.uk website: tinyurl.com/IHT-Toolkit.

HMRC have also published an 'online bereavement guide questionnaire', which is aimed at unrepresented individuals with a simple estate to administer and distribute. It covers income tax, child benefit and tax credits, as well as IHT and probate, and provides tailored, basic guidance (www.hmrc.gov.uk/tools/bereavement/index.htm). Improvements to HMRC's bereavement service were announced in its Trusts & Estates Newsletter for December 2014 (tinyurl.com/TEN-Dec14).

Subsequently, HMRC announced (in its Trusts & Estates Newsletter for April 2017) that it was developing 'IHT online', which would (among other things) assist in applying for grant of probate in England and Wales. HMRC would also be continuing work on expanding the service (tinyurl.com/TEN-Apr17).

In a special edition of the Trusts & Estates Newsletter (April 2018), HMRC announced improvements to its IHT process and timescales, including changes to the process for clearance, and a timetable indicating when HMRC can be expected to deal with submitted forms IHT400 (tinyurl.com/TEN-Spec-Apr18).

Chapter 6

Valuation of assets

SIGNPOSTS

- **Valuation principles** – An 'open market value' rule generally applies for IHT purposes. However, a transfer of value is broadly measured by the reduction in a person's estate, which may differ (see **6.1–6.5**).
- **Related property** – The value of 'related property' must be taken into account if this results in a higher valuation. However, related property relief may be available if related property is sold to an unconnected person within three years of death for less than the related property valuation (see **6.6–6.10**).
- **Particular assets** – Certain assets are subject to particular valuation rules and principles. These include life policies, unquoted shares and securities and debts (see **6.11–6.35**).

GENERAL

6.1 IHT is charged on the value transferred by a chargeable transfer (*IHTA 1984, s 1*).

As a general rule, the value of property for IHT purposes is the 'open market value', ie the price which the property might reasonably be expected to fetch if sold in the open market at that time. The price is not reduced on the basis that selling the property on the hypothetical open market at the same time would flood the market (*IHTA 1984, s 160*), and assumes a willing seller and a willing buyer, and sometimes a special buyer.

A 'special buyer' is a person prepared to pay more for an asset than anyone else. For example, a 49% shareholder in a company wishing to acquire a further 2% of the company's shares to assume a controlling interest would probably be willing to pay more for those shares than another person acquiring the 2% holding in isolation.

A restriction or fetter on the freedom to dispose of property (eg a provision in a partnership agreement stating that a deceased's partnership interest passes on death to the retiring partners without cost) can reduce the value of a person's estate. However, the property is valued ignoring restrictions unless certain conditions are satisfied, including that consideration was given for the restriction or exclusion in money or money's worth (*IHTA 1984, s 163*).

For example, a stipulation in a testator's will that the grounds of his house are 'never to be sold for building land but always kept with the house' cannot restrict the value of that land if, at the date of death, it has 'hope value'. This is because the testator has received nothing as consideration for the restriction. It would be different if, for example, the testator had given the National Trust covenants over the land for the benefit of some property belonging to the Trust.

Other valuation principles also need to be considered for IHT purposes, which are outlined below.

HMRC's approach

6.2 HMRC considers valuation to be an area of 'high risk' in terms of the potential loss of IHT. This increases the possibility of challenge, where the valuation appears to HMRC to be too low (*Hatton v Revenue and Customs Commissioners* [2010] UKUT 195 (LC); although by contrast, see *Chadwick and another v Revenue and Customs Commissioners* [2010] UKUT 82 (LC)). In addition, a material undervaluation may result in the imposition of penalties. However, the tribunal decision in *Cairns v Revenue and Customs Commissioners* [2009] UKFTT 67 (TC) might offer some comfort in this context.

The generally preferred approach from HMRC's perspective is that taxpayers etc refer valuations to a qualified, independent valuer. However, this of itself may not be sufficient to satisfy HMRC that an asset has been valued satisfactorily. In its 'Inheritance Tax Toolkit' (tinyurl.com/IHT-Toolkit), HMRC advises (subject to certain exceptions – see below) as follows:

> 'For assets with a material value you are strongly advised to instruct a qualified independent valuer, to make sure the valuation is made for the purposes of the relevant legislation, and for houses, land and buildings, it meets Royal Institution of Chartered Surveyors (RICS) or equivalent standards.'

In terms of engaging a qualified independent professional valuer, HMRC strongly advise that this is done 'properly', and recommends the following:

- 'Explain the context and draw attention to the definition in section 160 Inheritance Tax Act (IHTA) 1984 (market value).
- Provide all the relevant details concerning the asset, in particular ensuring the valuer is aware of the need to take into account any points in the bullet points under 'Risk' above.
- Ensure that copies of relevant agreements, or full details where only an oral agreement exists, are provided so misunderstandings do not arise.'

The importance of professional valuations was further emphasised in HMRC's Trusts and Estates Newsletter (August 2010), in the context of land and buildings (see **6.22** and subsequent paragraphs below). In a subsequent Trusts and Estates Newsletter (April 2011), HMRC also stated that it will take an 'appropriate penalty' if an application for a grant of probate is made as an excepted estate, but the discovery of an undervaluation (or omission) leads to IHT being payable, where it is shown that personal representatives have failed to take reasonable care (or worse).

However, HMRC does not consider professional valuations to be necessary in all cases. The IHT toolkit also states:

> 'In limited circumstances you can provide self valuations for assets. For example, ordinary household goods where individual items have a value of no more than £500, and the use of publicly available data to obtain a valuation for second hand cars. Where you have provided a self valuation, explain how you have arrived at that value and why, if appropriate, a low or "nil" valuation has been returned. Where there are antiques or collections and you are not obtaining a professional valuation provide us with a full description of the items and details of any sales proposed.'

6.3 Aside from this Chapter and HMRC's IHT Toolkit, further guidance on valuations for IHT purposes is available as follows:

- HMRC's guidance on the work of its Shares and Assets Valuations (SAV) specialists, including the approach of SAV in valuing various categories of assets, such as unquoted shares and goodwill (tinyurl.com/HMRC-SAV-Guidance);
- HMRC's notes to form IHT400 ('IHT400 Notes – Guide to completing your Inheritance Tax account') (tinyurl.com/HMRC-IHT400-Notes);
- HMRC's Inheritance Tax Manual (eg at IHTM09701 onwards);
- HMRC's Shares and Assets Valuation Manual (eg at SVM113000 onwards in the context of 'The statutory open market, and SVM114000 in relation to 'Information standards'); and
- The Valuation Office Agency's (VOA) IHT manual: (tinyurl.com/VOA-IHT-Manual).

The 'loss to estate' principle

6.4

> **Focus**
>
> The value transferred by a transfer of value is the amount by which a person's estate is reduced as a result (*IHTA 1984, s 3(1)*).
>
> This value will not necessarily be the actual value of an asset.

Example 6.1—Loss in value of estate

ABC Ltd has 100,000 issued ordinary £1 shares. The shares (shown as a percentage of the company's overall issued share capital) are valued as follows:

51%–75% = £25 per share

26%–50% = £14 per share

25% or less = £8 per share

Mr Scott owns 60,000 shares (ie 60% of the shares). He makes a gift of 20,000 shares to his daughter. The transfer of value for IHT purposes is as follows:

	£
Before (60,000 × £25)	1,500,000
After (40,000 × £14)	(560,000)
Value transferred	940,000

Note that although the value of 20,000 shares in isolation is £160,000 (ie 20,000 × £8), for IHT purposes the reduction in Mr Scott's estate is higher as the result of losing his controlling interest in the company.

HMRC's IHT Toolkit lists the 'loss to the estate principle' as a 'risk' area for valuation purposes in respect of gifts, and sums up the principle as follows:

'When looking at the value of gifts you need to consider the "loss to the estate" principle. This means that you look at the value of the estate before and after the gift was made. The difference between those two figures is the loss to the estate and is the figure that needs to be included on the form IHT400'.

The 'estate concept'

6.5 A person's estate includes all the property to which he is beneficially entitled (but not excluded property or a foreign-owned work of art situated in the UK only for the purpose of public display, cleaning and/or restoration) (*IHTA 1984, s 5(1)*).

The estate generally also includes property over which a person has a general power (*IHTA 1984, s 5(2)*), together with certain settled property in which the person is beneficially entitled to an interest in possession (see **5.2** and **Chapter 9**).

A beneficial interest in the net assets of an unadministered residuary estate also forms part of the estate for IHT purposes (*s 91*), together with property subject to a 'gift with reservation' (*FA 1986, s 102(3)*).

Example 6.2—Estate assets

On Mr Johnson's death, his free estate included 2,000 ordinary £1 shares in XYZ Ltd, representing 20% of the company's issued share capital. He also had an immediate post-death interest created by will on his wife's death. The trustees held a further 6,000 ordinary shares in the company.

In valuing Mr Johnson's estate for IHT purposes, it is necessary to value 8,000 shares in XYZ Ltd, out of the company's issued share capital of 10,000 ordinary shares.

There is case law authority for the treatment of valuing property together (*Gray (surviving executor of Lady Fox) v IRC* [1994] STC 360), and for dividing estates into 'natural' or appropriate units (*Buccleuch v IRC* [1967] 1 AC 506) if doing so results in higher valuations.

When considering the value of land or buildings, the Valuation Office Agency will normally divide the estate so as to provide the highest value. HMRC may similarly seek to decide how to divide certain other assets (eg art and wine collections) for estate valuation purposes (IHTM09715). In the context of wine cellars, HMRC have stated that the valuation must be open market value (under *IHTA 1984, s 160*) at the time of the relevant occasion of IHT charge, and not (as some had apparently thought) at the purchase price (HMRC Trust & Estates Newsletter, August 2010).

A person other than the sole legal owner of an asset such as land and buildings may claim to have a beneficial interest in that asset. Alternatively, property may be registered in joint names (eg unmarried co-habitants), but one of the parties may have a greater beneficial interest than the other, perhaps having contributed a larger proportion of the purchase price. In such cases, the parties may prefer the asset to be treated as owned by them in accordance with their respective beneficial shares.

This principle is derived from two non-tax cases, *Oxley v Hiscock* [2004] EWCA Civ 546, [2005] Fam 211 and *Stack v Dowden* [2007] UKHL 17. In the latter case, Baroness Hale commented:

> 'The burden will therefore be on the person seeking to show that the parties did intend their beneficial interests to be different from their legal interests, and in what way. This is not a task to be lightly embarked upon.'

Following those cases, HMRC stated that the onus is upon the non-legal owner to demonstrate that they have any interest in the property, as if the claimant was presenting their case to a court of law (IHT & Trusts Newsletter – December 2007).

Subsequently, in *Pankhania v Chandegra* [2012] EWCA Civ 1438, the Court of Appeal had to consider whether an express declaration of trust was conclusive, or whether the rules of implied, resulting or constructive trusts in *Stack v Dowden*, as reviewed in *Jones v Kernott* (see below), applied instead. In *Pankhania v Chandegra*, C and D purchased a property in 1987, which was the subject of an express declaration that C and D held the beneficial interest in the property as tenants in common in equal shares. The Court allowed an appeal from the High Court, and confirmed that an express declaration of trust is conclusive, unless it is set aside, varied or rectified.

In *Wade v Baylis* [2010] EWCA Civ 257, a couple commenced living together as man and wife in 1982, but separated in 2005. Following the split, Mr Wade claimed a 50% beneficial interest in the property, even though he had been removed from the deeds in 1986 at his own request. He had apparently made no contribution to the capital cost of the property, and contributed little to the mortgage repayments, although he had worked for free in a business run by Ms Baylis. The Court of Appeal dismissed Mr Wade's appeal against an earlier decision that Ms Baylis was the sole beneficial owner of the property in question.

Subsequently, in *Jones v Kernott* [2011] UKSC 53, the Supreme Court unanimously held that the beneficial interests of co-habitants in a property can change without their explicit intention. In that case, the co-habitants bought a house in 1985, and jointly owned it, without making any declaration as to how their beneficial interests should be apportioned. The relationship ended, and Mr Kernott moved out after the parties had lived in the property together for more than eight years. Ms Jones had originally contributed £6,000 of the £30,000 purchase price, and the balance had been funded by an interest-only mortgage. Following the separation, Ms Jones continued to live in the property, and assumed sole responsibility for the mortgage and outgoings, including repairs and maintenance. Mr Kernott later demanded a half-share of the house. However, the county court awarded Ms Jones 90% of the equity. Mr Kernott unsuccessfully appealed to the High Court. Subsequently, the Court of Appeal ([2010] EWCA Civ 578) held (by majority) that Mr Kernott and Ms Jones each had a 50% beneficial interest in the property. However, the Supreme Court overturned that decision, stating that an initial presumption of joint tenancy in law and equity can be displaced if the parties changed their intentions, and that a court can deduce their common intention from their conduct.

In *O'Kelly v Davies* [2014] EWCA Civ 1606, an individual who was the legal owner of a house was found on the facts to have held the beneficial ownership of the property on constructive trust for herself and her former co-habiting partner in equal shares.

A common intention to vary beneficial interests of the parties was subsequently inferred in *Barnes v Phillips* [2015] EWCA Civ 1056, such that the respondent was held to own an 85% interest and the appellant an interest of 15%.

In *Marr v Collie (Bahamas)* [2017] UKPC 17, it was concluded that (taking into account cases including *Stack v Dowden*) where assets are held in the joint names of parties who are not married or civil partners, but the parties contributed unequally to the purchase price, the outcome should depend on the context in terms of the parties' common intention (or the lack of it), unless the intention at the time of purchase changed.

There are specific IHT valuation rules, such as for quoted shares and life assurance policies, and also in the case of property that is related to property in the estate of a spouse or civil partner or the property of a charity.

RELATED PROPERTY

Rule of valuation

6.6

> **Focus**
>
> The value of 'related property' must be taken into account when valuing a person's estate if this results in a higher valuation (*IHTA 1984, s 161*).
>
> This rule applies to lifetime and death transfers, and prevents the division of an asset into less valuable parts by means of exempt transfers to reduce overall IHT liabilities.

Property is broadly 'related' for these purposes if it is:

- in the spouse's or civil partner's estate; or
- is (or was during the preceding five years) the property of a charity (or held on trust for charitable purposes only) or a qualifying political party, housing association or national or public body, to which exempt transfers may be made as the result of an exempt transfer (after 15 April 1976) by the individual, spouse or civil partner (*IHTA 1984, s 161(2)*).

The transferor's property and the related property are combined and valued as a single unit. The combined value of the estate property and related property is then apportioned to the estate property in the proportion that its value in isolation bears to the separate values when added together.

The related property rules are mostly used in practice to value transfers of unquoted shares and jointly owned property. They are one of the 'risk' areas for valuation purposes listed in HMRC's IHT Toolkit (tinyurl.com/IHT-Toolkit): 'Where there is "related property" ensure that this has been taken into account in the valuation following a lifetime event or on death.'

It should be noted that, for the purposes of determining whether shares or securities are deemed to give a person control of a company, shares or securities which are related property (within the meaning of *IHTA 1984, s 161*) are taken into account (*IHTA 1984, s 269(2)*).

How does the rule apply?

6.7 In the case of jointly owned property, the value of the combined unit is apportioned between the property in the individual's estate and the related property according to their separate values (*IHTA 1984, s 161(3)*). This general rule also applies for valuing other assets (but see below for a special rule in respect of shareholdings).

Example 6.3—Related property (land)

Derek owns land worth £15,000 and his wife Lisa owns adjoining land worth £25,000.

The combined value is £80,000.

The related property value of Derek's land is:

$$\frac{15{,}000}{15{,}000 + 25{,}000} \times £80{,}000 = £30{,}000$$

6.8 Should the value of jointly owned property be discounted to take into account the rights of the co-owner? The Inheritance Tax Manual (at IHTM04045) states HMRC's view as follows:

> 'It is often said that in order to sell either half share, the co-operation of the other joint owner is required and so a discount should be allowed to compensate for the uncertainty involved. Whilst in reality this may be true, for IHT purposes the statute imposes the hypothesis that the deceased is beneficially entitled to the whole and it is the whole that is valued in accordance with Section 160 IHTA 1984. If tax is only chargeable on a fractional share (because, say, the other share is exempt) it is the arithmetic proportion that is taxed and not the value of the share involved.'

In the context of real, heritable or leasehold property, HMRC also comments as follows (at IHTM09739):

'The related property rules apply because the interests of the spouses/civil partners are together worth more than the sum of their separate interests – the separate interests would normally be subject to a discount for joint ownership. The interests of the husband and wife, or civil partners, will normally be identical and will extend to the whole of the land and property so the value of the deceased/transferor's interest will be the appropriate proportion of the entirety value.'

The value to be included in the estate is the 'appropriate portion' of the value of the combined property (*IHTA 1984, s 161(1)*). There are two methods of calculating the appropriate portion: what HMRC refers to (in IHTM09734) as the 'general rule' (*IHTA 1984, s 161(3)*; see **6.7**); and the 'special rule' (*IHTA 1984, s 161(4)*; see below). HMRC's guidance indicates that the general rule is used where the items of property being aggregated for valuation purposes are different (eg see **Example 6.3**). The special rule is mainly used for calculating the value of shareholdings where the value of the same shares can vary with the size of holding. However, HMRC may seek to use the special rule in other situations as well.

For example, in *Arkwright and another (Personal Representatives of Williams, deceased) v IRC* [2004] EWHC 1720 (Ch), Mr and Mrs W owned a freehold property as tenants in common. On Mr W's death, HMRC determined that IHT was due on 50% of the property's agreed open market value. The personal representatives appealed, contending that Mr W's interest should be valued at less than 50% of the vacant possession value, because his widow had the right to occupy the property and could not have it sold without her consent.

The Special Commissioner accepted this contention and allowed the appeal in principle, holding that the value of Mrs W's interest should be determined in accordance with *IHTA 1984, s 161(3)* (ie on the basis that both shares in the property were related, and that their values should therefore be aggregated, with the value of each property share being determined as if it did not form part of that aggregate). The High Court subsequently held that the Commissioner was entitled to conclude that the value of the deceased's interest in the property was not inevitably a mathematical one-half of the vacant possession value, rejecting HMRC's argument that *IHTA 1984, s 161(4)* applied to treat the land as 'units' and that the valuation ratio was one-half. However, the court considered that the value of Mr W's interest was a question for the Lands Tribunal to determine. The appeal was eventually settled by agreement.

HMRC subsequently stated (in Revenue & Customs Brief 71/07) that, following legal advice, they would apply *IHTA 1984, s 161(4)* when valuing shares of land as related property in cases received after publication of that Brief (27 November 2007) and would consider litigation in 'appropriate cases', but that any existing cases would be dealt with on the basis of the Special Commissioners' decision in the *Arkwright* case as it relates to the interpretation of *IHTA 1984, s 161(4)*.

The 'general rule' was applied in *Price v Revenue and Customs Commissioners* [2010] UKFTT 474 (TC). In that case, the appellant (the executor and trustee of his late wife's estate) appealed against an IHT determination in respect of a property owned in equal half shares by husband and wife as tenants-in-common. The entire property was valued at £1.5 million, whereas the half shares of the property, valued independently, amounted to £637,500 each. The appellant argued (among other things) that 'the value of that and any related property' in *IHTA 1984, s 161(1)* meant the value of the two property interests valued independently of each other. HMRC argued that the above expression meant the totality of both interests treated as a single item of property. The tribunal held that the related property provisions hypothesise a notional sale and that the property interests were to be valued on the basis that they are offered for sale together and at the same time. If this resulted in a greater price than if the interests had been offered individually, then (if the sale would not have required undue effort or expense) the greater price must be attributed to the two items by applying the formula in *IHTA 1984, s 161(3)*. The appeal was therefore dismissed.

6.9 As indicated at **6.8** above, the 'special rule' generally applies for the purposes of valuing shares and other securities of the same class (*IHTA 1984, s 161(4), (5)*). In that case, the apportionment of the combined value is based on the number of shares, not the value of the different holdings.

Example 6.4—Related property (shares)

On the husband's death on 31 October 2018, the share capital of a private company was held as follows:

Issued share capital – 10,000 shares

Husband	4,000	40%
Wife	4,000	40%
Others (employees)	2,000	20%
	10,000	100%

The value of an 80% holding is £80,000, while the value of a 40% holding is £24,000. In his will, the husband left his 4,000 shares to his daughter. The related property rules apply to aggregate the shares of:

Husband	4,000
Wife	4,000
Related property	8,000 shares

Chargeable transfer on legacy to daughter:

IHT value of 8,000 shares (80%)	£80,000
IHT value attributed to legacy of husband's shares	$\frac{4,000}{8,000} \times £80,000 = \underline{£40,000}$

This special rule applies not only to shares of the same class, but also to stock, debentures and other 'fungible' property, ie that which is capable of being divided into units of an identical nature, such as unit trusts or bottles of wine of the same vintage.

In the case of lifetime transfers, both the 'loss to estate' principle and the 'related property' rule apply in arriving at the value transferred (ie the related property rules are used to calculate the 'before' and 'after' estate values).

Related property relief

6.10 If related property is sold to an unconnected person within three years of death for less than the related property valuation, a claim is available to recalculate the tax at death without reference to the related property (*IHTA 1984, s 176*). The relief is subject to certain conditions, and applies to a 'qualifying sale' as defined (*IHTA 1984, s 176(3)*; see IHTM09754).

The relief must be claimed (*IHTA 1984, s 176(2)*). Relief is also available if the property was valued with other property in the estate (eg if the deceased held property absolutely, together with property subject to an interest in possession (ie within *IHTA 1984, s 49(1)*)).

Note that related property relief does not substitute the value of the property at the date of sale. The valuation date is immediately before the death.

See **Chapter 12**.

PARTICULAR ASSETS

6.11 Certain assets have their own valuation rules. Some of the more common assets and situations are outlined below.

In some cases, the uncertain nature of an asset at a particular point in time can cause difficulties in its valuation. One such example is compensation payments received after the date of death. The right to pursue a compensation claim is an asset of the estate. The personal representatives should therefore disclose full information about the claim on form IHT400, together with a 'reasoned estimate' of the open market value of the right where they are able to do so (HMRC Trusts and Estates Newsletter, August 2013).

A list of specific types of property is contained in the Inheritance Tax Manual (at IHTM09702), together with references to detailed guidance elsewhere in the manual on HMRC's approach to valuing them.

Life policies

Lifetime transfers

6.12 The lifetime gift of a life policy or annuity (ie by assignment or declaration of trust) from one person to another constitutes a transfer of value. The value transferred is broadly the greater of the premiums paid (less any proceeds received under the policy or annuity contract prior to the transfer, eg on a partial surrender) and the open market value of the policy (ie normally its surrender value) (*IHTA 1984, s 167(1)*).

It should be noted that the above valuation rule does not apply to transfers of value on death (*s 167(2)(a)*) (see **6.13**), or any other transfer of value which does not result in the policy etc ceasing to be part of the transferor's estate (*IHTA 1984, s 167(2)(b)*), except in both cases where the death or transfer was before 11 April 1978 (IHTM20242).

In addition, term assurance policies are excluded if the sum assured becomes payable only if the life assured dies before the expiry of a specified term (or before the expiry of a specified term *and* during the life of a specified person). If the specified term ends, or can be extended to end, more than three years after the policy is made and if neither the life assured nor the specified person dies within the specified term, the premiums must be payable during at least two-thirds of that term and at yearly or shorter intervals, and the premiums payable in any one period of 12 months must not be more than twice the premiums payable in any other 12-month period, for this exclusion to apply (*IHTA 1984, s 167(3)*).

A separate rule applies for the purpose of valuing unit-linked policies. This broadly provides for a reduction in the value of the policy if the value of the units has fallen since the date of their allocation (*IHTA 1984, s 167(4)*; see HMRC's example at IHTM20244).

A policy taken out for another person is a transfer of value, normally based on the amount of the first premium, and on any subsequent premiums. If premiums are paid on a policy owned by somebody else, the amount of each premium is a separate transfer of value, subject to any exemptions due (eg the annual exemption (*IHTA 1984, s 19*) or the normal expenditure out of income exemption (*IHTA 1984, s 21*)).

Transfers on death

6.13 The proceeds of a policy taken out on the person's own life or for his own benefit, which are payable on death to the deceased's personal representatives are taken into account as part of the estate, based on the policy's open market value (*IHTA 1984, s 160*). The open market value will be the amount for which the policy could be sold, and might exceed its surrender value (IHTM20231).

If the proceeds from the life policy are payable to someone other than the life assured, and if that beneficial owner dies before the life assured, there will be a transfer on their death based on the value of the life policy.

'Back-to-back' arrangements

6.14 An anti-avoidance rule applies to circumstances in which an individual (who may be in poor health) purchases one or more annuities to enable him to take out one or more life policies written in trust for someone other than the life assured, and where the annuity payments feed the premiums for the life policy. If the life policy was taken out (or varied) since 26 March 1974 and the two events are associated operations, the IHT exemption for normal expenditure out of income does not apply to the payment of the premiums (*IHTA 1984, ss 263, 21(2)*).

In addition, unless it can be shown that the purchase of the annuity and the taking out of the life insurance policy are not 'associated operations' (as defined in *IHTA 1984, s 268*), the purchaser of the annuity is treated as having made a transfer of value when the policy became vested in the other person. The amount of the transfer of value is the lower of the following:

- the cost of the annuity and any premiums (or other consideration) paid on or before the transfer; and
- the value of the greatest benefit capable of being conferred by the policy, calculated as if that time was the transfer date (*IHTA 1984, s 263(2)*).

However, HMRC should accept that the two contracts are not 'associated operations' if the policy was issued on full medical evidence of the assured's health, and it would have been issued on the same terms if the annuity had not been bought (Statement of Practice E4; see IHTM20375). The easiest way to demonstrate that the two contracts were not 'associated' would probably be to take up the annuity and the policy with separate, unconnected life offices. If the same life office is used, the policy should be issued and the premiums fixed on the basis of full medical evidence.

In the case of joint life assurance policies (eg between husband and wife) full medical evidence is required in respect of both lives assured. In *Smith v Revenue and Customs Commissioners* [2008] STC 1649, it was held that Statement of Practice E4 did not apply to a joint life policy, where a medical report had not been obtained in respect of the wife's health. The Court upheld the earlier decision of the Special Commissioner that the purchase of the annuity and making of the life assurance policy were associated operations.

Discounted gift schemes

6.15 A discounted gift scheme broadly involves the gift of a bond, subject to retained rights such as withdrawals or successively maturing reversions. The retained rights are such that the 'gift with reservation' anti-avoidance rules (*FA 1986, s 102*) ought not to apply. The gift of the bond is a transfer of value, based on the difference between the amount invested in the bond and the open market value of the retained rights (*IHTA 1984, s 160*).

In May 2007, HMRC issued a Technical Note concerning the valuation and other issues relating to discounted gift schemes, which stated HMRC's view, *inter alia*, that if the settlor was uninsurable for any reason at the date of gift the open market value of the retained rights would be nominal, and the gift would be close to the whole amount invested. HMRC also stated that settlors older than 90 years of age would be considered uninsurable (tinyurl.com/DGS-HMRC-TN).

However, in *Bower v Revenue and Customs Commissioners*, a 90-year old lady in relatively poor health took out a life annuity policy. She paid a premium of £73,000, and the policy was issued to a settlement she created, subject to the reserved right to a 5% life annuity. Mrs Bower died five months later. HMRC valued the reserved right at only £250, whereas the insurance company had valued the rights at £7,800. Her executors appealed. The Special Commissioner ([2008] SpC 665) considered that the open market value of the reserved rights to the annuity was £4,200. HMRC appealed.

In Business Brief 23/08, HMRC stated an intention to appeal to the High Court against the decision in the above case, and indicated that in the meantime new cases would continue to be dealt with in accordance with the May 2007 Technical Note mentioned above. Subsequently, the Court allowed HMRC's appeal in the *Bower* case ([2008] EWHC 3105 (Ch)), on the grounds that the Commissioner erred in law in concluding that he was required or entitled to assume hypothetical speculators or to indicate the price that the hypothetical buyer was assumed to have paid.

HMRC subsequently issued Revenue & Customs Brief 21/09 (dated 2 April 2009), confirming that cases would be dealt with in accordance with its technical note issued in 2007. The Brief also stated that '... there is nothing in the Inheritance Tax legislation which allows any withdrawals actually taken between the gift date and the date of death of the settlor to be offset against the sum invested'.

In *Watkins and another v Revenue & Customs* [2011] UKFTT 745 (TC), the deceased had created a discounted gift trust in December 2004, and settled a redemption bond obtained for a premium of £340,000. She died in March 2006, aged 91 years. The deceased's retained right in the settlement to an income stream was valued at approximately £49,033, but HMRC determined the value to be £4,250. The tribunal dismissed the appeal against HMRC's Notice of Determination, and held that although the appellants' formulations were 'ingenious' they were not identifiable with any type of open market which exists. The burden of displacing HMRC's valuation was on the appellants, and the tribunal held that this burden had not been discharged.

The ability of UK life insurers to charge different premiums (or determine different benefits) for males and females based on gender-related factors was removed following a legal challenge to the European Court of Justice by the Belgian consumer's association Test Achats. HMRC subsequently stated (in its Trusts and Estates Newsletter for April 2011) that if the *Test Achats* decision resulted in changes from the market practice of life companies to take into account the gender of the life assured, HMRC would consult on how best to incorporate that change into its practice of valuing retained rights under discounted gift schemes.

HMRC later pointed out that, following the *Test Achats* case, the use of gender as a factor in setting insurance premiums is not permissible from 21 December 2012. HMRC therefore altered the mortality basis used in the calculation of the open market value of the retained rights, to reflect the change in open market premium rates. It also revised the current interest rate assumption within the calculation. The revised mortality (80% of AFC00 select mortality) and interest rate (4.5% per annum) basis would apply to transfers (or ten-year anniversaries, in respect of relevant property trusts) from 1 December 2013 (Revenue and Customs Brief 22/13).

Quoted shares and securities

6.16 HMRC's IHT400 Notes state (tinyurl.com/HMRC-IHT400-Notes) (on p 67):

> 'You don't have to get a professional valuation for quoted stocks and shares. You can value shares quoted on the London Stock Exchange by finding the price of the shares in the financial pages of a newspaper'.

Further HMRC guidance on the basis of valuation is included in the IHT manual (at IHTM18091 and following).

Quoted investments must be valued based on the general rule regarding open market value in *IHTA 1984, s 160.*

There is no special statutory basis (in *IHTA 1984, s 160* or otherwise) for valuing quoted shares and securities for IHT purposes. Historically, capital gains tax valuation rules were generally used in practice to ascertain the value of stocks and shares for IHT purposes (*TCGA 1992, s 272*).

Prior to 6 April 2015, the same valuation basis therefore applied for both capital gains tax and IHT purposes. However, the basis of valuation for listed shares, securities and strips for capital gains tax purposes was changed by statutory instrument from that date (see below); however, the statutory instrument does not apply for IHT purposes as well. At the time of writing, the valuation bases have not been aligned, so the pre-6 April 2015 basis of valuation for capital gains tax purposes continues to apply to IHT valuations (see IHTM18093).

From 6 April 2015, the market value of UK quoted stocks and shares for capital gains tax purposes is generally the lower of the two prices shown in the Stock Exchange Daily List as the closing price, plus one-half of the difference between those two figures, or (if the Stock Exchange was closed that day) that value on the last day on which it was open, unless the closing prices are not a proper measure of market value due to special circumstances (*Market Value of Shares, Securities and Strips Regulations 2015, SI 2015/616, reg 2*). Different valuation rules apply to securities or strips (but not shares) listed on a foreign exchange (*SI 2015/616, reg 3*).

For IHT valuations (and for capital gains tax valuations prior to 6 April 2015), the lower of two figures is normally applied:

- The 'quarter-up' method, ie the lower closing Stock Exchange price plus one-quarter of the difference between the lower and higher closing prices (this can normally be obtained, for example, from a *Financial Times* or similar periodical for the day following the valuation date).

Example 6.5—Valuation of quoted investments: 'quarter-up' method

James owned 5,000 shares in Widgets plc at the date of his death. Their price range on that date was 110–122 pence. The valuation would be:

$$110 + \frac{1}{4}(122 - 110) = \underline{113 \text{ pence}}$$

The value of 5,000 shares would therefore be 5,000 × 113p = £5,650.

- Mid-price between the highest and lowest recorded bargains for the day of valuation. This is sometimes referred to as the 'mid-price bargain' or 'average bargain' rule.

If the transfer takes place on a day that the Stock Exchange is closed, HMRC accepts (in its IHT400 Notes, on p 68) that the market value can be ascertained by reference to the previous day or the following day, and the lower valuation is taken.

If shares are transferred 'ex-dividend' (ie broadly dividends declared but not yet paid at the date of valuation), the right to the dividend represents an asset of the estate, which should therefore be taken into account unless the right to receive it is transferred.

These valuation rules can be applied both to lifetime transfers and for the purposes of valuing the death estate.

The approach to valuation may depend on the circumstances. For example, a special rule was applied to holdings in Bradford & Bingley (B&B), in relation to former shareholders who died on or after 29 September 2008 and no longer held the shares but were entitled to compensation for the loss of them. Where the right to compensation was for a holding of 1,000 shares or less in B&B, HMRC indicated that the value offered may be accepted without enquiry. For holdings of more than 1,000 shares, any valuation is likely to be referred to HMRC Shares and Assets Valuation (IHTM10073).

Unit trusts

6.17 The market value of unit trusts is the buying price, being the lower of two published values (ie the buying and selling price) for the date in question, or on the last previous business day if the transfer does not take place on a business day (*TCGA 1992, s 272(5)*; see also IHTM18095).

Unquoted shares and securities

6.18

Focus

Unlike quoted shares and securities, there is normally no ascertainable or readily available value for unquoted shares and securities. The valuation of unquoted shares and securities is based on the price that they might reasonably be expected to fetch when sold in the open market (*s 160*).

For the purpose of determining this price, it is assumed that a prospective purchaser possessed all the information that might reasonably be required if the purchase was from a willing vendor at arm's length (*s 168*).

Valuations may take into account relevant factors, such as the size of the company and shareholding, its activities and profit levels, asset backing and dividend history. In practice, the IHT value is generally subject to negotiation with HMRC Shares and Assets Valuation.

HMRC guidance on valuation issues regarding unquoted shares is included in the Shares and Assets Valuation Manual (see SVM113000 and following in connection with the statutory open market, and SVM114000 and following concerning information standards).

If a valuation cannot be agreed, it will be subject to appeal before the Tax Tribunal.

6.19 In practice, HMRC Shares and Assets Valuation will not always consider and formally agree a valuation (eg if the share value is likely to be well within the transferor's available nil rate band, or if the shares qualify for 100% business or agricultural property relief (see **Chapter 13**)).

In the latter case, if HMRC agree that full relief may be deducted, this is not an indication that the share value has been accepted (*Note*: in those circumstances, the value has not been 'ascertained' for IHT purposes, and therefore cannot be relied upon in any subsequent CGT computations (*TCGA 1992, s 274*)). It should be noted that such share transfers are subject to the same reporting requirements as other types of assets, and that a reasonable valuation should still be advanced (see **6.2**).

Joint property

6.20 Jointly owned property can be held either as 'joint tenants' or as 'tenants in common'. Ownership will be as joint tenants (in equal or identical interests) unless the owners declare otherwise. The interest of a joint owner passes upon death by survivorship to the remaining owner.

However, joint tenancies can be severed, with the owners holding the asset as tenants in common. An important consequence of ownership as tenants in common is that the interest or share of any owner passes on death under their will (or, if there is no will, under the rules of intestacy).

Under Scots law, the two main categories of joint ownership are 'common property' (ie joint owners have separate title to a specific share, which they can transfer separately) and the joint property rights of trustees and partners (which automatically accrues on death to the survivors) (see IHTM15091 and following).

Money accounts

6.21 Joint money account holders (eg with banks, building societies, etc) are normally regarded as beneficially entitled to the proportion of the account attributable to their contributions. In addition, HMRC accept that, as a general rule, if one individual places money in a joint account with another as joint tenants and retains the right to withdraw the whole of it, there will not be a lifetime transfer when the money is paid into that account (although there may be a transfer on a later withdrawal of funds for the other joint owner) (IHTM15042–3). As to the position under Scots law in respect of joint money accounts, see below.

However, care should be taken when one or more beneficial interests in joint accounts are gifted to other individuals (particularly if those individuals are not exempt beneficiaries), to avoid the whole account being included in the transferor's estate (*O'Neill & O'Neill's Executors v CIR*, SpC [1998] SSCD 110; *Sillars v IRC* [2004] SSCD 180).

In *Taylor and another v Revenue and Customs Commissioners* [2008] SSCD 1159, the deceased was held to have a general power enabling her to dispose of the whole of two joint accounts. This was on the grounds (among other reasons) that there was no evidence that the other joint account holder was to benefit from the accounts on the particular facts of the case, and that the deceased was able to dispose of the whole balance in those accounts.

In *Matthews v Revenue and Customs Commissioners* [2012] UKFTT 658 (TC), Mrs Matthews died in January 2007. She initially held funds in an account in her sole name. In 1999, she opened a new account with her son at Abbey plc. Mrs Matthews withdrew all the monies in the account in her sole name, and deposited them in the new joint account. The account instructions included that either Mrs Matthews or her son could withdraw monies from the account without the other's signature being required, although no withdrawals were actually made prior to Mrs Matthews' death. The only deposits after the deceased's initial transfer into it consisted of interest credited, and small account bonuses. Each account holder declared half of the interest earned in their income tax returns each year. In addition, the IHT account on Mrs Matthews' death indicated that her share of funds in the account passed by survivorship to her son. The tribunal held that the whole of the funds in the account were liable to IHT as part of the deceased's estate under *IHTA 1984, s 5(2)*, or alternatively under the gift with reservation anti-avoidance provisions (*FA 1986, s 102*).

In *Lidher v Revenue and Customs* [2017] UKFTT 153 (TC), the tribunal held that 50% of the funds in a joint bank account that a deceased individual had held with his son (the deceased's personal representative) should be included in the deceased's estate, despite a submission that his son had provided all the capital in the account. The lack of reliable evidence was a significant factor in the tribunal's decision.

HMRC guidance points out that under Scots law, where bank or building society accounts are held in joint names, the special or survivorship destination does not by itself pass the ownership of the money in the account to the survivor.

An account with a bank or building society is not a document of title (ie it is not a deed of trust in terms of the *Blank Bonds and Trusts Act 1696*). It is a contract between the bank and the customer. The question of the ownership of the funds in the account therefore falls to be determined according to the ordinary principles of ownership. The individual who deposited funds in the account remains the owner, unless a transfer of ownership has occurred. This applies to all bank or building society accounts governed by Scots Law, and therefore applies to taxpayers living in England, Wales and Northern Ireland with an account governed by Scots Law (IHTM15054).

On the legal question of beneficial ownership of joint money accounts, in *Whitlock & Anor v Moree (Bahamas)* [2017] UKPC 44 (a non-IHT case), an individual (FL) contributed all the funds held in a joint bank account with his friend (DM). On setting up the joint account, FL and DM signed the bank's standard joint account opening form, which included a clause headed 'Joint tenancy'. FL died in February 2010. The Privy Council held (by a majority) that upon FL's death the beneficial interest in the account passed to DM by survivorship and did not by reason of the operation of the doctrine of presumed resulting trust (since FL provided all the money) remain part of FL's estate. Both parties had expressly signed a declaration as to the beneficial interests in that joint account which, on its true construction, provided for any balance on the account to be the beneficial property of the survivor upon the death of the other account holder, regardless of who contributed the money to the credit of the account before that date.

Land

6.22 As indicated at **6.2** above, HMRC consider land and property valuation to be an area of high risk in terms of the potential loss of IHT, particularly where the valuation is not undertaken by a qualified, independent valuer. However, even if a professional valuation is obtained, HMRC may expect it to be revisited in certain circumstances.

HMRC's Trusts & Estates Newsletter (August 2010) states the following:

> 'If, having obtained a valuation and before you apply for a grant, you find out about other information that casts doubts on the initial valuation, you must reconsider it. For example, if you have a valuation that shows the property was worth £250,000, but when you try to sell the property you market it at £270,000 and receive some offers at that figure or more, it suggests that the open market value for the property may be more like £270,000.
>
> In these circumstances, HMRC recommends that you ask the valuer to reconsider and, if appropriate, amend the date of death value, taking into account such things as the length of time since the death and movements in the property market.'

However, in the case of excepted estates where property is sold some time after the date of death for a higher sale price than the figure reported on form IHT205, HMRC has indicated that it will not amend the value of the property previously reported for the subsequent sale price unless IHT is due. Thus, as the deceased's personal representatives have not agreed the value of a property for IHT purposes at the date of death, they do not have an agreed value for the purposes of calculating whether there is any capital gain between the date of death and the date of the eventual sale (HMRC Trusts Estates newsletter: December 2016).

6.23 If joint tenants (see above) purchase land with the help of a mortgage, unless there is an agreement to the contrary, their beneficial interests will generally equate to their respective shares of the mortgage. In addition, as indicated on the death of a joint owner of property (eg the family home) the survivor takes absolutely and by operation of law. Hence, it is impossible to make testamentary or lifetime dispositions to third parties.

If the beneficial interests in land vary from the legal title, HMRC will require evidence of the parties' beneficial ownership (IHTM15044). See **6.5** above.

In the case of a tenancy in common, disposals of interests in the property during lifetime or by will are possible. A tenant in common of an interest in the family home would entitle that co-owner to occupy the whole property. On the transfer of an interest by a tenant in common (eg on death), that person's share could be eligible for a discount, generally of between 10–15%, although the actual level of discount will be subject to the Land Tribunal's agreement based on the particular facts and circumstances (see the Valuation Office Agency's guidance 'Inheritance tax: undivided shares' at: tinyurl.com/VOA-IHT-Manual-s18).

However, in the case of property held by spouses or civil partners (whether as joint tenants or tenants in common, albeit that joint property passing by survivorship may be subject to the spouse exemption in any event), HMRC may seek to challenge any discount claimed, based on the related property provisions (see **6.8** above).

6.24 In *Wight v IRC* 264 *Estates Gazette* 935/82, the value of an interest in a dwelling house owned as tenants in common in equal shares was held by the Lands Tribunal to be its vacant possession value less a discount of 15% to reflect the restricted demand for this type of interest.

In *Price v Revenue and Customs Commissioners* (see **6.8** above), HMRC acknowledged that such a discount is appropriate when the interest being valued is an undivided share in property (but not if the valuation involves aggregating two undivided shares in property, when considering a valuation under the related property provisions in *IHTA 1984, s 161*).

In *Charkham v IRC* [2000] RVR vol 40, p 7, an individual held minority interests in a number of investment properties. The Revenue considered that the value should be discounted overall by between 10–15%. The taxpayer appealed. The Lands Tribunal held that there should be a single discount on each property, and that the appropriate discount should be 15% on some properties, and 20% or 22.5% on others. However, these larger discounts are exceptional: see **6.28** below.

6.25 As mentioned previously, HMRC's IHT Toolkit highlights valuations as a potential risk area. In the context of farms, it emphasises 'the need for separate valuations and details for the farmhouse, any other dwellings, any farm/outbuildings and their usage, the land and any amenity land and their rights such as fishing, shooting, mineral'. It also encourages the submission to HMRC of plans and photos of the farmhouse, buildings and land, in addition to copies of any professional valuation reports obtained.

Development value

6.26

> **Focus**
>
> HMRC made their view of development value clear in their IHT Newsletter of 28 April 2006. The potential for development value must be accounted for where an estate contains land or buildings. The personal representatives should take all appropriate steps to disclose the value that the land may expect to achieve if sold on the open market and that must take account of any feature that may make it attractive to a builder or developer, for example a large garden or access to other land.

HMRC's guidance adds (at IHTM36275): 'Where professional values are obtained we expect … the valuer to consider whether there is any potential for development and if so to ensure that it is taken into account and reflected in the valuation ("Hope" value is a component part of the open market value in appropriate cases, whether or not planning permission has been sought or granted).'

The personal representatives should consider all the evidence available when completing the IHT account. It is not enough just to obtain a professional valuation. If further information then comes to light, for example on advice about marketing the property, and if that later advice casts some doubt on the original valuation, the extra information should be disclosed.

In the IHT Toolkit, HMRC state that a 'risk' area in respect of land and buildings is 'the potential for the development of the land (in particular large gardens) and buildings (in particular dividing buildings into flats), the existence of tenancies, or occupation by people other than the deceased'.

6.27 It may happen that after the personal representatives have lodged form IHT400 based on the situation as they saw it as at the date of death, new information will come to light during the administration of the estate and before winding up the estate. If that affects the value as at the date of death, HMRC would expect to be notified as quickly as possible. Where it is clear that reasonable and adequate steps have not been taken to ascertain the open market value based on all the information that was available, the personal representatives may be liable to penalties.

That does not necessarily mean that the full development value is taxable. In *Prosser v IRC* DET/1/2000 [2001] RVR 170, it was realised that a house enjoyed a garden big enough to serve as an extra building plot. The district valuer suggested a figure as at the date of death of 80% of the value that the plot would have with planning consent, allowing for the fact that no application for planning permission had yet been made. That was considered to be wrong. The Lands Tribunal held that, at the date of death, there was a 50% chance of obtaining planning permission and that a speculator, in the absence of permission, would not offer 80% of the development value but would offer only 25%.

More recently, in *Palliser v Revenue and Customs* [2018] UKUT 71 (TC), an individual's interest in a maisonette was originally valued on his death in June 2012 without reflecting any 'hope value' for future development of the property or change of use. HMRC served a notice of determination on the deceased's personal representative under which the property interest was valued at £1,829,880. The personal representative appealed, on the basis that the correct valuation was £1,113,840. The property was eventually sold for £2.525 million in March 2014. The Upper Tribunal considered that insofar as the property's potential for improvement had not been crystallised by planning permission its value would be hope value rather than development value, but either way it was not an element of value that fell to be ignored under *IHTA 1984, s 160*. In arriving at a value of £1,603,930 for IHT purposes, the tribunal included 50% of the difference between the net value of the property with and without extension as representing the hope value of extending the floor area of the property.

Discounts

6.28 The Valuation Office Agency (VOA) generally applies discounts when valuing an undivided half-share interest in accordance with the table below (Valuation Office Agency Inheritance Tax Manual, Practice Note 2, para 9.7, which can be viewed online at: tinyurl.com/VOA-IHT-Manual-PN2-9-7):

Table 6.1—Discounts re undivided half-share interest in land

(a)	where the other co-owner(s) is (are) not in occupation and the purpose behind the trust no longer exists	10%
(b)	where the other co-owner(s) is (are) not in occupation but they have a right to occupy as their main residence and the purpose behind the trust still exists	15%
(c)	where the other co-owner(s) is (are) in occupation as their main residence	15%

The VOA Inheritance Tax Manual also indicates that a discount may be appropriate for a minority share, and even for a majority share. Practice Note 2, para 10.9 states:

> 'When valuing a minority share a larger discount than 10% may be appropriate in cases where
>
> i it is felt unlikely that a potential purchaser would seek an order for sale (under Section 14 TLATA 1996 or Section 30 LPA 1925) or, there is evidence that the majority of the share owners under a trust of land would oppose an application for an order for sale by a minority shareholder, and
>
> ii it is felt that there is potential for dispute concerning how the property is managed,
>
> However, the discount should not normally exceed 20%.'

The guidance goes onto state (at para 10.10):

> 'Clearly even a majority share has disadvantages compared with ownership of the entirety. There will be circumstances however, where a discount of less than 10% share should be considered – e.g. where it is known the co-owner(s) is/are keen to place the entirety interest on the market, or in cases involving large majority shares, such as a share of over 90% in a high value property.'

The extent of any discount will therefore depend on the circumstances of each case.

HMRC guidance points out in relation to the law of special (or survivorship) destination in Scotland that if an asset is purchased jointly under which there is a contractual agreement that on death the property passes to the survivor and they have paid equally for the asset, the survivor will be entitled to the whole on the death of the first to die. If the price was not provided equally, the donor can revoke the survivorship destination by will. If one party provided the whole property, he retains ownership unless there is indication of intention to make an immediate gift to the joint owner (see IHTM15050).

Settled property

6.29 The value of settled property in which an individual has an interest in possession generally forms part of the estate on death, if he became beneficially entitled to it before 22 March 2006, or alternatively if he became beneficially entitled to an 'immediate post-death interest', a 'disabled person's interest' or a 'transitional serial interest' on or after that date (*IHTA 1984, s 49(1), (1A)*) (see **Chapter 9**).

If an interest in possession falls within one of the above categories, the individual is effectively treated as the absolute owner of that property, or the relevant proportion of it. The value of the life interest for IHT purposes is the value of the settlement property in which the individual's life interest subsisted.

An exception to this rule applies if the interest in possession is acquired for money or money's worth, ie the extent (if any) to which the giving of consideration is a transfer of value falls to be determined without regard to that valuation rule (*IHTA 1984, s 49(2)*).

6.30 The lifetime cessation of the above interests in possession is usually a PET, which becomes chargeable on the individual's death within seven years. If an immediate IHT charge arose at lifetime rates (eg if the settled property went into a discretionary trust) further IHT may become due at the rate on death, upon the individual's death within seven years.

Scots law has always had a unified system of law and equity and therefore does not recognise the principles of legal and beneficial estates (ie it does not recognise that the beneficiary could have real rights in trust property). Specific IHT legislation therefore applies in respect of proper life-rents (*IHTA 1984, ss 43(4), 46, 47*) (see IHTM16072).

If the individual's estate was increased by an earlier chargeable transfer of the settled property within the previous five years, 'quick succession relief' is available (**Chapter 12**). The IHT charged on death falls to be reduced by a percentage of the tax charged on the earlier transfer (*IHTA 1984, s 141*).

Gifts with reservation

6.31 Property may fall to be treated as forming part of a donor's estate for IHT purposes if the 'gifts with reservation' (GWR) provisions apply (see **Chapter 7**).

For example, a parent may transfer his home into joint ownership with his adult daughter, but continue living there. Unless the parent pays a market rent for his continued occupation, or unless his daughter takes up co-occupation, there is a GWR.

A gift caught by the GWR rules at the individual's death is treated as part of the donor's estate, and is liable to IHT accordingly. In addition, where the gift was made within seven years prior to the transferor's death, or the reservation ended within that period, there is a further chargeable transfer in respect of the same gift. However, there are regulations to eliminate this double tax charge (*FA 1986, ss 102, 104*; *IHT (Double Charges Relief) Regulations, SI 1987/1130*), which effectively determine the value of the gift to be taken into account on the donor's death.

The lifetime termination of an interest in possession falling within the categories mentioned in **6.29** above is treated as a gift for GWR purposes. If the individual retains use or enjoyment of the settled property after their interest has ended, it remains part of their estate under the GWR rules as if they had owned the property outright and gifted it when the interest ended (*FA 1986, s 102ZA*).

Other assets

Debts

6.32 It is generally assumed that the right to receive a sum due under any obligation will be paid in full (ie the face value of the debt is included in the creditor's estate), unless recovery of the debt is impossible or not reasonably practicable (eg if the debtor is insolvent).

It may be possible to include a reduced value on the death estate if either title to the debt or the amount due is in doubt. However, if a reduced figure is used, HMRC will probably require an explanation, including how that amount has been calculated and any evidence in support of the reduced amount shown.

No allowance is made if the recovery is in doubt because of any act or omission by the creditor (eg failing to enforce collection) (*IHTA 1984, s 166*).

The amount to be included in the death estate also includes interest due up to the date of death. If some or all of the debt has been written off, that amount is treated as a gift.

If the lender waives a loan (voluntarily and not for consideration), HMRC will generally expect the debt release to be effected by a deed before allowing a reduction in the lender's estate, clearly indicating that it is intended as a deed by the parties involved. The deed must be validly executed (usually by signature) by those persons. However, in Scotland the release of a debt does not need to be effected by deed (IHTM19110).

Household goods and personal effects

6.33 Household and personal goods are subject to the 'market value' rule (*IHTA 1984, s 160*), ie 'the price which might reasonably be expected to fetch if sold in the open market …'

In its *IHT Newsletter* (December 2004), Inland Revenue Capital Taxes (as it then was) stated:

> '... we will be paying particularly close attention to the values included for household and personal goods. In appropriate cases we will open an enquiry and ask you for further information to satisfy ourselves that all of the goods have been included and that they have been valued on the statutory basis.'

HMRC may seek to impose a penalty if the value of household or personal goods as returned for IHT purposes is estimated inaccurately, or if incorrect information is not corrected within a reasonable time. If preparing an IHT account (ie form IHT400 or IHT100) which includes the value of household and personal goods, it would therefore clearly be advisable to provide the fullest information possible in the circumstances. This should also reduce the possibility of enquiry by HMRC. In particular, references in the account to the valuation being made 'for probate purposes' or for 'IHT purposes' should be avoided.

Whilst it is generally good practice to obtain professional valuations of assets, it is not considered necessary to do so in all cases, such as in respect of ordinary household goods where individual items have a value of no more than £500 (see **6.2** above).

Note that HMRC do not accept that the value of jointly owned household goods should be discounted as a matter of course, where the related property provisions (see **6.6** above) do not apply. HMRC's guidance states (at IHTM21043):

> 'Although we allow a discount as a matter of course for jointly owned land, we do not do this automatically for jointly owned chattels. This is because any discount is to reflect problems with disposing of less than a full share and, for chattels, the circumstances in which a sale could be obtained may vary.'

Values 'ascertained'

6.34 As explained in *Capital Gains Tax 2018/19* (Bloomsbury Professional), and as indicated at **6.19** above, if IHT was chargeable on the value of a person's estate immediately before death and the value of an asset forming part of that estate has been 'ascertained' for IHT purposes, that value is taken to be the market value for CGT purposes at the date of death (*TCGA 1992, s 274*).

However, where a value has been ascertained solely for the purpose of establishing the amount of transferable IHT nil rate band between spouses or civil partners, that value will not similarly apply for CGT purposes (see **Chapter 3**).

Valuation of liabilities; guarantees

6.35 It was noted at **5.9** that a liability may be taken into account to reduce the chargeable estate only to the extent that it was incurred for money's worth and is enforceable.

One area of regular difficulty is the valuation of a guarantee given by the deceased that has not been called upon at the date of death. HMRC may strongly resist an allowance of the full value guaranteed. For HMRC's approach on the calculation of allowable deductions for guarantee debts, see IHTM28355.

The negotiation of that valuation generally involves considering:

- what security was given by the deceased to support the guarantee;
- the likelihood that the guarantee will be called upon; and
- the amount by which the original debtor will default, such that the guarantor must make it good.

This is unsatisfactory from the point of view of the guarantor, because an obligation has been assumed that no doubt restricts his freedom to deal with certain assets because they support the guarantee. It will often be better, from a tax point of view, simply to provide the money rather than a guarantee; but in family situations the donor/lender may be reluctant to do so.

Chapter 7

Gifts with reservation of benefit

SIGNPOSTS

- **Scope** – The 'gifts with reservation' (GWR) provisions are anti-avoidance rules, which apply to property given away from 18 March 1986. Gifts 'caught' by the GWR provisions are generally treated as remaining part of the donor's estate for IHT purposes (see **7.1–7.9**).
- **Interests in land** – The GWR provisions were extended in relation to gifts of interests in land for disposals from 9 March 1999 (see **7.10–7.15**).
- **Specific issues** – A GWR can be 'traced' in some cases by special rules ('substitutions and accretions'). The GWR rules can also apply to gifts into settlement, and specific rules apply in respect of insurance policies, and business and agricultural property (see **7.16–7.23**).
- **Exceptions and exclusions** – The general rule that gifts 'caught' by the GWR provisions are treated as remaining part of the donor's estate (**7.7**) is subject to various exceptions and exclusions (see **7.24–7.37**).
- **Double IHT relief** – The GWR provisions could result in a double IHT charge on the same property. However, relief from a double IHT charge applies in various circumstances (see **7.38–7.39**).
- **Separating income and capital** – Certain trust arrangements have been argued to escape the GWR rules (see **7.40**).

INTRODUCTION

7.1 An individual who gives away property (on or after 18 March 1986) makes a 'gift with reservation' (GWR) broadly if:

- the recipient does not immediately enjoy possession and enjoyment of the property; or
- the donor continues to enjoy, or benefits from, the property gifted.

As indicated at **4.22**, the GWR rules (*FA 1986, ss 102–102C, Sch 20*) are anti-avoidance provisions designed to prevent 'cake and eat it' situations whereby an individual makes a lifetime gift of an asset (which they hope to survive by at least seven years), but continues to have the use or enjoyment of it.

Property subject to the GWR rules on the individual's death is treated as part of the donor's estate, and charged to IHT accordingly. If the reservation ends during the individual's lifetime and before the end of the 'relevant period' (see **7.5**), the gift is generally treated as a PET at that time, which is subject to IHT upon death within seven years (*FA 1986, s 102(4)*).

The annual exemption cannot be used against the value of the 'deemed' PET (*IHTA 1984, s 19(5)*). In addition, the 'normal expenditure out of income' exemption does not prevent a gift being chargeable under the GWR rules (*IHTA 1984, s 21(5)*). HMRC regard the small gifts exemption (*IHTA 1984, s 20*) as strictly only applying to outright gifts (IHTM14319).

Despite property subject to the GWR provisions being treated as part of the donor's estate on death for IHT purposes, the normal capital gains tax uplift in the value of the property (*TCGA 1992, s 62(1)*) does not apply on the donor's death. Furthermore, the same property will generally form part of the donee's IHT estate as well. The implications of the GWR provisions applying are therefore potentially wide ranging.

7.2

Focus

- If the transferor pays a full market rent for continued enjoyment or benefit of land or a chattel, the gift is not treated as a GWR (*FA 1986, Sch 20, para 6(1)(a)*). Note that this GWR exception applies specifically to land and chattels. Care should therefore be taken with other assets (see **7.29**).
- A gift which is an exempt transfer (eg a straightforward transfer to a UK-domiciled spouse or civil partner, or a transfer subject to the small gift or marriage gift exemption) cannot normally be a GWR (*FA 1986, s 102(5)*).

Special rules apply if an individual disposes of an interest in land by gift (on or after 9 March 1999), where the donor or his spouse enjoys a 'significant right or interest', or is party to a 'significant arrangement' in relation to the land. In such cases, the gifted interest in the land is treated as a GWR, unless certain specific exceptions apply (see **7.10**ff).

Relief is available in certain circumstances where a double IHT charge would otherwise arise in respect of the same property (ie where the original gift was immediately chargeable), or as the result of a PET becoming chargeable within seven years of death, where that property is also included in the death estate for IHT purposes because it was a GWR (*Inheritance Tax (Double Charges Relief) Regulations, SI 1987/1130*) (see **7.38** below).

Pre-owned assets

7.3 The 'pre-owned assets' income tax charge (ie the 'charge to income tax on benefits received by former owner of property') was introduced (by *FA 2004, s 84*, and *Sch 15*, and underpinned by subsequent Treasury Regulations) in response to certain IHT planning arrangements. The charge operates for 2005/06 and subsequent years, but applies with retroactive effect to 18 March 1986.

It should be noted that there is no 'pre-owned assets tax' charge if the GWR provisions apply (*FA 2004, Sch 15, para 11(5)*), or if an election is made (under *FA 2004, Sch 15, para 21*) to effectively 'opt out' of the income tax charge and into the GWR rules for IHT purposes.

A double IHT charge could arise if an election is made and the taxpayer dies within seven years of the original gift (ie both on the original transfer that must now be aggregated with the death estate, and on the property subject to the reservation). Double charge regulations (*Charge to Income Tax by Reference to Enjoyment of Property Previously Owned Regulations, SI 2005/724*) therefore prevent a double liability (ie on the original gift and the GWR); the higher amount of tax is charged (*SI 2005/724, reg 6*).

HMRC have published a section on pre-owned assets in their Inheritance Tax Manual (IHTM44000–IHTM44128), albeit that the pre-owned assets regime relates to income tax, as opposed to IHT.

For further commentary on pre-owned assets, see **Chapter 17**.

SCOPE AND EFFECT OF THE GWR RULES

Scope of GWR rules

7.4 The GWR provisions are anti-avoidance rules designed to stop taxpayers decreasing the value of their IHT estates by making gifts whilst leaving their overall circumstances effectively unchanged.

The rules apply to gifts of property on or after 18 March 1986 by an individual ('the donor') if:

- possession and enjoyment of the property is not assumed ('bona fide' as the legislation puts it) by the recipient of the gift ('the donee') at or before the beginning of the 'relevant period' (see below); or

- at any time in the relevant period the property is not enjoyed to the entire exclusion, or virtually to the entire exclusion, of the donor and of any benefit to him by contract or otherwise (*FA 1986, s 102(1)(a), (b)*).

The above requirement that the donee must assume 'bona fide' possession and enjoyment of the gifted property to prevent a GWR means that the beneficial interest in the gifted property must be duly transferred, and the donee must have had actual enjoyment of that property (eg through physical occupation, or the receipt of income generated therefrom), instead of just the legal right of enjoyment.

Chattel gifts are usually perfected by the delivery of the item to the donee. Several cases have examined what constitutes a valid gift, and from these we may perhaps see what amounts to the assumption of possession and enjoyment of the thing given. For example, in *re Cole (a bankrupt)* [1964] Ch 175 as between husband and wife, the gift of such chattels as remained in the house was not a gift by delivery. The gift, in *re Lillingston* [1952] 2 All ER 184, of a key to a box was the gift of the contents of that box. Where the claimant had lived in a house where some furniture was situated, and there was a verbal gift of the furniture, that amounted to a valid gift because the donee lived there: *re Stoneham* [1919] 1 Ch 149. The question of whether gifts of assets (ie paintings) were effected by delivery was considered more recently for IHT purposes in *Scott v Revenue & Customs* [2015] UKFTT 266 (TC). In practice, the 'delivery' problem can generally be addressed by means of a straightforward deed of gift.

The gift of a chattel to a person living in the same house may be challenged on the ground that the donor can still use it. Only special circumstances, such as if the item is stored in the attic and the donor is too frail to have access to it, may displace the GWR argument.

7.5 The GWR rules can apply if the donor derives a benefit 'at any time' during the relevant period. The 'relevant period' is the period ending on the date of the individual's death and beginning seven years before that date, or (if later) on the date of the gift (*FA 1986, s 102(1)*).

For example, if the donor makes a gift eight years before his death (which satisfies condition *(a)* or *(b)* in *FA 1986, s 102(1)*), the relevant period is seven years before his death. However, if the gift was made four years prior to death, the relevant period is four years.

HMRC's view (at IHTM14333) is that 'virtually' intends to take gifts outside the reservation of benefit rules if the donor's benefit is 'insignificant' in relation to the gifted property. HMRC's guidance also identifies two separate and distinct limbs to the condition in *FA 1986, s 102(1)(b)*). The GWR rules require (in the context of the donor's exclusion) that the gifted property is enjoyed:

- to the entire exclusion, or virtually to the entire exclusion, of the donor; and

- to the entire exclusion, or virtually to the entire exclusion, of any benefit to the donor by contract or otherwise.

Both limbs need to be complied with to prevent a possible GWR. It should be noted that a benefit obtained by the donor through 'associated operations' of which the gift is one is treated as a benefit to the donor 'by contract or otherwise' (*FA 1986, Sch 20, para 6(1)(c)*). See **4.23**.

In *Buzzoni and others v Revenue & Customs* [2013] EWCA Civ 1684, the Court allowed an appeal by the deceased's executor and others against the conclusions of the First-tier Tribunal and Upper Tribunal that the grant in 1997 of a future underlease to a trust (Legis) out of a headlease was a gift with reservation (within *FA 1986, s 102(1)(b)*). The decisions of the Tribunals had been on the basis that the underlease was not enjoyed to the entire exclusion, or virtually the entire exclusion, of a benefit to the donor (Mrs Kamhi) by reason of positive covenants in the underlease which mirrored the covenants in the headlease.

The Court had to consider whether the benefit Mrs Kamhi obtained from the positive covenants affected Legis' enjoyment of the flat, but concluded that it made no difference whatsoever to their enjoyment of the underlease. The obligations in the positive covenants did not detract from the enjoyment of the underlease because the obligations imposed by those covenants did not add to the obligations already imposed. Even if it could be said that Mrs Kamhi obtained a benefit she had not previously enjoyed, it was not obtained at the expense of the donees' enjoyment of the underlease.

In allowing the appeal, Moses LJ commented as follows:

> 'To persist in the possibly over-baked metaphor, the size of the cake remained unaffected, because the portion Mrs Kamhi is said to have eaten had already been consumed by the Head Landlord. She gifted a property, the enjoyment of which was already subject to obligations which mirrored the obligations contained in the positive covenants which are said to constitute her benefit. The imposition of duplicate obligations on that property merely mirrored but did not add to the obligations which the Underlease already bore under the Licence to Underlet.'

By contrast, in *Hood v Revenue & Customs* [2017] UKUT 0276 (UT), at her death Lady Hood (LH) was entitled to the head lease of a property in London dated 21 September 1979, which expired in December 2076. A sub-lease was granted in June 1997, by which the property was sub-let for a term of years commencing on 25 March 2012 and expiring on 22 December 2076. The sub-lease was subject to the same terms, covenants, provisos and conditions as were contained in the head lease. LH (as sub-lessor) and her three sons (as sub-lessees) respectively covenanted to perform and observe those provisions as if they had been repeated in full in the sub-lease. LH died in March 2008. HMRC considered that the creation of the sub-lease was a GWR, and LH's executor appealed against HMRC's determination.

The dispute concerned *FA 1986, s 102(1)(b)*, and particularly the second limb of that provision, which the First-tier Tribunal ([2016] UKFTT 59 (TC) expressed as: 'at any time in the relevant period the property is not enjoyed to the entire exclusion, or virtually to the entire exclusion, of any benefit to the donor by contract or otherwise'. The tribunal noted that, in contrast to the position in *Buzzoni*, the sub-lessees in the present case gave no direct covenants to the head lessor. The only positive covenants from the sub-lessees were those given in the sub-lease in favour of the sub-lessor (LH). Unlike the position in *Buzzoni*, the sub-lessees were under no obligation to the head lessor in respect of the covenants.

Furthermore, the tribunal did not accept that the circumstances of the present case were economically equivalent to those in *Buzzoni*. Nor did the tribunal accept that, as a matter of property law, the benefit of the sub-lessees' covenants formed part of LH's retained proprietary interest under the head lease, and not the donated property (ie such that LH was not enjoying any part of the donated property, and the case was thus outside *s 102(1)(b)*). The appellant's appeal was dismissed. The Upper Tribunal upheld the findings of the First-tier Tribunal, and dismissed the appellant's subsequent appeal.

The scope of the GWR rules was extended in 1999 and again in 2003, to counteract IHT avoidance arrangements designed to exploit loopholes in the GWR provisions in connection with interests in land and the spouse exemption. Those provisions are considered later in this chapter.

'Property' and 'gift'

7.6 To determine whether a gift is subject to the GWR rules, it is first necessary to ascertain the property given away.

For example, if Mr X gave his home to Miss Y (his daughter) in 1998, and Miss Y immediately decided to lease the house back to Mr X at a nominal rent, the 'property' would be the house, and the reserved benefit (subject to the GWR rules) would be the lease.

It was previously possible to make arrangements for gifts of an interest in land whilst continuing to enjoy a benefit from it. However, changes to the GWR rules were introduced (with effect from 9 March 1999) with the intention of blocking such arrangements (see **7.12**).

The GWR rules apply to 'gifts', which can include sales at undervalue. HMRC's view is that a sale for less than full value arising from a 'bad bargain' is not necessarily a gift with reservation. However, where the GWR provisions do apply to a sale at undervalue, they only apply in respect of the undervalue proportion (see IHTM14316 at Example 1).

It is arguably possible to reach the alternative conclusion that any element of undervalue is sufficient for the entire property to be 'caught' under the GWR rules. However, taxpayers and their advisers will no doubt wish to apply HMRC's more generous view.

Example 7.1—GWR: sales at undervalue

Henry sold his home to his daughter Daphne on 1 September 2004 for £10,000, when the value of the property was £100,000. Henry continued living at the house rent-free until his death on 15 June 2018, when the property had increased in value to £600,000.

Henry's sale of the property to Daphne at undervalue is a GWR. The value of the property disposed of by way of 'gift' was 90% of the value of the whole property. Therefore, 90% of its death value is treated for GWR purposes as property to which Henry was beneficially entitled, ie £600,000 × 90% = £540,000.

Effect of GWR rules

7.7 Without the GWR rules, if an individual could make a PET of property and survive at least seven years, the property would fall outside his estate and he could continue to enjoy or benefit from the gifted asset with impunity for IHT purposes.

The GWR rules therefore provide that if property subject to a reservation *would not otherwise* form part of the donor's estate immediately before his death, it will be treated as such (*FA 1986, s 102(3)*). The gift is deemed for IHT purposes to be property to which the individual was beneficially entitled immediately before his death, and is therefore ineffective to reduce the value of his IHT estate. However, this GWR treatment does not apply to excluded property (IHTM04072). See **7.33**, but see also **7.37** for a possible exception to excluded property status in relation to certain overseas assets whose value is attributable to UK residential property.

Following the introduction of extra (or 'residence') nil rate band where a home is passed on death to lineal descendants of the deceased from 6 April 2017 (see **16.55–16.77**), if the property has been given to a person but is treated as forming part of the deceased's estate by reason of the GWR rules (under *FA 1986, s 102(3)*), the recipient will have 'inherited' the property for the purposes of the residence nil rate band (*IHTA 1984, s 8J(6)*).

Example 7.2—'Caught' by GWR rules (1)

On 5 September 2010, Derek gave his house and its contents to his nephew Gerald, but continued to live in it with his wife Fiona, paying no rent. The house and contents were valued at £400,000 (after annual exemptions).

On 3 July 2018, Derek died leaving his estate of £400,000 by way of a specific legacy of £200,000 to Fiona, with residue to his niece Hannah. The value of the house at that time was £600,000.

The IHT position is as follows:

5 September 2010 – Gift

Derek's original gift of the house to Gerald is a PET. However, the property is subject to the GWR rules.

3 July 2018 – Death

Derek's gift of the house to Gerald on 5 September 2010 is a PET which has become exempt, because it was made more than seven years before Derek's death.

However, the GWR rules apply to treat the house as forming part of Derek's death estate. IHT is charged on the value of the house on death. The chargeable estate is therefore £800,000 (ie the house worth £600,000, plus his other chargeable estate of £200,000; the other £200,000 passing to his wife is exempt).

	£
Chargeable transfer	800,000
IHT thereon:	
£325,000 × nil	NIL
£475,000 × 40%	190,000
	190,000

As indicated above, if the property had been gifted to a lineal descendant, the residence nil rate band could be taken into account in calculating the IHT liability on the value of the house, upon a successful claim being made.

7.8 In the above example, the original gift of the property was a PET made more than seven years before Derek's death. Had the gift been a chargeable PET made within seven years before his death, a double IHT charge would arise (ie on the original gift, and on the property forming part of Derek's estate under the GWR rules).

Special rules therefore apply to prevent double taxation in such circumstances (*FA 1986, s 104*; *Inheritance Tax (Double Charges Relief) Regulations, SI 1987/1130*). The rules as they apply to a GWR are discussed at **7.38** below.

Example 7.3—'Caught' by GWR rules (2)

The facts are as in **Example 7.2**, except that the date of the GWR is 5 September 2015.

5 September 2015 – Gift

Derek's original gift of the house to Gerald (see previous example) is a PET. The property is subject to the GWR rules.

3 July 2018 – Death

Derek's gift of the house to Gerald on 5 September 2015 is a PET which becomes chargeable, because it was made within seven years of Derek's death. The house also forms part of Derek's death estate, so it is necessary to consider the double charges relief regulations.

Calculation (a) – Ignore PET and charge house in death estate

5 September 2015 – gift ignored: IHT = nil.

3 July 2018 – tax on chargeable death estate of £800,000 = £190,000 (see **Example 7.2**)

Calculation (b) – Charge PET and ignore house in death estate

5 September 2015 – Gift: IHT on £400,000:

	£
IHT thereon:	
£325,000 × nil	NIL
£75,000 × 40%	30,000
	30,000

3 July 2018 – tax on chargeable death estate of £200,000 (no nil rate band available):

£200,000 × 40% = £80,000

Total IHT (£30,000 + £80,000) = £110,000

Conclusion

A higher amount of IHT is payable on calculation (a) by charging the house as part of Derek's death estate. This amount (£190,000) is therefore charged, and the second IHT charge (£110,000) is reduced to nil (*SI 1987/1130, reg 5(3)*).

GWR and spouse exemption

7.9 As mentioned at **7.2** above, certain exempt transfers (eg to a spouse or civil partner) cannot generally be a GWR. However, legislation was introduced in *Finance Act 2003* (inserting *FA 1986, s 102(5A)–(5C)* into the GWR rules) to block '*Eversden* schemes' resulting from the Court of Appeal's decision in *IRC v Eversden (exors of Greenstock, decd)* [2003] EWCA Civ 668.

In that case, a married woman (W) settled a 5% interest in the family home she owned for herself absolutely. The other 95% was settled on an interest in possession trust to benefit her husband (H) for life, following which the trust fund would be held on discretionary trusts for a class of beneficiaries including W. They continued to occupy the property until H's death four years later. The property was sold a year later, and a replacement property was bought together with an investment bond. The interests held by W and the settlement remained unchanged. W died five years later. The Court of Appeal held that the original gift of the property was an exempt transfer between spouses under *IHTA 1984, s 18.*

The effect of the GWR rules (following *FA 2003*) is that the donor is treated as making a gift when the life interest of their spouse or civil partner terminates. This means that if the donor subsequently occupies or enjoys a benefit from the settled property, the gift is one to which the reservation of benefit rules apply. For example, the rules affect a husband making a gift to a trust under which his wife takes an initial interest in possession, which is subsequently terminated in favour of a discretionary trust in which the husband is a potential beneficiary.

However, following changes to the IHT treatment of interest in possession trusts introduced in *FA 2006*, these anti-avoidance rules are generally more likely to be relevant to interests in possession before 22 March 2006 (see **Chapter 9**).

Gifts of interests in land

7.10 As indicated at **7.6**, previously (ie prior to 9 March 1999) it was possible to make arrangements for gifts of an interest in land whilst continuing to enjoy a benefit from it.

Ingram schemes

7.11 A 'loophole' in the GWR rules at that time was highlighted in *Ingram and Another v IRC* [1998] UKHL 47.

In that case, Lady Ingram gifted to her children the freehold interest in a property, subject to a leasehold interest which she retained. The leasehold interest was created by the conveyance of the property to a nominee, followed by the grant of a lease to Lady Ingram for 20 years. The purpose was to enable

Lady Ingram to continue occupying the property by reason of the lease, without making a gift of the freehold subject to the GWR provisions.

The House of Lords held that Lady Ingram had made an effective gift of the freehold reversion, in which no benefit had been reserved. She had simply gifted one property interest in which she reserved no benefit, and retained (or 'carved out') another interest which entitled her to remain in residence. Lord Hoffmann described the position in the following terms;

> '... although [section 102] does not allow a donor to have his cake and eat it, there is nothing to stop him from carefully dividing up the cake, eating part and having the rest. If the benefits which the donor continues to enjoy are by virtue of property which was never comprised in the gift, he has not reserved any benefit out of the property of which he disposed ...'

Following the decision by the House of Lords in Lady Ingram's favour, changes to the GWR rules were quickly introduced by *FA 1999* with the intention of countering the effects of that decision (*FA 1986, ss 102A–102C*). The provisions apply to gifts of interests in land from 9 March 1999.

It should be noted that pre-9 March 1999 *Ingram* schemes considered effective for IHT purposes are generally subject to a pre-owned assets income tax charge (see **7.3**).

In addition, the general GWR provisions (*FA 1986, s 102(3), (4)*) discussed earlier are still capable of applying to 'straightforward' gifts of land (*s 102C(7)*).

The 'interests in land' rules

7.12 The GWR rules for gifts of interests in land (from 9 March 1999) provide that if the donor or spouse (or civil partner) enjoys a 'significant right or interest', or is 'party to a significant arrangement' in relation to the land during the 'relevant period' (as defined; see **7.5**), the gifted land interest is a GWR.

A right, interest or arrangement is 'significant' only if it entitles or enables the donor to occupy all or part of the land, or to enjoy some right in relation to all or part of it, otherwise than for full consideration in money or money's worth (*FA 1986, s 102A(2), (3)*).

Thus, no GWR arises if, for example, a donor gifts the freehold interest in a house to another individual (a PET) but retains, or is immediately granted, a lease at a full rent.

There are exceptions from the GWR rule if the right, interest or arrangement (as appropriate) is not 'significant', ie if:

- it does not and cannot prevent the enjoyment of the land to the entire exclusion, or virtually to the entire exclusion, of the donor (*FA 1986, s 102A(4)(a)*); or

- it does not entitle or enable the donor to occupy all or part of the land immediately after the disposal, but would do so but for the interest disposed of (*FA 1986, s 102A(4)(b)*);
- the right or interest was granted or acquired before the seven-year period ending with the date of the gift (*FA 1986, s 102A(5)*).

An example of the second exception above is where the donor gifts a 20-year rent-free leasehold interest and retains the freehold reversion, as those rights do not entitle or enable the donor to occupy the land immediately after the disposal, but would do so but for the interest disposed of.

The third exception above means that a *Lady Ingram* type scheme is not caught by *FA 1986, s 102A* as a 'significant right or interest' in those circumstances if there is a gap of at least seven years between the creation of the lease and the gift of the freehold reversion. However, note that this exception does not preclude a 'significant arrangement' in relation to the land from being a GWR.

Reversionary lease schemes

7.13 IHT avoidance arrangements involving reversionary leases in land originally came into being before 9 March 1999. The 'reversionary lease scheme' typically involves a donor granting a long lease for (say) 999 years to the proposed donee. The lease would not commence until a future date (ie normally beyond the donor's life expectancy, but less than 21 years to avoid problems under the *Law of Property Act 1925, s 149(3)*).

To fall within the GWR exception in *FA 1986, s 102A(5)* mentioned at **7.12**, a gap of at least seven years would need to be left between the date of purchase of the land and the date of the grant of the lease.

HMRC state (in the Inheritance Tax Manual at IHTM14360) that reversionary lease schemes entered into before 9 March 1999 avoid the GWR provisions provided that the lease contains no covenants of benefit to the donor (eg to keep the property in full repair). However, reversionary lease schemes were one of the targets of the 'pre-owned assets' income tax provisions covered in **Chapter 17**.

HMRC's guidance on pre-owned assets in the Inheritance Tax Manual confirms this approach (at IHTM44102):

> 'Where a reversionary lease scheme is established before 9 March 1999 … the arrangement succeeds in avoiding the reservation of benefit provisions so long as the lease does not contain any terms that are currently beneficial to the donor, such as covenants by the lessee to, say, maintain the property. Consequently, the donor will be subject to the POA charge under FA04/Sch15/Para3(2).'

With regard to reversionary lease schemes established on or after 9 March 1999, HMRC's guidance distinguishes between situations where the donor grants a reversionary lease more than seven years after acquiring the freehold interest, and where the reversionary lease is granted within that seven-year period:

> 'Where a reversionary lease scheme is established on or after 9 March 1999 it was originally considered that FA86/S102A … would apply because the donor's occupation would be a "significant right in relation to the land". If that were correct, the reservation of benefit rules would apply and there would be no POA charge.
>
> However, where the freehold interest was acquired more than 7 years before the gift … the continued occupation by the donor is not a significant right in view of FA86/S102A(5), so the reservation of benefit rules cannot apply and a POA charge arises instead.
>
> It follows that if the donor grants a reversionary lease within 7 years of acquiring the freehold interest, FA86/S102A may apply to the gift depending on how the remaining provisions of that section apply in relation to the circumstances of the case – for example, if the donor pays full consideration for the right to occupy or enjoy the land, that would not be a significant right in view of FA86/S102A(3), so the reservation of benefit rules cannot apply and a POA charge arises instead.'

Where the pre-owned assets provisions apply, it may nevertheless be possible to elect out of an income tax charge and into the GWR provisions instead.

The GWR provisions will apply in any event if the lease contains terms which are currently beneficial to the donor. However, the decision in *Buzzoni and others v Revenue & Customs* [2013] EWCA Civ 1684 should be noted. There was no reservation of benefit in that case, on the basis that the covenants given by the donee that benefited the donor did not adversely affect the donees' enjoyment of the gifted property.

By contrast, in *Hood v Revenue & Customs* [2017] UKUT 0276 (UT), the grant by an individual to her sons of a sub-lease of premises was held to be a GWR on the particular facts of that case (see **7.5**).

Share of interest in land

7.14 The GWR rules were extended in *FA 1999* to cover gifts of an undivided share of an interest in land (from 9 March 1999), such as where a sole freeholder gifts a half interest to another individual (*FA 1986, s 102B*). The share disposed of is a GWR, and the general GWR provisions in *FA 1986, s 102(3)* and *(4)* apply.

There are exceptions from this GWR rule if:

- the donor does not occupy the land (*FA 1986, s 102B(3)(a)*); or
- the donor occupies the land to the exclusion of the donee for full consideration in money or money's worth (eg a full market rent) (*FA 1986, s 102B(3)(b)*); or
- both donor and donee occupy the land, and the donor receives no (or negligible) benefit from the donee in connection with the gift (*FA 1986, s 102B(4)*).

Focus

- The first exception above means that, provided the donor does not occupy the land, there is no reservation of benefit even if the donor otherwise benefits from the gifted interest (eg the gift is of a share in an investment property).
- The third exception above means that if, for example, an individual gifts an interest in the property to his daughter who lives with him and shares the property outgoings, there is no GWR (*Note*: the daughter should not contribute in any way to the father's share of the household upkeep and running expenses. There is nothing to prevent the father continuing to pay all such costs of the property).
- There is also an exemption from the 'pre-owned assets' income tax charge in circumstances such as those described in the previous bullet point (*FA 2004, Sch 15, para 11(5)(c)*); see **Chapter 17**.
- If *FA 1986, s 102B* applies, the other GWR rules (*FA 1986, ss 102* and *102A*) do not (*FA 1986, s 102C(6)*).

Other points

7.15 Supplemental provisions (*FA 1986, s 102C*) linking the 'interests in land' rules with the general GWR rules provide that exempt gifts (listed at **7.25**) fall outside both *FA 1986, ss 102A* and *102B* (*s 102C(2)*).

In addition, the donor's occupation of land (or an arrangement which enables it) is expressly disregarded in applying *ss 102A* and *102B* if certain conditions are all satisfied (*FA 1986, s 102C(3)*, and *Sch 20, para 6(1)(b)*). See **7.31**.

As indicated above, the exception for exempt transfers to spouses or civil partners in *FA 1986, s 102(5)* is applied to the GWR land rules (*FA 1986, s 102C(2)*). However, the spouse exemption is limited in its application for GWR purposes (*FA 1986, s 102(5A)–(5C)*) (see **7.9**).

It should be noted that the provisions in *FA 1986, ss 102A–102C* apply to interests in land (including a share in land); they do not apply to chattels.

However, the general GWR provisions (*FA 1986, s 102, Sch 20*) are still relevant to chattels.

'Tracing' GWRs

7.16 There are complicated GWR rules dealing with situations whereby the donee does not retain the gifted property until the donor's death or until the benefit ends (eg the property is sold, exchanged or otherwise disposed of) (*FA 1986, Sch 20, paras 2–4*).

For GWR purposes, it is necessary to determine whether the original subject matter of the gift can be traced and substituted. These rules (ie 'substitutions and accretions') prevent what might otherwise be simple IHT avoidance.

For example, a mother may give Property A to her daughter, who exchanges it for Property B, and allows her mother to live there rent free. The tracing rules mean that the mother has reserved a benefit by occupying Property B.

7.17 The tracing rules do not apply to absolute gifts of cash (*FA 1986, Sch 20, para 2(2)(b)*).

However, HMRC consider that if individual A gives £250,000 cash to B, which B uses to purchase A's residence (worth £250,000), with A remaining in occupation rent free until his death, this may constitute a GWR of the residence, under the 'associated operations' rules in *IHTA 1984, s 268* (see **4.23**) (note HMRC's example 'Anna' at IHTM14372, which states that there 'may' be a GWR of the residence in such circumstances).

The scope of the associated operations rules was effectively diminished (albeit in a different context) by the Court of Appeal in *Rysaffe Trustee Co (CI) Ltd v IRC* [2003] EWCA Civ 356. Nevertheless, this remains a point that HMRC appear to take.

The GWR provisions only apply to the property originally given. Thus if, for example, individual C gives land to individual D, and individual D builds a house on that land, if the GWR rules are in point they apply only to the extent of the gifted land, though interesting valuation issues may arise where the development has increased the value of the subject matter of the gift.

If the donee gifts the relevant property to someone else, or voluntarily disposes of it for less than full consideration (other than back to the donor), the donee is generally treated as continuing to have possession and enjoyment of the property (*FA 1986, Sch 20, para 2(4), (5)*).

If the gifted property was shares or debentures, any bonus and rights issues are generally treated as comprised in the gift (*FA 1986, Sch 20, para 2(6), (7)*), subject to a deduction for consideration paid by the donee for the shares in valuing the property comprised in the gift (*FA 1986, Sch 20, para 3*).

If the donee predeceases the donor, or dies before the benefit ends, then unless the property is settled by will or intestacy (see **7.18**), the GWR tracing rules (in *FA 1986, Sch 20, paras 2, 3*) apply as if he had not died, and the actions of his personal representatives are treated as his own. Any property taken under the donee's will or intestacy is treated as a gift made by him on death (*FA 1986, Sch 20, para 4*).

Settled gifts and GWR

7.18 The GWR rules also potentially apply to settled property. However, a pre-18 March 1986 settlement is not subject to the rules (even if it would have been caught if made after 17 March 1986), unless further gifts into settlement are made after that date, in which case the GWR provisions will only apply to the property settled by those further gifts (IHTM14311).

If a donor makes a gift by way of settlement, the type of property is immaterial. The property comprised in the settlement needs to be considered instead. The normal 'tracing' rules (described at **7.16-7.17**) do not apply to a gift of settled property, although the GWR rules potentially apply instead to the settled property at the date of the donor's death (or when the GWR ceased), unless it is unrelated to the original gifted property (*FA 1986, Sch 20, para 5(1)*) (see **7.20**).

The donor should be excluded from being a beneficiary, in terms of avoiding a GWR (for example, see *Lyon's Personal Representatives v HMRC* ([2007] SSCD 675). Furthermore, if there is a settlement power to add beneficiaries, any argument by HMRC that the GWR rules apply can be avoided if the trustees are expressly prevented from adding the donor as a beneficiary.

In addition, it may be good practice to ensure that the trust deed is drafted so as to ensure that there is no possibility of the settled property reverting to the settlor by default, in terms of preventing any contention that the settlor can benefit under a resulting trust. Whilst HMRC (or the Inland Revenue, as was) previously indicated (in a letter dated 18 May 1987) that no reservation of benefit is considered to arise in such circumstances, there may be other issues to consider, such as whether any income tax implications arise.

Focus

- If the donor creates a discretionary settlement in which the donor's spouse or civil partner (but not the donor) is a potential beneficiary, this is not, of itself, a GWR.
- However, a trust distribution to the spouse or civil partner may be a GWR, if the donor can share in the benefit of that distribution (IHTM14393).

- The GWR rules can apply not only if the donor is a beneficiary of the settlement, but also if a gift is made into trust for others, to the extent that the donor's beneficial interest is not completely lost, or if the property can revert back to the donor.

Interests in possession and GWR

7.19 GWR rules dealing with the lifetime termination of interests in possession were introduced by *FA 2006* (*FA 1986, s 102ZA*). The rules apply to:

- pre-22 March 2006 interests in possession; or
- a post-21 March 2006 interest in possession which is an immediate post-death interest, disabled person's interest or a transitional serial interest (for further discussion, see **Chapter 9**).

The GWR rules apply to gifts, whereas the lifetime termination of an interest in possession is a transfer of value. The effect of these rules is that the lifetime termination of the interest is treated as a gift of the settled property (*FA 1986, s 102ZA(2)*). See **15.16–15.18**. If the individual retains use of the settled property after their interest in possession has ended, the property remains part of their estate under the GWR rules as if they owned it outright.

The lifetime creation of an interest in possession trust on or after 22 March 2006 is not normally a potentially exempt transfer (*IHTA 1984, s 3A(1A)*), with the trust entering the 'relevant property' regime as for discretionary trusts.

If the trust is settlor-interested, there is arguably no GWR on the value of the settled property upon the settlor's death under *FA 1986, s 102(3)*. This is on the basis that the settlor has given away the remainder interest in which no benefit is reserved, but there is no gift of the right to receive the income because the donor has always had it, ie there is no GWR but rather a 'carve-out' (*Trust Taxation and Estate Planning* 4th Edition by Emma Chamberlain and Chris Whitehouse (Sweet & Maxwell) at 39.32).

As to the tracing of property on the lifetime termination of an interest in possession (that constitutes a deemed disposal under *FA 1986, s 102ZA*) where the property continues to be settled immediately after the disposal (under *FA 1986, Sch 20, para 4A*), see **7.20**.

'Tracing' the settled GWR

7.20 There are also 'tracing' provisions under which the GWR rules may apply if the property subject to the deemed gift continues to be settled property immediately thereafter and is replaced by other assets; or if all or part of the settled property ceases to be settled while the reservation still exists; or if gifted property is not settled directly by the donor but subsequently becomes settled by the donee (*FA 1986, Sch 20, para 5(1)–(3)*).

In the latter case, the period between the original gift and settlement by the donee is subject to the normal tracing rules, but from the date of settlement by the donee, the tracing rules for settled property apply instead (see IHTM14403).

The tracing provisions can also apply to loans to the trustees, broadly where a donor has made a gift to the trust, and any property comprised in the settlement is derived (directly or indirectly) from a loan made by the donor to the trustees of the settlement. In such circumstances, the property deriving from the loan is treated for tracing purposes as derived from property originally comprised in the gift (*FA 1986, Sch 20, para 5(4)*). This provision relates to both interest-free and interest bearing loans, but does not apply to someone other than the donor (eg the donor's spouse) (IHTM14401).

In addition, accumulations of income arising before the reservation ceased (but not subsequently) are treated as derived from the settled property (*FA 1986, Sch 20, para 5(5)*).

Similar tracing provisions to those for settled gifts apply on the lifetime termination of an interest in possession to which *FA 1986, s 102ZA* applies (see **7.19**). If the property continues to be settled, the individual's deemed gift for GWR purposes is broadly the settled property at the 'material date' (as defined in *FA 1986, Sch 20, para 1(1)*), or property representing or derived from it. Furthermore, any property comprised in the settlement on the material date which is directly or indirectly derived from a loan by the individual to the settlement trustees is treated for these purposes as derived from the property comprised in the original gift. However, accumulated trust income arising after that time is not treated as derived from that settled property (*FA 1986, Sch 20, para 4A*).

Settlor as trustee and GWR

7.21 A trustee's duties are of a fiduciary nature (ie to safeguard the interests of the beneficiaries). Thus, as a matter of trust law, and for GWR purposes, there is normally no objection to the donor (or spouse or civil partner) being one of the trustees, as long as he acts in the interests of the beneficiaries and not himself.

In addition, HMRC accept that a donor can receive reasonable remuneration for his duties as a trustee without constituting a GWR (IHTM14394). This is despite the decision in *Oakes v Comr of Stamp Duties of New South Wales* [1954] AC 57, an Australian case in which it was held that remuneration paid to the settlor as trustee was a benefit.

If company shares are settled and the settlor is a trustee and also a paid director of that company, the gift does not, of itself, constitute a GWR. There is a possible GWR argument if the settlor settles shares onto a trust and *then* obtains a paid position as director or employee of the company. In that situation, the settlor should obtain no more than reasonable remuneration for the work done.

HMRC accept that the continuation of reasonable commercial remuneration arrangements entered into before the gift does not of itself constitute a reservation, provided that the benefits were in no way linked to or affected by the gift. However, a new remuneration package may be challenged as a GWR 'by contract or otherwise' if the gift was taken into account as part of the arrangements (IHTM14395).

Insurance policies

7.22 There are also GWR rules specifically in respect of insurance policies, which can apply if there is a gift relating to a policy of insurance on the life of the donor, their spouse or civil partner or on joint lives, where the resulting benefits to the donee vary according to benefits to the donor, spouse or civil partner.

If those GWR provisions apply, the property comprised in a gift relating to the insurance policy is treated as a reserved benefit for the donor (*FA 1986, Sch 20, para 7*).

Note that this rule can apply to policies from which the donor's spouse (or civil partner) can benefit. This is an exception to the general scope of the GWR provisions that a gift of property from which the donor's spouse (but not the donor) can benefit or enjoy is not necessarily property subject to a reservation in relation to the donor (although see also **7.12** as to the scope of *FA 1986, s 102A(2)* in relation to gifts of interests in land).

However, if a donor effects a whole life policy on his own life *in trust*, and the trustees' power of appointment over the trust fund can be exercised in favour of the donor's spouse (but not the donor), HMRC's position is that *FA 1986, Sch 20, para 7* does not apply (see Example 2 at IHTM14453). This is on the basis that the provision is only relevant if benefits can accrue to the donor or spouse under the policy itself, not where the spouse can only benefit under the trust (even though the trust assets include the insurance policy).

If an insurance policy is taken out, the date of gift is the date on which the insurance contract is taken out. Gifts made before 18 March 1986 are not subject to the GWR rules (*FA 1986, s 102(6)*). However, HMRC consider that if the policy is varied on or after that date, all premiums paid after 17 March 1986 (not just those paid after the variation) are generally subject to the GWR rules (IHTM14433).

Business and agricultural property

7.23 The availability of business property relief (BPR) or agricultural property relief (APR) (see **Chapter 13**) on gifts charged as a GWR depends on whether the property is qualifying business or agricultural property (eg land or buildings) or qualifying shares or securities in a company (*Note*: if the shares or securities subject to the GWR charge do not qualify for APR, they may qualify for BPR instead).

HMRC will consider whether the BPR or APR conditions were satisfied at the date of gift (and by reference to the donor's ownership history), and also when the GWR charge arises, ie on the death of the donor, or when the benefit ceases (IHTM25381, IHTM24201).

Subject to a deemed ownership rule for BPR purposes regarding the rate of relief on shares and securities (in *FA 1986, Sch 20, para 8(1A)(a)*; see below), the question whether BPR or APR is available (and, in the case of APR, at what rate) is determined on the basis that a notional transfer of value had been made by the donee (*FA 1986, Sch 20, para 8(1A)(b)*). As to the availability of APR for shares or securities in farming companies, see below.

For the purposes of establishing entitlement to BPR or APR on the transfer of value the donee is assumed to make (under *FA 1986, Sch 20, para 8(1A)(b)*) in terms of the minimum period of ownership requirement (*IHTA 1984, ss 106, 117*), ownership by the transferor before the gift is treated as ownership by the donee (*FA 1986, Sch 20, para 8(2)(a)*), and occupation by the transferor (ie before and after the gift) is treated as occupation by the donee (*FA 1986, Sch 20, para 8(2)(b)*).

For shares or securities in farming companies, if the GWR rules apply, the availability of APR is subject to separate requirements (*FA 1986, Sch 20, para 8(3)*). These are, broadly, that the shares or securities qualified for relief when the GWR was made, the donee has retained ownership of the shares between the dates of the gift and GWR charge, and the shares or securities qualify for relief on the basis of a notional transfer of value by the donee.

As indicated above, the conditions for APR (or BPR) in respect of shares or securities must be satisfied at the time of gift, and also when the GWR charge arises (*FA 1986, Sch 20, para 8(1A)(b)*). In addition, for controlling holdings of shares within *IHTA 1984, s 122(1)* ('Agricultural property of companies') the donee must retain ownership of the shares between the date of gift and the date of the GWR charge (*FA 1986, Sch 20, para 8(3)(b)*).

The availability of BPR on shares or securities is generally determined on the basis that they remained in the donor's ownership, ie as if the gift had never been made (*para 8(1A)(a)*). The normal requirement that the donee must retain the gifted property until the time of the GWR charge is subject to tracing provisions, as discussed above. However, if the gifted property is shares or securities constituting a control holding in a company with agricultural assets within *IHTA 1984, s 122(1)*, HMRC state that any substitute property will not qualify for APR (or BPR) due to the ownership requirement in *FA 1986, Sch 20, para 8(3)*. HMRC guidance to its officers instructs (at IHTM24206 and IHTM25384): 'advice should be taken on any case where it is claimed that agricultural or business relief should apply in respect of substituted property'.

If the donee dies prior to the GWR charge, the donee's personal representatives or beneficiaries (under a will or intestacy) of the GWR property are treated as the donee for the above purposes (*FA 1986, Sch 20, para 8(5)*).

EXCEPTIONS AND EXCLUSIONS FROM CHARGE

Gifts made before 18 March 1986

7.24 The GWR rules do not apply to gifts before 18 March 1986, even if there is a reservation of benefit thereafter.

For example, a pre-18 March 1986 discretionary trust which would have been caught by the GWR provisions had it been made after 17 March 1986 will escape the GWR charge, unless further gifts into trust are made after that date (in which case the GWR rules will apply to those later gifts).

Gifts which are exempt transfers

7.25 The GWR rules do not apply to certain exempt transfers (*FA 1986, s 102(5)*). The exemptions are listed below:

- transfers between spouses or civil partners (but see **7.26**) (*IHTA 1984, s 18*);
- small gifts (*IHTA 1984, s 20*);
- gifts in consideration of marriage or civil partnership (*IHTA 1984, s 22*);
- gifts to charities or registered clubs (*IHTA 1984, s 23*);
- gifts to political parties (*IHTA 1984, s 24*);
- gifts to registered housing associations or registered social landlords (from 14 March 1989) (*IHTA 1984, s 24A*);
- gifts for national purposes etc (*IHTA 1984, s 25*);
- maintenance funds for historic buildings, etc (*IHTA 1984, s 27*);
- employee trusts (*IHTA 1984, s 28*); and
- employee ownership trusts (*IHTA 1984, s 28A*).

7.26 Before changes to the GWR rules were introduced (*FA 1986, s 102(5A)–(5C)*), arrangements were possible to take advantage of the exception from the GWR provisions for exempt gifts between spouses. *Eversden* schemes (such as outlined at **7.9**) used the spouse exemption (*IHTA 1984, s 18*) to avoid a GWR on the gift of an asset to a trust. Such schemes were blocked by the above GWR changes (with effect for disposals from 20 June 2003), and pre-existing schemes are potentially subject to an income tax charge under the pre-owned assets regime (see **Chapter 17**).

Whilst the GWR rules do not necessarily apply to a gift (eg to a discretionary trust) in which a benefit is enjoyed by the donor's spouse or civil partner (ie as a potential beneficiary), if enjoyment of the gift is effectively shared by the donor (eg if distributions from the discretionary trust are paid into a joint bank account of the donor and spouse/civil partner), the GWR provisions will need to be considered.

In the context of joint money accounts (eg between mother and son), care is needed if the funds were provided by one of the parties. Otherwise, the whole of the funds may be treated as part of the donor's estate on death, either under *IHTA 1984, s 5(2)* or the GWR provisions (*Matthews v Revenue and Customs Commissioners* [2012] UKFTT 658 (TC); see **6.21**).

7.27 It should be noted that the following categories of exempt gift can fall within the GWR rules:

- PETs made more than seven years before the donor's death (*IHTA 1984, s 3A(4)*);
- the £3,000 annual exemption (*IHTA 1984, s 19(5)*); and
- the normal expenditure out of income exemption (*IHTA 1984, s 21(5)*).

For example, if there is a GWR and the reservation ceases with the gift becoming a PET, there can be no £3,000 exemption when the reservation ends, as *IHTA 1984, s 19(5)* effectively precludes the annual exemption from applying to the resulting deemed transfer (IHTM14343). This exclusion is perhaps logical in the sense that the gifted property actually passed to the donee at the time it was made, not when the reservation ceased.

De minimis exceptions

7.28

> **Focus**
>
> As indicated at **7.4**, one of the conditions to avoid a GWR is that the gifted property must be enjoyed by the donee to the entire exclusion, or virtually to the entire exclusion, of the donor (*FA 1986, s 102(1)(b)*).
>
> There is no definition of 'virtually' in the legislation. However, in HMRC's view, the expression 'virtually to the entire exclusion' covers cases in which the benefit to the donor is 'insignificant' in relation to the gifted property.

Examples of situations in which HMRC consider that the donor can benefit to some extent without the GWR rules applying are illustrated in *Revenue Interpretation 55*, and are reproduced below:

Table 7.1—GWR: *de minimis* exceptions (RI55)

- A house which becomes the donee's residence but where the donor subsequently:
  - stays, in the absence of the donee, for not more than two weeks each year; or
  - stays with the donee for less than one month each year.
- Social visits, excluding overnight stays made by a donor as a guest of the donee, to a house which he had given away. The extent of the social visits should be no greater than the visits which the donor might be expected to make to the donee's house in the absence of any gift by the donor.
- A temporary stay for some short-term purpose in a house the donor had previously given away, for example:
  - while the donor convalesces after medical treatment;
  - while the donor looks after a donee convalescing after medical treatment;
  - while the donor's own home is being redecorated.
- Visits to a house for domestic reasons, for example babysitting by the donor for the donee's children.
- A house together with a library of books which the donor visits fewer than five times in any year to consult or borrow a book.
- A motor car which the donee uses to give occasional (ie fewer than three times a month) lifts to the donor;
- Land which the donor uses to walk his dogs or for horse riding provided this does not restrict the donee's use of the land.

The above guidance warns taxpayers that if a benefit escalates into something more significant, the GWR provisions may apply (eg a house in which the donor then stays most weekends, or for a month or more each year).

Full consideration

7.29 If the donor gives full consideration in money or money's worth there should generally be no reservation in the case of land and chattels. The retention of a benefit by the donor is disregarded if the donor is in actual occupation or actual enjoyment and pays full consideration in money or money's worth (*FA 1986, Sch 20, para 6(1)(a)*), eg a 'commercial lease' pursuant to which the donor pays a full arm's-length rent for the lease or tenancy retained.

Full consideration is required throughout the period, and regular rent reviews should take place to ensure that this condition continues to be satisfied. HMRC accept that 'full' consideration falling within 'normal' valuation tolerances will be acceptable (*Revenue Interpretation 55*), although there is no statement of what is regarded as 'normal' in this context.

Note that the above GWR exception applies specifically to land and chattels. Care should be taken with other assets. HMRC's Inheritance Tax Manual (at IHTM14336) cites an example in which Alex, who is a partner, withdraws capital from his partnership capital account and gives it to Bella. Bella then lends the partnership an equivalent cash sum. HMRC consider that this is a GWR, and state that even though Alex may pay Bella a commercial rate of interest for the loan, this payment will not prevent the loan being a reservation (NB in the context of partnerships, see also *Chick v Commissioner of Stamp Duties of New South Wales* [1958] AC 435).

7.30

> **Focus**
>
> To reduce the possibility of a GWR challenge by HMRC, the 'full consideration' in relation to land or chattels should be negotiated at arm's length between parties with separate professional advisers in accordance with normal commercial criteria at the time.

HMRC guidance on 'full consideration' can also be found in *Revenue Interpretation 55* (see **7.28**), and specific examples are included in the Inheritance Tax Manual (at IHTM14341).

There is a similar full consideration let-out from the pre-owned assets income tax charge (see **Chapter 17**) in relation to land and chattels (ie where the consideration is paid under a legal obligation), but not intangible property (*FA 2004, Sch 15, paras 4(1), 7(1)*).

The donor's occupation of gifted land is not a GWR if it represents reasonable provision for an infirm relative, if certain conditions are all satisfied (*FA 1986, Sch 20, para 6(1)(b)*) (see **7.15** and **7.31**). There is also an exemption from a pre-owned assets income tax charge in those circumstances (*FA 2004, Sch 15, para 11(5)(d)*).

Provision for old age and infirmity

7.31 As indicated at **7.15**, the donor's occupation of *land* is expressly disregarded if the following conditions are all satisfied (*FA 1986, s 102C(3)*, and *Sch 20, para 6(1)(b)*):

- it results from unforeseen changes in circumstances of the donor since the gift (eg a sudden serious illness, but not merely getting old); *and*
- the donor has become unable to maintain himself through old age, infirmity, etc; *and*
- it represents a reasonable provision by the donee for the donor's care and maintenance; *and*
- the donee is a relative of the donor or his spouse (or civil partner).

It should be noted that the above conditions are cumulative, and therefore potentially onerous.

In addition, it may be difficult in practice to determine what constitutes a 'reasonable' provision by the donee for the donor's care and maintenance; this will depend on the particular facts of the case.

Instruments of variation

7.32 The GWR rules cannot apply to a disposition which is subject to a variation by the beneficiary (ie within *IHTA 1984, s 142*).

The variation is treated for IHT purposes as having been made by the deceased person whose estate is the subject of the variation, not the persons entitled under his will.

Example 7.4—GWR exception: deed of variation

Mr Baker died on 2 January 2017, leaving property under his will to Mrs Baker.

On 1 June 2018 (ie within two years), Mrs Baker varied her late husband's will (ie by an instrument of variation within *IHTA 1984, s 142*), so that the property became settled on a discretionary trust for Mrs Baker and her adult children.

The discretionary trust is treated for IHT purposes as having been made by the deceased, Mr Baker. Therefore, the GWR rules cannot bite.

The government announced at summer Budget 2015 that it intended reviewing the use of DOVs for tax purposes, due to concerns that the tax rules are being abused. Following that review, the government stated that it would not be introducing new restrictions on how DOVs can be used for tax purposes. However, the government also pointed out that it would continue to monitor the use of DOVs for such purposes, and therefore future changes cannot be ruled out.

Non-UK assets of non-UK domiciliary

7.33 The 'excluded property' of a non-UK domiciled person (see **1.13**) is generally not subject to the GWR rules (NB: see **7.37** below for an exception to excluded property status in relation to UK residential property interests held indirectly, such as by an offshore company).

Example 7.5—GWR exception: excluded property

James was born and domiciled in New Zealand. In 2009, he gave away a commercial property portfolio in Wellington to his daughter Mary. The rental income was shared equally between them. James died in 2018, still domiciled in New Zealand.

The gifted property was subject to a reservation at James' death. However, it was situated outside the UK, and James remained domiciled outside the UK throughout. The property is therefore excluded property (*IHTA 1984, s 6(1)*), and the GWR charging provisions do not apply.

However, HMRC's view (see IHTM14318, at Example 3) appears to be that if the donor makes a gift subject to a reservation and subsequently becomes UK domiciled, there may be a GWR claim on death; or alternatively if the reservation ceased in the donor's lifetime, a deemed PET may be treated as being made. This is on the basis that the donor is domiciled in the UK when the GWR charge arises, and that the excluded property rule in *IHTA 1984, s 6(1)* does not then apply.

As to domicile generally, see **Chapter 2**.

It should be noted that the scope of deemed domicile for IHT purposes was extended (by *IHTA 1984, s 267(1)(aa)*) to include a 'formerly domiciled resident' in relation to times from 6 April 2017 (see **2.13**).

7.34 A popular IHT planning point has been that if a non-UK domiciliary held assets abroad, those assets could be gifted into trust if there was any possibility of the individual becoming actually or deemed domiciled in the UK (eg settling non-UK situs assets on discretionary trust with the settlor as a possible beneficiary), in order to continue benefiting from excluded property status. It was commonly thought that the GWR rules could not apply, because the excluded property rules prevailed. HMRC's guidance in the Inheritance Tax Manual created uncertainty on this issue for some time.

However, HMRC's guidance (at IHTM14396) was subsequently amended, and now states the following:

> 'Where the settlor was domiciled outside the UK at the time a settlement was made, any foreign property within that settlement is excluded property and is not brought into charge for inheritance tax purposes.
>
> This rule applies where property is subject to a reservation of benefit even though the settlor may have acquired a domicile of choice in the UK, or be deemed to be domiciled in the UK, at the time the GWR charge arises.'

7.35 The rationale for HMRC's approach in the above circumstances is that the property is comprised in a settlement when the GWR charge arises. If property comprised in a settlement is situated outside the UK, it will generally be excluded property if the settlor was not domiciled in the UK when the settlement was made (*IHTA 1984, s 48(3)(a)*).

However, this general rule is subject to certain exceptions, one of which is that (in relation to times after 5 April 2017) the property is not excluded property (by virtue of *IHTA 1984, s 48(3)* or *(3A)*) at any time in a tax year if the settlor was a 'formerly domiciled resident' (see **2.13**) for that tax year (*IHTA 1984, s 48(3E)*).

The HMRC guidance goes on to provide the following example:

> '*Example*
>
> Henry, who is domiciled in New Zealand, puts foreign property into a discretionary trust under which he is a potential beneficiary. He dies five years later having acquired a domicile of choice in the UK and without having released the reservation. The property is subject to a reservation on death but it remains excluded property and is outside the IHT charge.'

However, if the trustees in the above example had sold the foreign property and invested the proceeds in UK situs assets (eg office buildings), the property comprised in the trust on Henry's death would no longer be situated outside the UK, and the excluded property treatment in *s 48(3)* would not then apply.

If the individual becomes domiciled in the UK and adds property to the settlement, HMRC will regard the donor as creating a separate settlement. Thus the foreign assets settled when the donor was non-UK domiciled continue to be excluded property (subject to the above exception if the settlor is a formerly domiciled resident), but all assets (UK and foreign) settled when the donor was domiciled in the UK will be subject to IHT under the GWR provisions.

7.36 If gifted assets are subject to a reservation which is subsequently ended during lifetime, the donor is treated as making a PET at that time (*FA 1986, s 102(4)*).

HMRC's view (at IHTM14396) is that no account is taken of excluded property which ceases to form part of the person's estate as the result of a disposition (*IHTA 1984, s 3(2)*), and therefore provided the assets were still excluded property when the deemed PET was made, they are excluded from an IHT charge. This is subject to exceptions, such as if the foreign assets had been replaced by UK situs property.

The GWR provisions are anti-avoidance rules. It should be noted that other anti-avoidance rules may treat excluded settled property as forming part of an individual's estate. An anti-avoidance provision was introduced in *Finance Act 2006* to counteract 'deathbed' IHT planning. This planning broadly involved an individual purchasing an interest in a pre-existing settlement created by a non-UK domiciled individual. Prior to 5 December 2005, a purchased interest in settled property was not precluded from being excluded property. However, the effect of the anti-avoidance rule is broadly that the exemption in *IHTA 1984, s 48(3)* is removed if a UK-domiciled individual's beneficial interest in excluded trust property has been purchased on or after the above date (*IHTA 1984, s 48(3B)–(3C)*).

Further anti-avoidance provisions (subsequently added by *Finance Act 2012*) affect certain arrangements in respect of settled excluded property (from 20 June 2012). The provisions are broadly aimed at avoidance schemes involving a UK-domiciled individual acquiring an interest in relevant settled property that would otherwise be excluded property, where there is a 'relevant reduction' in the value of the individual's estate. The scope of the legislation includes arrangements where a UK corporate settlor has settled assets as part of an avoidance scheme, and where individuals retain the interests in settled property they have acquired. The effect of the provisions is broadly that the relevant settled property is no longer treated as excluded property, ie it is treated like a UK trust (*IHTA 1984, s 48(3D)*). Furthermore, the reduction in value of the individual's estate falls to be charged to IHT as if a transfer of value had been made directly to a relevant property trust (*IHTA 1984, ss 74A–74C*).

7.37 Provisions were introduced (in *Finance (No 2) Act 2017*) to ensure that, from 6 April 2017, IHT is chargeable on UK residential property owned directly or indirectly by non-UK domiciliaries. The measures (in *IHTA 1984, Sch A1*) are aimed at blocking the holding of such property indirectly through offshore structures (or what HMRC has described as 'enveloping').

For example, the above measures broadly provide that an interest in a close company is not excluded property to the extent that the value of the interest is directly or indirectly attributable to a UK residential property interest. However, an interest in a close company is disregarded for these purposes if the value of the interest (also including the value of any connected person's interest) is less than 5% of the total value of all the interests in the close company A similar exclusion from excluded property status relates to interests in partnerships.

A further exception from excluded property status applies in respect of 'relevant loans' (as well as security, collateral or guarantees for such loans). There are also exceptions for certain disposals and repayments in respect of property within the above categories (see **1.18**).

The GWR provisions will need to be considered in some instances, such as if a non-UK domiciled individual has retained a benefit in UK residential property gifted to an offshore company. Similarly, if (for example) shares in an offshore company owning UK residential property are held by a discretionary trust, the GWR provisions may be in point in respect of the shares on the non-UK domiciled settlor's death, unless he was excluded from any benefit (NB: see **7.1** where a reservation is ended during an individual's lifetime).

GWR AND DOUBLE IHT RELIEF

7.38 As indicated at **7.2** above, the GWR rules give rise to the possibility of a double IHT charge in respect of the same property. However, there are provisions (*FA 1986, s 104*; the *Inheritance Tax (Double Charges Relief) Regulations, SI 1987/1130*) which provide for relief in those circumstances.

The regulations provide for the avoidance of a double IHT charge in the following circumstances involving a GWR (*SI 1987/1130, reg 5*):

- an individual makes a gift caught by the GWR rules (which may be a PET or a chargeable lifetime transfer) and the property is (by reason of the GWR rules) also subject to a deemed transfer which is chargeable as a result of the transferor's death; or
- facts as above, except that the donor's benefit ends before death (ie a deemed PET under the GWR rules), which becomes chargeable on the donor's death within seven years.

In both cases, two calculations are performed as a consequence of the death:

- charging the GWR in the death estate, and ignoring the lifetime transfer (*SI 1987/1130, reg 5(3)(a)*); or
- charging the lifetime transfer and ignoring the GWR (*SI 1987/1130, reg 5(3)(b)*).

7.39 Whichever transfer produces the higher amount of tax remains chargeable. However, provision is made for credit to be given for any lifetime tax already paid (*SI 1987/1130, reg 5(4)*). See the example (**Example 7.3**) at **7.8**. In addition, the regulations include a schedule with worked examples of the double IHT relief rules as they apply to GWRs, although the examples do not prevail over the rules as stated in the regulations (*SI 1987/1130, reg 9*).

It should be noted that (as indicated at **7.3**), the 'pre-owned assets' income tax legislation (see **Chapter 17**) also provides a measure of relief from IHT in certain very specific circumstances, where the taxpayer elects for those provisions not to apply and if two IHT charges otherwise arise on the same underlying asset value (*Charge to Income Tax by Reference to Enjoyment of Property Previously Owned Regulations, SI 2005/724, reg 6*). The double charges relief provisions effectively retain the charge on the transfer that produces the higher overall amount of IHT, and reduce the other transfer to nil.

Further provisions (*Inheritance Tax (Double Charges) Regulations, SI 2005/3441, reg 4*) were designed to deal with the double IHT charges that may arise for taxpayers who decide to dismantle a 'double trust' arrangement and return to the position they were in previously. Once again, IHT is charged on the transfer producing the greater amount of tax, with the other transfer being reduced to nil. The introduction of the residence nil-rate band (see **16.55–16.77**) provides an additional incentive for some people to 'unravel' these schemes in some cases, but it is worth noting that unravelling is not always easy and involves a consideration of relevant tax and trust issues based on the particular circumstances. HMRC guidance on the unwinding of home loan or double trust schemes is included in the Inheritance Tax Manual at IHTM44120-IHTM44128.

GWR AND 'SHEARING' ARRANGEMENTS

7.40 There is always a fine line to be drawn between 'shearing' (or 'carving out') and GWR. At its simplest, shearing has been described thus: if Mr A owns three assets and gives two of them away, he does not reserve a benefit out of the third; he simply does not give it away.

Focus

In the context of more subtle arrangements, it has been suggested that it may be possible to separate capital from income, such as by a settlement in which the settlor retains a right to income but excludes himself from the possibility of benefiting from the capital.

Some commentators have suggested that such a trust might hold an interest in commercially let property, with the settlor retaining an interest by receiving the income stream.

HMRC may consider this to be fairly aggressive tax planning: the draftsman should issue the client with a suitable 'health warning'. Note that the section in HMRC's guidance concerning 'carve-out arrangements' (at IHTM14314) in relation to commercial property has been withheld from public access under the Freedom of Information Act 2000.

Chapter 8

Compliance

SIGNPOSTS

- **IHT: Interest** – Amendments have been made to the IHT late payment interest provisions, to complement future changes in secondary legislation to support the digitisation of IHT and the introduction of an online IHT service (see **8.2**).
- **Accounts and returns** – IHT100 and its supplementary forms reporting lifetime gifts need to be filed in certain circumstances (see **8.4–8.9**).
- **Accounts and returns** – IHT400 and its supplementary forms report transfers on death (see **8.10–8.15**).
- **Excepted estates** – In certain circumstances the completion of Forms IHT100 and IHT400 can be dispensed with (see **8.16–8.20**).
- **Payment of IHT** – Due dates and instalment options explained (see **8.25–8.36**).
- **Penalties** – An explanation of HMRC's new tougher approach to penalties and the potential pitfalls for advisers (see **8.38–8.54**).
- **Determinations and appeals** – An outline of 'what to do' if a dispute with HMRC arises (see **8.56–8.67**).

LIABILITY AND INCIDENCE OF TAX

8.1 The difference between 'liability' and 'incidence' is similar to the difference between legal and equitable interests. Liability is the duty to pay the tax from the assets that lie to hand and it concerns the relationship between HMRC and the accounting party. Incidence is the allocation of the burden of that tax between beneficiaries; thus an executor or trustee will be concerned with the rules as to incidence when administering an estate where, for example, the residue passes partly to non-exempt persons and partly to charity. In that situation the executor is liable for the tax but must apply the rules of incidence to ensure that, subject to the terms of the will and to the rules in *Re Benham's*

Will Trust [1995] STC 210 and *Re Ratcliffe* [1999] STC 262, the tax is actually suffered by the non-exempt persons. For analysis of these decisions, see **5.40–5.41**. *Finance Act 2006* has thrown up some anomalies in this area and reference should be made to 'A sting in the tail' at **9.42**.

ACCOUNTS AND RETURNS

The forms

8.2 The main control documents are:

- IHT100, the account for the lifetime transfer of value; and
- IHT400 (which replaced IHT200) the HMRC Account for IHT at death.

These are supplemented by administrative forms that apply in situations, especially on death, where an estate is of substantial size but where no tax is in fact chargeable (and the estate does not fall with any of the exempt estate categories). The forms are updated regularly and there have been several changes in the last few years alone, so it is important always to use the most recent version which can be downloaded from the HMRC website at www.hmrc.gov.uk.

> **Focus**
>
> To use the website forms to best advantage, practitioners should give serious thought to the purchase of editing software. Alternatively there is now a range of bespoke software developed by commercial providers.

The IHT400 series takes account of common practices such as the gift of personal possessions/chattels to charity, which is dealt with in form IHT408 – this is actually a 'one-off' variation of the dispositions of the estate and as such should be read in conjunction with any other variation contemplated by the personal representatives. Extra information, which was hitherto set out in a supplemental sheet, may now be entered at pages 15 and 16 of form IHT400.

The schedules, to include the main control document IHT400, are regularly amended and in February/March 2016 minor adjustments were made specifically to forms IHT 403, 408 and 421. Current versions of the full suite of forms are available from the HMRC website.

It should be noted that HMRC have identified an increasing number of errors made in completing form IHT403 where reliance is placed on securing the gifts out of income exemption. HMRC have stated that where the exemption is being claimed:

- full details of the gift must be included;

- full details of the deceased's income and expenditure during the period the gifts were made must be included on the form or be supplied by separate attached schedule; and
- relevant documents should be sent in support of the information stated on the form.

HMRC have made it clear that they will and do pursue tax geared penalties for careless errors (or more serious misdemeanours) in the event of any loss of tax.

The current Form IHT407, formerly IHT409 'Household and personal goods', is more user friendly than its predecessor but its proper completion will be much more demanding than most families will expect or enjoy.

Form IHT409, Private and occupational pensions on death, now asks more pertinent questions particularly concerning binding nominations that oblige pension scheme trustees to make a payment to a nominee where trustee discretion may be effectively overridden.

HMRC have issued two new forms IHT435 and IHT437 to the IHT400 series, which deal with the residence nil rate band (RNRB) and the transferable residence nil rate band (TRNRB) to the IHT 400 series. Updated HMRC guidance is also available at IHTM 46001 et seq and the IHT gross-up calculator has also been amended to reflect the impact of the RNRB.

The useful DX facility previously available was withdrawn on 1 April 2016. However, the government commitment to a 'digital strategy' to improve the process of interaction between HMRC and their 'customers' and HMRC's administration of taxes generally, including IHT continues to be rolled out. The service is now available for use by personal representatives, trustees, agents and other persons who are liable to IHT and/or who need probate to administer an estate and from 6 March 2017 the service was extended to simple estates (those subject to the less onerous IHT205 return completion). HMRC have commenced to carry out their previously announced intention to verify the source identity of the online IHT filer by sending an access code to their mobile phone and have also added the following safeguards requiring the filer to also:

- enter a User ID and password as noted on the Government Gateway service;
- on first registration only, answer a series of identity verification questions.

Having registered for electronic filing, any request to withdraw consent for HMRC to communicate via electronic means must be made in writing.

Prior to 2 November 2015 any person delivering the online account had to declare that the information was correct and complete to the best of their knowledge and belief. As a result of adverse comments from the professional bodies, HMRC issued revised directions effective from 2 November 2016 which make it clear that where an agent is submitting electronic IHT information on behalf of the client, the agent is confirming that the client, not the agent, has approved the information of a return– the relevant wording on the submission document has been amended to this effect.

To support the introduction of the IHT online service, various legislative changes were necessary in the primary and secondary IHT legislation to facilitate online processes and align the treatment of interest and penalties for IHT purposes with other taxes. As part of the above changes, amendments to the legislation concerning late payment interest were included in the *Finance (No 2) Act 2015*, to come into force from a date to be specified in regulations. In particular, the changes extend the power to make regulations (under *FA 1986, s 107(4)* and *(5)*) to the late payment interest provisions where IHT is payable by instalments in *FA 2009, Sch 53* (*para 7(7)* and *(8)*) and update the provisions relating to financial institutions and companies. The changes will enable regulations to be made so that the late payment interest provisions in *FA 2009, Sch 53* relating to IHT instalment payments can be updated.

In addition, the period from which late payment interest is charged (in *FA 2009, Sch 53, para 9*) on amounts payable under *IHTA 1984, s 147* (Scotland: legitim, etc) in sub-para (4) is corrected by the changes, so that it refers to the end of the month in which the testator died (as opposed to the date of the testator's death). This amendment aligns the date with the late payment interest provisions in *IHTA 1984, s 233(1)(b)*. Other legislative changes are expected to be made by later regulations and appointed day orders to support the digitisation of IHT, with a view to ensuring that the relevant late payment interest provisions are updated and apply correctly to the online service.

It is important that the duty of notification on creation of offshore trusts stipulated by *IHTA 1984, s 218* should not be overlooked. Those concerned with the creation of such trusts, with the exception of barristers, must inform HMRC within three months. There is no prescribed format and such notifications can be made by way of simple letter.

Introduced in October 2017, the digital IHT service has been extended to replace the (paper) IHT205 application process for a grant of probate in England and Wales. HMRC consider that the new service:

- is quicker and easier to follow than the paper IHT205 form;
- only displays questions that are relevant;
- indicates what information needs to be provided to the probate office; and
- has online help and guidance to assist in completing the details and helpful links to supporting information.

Those eligible to use the service include:

- the personal representative of the person who has died (for example, the executor);

- those applying for a grant of representation (for example, probate) in England and Wales; and
- those for whom no IHT is payable.

The service is not available to a professional agent.

Compliance

8.3 Legislation was introduced in *Finance Act 2008, Pt 7* ('Administration') and *Schedules 36, 37, 39* and *40* (dealing with inspection powers, record keeping, time limits for assessments, claims etc and amendments to the rules on penalties for errors etc). *Finance Act 2009, s 96* and *Sch 48 (Appointed Day, Savings and Consequential Amendments) Order 2009 SI 2009/3054,* applicable from 1 April 2010, extended the rules as to information and inspection powers to IHT: see CH20150 and for a useful summary of commencement dates, follow the links there set out.

The general scope of the legislation is to amend the rules on record keeping and the information and inspection powers. The general thrust of the more readily seen compliance checks is to reassure the majority who do comply that the system is fair and to ensure that taxpayers know what their obligations are in relation to registration for tax.

Taxpayers should understand what records are needed in order to calculate the tax due and, in the context of the administration of estates, the preparation of proper executorship accounts must come high on the list. The checks are also intended to clarify where people are unsure of the law, to eradicate weaknesses in the systems and processes which are used by taxpayers, correct mistakes and discourage people from non-compliance.

The checks also operate to expose the deliberate understatement of tax and that approach is driven by what HMRC perceive to be the risk involved. As for example with valuation of chattels, the risk may only involve a small amount of tax each time, but errors may be widespread. Alternatively, there may be segmental risk where, for example, taxpayers in a particular category or holding a particular type of asset may exhibit behaviour leading to risk which can be addressed through work with representative bodies or trade organisations.

The new basis includes the following features:

- flexibility according to the way taxpayers behave;
- going easy on the compliant majority;
- cracking down on the minority who deliberately understate their tax;
- greater clarity and consistency across the various taxes;
- clear definitions of HMRC powers and safeguards against inappropriate use.

To some extent, none of this is really new but rather it underpins HMRC's approach. For example, HMRC were able to use existing legislation very effectively against the taxpayer in *Smith v HMRC* [2008] SpC 680, where the Inspector examined private bank accounts to trace credit card expenditure of £47,500 and other unexplained transfers of £410,000 from companies controlled by the taxpayer. He extrapolated backwards into (more than six) earlier years to estimate the full level of under-disclosure of tax.

In *Sokoya v HMRC* [2008] ChD STC 3332, the taxpayer complained unsuccessfully against the decision of the Special Commissioner to allow an HMRC request for certain documents to check 'nil' entries in his return. The burden of proof to be satisfied by HMRC is not that of the criminal courts: see *HMRC v Khawaja* [2008] ChD STC 2880. The HMRC Inspector need not be clairvoyant, so the inclusion of a round sum as a loss is not sufficient notice that the taxpayer has been using a tax scheme to create an artificial loss, such that time runs against HMRC in discovering it: *Corbally-Stourton v Revenue and Customs Commissioners* [2008] STC (SCD) 907 (SpC 692).

Note, however, that the First-tier Tribunal can take a refreshingly robust and practical line, as it did in *Cairns v Revenue & Customs* [2009] TC00008, an investigation into the estate of a former Chief Examiner within the Estate Duty Office. The deceased's house was in extremely poor condition and had been valued shortly before death at approx £400,000. The personal representative adopted that figure in the IHT account (form IHT200, as it then was), not considering it necessary to revalue since on sale the price achieved would very likely be substituted. Following a sale for £600,000, which was then agreed to be the value at date of death, HMRC pressed for penalties for delivery of an incorrect account. Fraud was not alleged but instead HMRC alleged negligence on the basis that the personal representative should have obtained a proper date of death valuation.

Not so, held the Tribunal which found that the account was not negligently delivered. The value specified should have been shown as provisional but that was a mere technical error which had no consequence whatsoever. There was no loss to the public purse because in fact IHT had been overpaid and was later repaid. Any finding of negligence would have been the merest technicality and a proportionate approach would have been a nominal penalty.

A detailed consideration of the legislation, which appears at *Finance Act 2008, ss 113, 115-117* and *Schs 36–37* is beyond the scope of this book, but is included in Chapter 1 of *Capital Gains Tax 2018/19* (Bloomsbury Professional). In practical terms, help has been rolled out to practitioners by HMRC in the form of 'checklists' for various taxes.

HMRC have published an 'Inheritance Tax Toolkit', which it is stated is aimed at 'helping and supporting tax agents and advisers in completing Inheritance Tax account form IHT400, although it may be of use to anyone, including trustees and personal representatives, in completing this form'.

The Toolkit, updated as at 4 August 2017, is quite simply an aide memoire and thus does not need to be used in order to demonstrate that 'reasonable care' has been taken, if the matter of penalties arises due to an error in the IHT400 account. However, HMRC's website states that use of the Toolkit '... can also be used to help demonstrate that "reasonable care" has been taken' (www.hmrc.gov.uk/agents/toolkits-background.htm).

HMRC announced changes to their compliance checks in their December 2013 Trust and Estates Newsletter. If a case has been selected for a compliance check, an initial letter will be sent to the practitioner explaining that a case has been so selected. HMRC stated that they will aim to complete the check within eight to ten weeks of receipt of the IHT account. The investigator will make contact with the practitioner by phone, with the aim to agree a case plan to resolve the matter more quickly. Sadly, in practice such suggested timeframes are not always met in such a timely way.

Finance Act 2014 contains legislation which imposes up-front penalties on taxpayers who have used marketed tax avoidance schemes that are under open investigation or litigation. Taxpayers who have used an avoidance scheme similar to one that a court has already overruled will have to pay the amount HMRC say they owe. Taxpayers who continue the dispute will incur penalties, unless they ultimately win their case. The accelerated payment scheme applies to tax in dispute under arrangements which fall within the Disclosure of Tax Avoidance Scheme (DOTAS) rules and cases challenged by the new General Anti-Abuse Rule (GAAR).

Lifetime transfers

8.4 The requirement as to when to deliver an account of a lifetime transfer is not sufficiently well known, and although HMRC have issued reminders of the rules from time to time (see **4.28**) there is still far too much confusion and misunderstanding. To be clear, no account is needed for a PET at the time when made (irrespective of its monetary value) but there may be a requirement to later report a PET (which is re-categorised as a lifetime chargeable transfer) which fails by reason of the donor's death within seven years.

Where the transfer is immediately chargeable and not otherwise exempt from reporting under the rules described below, the account is to be delivered by the transferor. If he does not pay the IHT by the due date, other persons (to include the donees, trustees and beneficiaries under settlements) become liable for that IHT payment though they do not have to deliver the account themselves. In those rare cases where a close company makes a transfer of value, IHT is calculated as if the participators in the company had made the transfer; nonetheless the company is liable for IHT thereon but it has no requirement to deliver an account: see *IHTA 1984, ss 94* and *202* and the commentary at **1.27** (all subsequent statutory references are to *IHTA 1984*, unless otherwise stated).

Finance Act 2006 greatly increased the number of transactions that now fall to be chargeable transfers, even though in a great many cases, the availability of exemptions, reliefs (ie APR/BPR) and the unused nil rate band often result in no immediate tax exposure. As a consequence the reporting requirement was revised and relaxed by the *Inheritance Tax (Delivery of Accounts) (Excepted Transfers and Excepted Terminations) Regulations 2008, SI 2008/605* and the *Inheritance Tax (Delivery of Accounts) (Excepted Settlements) Regulations 2008, SI 2008/606*. These regulations, which came into force on 6 April 2008, apply in the case of the former with regard to chargeable events occurring on or after 6 April 2008 and in the latter with regard to chargeable events occurring on or after 6 April 2007. These are discussed in more detail below.

The changes caught many taxpayers out but not (see *Marquess of Linlithgow and Earl of Hopetoun v HMRC* [2010] CSIH 19) those who acted promptly (or with prescience). That case turned on the effective date of a transfer of land under Scots law. Two documents detailing dispositions to an accumulation and maintenance trust, were executed on 15 March 2006, so just days before the changes; but they were not recorded in the Register of Sasines until October and November of that year. An attempt by HMRC to treat the transfers of value as chargeable failed. Following the estate duty case of *Thomas v Lord Advocate* [1953] SC 151, the date of transfer was that of the disposition, not registration.

Excepted transfers and terminations

8.5 The regulations as to excepted transfers and excepted terminations remove the obligation to deliver an account for those transactions covered by the regulations unless HMRC has served a notice requiring one. However, there is a duty:

- in a trust scenario, on trustees to file an account in respect of failed PETs; and
- in a trust scenario, on trustees and others to file an account on the termination of a settlement which would have been a PET, but fails under the seven-year rule; and
- on other lifetime gifting, to file a return where the parties thought that the transfer was excepted within the new rules and it turned out not to be.

Excepted transfers

8.6 An excepted transfer under the *Inheritance Tax (Delivery of Accounts) (Excepted Transfers and Excepted Terminations) Regulations 2008, SI 2008/605* must be one made by an individual and must be an actual transfer, not a deemed transfer as defined for IHT purposes. There are two categories.

(a) Fixed-value transfers

Where the transfer is either cash or quoted shares or securities that transfer will be excepted if the value transferred, together with values of chargeable transfers made by that transferor in the preceding seven years, do not exceed the current nil rate band (£325,000 for 2018/19).

(b) Transfers of uncertain value

Where the transfer includes assets other than cash or quoted shares or securities (ie realty) that transfer is exempt where:

- its value, together with other transfers by that transferor in the preceding seven years do not exceed 80% of the nil rate band (upper level of £260,000 based on the 2018/19 nil rate band of £325,000); and
- the value transferred by this particular transfer does not exceed the nil rate band after deducting the value of all the previous chargeable transfers.

For this purpose neither BPR nor APR is to be taken into account, so to be excepted the entire value must be within the limits prescribed.

Example 8.1—Gift of a share in a flat

Louis wishes to give his grandchildren a one-third interest in a flat in London which is let. The flat as a whole is worth £660,000. On 30 June 2018, he settles that one-third interest, which might seem to be a gift of £220,000 (ie £660,000 × 1/3) but the value for the lifetime transfer must be calculated on the loss to estate rule. Before the transfer his estate includes the full (100%) value of the property but post transfer his estate holds a 67% (two-thirds share) which should be discounted by say 15% to reflect multiple ownership and is therefore worth £374,000 ((660,000 × 2/3) × 85%). The loss to his estate is £286,000 (660,000 – 374,000).

Given the current 2018/19 nil rate band of £325,000 the limit above which the transfer must be reported is £260,000 namely 80% of £325,000. Louis' transfer must be reported; it is not £220,000, which would have been within the limit, but £286,000. Even the availability of two annual exemptions (current and prior year) would not help here.

Example 8.2—Excepted transfers: generous grandfather

Harry, having used his annual exemptions, set up a series of small discretionary trusts totalling £39,500 in the years 2012 to 2015. Some were of cash, some of assets but all of that was below the filing threshold. In November 2018, he proposes to settle another £150,000 in cash and quoted securities (he has already utilised his annual exemption such that this is no longer available). This will bring his cumulative total to £189,500 (150,000 + 39,500) which is less than the 80% limit.

Harry also has a remaining nil rate band pre transfer of £285,500 (325,000 – 39,500). Harry need not file an IHT100.

Excepted terminations

8.7 The rules as to excepted terminations apply only to 'specified' trusts, ie:

- interest in possession trusts (qualifying interest) that existed before 22 March 2006;
- trusts for bereaved minors under *IHTA 1984, s 71A*;
- IPDI trusts within *IHTA 1984, s 49A(1)(d)*;
- disabled persons trusts; or
- TSI trusts within *IHTA 1984, ss 49B–49E.*

The termination of a qualifying interest in possession in a trust can be a chargeable transfer, but it need not be reported if it falls within any one of the three circumstances described below:

(a) Small or exempt transfers

The transfer may be small, for example within the annual exemption, and the life tenant may have served notice under *IHTA 1984, s 57(3)* that an exemption is available. If the amount of the transfer is within the specified exemption, there is no need to submit an account.

(b) Nil rate band: fixed-value fund

Where the trust property is cash or quoted securities and the total of the value of the fund in respect of which the termination takes place and the value of other chargeable transfers made by the life tenant in the seven years preceding the event are within the nil rate band, there is no need to submit an account.

(c) Variable value funds

Where the trust fund does not consist wholly of cash or quoted securities there is still no need to submit an account if the value of the 'termination fund' and of previous chargeable transfers by the life tenant in the prior seven years do not exceed 80% of the nil rate band in force at time of termination. As with the rules for excepted settlements, these termination rules take no account of APR or BPR.

The 2008 Regulations replaced those made in 2002 in relation to lifetime transfers made on or after 6 April 2007.

Excepted settlements

8.8 The *Inheritance Tax (Delivery of Accounts) (Excepted Settlements) Regulations 2008, SI 2008/606* reduce the filing requirements in respect of pilot trusts and small settlements in which no qualifying interest in possession subsists (ie where the settlement is a relevant property trust). As such there is no need to file an account in respect of such trusts where the transfer is of cash of no more than £1,000 to a UK-resident settlement and there are no related settlements.

Apart from such pilot trusts the regulations have also removed the obligation to file a return in respect of:

- UK trusts (which continue to remain UK resident); by
- settlors domiciled in the UK at the time the settlement is made; who
- remain domiciled here until either the chargeable event or the death of the settlor whichever first happens; where
- there are no related settlements;

in any circumstance in which one of the following conditions apply:

Extra condition 1 – The ten year charge: The trust is excepted where the value in the trust is not more than 80% of the available trust nil rate band at the event date (disregarding liabilities or reliefs such as APR or BPR).

Extra condition 2 – The exit charge in the first ten years of the trust: The language of the *Inheritance Tax (Delivery of Accounts) (Excepted Transfers and Excepted Terminations) Regulations 2008, SI 2008/605, reg 4(5)* is somewhat obscure but it concerns the value that is transferred by the notional chargeable transfer which is one element of calculating the exit charge in the first ten years of the relevant property trust. For a transfer to be 'excepted' the calculation of value disregards liabilities or reliefs such as APR and BPR. On an exit charge in the first ten years of a relevant property trust, there is no need to submit an account if the value released from the trust does not exceed 80% of the available trust nil rate band in force at the event date.

Extra condition 3: The exit charge after the first ten-year anniversary: There is no need to submit an account if the value of the transfer does not exceed 80% of the available trust nil rate band in force at the event date.

Extra condition 4: *The exit charge from an 18-to-25 trust*: There is no need to submit an account where the chargeable transfer is within 80% of the available trust nil rate band in force at the event date.

A trap for unwary trustees

8.9 There is one circumstance that could easily catch trustees out which is described in IHTM06130 and arises on the death of a transferor. Trustees may have received sums which are well within the settlor's nil rate band and may have appointed funds out, again well within the levels that are now exempt from reporting. If this is the only chargeable transfer made by the settlor, there is no problem, but if the settlor had made PETs which now fail by reason of his death within seven years there will be a 'knock-on' effect for the trust. This is because, when seen in the context of the failed PETs, the transfers that were previously exempt from reporting must now be shown in an account. Depending on the value there might not be any extra tax to pay, but an account must be filed.

Example 8.3—Death affecting prior transactions

In 2013, Jessica gave her daughter Celia a plot of land. This was a PET, so there was no requirement to submit an account. There was some prospect that Celia could get planning permission on the land, but she and her mother assumed that the value of the gift was £60,000.

On 1 July 2016, Jessica settled £235,000 on trust being partly cash and partly quoted securities. Seen in isolation that was an 'excepted transfer' and there was no need to submit an account.

On 15 May 2017, the trustees advanced £80,000 to John, a beneficiary, to help him buy a house. The settlement had been within the nil rate band on creation so there would be no exit charge under normal principles. Applying the rules, 80% of the nil rate band at that time was £260,000 so an appointment that could conceivably give rise to an exit charge need not be reported because in this example the original fund, at £235,000, is well within the reporting limits.

On 6 August 2017, Jessica died, causing the 2013 PET to Celia to fail triggering a review of the tax charges on the settlement. The end effect will depend on the value finally agreed for the transfer of the land. If the value is, as claimed, £60,000, the notional aggregate of chargeable transfers goes up to £295,000 (£60,000 + £235,000). That is still within the nil rate band, so there will be no exit charge on the appointment made by the trustees, but the figures now exceed the limits in the new regulations so the trustees will have to deliver an account.

Greater difficulties will arise if it transpires that the likelihood of planning permission was so great at the time of the gift that the true value of the land was much more than £60,000. A significant increase in the valuation of the gift of the land could easily bring the tax rates applicable to the trust up to the level where an exit charge would be due on the £80,000 that was advanced to John.

Practitioners should read the detailed and useful guidance, with further illustrations, inserted into the IHT Manual at IHTM06100 to IHTM06130. See for example the detailed guidance on discounted gift schemes and their valuation at IHTM06105: where the discount is later found to be set at too high a level, a duty to file may arise on discovery within six months.

Settlors sometimes try to circumvent the chargeable transfer rules using the *IHTA 1984, s 21* 'normal expenditure out of income' exemption. Under the 2008 Regulations, there is no duty to submit an account if the transfers are covered by exemptions but the position is not so straightforward in the case of the normal expenditure out of income exemption (IHTM14231) where the exemption is only available '… to the extent that it is shown…' that the exemption applies. For this purpose HMRC interpret 'shown' as meaning 'shown to the satisfaction of HMRC' although there is no statute authority for this view. Where denial of the exemption does not cause a breach of the limits for a cash transfer it is not necessary to submit an account. HMRC will consider whether the *IHTA 1984, s 21* exemption is due if the matter is material when a later transfer is made or on death. However, in other cases where denial of the exemption in respect of the transfer would mean that there is a liability to IHT, an account should be delivered so that the availability of the exemption could be agreed: see IHTM06106.

There are often instances of discovery and catch-up whereby a taxpayer may have thought that a transfer was outside the filing rules and only realises the error later. If so, he has six months to put things right.

Transfers on death and failed PETs

8.10 **Chapter 1** explained how a lifetime transfer which was not otherwise immediately chargeable (a PET) might become chargeable if death occurred within seven years (a failed PET). The primary duty to complete returns rests with the personal representatives, who owe a duty of care to complete the return to the best of their knowledge and belief, subject to a test of reasonableness. HMRC's 'Inheritance Tax: Customer Guide' contains guidance to encourage consistency between HMRC's approach to the penalty legislation for IHT (www.hmrc.gov.uk/cto/customerguide/page22.htm).

Example 8.4—Accounting for a gift (and illustration of some rules)

On 17 May 2018, Joe died, leaving his estate to his daughter Emma. He had made simple, outright, cash lifetime gifts as follows:

1: January 2011	£20,000 to Emma
2: June 2011	£16,000 to his son Philip
3: December 2011	£3,000 between his grandchildren
4: December 2012	£3,000 as before
5: December 2013	£3,000 as before
6: May 2014	£10,000 to the National Trust
7: December 2014	£3,000 as before
8: December 2015	£3,000 as before
9: May 2016	£20,000 to Philip
10: December 2016	£3,000 as before

Under a lasting power of attorney (LPA), Philip continued the established pattern of gifts at Christmas and also made, on behalf of his father, gifts as follows:

11: January 2017	£15,000 (personal effects to Emma)
12: May 2018	£25,000 between grandchildren

The executors can likely claim relief under *s 21* (ie normal expenditure out of income) for all the Christmas gifts up to 2017.

Gift 1 is more than seven years before death and out of the reckoning. The gift, even though made outside the seven-year period, will none the less absorb the annual exemption for that year, leaving less to set against gifts that do fall within the seven-year period.

Gift 2 enjoys £3,000 of annual exemption, so is a failed PET of £13,000 net. It is set against the nil rate band. *Gift 6* is to a charity and exempt. *Gift 9* benefits from two annual exemptions, leaving £14,000 to go against the nil rate band.

Of the gifts under the power of attorney, those at Christmas are probably exempt both under *s 21* and because they were habitual and therefore reasonable for the attorney to continue.

Gift 11 may also have been reasonable within the terms of the power, if Joe was moving into a nursing home and the alternative was to sell the chattels.

Gift 12 fails in every sense. It goes beyond what is reasonable under a power, unless there was specific authority, and (as it turns out) half the cheques were in fact still unpresented at the date of death and thus, not effective gifts.

The power of an attorney under a Lasting Power of Attorney (LPA) is more closely defined than used to be the case under an Enduring Power of Attorney (EPA): see *MCA 2005, s 12*, which provides that there is no general power to make gifts but that, subject to any express limitation in the power, the attorney may make gifts on customary occasions to persons related to or connected with the donor, including the grantee of the power; and may make certain charitable gifts. 'Customary occasion' means births, birthdays, marriage, and formation of civil partnership or any other customary occasion, which allows cultural flexibility.

Reporting lifetime transfers after death: the duty of care

8.11 Personal representatives should enquire into the history of lifetime transfers by the deceased but how far they should pry depends on the circumstances. Having established the extent of the property remaining in the estate at death, executors should call for back statements on bank and similar accounts to check the pattern of withdrawals. They should make enquiries of relatives, professional advisers and close business colleagues. If, in the course of those enquiries, suspicions are raised that gifts may have been made that were not disclosed by other papers of the deceased, their enquiries should continue until they are reasonably sure that they have identified all the gifts made by the deceased.

A particular problem concerns the date and nature of the gifts. In relation to 'old' gifts, the date will be material not least to show that a gift was made more than seven years before death. Equally, a gift may have been made out of property that was at that time held jointly with some other person who has since died and that gift may therefore have been of only one half or some other fraction of the property.

Lifetime gifts may qualify for exemption under *IHTA 1984, ss 18, 19, 20, 21, 22* or *23* and following. Form IHT403 suggests a checklist of information that should be supplied and if correctly completed it could avoid an enquiry into the return. The difficulty, which has been noted before, lies in page six of IHT403, which attempts to help the personal representative to claim relief under *IHTA 1984, s 21* by setting out columns for each tax year prior to the death to show the surplus income so that gifts may be allocated to tax years and set against that surplus. If the deceased died on 5 April, the form works fine; but if on any other day in the year an extra column may be needed, if the deceased made gifts on a regular basis – as is implied by reliance in *IHTA 1984, s 21* anyway. As an alternative for the practitioner's own use, the following (partly completed) table may be prepared as a spreadsheet to help to calculate the amount of nil rate band available after the lifetime gifts have been brought into account on death.

Focus

Rules introduced by *Inheritance Tax (Delivery of Accounts) (Excepted Estates) (Amendment) Regulations 2011, SI 2011/214* provide that where someone dies after 1 March 2011, an account may have to be delivered, even though the value of the estate is below £150,000, if reliance is sought on *IHTA 1984, s 21* (see **8.18**).

Example 8.5—Checking lifetime gifts

On 17 December 2018, Susan died having made the following lifetime gifts:

- June or July in each year: £2,000 to her niece;
- 1 September 2011: 12,000 to her godson;
- 1 February 2012: £10,000 to a niece;
- 1 May 2013: £5,000 to her nephew;
- 1 September 2014: £4,000 to a friend;
- 1 December 2018: £1,000 (effected by her attorney, also named as her executor in her will) to each of five beneficiaries named in her will, 'to save trouble'; three of the cheques remained uncashed at the date of death.

Her income was steady, at about £30,000 per annum after tax. She lived frugally, taking a holiday (cost £3,000) only in alternate years. Her living expenses were £15,000 per annum in the 'non-holiday years'. The table, which should be created as a spreadsheet, can be used to sort the gifts and to claim the reliefs before completing IHT400. Note that gifts that are clearly exempt need not be set out in IHT400 itself but this form ensures that none are forgotten.

Period	*Income** *See note below*	*Gifts*	*Annual Exemption*	*s 21 Claim*	*Other Claims*	*Chargeable*
Part year 18.12.2011 – 5.4.2012	4,375	10,000				10,000

Year to 5.4.2013	12,000	2,000	3,000	2,000	
Year to 5.4.2014	15,000	7,000	5,000	2,000	
Year to 5.4.2015	12,000	6,000	3,000	2,000	1,000
Year to 5.4.2016	15,000				
Year to 5.4.2017	12,000				
Year to 5.4.2018	15,000				
Part year 6.4.2018 –17.12.2018	8,500	None**			
Total chargeable					11,000
NRB unused					314,000

*For this purpose 'income' means disposable income not necessarily taxable income, thus will income for example ISA income, and a preliminary filter or table is needed to establish the sum each year or part year that was truly available to fund gifts.

The table is an example of the situation where there are actually eight periods for consideration, as noted above. The nil rate band at date of death was £325,000. The regular gifts form part of a pattern and are exempt under *s 21*. The isolated gift of £12,000 in September 2011 falls entirely out of account, but the annual exemption for that year and for the previous year will have been used up. Therefore, the gift in February 2012 of £10,000 has to be set against the nil rate band.

**Gifts by attorneys should be examined with care. Cheques uncashed at death are not effective gifts and their value is still part of the estate at death. An attorney may not make gifts over and beyond the limits set out in *Mental Capacity Act 2005*, whereas seasonal gifts (birthday/Christmas etc.) are permitted up to reasonable limits. However, merely accelerating bequests does not fall within that category and the value must be added back to the estate.

In real life there may be formidable obstructions to the proper performance by the executors of their duties and this should not be underestimated. Families may be secretive, especially where one sibling knows that they have received more by way of lifetime gifts than the others or chattels may be taken from the residence to avoid burglary during the funeral and somehow are not returned to be included in the inventory or probate valuation (if indeed there is one). All of this will place an extra burden on the executor who must be seen to and indeed undertake 'reasonable care' so as to avoid penalties.

Normal expenditure out of income

8.12 Claims under *IHTA 1984, s 21* (normal expenditure out of income) meet resistance from HMRC where the evidence is, frankly, thin and without foundation. The evidence must show that:

- the gift was made of part of normal expenditure;
- it was made out of income; and
- the transferor was left with enough to live on and maintain his normal lifestyle.

Note that form IHT403 ('Gifts and other transfers of value') includes nursing home fees as an expense to be met out of income. This is consistent with the decision in *Nadin v IRC* [1997] STC (SCD) 107, but takes no account of the views expressed in *Stevenson (Inspector of Taxes) v Wishart* [1987] STC 266, where nursing home fees were substantial and accepted as made from capital. The issue causes regular difficulty and is discussed at **1.30** and **4.3**.

It is not necessary to set gifts against the annual exemption in priority to making an *s 21* claim: thus, in the example above, where Susan made a gift in May 2013 that used up the annual exemption for that year, she could make gifts in the following year of £3,000 and still have available £15,000 (more or less) to set against gifts in respect of which an *IHTA 1984, s 21* claim was made.

8.13 To satisfy the test as to normal expenditure there must be:

- regularity;
- a pattern of gifts; or
- a commitment to make regular gifts; and preferably all three.

The scope for 'overs and shorts' under *IHTA 1984, s 21(1)(b)* is interpreted narrowly by HMRC. They will, to a limited extent, permit 'storing up' of surplus income to support later gifts but will still deny claims to relief unless there is evidence of intention to make particular gifts. HMRC strongly resist a claim based on averages which relies on bringing back into a year the surplus income of a later period but the legal authority for this resistance is unclear and should be challenged: the legislation only requires the taxpayer to show 'that (taking one year with another) [the gift] was made out of [the taxpayer's] income'. The leading case on the allowability of exemption under *IHTA 1984, s 21* is *Bennett v IRC* [1995] STC 54 and it requires careful reading as it is more generous to the taxpayer than generally realised. That having been said, each case will turn on its own facts and on the quality of records which in many cases are seldom complete or even available.

HMRC have in recent years substantially re-written their guidance on gifts out of income (IHTM14231 to IHTM14255), which reflects their approach to closer scrutiny of this exemption – see **8.2**.

Focus

- Where reliance is placed on the exemption under *IHTA 1984, s 21*, it is strongly recommended that an annual record of income and expenditure is kept. This can be recorded either by using a spreadsheet or form IHT403.
- It is recommended that a record is made of the date and value of the gift.

Personal effects

8.14 Another area of difficulty is personal effects, where HMRC consider that there may previously have been insufficient or somewhat superficial disclosure. The true value to be shown is governed by the market value rule in *IHTA 1984, s 160* and there is simply no such thing as a formulaic 'probate value': the value to be disclosed is 'the price which the property might reasonably be expected to fetch if sold in the open market' at the date of death and that is the gross selling price, not the net. Here, in particular, Form IHT407 asks searching questions such as:

- the registration number of the deceased's car;
- whether chattels that have been sold were purchased by relatives;
- how the value of other chattels was arrived at.

Estimates

8.15 There is statutory authority in *IHTA 1984, s 216(3A)* for the use of estimates. The personal representatives must make very full enquiries but, if unable to arrive at the exact value, they must:

- say that they have made full enquiries;
- supply a provisional estimate of the value; and
- undertake to deliver a further account as soon as the value is ascertained.

For an example of litigation on these issues and on the costs of the litigation itself, see *Robertson v CIR* [2002] STC (SCD) 182 and *Robertson v CIR (No 2)* [2002] SSCD 242. For a case that highlighted the duty, see *Cairns v Revenue & Customs* [2009] UKFTT 67 (TC) TC00008, noted at **8.3** above.

> **Focus**
>
> HMRC are taking a noticeably much more aggressive stance on the use of estimates.
>
> - It is advisable, if not a necessity, to obtain robust valuations from qualified professionals ideally so called 'Red Book Valuations'. This is more so now given the introduction of the new penalty regime (see **8.38–8.45**).
> - In relation to land, 'development value', 'hope value' and the state of repair of a property all need to be addressed and recorded. In such situations photographic evidence is particularly useful.
> - As of April 2011 it became mandatory for chartered surveyors who provide 'Red Book Valuations' to sign up to a registration scheme. Alternatively a member of the Institute of Rating, Revenue and Valuation will comply with the requirement of The Red Book.

EXCEPTED ESTATES

Bare trusts

8.16 Following *FA 2006*, there was a resurgence in the popularity of bare trusts, since these were outside the scope of the relevant property regime but, as is always the case, some advisers pushed the boundaries of what might be considered to be a bare trust. Perhaps in response to this, HMRC revealed that they were considering one analysis of such trusts where there was, either expressly or by implication, a duty on the trustees to accumulate the income where such arrangements might be thinly disguised substantive trusts caught by *FA 2006*. A second issue was whether the power of advancement under *Trustee Act 1925, s 32* might be used to make settled advances, which would again allow ongoing trusts of precisely the kind eschewed by *FA 2006*.

This suggestion provoked a quick riposte from professional advisers who considered it to be wrong in law. The core of the HMRC argument turned on the effect of *IHTA 1984, s 43(2)(b)* and its reference to accumulations. There is perceived to be inconsistency between the established treatment of bare trusts for income tax (see TSEM1563) and as proposed for IHT thus cautious advisers may decide to exclude *TA 1925, s 31* to weaken the suggestion that there is a substantive trust.

The issue now seems to have been resolved and it is accepted that a simple bare trust of capital for a minor beneficiary is not settled property and thus cannot be relevant property. HMRC have formally commented:

'…We confirm that our view is that where assets are held on an absolute trust (ie a bare trust) for a minor the assets so held will not be settled property within the meaning of section 43 IHTA 1984 and that this will be the case whether or not the provisions of section 31 Trustee Act 1925 have been excluded….'

Transfers on death

8.17 There are now three categories of excepted estate, see *Inheritance Tax (Delivery of Accounts) (Excepted Estates) Regulations 2004, SI 2004/2543*. Many practitioners fail to take advantage of the regulations, preparing form IHT400 where it is not needed thereby incurring additional administration, cost and time which could all have been avoided. This apparent ignorance of the regulations is not encouraged by HMRC, because it just makes for unnecessary work that yields no tax. The reporting levels were increased by *Inheritance Tax (Delivery of Accounts) (Excepted Estates) (Amendment) Regulations 2006, SI 2006/2141* with effect from 1 September 2006 and *Inheritance Tax (Delivery of Accounts) (Excepted Estates) (Amendment) Regulations 2011, SI 2011/214* with effect from 1 March 2011.

Category One: small estates: the traditional form

8.18 The conditions are:

(1) The deceased was UK domiciled and died on or after 1 September 2006.

(2) The value of that person's estate is attributable wholly to property passing:

- under the will of the deceased or on his intestacy;
- under nomination taking effect on death;
- by a single settlement in which the deceased had a qualifying interest in possession; or
- by survivorship in a beneficial joint tenancy or, in Scotland, by survivorship in a special destination.

(3) Of the property passing on death:

- no more than £100,000 was situated overseas; and
- no more than £150,000 was trust property.

(4) In the seven years before death the deceased made transfers which, before deduction of business or agricultural property relief, did not exceed £150,000.

Note: For deaths on or after 1 March 2011 gifts under *IHTA 1984, s 21* (normal expenditure out of income) in excess of £3,000 in any one tax year will be treated as chargeable gifts for reporting purposes.

(5) The whole estate, including certain categories of transfer, did not exceed the IHT threshold which for this purpose means:

   (a) where death occurred on or after 6 April and before 6 August or where an application for a grant of representation (or in Scotland, an application for confirmation) is made after 5 April and before 6 August in that year, the nil rate band applicable in the prior tax year; or

   (b) in any other case the nil rate band in force for the year in which death occurred.

(6) The deceased had not made a gift with reservation of benefit, nor had an IHT charge arisen on an alternatively secured pension.

There are two categories of transfers referred to in this last condition. 'Specified transfers' are defined in *SI 2004/2543, reg 4(6)* to mean chargeable transfers in the seven years up to death consisting only of:

- cash;
- personal chattels or moveable property;
- quoted shares or securities; or
- interest in land (with qualifications).

The same regulations define 'specified exempt transfers' as those made in the seven years up to death which are exempt under one of the following headings:

- transfers between spouses;
- charities;
- political parties;
- gifts to housing association;
- gifts to maintenance funds for historic buildings;
- employee trusts.

Category Two: estates: spouse/charity exemption

8.19 *SI 2004/2543* created a new category of excepted estate of a gross value of up to £1 million where, post offset of the spouse or charity exemption, the estate was still within the IHT threshold. To comply with this category the following conditions must be satisfied.

(1) The deceased was UK domiciled and died on or after 6 April 2004.

(2) The value of that person's estate is attributable wholly to property passing:

- by will or on intestacy;
- under a nomination taking effect on death;
- under a single settlement of which the deceased was tenant for life; or
- by survivorship in a beneficial joint tenancy or, in Scotland, by survivorship in a special destination.

(3) The estate included:

- not more than £100,000 foreign property;
- not more than £150,000 of settled property but ignoring settled property that on death passes to a spouse or to charity; and
- that in the seven years leading up to death the deceased did not make chargeable transfers other than specified transfers not exceeding £150,000 before deduction of business or agricultural relief.

(4) The estate did not exceed £1,000,000, including within that figure:

- the gross value of the estate;
- the value transferred by specified transfers;
- the value transferred by specified exempt transfers.

(5) Applying the formula A – (B + C), the total does not exceed the IHT threshold. For this purpose:

- A is the aggregate of the estate, specified transfers and the specified exempt transfers.
- B is the total value transferred on death that qualifies for exemption as passing to a spouse or charity, but subject to qualification of that rule in relation to Scotland.
- C is the total liabilities of the estate.

IHT threshold: transferable nil rate band

8.20 *SI 2011/214* allows personal representatives to claim the benefit of the transferable nil rate band (TNRB) and apply for a grant as an excepted estate provided that a number of conditions are met. The TNRB in an excepted estate must be claimed using form IHT217. The conditions that must be met are:

- the deceased survived the earlier death of their spouse or civil partner and was married to, or in a civil partnership with, them at the earlier death;
- importantly, none of the nil rate band must have been used by the earlier death, so that 100% is available for transfer;
- a valid claim is made and is in respect of one earlier death only;
- the first deceased person died on or after 13 November 1974, where the deceased was the spouse of the first deceased, or on or after 5 December 2005, where the deceased was the civil partner of the first deceased person.

The estate of the first deceased person must also meet the following conditions:

- the first deceased person died domiciled in the UK;
- their estate consisted only of property passing under their will or intestacy and jointly owned assets;
- if their estate included foreign assets, their gross value did not exceed £100,000;
- agricultural and business relief did not apply.

Where an estate meets the above conditions and a valid claim is made:

- in a 'standard' excepted estate, the gross value of the estate must not exceed double the applicable nil rate band; or
- if the estate is an exempt excepted estate, the gross value of the estate must not exceed £1 million and the net chargeable value of the estate (after deduction of liabilities and spouse or civil partner exemption and/or charity exemption) must not exceed double the applicable nil rate band.

Category Three: small foreign estates

8.21 This category of estate is one where the deceased was never domiciled or deemed domiciled in the UK for IHT purposes and the UK estate comprises only cash or quoted shares or other securities with a total value not exceeding £150,000. It is necessary to state the value of worldwide estate and if the level is below the IHT threshold, domicile is less likely to be examined in detail as there is no tax at stake.

The personal representatives of an excepted estate are not entirely excused from supplying information and in all such cases they must complete the short form IHT205. This may in any event serve a separate function by offering some protection to beneficiaries, especially charities, because without IHT205 there might actually be no formal inventory of the estate.

PARTICULAR COMPLIANCE POINTS

Development value of land

8.22 Cases such as *Prosser v IRC* (DET/1/2000) have shown that the value of land for IHT must reflect some, but not necessarily full, account of 'hope' value where appropriate. In that particular case a garden plot in respect of which planning permission was eventually obtained, was held to be worth 25% of its ultimate value for probate purposes. The IHT Newsletter of 28 April 2006 stressed that development value must be accounted for, and that the value of a house should reflect any feature that makes it attractive to a builder or developer. If new information comes to light that enhances the value, the personal representatives should declare it, on pain of penalties for failure to do so.

Note that HMRC no longer automatically adopt the view that if an asset is sold relatively soon after the death for substantially more than probate value the personal representatives may have failed in their duty of disclosure prompting imposition of penalties. Having said that, certainly such a disparity in values will invite HMRC interest.

Focus

- In 2012/13 HMRC saw a 23% rise in the amount of money raised by challenging the valuation of estates. Such HMRC challenges into land valuations increased the IHT total to £108 million.
- HMRC are now asking PRs how much care they took when getting an independent valuation – see earlier reference to 'Red Book' valuations on property.
- HMRC now consider that PRs have a duty to draw the valuer's attention to specific features of the property that may affect its price.

Annuities

8.23 There will seldom be any residual value of an annuity, but where payments do continue after death, as where the annuitant dies before the end of the guaranteed period, that right to the income stream must be valued. Whilst personal representatives may value as they think fit, many will want to make use of the HMRC calculator on their website, giving a reasonable estimate of the value under *IHTA 1984, s 160*; see www.hmrc.gov.uk/cto/forms/g_annuity.pdf

Joint property

8.24 Property owned as joint tenants passes to the survivor outside the will by the *ius accrescendi*, without the need for a grant of representation. However, that does not mean that no IHT is due and if the surviving joint owner is neither the spouse nor the civil partner, the value may attract an IHT charge. Form IHT400 will be appropriate, with form IHT404 annexed.

The deceased may have opened an account jointly with an adult child, perhaps for convenience through frailty or failing capacity. Payment of money into such an account by the deceased is not necessarily a gift of half to that child: but the withdrawal of funds by the child for their own purposes will usually be a transfer of value for IHT and should be brought into account. HMRC explained, in IHT Newsletter for December 2006, that they, not surprisingly, look critically at accounts opened shortly before death. See also *Taylor & Another v RCC* [2008] SSCD 1159 (SpC 704).

PAYMENT OF IHT

8.25 In the past, the main IHT event was triggered by death with tax payable on the death estate whilst bringing into account failed PETs made within the previous seven years. *FA 2006* has now caused that position to quietly shift as a direct consequence of the new rules which bring most lifetime trusts and caused many existing settlements to migrate into the relevant property regime of exit charges and periodic charges.

Lifetime transfers

8.26 Hitherto most transfers, by number and possibly by value, have been PETs, so that tax on them would arise only if they failed by reason of the donor's death within seven years. The 'top-up' death levy that arises on the failure of a PET is charged, see *IHTA 1984, s 199(1)*, on:

- the transferor;
- the transferee whose estate is increased by the transfer;
- the recipient of the property in whom it is vested, whether for his own benefit or not, at any time after the transfer;
- anyone enjoying a qualifying interest in possession in the transfer;
- anyone for whose benefit the property or its income is applied where the property has become settled.

8.27 On death of the donor, the first in line is the donee but, if he does not pay the tax within 12 months of the end of the month in which the donor died, *IHTA 1984, s 204* transfers that liability to the personal representatives. That can cause a real problem for executors, who may not know the full facts. HMRC have indicated (in a letter dated 13 March 1991 addressed to the Law Society) that they will not normally pursue personal representatives who have made the fullest enquiries as reasonably practicable, to discover lifetime transfers; have done all they can to make full disclosure; have obtained the certificate of discharge and have distributed the estate all before a chargeable transfer comes to light.

There is a special rule for woodlands: see *IHTA 1984, s 208*.

Due date: lifetime transfers

8.28 The filing deadlines for lifetime chargeable transfers that were made prior to 6 April 2014 were:

- for chargeable events occurring after 5 April but before 1 October the due date was 30 April in the following year; and
- for chargeable events occurring after 30 September but before 6 April the due date was six months after the end of the month in which the chargeable event occurred.

Finance Act 2014 addressed the issue that the time limits for reporting IHT periodic and exit charges for relevant property trusts differed from the time limits for paying any IHT due. Therefore for chargeable events occurring within a trust scenario on or after 6 April 2014, the time limit for both submitting an account and paying any IHT due is fixed at six months from the end of the month in which the transfer was made.

Payment by instalments

8.29 The tax may be paid by ten equal annual instalments on 'qualifying property' where certain conditions apply. 'Qualifying property' for this purpose means:

- land;
- shares or securities within *IHTA 1984, s 228*; or
- business or an interest in a business.

The conditions are:

- the transfer is made on death; or
- the tax is being paid by the person who benefits from the transfer; or
- the transfer comes within the relevant property regime (which will be more common in the post-*FA 2006* era) and either the tax is borne by the beneficiary or the property remains in the settlement.

At first sight this would seem to exclude IHT due on failed PETs but actually the instalment option is available, see *IHTA 1984, s 227(1C)*, where:

- the property was owned by the transferee from the date of the transfer to the death of the transferor (or if earlier of a transferee); or
- the charge arises under clawback of APR or BPR following the death of the transferor.

'Section 228' shares

8.30 Four categories of shares or securities of a company qualify for the instalment option:

- shares giving control;
- unquoted shares which attract (together with tax due on other instalment assets for which the same person is liable) not less than 20% of the tax chargeable by that person in the same capacity;
- unquoted shares where the tax cannot be paid without undue hardship; and
- other shares neither giving control nor unquoted but where the value of the transfer is over £20,000 and the shares are at least 10% of the nominal value of all the shares in the company at that time, or they are ordinary shares and their nominal value is at least 10% of the nominal value of all the ordinary shares of the company at that time.

Interest

8.31 Interest is added to each instalment, running from the date at which the instalment is payable if the property is land (excluding a business asset qualifying for BPR or agricultural property qualifying for APR) or shares/securities in companies whose business is wholly or mainly dealing in securities, stocks or shares, or making or holding of investments: see *IHTA 1984, s 234(2)*.

Loss of the instalment option

8.32 Curiously, advance payment of more than the instalment currently due can cause the loss of the instalment option in total. In the past, if it suited the taxpayer to pay extra at any time, the recommended action was to do so using the certificates of tax deposit scheme (CTDs) – however, the CTD scheme was withdrawn in its entirety on 23 November 2017. It should also be remembered that the right to pay by instalment belongs to the beneficiary, who can claim against an executor or trustee in circumstances where the latter have caused the instalment basis to be forfeit by early settlement of instalment payments.

However, if the executor releases property to the beneficiary in advance of the instalment payment he remains liable: see *Howarth's Executors v IRC* [1997] STC (SCD) 162, where a lawyer was personally liable for the outstanding and unpaid instalments of tax due on property that he had earlier released to the beneficiaries.

The 'Inland Revenue' charge

8.33 Where tax charged on the value of a chargeable transfer is unpaid *IHTA 1984, s 237(1)* imposes a charge in favour of HMRC on the relevant property. It is known by statute as the 'Inland Revenue charge', see *IHTA 1984, s 237(1)*, rather than the 'HMRC charge'. The rules were updated by *IHTA 1984, s 237(3C)* in relation to certain specialised forms of charge.

Payment of IHT on death

8.34 The personal representatives are liable and the tax is treated as part of the administration expenses of the estate. The *Administration of Estates Act 1925* sets out the order in which the tax is charged against the assets in the estate but that rule is limited by *IHTA 1984, s 211* to the value of property in the UK that vests in the personal representatives of the deceased and was not comprised in a settlement immediately before the death. There are separate rules for recovery of tax where property is vested in another person.

IHT direct payment scheme

8.35 Since 31 March 2003, by arrangement between HMRC and certain financial institutions, it has been possible for personal representatives to access funds in the name of the deceased before the grant of representation is issued. This is a great help because tax must be paid 'up front' on all property except that which qualifies for the instalment option. Where, for example, a dispute about the will prevents the issue of a grant of representation, this facility still allows the tax to be timely paid whilst avoiding the need to raise loans from third parties (ie banks).

The scheme is voluntary, so whilst most of the mainstream organisations do, certainly not all financial institutions (to include some banks) participate. It applies only to accounts held in the sole name of the deceased and, if the deceased has several accounts, the institution will not release more than the net value (ie after setting off overdrafts or credit card liabilities). The number of the account must be nominated on the form IHT423 using a separate form for each financial institution from which the funds will be applied.

Acceptance of property in lieu of tax

8.36 This is a specialist topic, but in outline it is possible to offer heritage property in satisfaction of tax liabilities. It must be of outstanding quality but the procedure is protracted, although it does secure for the nation valuable objects that might otherwise have been sold to overseas buyers to pay tax. As an incentive, the taxpayer receives a credit that slightly exceeds the net of tax commercial value of the item. This is known somewhat archaically as the 'douceur' (under a tax law rewrite it would perhaps be better described as a 'cashback'). For more guidance see *Agricultural, Business and Heritage Property Relief (7th edn) (Bloomsbury Professional).*

DISCLOSURE OF TAX AVOIDANCE SCHEMES (DOTAS)

8.37 In January 2011 the *Inheritance Tax Avoidance Schemes (Prescribed Description of Arrangements) Regulations SI 2011/170* were published and had the effect of bringing transfers into trusts within the DOTAS regime for IHT from 6 April 2011.

A useful flowchart to determine whether a particular scheme is subject to DOTAS was published by HMRC in their guidance notes (see www.hmrc.gov.uk/aiu/dotas.pdf). To determine whether DOTAS applies HMRC published a four-stage test in their guidance:

- **Test 1**: Are there arrangements or proposals for arrangements which result in property becoming 'relevant property'?
- **Test 2**: Are those arrangements or proposals for arrangements such that they enable a 'relevant property charge advantage?
- **Test 3**: Is the tax advantage a main benefit of the arrangements?
- **Test 4**: Is the arrangement on the list of grandfathered schemes and schemes that are not within the regulations. If so it may have to be disclosed. The list of grandfathered schemes can be found in the guidance.

The main aim of the extension of the disclosure rules was to restrict disclosure to those schemes which were new or innovative. This was achieved by exempting from disclosure those schemes which were the same or substantially the same as arrangements made available before 6 April 2011.

Legislation was included in *FA 2014* to impose advance penalties on taxpayers who entered into a tax avoidance scheme. In such cases where the tax avoidance scheme involved is notifiable to HMRC under DOTAS, or is counteracted under the GAAR, HMRC have (from 17 July 2014) the power to issue a Notice to Pay. This requires the taxpayer to pay the tax that HMRC consider to be due, even though the taxpayer has appealed against the assessment and does not believe that he will owe any tax. Controversially this also applies to those who entered into tax schemes many years ago where the dispute has not yet been settled. It was further announced that users of defeated avoidance schemes will be required to disclose their use to HMRC and pay any tax in dispute upfront. Penalties will apply for non-compliance.

Finance Act 2014 also included measures against so-called high-risk promoters of tax avoidance schemes awarding HMRC two new powers. The first power enables HMRC to issue a promoter a 'conduct notice', demanding full details about a particular tax planning product and its intermediaries and users. The second power allows HMRC to issue 'monitoring notices' to selected promoters to provide details of all their products, intermediaries and users within five days of being asked to do so – all such 'Monitoring notices' require the approval of the First-tier Tribunal. On 31 July 2014 HMRC issued a consultation document 'Strengthening the Tax Avoidance Disclosure Regimes' and a summary of responses was later published in December 2014. The 2014 Autumn Statement contained a proposal for the introduction of a new threshold condition to ensure that promoters do not use the DOTAS regime as a way of obtaining advance clearance by repeatedly tweaking schemes and re-submitting them for consideration. The new threshold condition would consider how often a promoter contacts HMRC to gain approval of a scheme.

Specifically aimed at IHT which hitherto had been largely unscathed by the DOTAS rules, it was intended that the disclosure requirements would be more keenly focused on those IHT avoidance schemes which operate outside the normal planning routines involving available reliefs and exemptions. Accordingly, on 2 September 2015 HMRC issued fresh Guidance Disclosure of Tax Avoidance Schemes which consolidated the changes introduced in *FA 2014* and *FA 2015* to include:

- increasing the penalty for persons using schemes which do not comply with reporting requirements;
- protecting persons who voluntarily provide information about potential failures to comply with DOTAS;
- requiring promotors to notify HMRC if their details or those of one of their schemes change;
- enabling HMRC to publish information about schemes and promoters that it receives under the DOTAS rules;
- giving HMRC powers to obtain details of users of undisclosed schemes from introducers; and
- creating a new power requiring additional information to be sent to clients.

Following responses made to the consultation on its proposed draft changes to the hallmark regulations, which closed in September 2015, HMRC made a number of amendments which changes became effective from 23 February 2016. In April 2016 HMRC issued a further consultation document which provided welcome examples of ordinary IHT planning which could secure a tax advantage but which HMRC considered to be nonetheless outside the DOTAS hallmark because such tax planning was neither contrived nor abnormal – these included:

- straightforward outright gifts;
- lifetime transfers into flexible or discretionary trusts;
- investment into assets that qualify for IHT reliefs;
- arrangements that are within a statutory exemption, ie paying full consideration for the continued use of a gifted asset; and
- certain routine insurance-based arrangements, ie loan trusts.

HMRC considered all comments received in response to that consultation and held meetings with stakeholders to help develop the new 'hallmark' now consolidated in the *Inheritance Tax Avoidance Schemes (Prescribed Descriptions of Arrangements) Regulations 2017 (2017/1172)* which will come into force on 1 April 2018. The wording has been refined to ensure the new 'hallmark' is appropriately targeted to IHT avoidance schemes whilst leaving the straightforward use of reliefs and exemptions or ordinary tax planning arrangements unaffected.

The new regulations replace the previous regulations (SI 2011/170) with new descriptions of disclosable arrangements designed to reduce the value of an estate on death or those which seek to avoid certain other IHT charges in addition to 'entry charges' on relevant property trusts. The new 'hallmark' also ensures that established retail products, which accord with established practice that HMRC has previously accepted, do not have to be disclosed if they were first made available and entered into before 1 April 2018. HMRC will also be publishing guidance to explain how the new DOTAS hallmark works, the conditions to be met for arrangements to be notifiable, and the circumstances for certain arrangements to be excepted from disclosure. The guidance will be published before the new hallmark comes into force.

PENALTIES

A new (and tougher) approach

8.38 Another part of the modernisation of powers, deterrents and safeguards was the reform of penalties. Whereas other aspects of the modernisation did not specifically concern IHT, as was noted at **8.3** above, IHT was included in *Finance Act 2008*. The intention of the new legislation was described during the HMRC consultation as being to influence behaviour, to be effective and to be fair. There are five areas of concern:

- incorrect returns;
- failure to notify a new taxable activity;
- late filing and late payment;
- record keeping and information powers failures; and
- other regulatory failures.

The legislation in *Finance Act 2008* is not the end of this particular story. It concerns failure to notify and understatement and does not fully address the issue of the failure to submit returns at all. The structure of the legislation was to amend *Finance Act 2007, Sch 24. Finance Act 2008,* extended the existing schedule of taxes affected so as to include for IHT purposes accounts under *IHTA 1984, ss 216* and *217*, information or documents required by *IHTA 1984, s 256* and statements or declarations in connection with deductions, exemptions or reliefs. Beyond that, legislation was included in *Finance Act 2009, s 106* to impose penalties for late filing and, as a separate matter in *Finance Act 2009, s 107*, to penalise late payment of tax.

In IHT situations, there is often shared responsibility for information gathering. The most obvious example concerns lifetime gifts.

The penalty rules for inaccuracies generally apply for IHT purposes in respect of the following (see *The Finance Act 2008, Schedule 40 (Appointed Day, Transitional Provisions and Consequential Amendments) Order 2009 SI 2009/571*):

- documents relating to periods commencing from 1 April 2009, for which the filing date is on or after 1 April 2010; and
- relevant documents produced under regulations under *s 256* ('Regulations about accounts etc'), where the date of death is on or after 1 April 2009.

Example 8.6—Penalties: a difficult estate to administer

Philip had led a long and colourful life and a relationship whilst at medical school produced a daughter, Alice. He paid for her upkeep for a few years before leaving the UK to practise medicine in Africa, where his first marriage brought him a son, Brian, and daughter, Celia. That marriage ended in divorce and he returned to the UK. The length and bitterness of his divorce was exacerbated by a relationship with Dorothy, with whom Philip lived until his death.

Philip's will was prepared whilst he was still in Africa and named two of his then colleagues as executors. The terms of the will were affected by the *Law Reform (Succession) Act 1995*, in that they took effect as if the former wife had died on the date of decree absolute, but the rest of the will was still valid and made no provision for Dorothy.

In his last years, Philip sought some reconciliation with each of his children, in particular Alice who (she said) cared for him in his later years. His mental powers were failing; he signed an enduring power of attorney in favour of Alice. By the time of his death serious difficulties had arisen between Alice, Brian, Celia and Dorothy. The estate was complicated, involving assets in Africa and in the UK and serious issues arose as to whether certain gifts had or had not been made and whether, at the time of gifts, Philip had had capacity to make them.

The executors in Africa face very significant difficulties in discharging their obligation under *IHTA 1984, s 216* to deliver an account that specifies all the appropriate property and its value.

This situation is addressed by *paragraph 1A* inserted into *Finance Act 2007, Sch 24*. Most of the schedule centres on the obligations of a person identified in *para 1(1)* of the schedule as P. The penalties in *para 1A* concern a different person, T, and address the situation where the inaccuracy in the return made by P is attributable to false information that is deliberately supplied, either directly or indirectly to T or where T deliberately withholds information from P.

The inaccuracy is one which results in:

- an understatement by P of the liability to tax; or
- a false or inflated statement of a loss (which would not normally apply to IHT though debts at death have a similar effect); or
- a false or inflated claim to repayment of tax.

Thus, in the example of Philip the obligations would be shared by the executors and the family and if, for example, it transpired that Philip had made a substantial gift to Alice which Alice kept quiet about, the burden would lie on Alice.

Degrees of culpability

8.39 *Finance Act 2007, Sch 24* had already set out the classifications, but the wording is tidied up by the amendments in *Finance Act 2008, Sch 40*.

Penalties may arise if 'reasonable care' has not been taken in preparing an IHT account or excepted estate return, or if any inaccuracy is discovered but reasonable steps are not taken to inform HMRC about it. HMRC consider that personal representatives will have taken reasonable care in the following circumstances (see HMRC Inheritance Tax and Trusts Newsletter, April 2009):

- The personal representatives follow the guidance provided about filling in forms such as the IHT400 and IHT205/207/C5.

- They make suitable enquiries of asset holders and other people (as suggested in the guidance) to establish the extent of the deceased's estate.
- They ensure correct instructions are given to the valuer when valuing assets.
- They seek advice about anything of which they are unsure.
- They follow up inconsistencies in information they receive from asset holders, the valuers and other people.
- They identify any estimated values included on the form.

If the personal representatives leave the account or return to an agent, they are nevertheless required to check the entries carefully. Merely signing a form completed by an agent is not reasonable care.

The penalty regime identifies three categories of behaviour that can give rise to penalties for an inaccuracy in an account or return:

- The lowest level of culpability, described as 'careless', is where the taxpayer fails to take reasonable care in completing the return.
- The 'middle' level of culpability is 'deliberate but not concealed' where the return is wrong and it results from the deliberate action of the taxpayer, but the taxpayer makes no arrangements to conceal the inaccuracy.
- Finally, the most serious level of wrongdoing is that which is 'deliberate and concealed' where the taxpayer has deliberately sent in a wrong return and deliberately tries to conceal the parts of the return that are wrong, for example by submitting false evidence in support of false figures.

When it is established that a return was inaccurate, the taxpayer will be treated as careless, even though he may not have been at the time of the return if he discovers the inaccuracy some time later and does not take reasonable steps to inform HMRC.

In this summary of the law, the word 'return' has been used but the rules apply in the much wider context of documents that, whether or not returns, fix the liability to tax.

The level of penalties

8.40 These maximum levels were established by *Finance Act 2007, Sch 24*, but their scope was extended by *Finance Act 2008*:

- The 30% rate: a penalty of 30% of the potential lost revenue applies where the taxpayer was careless.
- The 70% rate: a penalty of 70% applies where the action of the taxpayer was deliberate but not concealed.

- The 100% rate: a penalty of 100% applies where the action of the taxpayer was deliberate and concealed. This can apply in two circumstances. Under *Finance Act 2007, Sch 24, para 4(C)* the full penalty could apply to 'deliberate and concealed action'. That penalty still stands but is extended to cover 'third party' acts such as might apply to the family of Philip in **Example 8.6** above. The collection of tax lost through third-party inaccuracy was extended by *Finance Act 2008,* so that it includes any inaccuracy that results from the supply of false information or the withholding of information.

The penalty regime in *Finance Act 2007, Sch 24* did not previously apply to IHT, so specialists in that area of practice may not have become familiar with the scheme of that schedule. In a situation where there are various errors, such as could easily apply in the administration of an estate, careless inaccuracies are corrected before deliberate inaccuracies; and deliberate but not concealed inaccuracies are corrected before deliberate and concealed inaccuracies. In calculating the lost tax, account is taken of any overstatement in any document given by the taxpayer that relates to the same tax period.

The case of *Timothy Clayton Hutchings v HMRC* [2015] UKFTT 9 (TC) is a stark lesson in the manner in which the penalties operate and it highlights HMRC's significantly tougher approach. In that case, the taxpayer deliberately withheld information relating to a substantial gift of an offshore bank account and as the disclosure was prompted, a hefty penalty of 35% was imposed on the taxpayer.

Example 8.7—Penalties: too casual an approach to compliance

Henry, a widower whose late wife had used her nil rate band, died on 1 January 2018, leaving a house, a share in an investment partnership and personal effects. There were no liabilities, Henry having taken out funeral costs insurance. His son John as sole executor knew that Henry had always used his annual exemption and was aware of lump-sum gifts of £70,000. John completed IHT400 thus:

	£
House	313,000
Partnership share	100,000
Personal effects	12,000
Gifts	70,000
	495,000
Less nil rate band	325,000
Taxable	170,000
Tax liability	68,000

John had been in a hurry to get a grant of probate, anxious to catch the property market before his father's house fell in value. He did not get a professional valuation but he did not use the 'estimates' box in the return as he thought he knew property prices in the area. Actually, it turned out that an area of land to the side of the house had realistic prospect of development and that, if sold separately, with the benefit of planning permission, it might realise £100,000 without taking any value off the house. Applying the valuation rule in *Prosser v IRC*, this added £25,000 to the estate and £10,000 to the tax liability.

It also transpired that the investment partnership had made certain losses in respect of which it was entitled to a refund of tax, so £20,000 would be added to the value of the estate when the returns were settled. John told HMRC as soon as he had the right figures. No business relief was available in respect of the investment partnership, so this added £8,000 to the eventual liability.

John knew that his father had given his sister, Sarah, the family yacht, some eight or nine years before his death. It had then been worth £30,000. John had not the slightest interest in sailing and had never been concerned with the arrangement between his father and his sister, and assumed that the gift need not be disclosed because it was outside the seven-year period. He did know that his father continued to sail with his daughter, but it never occurred to him that that might constitute a reservation of benefit out of the gift within *Revenue Interpretation 55*. Sarah complained occasionally that she had to bear all the costs of running the boat whilst her work as a matrimonial lawyer prevented her from taking time off to sail, whereas her father in retirement made extensive use of the vessel. When the reservation of benefit point was raised in correspondence on another aspect of the estate, John immediately realised that there was a problem and disclosed the gift.

John was less forthcoming about the cheques that he had signed in his capacity as attorney for his father. For the last four years of his father's life, acting under an enduring power of attorney which had not been registered despite his father's failing powers, John had regularly drawn off £1,000 per month into a separate account and had used the money towards the cost of his children's education. He thought that the gifts would be covered by *IHTA 1984, s 21* relief for normal and reasonable expenditure of the deceased, even though the gifts went well beyond what John had power to make under (what was then) *Enduring Powers of Attorney Act 1985, s 3(5)*. It was only when HMRC called for copy bank statements that the £48,000 of gifts were discovered and even then John offered a number of implausible reasons that the sums should not be taxable. Adding them back to the estate increased the tax liability by £19,200.

The valuation error was careless. It was held in *Robertson v CIR* [2002] STC (SCD) 182 that a material understatement of value did not trigger penalties, but in that case the executor had indicated in the return that the value was an estimate and was therefore, in *Robertson v CIR (Number 2)* [2002] SSCD 242, able to recover handsomely from HMRC. In the present case, a penalty of up to £3,000 arises because the error is not simply the difference between one person's view of a value and that of another; there is a fundamental error in the basis of valuation which would have been avoided if John had been in less of a hurry and had obtained a proper valuation in the first place.

The restatement of value of the partnership interest probably does not attract a penalty at all. John showed the value of the partnership as he understood it at the date of death, and it is only after some negotiation with another branch of HMRC that the tax refund materialises. John has disclosed the change as soon as aware of it, so it is simply a case of paying the tax and interest, but not a penalty.

John did not disclose the reservation of benefit in connection with the boat, which was careless because he should have thought about the issue and the form of the return contains ample prompts on the issue. Sarah has made no secret of the fact that her father has had some benefit from the boat that he has given away, so she is not to blame. Tax is chargeable subject to negotiation as to value, remembering the option of HMRC to treat the gift as a chargeable transfer or to treat it as part of the estate at death. Where an asset falls in value, HMRC will probably prefer to treat the gift as a failed PET and tax the value at the time of the gift. On that basis, there is extra tax of £12,000 to find and the penalty could be another £4,000, subject as below.

In relation to the school fees, John's action is deliberate and concealed, so the penalty (subject to the observations below) is 100% of the tax: an extra £19,200.

Finance Act 2007, Sch 24, para 6 requires an initial calculation of the careless inaccuracies, here the £10,000 on the valuation issue and possibly the £8,000 in respect of the business. Next in gravity comes the £12,000 on the boat and finally the £19,200 on the school fees. As to mitigation, see below.

Strengthening civil deterrents for offshore tax avoidance

8.41 The offshore penalty regime strengthens existing penalties for:

- failure to notify;

- inaccuracy on a return; and
- failure to file a return in time.

There are three penalty levels, which depend on the territory in which the income or gain arises:

- Where the income or gain arises in a territory in 'Category 1' (which includes most of Europe and the United States), the penalty regime will be up to 100% of the tax involved.
- Where the income or gain arises in a territory in 'Category 2', the penalty rate will be up to 150% of the tax involved.
- Where the income or gain arises in a territory in 'Category 3', the penalty rate will be up to 200% of the tax involved.

There are no penalties for those who have taken and can demonstrate reasonable care or have a reasonable excuse for the failure to notify taxable income and gains. However, HMRC announced that consultation will take place on further proposals for a 'strict liability' rule for offshore under-declarations which would provide:

- an automatic assumption of tax evasion without the need to establish fraud;
- enhanced penalties linked to the value of the overseas asset rather than the tax involved;
- new and wider penalties to include criminal sanctions aimed at 'enablers' of tax evasion and organisations who facilitate or fail to prevent such evasion.

The *Finance Act 2015* extended the offshore penalty regime to:

- include IHT;
- apply to domestic offences where the proceeds of UK non-compliance are hidden offshore;
- update the territorial classification system; and
- introduce a new aggravated penalty, up to a further 50% of tax lost, for moving hidden funds to circumvent international tax transparency agreements.

However, *FA 2015* also increased the level of penalties for offshore tax avoidance from 30% to 37.5%, 70% to 87.5% and 100% to 125% respectively (see **8.40** above) and introduced a new country category known as 'category 0'. This includes countries previously in category 1 that have since adopted the common reporting standard (CRS), a process by which countries automatically provide to HMRC annual information on offshore bank accounts, investments and structures. Irregularities relating to 'category 0' countries are liable to the normal penalty regime associated with domestic misdemeanours. For IHT purposes, the territory where the assets are situated immediately after the transfer of value that gives rise to the IHT is the determinant for the relevant categories 0 to 3. If more than one territory is involved in an offshore transfer the penalty is determined by reference to the territory in the highest category, thus maximising the penalty.

On 11 October 2017, regulations were made amending the *Offshore Asset Moves Penalty (Specified Territories) Regulations 2015 (SI 2015/866)*. The regulations remove Albania and the USA (not including overseas territories and possessions) from the list of specified territories, and incorporate Bahrain, the Cook Islands, Ghana, Kuwait, Lebanon, Nauru, Panama and Vanuatu as specified territories. The amendments reflect the jurisdictions that have committed to implementing the Common Reporting Standard. The regulations come into force on 3 November 2017.

There are three conditions for the new penalty regime to apply:

1 A penalty for deliberate behaviour is due, known as the 'original penalty'.

2 There is a 'relevant offshore asset move' after the 'relevant time'.

3 The main purpose of the offshore asset move, or at least one of them, is to prevent or delay HMRC discovering the asset.

Where:

- A relevant offshore asset move is triggered where the person, in reality, remains the beneficial owner of the asset and:
  - the asset is moved from a specified to a non-specified territory;
  - the owner ceases to be resident in a specified territory and becomes resident in a non-specified territory;
  - ownership appears to change.
- The relevant time for IHT purposes is when the liability for the tax first arises.

The penalty itself is a flat rate of 50% of the original penalty, but it is nonetheless regarded as an entirely separate penalty to which the normal rules apply regarding HMRC's ability to assess, time limits and appeals etc.

In December 2016, HMRC issued an initial consultation document on the requirement for intermediaries/professionals involved in the creation of and/or promotion of complex offshore structures to notify details of the financial arrangements and the clients involved. Following this consultation, the European Union (EU) and the Organisation for Economic Co-operation and Development (OECD) collaborated on and published guidance setting out a multinational standard on the reporting and exchanging of such information between jurisdictions. Stemming from this, on 1 December 2017, HMRC published the response to its consultation document 'Tackling evasion: A requirement to notify HMRC of offshore Structures', which will be used to develop a revised draft to the current widely-drawn IHT hallmark. The *Finance (No 2) Act 2017* contains legislation in response to the outcome of the HMRC consultation document 'Tackling Offshore Tax Evasion: a requirement to correct'. The thrust of the 'requirement to correct' (RTC) provisions is to encourage taxpayers to update their tax affairs on or before 30 September 2018, with the imposition of heavy penalties for those who failed to do so by the 2018 deadline. In January 2018 HMRC updated its guidance on offshore disclosure facilities: See tinyurl.com/nezhrfn.

Reduction in penalties for disclosure

8.42 The purpose behind *Finance Act 2007, Sch 24, para 9* is to set bands of penalties and to allow some reduction within the band but, which is an important departure from previous practice, not total reduction in the more serious cases. *Paragraphs 9* to *12* of *Sch 24* were updated by *Finance Act 2008*. There are reductions in penalties where a person, including a third party, discloses inaccuracy in a tax document. This may be by simply telling HMRC about the situation; or giving HMRC reasonable help to quantify the inaccuracy; or giving HMRC access to records to enable the inaccuracy to be corrected.

Where the disclosure is made by the taxpayer at a time when he has no reason to believe that HMRC have discovered or are about to discover the inaccuracy, that disclosure is classified as 'un-prompted'. The effect of this is that an un-prompted disclosure of a careless error can reduce the penalty to nil. Applying the example of John's estate, the revaluation of the business following the obtaining of the tax refund, if disclosed promptly, may avoid a penalty entirely.

Mitigation of 30% penalties

8.43 Where the disclosure is prompted, a careless error, attracting a penalty of 30%, may be reduced, but not below 15%. The error by John in valuing his father's house was careless – see **Example 8.7** above. If he had notified HMRC as soon as he discovered that the property was significantly more valuable than he thought, that might have been treated as an unprompted disclosure. However, the mechanism of valuation in deceased estates relies on disclosure which in turn includes answering the question whether the property is to be offered for sale. The value of the property is routinely referred to the Valuation Office. If it is known that a property is to be sold within a reasonably short time of the death, then it is quite common for the gross sale proceeds to be taken as the value at the date of death. There is scope for arguing that John, in **Example 8.7** above, merely put forward an opinion of the value of the property that turned out to be wrong and that he was, in effect, disclosing as part of the estate whatever price would eventually be received on sale, on the basis that the sale price would be substituted for the valuation. However, that is a weak argument and by his carelessness John has certainly risked a penalty of at least £1,500.

Mitigation of 70% penalties

8.44 Where the action of the taxpayer was deliberate but not concealed the starting point for penalties is 70% but it may be reduced to a minimum of 20% (*Finance Act 2007, Sch 24, para 10(3)*). The mitigation will depend on the 'quality' of the disclosure, which is defined by *Finance Act 2007, Sch 24, para 9(3)* as including timing, nature and extent.

In the case of Henry's estate in **Example 8.7** above the failure to disclose the gift with reservation was careless; however, it was not actually concealed but neither was it unprompted. It arose only from the detailed correspondence on the administration of the estate. Had John volunteered details of the gift, the penalty could have been reduced to 20% but under *Finance Act 2007, Sch 24, para 10(4)* a penalty that is otherwise chargeable at 70% cannot be reduced below 35%. On the face of it, therefore, John is at risk of a penalty of £4,200 in respect of the boat.

Mitigation of 100% penalties

8.45 Similar, but sharper rules apply to errors that fall into the 100% regime. Where disclosure is unprompted the minimum penalty is 30%, but where the disclosure arises only after HMRC have raised questions the penalty cannot be less than 50%. In relation to the undisclosed, unauthorised transfers to pay school fees from Henry's estate John has done nothing much to help HMRC. He did finally supply copies of his father's bank statements, but only after he had been asked a couple of times. He attempted to 'explain away' the payments. He will be lucky to escape with a penalty of much less than £18,000.

There is facility for 'special reduction' of a penalty in *Finance Act 2007, Sch 24, para11* if HMRC think it right to reduce a penalty because of 'special circumstances', but that does not include inability to pay, nor the fact that the increased liability of one taxpayer may reduce the liability of another.

There is a 100% cap on penalties, introduced by *Finance Act 2008*, which inserts the limitation into *Finance Act 2007, Sch 24, para 12*. This is necessary where, for example, a penalty could be charged against both the taxpayer and a third party. Thus, in the example of Henry's estate in **Example 8.7** above if Sarah had kept quiet about her father's use of the boat and John had been careless about the issue of reservation of benefit, a penalty could apply to both of them but either way it would not exceed 100% of the tax in issue.

Failure to file

8.46 A penalty of £100 applies for failure to deliver an account on time, and is now routinely imposed (*IHTA 1984, s 245(2)*). A further penalty of not more than £60 per day may be claimed, though this is much less common. This is per day of default running from the day on which the failure to deliver the account has been declared as a default, either by a court or by the Special Commissioners. The daily charge runs up to the day on which the account is delivered. Usually, HMRC will give notice of an action to seek penalties so the taxpayer has one last chance to comply. If an account is delivered more than six months after the due date but before HMRC have taken proceedings before the tribunal the penalty is increased to £200. If the account is delivered more than 12 months after the due date a penalty of up to £3,000 may be charged.

The penalty is not imposed where the taxpayer can show reasonable excuse. The procedure involves the simple completion of a form setting out the circumstances, but the penalty will be charged unless the taxpayer delivers the account without unreasonable delay after the excuse has ceased: see *s 245(7)*. The mere fact that the estate is complicated is not itself a factor: there must be some other element.

Example 8.8—Late filing of return

Josiah's estate comprised his many business interests, investments and properties, all in the UK. His will appointed as executors his daughter, who had worked in the businesses with her father; and his friend, who was qualified as a registered trust and estate practitioner.

On 1 September 2017 Josiah died and the normal filing date under *IHTA 1984, s 216(6)(a)* for form IHT400 was therefore 12 months from the end of the 'death month' ie 30 September 2018.

The account was late. It seemed for a time that, by a codicil, Josiah's estranged wife might be appointed executrix, but the difficulty was resolved by 7 May 2018 without her having to act. Had she become an executrix, she could have argued, under the 'three-month' rule in *s 216(6)(a)*, that time did not run against her until appointed, but: (a) she did not act anyway; and (b) the executors as a body are jointly liable for penalties, so the daughter and friend had no excuse. The size and complication of the estate are not excuses *per se*: the daughter knew all about the assets and the TEP had the specialist knowledge to deal with the account.

Where the failure relates to non-resident trustees the risk is perceived to be higher and as a consequence, the penalties greater. The rules as to disclosure are in *s 218* and failure to make a return may trigger a penalty of up to £300 plus £60 per day of default (*IHTA 1984, s 245A*).

Penalties will not be claimed from a deceased person who had not been compliant, but that in no way exonerates delinquent personal representatives as confirmed in HMRC Enquiry Manual EM1395 which states: 'Where an error or failure offence has occurred after the date of death in respect of the deceased's estate and this offence is attributable to the personal representatives you should seek to impose a penalty on the personal representatives.' The Compliance Handbook, at CH402000 also adds:

> 'If a penalty assessment, raised prior to a person's death, remains under appeal then negotiations to conclude any appeal must continue with personal representatives.'

Incorrect returns

8.47 The penalties for failure to make returns are modest by comparison with those where incorrect information is supplied. Under *IHTA 1984, s 247(4)*, any person assisting in the production of an account that he knows to be incorrect is liable to a penalty of up to £3,000. The person who actually makes the return wrongly may be liable for a penalty of up to 100% of the tax in issue, where the inaccuracy is both deliberate and concealed. If that person makes the return, but is not himself liable for the tax he may still be liable to a penalty of up to £3,000.

Errors are particularly prevalent in completing form IHT404 (joint property) with approximately 10% of IHT return forms IHT400 meriting detailed examination. Form IHT407 (chattels) and IHT405 (property) are also often a fruitful source of enquiry for HMRC.

8.48 It is in the nature of probate work that the full story does not emerge immediately but is drawn together over time. That is recognised (see **8.15** above) in the provisions for the use of estimates but it is also considered by HMRC in connection with the delivery of an account which is later found to be incorrect. In such cases errors must be corrected without 'unreasonable delay' (see *IHTA 1984, ss 217* and *248(1)*), otherwise the person liable to deliver the account will suffer the same penalty as someone who delivers an account negligently. Correction may be made on form C4 but, if there are a number of small changes and the overall value is not significant, the changes can be dealt with more swiftly by correspondence.

The pre-*FA 2007* rules as to calculation and mitigation of penalties allow practitioners to negotiate mitigation of the penalty by up to 30% for disclosure, up to 40% for co-operation and up to 40% in respect of seriousness (ie size and gravity), but all that changes for inaccuracies in returns for periods covered by the new rules described in this chapter.

Interest

8.49 Traditionally, it must be said that probate lawyers would appear untroubled over the imposition of interest on late paid IHT. It would seem to be regarded as a normal expense of administration and the work would be done as the work schedule permitted. Until the changes in *Finance Act 2009* (*s 101, Sch 53*) the level at which interest was charged on IHT was less than that charged in respect of other taxes. That helped advisers, but personal representatives and beneficiaries are now much less tolerant of this easy-going attitude on the part of lawyers. Clients are aware of the due dates and expect lawyers to administer estates more promptly to mitigate the burden of interest and in many cases it can be avoided by the use of the direct payment scheme mentioned at **8.35** above. Under *Finance Act 2009, s 101(1)* the rate applies to any tax, so the rate of interest for IHT is aligned with that for other taxes (currently 3% with effect from 21 November 2017) and will track Bank of England Base Rate. The new rules also set the late payment start dates for certain IHT instalments (ie under *IHTA 1984, ss 227, 229*). In consultation the professional bodies argued that the same rate should apply to repayments as to late payments, but the government have rejected that idea.

Interest is inevitable where payment of the tax itself is made by instalments on certain designated assets (see **8.31**). Where tax and interest arise on death, *s 233(1)(b)* charges interest from the day after the end of six months running from the end of the month in which the death occurred, but there are special rules in relation to certain types of property. Interest charged by HMRC is not allowable as a deduction in calculating any income profits or losses for any tax purposes.

That, however, is different from the situation where the executors have taken out a loan specifically in order to pay IHT (ie where they have not used the direct payment scheme). Where a specific loan account is taken out (not merely an overdraft) the interest paid for the first year may be deductible in calculating the income tax liability of the executors on untaxed estate income arising during the administration period (*ITA 2007, s 403*). This facility relates only to the initial loan to fund the tax payable before a grant of representation can be issued and does not relate to any further loans taken out by the personal representatives at any other time.

Suspension of penalties

8.50 The new penalty regime includes an 'enabling' facility to encourage better compliance, where the error in a return is careless, but results from a faulty procedure or misunderstanding on the part of the taxpayer that can be put right. Penalties can be suspended where, by notice under *Finance Act 2007, Sch 24, para 14*, HMRC specify the action to be taken and the period for which it must be taken. This is unlikely to apply to family members who act as executor.

Shifting the blame onto the adviser

8.51 It has long been the complaint of taxpayers that 'I left it to the accountant/solicitor/adviser to get the forms right'. This all too prevalent reluctance of taxpayers either to pay tax or to give sufficient time to form filling suggests that sometimes such a complaint is unjustified, but *Finance Act 2007, Sch 24, para 18(3)* only exonerates the taxpayer who can show that he took reasonable care to avoid inaccuracy or unreasonable failure.

Penalties for late payment

8.52 *Finance Act 2009, s 106, Sch 56* introduced a more sophisticated penalty regime to tackle the issue of late payment. No doubt it will mainly affect 'ordinary' taxpayers more than trusts and estates, but the regime will be tougher. Where, as for IHT, the obligation to file is occasional rather than annual, the regime provides:

- 5% of the tax penalty one month after the filing date;
- 5% more at six months;
- 5% more at 12 months; but
- suspension where the taxpayer agrees an arrangement for time to pay (though that does not apply to IHT, being inappropriate).

For a tax on capital, where there may be little liquidity, these are potentially serious amounts of extra money to find.

Penalties for late filing

8.53 *Finance Act 2009, s 105, Sch 55* applies penalties simply for late filing, something that has hitherto been almost routine in probate work. The regime, which already applied to certain taxes, is now extended to IHT. It is routinely applied in practice thus:

- £100 straight after the due date;
- £10 for each day that the failure to submit a return continues, for up to 90 days (but only if HMRC 'decide' that the penalty should be payable and issue a notice to that effect;
- 5% of the tax due (or £300, if greater) for prolonged failure (ie at six months);
- 5% more (or £300, if greater) at 12 months;
- 70% of the tax due where a person fails to submit a return for over 12 months and has deliberately withheld information that HMRC need to assess the tax due; and
- 100% where there has been concealment.

The latter two tax-based penalties are subject to potential reduction for disclosure. It is not uncommon for family to be so affected by bereavement that there is a delay before the formalities of probate are even approached, let alone tackled. Where the estate is complex, these new penalties in effect force the family to begin the task of gathering information with what may feel like unseemly haste.

TIME LIMITS FOR HMRC ASSESSMENTS

8.54 *FA 2009, s 99* and *Sch 51* introduced extended powers for HMRC to issue assessment notices in relation to IHT matters.

They are as follows:

	IHT (account and payment submitted)	IHT (no account and payment submitted)
Careless loss of tax	6 years	20 years
Deliberate loss of tax	20 years	No limit
Other reason	4 years	20 years

If there is deliberate loss of tax and no account and payment has been submitted, the legislation is silent on time limits for an assessment notice. It is therefore implied that there is no time limit.

RECORD KEEPING

8.55 The absence of records can be a major problem for personal representatives. Specific instances have already been described at **8.8** where the executors have a duty to notify HMRC of events of which they have had no personal knowledge before taking office. It is of course good practice for any person who has an estate that may on his death become taxable to maintain personal records of gifts etc in a form that will be intelligible to the personal representatives. That has become more important as many more transfers (notably those into/out of trust) have been treated as immediately chargeable since 22 March 2006.

Capital taxation long enjoyed a separate and more relaxed compliance regime than now applies, for example under self-assessment. However, prior to the changes introduced in *FA 2008* (*s 113* and *Sch 36*), the information-gathering powers of HMRC were just as strict as the corresponding provisions under self-assessment. There were previously powers to require information under *IHTA 1984, s 219*, to call for documents under *IHTA 1984, s 219A* and to inspect property under *IHTA 1984, s 220*. However, the information and inspection powers in *FA 2008, Sch 36* were extended to apply for IHT purposes by *FA 2009* (*s 96* and *Sch 48*), with effect from 1 April 2010.

Practitioners will usually keep probate and trust files for a very long time. In relation to trusts the papers will be kept because of the ongoing nature of the matter and because of the record-keeping requirements under self-assessment. In relation to estates, it is not uncommon that queries will arise some time later, for example where assets have been appropriated to beneficiaries *in specie* and where the probate value has not been notified to the beneficiary or, if it has, the beneficiary has lost the record. The value for tax purposes at which the beneficiary acquired the asset will normally be its probate value under the rule in *TCGA 1992, s 274* (where the value was 'ascertained' for IHT).

Finance Act 2008, Sch 37 contains new obligations as to record keeping, but they do not affect IHT. There were proposals for this in the initial consultation, but the professions doubted the validity of a proposal for documents to be kept for two years from the date of preparation of returns because (a) the time limit did not sit easily with others; and (b) most papers were retained anyway, so there was no need to legislate. Budget Note 89 to the Budget 2009 confirmed that in the light of these comments the government would not pursue the idea of special record-keeping requirements for IHT, so the more general IHT rules set out in *IHTA 1984, ss 254–261* continue to apply.

DETERMINATIONS AND APPEALS

Procedure

8.56 In practice, the issue of a Notice of Determination will rarely come as a surprise to the taxpayer. After the usual examination of a return and correspondence about matters such as value, a disagreement as to treatment will arise where the positions of HMRC and the taxpayer are so far apart that they cannot be reconciled. There is a review procedure, under which the taxpayer may ask for the HMRC file to be passed to a separate officer to consider the issues in dispute: see **8.62** below. This can result in agreement without formal proceedings, so it should be considered in the first instance.

Example 8.9—Progress of a dispute with HMRC (I)

John Davis was an engineer working in the Middle and Far East. At the age of 45 he returned to his native East Anglia and purchased a smallholding. Adjoining the house were a range of farm buildings and 50 acres of land which he put to profitable use. He kept sheep and poultry but in later life he discontinued the poultry operation because it was no longer profitable. Age and infirmity eventually forced him to take on help with the flock, which he sold to a neighbour who continued to graze them on his land on an arrangement which, if it had been committed to writing, would have been more like a partnership or contracting agreement than a tenancy or licence. Those farm buildings that had not fallen into disrepair were used partly by his grandson for the repairing of vehicles but otherwise for the management of what remained of the farming business. There was some development value on part of the land.

Following his death his executors claimed that the house, buildings and land were a farm and that agricultural property relief should be available on the entirety. Mindful of the decision in *McCall v Revenue and Customs Commissioners* [2008] STC (SCD) 752, it was agreed that no BPR would be available, but the claim to APR was pursued.

HMRC quoted *Re Antrobus (No 2)* [2005] Lands Tribunal DET/47/2004: buildings used for car repairs are not occupied for the purposes of agriculture. They were willing to allow APR on the land, and on one of the farm buildings, but not on the house, nor on the remainder of the property because, in effect, the deceased had given up farming some years before he died. His residence was merely a house with land rather than a farm. Correspondence ensued: see continuation of this example at **8.64** below.

The form of the notice

8.57 There is some latitude: it can include:

- the date of the transfer;
- the value transferred;
- the value of any property to which the value transferred relates;
- the transferor;
- the tax chargeable;
- the person liable to tax or part of it;
- the amount that anyone has overpaid tax and the date from which that overpaid tax carries interest;
- 'any other matter that appears to the Board to be relevant for the purposes of [*IHTA 1984*]'.

The notice specifies a time limit for appeal and the way in which the appeal can be made. Essentially, this makes the taxpayer decide exactly what to appeal against and why. That appeal is covered by *IHTA 1984, s 222* and must be made within 30 days by notice in writing given to the Board. Since 1 April 2009, appeals have normally proceeded to the First-tier Tax Tribunal.

8.58 Under the new appeals process introduced by the *Tribunals, Courts and Enforcement Act 2007* there is a primary filter in *rule 23* under which all cases must be allocated to a category, viz:

- default paper;
- basic;
- standard; or
- complex.

The treatment of a 'default paper' appeal

8.59 Within this category will come late returns and fixed percentage surcharges for late payment, so this may affect few IHT situations. There will be a statement of the case, which can include a request for an oral hearing; a reply, which likewise could request a hearing; possibly listing for hearing but otherwise consideration of the papers and a decision.

The treatment of a 'basic' appeal

8.60 'Basic' will include appeals: from penalties; from information notices; for leave to appeal late; to postpone payment of tax pending appeal; or to close an enquiry; so again not really affecting many IHT situations. These will just be listed for hearing without statement of case or reply.

The treatment of a 'standard' appeal

8.61 This is the more likely territory for IHT practitioners, where say such a question as 'is it a farmhouse?' is considered. There will be a statement of case, and at that point the case may be designated as 'complex'. A list of documents must be produced. There may be a case-management hearing but in its absence the case will be listed for hearing. It is likely that many cases that would in the past have gone to the Special Commissioner will follow this route to a hearing.

The treatment of a 'complex' appeal

8.62 These will be rare. They will be treated like standard cases, but may enjoy specific directions before any case management hearing or the hearing itself.

Internal reviews

8.63 A system of 'internal reviews' by HMRC was introduced to coincide with the Tax Tribunals regime from 1 April 2009. Internal reviews broadly provide an alternative means for taxpayers and HMRC to resolve disputes by agreement, rather than through the auspices of a tribunal hearing. If an appeal has been submitted to HMRC and the issue cannot be settled, the taxpayer can notify the appeal to the Tribunal. Alternatively, the taxpayer may ask HMRC to review the point at issue, or HMRC may offer the taxpayer a review (*TMA 1970, s 49A*).

If the taxpayer requests a review, HMRC must respond by stating their original view within 30 days, or possibly a longer period if this is reasonable. If HMRC offer a review, the taxpayer has 30 days in which to accept. Otherwise, HMRC's original view generally stands (*TMA 1970, s 49C*).

If a review takes place, HMRC may uphold, vary or cancel their original view of the case, and notify the taxpayer of their conclusion within the following 45 days, or other agreed period (*s 49E*). If HMRC's review is unfavourable, the taxpayer may notify an appeal to the Tribunal within 30 days, or outside this period with the Tribunal's permission.

Appeal

8.64 Appeals may be brought out of time with the consent of HMRC if there is reasonable excuse – see *IHTA 1984, s 223*. Equally, the taxpayer may have second thoughts about the grounds for appeal. The Special Commissioners could, under the old rules, allow him to put forward ideas that were not specified in the notice of appeal provided that the omission was neither wilful nor unreasonable and could then decide the matter.

Under the new system, which is designed to be seen to be totally independent of HMRC, it is likely that that facility will continue, but it is necessary to wait and see how the new tribunals exercise their powers.

Example 8.10—Progress of a dispute with HMRC (II)

[Continuing from **Example 8.9** above]

Following a review of the facts, the executors give up the claim to relief on the farm buildings that were virtually empty but pursue the main claim, relief on the house which has not yet been sold. A meeting is fixed between HMRC, the Valuation Office, the valuer acting for the executors and the executors themselves. At that meeting the respective valuers agree the open market value of the farm house, the value of the buildings in respect of which no relief is claimed, and without prejudice to the dispute also agree the value of the house for the purposes of agricultural property relief. They also agree that, if the arrangement for sheep farming really was a partnership rather than a tenancy, there was enough agricultural land to support the claim that the house was a farmhouse; and that, on that basis, the house was of 'character appropriate'. That just leaves one issue to be decided: quite what was the arrangement between the deceased and his neighbour? On that now hangs the entire claim to APR on the house.

One week later, whilst still under the 'old' regime, HMRC issue the Notice of Determination. One week after that the executors appeal, arguing that the deceased was a farmer to the date of his death. The case is designated a 'standard' appeal because it turns entirely on questions of fact; but see below as to the progress of the matter. See continuation of this example at **8.66**.

Costs

8.65 The main concern of taxpayers, apart from the decision itself, is costs. This is currently the subject of informal consultation, to see if the present arrangements work fairly. Following the introduction of the First-tier and Upper Tax Tribunal regime from 1 April 2009, there are provisions for the award of costs in certain specific circumstances. The rules for the First-tier Tribunal (*The Tribunal Procedure (First-tier Tribunal) (Tax Chamber) Rules, SI 2009/273*) provide for costs if (among other circumstances) a party to the appeal (or their representative) has acted unreasonably in bringing, defending or conducting the proceedings. In addition, if a case falls into the 'complex' category, the taxpayer may effectively 'opt out' of costs or expenses by written request to the Tribunal within 28 days (*rule 10*). The Upper Tribunal Rules also make provision for the award of costs following unreasonable behaviour, but do not include an 'opt out' facility.

Under the previous appeals regime *SI 1994/1811, reg 21* provided, in relation to the old tribunals, that a tribunal might award costs against any party to the proceedings including one who has withdrawn his appeal if that party had acted 'wholly unreasonably'. For an example of this rule applied in favour of the taxpayer, see *Robertson v CIR (No 2)* SpC [2002] SSCD 242 (SpC 3130). The Revenue won, however, against an unreasonable taxpayer in *Phillips v Burrows* SpC [2000] SSCD 112 (SpC 229, 229A).

Costs were an issue in the case of *Wells (Personal Representative of Glowacki (deceased)) v Revenue and customs Commissioners* [2008] STC (SCD) 188, which decided in favour of HMRC that a slightly curiously drafted deed of variation did not have the effect of removing a house from the estate of the deceased by means of a non-chargeable deemed lifetime transfer. In the event,

Malcolm Gammie QC as Special Commissioner quashed the determination that was the subject of the appeal but acknowledged (see para 48 of the decision) that the next step would be a further determination, based on his decision in the instant case. He ruled that neither party had acted unreasonably and that he could therefore make no order as to costs.

No order for costs is made without giving that party a chance to make representations. The tribunal can order one party to pay all the costs of the other. If not agreed they are taxed in the county courts like county court costs. There are special rules in Scotland.

The Special Commissioner appeal procedure has in the past been helpful both to HMRC and to the profession. It was very appropriate in deciding how the law should be applied in particular circumstances where the law was unclear. Strictly speaking, the decision of a Special Commissioner bound neither him in a subsequent case nor any other commissioner nor any court. However, the costs of an appeal are such that taxpayers, and no doubt HMRC and the new tribunals, will be guided by previous decisions of the Special Commissioners where the facts of the current case are broadly similar to one that has already been decided.

Do the changes represent a better way?

8.66 Classification of cases as 'default paper' or as 'basic' should allow for cheaper decisions. There is virtually no risk that precedents will be set, whether good or doubtful.

HMRC hope that their introduction of the internal review process mentioned above will reduce the number of disputes that go to appeal. The review will be done 'at a distance from caseworkers', something no doubt harder to achieve within the fairly narrow compass of IHT officers. Taxpayers can appeal from what they see as an unsatisfactory review.

Example 8.11—Progress of a dispute with HMRC (III)

Continuing from **Example 8.10** above, the executors correspond with HMRC to identify the issues that are relevant to the hearing and, where possible, to agree the facts of the case. The executors obtain a proof of evidence from the neighbour and research the financial transactions between the deceased and the neighbour. It turns out that a diligent junior employee of the accountants had attended a meeting between the deceased and the neighbour some time previously, at which the basis of the farming arrangements was discussed. Prompted by the employee, a contemporaneous note was made of the arrangement, initialled by both parties and the accountant!

This shows that in fact the deceased remained the main decision maker, that he was responsible for various aspects of management of the flock and that the neighbour provided occasional help when required.

The tax in issue is not substantial. There is an internal review by the dedicated HMRC review team, whose decision can bind their case workers. After discussion between the executors and HMRC the matter is compromised on terms that require the taxpayer to pay some money, but not as much as tax on the entire farmhouse.

Chapter 9

Trusts: interest in possession

SIGNPOSTS

- **Substance v form** – The formal title of an interest in possession can be subject to HMRC challenge in light of the action or indeed lack of action, by the trustees. This is particularly relevant where the main trust asset is the whole or a share of the former home (see **9.1–9.6**).
- **The old-style trust interest** – The full impact of the *FA 2006* trust reforms must be considered in the context of any IHT planning routine involving variation or termination of an established (qualifying) pre-22 March 2006 interest in possession or A&M trust (see **9.10–9.13** and **9.27**).
- **The post-*FA 2006* trust interest** – The trust reforms principally affect the IHT code with a beneficial knock-on effect for CGT – the income tax treatment remains unaffected. The current categories and restrictive use of the IPDI, BMT and 18-to-25 must be distinguished from their predecessors (see **9.7–9.10**; **9.19–9.21**; **9.31**).
- **Reversionary interests** – The penal anti-avoidance rules can produce costly and unintended results for the reversionary and purchased interests (see **9.22–9.26**).
- **Excluded property** – The application of the rules can still work in the taxpayer's favour but great care must be taken to avoid the not so obvious pitfalls (see **9.32–9.35**).

IHT TREATMENT

The old law: how an interest in possession was taxed

9.1 The 'old law' refers to the position that applied before the trust reforms introduced in *FA 2006*.

IHTA 1984, s 49 treated a person who was entitled to an interest in possession in settled property as if that person was beneficially entitled to the property in which that interest subsisted. This had IHT consequences (particularly on the partition of a fund between the life tenant and the remaindermen) that were difficult to explain to the lay client. One illustration of the difficulty is *Executors of Patch deceased* [2007] SpC 600, which is reviewed at **15.51**. The issue of the existence of an interest in possession (such term to include an Immediate Post Death Interest (IPDI)) is frequently litigated.

Note: All statutory references in this chapter are to *IHTA 1984* unless otherwise stated.

Example 9.1—Half share of a house in a trust

Spouses Chris and Les, owned the family home as tenants in common in equal shares. Each made a will in 2006 leaving their half share in the house to their adult children without any restriction on use or alienation in the hope that there would be no interest in possession in that half share by the surviving spouse given that the latter would be occupying the property by virtue of their own half share. When the will was drawn up it was intended that the value of the legacy to the children would use all or part of the nil rate band of the first spouse to die. (*Note*: the benefit of this tax planning routine has been largely eroded by the introduction of the transferable nil rate band effective from 9 October 2007– see **Chapter 15** for existing schemes and **Chapter 3** for the position going forward.)

Whilst there is no case directly in point, the robust view is that there is no interest in possession by the surviving spouse in the half house owned by the children as the former's continued occupation is by virtue of their own half share. The downside is that the CGT principal private residence relief is not available on the children's share if the house is later sold at a profit.

9.2

Focus

Exercise of trustees' discretion to permit beneficiary occupation of a trust property does not necessarily create an interest in possession.

In *IRC v Lloyds Private Banking Ltd* [1998] STC 559, considered further at **16.45**, a mother gave her share in the house to her daughter but contrary to Example 9.1 above, out of natural caution the will contained provisions restricting the daughter from disposing of that half share in the house during the father's lifetime. The daughter successfully argued before the Special Commissioner that her father did not gain significant advantage from the will because he was now responsible for all the outgoings instead of only half as before. However, on appeal, the High Court held that the father had, during widowhood, enjoyed the exclusive use of the mother's half share in the house and therefore had an interest in possession in it, thereby nullifying the intended tax advantage.

Interpretation of the law in Judge v HMRC

9.3 In *Judge (personal representatives of Walden deceased) v Revenue and Customs Comrs* [2005] SSCD 863 (SpC 506), the Special Commissioner had to consider a badly drawn will. The case, which is analysed in more detail at **16.34**, is of particular interest because it reviews several important and practical issues. The material part of the will gave an interest in a property:

> '... free of tax ... upon trust with the consent in writing of my wife during her lifetime... to sell the same with full power to postpone the sale for so long as they shall in their absolute discretion think fit ... and I declare my trustees during the lifetime of my Wife shall permit her to have the use and enjoyment of the said property for such period or periods as they shall in their absolute discretion think fit pending postponement of sale she paying the rates taxes and other outgoings and keeping the same in good repair and insured against fire to the full value thereof ...'.

9.4 The question posed was, did this give the widow an interest in possession? Clearly she had a substantial economic interest because she could effectively restrict sale. On her death her executors considered that the widow did not have an interest in possession as her interest could have been terminated at any time by the trustees and thus they concluded that the property was held on discretionary trust.

The Commissioner agreed.

Had the trustees required the widow to vacate, they still could not have sold the house but they could have perhaps let it. The Commissioner disregarded the external evidence of the way that the advisers had treated the trust and looked only at the (unsatisfactory) terms of the will, inserting one or two words to complete its sense but giving effect to the intention of the testator as expressed in the terms of the whole will. There was nothing to go on as far as extrinsic evidence of the intentions of the testator was concerned.

9.5 An 'interest in possession' was defined adopting the tests in *Gartside v IRC* [1968] AC 553 and in *Pearson v IRC* [1980] STC 318. In *Pearson* it was described as '...a present right to the present enjoyment ...' of something. Later cases such as *Woodhall (Woodhall's Representative) v IRC* [2000] SSCD 558 (SpC 261) and *Faulkner (Adams Trustee) v IRC* [2001] SSCD 112 (SpC 278) have shown that a right of occupation could constitute an interest in possession. In the *Judge* case the widow's right to occupation could be terminated by the trustees, so she did not have an interest in possession but it should be carefully noted that the *Judge* case is limited to its specific facts and for that reason it should not be regarded as a blueprint for all cases. In particular it does not indicate whether Statement of Practice 10/79, reviewed below, is good law, nor does it comment on the effectiveness of the 'debt or charge' scheme – the latter is examined in detail at **16.48**.

One more 'finding' of an interest in possession was in *Smith and others v HMRC* [2009] SpC 742, where an account formerly held in the name of the late husband of the deceased had been transferred into the joint name of the son and the deceased. The intended purpose (but never committed to writing) was that the deceased would receive the interest during her lifetime but on her death the capital would belong to the son – the reasoning was that the son helped his parents with both time and money. The account funds were not included in the estate of the deceased but its existence was later notified to HMRC, who issued a Notice of Determination which held the executors liable for IHT on its value. The son was assessed in his separate capacity as both executor and the recipient of the funds. The other executor appealed, partly because he had not received nor benefited from the funds.

The Commissioner found that the account had become settled property before the mother's death, being held for her and then the son in succession within *IHTA 1984, s 43(1)(a)*. As a result, the executors were not liable to IHT on the fund itself, so to that extent their appeal succeeded; but the son was liable as trustee. The executors were liable, however, for additional tax as adjusted for the amount due on the fund itself (ie the increase that resulted from aggregation of the settled fund with the free estate).

This outcome should be contrasted with the decision in *Davies and Rippon v HMRC* [2009] UKFTT 138 (TC) TC00106, where the existence of an interest in possession was asserted but not proved to the satisfaction of Judith Powell, sitting as judge in the First-tier Tribunal. The nature of the case is such that perhaps it is of greater interest to lawyers and will writers than to tax specialists, but it nonetheless establishes a useful reference point. The key facts are set out below.

Mrs Rhona Goodman, the mother of the appellants, was the widow of Geoffrey Goodman, who had died in 1969. Following the death of Mrs Goodman, it was argued that estate duty surviving spouse relief should apply to certain assets, though HMRC considered that they were part of Mrs Goodman's estate for IHT. The taxpayers argued that, by his conduct, Mr Goodman had, in effect, settled certain property on his wife for life, with remainder to his daughters; an alternate argument ran that Mr and Mrs Goodman had executed mutual wills, with the result that property later inherited by Mrs Goodman on her husband's death was held under trust and could not be alienated by her except in accordance with that mutual agreement.

The evidence supported that the wills of husband and wife were similar but not identical; during her widowhood Mrs Goodman formed a friendship with a

Mr Dodd but was concerned to protect her daughters' inheritance; she did not spend the capital that she also inherited from Mr Dodd when she survived him.

The judge held that, for the claim to succeed, the appellants must show that the property had been settled and that the surviving spouse must not have been competent to dispose of it. The burden of proof of a secret trust is on those who assert it; see *re Snowden Deceased* [1979] Ch 528. Past evidence is admissible: see *Blackwell v Blackwell* [1929] HL 318. There must be 'clear and satisfactory evidence' to support mutual wills: see *re Cleaver* [1981] 2 All ER 1018. The judge considered the arguments as to a secret trust and as to mutual wills but found no evidence to support either contention. There was no written or implied trust and accordingly, all the property was taxable as part of Mrs Goodman's free estate.

Statement of Practice 10/79

9.6 Statement of Practice 10/79 has never been tested in court. Put simply, it states that where, pursuant to their powers, trustees of a discretionary trust permit the trust beneficiary to rent trust property or to have non-exclusive occupation of it that occupation does not create an interest in possession if full rent is paid or even if the tenancy is for less than full consideration. If, in the exercise of a power drawn widely enough, the trustees use that power so as to provide a beneficiary with a permanent home, HMRC will treat that as creating an interest in possession.

In *Judge*, Statement of Practice 10/79 was not in point because the trustees had not exercised any power. In *IRC v Eversden (exors of Greenstock, decd)* [2002] EWHC 1360 (Ch), [2002] STC 1109 there was an opportunity to rely on SP 10/79 which was not taken by the court. *Eversden*, which is discussed at **7.9**, went in favour of the taxpayer but was nullified by *FA 2003, s 185*, which inserted *sub-s (5A)* into *FA 1986, s 102* (the 'gifts with reservation' legislation).

Changes under FA 2006

9.7 *Section 156* of the *Finance Act 2006* introduced amendments to *FA 1986, Sch 20,* which changed the IHT treatment of many forms of interests in possession. It had become common, in settlements and even more so in wills, for any life interest to a spouse or civil partner to be subject to overriding powers of appointment. Occasionally, these powers were included for family reasons, such as where, following second marriage, the testator had strong reasons to protect the capital of the fund from access by the second spouse to instead preserve for the benefit of children of the first marriage. Whilst that might have been unobjectionable, one very common result of the structure was that, during widowhood, the trustees could exercise their powers to terminate the interest in possession and yet allow the widow(er) to continue to live in trust property but not by any right as a beneficiary.

Equally, where a wealthy man had late in life married a much younger woman, he could effectively use her as a 'peg life' or 'bridge' for substantial gifts to his children from a prior relationship. Whilst he might not meet the required seven years survival period, giving the new wife a short-term interest in possession could provide that the indirect gifts to his children in remainder would likely escape tax assuming that their stepmother would live seven years from the date on which her interest in possession ceased. This manoeuvre is specifically countered by *FA 1986, s 102ZA*, though some doubts have been expressed as to whether that section in fact closes all possible loopholes in this area.

9.8 With effect from 22 March 2006 most lifetime interest in possession trusts attract the IHT (and hence CGT) treatment always afforded to the discretionary trust – for IHT purposes only the correct term for such a trust is a 'relevant property' trust. Transitional rules were introduced in respect of pre-March 2006 trusts, most of which applied up to 5 April 2008. This chapter does not attempt to do justice to all the issues that have been raised, particularly since some are unresolved, though *Finance Act 2008, s 140* did contain some amending legislation (see at **9.27** below).

IPDI

9.9 An interest in possession trust created on death will generally continue to be taxed under the old rules by virtue of *IHTA 1984, s 49A* – it will be a qualifying interest. This preserves most of the hallmarks of the pre-22 March 2006 treatment in that the spouse or civil partner exemption will continue to be available to shelter life interests under wills.

The conditions of *IHTA 1984, s 49A* ('Immediate post-death interest' (IPDI)) are as follows:

(1) The settlement must be effected by will or on intestacy.

(2) The tenant for life must become beneficially entitled to an immediate interest in possession on the death of the testator or intestate.

(3) The trusts must not currently be for bereaved minors and the interest must not be that of a disabled person.

(4) Condition (3) must have been satisfied at all times since the life tenant became entitled to that interest in possession.

The concept of the IPDI is retained as part of the overall anti-avoidance scheme of *FA 2006*. Thus, if the trustees use overriding powers to terminate the life interest of the spouse or civil partner to create ongoing trusts for adult beneficiaries, that will trigger an IHT charge and the funds will then migrate to the relevant property IHT regime described in **Chapter 10**. The specific target of abuse of 'peg lives' was countered by *FA 1986, s 102ZA*. This treats the termination of an interest in possession as a 'gift' by the life tenant, thus bringing the 'gift with reservation rules' into play.

Example 9.2—House in a nil rate trust

Under her will Sarah left her house to a discretionary trust, the class of beneficiaries of which includes her friend John. Within two years of Sarah's death the trustees allow John to occupy the property. That does not automatically give John an interest in possession: it will depend on the facts, as it did in *Judge v HMRC*, reviewed at **9.3–9.5**.

If more than three months but less than 24 months from the date of Sarah's death, the trustees appointed the house to John absolutely, then for IHT purposes alone *s 144* would treat that appointment as effective from Sarah's death and hence as if read back into the will. Equally if they gave John an IPDI within 30 days of Sarah's death that would be effective in the same way but note there is no three-month waiting period for the latter IPDI creation, thus the impact of *Frankland v IRC* [1997] STC 1450 is neatly avoided.

If, however, John was residing in the house before Sarah's death and had just never moved out, but the trustees did nothing and simply allowed the situation to continue, the trustees could not be said to have exercised their powers to create an IPDI.

But consider what if John was a part owner of the house – how could the trustees throw him out? In such a case, HMRC would look carefully and decide the case on its specific facts.

Although the more common case will be that of beneficial ownership of a house which passes into trust under the terms of a will, some property is held within trusts that give a general power of appointment and usually to the incumbent life tenant. The exercise of that power to create an immediate interest in possession can be an IPDI.

Example 9.3—IPDI by default

Ursula's will leaves shares in the family property company to her nephew, Tom and the residue of her estate to her niece Yolande for life, with remainder to her great-nieces. Tom promptly disclaims his gift such that the shares fall back into residue. Yolande's resulting interest in the increased residue is an IPDI.

Example 9.4—Pilot trust

During his lifetime, Hank set up a pilot trust of £100 for his son for life with remainder to the grandchildren. By his will Hank left his estate to that pilot trust. The net estate passing under the will and now held on the trust is an IPDI: it was in effect settled on death, not when the pilot trust was formed (though if it should ever be relevant, the trust began when the £100 went in).

'Old' interests in possession

9.10 Questions arise as to whether an interest in possession that existed before 22 March 2006 (an 'old-style' IIP or more correctly qualifying IIP) remains within *IHTA 1984, s 49(1)*, ie is it treated today in the same way it always was? The issue is whether, by virtue of *IHTA 1984, s 49(1A)* that old treatment is displaced where the interest in question is one to which the beneficiary first becomes entitled after that date. Is it a new interest? The problem may gradually cease to be relevant but is best understood by illustrative examples.

Example 9.5—'Old' interests in possession: coming of age

A trust was created in 2002 giving Bill, who was born on New Year's Day 1988, the capital if he should attain age 35 – the gift carries the intermediate income and, under *s 31* of the *Trustee Act 1925*, an income entitlement arises at age 18. Bill reached age 18 on 1 January 2006 and the trustees, in making their return to 5 April 2006, showed that for part of the year (the period from New Year's Day 2006) Bill had an entitlement to that income. This situation continues even when Bill reaches age 30 in 2023 – he has no different interest from that held on 22 March 2006: there is only one interest.

It follows that, if he had wished, Bill could have created a 'transitional serial interest' (TSI; see below) in favour of A N Other before 6 October 2008 and could even after then give away his interest which would be treated as a potentially exempt transfer (PET).

Example 9.6—'Old' interests in possession: protected heiress

A trust fund created in the same year (2002) is also held for Bill's twin Celia on terms where, if she attains age 35, the capital is applied for her benefit, but only for life, with remainder for any children she may have.

The trust carries the intermediate income and similarly *Trustee Act 1925, s 31* applies.

Celia, like her brother Bill, also has an entitlement to income at age 18 on New Year's Day 2006. In 2023 she will still have a qualifying IIP, even though the particular trust provision under which income is paid to her is actually one that becomes operative only then. This would still be the case if the further trusts were in a separate clause in the trust document: Celia has an old IIP.

Example 9.7—'Old' interests in possession: long-delayed enjoyment of the fund

David was 25 early in 2006 and had an established qualifying IIP (QIIP) by 22 March in that year. However, the trust ties up the capital so that, even though David becomes entitled to it at age 40, the trustees can at any time take it away from him by exercising a power of appointment in favour of his younger sister, Emma.

What is David's interest at age 40 in 2021? His qualifying IIP is, in one sense, replaced by a new but precarious capital interest that can be withdrawn at any time. The trust fund is still settled because the trustees could take the capital away. It is a defeasible interest in the capital. *IHTA 1984, s 49(1)* still applies: he still has a qualifying IIP.

Example 9.8—Using the TSI facility but still controlling the capital

Frances had a qualifying IIP (QIIP) and once the terms of *FA 2006* became clear she agreed to the creation of a Transitional Serial Interest (TSI) on terms that the fund was to be held to pay the income to her daughter Harriet, now 21, until age 35. At 35, Harriet is not to get the capital outright: there are overriding powers that could take the capital away.

Harriet has a TSI now and will still have a TSI once she is 35.

The common thread running through these examples, which are taken from an exchange of questions and answers between STEP/CIOT and HMRC (available via the STEP website: www.step.org/default.aspx?page=955), is that the interests stem from the original trust instrument and not from action taken by the trustees at some later point. The parties are not artificially prolonging the trust beyond what was originally provided.

DISPOSAL OF A QUALIFYING INTEREST IN POSSESSION

The basic rule

9.11 *Section 51(1) of IHTA 1984* provides that the disposal of a qualifying interest in possession by the person who is entitled to it is not the transfer of money/assets but instead is to be treated as the termination of the interest in possession, triggering the provisions of *s 52*. The single exception, see *s 51(2)*, is a disposition for the maintenance of a family member under *IHTA 1984, s 11* but in practice, claims that dispositions are covered by *IHTA 1984, s 11* are rare.

The *IHTA 1984, s 52* charging regime imposes a tax charge on the capital of the fund in which the interest in possession subsisted. If, for example, the person disposing of the interest was entitled to half the income, it is half the trust capital that is taxed. If the tenant for life sells his interest for money, the money is then part of his estate and the tax on the fund is reduced by the amount of that money. However, that does not affect the valuation of a reversionary interest in the property.

Example 9.9—Partition of a life interest fund

Sally, aged 60, enjoys a qualifying life interest under the will of her late husband and on her death the property will pass to her daughter Jane. Given Sally's life expectancy, actuaries determine that the commercial value of her interest is equal to 55% of the fund. Sally and Jane agree to divide the fund equally between them with Jane paying Sally cash equal to 5% by way of equalisation.

The IHT treatment is not what they might expect. Sally and Jane, having read about *IHTA 1984, s 10*, thought that this was a transaction at open market value and was not a gift at all. *Section 52 of IHTA 1984*, however, treats the entire fund as belonging to Sally and not just the actuarial 55% element. There is therefore a transfer by her to Jane of 45% after taking account of what Jane has paid her (100% less 50% retained by Sally = 50% less 5% purchased by Jane = 45%). This was the very point in issue in *Executors of Patch deceased* [2007] SpC 600: see **15.51**.

Exceptions from charge on disposal

Focus

FA 2006 radically altered the IHT position on the termination of an interest in possession and its impact must be fully understood when considering any trust tax planning routine.

9.12 There are exceptions from the *IHTA 1984, s 52* charge and these are examined in more detail when considering the 'true' termination, rather than the 'deemed termination', of an interest in possession, but are:

- excluded property (see **9.32** and following below);
- exchange of one interest in possession for another;
- reverter to settlor;
- spouse/civil partner relief.

Under the current rules virtually all post-21 March 2006 lifetime life interests will fall to be treated under the relevant property regime for IHT purposes. Accordingly, *FA 2006, Sch 20, para 15* restricted the application of *s 52* so that the charge is confined to the coming to an end of an interest which is within the FA 2006 restricted class of favoured life interests (those which fall outside the relevant property regime), namely:

- an IPDI;
- a disabled person's interest (see **Chapter 10**); or
- a transitional serial interest (see **9.27** and **9.29** below).

Similarly, *FA 2006, Sch 20, para 14* amended *s 53* so that tax is no longer chargeable under *s 52* where:

- the tenant for life was entitled to the interest before 22 March 2006;
- that life interest was terminated after that day; and
- immediately before the termination of that life interest, the *IHTA 1984, s 71A* (bereaved minors) or *IHTA 1984, s 71D* (18-to-25 trusts) provisions applied to the property in which the interest subsisted.

This is part of the regime that limits favoured life interests to 'simple' life interest for spouses followed by absolute interests for children on attaining the age of 18 (bereaved minors trust) or by short-term follow on trusts that end by age 25 (18-to-25 trust). *IHTA 1984, Sch 20, para 14* made consequential amendments where a person becomes entitled to an interest in settled property on or after 22 March 2006 and the interest is not that of a disabled person and therefore not favoured under the current regime.

Finance Act 2010 introduced legislation that contains anti-avoidance measures to combat the exploitation of the rules as to excluded property trusts. This is discussed in greater detail at **9.24** below.

TERMINATION OF INTEREST IN POSSESSION

The old law

9.13 *Section 52 of IHTA 1984* provided for a deemed transfer by the life tenant of the property in which they had a qualifying interest in possession. The exceptions from charge on a disposal of qualifying interest in possession have been noted at **9.12**. There are also exceptions from charge when such an interest in possession comes to an end in circumstances where:

- the life tenant becomes absolutely entitled to the property;
- the life tenant obtains some other interest in possession in the property;
- the capital of the fund reverts to the settlor;
- the capital of the fund passes absolutely to the spouse of the settlor; the capital of the fund passes absolutely to the widow or widower of the spouse of the settlor where that settlor has died within two years earlier and the widow or widower is domiciled in the UK.

There are qualifications to these rules in certain specified circumstances: see *IHTA 1984, s 53(5)–(8)*.

9.14 In addition to the general exceptions from the charge on deemed termination there were, under the old law, other exceptions in *IHTA 1984, s 54* which broadly mirrored the *IHTA 1984, s 53* exceptions thus:

- reversion of the fund to the settlor during the lifetime of the settlor – the value of the fund is not to be included as part of the estate of the life tenant;
- the passing of the fund on the death of the life tenant to the UK-domiciled spouse of the settlor absolutely – again, the capital of the fund is to be left out of account through availability of the spousal exemption;
- the passing of the fund to the UK-domiciled widow or widower of the settlor where the settlor had died less than two years earlier – the capital of the fund is left out of account.

These exceptions are subject to qualification in the (somewhat rare) circumstances provided by *IHTA 1984, s 53(5)* and *(6)*. The even rarer situation of *commorientes* will also apply here.

Reverter to settlor

> **Focus**
>
> *FA 2006* has negated the benefits previously enjoyed under the reverter to settlor rules.

9.15 This type of settlement has long been popular in appropriate circumstances. At its simplest consider A settled funds on B for life, with remainder to A. There was no IHT charge on B's death if A was still alive, which was logical because the property was returning to its original owner, A. However, this device was often used in relation to the family home or a share in it thus consider A, married to B, left his share of the house to their child, C, absolutely. Following A's death C would settle the share of the house on B for life, with remainder back to C and again there was no IHT charge on B's death if C was still alive, which was logical because the property was returning to its original owner, C. Thus, a share in the house might pass down the generations whilst still being occupied by the surviving parent without being taxed on the second death.

This did not always work for CGT. If the house was sold during B's lifetime, any gain might be sheltered by the principal private residence exemption under *TCGA 1992, s 225*; but if it was unsold at the time it reverted to C there was no tax-free uplift on B's death because of *TCGA 1992, s 73*. To avoid that situation arising, the settlement was drafted so that it did not end on B's death, but the fund passed to C for life with gifts over and powers of appointment of capital. That sidestepped *TCGA 1992, s 73* and, instead, *TCGA 1992, s 72* gave the desired uplift on B's death.

Finance Act 2006 spoilt this structure. On B's death a relevant property trust will now arise unless, to avoid that, it is arranged that the property is to vest absolutely in C; but if it does the CGT problem revives. The trustees, with the concurrence of the parties, must do their sums. Which is the greater evil, CGT or IHT? Action must be taken whilst B is still alive or it will be too late. These things cannot always be engineered, but a good solution might be to crystallise the gain whilst it is still protected by *TCGA 1992, s 225*. That would be possible if B was willing to move house, perhaps to sheltered accommodation or even to a place offering substantial care but of course practicality must take precedence over tax savings.

There can be no tax-free uplift on B's death although if the trustees leave the ongoing trusts in place, a sale soon after B's death might be substantially sheltered from CGT by *TCGA 1992, s 225*. However, as mentioned above the old IHT exemption secured under the reverter to settlor trust rule cannot apply because a relevant property trust has arisen, but if the funds are promptly appointed out to C, the IHT charge may be moderate, even nil.

There is still one occasion where the CGT uplift may be achieved. This arises under *IHTA 1984, s 53(4)*, which provides that there is no *IHTA 1984, s 52* charge on termination of a qualifying interest in possession if, on that termination, either the:

- UK-domiciled spouse or civil partner of the settlor; or
- UK-domiciled widow/former civil partner, if the settlor has died

becomes beneficially entitled to the settled property. In these circumstances the property is still in trust, so it is *IHTA 1984, s 72* that is in point rather than *IHTA 1984, s 73*; and *IHTA 1984, s 72(1)(b)* excludes a chargeable gain.

FA 2006, s 80 changed *para 11(9)* and inserted *sub-paras (11)–(13)* into *FA 2004, Sch 15. Paragraph 11(12)* prevents relevant property from being treated as comprised in the taxpayer's estate for the purposes of the *para 11(1)* or *para 11(2)* exemptions 'at that subsequent time'. The situation may not often arise and it is accepted that the new rules are difficult to follow.

No qualifying interest in possession trusts can be created post 21 March 2006 (except for disabled persons or on death), so maybe this point is merely academic. One specific, but rarefied, problem arises where a settlor-interested trust owns a company that in turn owns a residence where a POAT election would cause the assets to be treated as part of the taxpayer's estate. It could bring assets within the IHT net which previously may have been sheltered from IHT exposure under the situs rules.

Some of the heat has now been taken out of the problem as HMRC comment that the words 'at any subsequent time' in *FA 2004, Sch 15, para 11(11)* do not literally mean 'at any later occasion'. Instead this should be interpreted more 'at any later time after value leaves the donor's estate, thereby reducing his estate, but returns to it because property is purchased with that value and the taxpayer has an interest in possession in the property'.

As a result there should be no difficulty where:

- X settled cash on himself before 22 March 2006; or
- Y, being a disabled person, did the same on/after that date,

and in either case, the trustees:

- bought a house for X (or Y, as the case might be) to live in; or
- sold that house and bought another; or
- used some of the proceeds of the house to buy shares, etc.

That leaves only the problem of the discretionary trust that was later appointed onto interest in possession trust. In this latter instance, an election is the only way to avoid POAT.

Anti-avoidance rule

9.16 As will be seen in **Chapter 10**, the creation of a discretionary trust is a chargeable lifetime transfer and thus elaborate provisions are included to prevent taxpayers deliberately inserting steps with the sole aim of avoiding this charge.

Consider the actions of a taxpayer who had already made substantial chargeable lifetime transfers and now wished to set up a further discretionary trust, but realised that this would trigger an immediate and unacceptable IHT charge. Under the pre-FA 2006 law without legislative intervention the device employed could see the settlor create a short-term interest in possession trust in favour of a person (the 'poor relation') who still had the full use of their available nil rate band; and thereafter for the fund to be held on full discretionary trusts (the intended aim from the outset). The purpose of this routine would enable the new trust to be chargeable to IHT by reference to the poor relation, under the rules described in **Chapter 10**, and at much lower rates than are otherwise the case.

The language of *IHTA 1984, ss 54A* and *54B* is obscure and not easily understood at first sight but it is very much designed to frustrate this tactic. *Finance Act 2006, Sch 20, para 16* introduces changes that give effect to the post 21 March 2006 regime.

Use of annual exemption

9.17 Pre *FA 2006*, the release by the life tenant to another of their qualifying interest in part of the trust fund was a potentially exempt transfer (PET). Accordingly, if not used elsewhere, the life tenant's annual exemption may be set against this transfer, provided that they notify the trustees that they wish to do so. *Section 57(4)* of *IHTA 1984* seems to suggest that such notice should be in some special form but that is misleading and although there was originally a form for this purpose its use has long since been discontinued. All that is currently required is a letter from the life tenant to the trustees indicating that the former has available an annual exemption (or two, if the prior year's allowance is also available) and that they wish to set it/them against the intended transfer.

Maintenance funds

9.18 There are special provisions where, on the termination of a qualifying interest in possession, property passes to a designated maintenance fund. Such a fund is connected with the maintenance of heritage property and use of the relief is, as a consequence, very rare (for a more detailed discussion see: *Agricultural, Business and Heritage Property Relief 7th edition (Bloomsbury Professional)*). Notwithstanding, the anti-avoidance measures in *FA 2010*, described at **9.25** below, contain a 'let out' for transfers to maintenance funds.

The law since 22 March 2006

9.19 *FA 2006, Sch 20* redefined the classification of potentially exempt transfers (PETs) made on or after 22 March 2006 so that lifetime transfers which can be PETs are henceforth limited to outright gifts to individuals or gifts into trusts for the disabled (DPI), namely those falling within the definition in *IHTA 1984, s 89)*.

This is a fundamental change which must be fully embraced as part of IHT planning through the use of trusts. Effectively all lifetime gifts into trust are now immediately chargeable (excluding a DPI) unless covered by exemptions or other pertinent reliefs (ie business property relief). As a result, those lifetime trust interests that confer a life interest and thus come under the category of an IIP trust are now within the relevant property regime for IHT purposes. The death of the life tenant no longer triggers a charge to IHT through aggregation with their estate – there is no need as the trust is now within the scheme of periodic and exit charges described in **Chapter 10**. The exceptions are:

- an IPDI;
- a DPI;
- a transitional serial interest (see **9.27** and **9.29** below).

Termination of IPDI

9.20 The termination of a qualifying IPDI is governed by the normal rules which applied to the old-style qualifying interest in possession. Tax is charged under *IHTA 1984, s 52* on the whole or any part of the fund affected. The same rule applies to a disabled person's interest or, see **9.27** below, to a transitional serial interest.

Under the new rules there is, however, an exception from the *IHTA 1984, s 52* charge where:

- the interest of a person who was entitled as life tenant before 22 March 2006 now comes to an end; and
- immediately before it does so, the fund is within the provisions of *IHTA 1984, s 71A* (trusts for bereaved minors); or
- the fund is within *IHTA 1984, s 71D* (18-to-25 trusts); see again *FA 2006, Sch 20, para 13*.

Prior to 22 March 2006, accumulation and maintenance (A&M) trusts for children were (perhaps simplistically) treated by practitioners as if they were within the IHT regime applied to the old interest in possession trusts. That is certainly no longer the case and A&M trusts are therefore examined in detail in **Chapter 10**.

Exceptions from charge under the rules from 22 March 2006

9.21 The exceptions from charge that were noted at **9.12** are now restricted. They apply only where the interest concerned is a DPI or a transitional serial interest (TSI). A modified version of the exception from charge is now specified by *IHTA 1984, s 54(2B)* whereby the value of the fund is left out of account in fixing the value of the estate of the life tenant where:

- the life tenant was entitled to the interest in possession on or after 22 March 2006 and dies thereafter; and
- the interest in possession held by the life tenant was an IPDI; and
- the settlor of the IPDI died before the life tenant but less than two years before; and
- on the death of the life tenant the fund passes to their or the settlor's UK-domiciled widow or widower or surviving civil partner.

The anti-avoidance rule noted at **9.15** is adapted so that it applies only to a disabled person's interest or a transitional serial interest.

The rules relating to maintenance funds for heritage property are adapted so as to apply only to an IPDI, a disabled person's interest or a transitional serial interest.

REVERSIONARY AND PURCHASED INTERESTS

The general rule

9.22 The basic rule is that a reversionary interest is not part of the estate of the person who holds it because for a qualifying interest in possession or later IPDI trusts, it is already treated as part of the estate of the life tenant. However, the market value rule in *IHTA 1984, s 10*, which would normally exclude a transaction from being a transfer of value, does not apply to an acquired or purchased reversionary interest. The law has been made a good deal more complicated by anti-avoidance rules introduced by *FA 2010, s 53* and described at **9.24** below.

The rule in Melville v IRC and its aftermath

9.23 *Section 55A* of *IHTA 1984* was introduced (in *FA 2002*) to counter a perceived abuse in relation to purchased settlement powers. It applies where a person becomes entitled to a 'settlement power' or has the right to exercise a power over a settlement or the ability to restrict such a power. The disposition, by which the taxpayer acquires that power, for money or money's worth, does not qualify for the market value rule in *IHTA 1984, s 10*, nor can it be treated as exempt by virtue of spouse relief or the reliefs relating to charities and other gifts for public benefit.

The use and retention of settlement powers is less common in UK-based trusts than in trusts for certain non-UK domiciliaries (especially US citizens), but even so this is a powerful anti-avoidance provision. The legislation arises out of the decision in favour of the taxpayer in *Melville v IRC* [2001] EWCA Civ 1247, [2001] STC 1271. The case turned upon a scheme involving a gift of a substantial portfolio of securities. A simple outright gift without a trust structure would have triggered an unacceptably large CGT charge but no immediate IHT consequence (by reason of its PET status). In contrast, the transfer to a discretionary trust would have paved the way for CGT holdover but would have triggered an exceptionally large IHT charge (immediate chargeable lifetime transfer). The scheme pivoted on the use of a discretionary trust, enabling the capital gains to be held over but with the trust terms crucially including a power over the settlement for the benefit of the settlor. This power had the effect of devaluing/depressing the chargeable transfer, thus mitigating the IHT charge. The scheme was nullified by *IHTA 1984, s 47A*, which defined 'settlement power', and by *IHTA 1984, s 55A*, which addressed the scheme itself.

Purchase of interests in trusts

9.24 *Finance Act 2010, s 52* inserted *s 81A* into *IHTA 1984* with the sole intention of preventing perceived abuse of trusts. Where a person:

- transfers property into a trust in which they or a spouse or civil partner has a future interest in reversion; or
- buys a reversionary interest,

the new legislation imposes an IHT charge when that future interest comes to an end and the property vests.

The guidance notes to the legislation employ the term 'future interest' interchangeably with 'reversionary interest'. When the interest comes to an end and the person becomes actually entitled to the trust interest there is a charge if that person:

- actually bought the reversionary interest; or
- is the settlor of the trust or the spouse or civil partner of the settlor and becomes entitled to the reversionary interest.

By *IHTA 1984, s 81A(2)*, the gift of a reversionary interest in this situation as defined in *IHTA 1984, s 81A(1)* is a chargeable lifetime transfer, not a PET. These rules are effective as from 9 December 2009, being the date of the Pre-Budget Report which first announced the rules. The rationale for the new legislation is that neither a purchased reversionary interest, nor a settlor's reversionary interest in trust property is excluded property. Each forms part of a person's estate whereas since *FA 2006* an interest in possession does not normally form part of his estate by virtue of *IHTA 1984, s 5(1A)*. A possible IHT saving could arise on the vesting of an interest in possession because the reversionary interest was no longer held. As a result of the changes it will no longer be possible to avoid an IHT charge by making a gift of a purchased reversionary interest before the interest actually vests. These rules do not apply to those interests in possession which are protected by *FA 2006* and do not form part of the relevant property regime thus for example a disabled person's interest (DPI) is outside the scope of these changes.

Changes to the tax treatment of interests in possession

9.25 *Finance Act 2010, s 53* expands on *IHTA 1984, s 3A* which sets out which transfers are potentially exempt (PET) and which are not a chargeable lifetime transfer. A purchased interest in possession is, by *FA 2010, s 53*, treated as part of the estate of the person who buys it. Whereas normally under *IHTA 1984, s 3A* dealings with an interest in possession fall within the PET category, *FA 2010, s 53(2)(a)* alters the thrust of *IHTA 1984, s 3A* by removing the reference to *IHTA 1984, s 52* and by inserting *IHTA 1984, s 3A(6A)*. As will be seen from the account that follows as a general rule purchased trust interests are best avoided.

The result of the *FA 2010* legislative amendments is that a transfer of value under *s 52* will be a PET except where it arises in respect of an interest that, under the new rules, is treated as part of a person's estate (ie by virtue of *IHTA 1984, s 5(1B)*). Therefore, where such a trust comes to an end and the capital is paid out, the transfer of value is treated as a chargeable transfer for IHT and no longer a PET.

Section 5(1)(a)(ii) of *IHTA 1984* is also amended so that where an interest in possession falls within the current definition in *IHTA 1984, s 5(1B)*, it will be treated as part of a person's estate. *Section 5(1B)* of *IHTA 1984* sets out a fresh category of interests in possession. These are interests that are included as part of a person's estate, being:

- those to which a person is entitled;
- who is domiciled in the UK;
- where that person acquired the interest in a transaction at arm's length.

For this purpose 'arm's length' is as defined in *IHTA 1984, s 10*. Thus the holder of a purchased interest in possession within *IHTA 1984, s 5(1B)* is now treated as entitled to the property, as under, *IHTA 1984, s 49(1A)*, so on death the value of the fund will be aggregated with the free estate.

There is, as a result, a change to *IHTA 1984, s 51(1A)*, which section normally provides that where a person disposes of an interest in possession it is not regarded as a transfer of value, though an IHT charge could arise under *IHTA 1984, s 52*. However, that does not apply to all interests but by virtue of *FA 2010*, it does now apply to purchased life interests within *IHTA 1984, s 5(1B)*.

The regime for IHT charges when an interest in possession comes to an end during the lifetime of a beneficiary is mainly regulated by *IHTA 1984, s 52(2A)* and *(3A)*. Those charges now apply only to certain qualifying interests in possession, but the category of interest to which the charge can apply is now extended to include purchased qualifying interests within *IHTA 1984, s 5(1B)*. The gift of a purchased life interest or its termination will trigger a chargeable event for IHT.

And still the changes go further. There can be relief under *IHTA 1984, s 57A(1A)* in relation to the IHT charge on a qualifying interest in possession where, somewhat unusually, the trust property is transferred to a heritage maintenance fund within two years of the death of the life tenant (for a more detailed discussion see: *Agricultural, Business and Heritage Property Relief (7th edn) (Bloomsbury Professional)*). There are actually very few heritage maintenance funds in existence, so the point is somewhat esoteric, but the relief is now extended by *IHTA 1984, s 5(1B)* to purchased life interests. There is a similar extension by way of an amendment to *IHTA 1984, s 100(1A)* in relation to reconstruction of the share capital of a close company and to slightly similar changes to company capital contemplated by *IHTA 1984, s 101(1A)*.

Section 102ZA(1)(b)(ii) of *FA 1986* builds on the gift with reservation rules as they apply to the holder of an interest in possession. This provision is changed by *FA 2010, s 53(8)* so as to include purchased life interests within *IHTA 1984, s 5(1B)*.

This extremely complicated anti-avoidance legislation is designed to frustrate the exploitation of the excluded property rules as they apply to trust interests that are not subject to IHT charges in the UK. Simply put, if a non-UK domiciled person sets up a trust of foreign property which includes an interest in possession, that interest is excluded property; but if a stranger buys that interest that stranger will come within the new regime and will not reap any of the benefits of the excluded property regime.

Purchase of interests in offshore trusts

9.26 The excluded property rules (which are considered below) do not apply where:

- a person is entitled to an interest in possession; and
- that person is domiciled in the UK; and
- the trust interest was purchased on or after 5 December 2005 (*s 48(3B)*).

It matters not whether the interest was paid for by the life tenant or another. The purchase may be direct or indirect (perhaps by way of inheritance from the purchaser). These rules are expanded by *FA 2010, s 53*, amending *IHTA 1984, s 5* to introduce *IHTA 1984, s 5(1B)* and making amendments where necessary so as to include reference to *IHTA 1984, s 5(1B)*. *Finance Act 2012* includes draconian legislation intended to target perceived abuse through acquisition of interest of settled property in offshore trusts.

TRANSITIONAL PROVISIONS: MARCH 2006 – APRIL 2008

Transitional serial interests: property other than life policies

Focus

The IHT treatment of a pre-22 March 2006 (qualifying) interest in possession can be preserved under the TSI rules but the conditions are tightly drawn with narrow application.

9.27 *Section 49C* of *IHTA 1984* sets out four conditions under which an interest in possession could benefit from the tax treatment that applied to an old-style interest that was in existence before 22 March 2006. However, the rules relate to transactions before 6 October 2008 and for a fuller account, readers are referred to earlier editions of this work.

The *IHTA 1984, s 49C* conditions are:

(1) The trust began before 22 March 2006 and immediately before that date the property was subject to an interest in possession ('the prior interest').

(2) The prior interest came to an end at some time between 22 March 2006 and 5 October 2008.

(3) The beneficiary became entitled to an interest in possession ('the current interest') at the time that the prior interest ended.

(4) This was not the settlement for a disabled person nor for a 'bereaved minor' (see below).

Care had to be taken in creating successive interests, perhaps for children, to ensure that the original life tenant was excluded from further benefit otherwise the termination of an interest in possession after 21 March 2006 could be a gift with reservation even if the interest in possession arose after that date.

Illustrative examples are as follows.

Example 9.10—TSI: making the beneficiary wait for the capital

Reginald had an established qualifying (pre-22 March 2006) life interest in the family trust which terms provided for entitlement to capital at age 30. The trustees doubted his business acumen and before 6 October 2008 exercised their power under *Trustee Act 1925, s 32* to advance the fund onto a fresh trust which would give Reginald direct access to capital only when he attained 50, long after 5 April 2008. This is a valid TSI.

Example 9.11—No TSI: spinning out the fund

Susan enjoyed the income of the trust, the terms of which provide that on her death the capital would pass to her brother Tom absolutely. Tom is wealthy and has assigned his interest to another established trust in which his own sons have life interests. Susan's interest was terminated before 6 October 2008, whereupon the fund came to be held on interest in possession trusts for her nephews. They do not have a TSI as their interest is in another trust.

Example 9.12—Continuing interest: sharing out the fund

The Goldsworthy fund, invested in stocks and shares, was held for Mike and Jim in equal shares, each having a life interest. The trustees created sub-funds by dividing the portfolio down the middle. That operation did not bring to an end the interest of either Mike or Jim.

One issue that could cause difficulty was deciding when an existing interest had been replaced by a new interest for the same beneficiary. There were many issues of detail to clarify and the professional bodies of CIOT and STEP collectively led the process of elucidation of the most difficult areas, of which the examples above are good illustrations.

One particular anomaly, which arose where a qualifying IIP was replaced by a new IIP for the same beneficiary, was addressed in *Finance Act 2008, s 140* and resulted in the rewriting of *IHTA 1984, s 53(2A)* retrospective to 22 March 2006. It provided that the exception from an IHT charge under *IHTA 1984, s 52* on termination of an interest in possession, which could apply if the person became entitled to another interest in the same trust, was available where a person became entitled to a new trust interest but only if that new interest was a disabled person's interest or a TSI. That would apply regardless of whether the original interest, which terminated, was a qualifying IIP, or an interest that came into being on or after 22 March 2006.

Example 9.13—Simple creation of a TSI

Under the will of Leonard, who died on 1 December 2005, his widow Marian became entitled to the income of the residue of his estate for life (an IPDI), with remainder to their grandchildren for life. The will gave the trustees power to advance capital in favour of any beneficiary who had a life interest and the remainder would pass to the great grandchildren insofar as capital had not been advanced to grandchildren during their lifetimes.

Marian was well provided for in other ways and hoped to live at least another seven years and thus on 17 May 2006, she surrendered her life interest in favour of her grandchildren. Her interest was the 'prior interest'. The new life interests that then arose in favour of the grandchildren are 'current interests'. Those current interests fall to be treated as interests in possession under the old rules by virtue of the TSI provisions.

The youngest grandchild, Zac, is now five years old. The treatment of interests in possession as it was before 22 March 2006 could therefore continue for many years. If in due course Zac were to marry, the trustees could, no doubt with his consent, appoint capital to him which he could then give to his wife, enabling them to enjoy a fund equal to twice the nil rate band then in force without risk of an IHT charge on it. Other possibilities may be imagined.

Section 49D of *IHTA 1984* contained special rules to apply where a person becomes entitled to an interest on the death of a spouse or civil partner. The conditions are:

- the trust was in being before 22 March 2006;
- before 22 March 2006, there was a prior life interest;
- the prior interest ends on the death of its holder on or after 6 October 2008;
- the prior holder was the spouse or civil partner of the present life tenant;
- the present life tenant becomes entitled to the life interest as soon as the prior interest ceases;
- it is not a bereaved minor trust (BMT) (see below), nor a disabled person's interest.

Example 9.14—Availability of spouse relief

George was already life tenant of his father's will trust as at 22 March 2006 and thus had a qualifying interest. On his marriage to Celia in September 2007 he gave up an interest in half of the trust fund in her favour, so that Celia became entitled to an interest in possession. That transfer was covered by the spouse exemption and was a TSI.

In May 2018 George inherited funds from another family trust and decided to give up the remainder of his original life interest in favour of Celia.

He surrendered it to her so that she became entitled to the income of the whole of the fund. Although in trust law Celia is entitled only to income, the second transfer is outside the transitional rules as it took place after 5 October 2008. It is not an IPDI, being a lifetime settlement and under the rules from 22 March 2006 it is treated as a relevant property trust, thus a chargeable transfer; and since the fund does not increase Celia's estate it is not covered by spouse relief.

Addition of funds to existing trusts: special rules for policy trusts

9.28 The transitional provisions did not generally allow qualifying interest in possession funds to be augmented and remain within the old regime. The addition of new assets to an existing trust is, for one exception, instead treated as the creation of a new settlement falling under the relevant property regime. This might simply be the transfer of extra funds by the settlor or an indirect benefit, such as the release by the settlor of a debt owed to him by the trustees.

On 29 October 2013, HMRC published updates to its IHT Manual (IHTM) which, amongst other items, included then fresh guidance on additions of property or value to qualifying interest in possession trusts (see IHTM16074–16078). The guidance contains useful examples of the HMRC approach to the additions. Thus, on the case of mixed funds, HMRC will consider: an apportionment of values determined on a just and reasonable basis; an outline of circumstances in which HMRC may investigate loans made to the trustees after 21 March 2006; and clarification on the treatment of third-party settlement of trust expenses where the trust lacks liquid funds.

The one exception relates to insurance policies. The payment of premiums simply to keep an existing policy in place is not regarded as the creation of a new settlement. Even so, depending on the circumstances, the payment of policy premiums may be exempt falling within *IHTA 1984, s 21* under the normal expenditure out of income rule.

9.29 *Section 49E* of *IHTA 1984* provides a special form of TSI for existing, but not new, trusts of insurance policies. For example, it can apply where 'C' has an interest in possession in a policy 'the present interest', before 22 March 2006 and certain conditions apply:

(1) It is a trust created prior to 22 March 2006; before 22 March 2006 the property in the trust was a policy; and C (or perhaps more likely some other person) had a life interest ('the earlier interest').

(2) The earlier interest ended on or after 6 October 2008 ('the earlier interest end-time') on the death of whoever was entitled to it and C became entitled to the interest on one of the following occasions:

- at the earlier interest end-time;
- at the end of an interest in possession occurring on the death of the previous life tenant; or
- when one of a series of interests in possession ends, where the first belonged to someone who became entitled to it at the earlier interest end-time and where each life interest came to an end when the holder of that interest died; or alternatively
- C became entitled to the interest that C now has on one of the following occasions:
  - when a transitional serial interest ends by death; or
  - when the last of several consecutive interests ends and the first of them was a transitional serial interest, each ending by death.

There are two further conditions:

(3) The policy rights were in the trust from 22 March 2006 until C became entitled.

(4) This is neither a bereaved minor's trust nor one for a disabled person.

Associated operations

9.30 The use of insurance policies was examined in the case of *Smith v Revenue and Customs Commissioners* [2008] STC 1649, where husband and wife took out 'back-to-back' annuity and life policies with the same insurer in circumstances where the annuity income funded the life policies, which in turn were gifted to their children. There was no express reference in any policy to any other, but the total package of documents provided by the insurer made the connection plain. It was held that the policies taken together were a transfer of value.

Bereaved minors and age 18-to-25 trusts

9.31 The provision of funds for young people in the context of the post March 2006 treatment of A&M trusts is dealt with more fully in **Chapter 10**. *Section 71C* of *IHTA 1984* defines 'bereaved minor' as a person not yet 18 and in respect of whom at least one parent (or guardian in loco parentis) has died. This definition is central to the *FA 2006* IHT regime. As a result of strong professional representations that the age of 18 was perceived as far too young to manage substantial capital, the original structure of IHT, which would have made the tax treatment of capital much more favourable where the young person became absolutely entitled at 18, is toned down albeit marginally.

The introduction of *IHTA 1984, s 71D* for 'Age 18-to-25 trusts' has given parent settlors and indeed trustees a choice. These trusts are considered in detail at **10.7**. It seems likely that many families will accept the burden of the IHT regime for relevant property trusts as the price to be paid for securing the capital in the short to medium term.

Wills can be drafted with flexibility to take advantage of the new rules.

Example 9.15—Trusts for bereaved minors: 'wait and see how they turn out'

On 31 January 2017, Betty died leaving funds to her husband Alfred for life (an IPDI) with remainder on discretionary trust for her children. The trustees appoint the reversionary discretionary fund onto a trust that complies with *IHTA 1984, s 71A*. That will be good enough: the *IHTA 1984, s 71A* trusts need not actually be set out in the will. Furthermore, it does not matter that capital might be appointed out to Alfred: whilst he has an IPDI the trusts of the reversion are not tested.

EXCLUDED PROPERTY TRUSTS

Focus

The valuable IHT benefits secured through the use of an excluded property trust must form a central part of IHT planning routine for the non-domiciliary. However, the complexity of the rules, the increasing raft of anti-avoidance legislation and the impact of the *FA 2008* changes which paved the introduction of the remittance charge mean that the position must be constantly monitored. The impact of *IHTA 1984, s 80* should not be underrated (see **9.35** below).

Reversionary interests

9.32 These have already been considered at **9.22**. A reversionary interest is excluded property unless (see *IHTA 1984, s 48(1)*) it is:

- purchased; or
- one to which either the settlor or his spouse is beneficially entitled; or
- an interest expectant on the determination of a lease where that lease is treated as a settlement by virtue of the special rules in *s 43(3)*.

In the case of purchased reversionary interests, careful note should be taken of the anti-avoidance provisions of *FA 2010, s 53* described at **9.24** and **9.25** above.

Foreign assets

9.33 The other more common category of excluded trust property is described in *s 48(3)* and concerns property situated outside the UK. There are two conditions:

- The property itself, but not a reversionary interest in it, is excluded provided that the settlor was not domiciled in the UK when the settlement was made.
- The rules in *s 6(1)IHTA 1984* apply to a reversionary interest in the property, but do not otherwise apply to it (see below).

Section 6(1) states: '… Property situated outside the United Kingdom is excluded property if the person beneficially entitled to it is an individual domiciled outside the United Kingdom…'. The conditions required for property to be excluded within *s 48(3)* would therefore be satisfied if the present life tenant was domiciled in the UK, but the remainderman was not so domiciled.

In the case of *Bowring v HMRC* [2015] UKUT 550, the Upper Tribunal decided that capital payments made to UK beneficiaries of a UK trust that had in turn received funds from an offshore trust were free of the capital gains that had originated in that offshore trust. This overturned the decision of the First-tier Tribunal that interpreted *TCGA 1992, s 97(5)* so widely as to apply to beneficiaries who received distributions from the UK trust were subject to tax under *ss 87* and *91 TCGA 1992* because they had received the capital payments indirectly from the offshore trust.

Prior to *Finance (No 2) Act 2017*, an otherwise relevant property trust which comprised solely excluded property was outside the scope of IHT and thus did not attract either exit of or ten-year anniversary charges even if the trust was settlor interested. *Finance (No 2) Act 2017* now includes measures which provide that from 6 April 2017 all UK residential property owned directly or indirectly by non-UK domiciliaries will be within the scope of IHT.

The new provisions will have a direct impact on the traditional non-resident relevant property trust structure which owns shares in an underlying offshore company that in turn owns UK residential property – the value of the shares attributable to that UK property asset will fall within the scope of IHT and will potentially thereafter attract ten-year anniversary charges/exit charges. Furthermore, the trust's indirect ownership of the UK residential property will deny the latter's access to excluded property status and where the settlor is a potential beneficiary of the trust, the protection previously afforded from attack under the gift with reservation rule (previously overridden by the excluded property status) will be withdrawn unless the trust falls within the complex 'protected settlements' provision.

For established mixed use property, the element subject to IHT is determined on a pro rata basis. However, where the use of the UK property subsequently changes from residential to non-residential (or vice versa) the property is within the scope of IHT if it has been a residential property at any time within the two years immediately preceding the chargeable event. Other UK situs assets (ie non UK residential property etc) owned directly or indirectly by offshore trusts created by non UK domiciliaries continues to remain outside the IHT net.

On 31 January 2018, the existing HMRC guidance set out in RDR1 was updated and expanded to incorporate the *Finance (No 2) Act 2017* provisions regarding the deemed domicile rules which took effect from 6 April 2017.

9.34 The excluded property rules may seem to be something of an anomaly.

Example 9.16—Excluded property trust: benefiting from the rule years later

Anton fled to the UK during the Hungarian uprising in 1956. He had been a successful engineer and on arrival in the UK settled his commercial interests in both Hungary and in Switzerland on trust for the benefit of his wife Josefina for life with remainder to their son Maxim for life with gifts over in remainder. All this happened at a time when Anton still hoped eventually to return to the country of his birth and when he had been in the UK for only three years – thus Anton had non-UK domicile status at that time of trust creation.

Although Anton remained in the UK for many years after making the trust, such that he became deemed domiciled here (under the then '17/20 year' rule under *s 267)* he did not add any further funds to the trust. In due course the composition of the trust fund changed and included indirect holdings in UK companies but the rules of situs were observed in such a way that at all times the trust property was situated outside of the UK. Anton died before 22 March 2006.

Josefina became deemed domiciled in the UK some years ago, but on her death in 2018 it was acknowledged that the fund was excluded property.

Maxim was born in the UK and on reaching late teens made it clear that he adopted the UK as his country of domicile. For IHT purposes, that does not matter – the trust is still outside the IHT regime because of the circumstances of its creation and it has avoided later tainting because there has been no addition to the fund at a time when the settlor was domiciled in the UK.

In **Example 9.16**, the tax treatment would be different if Anton had instead purchased the trust interest after 5 December 2005 (see *IHTA 1984, s 48(3B)*).

Professional advisers have long debated the precise relationship between the rules as to excluded property and those for gifts with reservation, and with good reason. A non-UK domiciliary ('the settlor') may set up a trust of offshore assets ('the excluded property') from which they continue to benefit by drawing the income ('settlor interested'). If the excluded property rule takes priority over the gift with reservation rule, the excluded property is not aggregated with their estate on death – this would also be the case should they later become deemed domiciled here under the 17/20 year residence rule. The current version of IHTM14396 makes it very clear that the excluded property provisions do indeed take priority over the gifts with reservation code (see **7.34**). However, in recent years the legislative spotlight on the non-domiciliary has become noticeably more focused which must make this an area to carefully watch and monitor.

In the past it was always considered that the difficulty could come from a non-fiscal source. By a press release dated 14 October 2009, the European Commission published proposals that if enacted, had the potential to impact directly on the procedures for inheritance within the EU through international recognition of rights to succession. This proposal posed fundamental problems for the UK with its concepts of domicile, executors, trusts and most importantly, testamentary freedom – from a planning perspective there would need to be certainty that lifetime gifts could not be clawed back to satisfy 'forced heirship' rules. It is considered that the French would not lightly give up rules that protect children from disinheritance whilst current English law does not accept 'habitual residence' as determinative of the legal system that should govern inheritance. These deep-rooted traditions were set on a collision course with the EU when the UK made known that it was unwilling to be bound by the new rules if enacted. Given the June 2016 Brexit decision it might be thought that this threat has gone away but of course at time of publication the precise terms of the UK exit and the structure of its future relationship with the EU have yet to be agreed. Accordingly, this area remains fluid and developments should be closely monitored as they unfold.

What should settlors and their trustees do now? *Finance Act 2008, ss 24* and *25* and *Sch 7*, introduced a much sharper regime for the taxation of the non-UK domiciled taxpayer by raising the financial stakes on the favourable remittance basis, although that mainly affects income tax and CGT rather than IHT. The law is in a state of flux: there are cases on residence that declare the law as it applied to past situations but none reflect the current position. HMRC6 ('Residence, Domicile and the Remittance Basis') which replaced Booklet IR20, set out revised guidance for income tax and CGT bolstered by HMRC victory in the now infamous Supreme Court decision against Gaines-Cooper, Davies & James (*R (on the application of Davies) v Revenue and Customs Commissioners* [2011] UKSC 47). In the case of *Peter Daniel v HMRC* [2014] UKFTT 173 HMRC's inconsistent application of the then IR20 residence rules was challenged but failed mainly due to the lack of credibility of the taxpayer, a senior banker with Morgan Stanley – the Tribunal stated it was '... surprised and troubled that every piece of objective evidence in this case, such as fax and email correspondence, presentations, letters and the very existence of at least three computers...' was unavailable. This case underpins the view that the strength of the technical argument must be supported by facts rather than statements.

Some progress has been made with the long-awaited statutory residence test brought into effect on 6 April 2013. Nevertheless, whilst time will bring familiarity with the rules, they remain complicated and involve the application of a raft of automatic tests with particular unexpected twists dependent on personal factors. Despite the issue of initial HMRC guidance (RDR3), last updated in August 2016, it will still be some time before the new framework becomes or feels comfortable.

The statutory residence rules affect IHT through the test for 'deemed domicile' in *IHTA 1984, s 267(1)(b)*, which turns on residence: *Finance Act 2008,Sch 7* adjusted the 'day counting' rules.

Domicile rulings are less frequent but a very aptly named and high profile case to read is that of *Stuart Gulliver v HMRC [2017] UKFTT 0222* (http://tinyurl.com/kmlyfn9). This concerned the domicile status of the then current high profile HSBC chief born in the UK of UK parents and has led some professionals to speculate this was the catalyst for the (suspended) Finance (No 2) Bill 2017 regime proposals for those born in the UK with a UK domicile of origin who acquire a different domicile of choice but then become UK resident.

The residence of trustees for CGT was reviewed in *Smallwood and another v HMRC* [2010] EWCA Civ 778. The case turned on exactly where the trust was resident when gains were made; on the facts, that was Mauritius, which had sole taxing rights under the double taxation agreement then in force. The appeal by Mr Smallwood and the trustees was allowed in the High Court ([2009] EWHC 777 (Ch)), but that decision was subsequently overturned in the Court of Appeal.

This same theme was echoed in the more recent case, in which the Smallwood case was cited, of R Lee; N Bunter (TC5757). The taxpayers used the 'round the world scheme' to mitigate the trust CGT liability by exploiting the double tax treaty between the UK and Mauritius. The main issue centred on the place of effective management of the trust which the Tribunal determined rested in the place where those most important decisions were taken and not, as argued, where the relevant share sale documentation was executed. It was determined 'the shots were called in the UK'.

Loss of excluded property status: the s 80 problem

9.35 *Section 80* of *IHTA 1984* ('Initial interest of settlor or spouse or civil partner') imposes a primary fiction on all trusts set up since 27 March

1974, where a settlor or his surviving spouse ('spouse' means spouse, widow, widower or civil partner of a settlor (*IHTA 1984, s 80(2)*)) is entitled to a prior qualifying interest in possession which continues on (relevant property) trust terms on the death of that settlor/surviving spouse. For IHT purposes the property contained in that qualifying interest is not initially treated as joining the trust fund of the relevant property trust rather its joinder is postponed. However, once the qualifying interest of the settlor/surviving spouse comes to an end and the property moves onto a fresh trust interest (ie discretionary), it is treated as joining a separate trust, made by the person who last held the qualifying interest.

The wording of *s 80* was amended and tightened by *FA 2014* such that the wider term 'an interest in possession' is replaced with the narrower and more precise term 'a qualifying interest in possession'.

Example 9.17—Disclaimed interest: trigger of relevant property trust regime

On 30 June 1979, Geoff (UK domiciled) settled £150,000 on trust for his wife Maud for life, with gift-over on discretionary trust for his children and grandchildren. Maud enjoyed the income until 31 May 2005, when she disclaimed her interest (at which time the trust fund was worth £700,000) with the intention that her family should benefit. There is an immediately chargeable lifetime transfer by Maud of £700,000. That would also be the result if the disclaimer took place after 21 March 2006.

Example 9.18—Pre-22 March 2006: side-stepping the relevant property trust regime

The facts are as in **Example 9.17** above, only instead of a simple disclaimer the change is effected, not by Maud but by the trustees (but still on 31 May 2005) under a power in the deed. They appoint funds onto a new life interest trust for the children and onto old-style A&M trust for the grandchildren. This time no discretionary trust arises, and as this occurred prior to 22 March 2006 there is no immediate chargeable transfer. It is a PET by Maud. However, see below as to the effect where the event occurs post 21 March 2006.

Under the post-*Finance Act 2006* regime, *s 80(4)* has the effect that, where the trigger event under *IHTA 1984, s 80(1)* happens on or after 22 March 2006, it will apply, not to the coming to an end of an interest in possession, as hitherto, but on the occasion of the ending of any 'postponing interest', by which is meant any type of qualifying interest in possession, even (see *IHTA 1984, s 80(4)(b)*), an IPDI or a disabled person's interest. This will severely cut down the freedom of trustees of offshore trusts for erstwhile non-UK domiciliaries to keep the fund outside the IHT net.

As mentioned above *F(No 2)A 2014* tightened the wording of *IHTA 1984, s 80* to correct an unintended effect which permitted a successive spousal non-qualifying IIP to potentially escape IHT charge because the trust assets were neither part of the successor's estate nor comprised within a relevant property trust. The term 'interest in possession' is now replaced with the term 'qualifying interest in possession' – the latter referring to an interest that is a pre-22 March 2006 established interest, an IPDI, transitional serial interest (TSI) or a disabled person's interest as set out in *IHTA 1984, s 59*. Accordingly, where one party to a couple succeeds to a life interest to which their spouse or civil partner was previously entitled during their lifetime, *IHTA 1984, s 80* will continue to apply at that time.

Example 9.19—Effect on an excluded property trust

The facts are as in **Example 9.17** except that: Geoff was domiciled in New Zealand in 1979 (and had been for more than three years); the disclaimer of Maud's interest occurred on 31 May 2018; and by this time both Geoff and Maud are both deemed to be domiciled in the UK. The fund loses its excluded property status, because it is retested as a transfer made on 31 May 2018 by Maud.

Thus, by stealth, the advantages of excluded property trusts will, for many families, disappear. Certainly all trustees of excluded property trusts must regularly consider their position and continue to monitor developments in this changing arena.

INSURANCE POLICY TRUSTS

Existing policy trusts

9.36 The scheme for trusts as finally enacted in *Finance Act 2006* imposed on professional tax advisers (to include financial advisors) a duty to understand the taxation of trusts and the ability to explain it. *Section 46A* of *FA 2006* now deals with existing life interest policy trusts. The conditions are:

- the settlement and the life policy both existed before 22 March 2006;
- premiums are payable, or there is a variation of the policy which is permitted by the new rules, some time on or after 22 March 2006;

- there were pre-existing settlement rights, now defined as a 'transitionally protected interest';
- by virtue of continued payment of premiums or of a variation of the policy, rights under the policy become settled as part of the transitionally protected interest; and
- the only variations to the policy are those allowed by the legislation in 2006.

For the purposes of the legislation a variation is 'allowed' only where it takes place by operation of the exercise of rights that existed before 22 March 2006. A 'transitionally-protected interest' means only a pre-existing life interest or a transitional serial interest. Where all of these conditions are satisfied, the payment of any more premiums on the policy is a transfer of value made by the individual who pays it and the transfer of value at that time is a PET.

Transitional provisions

9.37 The same treatment will apply in an existing situation where the policy is not held on life interest trusts but on old-style A&M trusts. The relevant legislation is *IHTA 1984, s 46B* and it adopts the pattern of *IHTA 1984, s 46A*, so the conditions are as follows:

- the settlement and the policy must have existed before 22 March 2006;
- a premium is paid on the policy after that date;
- rights under the policy were settled on A&M trusts established before 22 March 2006; and
- further rights (ie those attaching to the next premium) become settled after 21 March 2006 and there is a variation on or after that date of the policy so as to increase the benefits or extend the term of the insurance, but that variation is an 'allowed one'.

Where the conditions are satisfied, A&M provisions may continue notwithstanding the general changes to A&M trusts introduced by *Finance Act 2006* thus the payment of a further premium is treated as a PET. For the purposes of policies subject to A&M trusts a variation is 'allowed' only where it represents the exercise of pre-existing rights under the policy.

9.38 There is a further level of protection of pre-existing policy trusts. This protects the eventual release of funds. The conditions are:

- pre-existing settlements and life policies;
- premiums paid or allowed variation on or after 22 March 2006 where the trusts fall within the 'new' *IHTA 1984, s 71A* (bereaved minors) or *IHTA 1984, s 71D* (18-to-25) trusts which were previously A&M trusts and which became *IHTA 1984, s 71A* or *IHTA 1984, s 71D* trusts; and

- a further premium was paid, the policy was varied in an allowed manner so as to increase or extend the benefits but only by exercise of pre-existing rights.

These rules apply to property in an 18-to-25 trust only where that property was previously in an A&M settlement which migrated to *IHTA 1984, s 71D* whilst still in the same settlement. If the settlements are bereaved minor trusts then the transitional provisions apply only where they migrate from A&M trusts under the terms of *FA 2006* or where they would have been in 18-to-25 trusts, but cease to be held on those trusts because the trustees decided to modify the rights so as to comply with the restrictions for bereaved minors: in other words, they let the grandchildren have the money early, ie at age 18 rather than at the preferred age of 25.

New trusts

9.39 Post *FA 2006* the creation of insurance policy trusts, even if expressed to be interest in possession trusts, are treated as relevant property trusts for IHT purposes and will become subject to the regime of entry charges, periodic charges and exit charges. This regime is described in more detail in **Chapter 10**.

Pensions

9.40 The IHT treatment of pensions before 22 March 2006 was that benefits might be settled under a discretionary trust. The death benefits were not relevant property, during the lifetime of the policyholder by virtue of *IHTA 1984, s 58(1)(d)*, whether the pension was a regulated one or one within *ICTA 1988, s 615* (a '*section 615* scheme').

Equally, under *FA 2004, Sch 29*, the death benefit was 'a defined lump sum benefit' if paid out within two years of death, see *para 13(c)*; or 'a non-crystallised lump sum death benefit' if paid out within the same period: see *para 15(1)(c)*. The language of the pensions simplification legislation was itself anything but simple but the effect was that the tax treatment for discretionary trusts did not apply if the lump sum (a defined lump sum benefit or a non-crystallised lump sum death benefit) was payable at the discretion of the trustees and the funds were distributed within two years of the death. Where the funds were paid by the pension scheme trustees to a second trust, IHT became chargeable when the second trust released the benefits but again subject to the two-year rule. Where the life tenant was the former spouse or civil partner, the IHT treatment reflected that and usually the funds were released so as to take advantage of that exemption.

The tax treatment following *FA 2006* is that where the funds are transferred at the discretion of the pension scheme trustees to a second trust, that trust will be treated as a relevant property trust and the fund may therefore be subject to an exit charge on distribution – see **Chapter 10**. One particular difficulty may be in establishing whether the funds are released by the pension trustees to the second trust at their discretion, or whether effectively they have no choice.

There was a slight relaxation in *Finance Act 2007*. Lump sums, whether arising under regulated schemes or *s 615* schemes, would not come within the IHT rules for relevant property trusts if distributed within two years of the earlier of:

- the day on which the death was known to the trustees or those in charge of the scheme; or
- the day on which they could first be expected to have known of the death.

The taxation of pension savings was revisited in *Finance Act 2008, s 91* and *Sch 28*. These changes are considered in the context of 'lifetime planning' in **Chapter 14**.

For a long time there had been a difficulty for the owners of pension rights in deciding, on approaching retirement, whether or not to accept the annuity rates currently on offer; or to go into drawdown; or to carry on working. The last option might be in the hope of restoring the value of the fund to what it had been before the recession or other reason for depressed values. *Section 3(3)* of *IHTA 1984* imposed a charge to IHT where, by failure to exercise the right to draw the pension, the taxpayer brought about a situation where, on his death soon afterwards, the fund would otherwise pass free of IHT to close relatives.

This dilemma was keenly illustrated in *Fryer and others (PRs of Arnold Deceased) v HMRC* [2010] UKFTT 87 (TC) 00398. Mrs Arnold could draw her pension on 8 September 2002, her sixtieth birthday. She was at that time diagnosed with a condition likely to prove terminal. Although she received details of the pension choices open to her, she did nothing. She died in September 2009. The First-tier Tribunal held that Mrs Arnold deliberately omitted, at her 60th birthday and thereafter until her death, to exercise her pension rights. Her estate in her lifetime lost the value of those rights, so there was a transfer of value within *s 3(3)*. The value transferred was the loss to the estate, ie the value of the right to opt to take the benefits. A hypothetical purchaser of those rights would opt to take the lump sum plus a guaranteed annuity for ten years; taking into account Mrs Arnold's health: all of that to be discounted 25%.

Practitioners had long worried about this issue: when was the failure tested to exercise the right to take the pension? The most difficult outcome of the *Arnold* case was to answer this question 'anytime until death', with the result that, since such a time must fall within two years of death, all future failures to draw pensions would be caught. It seems it was necessary to begin to draw the pension before death; or risk its exposure to IHT later but that interpretation, if correct, was harsh.

However, as part of the wider pensions reform from 6 April 2011 a charge under *s 3(3)* is dis-applied (by *IHTA 1984, s 12(2ZA)*) where a member of a registered pension scheme (or qualifying non-UK pension scheme or *s 615(3)* scheme) omits to exercise pension rights under the scheme.

Life policies

9.41 There is no change to the treatment of discretionary trusts of life policies. Where the trusts are A&M trusts, care should be taken to note the identity of the beneficiaries as at 6 April 2008 because after that date a variation can bring the fund within the relevant property regime. As was noted at **9.28** above, there should be little difficulty with existing (pre 22 March 2006) trusts. The main problems concern the post 21 March 2006 policies, especially those where the premiums are substantial (see **Chapter 8** which outlines the relaxation of the reporting requirements for new discretionary trusts). Once the policy trusts are in being, the usual regime described in the next chapter will apply.

It is of course part of the nature of a life policy, especially one of term assurance, that its value reflects the state of health of the life assured. As will be seen in **Chapter 10** the charging regime of relevant property trusts requires valuation of the fund on the eve of the tenth anniversary of creation. If at that date the life assured is seriously ill the value of the trust may exceed the nil rate band. The same could apply if death occurred just before a tenth anniversary. In relation to particular schemes, such as discounted gift schemes and loan trusts it will be necessary to go back to first principles and establish the exact nature of the rights under the policy and under the trusts before applying the charging provisions.

A sting in the tail

9.42 Finally, there is an anomaly of which both trustees and beneficiaries should take note. The issue of burden and incidence of tax was discussed at the beginning of **Chapter 8**. On death, liability for IHT is, see *IHTA 1984, s 200(1)*, on:

- the personal representatives, for the free estate;
- the trustees, for trust property;
- any person in whom the property is vested, whether beneficially or not, or who has an interest in possession; or
- anyone for whose benefit a trust fund is held.

Section 201 of *IHTA 1984* deals further with trust property and *IHTA 1984, s 201(1)(b)* makes a person liable for tax if they are entitled to an interest in possession whether or not that interest is a qualifying interest.

These rules do not sit easily with the principle that many post-21 March 2006 life tenants will not have a qualifying interest and thus will not be treated as entitled to the underlying trust capital. Although they may have an interest in possession for the purposes of trust law and even for CGT, for IHT it will be taxed as the interest of a beneficiary of a relevant property trust. Why treat them differently from 'true' discretionary trust beneficiaries? HMRC do not really defend the situation: they have commented:

> 'Although an IIP holder whose interest arose before 22 March 2006 has been regarded as owning the underlying property for inheritance tax purposes, in reality he has only ever owned a limited interest. The FA 2006 changes do not alter the IIP owner's real position.'

This seems to recognise the anomaly but does not redress the balance.

Chapter 10

Relevant property trusts

SIGNPOSTS

- **Post-March 2006 categories** – Despite its rigid construction, the BMT and its more flexible 18-to-25 sibling present a more palatable IHT option to the full-blown discretionary trust when considering will provision for children. However, great care must be taken to avoid the less obvious pitfalls (see **10.6–10.8**).
- **Migration** – It is crucial to understand the impact of FA 2006 on the old-style trust, to appreciate the impact of transitional relief provisions, to be aware of tax treatment going forward and in particular to consider the impact of later funding (see **10.22–10.25**; **10.17**).
- **The relevant property regime** – Given the extent of the *FA 2006* trust reforms most lifetime trusts will now fall to be taxed under the IHT code of periodic and exit charges; thus familiarity with the charging provisions must now be a prerequisite rather than option for the trust practitioner (see **10.26–10.59**).
- **Relevant property trusts** – Earlier proposed reforms designed to simplify the periodic charge calculation and block the effective use of multiple trusts take effect for charges arising on or after 18 November 2015 (see **10.26**).
- **The 'Frankland' trap** – Appointments made out of trusts within three months of death in favour of the deceased's surviving spouse/civil partner will qualify for the spousal exemption (see **10.26**).
- **Interaction of APR and BPR** – The demarcation lines of myth and fact must be clearly drawn when considering the use of these valuable headline reliefs in the context of the charging regime applicable to relevant property trusts (see **10.60–10.65**).

TYPES OF DISCRETIONARY OR RELEVANT PROPERTY TRUSTS

Full relevant property trusts: history of the legislation

10.1 This book is mainly about IHT, but where trusts are concerned IHT and CGT closely interact and it is therefore necessary to comment on that interaction. Although at one time it was relatively easy to hold over gains on transfers into and out of trusts, this facility has been eroded in two ways:

- by *FA 2003* which restricts holdover in connection with settlor-interested trusts and trusts of real estate residence; and
- by *FA 2004* introducing *TCGA 1992, s 169B* in relation to trusts for minors which are treated as settlor-interested following *FA 2006*, so that in effect there can be no holdover on gifts to children by way of trust. This restricts the advantage that was previously available on transfers of business property under *TCGA 1992, s 165* and of property in general under *TCGA 1992, s 260*.

The oft-forgotten upside of the *FA 2006* changes that bring more trusts within the relevant property IHT regime is to make CGT holdover relief more readily available: see **10.6**. By *FA 2008*, some of the restrictions on settlor-interested UK-resident trusts were also removed because until 22 June 2010 a single CGT rate of 18% applied across the board. In the post-22 June 2010 era with a higher CGT rate applied to trusts, estates and higher rate taxpayers this may pave the way for the reintroduction of the settlor-interested rules formerly contained in *TCGA 1992, s 77*.

The individual as the taxable entity

10.2 The preferred subject matter for IHT is the individual and the size of their estate. Thus an outright transfer from one individual to another is taxed on a simpler, if not necessarily more favourable, basis than a transfer which reduces the estate of one person without at the same time increasing the estate of any other. The distinction between potentially exempt transfers (PETs) and chargeable lifetime transfers (CLTs) was examined in **Chapter 1**. The effect of *IHTA 1984, ss 3* and *3A* is that the transfer of funds to a relevant property trust (namely a trust subject to the IHT regime of periodic and exit charges) is a chargeable transfer. The amount of the transfer (net of available exemptions) will initially be set against the transferor's unused nil rate band. Any excess will be chargeable initially at the lifetime rate of 20% (or effective 25% rate if the IHT charge is not met out of the gifted funds) and, in the event of the death of the transferor within three years, at the unabated death rate of 40% or where the transferor's death occurs more than three but less than seven years, at the tapered death rate (effective rate of between 8% and 32%). *Note*:

- All statutory references in this chapter are to *IHTA 1984*, unless otherwise stated.
- For the purposes of calculations/illustrations the exit charge/periodic charge is set to three decimal places, which reflects current HMRC application.
- Tax liabilities have generally been rounded to whole numbers.

How discretionary and accumulation trusts work

> **Focus**
>
> For trusts created post 5 April 2010 there is now a single fixed trust period of up to a maximum of 125 years, whilst the standard 21-year accumulation period has been withdrawn.

10.3 The standard discretionary trust used to provide for a perpetuity period, which was usually 80 years and an accumulation period of usually 21 years. The *Perpetuities and Accumulations Act 2009*, which came into force on 6 April 2010, introduced a single perpetuity period of 125 years and removed the accumulation period in its totality – it also enabled a substitution perpetuity period of 100 years where the shelf life of a pre-6 April 2010 trust was either unclear or in doubt.

Once the discretionary trust is established, the settlor transfers assets to the trustees who then have complete freedom to decide which of the beneficiaries are to receive anything from the trust, whether it be capital, income or the benefit of the use of a trust asset.

It is most common and certainly recommended practice that the settlor will give the trustees (of whom they may be one) a letter of wishes and an example is included as Form A at the end of this chapter. The letter of wishes is not legally binding on the trustees but is a subsidiary reference document and has a definite purpose. Significant debate surrounds the issue of whether such a letter is actually a trust document: clearly, its content is of interest to all beneficiaries and so too for fiscal authorities in any jurisdiction.

Although many jurisdictions specifically protect such documents from prying eyes, there is some authority for the view that, if the disclosed principal trust document is so blandly or opaquely drawn as to render it meaningless without the content of the letter of wishes, then the latter must be a trust document and as such belongs to the beneficiaries as a body, so they can, in fact, demand to see it. Alternatively, the view advanced in some quarters is that disclosure might be forced under the *Data Protection Act 1998* and/ or the *General Data Protection Regulations* (applicable from 25 May

2018*)*, but most practitioners (including this author) disagree – certainly the Information Commissioner's Office (ICO) has not made a ruling on the point. Notwithstanding, most trustees will be guided by the letter of wishes and may find it useful in resisting repeated claims from one beneficiary in particular to preferential treatment. Good trustees can and should 'stand up to' the beneficiaries and preserve their independence. That having been said, the successful beneficiary's right to information on the trust composition was pivotal in the recent case of *Blades v (1) Isaac & (2) Alexander* (2016) which considered whether costs incurred by both the trust and plaintiff by reason of that action should be borne by the trust fund.

A discretionary trust comes to an end through the natural passage of time unless the trustees take earlier action to bring about its premature demise. Normally, the trust deed will provide that, in default of exercise of the trustees' discretion, the fund will at the end of the trust period be held for a particular person absolutely. However, the trustees can bring the trust to an end earlier simply by distributing all of the trust funds.

CGT and relevant property trusts

Focus

The *FA 2006* extension of the relevant property regime has provided a welcome CGT planning opportunity to secure access to general holdover relief on chargeable assets transferred into most post-21 March 2006 lifetime trusts.

10.4 Apart from the IHT impact, relevant property trusts do attract CGT benefits. *TCGA 1992, s 260* provides that general gains (as opposed to gains on business assets) may be held over, both on transfers into relevant property trusts (but beware the restriction for transfers into settlor-interested trusts) and transfers out.

Example 10.1—Tax charges on setting up a trust

Alice owns a small parade of shops with flats above which she inherited from her husband many years earlier and which have risen substantially in value since then. She wishes to benefit her grandchildren Bella, Catherine and David. The present value of the combined parade of shops and flats is £700,000 but considered separately, the flats are together worth £300,000 and the shops £350,000. Alice transfers the flats to a relevant property trust and although the flats are worth £300,000 the reduction in Alice's estate is £400,000 (£700,000 – £300,000) – that is the value of the transfer on the 'loss to the estate' principle. Alice utilises her nil rate band for 2018/19 of £325,000 and the annual exemption for this year and last, thus leaving a chargeable transfer of £69,000 ((£400,000 – £325,000) – (£3,000 + £3,000)). As the trust has no liquid assets from which to meet the IHT charge Alice agrees to settle the liability, thus requiring the net value of the asset to be grossed up for IHT purposes. The grossed-up value of £86,250 (£69,000 × 100/(100–20)) charged at 20% triggers an IHT charge of £17,250 (an effective rate equal to 25% of the net transfer).

Although the transfer to the trustees is a disposal for CGT purposes, Alice may avoid paying that tax herself by electing to hold over the gain – the trustees will acquire the flats at the adjusted base cost (the later of March 1982 value or Alice's original cost basis) rather than market value for the purpose of later disposal (that might be by sale or by transfer out to the beneficiaries). If the transfer out of trust ownership is itself a chargeable transfer (which in all normal circumstances it would be) the trustees could, subject to joint agreement with the beneficiary hold over the gain, so that the beneficiaries as the trustees before, acquire the asset at its adjusted base cost. If there are several beneficiaries, the fragmentation of the gain, the perhaps reduced rate of tax charged on individuals and the potential availability of the individual annual exemption may make for good planning.

Old accumulation and maintenance (A&M) trusts

10.5 These trusts in their original form no longer exist as a separate category, having become interest in possession trusts or relevant property trusts, according to the circumstances prevailing when *Finance Act 2006* came into force. All A&M trusts, whether established in lifetime or by will, have long since migrated to the FA 2006 regime albeit perhaps with modified IHT impact and all post FA 2006 lifetime trusts, with very few exceptions, are relevant property trusts. The exceptions to that rule are:

- disabled trusts (DPI);
- trusts for bereaved minors (BMT);
- age 18-to-25 trusts; and
- immediate post-death trusts (IPDI).

The regime of A&M trusts under *IHTA 1984, s 71* was terminated with effect from 6 April 2008, except as still provided for bereaved minors under *IHTA 1984, s 71A* and 18-to-25 trusts under *IHTA 1984, s 71D*.

Bereaved minors' trusts (BMTs)

> **Focus**
>
> The post-21 March 2006 BMT and its extended 18-to-25 sibling cannot be created in lifetime and thus can never be viewed as a modern version of the old-style A&M trust.

10.6 It is important to appreciate that the BMT does not replicate the old style A&M trust. The essential features of a BMT are:

- It can arise only on death.
- It may arise on intestacy or under deed of variation or by way of appointment under *IHTA 1984, s 144*.
- The only possible beneficiary is a minor child of the testator or where the testator is acting in *loco parentis*. A grandchild is not a child for this purpose. There is some provision for substitution of beneficiaries, but only under the rules of intestacy and not under the terms of a will.
- There is no need for an interest in possession in the income and thus income may be accumulated. However, the capital and all accumulations of income must vest at 18. It is not possible to exercise discretion between one beneficiary and another. Effectively, it is sub-funded for each beneficiary from the outset (though not in the full sense of that term).
- CGT holdover relief is available on vesting or asset appointment, as with any other relevant property trust (*TCGA 1992, s 260(2)(da)*).
- There must be no general power of advancement and in particular no power to make a 'settled advance'. This means that whilst *IHTA 1984, s 71A(4)(a)* allows the statutory power of advancement under *Trustee Act 1925, s 32*, effectively there may be no material extension of the powers in the *Trustee Act 1925*. Merely removing the 50% restriction from *Trustee Act 1925, s 32* is acceptable.

> **Example 10.2—Test of a BMT**
>
> Fred died intestate and was survived by his two children both under the age of 18. As each reach the age of 18 they become absolutely entitled under the general intestacy rules and the BMT requirements are satisfied.
>
> In the unlikely event that one of them married and died in childbirth before obtaining majority, the intestacy rules would provide that the grandchild would step into the shoes of their parent and again be entitled to capital at age 18. The BMT rules would be satisfied.

By contrast, if Fred had made a will that provided for his children at age 18 but with substitution clauses in favour of a grandchild that would not comply with the requirements of BMT and the funds would be treated as held on relevant property trusts.

Example 10.3—Further tests of a BMT

On her death, Celia left her house to her minor daughter Jessica absolutely on reaching age 18 but, if Jessica should die before that age then to Celia's brother David, currently aged 23. As a result, the gift is a BMT. The substituted beneficiary is an adult and the other requirements are satisfied.

However, if Celia had instead specified that the house was to go to her daughter at age 21, that would have breached the BMT requirements and the trust would instead become one that met the conditions of an 18-to-25 trust.

Returning to the original scenario, shortly before the daughter is 18 the trustees decide that she is too young to have control of the house. They use the statutory power of advancement and move half of the value of the house onto interest in possession trust terms. That goes beyond what HMRC approve, not being considered an appointment '… to the like effect …' as *TA 1925, s 32*. There is no precise or case-driven *dicta* as to interpretation of this latter phrase other than from Statement of Practice SP/E7, in the context of protective trusts. The appointment therefore triggers the special charge on an A&M trust (or indeed a BMT) under *IHTA 1984, s 70*: see **10.66** below.

If the will had included the usual clause extending *TA 1925, s 32* to the whole of the fund that would have likely satisfied '… to the like effect …' and there would have been no BMT from the outset.

Example 10.4—Wording to create a BMT or 18-to-25 trust

Beverley's will left property 'to such of my children as reach 18 and if more than one in equal shares'. One of her children, Alice, survived her but tragically died of leukaemia at 17. Alice's share passed to her siblings at 18.

HMRC consider that this does not prejudice the shares, which can be treated sibling by sibling. The same treatment would result for 18-to-25 trust purposes.

18-to-25 trusts (to include conforming A&M trusts): overview

10.7 Broadly, the flexibility of a vesting age between age 18 and age 25 comes at a tax cost. If the beneficiary becomes entitled to the capital at age 18 then the fund is IHT neutral during its lifetime up to vesting. If the capital vesting is between age 18 but no greater than age 25 there will be a partial IHT exposure – no IHT charge will trigger before age 18 and that of course is an advantage over a fully relevant property trust, but thereafter the fund will attract a modified exit charge when capital vests (or on capital advancement) on or before age 25. In such circumstances, the benefit of the 'appropriate fraction', as described at **10.12** below, has the effect that the exit charge cannot exceed 4.2% (6% x 7/10) and in practice may well be very much less. If there is an income entitlement only at age 25 but capital does not vest until, say, age 28, the trust is not an 18-to-25 but rather is fully within the IHT rules for relevant property trusts from the outset and thus will attract both the periodic charge and exit charge throughout its life.

These rules apply to existing pre 22 March 2006 A&M trusts as well as to post 21 March 2006 will trusts. Importantly, no new lifetime trust can come within this narrow class which can only now be created on death: it will be a relevant property trust from the outset. However, an immediate life interest trust under a will may qualify as an IPDI and, if it does, it will be treated for IHT purposes as within the 'old' pre-March 2006 regime (see **Chapter 9**).

The conditions for 18-to-25 trusts

10.8 The conditions for an 18-to-25 trust are:

- property is held on trust for someone under age 25;
- a parent (or where *loco parentis* applies) of that person has died;
- the trust is in a will of the parent who has died, or is under the Criminal Injuries Compensation Scheme and meets the 'subsection 6' conditions (see below).

  The 'subsection 6' conditions are:

  (i) the beneficiary will, by age 25 or earlier, be absolutely entitled to the capital and all income arising and all accumulated income;

  (ii) their share of the trust fund has been sub-funded so that their fund has never been available to anyone else.

The 18-to-25 rules do not apply to other categories of trust property, such as that for BMTs, existing interest in possession trusts, IPDIs or trusts for the disabled (DPI). A difficulty had been noted where a trust was subject to the *Trustee Act 1925, s 32* (powers of advancement) but this problem is now resolved by *IHTA 1984, s 71D(7)*.

Particular points of difficulty affecting BMTs and 18-to-25 trusts

10.9 HMRC guidance has clarified three troublesome issues:

- who is a 'the bereaved minor' (or 'B' in the legislation);
- how the legislation deals with the class closing rules; and
- the treatment of settled powers of advancement.

In *IHTA 1984, s 71A* 'the bereaved minor' can mean all the beneficiaries in the class who are alive and under age when the trust takes effect. This will assist in the common form of bequest to all children who reach age 18 in shares appointed by the trustees, where the power of appointment is limited to prevent augmentation or depletion of a share of a child over 18. As a result the fund could be paid out in unequal shares; but age 18 is an effective cut-off point for the further exercise of the power of appointment to that child. Any further 'favouritism' is limited to the children under 18.

Example 10.5—Reallocation of capital share

Henry died young leaving his estate to such of his sons, Charles and Trevor and his daughter Alice as should survive him and attain age 18, but with power of appointment among them. Initially, the trustees treated all three children the same but Henry's brother Iain then died, leaving his estate to his nephews but nothing to Alice (at this point all three are still under age 18). To balance matters, the trustees now want (irrevocably) to allocate a nominal 1% of the fund each to Charles and Trevor with the remainder to Alice.

This will not prejudice the BMT status of the interests. Charles and Trevor could still, up to age 18, benefit if the power in favour of Alice were to be revoked, because they are still 'B' for the purpose of the legislation.

The mere existence of a power of advancement does not prevent a BMT or 18-to-25 trust classification: it is the exercise of that power in such a way as to defer the vesting of capital that will cause a relevant property trust to arise.

IHT charge on 18-to-25 trusts (including conforming A&M trusts)

10.10 The IHT charge on an 18-to-25 trust is set out in *IHTA 1984, s 71E*. It will not apply if the beneficiary takes absolutely at age 18, or dies under that age, or if the trust property becomes subject to the rules for a BMT before the beneficiary becomes age 18 (perhaps where the trustees vary it so that it will vest at age 18) or the fund is used for the beneficiary before he is aged 18 or as soon as he is aged 18. This allows the trustees to bring an otherwise non-compliant trust within the rules to escape IHT. In all other cases the charge will apply when the fund leaves the trust or the trustees enter into a depreciatory transaction. There is no tax charge on a depreciatory transaction if at arm's length or if it is the grant of an agricultural tenancy within *IHTA 1984, s 16*.

The tax itself is calculated under *IHTA 1984, s 71E* when property comes out of the trust, either by passing to the beneficiary absolutely or by being applied for his benefit after the beneficiary is 18; or he dies at a time when he is over the age of 18. The legislation uses a formula multiplying the 'chargeable amount' by 'the relevant fraction' and by the 'settlement rate'. To find the settlement rate the trustees must establish a notional transfer similar to that described later in this chapter in relation to periodic and exit charges.

Chargeable amount

10.11 This is the reduction in the value of the trust fund as a result of the transfer. Importantly, where the IHT is to be paid out of the remaining fund rather than out of the asset so released, the value of the transfer is the grossed-up amount.

Example 10.6—18-to-25 trust: simple release

On 31 May 2005, Cyril set up an A&M trust which provided for capital entitlement at age 25 such that in the post-21 March 2006 era it conforms to the 18-to-25 rules. It holds £1 million for Cyril's four grandchildren, hence £250,000 for each. Rachel, aged 22, needs money to pay off her student loan, so the trustees pay her £40,000 on the basis that she will meet any IHT due. The chargeable amount attracting the modified IHT exit charge is £40,000.

Example 10.7—18-to-25 trust: net release

Continuing the above example, Rachel's elder brother David (born on 6 April 1995 and now aged 23) would like £40,000 to assist with the purchase of a flat. On 6 April 2018, he asked the trustees for the funds and for the trust to pay any IHT exit charge that may be due on that sum. There is no income available to distribute thus the payment must come from capital which must be grossed up to bear its own tax. Assuming that the settlement rate is 18% and that the appropriate fraction is 20/40* the position would be as follows:

Tax rate –	(18 × 30)% × 20/40 = 2.700%.
Tax thereon –	£40,000 @ 2.700% = £1,080
Tax grossed up –	£1,080 @100/(100 – 2.700) = £1,110
Gross transfer –	£1,110 + £40,000 = £41,110

Thus a net transfer of £40,000 would attract a tax charge of £1,110:

£41,110 × (18 × 30)% × 20/40 = £1,110, leaving a net £40,000.00.

* Complete quarters counting from the date of David's 18th birthday on 6 April 2013 (being later than 6 April 2008) to 6 April 2018.

Example 10.8—18-to-25 trust: fall in value of the fund

Dimitri's fund holds only shares in the family investment property company. His son Alexei aged 22 is now joining the board of directors, so the trustees want him to have some shares in his own right.

Owing to the different values of holdings, the fall in value of the fund is in fact greater than the value of the shares themselves. Notwithstanding, it is that greater value that is the transfer value for IHT purposes (but not for CGT purposes).

Relevant fraction

10.12 The relevant fraction for the purpose of the exit charge calculation for an 18-to-25 trust (to include a pre-March 2006 conforming A&M trust) is dependent upon the time elapsed from the date on which the beneficiary reached age 18 (or 6 April 2008 if later) to the date of the chargeable event, reckoned in complete quarters (three-month period). The fraction is 30% of X/40 where X is the number of complete quarters counted from age 18 (or 6 April 2008 if later).

The position is different for a non-conforming pre-March 2006 A&M trust. Consider that an A&M trust was established on 1 March 1998 (no other trusts were created on the same day and there was no settlor cumulative transfer history) which provided for income only at age 25 with capital at trustees' discretion – this does not conform to an 18-to-25 trust under *FA 2006* and thus it formally 'migrated' to the relevant property regime on 6 April 2008 (when its value stood at £250,000) thereafter exposed to ten-year and exit charges. The next ten-year charge post-21 March 2006 fell on 1 March 2008, but the relevant property regime did not actively apply to the trust until 6 April 2008.

The trustees, having made no prior capital distributions, want to terminate the trust as soon as they safely may, but there are large gains and a simple chargeable asset appointment would trigger a CGT charge. How soon can they appoint assets and hold over the gains, relying on *TCGA 1992, s 260*?

The bold answer is 'as soon as they like', on the basis that any appointment that is a chargeable transfer qualifies as a chargeable transfer for the purposes of *TCGA 1992, s 260(2)(a)*. A chargeable transfer from a trust which is within the relevant property regime is still a chargeable transfer even if the exit charge rate is 0% and holdover relief is therefore in point. However, that is different to the position of an appointment where no IHT is due because that transfer is not an IHT event namely within the first quarter post a ten-year charge. The 'exit' charge is calculated under *IHTA 1984, s 65(1)*, but importantly such charge is disapplied (*IHTA 1984, s 65(4)*), if the appointment is made in a quarter beginning with the date of commencement or beginning with the date of the actual ten-year anniversary of the trust. Accordingly, even though the result for IHT in economic terms is the same as a charge at 0% ie no IHT due, holdover under *TCGA 1992, s 260* is no longer in point – there is no occasion of charge for IHT purposes.

In this case the trust entered the relevant property regime on 6 April 2008 pursuant to *Finance Act 2006, Sch 20, para 3. Section 69(2)(b)* of *IHTA 1984* provides for the situation where property was in a trust at the last ten-year anniversary (in this case as at 1 March 2008); but was not then relevant property (the trust was not within the relevant property regime on that anniversary date) but has since become relevant property (the trust entered the relevant property regime on 6 April 2008).

The exit charge in such a situation is charged at the 'appropriate fraction' of the rate, ie (X – Y)/40 where X is the number of complete quarters counting from the last ten-year anniversary (1 March 2008) to date of distribution and Y is the number of complete quarters during which the property was non relevant property in that same period from the last ten-year anniversary up to the date of the appointment (see *IHTA 1984, s 69(4)*). On that basis the trustees can safely distribute after 1 June (being the first day of the second quarter counting from 1 March 2008) and hold over the gain.

Most trustees and many advisers will play safe and let a further, clear, full quarter elapse, so as to avoid the complexities of this legislation. In any event the IHT charge may be very small compared with the CGT in issue.

Settlement rate

10.13 This is the effective rate, namely the tax expressed as a fraction of the notional chargeable transfer and it can be found only after other calculations have been performed. Although the multi-step calculation is difficult to grasp, it can be performed by using the form IHT100 with the working sheet IHT100 (WS) and the guide IHT113. These can be downloaded at the HMRC website: www.gov.uk/government/organisations/hm-revenue-customs.

The notional transfer

10.14 As with relevant property trusts generally, there are a number of components namely:

- the historic (original) value of the trust to include the value of non-relevant property contained therein (but with the latter excluded for chargeable events occurring post 17 November 2015);
- the historic (original) value of any related trust (with non-relevant property related trusts excluded for chargeable events occurring post-17 November 2015); and
- the value of any property added to the trust post creation and before the event now being taxed.

Example 10.9—Grandchildren's trust: the notional transfer

On 6 April 2017, Sean, who had only his current annual exemption available, divided £403,000 between two trusts: one providing a life interest for his daughter Megan (Megan's Trust) and the other a discretionary trust for the benefit of Megan's children (Grandchildren Trust). The IHT due on creation was met out of the funds passing into the respective trusts.

On 16 June 2018, having utilised his annual exemption but fearful of a rise in CGT, Sean added quoted shares/cash worth £26,500 into the grandchildren discretionary trust and the trustees agreed to meet any IHT thereon.

6 April 2017		£
Transfer to the grandchildren trust	201,500	
50% of 2017/18 annual exemption	(1,500)	
Chargeable transfer		200,000
Transfer to Megan's trust as above	201,500	
50% of 2017/18 annual exemption	(1,500)	
Chargeable transfer		200,000
Total chargeable transfers		400,000
Nil rate band (2017/18)		(325,000)
Balance		75,000
IHT thereon at 20% met by the respective trusts		15,000
IHT Allocable:		7,500
Grandchildren trust		7,500
Megan's trust		

16 June 2018

Addition to grandchildren trust		26,500	
Nil rate band (utilised)		Nil	
Balance		26,500	
IHT thereon @ 20% met by grandchildren trust		5,300	

Notional transfer as at 16 June 2018

Grandchildren trust	201,500		
Less: IHT borne by trust	(7,500)		
Net		194,000	(A)
Related settlement – Megan's trust	201,500		
Less: IHT borne by trust	(7,500)		
Net		194,000	(B)
Addition to grandchildren trust	26,500		
Less: IHT borne by trust	(5,300)		
Net		21,200	(C)
Notional transfer (A+B+C) of Grandchildren trust		409,200	

Note:

(i) In each case the gross value of the respective trust fund is reduced by the IHT paid by the trust.

(ii) Megan's trust, although an interest in possession, was created in lifetime post 21 March 2006 thus is a relevant property for IHT purposes.

Life interest trusts

Focus

Most lifetime interest in possession trusts created post-21 March 2006 will now fall within the relevant property regime.

10.15 Sometimes a change in tax law proves particularly difficult for practitioners/clients to grasp and there is a tendency to hearken back to the old law. A classic example is the treatment of gifts under estate duty where taper relief applied to reduce the value of the gift itself in order to arrive at the value on which estate duty was charged. This rule was changed to the point of complete reverse under IHT such that chargeable lifetime gifts are now set initially against the nil rate band with taper relief, where in point, applied to the tax rate and not to the value of the gift. Notwithstanding the nearly 40 plus year passage of time elapsed, there is still adherence to the memory of that old estate duty treatment. In this same way, there will be many practitioners/clients who will have a fundamental difficulty in accepting that a newly created life interest trust, treated as such for many purposes such as:

- matrimonial proceedings; or
- the taxation of income; or
- the taxation of gains where main residence may be in point;

is not treated as a qualifying interest in possession trust for IHT purposes but is instead treated as a relevant property trust. The difficulty may be compounded by anti-avoidance legislation, which often employs the concept of a double negative: see for example the complex changes introduced by *FA 2010, ss 52* and *53*, noted at **9.24** relating to reversionary interests and purchased life interests.

Except where it is a trust for a disabled person (DPI), a BMT, 18-to-25 or IPDI, an interest in possession trust will now fall within the relevant property trust regime unless saved by the pre-existing or transitional rules which afford it qualifying interest status. In this chapter unless preceded by 'qualifying' or 'old style', the term 'interest in possession trust' in which a beneficiary has a right to income is treated as a relevant property trust under the post-21 March 2006 regime. The conditions for an IPDI are set out in **Chapter 9**.

Post-21 March 2006 virtually any life interest trust established during the lifetime of the settlor and even if settlor interested will be treated as a relevant property trust for IHT purposes and thus its creation will be an immediate chargeable transfer (see **Example 10.9** above). The trust will be subject to the periodic (ten-year anniversary) charge described at **10.38** and may incur the proportionate (exit) charge described at **10.26** and following below. Contrary to the traditional treatment of qualifying interest in possession trusts, there will (except in relation to purchased interests and reversions of settlor-interested trusts) be no aggregation of the capital of a life interest trust with the estate of the life tenant. There will, for CGT, be some holdover relief such that there will be scope for tax planning opportunities.

Example 10.10—Life interest trust: lifetime transfer failing to comply with new rules

On 6 May 2017, Henry, who has made no previous chargeable transfers and has not used his current or prior year annual exemptions, settled £331,000 on trust for his wife for life with remainder to their children at 25.

This cannot be an IPDI because it is a lifetime settlement. The result is that it must be treated as a relevant property trust. That in turn means that Henry's wife is not deemed to be the owner of the trust fund for IHT purposes as would have been the case under the old rules. As a result, the spousal relief is not available. Fortunately, after taking account of the two annual exemptions, the amount of the settlement is (just) within Henry's unused nil rate band ((£331,000 – (£3,000 + 3,000) = £325,000), so its creation does not trigger an IHT charge. However, Henry must keep good records for the future in case he decides to make any other settlements later.

THE RELEVANT PROPERTY IHT REGIME

The range of charges

10.16 There are three main occasions of charge on a relevant property trust:

- Entry charges:
  - On creation: use event form IHT100a.
  - On any addition to the fund, other than an exempt addition such as one within *IHTA 1984, s 21* (normal expenditure out of income): use event form IHT100a.
- Exit charges:
  - Before the first ten-year anniversary: use event form IHT100c.
  - Between ten-year anniversaries: use event form IHT100c.
- Ten-year charges:
  - Use event form IHT100d.

Other charges to IHT can apply, when for example:

- a qualifying interest in possession comes to an end and a relevant property trust arises; or
- a special charge arises, for example on a heritage fund (See: *Agricultural, Business and Heritage property Relief (7th edn) (Bloomsbury Professional)*); or
- woodland that was previously exempt is felled; or
- a chargeable event arises on a pension that has been 'alternatively secured' (prior to the abolition of those pension rules in *Finance Act 2011*); or
- a purchased reversionary interest vests.

but these are all outside the scope of this chapter.

TRANSFERS INTO TRUST: THE ENTRY CHARGE

Simple cases

Commencement

10.17 For many of the IHT calculations involving relevant property trusts it is important to know the trust commencement date but that will not always be easy to establish. The legislation is brief: '… references to the commencement of a settlement are references to the time when property first becomes comprised in it …'. This rule is not subject to *de minimis*, so the creation of a pilot trust with an initial £100 will be the commencement of that trust even though the bulk of funds are not added until, say, a death many years later. The importance of the commencement date is highly relevant to those old A&M trusts which fall foul of the post-21 March 2006 trust regime and which from 6 April 2008 became subject to the ten-year anniversary charge.

A slightly different but important rule applies where a trust is initially 'favoured' in some way but becomes a relevant property trust at a later date. Under *IHTA 1984, s 80(1)* the property is treated as joining a new settlement at the time when the first (favoured) interest ends – unusually, the value of that fund is treated as a transfer made by the person holding the qualifying interest in possession at the time of change and not the original settlor. This does not affect the commencement date of the original trust which is relevant for counting of subsequent ten-year anniversaries. However, difficult questions arise where there has been more than one settlor and property has been added at various times. The general approach for the practitioner must be to recommend a new trust for each major transfer of property: the initial cost will be recouped in savings later.

Example 10.11—Transfer into trust: small family trust

On 15 March 2006, Hubert set up an old-style A & M trust for the benefit of his grandchildren providing for income at age 18 and capital at trustee discretion. A review of the trust in the light of the *Finance Act 2006* showed that, in the particular circumstances given the ages of the relevant beneficiaries, unless appointments were made promptly half of the fund would be held on relevant property trusts from 6 April 2008 onwards.

The trustees thought the risk of dissipation of the fund by young beneficiaries was much greater than possible IHT charges. They anticipated that the nil rate band would increase, so they did nothing before 6 April 2008. The first ten-year charge fell due on 15 March 2016 (but tax is calculated by reference to only part of the ten-year period namely for the total of part/complete quarters counting from 6 April 2008 when it first entered the new regime).

Example 10.12—Migration of a trust to relevant property regime

As at 21 March 2006, Iain was the established life tenant of a trust created by him (therefore settlor interested) on 31 December 1982. On 30 June 2018 the trustees at his request terminated his interest and relevant property trusts arose for his grandchildren. The capital of the fund is treated as passing to a new trust on 30 June 2018 and the event is a chargeable transfer by Iain, but the next ten-year anniversary will be on 31 December 2022 (anniversary of original trust creation) not 30 June 2028 (anniversary of creation of new trust).

Example 10.1 concerned the setting up of a relevant property trust by Alice and of the calculation of IHT on that occasion. The initial charge on establishing a settlement is relevant in later computations but at this stage is quite straightforward with PETs ignored because they may fall out of account if the seven-year survival test is met. The annual exemption (and that for the previous year if available) is set against the first transfer made in any given tax year: see *IHTA 1984, s 19(3)(b)* and where there are no earlier chargeable transfers the nil rate band is applied to the balance of the gift with the excess taxed at 20%. The only complicating issue is to observe whether the gift is gross, here meaning that the donee will pay any IHT on it, or net, in which case the donor will pay the extra tax on the grossed up gift.

Example 10.13—Simple gross gift

On 30 April 2018, Sandra settles investment properties worth £370,000 on relevant property trusts. She had already used her 2017/18 annual exemption against a PET made in that tax year but she has made no other gifts in the current 2018/19 year nor had she made any prior chargeable lifetime transfers. She tells the trustees that they must pay any IHT due.

	£
Value transferred	370,000
Exemption 2018/19	(3,000)
	367,000
Nil rate band 2018/19	(325,000)
Excess	42,000
IHT @ 20%	8,400

Grossing up

10.18 If the settlor agrees to pay the tax, that tax is established by grossing up the value of the intended net transfer by the IHT due thereon. On lifetime transfers the grossing-up fraction for the tax is one-quarter to give an effective rate of 25%; on death transfers the grossing-up fraction is two-thirds to give an effective rate of 66.66%. In calculating the tax any previous chargeable transfers must be taken into account.

Example 10.14—Net gift following previous chargeable transfer

On 4 April 2018, Tanya gives trustees £280,000 cash to hold on relevant property trust similar to the trust to which on 31 December 2016 she had made a chargeable transfer of £100,000. She has used her annual exemption on 6 April in each year so this was not available to set against either trust transfer and the current gift is to be 'tax free'.

		£
Value transferred		280,000
Annual exemption fully utilised		
Nil rate band 2017/18	325,000	
Less: previous chargeable transfer	(100,000)	
Remaining nil rate band		(225,000)
Net transfer		55,000
Gross transfer £55,000 × 100/80		68,750
IHT £68,750 @ 20%		13,750

10.19 Although the tax charged on the initial lifetime transfer is calculated at the lifetime rate, that rate is subject to review to take account of the higher death rate of 40% if the death of the settlor subsequently occurs within seven years. However, despite the disparity in the rates, the review may not result in an increased charge and this is typically the case where the available nil rate band has increased in the interim: to the extent that the review results in a lower charge then there is no refund of the earlier tax paid.

Example 10.15—Death within three years of a small chargeable transfer

On 4 April 2009, Una made a relevant property trust of £330,000 gross but had already used her annual exemption (current and prior year) – she made no prior chargeable transfers. When the trust was set up, the entry charge was:

	£
Value transferred	330,000
Nil rate band 2008/09	(312,000)
Excess	18,000
Tax @ 20%	3,600

Una died on 31 March 2012 and as this occurred within three years, it is necessary to recalculate using the 'death' rate as required by *s 7(4)*:

Value transferred	330,000
Nil rate band 2011/12 (year of death)	(325,000)
	5,000
Tax @ 40%	2,000
Deduct tax already paid	(3,600)
Additional tax charge	NIL

10.20 Where the figures are larger, it is much more likely that death within three years, where no taper applies, will trigger a charge to additional tax.

Example 10.16—Death within three years of a large chargeable transfer

On 5 April 2009, Victor made a relevant property trust of £750,000 gross but had already used his annual exemption (current and prior year) – he made no prior chargeable transfers. When the trust was set up, the entry charge was:

	£
Value transferred	750,000
Nil rate band 2008/09	(312,000)
Excess	438,000
Tax at 20%	87,600

Victor died on 31 March 2012 and as death occurred within three years it is necessary to recalculate using the 'death' rate as required by *s 7(4)*:

	£
Value transferred	750,000
Nil rate band 2011/12	(325,000)
	425,000
Tax @ 40%	170,000
Less tax paid earlier	(87,600)
Balance now payable	82,400

10.21 The final factor that can affect the entry charge is the existence of prior transfers which, though a PET when made, become chargeable (as a failed PET) because the settlor's death occurs within seven years thereof and thus have first call on the nil rate band.

Example 10.17—Review of earlier tax charge and re-computation at death rates

Willie, who always used his annual exemption on 6 April each year, made a number of additional lifetime gifts:

	£
31 March 2010: cash to his daughter (outright)	150,000
31 January 2012: cash to his son	172,000
28 February 2016: investment property to a relevant property trust	330,000

No IHT was paid on the cash gifts, being PETs.

Tax was paid by the trustees out of the funds settled on relevant property trust as follows:

	£
Value transferred	330,000
Nil rate 2015/16	(325,000)
Excess	5,000
Tax at 20%	1,000

On Willie's death on 31 December 2018, the gift in 2010 falls out of account as it was made more than seven years earlier but the PET in 2012 has now failed and is chargeable. The nil rate band otherwise available is first used towards and wholly covers this gift, so there is no tax to pay, but the position for the 2016 transfer into the relevant property trust must now be revisited following the repositioning of the nil rate band against the earlier gifts.

	£	£
Value transferred		330,000
Nil rate band 2015/16 (event date)	325,000	
Less: used for gift to son	(172,000)	
		(153,000)
Balance		177,000
Lifetime tax at 20% (but see below)	35,400	
Less paid earlier	(1,000)	
Payable now in respect of original event (subject as below)		34,400

Willie's death occurred within three years of the transfer into trust so it is necessary to adjust the calculation for the increased death rate.

	£	£
Value transferred		330,000
Nil rate band 2018/19 (date of death)	325,000	
Less: used for gift to son	(172,000)	
		(153,000)
Excess		177,000
Tax at 40%	70,800	
Less: paid originally	(1,000)	
Less: payable at lifetime rates	(34,400)	
Excess payable at death rates		35,400

In the above example it was not strictly necessary to recalculate the tax at the lifetime rates to establish the further burden of tax but circumstances may be imagined where, because of periodic changes in the rates, each step in the calculation is necessary.

Migrations from the pre-2006 regime: the general position

10.22 The intention of *FA 2006* was to extend the IHT relevant property regime to now apply to those various trusts that previously were outside that regime such as interest in possession trusts subject to overriding powers and A&M trusts where capital did not vest until post age 25. The position of a qualifying interest in possession trust is protected until that pre-March 2006 interest expires (or even longer where there is a transitional serial interest). On the termination of that interest there will be an IHT charge if the property remains settled and irrespective of whether it then falls, as it most likely, to be held on relevant property trusts or not.

By *IHTA 1984, s 51(1A)*, the disposal of a post-21 March 2006 interest in possession is a transfer of value unless that interest is an IPDI, a DPI or a TSI. By *IHTA 1984, s 51(1B)*, the disposal of a pre-22 March 2006 qualifying interest in possession is a transfer of value unless immediately before that disposal the trust as a whole complies with the requirements of *IHTA 1984, s 71A* trusts for bereaved minors or *IHTA 1984, s 71D*: in other words, that on the disposal the trust will become either the property of minors at the age of 18 or the property of others no later than age 25.

Migration of interest in possession trusts to the relevant property trust tax regime

10.23 *Section 52* of *IHTA 1984* provides the general rule that there is a charge to tax on the coming to an end of a qualifying interest in possession where the trust continues, but with the condition that where that interest is sold the proceeds of sale are set against the value that would otherwise be taxed. *Section 52(2A)* provides that in relation to 'new' interests in possession, *IHTA 1984, s 52(1)* and *(2)* apply only where the interest being terminated is an IPDI, or a DPI, or a TSI. The same applies to depreciatory transactions.

Section 53(1A) of *IHTA 1984* provides for an exception from the general charge to tax on the fund under *IHTA 1984, s 52* in relation to an established qualifying interest in possession which continues after 21 March 2006 where, on the later cessation of that interest, the requirements of a BMT or an 18-to-25 trust are met. The structure that results is that the termination of a qualifying interest in possession is still to be treated under the old pre-22 March 2006 rules thus:

- on that termination the fund becomes part of the estate of another person and it is a PET; and
- on that termination the trust continues and relevant property trusts arise (as is most likely the case) it is a chargeable transfer deemed made by the person giving up their qualifying interest, namely the life tenant.

On the other hand, the termination of an interest in possession which has only come into being after 21 March 2006 (thus a non-qualifying interest unless an IPDI) in circumstances where the trust continues will not be a chargeable transfer unless it is brought within the exceptional regime for a TSI or a BMT.

Migration of A&M trusts to the relevant property trust tax regime

> **Focus**
>
> Those old-style A&M trusts the terms of which were timely amended to provide for capital (as opposed to income) entitlement at age 25 will only attract a modified exit charge – they will not be subject to a ten-year charge irrespective of the passage of time post-5 April 2008 before entitlement occurs.

10.24 The beneficial IHT treatment previously enjoyed by the old-style A&M trust was terminated with effect from 22 March 2006.

Any beneficiary who had already obtained an interest in possession (a qualifying interest) at that date could happily continue to benefit from the old treatment.

However, a beneficiary who by accident of date of birth had not achieved an interest in possession by 22 March 2006 would henceforth be treated as a beneficiary of a relevant property trust, making their interest potentially subject to periodic and exit charges. This could cause significant disadvantage as between one beneficiary and another, thus the provisions were softened a little to provide the trustees with a limited range of options.

Example 10.18—A&M trust: no election by the trustees

Hannah had four grandchildren for whom, in 2000, she set up an A&M trust comprising a quoted share portfolio. The trust terms were straightforward such that the children became entitled to income at the age of 18 (because the provision of *Trustee Act 1925, s 31* had not been excluded) and to capital at age 25. The trustees were either unaware of the right to elect into the BMT regime or considered it unwise for family reasons.

By 22 March 2006 the eldest grandchild, Isaac, was 25 and had already received his one quarter capital share. Thus he was not affected at all by the post-21 March 2006 regime and there was no *TCGA 1992, s 260* holdover relief for CGT purposes.

Jessica was aged 24 on 21 March 2006 and thus had an established qualifying income entitlement. She did not suffer an IHT charge on her one-third share of the remaining fund when she became entitled to the capital in March 2007 as this occurred before the watershed of 6 April 2008. Conversely, there was no *TCGA 1992, s 260* holdover relief for CGT purposes.

Karen was 18 in January 2008 and as she had not established an interest in possession as at 21 March 2006, her one-half share of the remaining fund entered the relevant property regime on 22 March 2006. The delayed impact of the *FA 2006* measures until 6 April 2008 ensured that there was no IHT charge when she became entitled to that interest in January 2008. However, the original freedom from IHT exit charges enjoyed by her elder sisters was lost post-5 April 2008 such that her fund suffered tax on the 18-to-25 basis when she became entitled to the trust capital in January 2015. As a consequence there was *TCGA 1992, s 260* holdover relief for CGT purposes.

Jenny was age 18 in December 2011 and as she had not established an interest in possession as at 21 March 2006, the remainder of the trust fund comprising her share entered the relevant property regime on 22 March 2006. There was no IHT impact when she became entitled to her interest in December 2011 as the trust continued in existence but her fund suffers tax on the 18-to-25 basis when she becomes entitled to the trust capital in December 2018. As a consequence there will be *TCGA 1992, s 260* holdover relief for CGT purposes.

10.25 The transitional provisions were set out in *IHTA 1984, s 71(1A)* and *FA 2006, Sch 20, para 3*. If the terms of the trust were changed so that the age for vesting capital was reduced to 18 (akin to a BMT) its A&M status could be preserved. The time for this has long since passed but the following illustration may be relevant to understanding the tax treatment.

Example 10.19—Transitional provisions: action by the trustees

Referring back to the **Example 10.18** above, although the trust entered the relevant property regime on 22 March 2006 there was actually no exit charge when Jessica became entitled to the capital in March 2007 because of the transitional provisions of *FA 2006, Sch 20, para 3(3)* which deferred active entry into the relevant property regime until 6 April 2008. The reason is one of timing of charges. Under the transitional provisions the capital was not treated as being within a relevant property trust until 6 April 2008. Capital that vested before that date therefore escaped the charge. Interests in possession that arose after that date did so within the context of a relevant property trust; they were not an occasion of charge.

THE PROPORTIONATE OR 'EXIT' CHARGE DURING THE FIRST TEN YEARS

Focus

Whilst the exit charge is only applied to the capital distribution itself, the rate of that charge is dependent on a combination of established values and time elapsed between date of trust creation and date of distribution. A nil rate band trust can therefore still produce a positive exit charge.

General considerations and the procedure

10.26 The taxation of relevant property trusts could have been made very much simpler by applying a single tax rate to all such trusts, regardless of size. Instead, the deliberate intention to tax settlements that are larger or that are derived from a larger estate, more heavily than smaller ones, has led to the introduction of complex rules. A fund that is within the nil rate band and remains so is infinitely easier to manage than a larger fund. The rate of tax is stipulated in *IHTA 1984, s 68(1)*, referring to:

- 'the appropriate fraction' of
- 'the effective rate' applied to
- the type of transfer identified in *IHTA 1984, s 68(4)*, but as varied by
- *IHTA 1984, s 68(6)* in relation to old trusts.

Perseverance is demanded in order to grasp the principles and this is particularly difficult for lawyers who are not generally accustomed to multi-step computations. This is one of the few areas where HMRC will help with the calculation and as a consequence some practitioners will be less inclined to become involved in the actual computation. However, this approach will severely curtail the ability to check the accuracy of any HMRC assessment which is known to be prone to human error and that must remain a concern. This is recognised within the professional organisations, such that both the Chartered Institute of Taxation (CIOT) and the Society of Trust and Estate Practitioners (STEP) now require new members to demonstrate much more than a basic level of competence in dealing with this subject.

There is no doubt that the complexities of the charges triggered under the relevant property regime have been heightened by the *FA 2006* trust legislation. Responding to the concerns of professional advisers, it was announced in the March 2012 Budget there would be a consultative process launched to explore possible options for simplifying the calculation of the IHT periodic and exit charges on trusts that hold or dispose of relevant property. Later that year HMRC published a consultation document to which the various professional bodies' response was invited and the outcome of that consultation was published in March 2013. It identified a number of areas of concern, simplification and potential reform to include standard treatment of accumulations, problems with poor historic records and the need for a uniform approach to multiple trusts. However, whilst HMRC rejected out of hand some suggestions ie a reversion to the pre-March 2006 rules for old-style A&M trusts and exclusion of the non-qualifying IIP trusts and 18-to-25 trusts from the relevant property regime, HMRC did accept that there was a real need to make the system more workable and user friendly and acknowledged that more work was needed. It was intended that the consultation would concentrate on:

- a simplified method of calculating the ten-yearly and exit charges;
- clearer rules concerning the treatment and recognition of accumulated income; and
- the alignment of IHT trust charges, filing and payment dates.

In May 2013 HMRC released a follow-up consultative document (see '*Inheritance tax: simplifying charges on trusts – the next stage*', 31 May 2013) which provided more detail to the proposed method of reforms for the above three headings namely:

(i) Ten-year charge:

- dropping the seven-year settlor cumulative history;
- ignoring non-relevant property;
- dividing the nil rate band by the total number of settlements created by the settlor whenever created; and
- introduction of a standard 6% rate.

(ii) Accumulations:

Giving statutory recognition to capital status of accumulated income not distributed by the end of the second year in which the income arises.

(iii) Compliance alignment:

Alignment with the self-assessment framework for filing and payment dates.

In December 2013, HMRC formally advised that following representations made by the key interest groups who participated in the consultation process, changes had been made to the original proposals, namely:

(1) to introduce a new rule proposing to treat income that has remained undistributed for more than five years at the date of the ten-year anniversary as if it was part of the trust capital for the purposes of the ten-year anniversary charge;

(2) to align filing and payment dates to a uniform six months after the end of the month in which the event occurred;

(3) to consult further on alternative proposals to split the nil rate band that will meet trustees' concerns whilst maintaining tax revenues and as a result:

    - put the simplification of the calculations on a slightly slower track so that any new legislation would be introduced in the Finance Bill 2015; and

- defer the proposal to require trustees to 'self-assess' IHT due until Finance Bill 2015.

Finance Act 2014 gave statutory authority (ii) for accumulations and (iii) for compliance alignment introduced with effect from 6 April 2014 but it was intended that (i) would be subject to further consultation. However, in June 2014 HMRC published a third consultation document on IHT trust simplification which contained new proposals aimed at thwarting the popular use of pilot trusts by preventing taxpayers from reducing their IHT liability through setting up multiple trusts each using a separate nil rate band. HMRC proposed applying a single nil rate band (to be known as a 'settlement nil rate band') to all relevant property trusts created by the same settlor since 6 June 2014, but with the ability of the settlor to elect how that settlement nil rate band should be allocated. HMRC also restated their intention to introduce a standard fixed 6% charge to ease the complications of the current system.

These proposals were summarily 'scrapped' in the December 2014 Autumn Budget and in their place new measures were proposed, intended to remove the need to recognise the value of non-relevant property when calculating the ten-year charge/exit charge and introducing rules dealing with the same-day addition of later added property to multiple trusts. The measures also included changes to the relevant property trust legislation intended to provide more certainty and to ease the effect/complexity of the legislation – in particular it was proposed that *IHTA 1984, s 144* be amended so that the provisions of *s 65(4)* which prevent an IHT exit charge arising in the first three months after the will trust commenced (the '*Frankland*' trap) would not apply to appointments so made thereby allowing the appointment to be read back into the will and claim the benefit of the spousal exemption where appropriate. Further, it was proposed that the value of non-relevant property would no longer be included in the ten-year charge calculation.

The proposals were contained in the Finance Bill 2015, and were intended to apply to all charges arising on or after 6 April 2015 in respect of relevant property trusts created on or after the publication of draft legislation on 10 December 2014. To prevent any pre-emptive steps, it was also intended to apply to such trusts created before 10 December 2014 where additions were made to more than one trust on the same day. It was intended that this latter provision would not apply to transfers into pilot trusts on death occurring before 6 April 2016 (provided they were made under the terms of a will which was put in place immediately before 10 December 2014). This latter measure initially raised concerns that post-December 2014 codicils could result in a loss of protection but this was later clarified in subsequent HMRC exchange.

However, due to the general election in May 2015 affording little time to debate the spring Finance Bill provisions on its passage through Parliament, none of the above intended trust measures made their way into *FA 2015*. However, this was partially addressed by the summer *Finance (No 2) Act 2015* which provided for the following:

(i) Exclusion of non-relevant property

The calculation of the periodic and exit charges is simplified by removing the need to include the (historic) value of non-relevant property (namely that property not subject to the IHT system of ten-year and exit charges) within the notional transfer total. This applies to all chargeable events arising on or after 18 November 2015 (date of Royal Assent).

(ii) Same-day additions

Aimed at negating the benefit of multiple trusts (pilot trusts) use, the rule operates to ensure that where property is added to more than one relevant property trust on the same day (on or after commencement of those trusts) that added value together with the original value of that trust when first settled (to the extent not already recognised as a related settlement) is brought into account in calculating the rate of tax for the purpose of the ten-year and exit charges. There is a *de miminis* exemption where the same-day addition is £5,000 or less (*IHTA 1984, s 62(2)–(4)*). The new provision does not apply to a will executed before 10 December 2014 where the death occurs before 6 April 2017 and applies to all chargeable events taking place on or after 18 November 2015 (date of Royal Assent).

The above anti-avoidance legislation does not apply if either (or both) trust A and trust B is a 'protected settlement' (*s 62C*) namely a trust which commenced before 10 December 2014 and either of two conditions (A or B) is satisfied:

- Condition A is broadly that the settlor has not added value to the settlement since 10 December 2014.
- Alternatively, Condition B is that the settlor makes a transfer on or after 10 December 2014 resulting in the value of the property being increased, where the transfer arises (under *s 4*) on the settlor's death before 6 April 2017 by reason of a 'protected testamentary disposition' (ie under the settlor's will, where its provisions are substantially the same as they were immediately before 10 December 2014).

It should be noted that it still remains possible for the settlor to create a new relevant property trust every seven years, each with its own nil rate band (assuming that no other chargeable transfers or PETs have been made in the intervening periods). Furthermore, consideration could be given to adding business property to existing trust, although as indicated such additions should generally be made on different days.

(iii) The 'Frankland' trap

The three-month waiting period for an absolute appointment out of a will trust (in which no qualifying interest in possession exists) created on the testator's death on or after 10 December 2014 to the surviving spouse or civil partner is withdrawn paving the way for full spousal relief. This action reflects the treatment already afforded to the carve-out of an interest in possession in favour of the surviving spouse or civil partner.

(iv) *Section 80* rejigged

The wording of *IHTA 1984, s 80* is amended to correct an unintended effect which permitted a successive spousal non-qualifying interest in possession to potentially escape IHT charge because the trust assets were neither part of the successor's estate nor comprised within a relevant property trust. The term 'interest in possession' is replaced with the term 'qualifying interest in possession' – the latter referring to an interest that is either a pre-22 March 2006 established interest, an IPDI, transitional serial interest (TSI) or disabled person's interest as set out in *IHTA 1984, s 59*. Accordingly, where one party to a couple succeeds to a life interest to which their spouse or civil partner was previously entitled during their lifetime, *IHTA 1984, s 80* will continue to apply at that time.

10.27 Where the fund value is greater than the nil rate band but the circumstances are simple, the computation is still manageable. The legislation, which is contained in *IHTA 1984, ss 64–69,* delivers little practical guidance since it expresses the charge without the use of formulae or examples. A more helpful tool is the actual form IHT100 itself – this can be simply downloaded together with the related forms IHT100d and the more daunting IHT100 (WS) accompanied by completion instructions. In contrast, the similar calculation required for an 18-to-25 trust, is clearly set out in *IHTA 1984, s 71F*, it does use a formula and it is slightly easier to follow – perhaps this style has benefited from a more modern draftsman. However, despite HMRC assurances, form IHT100 has not yet been adapted to deal with the modified 19-to-25 calculation warranting the need to submit the form under cover of explanatory letter.

In a simple case, the settlor will not have added any funds to the trust since its creation. However, it is distressingly common for this 'rule' to be breached and this only serves to make the calculations more complicated –see **Example 10.28** below.

Further complications arise where the relevant property trust is also used as the vehicle for holding family assets which are the subject of pre-March 2006/ TSI or interest in possession trusts: see **Example 10.23** below. Following the changes in *FA 2006*, this is perhaps likely to be less of a problem in time because it will no longer be possible to create new lifetime interest in possession trusts outside of the relevant property regime.

Establishing the 'hypothetical transfer'

10.28 The complete calculation is dependent on a series of steps which taken together achieve a graduated tax burden. The first step in the calculation is to determine a hypothetical transfer as required by *IHTA 1984, s 68(4)*. The process may become clearer by working through several illustrative examples. Elements of the hypothetical transfer include (see *IHTA 1984, s 68(4)(b))*:

- the initial transfer into trust itself;
- the initial value of other settlements made on the same day (excluding non-relevant property settlements for chargeable events on or after 18 November 2015) and ignoring the availability of agricultural property relief (APR)/or business property relief (BPR); and
- funds added later.

In each case the value of the transfer/funds is the amount net of any tax met therefrom.

The following notes relate only to settlements established after 26 March 1974, thus avoiding the complexities of *IHTA 1984, s 68(6)*.

Example 10.20—Hypothetical transfer: simplest version

Alfred had used his annual exemptions and the other reliefs to the full but had made no chargeable transfers until 31 October 2017, when he put a small investment property, worth £260,000, into a relevant property trust for his grandchildren.

The hypothetical transfer comprises:

	£
• Value of property in trust at commencement	260,000
• Historic value of related relevant property trust	NIL
• Value of any added property	NIL
Total	260,000

This is within the nil rate band then in force (£325,000 for 2017/18) so, there was no entry charge and as will be seen later, no IHT will be payable on transfer out of the fund during the first ten years of its life (provided there are no later additions).

10.29 The transfer is made up of the full value of the property, even though reliefs or exemptions may apply to the settlor – it should be remembered that no tax is actually being paid at this stage thus the taxpayer is not disadvantaged. *Section 62* of *IHTA 1984* defines a 'related settlement' as one made on the same day by the same settlor (except where one is for charity or covered by the spousal exemption) but *Finance (No 2) Act 2015* disregards recognition for chargeable events occurring on or after 18 November 2015 where the related settlement is of non-relevant property.

Example 10.21—Hypothetical transfer: related settlement and business property

Bernard transferred a block of property to a relevant property trust (No 1) created on 31 October 2017. It comprised a factory occupied by Bernard's family company (in which Bernard has a controlling shareholding) and some terraced cottages adjoining. The factory was worth £200,000, the cottages £150,000. The same day Bernard settled £50,000 cash on a separate relevant property trust (No 2).

The hypothetical transfer comprises:

	£
• Value of the property in trust at commencement (No 1)	350,000
• Historic value of related relevant property trust (No 2)	50,000
• Value of any added property	NIL
Total	400,000

Following through the point mentioned at **10.28** above, although BPR at 50% is in point with regard to the factory, that relief is ignored when (and only when) calculating the initial value of the related settlement within the hypothetical transfer total.

10.30 Often overlooked is the need to take account of the tax borne by the trustees on the transfer in of trust property when considering the value of the trust fund for the purposes of the hypothetical transfer.

Example 10.22—Hypothetical transfer: allowance for tax debt

Celia owned a block of flats worth £415,000 and settled it on a relevant property trust on 31 October 2017 on terms that the trustees would pay any IHT due thereon. Earlier in that same tax year Celia had made one chargeable transfer of £50,000 (net of the current/prior year annual exemptions) which was not connected with the trust.

The IHT on the transfer into trust is calculated as follows:

	£
• The transfer itself	415,000
• The earlier 'unconnected' transfer	50,000
	465,000

Less: nil rate band 2017/18	(325,000)
Chargeable excess	140,000
20% of excess (the 'entry' charge):	28,000

The hypothetical transfer comprises:

	£
• Value of property in trust at commencement	415,000
• Less the entry charge	(28,000)
	387,000
• Historic value of related relevant property trust	NIL
• Value of any added property	NIL
Total	387,000

There is no statutory authority for the deduction of tax but it is a logical approach and it is accepted by HMRC – the value of the trust fund must be the actual value received. Note that at this point it is not necessary to consider the prior chargeable transfer (in this example £50,000) – that will be relevant later but is not a component of the calculation of the notional transfer and is not included within the elements set out in *IHTA 1984, s 68(5)*.

10.31 Where (in the case of a trust established before 22 March 2006) part of the trust fund was not held on relevant property trusts, logic suggests that value should be excluded when determining the notional transfer but this was not the case until 18 November 2015 (see **10.26** above). Of course in the post 21 March 2006 era virtually all lifetime trusts will likely be relevant property trusts, so this particular issue will disappear in time but it remained on the radar until 18 November 2015.

Example 10.23—Hypothetical transfer: mixed (but not exempt) settlement

On 1 March 2006, Dennis transferred £540,000 into a trust of which 50% of the fund provides a life interest for his niece whilst the other 50% is held on discretionary trust terms for his godchildren. The hypothetical transfer relevant for events (ie exit charge) which took place before 18 November 2015 comprised:

	£
• 50% value of relevant property in trust at commencement	270,000
• 50% value of non-relevant property in trust at commencement	270,000
• Historic value of related trust	NIL
• Value of any added property	NIL
Total	540,000

The fact that 50% of the trust was non relevant property which settled value was a PET on creation (under the old pre-22 March 2006 rules) does not impact on the hypothetical transfer in this example. However, by virtue of the new rules contained in *F(No 2)A 2015,* which excludes recognition of related non-relevant property, this does impact on events taking place after 17 November 2015.

Example 10.24—Trust migrating to the relevant property regime under the new rules

Doreen had made chargeable transfers totalling £75,000 in 1997 and having utilised her annual exemption, created two settlements on 31 July 1998. The first, of £100,000, provided for a life interest for her son Eric. The second, of £350,000, was an A&M settlement for her grandchildren providing for capital and income at age 25 thus post *FA 2006* it conformed to an 18-25 trust – it will not be subject to a ten-year charge but the capital entitlements at age 25 will attract an exit charge.

The hypothetical transfer for the A&M trust in respect of events taking place after 5 April 2008 and before 18 November 2015 comprises:

	£
• Value of property in A&M at commencement	350,000
• Historic value of property in non-relevant property related trust	100,000
• Value of any added property	NIL
Total	450,000

The hypothetical transfer for events taking place after 17 November 2015 but before the ten-year anniversary date of 31 July 2018 comprises:

	£
• Value of property in A&M at commencement	350,000
• Historic value of related relevant property trust	NIL
• Value of any added property	NIL
Total	350,000

10.32 Related settlements (but restricted to relevant property related settlements only post 17 November 2015) can greatly affect the rate and this will be relevant in relation to A&M trusts that migrated to the IHT regime under *FA 2006*, where it will now be necessary to look at the element that is caught by the new rules in the context of the trust as a whole – see **Example 10.24** above. However, by virtue of the new rules contained in *F(No 2)A 2015,* which excludes recognition of related non-relevant property, this will impact on events taking place on or after 18 November 2015 (date of Royal Assent).

Example 10.25—Hypothetical transfer: death same day as settlement

Eric made a relevant property trust (No 1) of £400,000 on 31 December 2017 and died later that day, leaving an estate of £500,000 on a separate relevant property trust (No 2). No reliefs were available on death.

The hypothetical transfer for trust (No 1) comprises:

	£
• Value of the fund at commencement (No 1)	400,000
• Historic value of related relevant property trust (No 2)	500,000
• Value of any added property	NIL
Total	900,000

10.33 An exemption is treated differently from a relief. Whereas reliefs do not affect the hypothetical transfer, exemptions may, as seen in the next example.

Example 10.26—Hypothetical transfer: death same day as settlement

On 31 December 2017, Frances settled £100,000 on an interest in possession trust (No 1) for her goddaughter. She died later that day having by her will left £100,000 on trust (No 2) for her local church, £200,000 to her husband absolutely and the residue of £350,000 on discretionary trust (No 3).

The hypothetical transfer for Trust (No 1) comprises:

	£
• Value of the fund at commencement (No 1)	100,000
• Historic value of related relevant property trust (No 3)	350,000
• Value of any added property	NIL
Total	450,000

10.34 Where on death funds are left on trust for a charity or on IPDI terms for the surviving spouse 'without limit of time' there is, as noted earlier, no aggregation: see *IHTA 1984, s 62(2)*.

Example 10.27—Hypothetical transfer: exempt share of the trust

On her death on 31 December 2017, Gina left £600,000 in trust as to one half on IPDI terms for her husband Gregory for life and as to the remainder on discretionary trust. She had made no previous chargeable transfers during her lifetime.

The hypothetical transfer for the discretionary trust comprises:

	£
• 50% value of relevant property fund at commencement	300,000
• Historic value of related relevant property trust	NIL
• Value of any added property	NIL
Total	300,000

This position, where the spousal exemption comes into play, should be contrasted with the example of Dennis above.

10.35 Curiously, even where an asset is added to the trust but is later distributed, it still affects the calculation. For valuation purposes it would seem that each asset is valued in isolation.

Example 10.28—Hypothetical transfer: extra funds for a while

On 30 November 2015, Henry settled a property worth £300,000 on discretionary trust. On 30 April 2016 he added £100,000 cash, of which £75,000 was distributed at Christmas 2017. The trustees paid the appropriate exit charge at that time. This calculation, like the others in this section, concerns only the hypothetical transfer which comprises:

	£
• Value of relevant property fund at commencement	300,000
• Historic value of related relevant property trust	NIL
• Value of added property	100,000
Total	400,000

Example 10.29—Failed PET coming to light

Celia (**Example 10.22**) died on 1 May 2018. It was established that she had made a PET of £100,000 (net of exemptions) on 31 August 2012 which now 'fails' and becomes chargeable by reason of her death within seven years. The calculation of the entry charge on her transfer into trust on 31 October 2017 is revised first to take account of the failed PET and secondly, to recognise the rebasing to the death rate of 40%.

The IHT entry charge on the transfer, to calculate the hypothetical rate for the later exit charge, is now:

	£
• The transfer in to trust	415,000
• The now failed PET	100,000
• The earlier recognised transfer	50,000
	565,000
• Less: nil rate band on trust creation (2017/18)	(325,000)
• Chargeable excess	240,000
• Tax at 40% of excess	96,000

All of this tax relates to the transfer into trust, because the earlier transfers (£100,000 + £50,000) have first bite of the nil rate band.

The hypothetical transfer comprises:

	£
• Value of property in trust at commencement	415,000
• Less IHT liability of trustees	(96,000)
	319,000
• Historic value of related relevant property trust	NIL
• Value of any added property	NIL
Total	319,000

Calculating the 'effective rate'

10.36 Even though the preceding examples involve a tax computation, they are but the first step in the overall process of establishing the final calculation. The second step is to now calculate the tax on the hypothetical transfer but again this is not real tax but merely part of the process.

The purpose of this particular set of sums is to fix the charge on assets leaving a relevant property trust. The rate of tax used is the rate in force at the time of the transfer, not at the time that the trust was set up. All that this computation achieves is to identify the 'effective rate' and even that is not the rate at which tax will be charged: only a proportion will be charged.

It is important to note that for this purpose the lifetime rate of 20% is always used even where the transfer was on death – the death rate of 40% is never a component of the ten-year exit charge.

Example 10.30—The 'effective rate' for distribution made 30 November 2018

	£
Alfred (Example 10.20):	
Value of hypothetical transfer	260,000
Nil rate band at time of exit charge (2018/19)	(325,000)
Notional chargeable transfer	0
Tax at 20%	0
Effective rate 0/260,000 × 100	0%
Bernard (Example 10.21):	
Value of hypothetical transfer	400,000
Nil rate band at the time of the exit charge (2018/19)	(325,000)
Notional chargeable transfer	75,000
Tax @ 20%	15,000
Effective rate 15,000/400,000 × 100	3.750%
Celia (original calculation at **Example 10.22**):	
Value of hypothetical transfer	387,000
Nil rate band (2018/19)	(325,000)
Notional chargeable transfer	62,000
Tax @ 20%	12,400
Effective rate 12,400/387,000 × 100	3.204%
Celia (revised calculation at **Example 10.29**):	
Value of hypothetical transfer	319,000

Nil rate band (2018/19)	(325,000)
Notional chargeable transfer	0
Tax @ 20%	0
Effective rate 0/319,000 × 100	0%

Eric (Example 10.25):

Value of hypothetical transfer	900,000
Nil rate band (2018/19)	(325,000)
Notional chargeable transfer	575,000
Tax @ 20%	115,000
Effective rate 115,000/900,000 × 100	12.770%

Frances (Example 10.26):

Value of hypothetical transfer	450,000
Nil rate band (2018/19)	(325,000)
Notional chargeable transfer	125,000
Tax @ 20%	25,000
Effective rate 25,000/450,000 × 100	5.555%

Gina (Example 10.27):

Value of hypothetical transfer	300,000
Nil rate band (2018/19)	(325,000)
Notional chargeable transfer	0
Tax at 20%	0
Effective rate 0/300,000 × 100	0%

Henry (Example 10.28):

Value of hypothetical transfer	400,000
Nil rate band (2018/19)	(325,000)
Notional chargeable transfer	75,000
Tax @ 20%	15,000
Effective rate 15,000/400,000 × 100	3.750%

In Dennis's case the distribution took place on 31 October 2015 thus:

Dennis (Example 10.24):

Value of hypothetical transfer	540,000
Nil rate band (2015/16)	(325,000)
Notional chargeable transfer	215,000
Tax @ 20%	43,000
Effective rate 43,000/540,000 × 100	7.960%

Calculating the 'appropriate fraction' and the actual tax charge

10.37 The 'effective rate' is not the final tax rate.

Property may not have been subject to relevant property trust regime for a full ten years: indeed it cannot have been for the proportionate charge to apply where the maximum quarter fraction can only ever be 39/40. Each period of ten years is divided into periods of three months – a quarter. A fraction is calculated based on the number of complete quarters during which the property has been subject to relevant property trust regime throughout that ten-year period (comprising 40 quarters). That fraction is applied to the effective rate: see *IHTA 1984, s 68(2)*.

The following principles should be applied:

- *Section 68(2)* of *IHTA 1984*: calculate the number of complete successive quarters from the commencement of the trust to the exit date = A.
- *Section 68(3)* of *IHTA 1984*: look for anomalies, such as a period (complete quarters) during which the property was not subject to relevant property trusts; or when the property was in a different trust = B.
- Calculate the period of that anomaly and exclude it from the earlier calculation = A – B.
- With regard to periods of anomaly, where A – B= 0, but A is at least 1, tax at 30% of the effective rate multiplied by 1/40.
- Assess accumulations of income disregarding income that has not been formally accumulated (see Statement of Practice 8/86) but (with effect from events occurring 6 April 2014) add back accumulations which arose more than five years prior to the ten-year anniversary date.
- Apportion the capital distribution that triggers the exit charge across the property that represents it.

- If the part now distributed was always subject to discretion then reduce it by the fraction A/40. *But*
- If, and to the extent that the above is not the case and an anomaly applies to part, apply the fraction (A – B)/40 to that part.
- Charge tax on the property at 30% of the effective rate, reduced by the A/40 or (A – B)/40 fraction, as appropriate.
- With regard to periods of anomaly, where A – B= 0, but A is at least 1, tax at 30% of the effective rate multiplied by 1/40.

Example 10.31—(Continued from the previous scenarios)—in each case, with the exception of Dennis's trust, there is a distribution of £50,000 cash on 30 November 2018 before the first ten-year charge

1. For two examples (Bernard and Celia) the period from the period 31 October 2017 to 30 November 2018 is 13 full months thus four complete quarters, as required by *s 68(2)*.

Thus the exit charge rate in each case is as follows:

Bernard –

(3.750 × 30)% × 4/40 = 0.112%

Celia (revised) –

(0.000 × 30%) × 4/40 = 0%

2. For three examples (Eric, Frances and Gina) the period from 31 December 2017 to 30 November 2018 is 11 full months thus only three complete quarters, as required by *s 68(2)*.

Thus the exit charge rate in each case is as follows:

Eric –

(12.777 × 30)% × 3/40 = 0.287%

Frances –

(5.555 × 30)% × 3/40 = 0.124%

Gina –

(0.000 × 30)% × 3/40 = 0.000%

3. For one example (Henry) the period from 30 November 2015 to 30 November 2018 is 36 full months thus 12 complete quarters, as required by *s 68(2)*. Thus the exit charge rate is as follows:

Henry –

(3.750 × 30)% × 12/40 = 0.338%

4. Doreen's example is omitted because it illustrates a slightly different point.

5. The example of Dennis relates to a distribution made in earlier year (31 October 2015) from a trust created at an earlier time (1 March 2006), so there are 38 quarters. Thus the exit charge rate is as follows:

Dennis –

(7.960 × 30)% × 38/40 = 2.268%

Alfred's trust (**Example 10.20**): £50,000 @ 0%	= £0
Bernard's trust (**Example 10.21**): £50,000 @ 0.112%	= £56
Celia's trust (**Example 10.29**): £50,000 @ 0%	= £0
Eric's trust (**Example 10.25**): £50,000 @ 0.287%	= £144
Frances' trust (**Example 10.26**): £50,000 @ 0.124%	= £62
Gina's trust (**Example 10.27**): £50,000 @ 0%	= 0
Henry's trust (**Example 10.28**): £50,000 @ 0.338%	= £169
Dennis's trust (**Example 10.23**): £50,000 @ 2.268%	= £1,134

Note:

The exit charge is rounded to whole figures but in practice this was be calculated in actual pence.

THE PERIODIC OR 'TEN-YEAR' CHARGE

Simple cases: first ten-year anniversary

10.38

Example 10.32—Reporting the charge

Om 1 January 1999, Sarah created a relevant property trust for her adult children and her grandchildren settling an amount equal to 75% of the then 1998/99 nil rate band – there are no related settlements. The trustees invest the fund on a fairly conservative basis such that its value on the second ten-year anniversary on 1 January 2019 equates to some 90% of the 2018/19 nil rate band. During that twenty-year period there have been distributions of income but not of capital. Although there is a duty on the trustees to complete form IHT100 in respect of the ten-year charge (as the fund exceeds 80% of the nil rate band the exceptions rule does not apply – see the *Inheritance Tax (Delivery of Accounts) (Excepted Settlements) Regulations), SI 2008/606, reg 4*)), there will be no tax to pay.

In complying with *IHTA 1984, s 64* and to the tax fund under *IHTA 1984, ss 66* and *67,* the completed form IHT100 must show the value of the fund on the eve of the tenth anniversary after taking account of any exemptions or reliefs applicable to the trust ownership. (Note that settlor additions to the trust exempted from entry charge under the regular gifts out of income rule does not carry across to the trust.) As would be the case with an estate on death, the fund is divided between assets on which tax must be paid immediately and those where the instalment option applies.

10.39 Form IHT100d identifies the date (see commentary at **10.16** above) on which property became subject to the relevant property trust regime and its value at the ten-year anniversary, again providing where appropriate for the instalment option. The form then puts the settlement into its gift context. In a simple case the transferor will have made no previous chargeable transfers in the seven years ending before the settlement was established and will have made no other settlements on the same day as the one which is the subject of the ten-year charge calculation.

In a process similar to that considered above for the exit charge, the ten-year charge involves a step-by-step calculation. It is again necessary to establish the 'hypothetical chargeable transfer' but in this case the component parts are different. The rate of charge established at the ten-year anniversary determines the rate of exit charge (subject to the quarter reduction) applied to interim capital distributions made in the following ten years up to the next ten-year anniversary. The tax rate is established by calculating tax on the hypothetical transfer (but adjusted for exclusion of non-relevant property where the ten-year anniversary takes place on or after 18 November 2015 (date of Royal Assent to *F(No 2)A 2015*)) and applying it to the amount on which tax is charged, producing the 'effective rate'. However, one particular difficulty is the need to put the settlement in the context of other gifts.

Establishing the 'hypothetical transfer'

10.40 Special rules apply, see *IHTA 1984, s 68(6)*, where the settlement commenced before 27 March 1974. The rules are merely mentioned here for completeness but are not included in or addressed in any of the illustrations. Those dealing with these old relevant property trusts are referred to the complex legislation in *IHTA 1984, s 68(6)*.

For all other settlements it is necessary to establish the cumulative total of the following (see *IHTA 1984, s 66(4)*):

- the transfer value (market value) for the periodic charge;
- the historic (original) value of funds not subject to the relevant property regime (note the comments at **10.26**), but see commentary above regarding *F(No 2)A 2015* where this rule is dis-applied in regard to non-relevant property for events taking place post 17 November 2015;
- the historic (original) value of property in related settlements but see commentary above regarding *F(No 2)A 2015* where this rule is dis-applied in regard to non-relevant property for events taking place post 17 November 2015.

The transfer value

10.41 This relates to the value that will attract the periodic charge (but see comment made in the next paragraph). It is the value of that part of the property in the settlement immediately before the ten-year anniversary which is regarded as relevant property – *market value basis*. For ease of identification this is called 'the relevant property trust fund' in the calculations that follow.

When calculating the relevant property trust fund, no account should be taken of excluded property (see *IHTA 1984, s 58(1)(f)*) or property passing to charitable and similar exempt trusts. Furthermore, favoured property qualifying for BPR or APR must be included at their value post relief.

Other non-relevant property funds within the trust

10.42 This now only applies to chargeable events taking place before 18 November 2015. This relates to the value of property that is neither not within the relevant property regime, nor has ever been subject to the relevant property trust regime, but which element is comprised within the main settlement. The value is taken immediately after that property joined the trust – *historic basis* and importantly, before the application of APR or BPR. For ease of identification this is called the 'sub-fund' in the computations that follow.

Related settlements

10.43 This relates to a separate trust which commenced on the same day as the main settlement and has the same settlor (but where it is a non-relevant property trust, this is excluded for chargeable events taking place after 17 November 2015). It will also take account of later added property – see **10.26** above. A charitable trust or other exempt trust (to include that covered by the spousal exemption) is not a related settlement for this purpose. The value is taken immediately after that property joined the trust but ignoring the availability of APR or BPR (see for example IHTM42165 for HMRC's view) – *historic basis*. For ease of identification, this is called 'the related fund' in the computations that follow. However, it should be noted that the impact of this factor has been severely affected by the *F(No 2)A 2015* legislation concerning the recognition of same-day funds added to existing settlements(see **10.26**). Developments in this area should be carefully monitored.

10.44 Importantly, there is one category of property that is specifically excluded from the hypothetical transfer cumulation. This is property in the settlement that was originally subject to the relevant property regime but which later became excluded or exempt without attracting any exit charge. A common but relatively rare example is relevant property that became held on permanent charitable trusts.

The following example is a model computation skeleton for the position post-17 November 2015 though in practice it is most likely that only some of the elements referred to will be needed.

Example 10.33—Form of computation of the hypothetical transfer required to calculate the ten-year charge occurring on or after 18 November 2015

Elements:

1 Market value of the relevant property trust fund, eg:

- quoted securities;
- cash (excluding accumulated undistributed income);
- unquoted securities;
- freehold residential property;
- business interests;
- business assets;
- farming interests. *Less*:
- liabilities set against the fund; and
- value of excluded property;
- assets held on charitable trusts;
- BPR or APR on qualifying fund assets.

2 Historic value of the related relevant property fund.

3 Hypothetical transfer = (1 + 2 + 3).

10.45 The following examples take each element of the computation in turn. The first is a simple situation, typical of that found in practice.

Example 10.34—Computation of the hypothetical transfer (for ten-year charge purposes)

On 28 February 2008, Elsie settled cash of £200,000 (which has never been invested by the trustees) and a holding of shares in an unquoted trading company qualifying for BPR, into a discretionary trust – she made no other settlements that day.

At the first ten-year anniversary on 28 February 2018 the shares are worth £75,000 and the cash remains at £200,000. The entire fund is held and has been held throughout on relevant property trusts for Elsie's grandchildren.

1 Value of 'the discretionary trust fund':

	£
Cash	200,000
unquoted securities	75,000
	275,000
Less:	
BPR (unquoted securities)	(75,000)
Hypothetical transfer	200,000

10.46 Matters become considerably more complicated where APR or BPR is involved, the fund included non-relevant property and the chargeable event takes place prior to 18 November 2015.

Example 10.35—Computation of the hypothetical transfer (for ten-year charge purposes) before 18 November 2015

On 28 February 2005, Yolande set up a trust of which 50% was held on interest in possession terms for her sister and 50% held on discretionary terms for the benefit of her grandchildren. She made no other chargeable transfers during her lifetime. Into the trust she transferred quoted securities valued at £160,000 and, now worth £220,000 (as at February 2015), a pair of cottages valued at £150,000 and now worth £180,000 (as at February 2015) and a share of some agricultural pasture (qualifying for APR) valued then and now at £20,000. The hypothetical transfer for the ten-year charge calculation as at 28 February 2015 is calculated as follows:

1. Value of 50% of the trust fund (the relevant property fund):

		£
	quoted securities	110,000
	freehold residential properties	90,000
	farming interests	10,000
		210,000
Less:		
	APR (pasture)	(10,000)
Total		200,000
2. Value of the related fund (historic value)		165,000*
Hypothetical transfer		365,000

- Note the availability of APR is ignored in establishing the historic value.

Had the trust instead been created one year later on 28 February 2006 with a ten-year charge triggered on 28 February 2016, the impact of the *FA 2015* exclusion of the non-relevant property element would have ignored the value of £165,000 and reduced the hypothetical transfer to £200,000.

10.47 Related trusts are not all that common but *Rysaffe Trustee Co (CI) Ltd v IRC* [2002] EWHC 1114 (Ch); [2002] STC 872 and on appeal [2003] EWCA Civ 356, [2003] STC 536 neatly illustrates the perils of related trusts and the tax planning routinely employed to avoid them. Where related trusts do exist (but restricted to related relevant property trust for chargeable events taking place post 17 November 2015), the hypothetical transfer is greater by reason of aggregation.

Example 10.36—Computation of the hypothetical transfer (for ten-year charge purposes) post 17 November 2015

On 28 February 2007, Grete created a discretionary trust (No 1) and at the first ten-year anniversary in February 2017 it comprised unquoted shares in a trading company worth £1 million, the premises from which the company trades worth £860,000 and cash of £100,000 (BPR is available at 100% on the shares but at only 50% on the building). On the same day in February 2007, Grete settled cash of £100,000 on a separate relevant property trust (No 2)– the value as at February 2017 is £120,000.

1. Value of the discretionary trust (No 1):	£
Cash	100,000
unquoted securities	1,000,000
business assets	860,000
	1,960,000
Less:	
BPR (at 100%/ 50% on shares/premises)	(1,430,000)
	530,000
2. Historic value of the related relevant property trust (No 2)	100,000
Hypothetical transfer	630,000

10.48 Excluded property is a complication but it does not increase the hypothetical transfer.

Example 10.37—Computation of the hypothetical transfer (for ten-year charge purposes) post 17 November 2015

On 28 February 2007, Walter, who was not domiciled in the UK, settled on discretionary trust, a German vineyard now worth £400,000 as at February 2017, cash now worth £600,000 as at February 2017 and a house in England now worth £150,000 as at February 2017 – he made no other settlements on that day.

1. Value of the discretionary trust fund:	£
Cash	600,000
Freehold residential property	150,000
Other property interests (the vineyard)	400,000
	1,150,000
Less:	
Value of excluded property (non UK situs)	(400,000)
Hypothetical transfer	750,000

Note: BPR (unlike APR, which until *Finance Act 2009* was restricted to the UK, Channel Islands and Isle of Man, and woodland relief, which until the same legislation was restricted to the UK) is available on worldwide qualifying assets and thus in this example might have been available in respect of the vineyard.

Example 10.38—Computation of the hypothetical transfer (for ten-year charge purposes) pre 18 November 2015

On 28 February 2005, Vera made two settlements – the first was held on discretionary Trust (No1); the second was held on qualifying interest in possession terms however, the life tenant died in 2008 after which the fund continued on discretionary trust (No 2). The current value (February 2015) of the discretionary Trust (No 1) is a share portfolio worth £360,000. The other former IIP trust (No 2) was valued at £50,000 on creation but has a current value (February 2015) of £80,000

1. Value of the discretionary trust (No 1):	£
Quoted securities	360,000
2. Historic value of the related property trust (No 2)	50,000
Hypothetical transfer	410,000

Example 10.39—Comparison of position of non-relevant property exclusion post-*F(No 2)A 2015*

On 30 November 2005, Thomas, having made no previous chargeable lifetime transfers in the previous seven years, settled cash of £1 million on A&M trust for his three grandchildren Albert, Betty and Carol which provided for income at age 25 and capital at trustee discretion. Under the pre-March 2006 rules that then prevailed this was a PET and hence no IHT fell due for payment and as Thomas survived the PET by seven years the transfer achieved full exempt status.

On 1 March 2006, Albert became entitled to an interest in possession (IIP) in one-third of the fund. As that IIP was established before 22 March 2006 it is a qualifying IIP.

On 22 March 2006, neither Betty (aged 10) nor Carol (aged 12) had an established IIP and since the trust terms did not provide for capital entitlement at age 25, it did not qualify as an 18-25 trust under the *FA 2006* provisions.

On 6 April 2008, Betty and Carol's remaining two-thirds of the fund entered the relevant property regime.

On 30 November 2015, the trust reached its ten-year anniversary and Betty/Carol's two-third share was valued at £1.5 million.

(i) 30 November 2015 – ten-year charge pre-*F(No2)A 2015* enactment

MV value of relevant property fund	1,500,000
Historic value of non-relevant property fund (Albert's one third IIP)	330,000
Hypothetical transfer	1,830,000
Nil rate band (2015/2016)	(325,000)
	1,505,000
1,505,000 @ 20%	301,000
301,000/1,830,000 x100	16.440%
(16.440 × 30)%	4.932%
Ten-year charge:	
1,500,000 @ 4.932% × (40 – 9*)/40	57,334

**Complete quarters before the trust became relevant property on 6 April 2008*

(ii) Ten-year charge post-enactment of *F(No 2)A 2015*

MV value of relevant property fund	1,500,000
Nil rate band (2015/2016)	(325,000)
	1,175,000
1,175,000 @ 20%	235,000
235,000/1,500,000 x100	15.666%
(15.666 × 30)%	4.699%
Ten-year charge:	
1,500,000 @ 4.699% × (40 – 9*)/40	54,625

**Complete quarters elapsed before the trust became relevant property on 6 April 2008*

Previous transfers

> **Focus**
>
> The total of chargeable transfers made by the settlor in the seven years prior to the original date of trust creation will, unless a greater figure can be substituted (see **10.51** and **10.52**) always be a constant of the calculation for both the first and subsequent ten-year anniversaries.

10.49 As to be expected at this stage, this computation is not straightforward and involves further considerations:

- bringing additions to the fund into account;
- transfers before the settlement was created;
- transfers preceding additions to the fund after the settlement was created; and
- bringing failed PETs into account.

Additions to the fund

10.50 The statutory authority for this part of the computation is *IHTA 1984, s 67(1)*. The legislation requires recognition of chargeable transfers made both after the settlement began and before the ten-year anniversary, as a result of which the value of any property in the settlement is increased, whether or not that property is subject to relevant property trusts.

A transfer that was not primarily intended to increase the value of the settlement and did not in fact increase the value of the trust property by more than 5% of its value immediately before transfer, is disregarded (*IHTA 1984, s 67(2)*). Furthermore, an exempt transfer is ignored, whether it is exempt by virtue of the small expenditure or annual exemptions or is made out of income within *IHTA 1984, s 21*. This is important where, for example, the settlor pays annual premiums on an insurance policy that is held by the trust.

Transfers by the settlor in the seven years before the trust

10.51 The total is required of any chargeable transfers (thus PETs excluded unless these later fail) made by the settlor in the period of seven years* ending with the day before the trust creation – this mirrors the seven-year backward shadow applied to lifetime gifts in the event of the donor's death. The statutory authority here is *IHTA 1984, s 66(5)(a)*. It is critical to note that this total will be a permanent inclusion in all future ten-year charges unless or until it is in turn replaced by a greater total – see **10.52** below.

**Before 18 March 1986, the relevant period was ten years.*

Transfers preceding additions to the fund

10.52 If there have been any additions to the trust post creation then the history of transfers by the settlor in the seven years before each addition must be re-examined and if this gives a greater total than the original seven-year cumulative figure (see **10.51**) then this former will be used going forward. This could cause an element of double counting therefore if there have been any chargeable transfers by the settlor in any such period of seven years, ending on the day before the addition to the trust, the amounts are excluded except in so far as they have already been brought into account in the computation of the hypothetical transfers (in other words where the value of that addition is already recognised in the value of the trust which will attract the ten-year charge).

Bringing failed PETs into account

10.53 As stated at **10.51**, only the seven-year history (or later substitution discussed in **10.52**) of the settlor's chargeable transfers are considered thus PETs are ignored. However, where such PETs become failed PETs (thereby now categorised as chargeable transfers) by reason of the settlor's death within seven years thereof, these must also be recognised with the transfer history adjusted accordingly. If the settlor's death, causing recognition of failed PETs, takes place after the ten-year anniversary it may still be necessary to consider the rule set out in **10.52**. The rules are complicated but in summary:

- If the death of the settlor took place less than seven years post creation of the trust to which no additions were made then any failed PETs made in that rump of the seven-year period prior to the trust creation must be brought into account (**10.51**).
- If the death of the settlor took place before the ten-year anniversary and additions were made to the trust before that death, and the settlor died within seven years of those additions, the history of his gifts before those additions must be re-examined (**10.52**).
- If the death of the settlor took place after the ten-year anniversary and additions were made to the trust before that anniversary, and the settlor died within seven years of those additions, the history of his gift before those additions must be re-examined (**10.52**) and the ten-year charge recalculated.

This can have the effect of increasing the aggregate of the transfer by the settlor which will feed through to a higher ultimate tax liability. In the example below, the 'aggregate transfer' is the extra value to be brought into the tax computation.

Example 10.40—Calculating the aggregate transfer: previous transfers

On 28 February 2013, Ulrich set up a relevant property trust of £300,000 (gross). He had made two earlier gifts of £56,000 to his daughter on 31 August 2011 and of £12,000 to his son on 31 May 2012. He died on 31 January 2018 without having added any funds to the settlement and the cash gifts, originally PETs, become chargeable:

	£
31 August 2011 (net of annual exemptions for 2011/12 and 2010/11)	50,000
31 May 2012 (net of exemption 2012/13)	9,000
	59,000
The aggregated transfer is calculated:	
Additions to the fund	NIL
Transfers seven years before the trust	59,000
Aggregate transfer	59,000

Example 10.41—Calculating the aggregate transfer: addition to a trust

On 31 January 2008, Tom, who made no previous gifts, settled £100,000 on relevant property trusts. On 31 August 2008 he gave his son £30,000 and on 31 May 2009 (having already utilised his annual exemption against a gift of equal value) he added £200,000 to the trust. He died within seven years of the gift to his son, so the PET became chargeable:

	£
Gift 31 August 2008	30,000
Less exemption (2008/09)	(3,000)
Failed PET	27,000
The aggregate transfer is calculated:	
Additions to the fund 31 May 2009	200,000
(Exemptions utilised)	
Transfers preceding addition to the fund	27,000
	227,000
Transfers in seven years before the trust:	NIL
Aggregate transfer	227,000

Note: this type of transfer may in certain circumstances be adjusted in accordance with *IHTA 1984, s 67(4)(b)* and *IHTA 1984, s 67(5)*. Those sections apply only to trusts created before 27 March 1974 and, as was noted at **10.28** above, this chapter concentrates on trusts created after that date. The section brings into account transfers in the seven years before the chargeable transfer but disregards any value already subject to an exit charge.

Distributions from the trust: special cases

10.54 There are additional rules to calculate the total distributions.

The first step requires a total of the amounts which attracted an exit charge during the first ten years of the life of the trust. However, this will exclude distributions which were otherwise exempt.

The second step requires a review of each occasion when property that was in the settlement at the ten-year anniversary had ceased to be subject to a discretion – prior to 22 March 2006 this situation could arise where funds were taken from the relevant property trust and set aside for a beneficiary to provide them with a qualifying interest in possession and that beneficiary died before the ten-year anniversary with the funds reverting to discretionary trust terms. Equally, it could have applied under the old rules where funds were appointed onto A&M trusts in favour of a beneficiary who then died. In such a case the total of distributions which is the subject of this part of the calculation must be reduced. The amount of the reduction is the lower of:

- the amount on which the exit tax was charged; or
- the value of the relevant fund on which the ten-year charge would otherwise be levied.

The purpose of this rule is to prevent double-counting of the same property.

10.55 The third step is rarely seen in practice but is included here for completeness. If the trustees have purchased heritage property and have obtained conditional exemption for it, the price paid for the heritage property must be included in the aggregate now being calculated as if it were subject to an exit charge (See: *Agricultural, Business and Heritage Property Relief (7th edn) (Bloomsbury Professional)*).

Calculating the 'effective rate'

10.56 The foregoing has been preparation of a hypothetical transfer so as to establish one component of the tax charge, the 'effective rate'. The notional transfer is:

- one made by a transferor immediately before the ten-year anniversary;
- who had in the previous seven years made other chargeable transfers that were equal in value to the aggregate brought forward from the earlier calculations in **10.49** to include substitution of a greater cumulation (**10.51**); and taking account of
- the distributions calculated by reference to **10.54**.

The result of the calculation is best illustrated as follows.

Example 10.42—The effective rate

On 31 January 2008, Sam made a relevant property trust (2008 No 2) of £250,000, having always used his annual exemptions on 6 April each year and having made a chargeable transfer to another trust (2007 Trust No 1) of £50,000 a year before. He did not add any funds to either trust, nor make any other PETs before his death on 28 February 2015. It is now necessary to consider the periodic charge on the 2008 Trust No. 2 as at 31 January 2018.

The 2008 trust (No 2) includes investments now worth £700,000 of which £100,000 are in unquoted trading companies, acquired more than two years before January 2018. Capital of £70,000 was distributed in December 2015.

Computation of the hypothetical transfer

		£
Value of the 2008 trust fund (No 2)		700,000
Less: BPR (unquoted shares)		(100,000)
Net value		600,000 (A)
Related settlement		Nil
Hypothetical transfer		600,000(B)
Settlor seven-year cumulative history	50,000	
Distributions	70,000	
Total		120,000
Notional transfer:		720,000(C)
Trust nil rate band at 31 January 2018		(325,000)
Excess		395,000
Notional tax @ 20%		79,000
Effective rate: 79,000/600,000(B) × 100		13.166%

Calculating the actual tax

10.57 In the above example it can be seen that the inclusion of the settlor's cumulative seven-year transfers together with account of the distributions in effect erodes the availability of the trust nil rate band and thus increases the charge levied on the hypothetical transfer.

Yet again, there is a need to review the history of the trust. It might be thought that it was enough merely for the trustees to maintain proper accounts of capital and income (though many trustees will not even do as much as that, until forced to review the situation by the need to complete tax returns). In addition to knowing which part of the fund is capital and which is income, for IHT purposes the trustees must also know which part of the trust fund at any one time was subject to their discretion and which was not.

Equally, the trustees must take a view on the subject of income. The traditional HMRC view is that any income which is accumulated is to be treated as comprised in the settlement from the date that the accumulation occurred: see Statement of Practice 8/86 which also notes that undistributed and un-accumulated income should not be treated as a taxable trust asset but will retain its income character. There is a fine distinction between income of a previous year that has simply not been distributed and income that has, by some action of the trustees or by virtue of the terms of the trust instrument, become accumulated into capital at some interval after it was received by the trustees. Fortunately, this is a somewhat rarefied area of the law but in practice HMRC appear to accept a reasonable computation put forward by the trustees that can be justified by the record of their actions.

However, this thorny issue and the complications that it raises was identified in the trust consultation process (see **10.26**) and *FA 2014* contains measures which for IHT purposes alone treat income which has remained undistributed for more than five years counting back from the date of the ten-year anniversary as trust capital for the purpose of computing the ten-year charge whether or not it is so regarded in the trust accounts. Harshly, tax is charged at the full rate without the proportionate reduction to reflect the period in which the income has been retained, thus where this is likely to apply the trustees should perhaps consider formally accumulating that income to ensure that the charge is scaled back to only apply from that date of that formal accumulation.

Problems of matching can occur where there is un-accumulated income but later income distributions have been made. HMRC have stated that in such circumstance a first in, first out (FIFO) approach should be adopted but such direction does not have statute authority and this would be welcomed.

For the purposes of this discussion of the taxation of relevant property trusts, it is assumed that any cash held by the trustees at the ten-year anniversary represents undistributed but capitalised income rather than retained accumulations of income.

10.58 Putting the income question to one side, there still remains the issue of whether capital has been subject to the discretion of the trustees throughout the whole ten years or whether, for example, it was added to the settlement at some interim point during that ten-year period. For each 'chunk' of capital so affected, it is necessary to calculate the appropriate fraction following a similar manner to that described at **10.37**. The result is to apply the tax charge only for the period during which the property was subject to the relevant property regime.

The effective rate multiplied by the fraction 3/10 (30%) is applied to the full value of the fund if it has been subject to the relevant property regime for the whole ten years or as reduced by the appropriate fraction otherwise. As can be appreciated this is not a straightforward calculation.

Example 10.43—Tax charge

Continuation of **Example 10.42** of Sam's 2008 trust No 2.

All the property in the trust at 31 January 2018 has been within the relevant property regime since the trust began.

	£
Value of the fund on 31 January 2018 (net of BPR)	600,000
Effective rate 13.166% (ie 79,000/600,000 × 100)	
Tax: £600,000 × ((30 × 13.166) = 3.949)%	23,694

Example 10.44—Tax charge where funds have been added to the trust

Referring back to the example of Tom (see **Example 10.41** above) it is noted that part of the fund has not been in the trust for ten years. At the date of the ten-year anniversary the fund is worth £600,000 of which only £200,000 can be identified with the original capital (and hence held within the trust for the full ten years) with the balance of £400,000 identified with the funds added later (and hence not held within the trust for the full ten years). All income has been distributed, but there have been no capital distributions.

Calculate the hypothetical transfer

	£
Value of the discretionary trust fund	600,000
Value of related fund	Nil
Hypothetical transfer	600,000(A)

Review of other transfers

Previous chargeable transfers	Nil
Aggregate transfer as previously calculated (see **10.42**)	227,000
Deduct the value attributable to property now in the fund (*s 67(3)(b)* read with *s 66(4)*)	(200,000)
	27,000(B)
Notional transfer: (A + B)	627,000
Nil rate band, 31 January 2018	(325,000)
Excess	302,000
Notional tax: 60,400 @ 20%	60,400
Effective rate: 60,400/600,000(A) × 100	10.066%
Charge on the initial fund (held for ten years):	
£200,000 × (30 × 10.066)%	6,038
Charge on the later added funds:	
Complete quarters elapsed before the property became relevant property thus from 31 January 2008 to 30 May 2009 = 5	
Fraction is therefore (40 – 5/40) = 35/40	
£400,000 × 35/40 × ((30 × 10.066) = 3.019%)	10,566
Total tax charge	16,604

Example 10.45—Ten-year charge where there has been a distribution

On 30 November 2007, Brian, who had made no earlier chargeable transfers, created a discretionary trust with cash of £270,000 gross but as the value fell within the 2007/08 nil rate band of £300,000 there was no IHT entry charge. No further funds have been added. There have been interim income distributions to the grandchildren with the tax credit wholly met from the tax pool and subject to later repayment in their hands because the payments were covered by their personal allowances.

On 10 June 2013, the trustees advanced capital of £60,000 to Sally to help her buy a flat.

At 30 November 2017 the trust fund comprised:

	£
Quoted stocks and shares	200,000

Dividends (ex-dividend)	1,000
Government stock	50,000
Unquoted shares	50,000
Dividends held by brokers	5,000
Property, let	175,000
Cash	30,000
Gross fund	511,000

The trustees had wisely arranged before the anniversary for valuations to be made. Their cost, at £275, was due at the valuation date. There was also income tax due on rental income of £400. The dividends held by the brokers are not relevant property unless appropriated to capital, which they have not been, because the trustees have pursued a policy of making regular distributions. Similarly, of the cash amount sum £13,000 is actually undistributed income which arose during the last five years. The unquoted shares are in a company that used to trade, but which now concentrates on property investment, so a claim for BPR is unlikely to pass muster.

A significant problem in dealing with the IHT liability on relevant property trusts is relating the text of the statute to the calculation and then to the return itself. In this example, reference is made to the various box numbers, with the intention that that will help in following the calculation. The fund is shown on the supplemental forms thus:

D32, stocks and shares:

SS1 total values £200,000 and 1,000 dividends (to boxes E1 and E5 in form IHT100);

SS2 total value £50,000 (to box E2);

Unquoted shares £50,000 (to box F10).

D36, land etc:

Value shown £175,000 (to box F1).

IHT100, the account:

Event form IHT100d will be appropriate, see below. After details of Brian's tax reference and that of the trust, the only supplementary pages used are as shown above plus perhaps D40. Cash is shown net of the undistributed income at £17,000 (box E8). The assets not qualifying for instalment relief are, gross, £268,000 (box E15) and after offset of the liabilities of £675 are £267,325. There are no exemptions, so the total appears at box E19. There are no liabilities to set against the instalment option property so the total at box F17 is £225,000. Thus:

	£
(a) Non-instalment option property:	
Stocks and shares:	200,000
Dividends	1,000
Gilts	50,000
Cash	17,000
Less liabilities:	
Valuation fee	(275)
Tax due	(400)
Sub-total (E19)	*267,325*
(b) Instalment option property	
Unquoted shares	50,000
Land	175,000
Subtotal (F17)	*225,000*

Event form IHT100d:

A proportionate charge has arisen in the preceding ten years in respect of the £60,000 distribution to Sally. However, the exit charge rate was set at 0% thus resulting in a nil tax charge (Q1.5) since Brian had made no prior chargeable transfers, had added no funds to the trust and its value on entry was wholly covered by the nil rate band. Nothing went into the trust that was not subject to the discretion of the trustees, so form IHT100d is fairly straightforward to complete.

Inheritance tax worksheet IHT100(WS):

There is no requirement to fill this in as already noted, HMRC will do the calculation, but that leaves the adviser vulnerable. In this example, the totals brought across from the main account (£267,325 + £225,000) yield a value for tax of £492,325 (box WSB7). In this (simple!) case the only extra item at this point is Sally's £60,000 (box WSB15) bringing the taxable total to £552,325 (box R12) against which may be set the nil rate band as at 19 November 2017 of £325,000 to leave tax (for the purpose only of calculating the effective rate) on £227,325 at 20% of £45,465 (box R16) which is not adjusted for Sally's £60,000 and therefore enters the fraction (45,465/492,325) × 30% to produce an effective rate (rounded to three decimal places) of 2.770% (box R24).

That rate, applied to the non-instalment assets of £267,325, yields tax of £7,404.90 (box TX41) and on the other assets, £225,000 of £6,232.50 (box TX48) to which must be added any interest now due; the detail can be calculated using the structure set out in boxes IT1 to IT9 of IHT100 (WS), but by now the reader must be tiring of this example, so the detail of that calculation, and its division between the different categories of property, is ignored for the present purpose.

The tax amounts to (£7,404.90 + £6,232.50): £13,637.40, which is a light burden for a fund of over £500,000 to bear.

To summarise:

Fund of non-instalment property:	£267,325
Real property – instalment property:	£225,000
Taxable fund:	£492,325
Distributions:	£60,000
Tax rate charged:	2.770%
Tax on non-instalment property:	£7,404.90
Tax on the land – instalment property:	£6,232.50

Later ten-year anniversaries

10.59 The legislation at *IHTA 1984, s 64* provides for an IHT charge in relation to any ten-year anniversary without distinction between the first and later anniversaries. It is (see *IHTA 1984, s 66*) charged at 30% of the effective rate on the chargeable transfer as described in *IHTA 1984, s 66(3)*. Importantly, the individual components of historic value of related settlements later added property to such related settlements and settlor's seven-year cumulative total of chargeable transfers (but see **10.52**) will always remain as a fixed part of the calculation irrespective of the passage of time but post enactment of *F(No 2) A 2015*, the previous historic value of non-relevant property is disregarded for events taking place after 17 November 2015.

Additions of property are covered by *IHTA 1984, s 67* except where within the *de minimis* 5% rule of *IHTA 1984, s 67(2)(b)* or where there was no intention to increase the value of the fund, within *IHTA 1984, s 67(2)(a)*. This can arise on, for example, the waiver by the settlor of a dividend which indirectly benefits the trust.

Prior to 6 April 2017, a relevant property trust which comprised excluded property was outside the scope of IHT and thus did not attract either exit or ten-year anniversary charges. This was also the case if the trust was settlor interested since the excluded property rules are considered to take precedence over the gift with reservation rules: see **Chapter** 9. *Section 48(3)* of *IHTA 1984* defines excluded property as property situated outside the UK where '…the property itself, but not a reversionary interest in it, is excluded provided that the settlor was not domiciled in the UK when the settlement was made…'.

However, *F(No 2)A 2017* now includes measures effective from 6 April 2017 which operate to bring all UK residential property owned directly or indirectly by non-UK domiciliaries within the scope of IHT. This will have a direct impact on the traditional non-resident relevant property trust structure which owned shares in an underlying offshore company that in turn owned UK residential property – the value of the shares attributable to that UK property asset will now fall within the scope of IHT and thereafter will attract ten-year anniversary charges/exit charges. Furthermore, in the case of settlor interested trusts which are otherwise 'tainted' the *F(No 2) A 2017* changes to the deemed domicile provisions (see **Chapter 2**) can impact on excluded property status thus withdrawing the protection previously afforded from attack under the gift with reservation rule.

F(No 2)A 2017 has addressed the position of mixed use property providing that the element subject to IHT would be determined on a pro rata basis, however, in a move intended to block repositioning to avoid the charge, the legislation also contains an avoidance measure. This will apply where that use subsequently changed from residential to non-residential (or vice versa) and that property had been a residential property at any time within the two years immediately preceding the chargeable event.

THE IMPACT OF APR AND BPR

Focus

Whilst BPR/APR can reduce the rate of charge (and hence exit charge) on the first and subsequent ten-year anniversaries, it is ignored in establishing the exit charge rate applied to capital distributions made in the first ten years alone. This can produce a distortive and unexpected tax charge.

Effect at commencement

10.60 As previously discussed, relevant property trusts benefit from APR and BPR so that, when applying tax to a transfer of value, the otherwise chargeable amount of that transfer is reduced by that relief. However, as was seen in the example of Bernard (**Example 10.21**), when calculating the exit charge in the first ten years alone, the availability of APR or BPR is wholly ignored in establishing the hypothetical transfer. Once the trust is established and the transfer to be considered is at the first tenth anniversary or later, APR or BPR can reduce the size of the hypothetical transfer which has the beneficial effect of reducing the exit charge for later capital distributions.

For determining satisfaction of the ownership period for APR or BPR, ownership is determined by:

- legal ownership of the trustees where there is no qualifying interest in possession; or
- beneficial entitlement where there is a qualifying interest in possession.

(See: IHTM25302)

Control

10.61 Control of a company can be relevant to BPR (see **Chapter 13**). Given that an unquoted shareholding of any size can potentially qualify for 100% relief, control is mainly important in determining access to relief under *IHTA 1984, s 105(1)(d)* in relation to land/other business assets personally owned by the shareholder and used in the business carried out by the relevant company, or under *IHTA 1984, s 122* in relation to farming companies, where control is essential for the relief to be available at all: see *IHTA 1984, s 122(1)(b)*. 'Control' of a company for IHT purposes is generally determined according to the specific provisions in *IHTA 1984, s 269.*

There is some difficulty in deciding whether trustees of a settlement have control of a company only by reference to the shares in that particular settlement or whether other settlements may be taken into account. This was one of the issues considered in *Rysaffe Trustee Co (CI) Ltd v IRC* [2003] EWCA Civ 356, [2003] STC 536.

Reduction in the tax charge

10.62 If a relevant property trust holds qualifying business or agricultural property, the exit charge post the first ten-year anniversary may be reduced (see **10.60**). If the occasion of the charge is the release of property which itself qualifies for APR and/or BPR, this will reduce the value on which the tax is charged but will not as such reduce the rate of tax established at the ten-year anniversary which is based on the position at that time.

Example 10.46—Release of farmland

Edward's relevant property trust holds farmland eligible for APR at 100%. The entire farm is worth £1.5 million and the records of the settlement show that the effective tax rate established at the previous ten-year anniversary was 4%.

The trustees transfer one-third by value of the farm to a beneficiary *in specie*. The remaining two-thirds of the farm is not devalued by this release, so the amount of the transfer, applying 'estate before less estate after' principles, is £500,000. The availability of APR reduces the chargeable value to nil and even though the exit charge is set at 4%, when applied to the nil chargeable value it still results in a nil IHT charge.

One capricious element of APR and BPR in the context of an exit charge post a ten-year charge is its effective cut-off date. If the conditions for that relief are satisfied at the time of the chargeable transfer in general terms, it does not matter that thereafter the transferee is not entitled to relief going forward. In the example just shown, post transfer the beneficiary could immediately sell the farm and there would be no tax clawback charge on the trustees. However, if the beneficiary died some three years later his estate would not include any property qualifying for relief – it should also be remembered that even if the property did continue to qualify by reference to the beneficiary's continued farming activities, a minimum two-year ownership period would be required to secure access to APR and/or BPR in his estate.

If the parties realise from the outset that it is likely that the relevant asset will be sold, it is better for it to be distributed *in specie* than for the trustees to make the sale.

Example 10.47—Distribution of cash

On its tenth anniversary on 31 March 2018 Daniel's relevant property trust comprised cash of £1,512,000 and unquoted shares (valued at £200,000) in the family trading company qualifying for 100% BPR – there are no other complicating factors (ie settlor's seven-year chargeable transfers or earlier capital distributions etc.). The ten-year charge rate is calculated as follows:

	£	£
Cash		1,512,000
Shares	200,000	
BPR	(200,000)	
Net		Nil
Fund value		1,512,000
Nil rate band (2017/18)		(325,000)
Taxable		1,187,000
Ten-year charge:		
1,187,000 × ((30 × 20) = 6.000%)		71,220

Exit rate:

71,220/1,512,000 × 100 4.710%

On 31 October 2018 the trustees distribute cash of £500,000. The tax payable (assumed met from the appointed cash) is calculated as follows:

£500,000 @ 4.710% × 2/40 = 1,177

Reduction in the rate of tax

10.63 The availability of APR or BPR can reduce the overall tax burden, not only by reference to specific release of property but to the overall context of the settlement. The rate of a periodic charge on a relevant property trust can be reduced as a result of the fact that the amount on which the charge is imposed is itself reduced by BPR or APR. The result will be that on any exit charge in the next ten years there will be a reduction whether or not the distribution that triggers the exit charge is of property that qualifies for APR or BPR. Contrast this with the exit charge triggered prior to the first ten-year anniversary.

Clearly, where the subject matter of the distribution itself qualifies for 100% relief, there will be no need for any calculations.

Clawback

Focus

The tax impact of clawback can be costly and great care should be taken to preserve the qualities of APR/BPR during the seven year run-off period.

10.64 The clawback rules are one of the more difficult features of the APR and BPR regime. The charge can affect trusts originally created by PETs under the old regime but which for IHT purposes have now become relevant property trusts by *FA 2006* (ie old-style A&M trusts). The later PET failure at a time when neither APR or BPR apply will cause the donor's cumulative history to be revised to reflect the PET value pre APR/BPR.

Often overlooked, it should be noted that the clawback rules also apply to transfers into relevant property trusts where that transfer was an immediate chargeable transfer. However, in that case the clawback impact is restricted to the additional tax due as a consequence of the loss of APR/BPR on the original chargeable transfer but the donor's cumulative history is not adjusted for the loss of that relief. This is because *IHTA 1984, ss 113A* and *124A* each refer to value transferred by a PET.

Consider that a settlor had transferred property into trust that would have originally qualified as a PET (pre 22 March 2006 IIP) in circumstances where APR or BPR would have been in point, but then died within seven years of that transfer. Clawback may apply if the trustees, who are the transferees for the purposes of the clawback rules, no longer own that property such that the potential to re-test that asset for BPR/APR is lost. This will have a double effect:

- the trustees will suffer IHT on the original transfer to them, except in so far as it was within the nil rate band; and
- there will be an increase in the calculations of exit charge and other transfers that have already been set out in this chapter.

Acquisition of relievable property

10.65 It is just as useful for trustees of a relevant property trust to acquire property that qualifies for APR or for BPR as it is for individuals in their later years. If trustees have invested the entire fund in assets that qualify for APR or BPR and have satisfied the period of ownership (two years (BPR) or two/seven years (APR)) appropriate for the type of property, the fund will escape the impact of the ten-year charge by reason of nil taxable value and as a consequence later distributions will also escape the impact of the exit charge by reason of this nil rate.

THE SPECIAL CHARGE UNDER SECTION 70

Background to the special charge

10.66 In certain cases, it was considered expedient for the legislation to include a special rate of charge which arises outside the usual regime of ten-year and periodic charges. Initially, the main trigger was the situation where property was settled for charitable purposes only until the end of some specific period but this scenario can now be extended to other situations – see **10.70** below. Since that period could be quite long, the rate of charge is expressed as a percentage which increases with the passage of time and which can relate to a period of 50 years or more.

The rate of charge

10.67 The charge is fixed by reference to the 'relevant period' which is usually a period that begins with the later of: the day on which the property came within *s 70*; or 13 March 1975; and ends with the day before the event that triggers the charge. The rate of tax is:

• For each of the first 40 complete successive quarters	0.25%
• For the next 40 quarters	0.20%
• For the next 40 quarters	0.15%
• For the next 40 quarters	0.10%
• For the next 40 quarters	0.05%

If the property was excluded property at any time during the period under consideration, then the period of one quarter during which it was excluded property is excluded from the calculation of the relevant period (*s 70(7)*) *IHTA 1984*.

10.68 The calculation is built up by applying the percentages set out above to the relevant period. For the first ten years, assuming that none of the property is excluded property, the rate, when expressed as a percentage, is the same as the period expressed as whole years and quarters. For other periods the following rate will apply:

• 15 years	14%
• 20 years	18%
• 25 years	21%
• 30 years	24%
• 35 years	26%
• 40 years	28%
• 45 years	29%
• 50 years or more	30%

Actually, these rates are in many instances higher than the normal rates of charge, but the fact that they can be calculated without the multi-step computations set out earlier in this chapter may be some compensation. There is however no election available to the taxpayer: the regime under *IHTA 1984, s 70* applies whenever the legislation states that it applies and not otherwise.

Variations on the rate of charge

10.69 Where a trust includes property qualifying for BPR or APR that relief can apply to mitigate the charge under *IHTA 1984, s 70*. There are also special provisions where property was previously in a maintenance fund for heritage property. Those special provisions are of limited application and the reader is referred to specialist works on the subject: see *Agricultural, Business and Heritage Property Relief (7th edn) (Bloomsbury Professional).*

When the special charge will apply following FA 2006

10.70 At **Example 10.3**, the example of Celia showed that trustees could use the statutory power of advancement. That triggered the special charge under *IHTA 1984, s 70*. It was always the case for A&M settlements that *IHTA 1984, s 70* would apply where property in an A&M settlement left it otherwise than in accordance with the main provisions of that section or where the trustees entered into a depreciatory transaction. Such occasions were rare and the application of *s 70*, as a result, is probably little known (and as a consequence perhaps of little interest) to general practitioners.

The position changed following *FA 2006*. *Section 71B* of *IHTA 1984* now applies where settled property ceases to qualify as being held for a bereaved minor under *s 71A*. Tax will not be charged where the property leaves the trust because:

- the bereaved minor becomes 18;
- or dies; or the property is applied for his benefit.

Similarly, although there is a general regime which has been described in this chapter for the charge under *IHTA 1984, s 71E* on 18-to-25 trusts, there is a residual basis of charge under *IHTA 1984, s 71G* which applies the rates in *IHTA 1984, s 70* where, see *IHTA 1984, s 71G(1)(b)*, tax does not fall to be calculated under the system set out in *IHTA 1984, s 71F*.

Letter of wishes

10.71 Often the settlor will also wish to be a trustee of their trust but in many cases perhaps due to age or disinclination, they may prefer to leave the task to others. In either case the settlor may wish to guide the trustees as to how to exercise their discretion. Detailed below are examples of the type of letter that might be appropriate in connection with lifetime settlements, discretionary will trusts of both the nil rate band and latterly of residue, as was common before the introduction of the transferable nil rate band that is described fully in **Chapter 3**.

All too often in the latter case, the family used the fund, by default, for the benefit of the surviving spouse, even mandating income to them. Such conduct would enable HMRC to argue that the widow(er) enjoyed a (qualifying) interest in possession thereby perhaps negating any tax planning routine, There is also a trap here for those who now release funds to the surviving spouse in the mistaken belief that this will retrospectively put them in the position of being able to claim two nil rate bands on the second death: this will not be the case unless that release is sheltered by *IHTA 1984, s 144*.

Sometimes a will contains precatory words and occasionally even, in effect, the text of a letter of wishes. This is bad practice: it denies the testator any flexibility later, and the words used may come back to haunt the draftsman; see for example *IHTA 1984, s 143*.

Example 10.48—Letters of wishes

Note: Form A is a (somewhat antiquated in its view) example for a standard lifetime settlement. Form B (albeit in modified form) is still often seen, dating back to the 'pre-*Finance Act 2008*' situation (ie prior to the introduction of the transferable nil rate band facility), such as an existing will; and Form C is more appropriate for a recently drawn will.

Form A

This letter is confidential to my Trustees and is not the property of the beneficiaries.

In the Trust Deed that I have made today I have created a discretionary trust for my immediate family. I am one of the trustees but this letter is intended to guide my trustees after I am no longer a trustee for any reason. The trustees can at their discretion at any time share out the trust fund, either capital or income, between my daughter Susan and my sons Peter and John, with provision for grandchildren. My thinking in setting up the trust was as follows.

Susan is not working at present and her husband will only with difficulty afford to cover their household bills, so I would like the trustees to provide for Susan and her family occasional 'extras', even luxuries such as holidays. They cannot afford private education but I would be happy to see money set aside for when their children go to university.

Peter is no better at managing money at the age of 40 than he was as a child. The trustees should only in exceptional circumstances release capital to him. Far better to make an allowance to his dear and long-suffering wife Sally, who I know will use it for the family's benefit.

John is too level-headed and successful to need much help from the trust but should not be penalised on that account. His children deserve a good start in life so the trustees should be willing to help, even with golf or flying lessons if that is what they want.

Of course, this is only a guide. The trustees must exercise their discretion as they see fit according to the circumstances prevailing at the time.

Dated this ….. day of September 2018

Signed

Form B

In my Will dated ….. September 2018 I have created a discretionary trust of 'the nil rate sum' for my immediate family. Apart from that, my Will gives my son Peter my interest in the family company and gives the rest of my estate to my wife Maureen for life. After Maureen's death, the trustees can at their discretion share out the rest of my estate between my daughter

Sarah and Philip, with a provision for grandchildren. None of us can know exactly what assets we shall have at the date of our death, but my thinking in preparing the Will this way was as follows.

I want Maureen to be well provided for but I appreciate that if I leave the whole of my estate to her I have effectively 'thrown away' the nil rate band. I therefore hope that the Trustees of the nil rate sum, whilst always having an eye to what Maureen needs, will try to avoid the situation where Maureen is regarded as effectively the only beneficiary of the discretionary trust. It will be wise to encourage Maureen to use up some of her own resources first, to reduce her estate, before the trustees come to her aid.

As to my personal effects, for example, which are part of the nil rate sum, if I still own the yacht at the date of my death, I would like Sarah to have it, if she would like it, whilst Peter and his growing family might like the Volvo estate. Otherwise I hope that Sarah and Peter will agree between themselves if they would like any of my personal possessions.

Apart from that, my gift to Peter recognises that he has given his life to working for the family business. Giving him my interest in the business will, I hope, give him some security. It is also my hope that he will effectively receive that benefit tax free, so that it would not form part of the nil rate sum.

It would therefore be my wish that the Trustees, in deciding whom to benefit when exercising their discretion over the nil rate sum, should first compensate Sarah and her family to even up the benefit between my two children.

I do not think that there will be a substantial balance of residue over and above the nil rate band after taking account of the gift of the business. However, if there is, again I would like the Trustees to compensate Sarah if, in terms of value, she has received less than Peter.

The Trustees have a complete discretion over the nil rate sum and over the residue of my estate. I leave it to them to exercise that discretion as they think best in the circumstances that arise. This letter is only intended as a guide to my thinking in making my Will.

Dated this day of 2018

Signed.......................

[Testator]

Form C

In my Will dated ....September 2018 I have created a discretionary trust of 'the nil rate sum' for my immediate family. Apart from that, my Will gives my son Peter my interest in the family company and gives the rest of my estate to my wife Maureen for life. After Maureen's death, the trustees can at their discretion share out the rest of my estate between my daughter Sarah and Philip, with a provision for grandchildren. None of us can know exactly what assets we shall have at the date of our death, but my thinking in preparing the Will this way was as follows.

I want Maureen to be well provided for and I appreciate that as far as I leave my estate to her I am preserving the nil rate band for use on her eventual death. I therefore hope that the Trustees of the nil rate sum, will always have an eye to what Maureen needs and in particular will consider, before the expiry of two years from my death, whether to release capital to Maureen.

As to my personal effects, which are part of the nil rate sum, Maureen should have anything she wants and needs but if I still own the yacht at the date of my death, I would like Sarah to have it, if she would like it, whilst Peter and his growing family might like the Volvo estate.

Apart from that, my gift to Peter recognises that he has given his life to working for the family business. Giving him my interest in the business will, I hope, allow him some security. It is also my hope that after business relief he will effectively receive that benefit tax free, so that it will not form part of the nil rate sum.

It would therefore be my wish that the Trustees, in deciding whom to benefit when exercising their discretion over the nil rate sum, should first compensate Sarah and her family to even up the benefit between my two children.

I do not think that there will be a substantial balance of residue over and above the nil rate band after taking account of the gift of the business. However, if there is, again I would like the Trustees to compensate Sarah if, in terms of value, she has received less than Peter.

The Trustees have a complete discretion over the nil rate sum and over the residue of my estate. I leave it to them to exercise that discretion as they think best in the circumstances that arise. This letter is only intended as a guide to my thinking in making my Will.

Dated this [day] of [month] 2018

Signed……………………

[Testator]

Chapter 11

Exemptions and excluded property

SIGNPOSTS

- **Lifetime exemptions** – The annual exemption of £3,000 (see **11.7**) and the normal expenditure out of income exemption (see **11.9–11.10**) can help to reduce a future IHT liability.
- **Dispositions that are not transfers of value** – Dispositions for the maintenance of family are often overlooked (see **11.12–11.15**).
- **General exemptions** – Spouse exemption and gifts to charities exemption offer a useful shelter for IHT (see **11.16–11.19**).
- **Death exemptions** – No IHT is payable on the death of a person whilst on active service, even if the death occurs many years later but somehow can be linked to injuries inflicted or a disease contracted during active service (see **11.26–11.28**).
- **Excluded property** – Assets situated outside the UK and owned by non-UK domiciled individuals and in some cases even assets situated in the UK and reversionary interest may escape a charge to IHT (see **11.29–11.40**).

INTRODUCTION

11.1 IHT exemptions can be divided into three categories, those that only apply on death, those that apply on lifetime transfers only and those that can apply during lifetime or on death, here called 'general' exemptions. A PET is not an exempt transfer, but may become one seven years after the gift is made (see **Chapter 4**). Some exemptions apply to lifetime transfers and death.

Lifetime exemptions etc

11.2 *Lifetime* exemptions only apply to lifetime transfers and they are examined in more detail below. These are (all references are to *IHTA 1984*, unless otherwise stated):

- potentially exempt transfers (*IHTA 1984, s 3A*; see **Chapter 4**);
- annual exemption for gifts not exceeding £3,000 in any tax year (*IHTA 1984, s 19*);
- small gifts in any tax year up to a total of £250 per donee (*IHTA 1984, s 20*);
- normal expenditure out of income with no upper limit, if certain conditions are satisfied (*IHTA 1984, s 21*; see **Chapter 1**);
- wedding or civil partnership gifts within certain limits (*IHTA 1984, s 22*).

Dispositions that are not transfers of value

11.3 Certain dispositions do not constitute transfers of value if certain conditions are satisfied, including the following (see **11.12**):

- dispositions for maintenance of family (*IHTA 1984, s 11*);
- dispositions allowable for income tax or conferring retirement benefit (*IHTA 1984, s 12*);
- dispositions by close companies for the benefit of employees (*IHTA 1984, s 13*).

General exemptions

11.4 *General* exemptions, ie those which apply to both lifetime and death transfers are as follows:

- gifts between spouses or civil partners (*IHTA 1984, s 18*);
- gifts to charities (*IHTA 1984, s 23*);
- gifts to qualifying Parliamentary political parties (*IHTA 1984, s 24*);
- gifts to registered housing associations (*IHTA 1984, s 24A*);
- gifts for national purposes (eg The National Gallery, National Museums and the National Trust) (*IHTA 1984, s 25*);
- transfers to maintenance funds for historic buildings, where HMRC so direct upon making a claim (*IHTA 1984, s 27*);
- transfers of shares or securities by an individual to an employee trust, subject to certain conditions (*IHTA 1984, s 28*);
- transfers of national heritage property may be exempt from IHT where certain conditions are satisfied, ie 'conditionally exempt transfers' (*IHTA 1984, ss 30–35*).

Death exemptions

11.5 *Death* exemptions: There are five exemptions which are only available on transfers on death:

- death on active service exemption (*IHTA 1984, s 154*);
- death of emergency service personnel (*IHTA 1984, s 153A)*;
- death of constables and service personnel targeted because of their status (*IHTA 1984, s 155A*);
- decorations for valour, if never transferred for consideration in money or money's worth (*IHTA 1984, s 6(1B)*); and
- wartime compensation payments (*IHTA 1984, s 153ZA* formerly ESC F20).

Excluded property

11.6 *Excluded property* is property which has been specifically excluded from IHT (see *IHTA 1984, s 6*). Following *IHTA 1984, s 3(2)* transfers of value do not take into account the value of any excluded property. Excluded property is also not included in a person's estate following *IHTA 1984, s 5(1)*. In determining whether property is 'excluded property', one not only has to look at the situs of the property and the domicile of the transferor, but also at the type of property transferred. Excluded property comprises two main types of property:

(a) non-UK situs property beneficially owned by a non-UK domiciled individual; and

(b) non-UK situs property settled in a trust made at the time when the settlor is a non-UK domiciled individual.

It also includes certain types of assets that are situated in the UK or described in **11.31–11.38**.

It is important not to confuse exempt property with excluded property. While 'excluded property' will not form part of a person's estate for inheritance tax purposes, the application of exemptions depends very much on the recipient of any transfer of value. Note however the amendment in *IHTA 1984, s 5(1B)* introduced by *FA 2010, s 53* in respect of purchased trust interests.

Finance Bill 2017 included legislation which provided that all UK residential property held through an offshore structure or trust will be chargeable to IHT from 6 April 2017 – this will be in addition to ATED introduced in 2013 – see **1.15**.

This was dropped prior to the General Election but it was re-introduced with retrospective effect in *Finance (No 2) Act 2017*.

LIFETIME EXEMPTIONS

Annual exemption

11.7 Transfers of value during the lifetime of a person up to a total of £3,000 per tax year are exempt from IHT (*IHTA 1984, s 19(1)*).

- Where the annual exemption is not used in any one tax year it can be rolled forward for one year only.
- Where a gift exceeds the £3,000 limit, the excess must:
  - if the gifts were made on different days, be attributed, so far as possible, to a later rather than an earlier transfer; and
  - if the gifts were made on the same day, be attributed to them in proportion to the values transferred by them.

Where a transfer is a PET, in the first instance the annual exemption is left out of account. However if the donor dies within seven years of making the gift, the gift becomes a chargeable transfer. If two transfers are made on different days in the same tax year, the annual exemption is first applied to the earlier transfer. It does not matter whether the transfers are PETs or chargeable transfers when made (IHTM14143).

Example 11.1—Annual exemptions and PETs

Mrs Smith died on 30 April 2018, having made the following gifts to her daughter:

	£
1 June 2016	2,500
6 April 2017	1,500
15 April 2018	4,000
IHT position of lifetime gifts on death	
1 June 2016 gift:	2,500
Deduct 2016/17 exemption	3,000
Chargeable transfer on death	NIL
£500 can be carried forward	
6 April 2017 gift	1,500
Deduct 2017/18 exemption	3,000
Chargeable transfer on death	NIL

Only £1,500 can be carried forward. The annual exemption for the current tax year must be used before any unused annual exemption brought forward from the previous year (IHTM14144). The £500 unused exemption from the previous year can only be used during the 2017/18 year. It cannot be carried forward.

	£
15 April 2018 gift	4,000
Deduct 2018/19 exemption	3,000
Deduct unused 2017/18 exemption	1,500
Chargeable transfer on death	NIL

Small gifts exemption

11.8 The small gifts exemption under *IHTA 1984, s 20* covers transfers of value to any one person up to a total of £250 per tax year. The gift can consist of settled property and it may include free use of property. This exemption applies to any number of gifts up to £250 to separate persons, but it cannot be used to cover part of a larger gift.

This exemption can be used in addition to the annual exemption of £3,000, as long as the gift of £250 is made to a separate person. The current rule means that where the only transfer of value made is an outright gift of £3,250, the small gifts exemption cannot be used on the excess over £3,000 (assuming no carry-forward of the annual exemption from a previous year). Therefore, £250 will be chargeable to IHT.

Normal expenditure out of income exemption

11.9 Under *IHTA 1984, s 21* a lifetime transfer is exempt from IHT if it can be shown that:

- it was made as part of the normal expenditure of the transferor; and
- it was made out of his income; and
- after allowing for all transfers of value forming part of his normal expenditure, the transferor was left with sufficient income to maintain his usual standard of living.

Generally, HMRC will judge each case on its facts, therefore evidence to support a claim for this exemption is essential. The case *Bennett v IRC* [1995] STC 54 considered *IHTA 1984, s 21* in detail and the court identified several points to consider:

- 'Normal expenditure' means expenditure that was part of the settled pattern of expenditure adopted by the donor.
- A 'settled pattern' can be shown from the expenditure of the donor over a period of time *or* by showing that the donor has assumed a commitment, *or* adopted a firm resolution, in relation to future expenditure *and* has then made gifts in accordance with that commitment. One payment will be viewed as sufficient if clear evidence can be shown to support the claim that regular payments were intended.
- There is no fixed minimum period to establish the relief.
- Where there is no formal commitment or resolution, it may be necessary to show a series of payments.
- There can be some variation in the pattern, but to claim the relief it must be shown that the donor intended a pattern to exist and remain for a period of time.
- The amount of the transfer does not have to be fixed; the amount may be fixed by a formula such as a percentage of earnings or a figure such as 'what is left after paying all my outgoings'.
- Tax planning does not disqualify the expenditure; in contrast, if the taxpayer entered into a series of payments after taking advice, it may support his claim.

11.10 Details of income and expenditure have to be listed to support a claim for this exemption on supporting schedule IHT403 to Form IHT400. It is seen as good practice, if someone wishes to rely on this relief, to prepare a short document which explains that the donor has surplus income and that he therefore intends to make regular gifts out of income. See **Chapter 8** as to duty of care.

A premium on a life insurance on the donor's life paid directly or indirectly by the donor will not qualify under the 'normal expenditure out of income' exemption if at any time an annuity was purchased on the donor's life, unless it can be shown that the purchase of the annuity and the making or varying of the insurance were not associated operations (see *IHTA 1984, s 21(2)*).

As long as the above conditions are satisfied, the donor can pass funds to a donee limited only to the extent of the donor's available surplus income (IHTM14231–14251).

In the case of *McDowall and others (McDowall Executors) v CIR* [2004] STC SCD 22 it was held that a power of attorney does not give the attorney an authority to make gifts out of income.

The introduction of the *Inheritance Tax (Delivery of Accounts) (Excepted Estates) (Amendment) Regulations 2011,SI 2011/214* at first sight looked as if the facility of making gifts out of income under *s 21* has been curtailed. This regulation is not a change in the law as such but a change in the reporting requirements of such gifts. The main regulations about whether an estate needs an inheritance tax return are the ones in 2004 which provide that the parameters for an excepted estate were satisfied (among other things) where a person died who had not made chargeable transfers in the period of seven years before death exceeding £150,000. The regulation says that certain gifts will be treated as chargeable transfers for reporting purposes. These are gifts that:

- in any year exceed £3,000;
- fall in the seven years prior to death; and
- are exempt only by virtue of *IHTA 1984, s 21.*

This means that under these rules, it might be necessary to complete an IHT return where previously that might not have been necessary.

HMRC have recently substantially re-written their guidance on gifts out of income – see IHTM14231 to IHTM14255. HMRC now advise staff to deny taxpayers' claims that the exemption applies on gifts made out of several years of accumulated income.

Partial withdrawals from investment bonds (even if they are within the 5% annual allowance), while they may assume the character of income, are now deemed to be capital payments and do not qualify for the exemption under *IHTA 1984, s 21.*

Focus

- Competent professional advisers advise their clients to keep records of such gifts – Form IHT403 is useful as an indication of the type of information HMRC require.
- It also is good practice to prepare a short document explaining that the donor has surplus income and that he intends to make regular gifts out of income.
- An annual ledger of income and expenditure which shows surplus income will assist.
- Regular withdrawals from investment bonds count as capital for the purposes of the normal expenditure out of income exemption.
- HMRC's IHT Manual has now been updated – IHTM14250 deals with the issue whether income may have lost its income nature.

Gifts in consideration of marriage/civil partnership exemption

11.11 Gifts in consideration of marriage are exempt from IHT on the value transferred up to the following limits (*s 22*):

- £5,000 by a parent of either party to the marriage/civil partnership. Each of four parents can give £5,000 (a total of £20,000) to the couple.
- £2,500 by one party to the marriage/civil partnership to the other or by a grandparent or remoter ancestor.
- £1,000 in any other case.

The gift must be made before, or contemporaneously with, the marriage/civil partnership. If it is made after the marriage/civil partnership it must be made in satisfaction of a prior legal obligation. If the marriage does not occur, the donor must have the right to recover the gift, otherwise a charge to IHT may occur.

The exemption applies to gifts to an illegitimate child, an adopted child and a stepchild.

This exemption can be used to settle property on trust, but only if the beneficiaries of the trust are limited to the couple, any issue and the spouses of such issue (*s 22(4)*).

DISPOSITIONS WHICH ARE NOT TRANSFERS OF VALUE

Disposition for maintenance of family

11.12 A disposition for the maintenance of family is not a transfer of value and it is therefore exempt from IHT (*IHTA 1984, s 11*). HMRC's view is that this exemption is limited to lifetime transfers only, so it is uncertain whether payments to the recipient would be covered under this exemption if the payer dies. The following payments are excluded from IHT:

- By one party to the marriage for the maintenance of the other party.
- By one party to a marriage for the maintenance, education or training of a child of either party. This includes stepchildren and adopted children. The maintenance can continue beyond 18 years, if the child is in full-time education.
- The provisions extend to the maintenance of an illegitimate child and to the maintenance of other people's children until they reach the age of 18 years.
- The exemption also covers reasonable provision made for the care or maintenance of a dependent relative who is incapacitated by old age or infirmity from maintaining himself. Mothers and mothers-in-law who are widowed or separated are always dependent relatives for this exemption. This has been confirmed in the case of *R McKelvey (personal representative*

of D V McKelvey) v HMRC [2008] SSCD 944 (SpC 694), where a terminally ill daughter transferred properties to provide for her elderly mother.

Unfortunately, 'maintenance' has not been defined and, until the *McKelvey* case, it was uncertain whether the transfer of capital assets (ie the former matrimonial home), would be covered by this exemption. As the above case illustrates, it can also be difficult in practice to quantify what constitutes 'reasonable provision' for care or maintenance, as this will often be a question of judgement.

Section 13 of *IHTA 1984* exempts dispositions of property to trustees in favour of employees of close companies.

Following concession ESC F12, a disposition has been treated as exempt under *IHTA 1984, s 11(3)* if the disposition is made for an unmarried mother, who is genuinely financially dependent on the child making the disposition. This concession has now been superseded by a change of definition of 'dependent relative' in *IHTA 1984, s 11(6)(b),* to include 'his mother or father or his spouse's or civil partner's mother or father'.

Example 11.2—Disposition for family

Susan, a young mother of two children, is terminally ill. Her main asset is the family home, which she inherited from her parents and a small share portfolio. Both assets push her above the available nil rate band. The previous year she separated from Simon, who now lives in rented accommodation.

Her main concern is to provide for her two children who would be forced to leave the family home if IHT were to become payable. By relying on *IHTA 1984, s 11*, she could transfer her assets to the children during her lifetime. As this will not be a transfer of value, the transfer will not become chargeable to IHT on her death.

Focus

This exemption has been used successfully where a terminally ill child has looked after an elderly relative.

Allocation of exemptions and interaction with reliefs

11.13 Where a transfer qualifies for any of the exemptions considered above, the question often arises how to apply these exemptions and how they interact with other reliefs.

First, there is the question of how business and agricultural reliefs (see **Chapter 13**) fit in with the exempt transfer rules such as those relating to the annual exemptions. This can best be illustrated by an example.

Example 11.3—Annual exemption and business property relief

Mr Miller died on 30 April 2018, having transferred a tenanted agricultural property, which qualifies for 50% relief, to his son in January 2016.

	£
1 January 2016 gift:	100,000
Deduct	
50% APR	50,000
Unused 2015/16 exemption	3,000
Chargeable transfer	47,000

APR and BPR are applied first and the annual exemption is then used to reduce the remaining chargeable transfer.

11.14 As indicated at **11.7**, there is an HMRC practice as to the allocation of exemptions where more than one of the exemptions as considered above are involved (see IHTM14143). Where tax is payable, if two transfers are made on different days in the same tax years, the exemption ought to apply first to the earlier transfer. If two transfers are made on the same day, apportion the exemption between them.

Example 11.4—HMRC's Inheritance Tax Manual, at IHTM14143

Ajani makes transfers of £4,000 and £8,000 on the same day. The total value transferred is £12,000.

£4,000/£12,000 × £3,000 = £1,000 exemption on the £4,000 transfer

£8,000/£12,000 × £3,000 = £2,000 exemption on the £8,000 transfer

11.15 Where a number of different exemptions apply, the order of applying the transfers is as follows:

- normal expenditure out of income;
- marriage gifts;
- £3,000 annual exemption.

This provides the transferor with the opportunity for some forward planning to use the exemptions in the most efficient manner. Should the transferor wish to allocate the exemptions in a different order, HMRC will consider the matter.

GENERAL EXEMPTIONS

Spouse or civil partnership exemption

11.16 Transfers of value between UK-domiciled spouses/civil partners are exempt from inheritance tax (*IHTA 1984, s 18*):

- where property becomes comprised in the transferee's estate, by the amount by which the transferor's estate is diminished; or
- in any other case (eg payment by the transferor of his spouse's/civil partner's debt) by the amount by which the transferee's estate is increased.

The spouse/civil partner exemption for IHT applies when property is held on trust for the transferee spouse/civil partner under an 'immediate post-death interest' (see **Chapter 9**). However, following changes introduced in *FA 2006*, the exemption does not apply to the lifetime creation of an interest in possession in favour of spouses or civil partners from 22 March 2006, as such transfers do not become comprised in that individual's estate.

The spouse/civil partner exemption is qualified where the transfer passes under a testamentary or other disposition, usually a will, and:

- the disposition takes effect on the termination, after the transfer, of any interest or period; or
- the disposition is conditional on the happening of some event that is not satisfied, or does not take place, within 12 months after the transfer (*IHTA 1984, s 18(3)*).

11.17 *Finance Act 2005* introduced the concept 'civil partnership' with the aim of granting equal rights to same-sex couples. A 'civil partnership' is one that exists by virtue of the *Civil Partnership Act 2004*. The spouse exemption applies to same-sex couples who have entered into a 'civil partnership'.

Following the *Marriage (Same Sex Couples) Act 2013*, which came into force on 13 March 2014, any reference to marriage, married couple, spouse, etc in existing legislation in England and Wales will be read as including marriage of a same sex couple. It will be possible for civil partners to convert their civil partnership into a marriage under a procedure established by regulations which are not yet in force at the time of updating this edition.

By contrast, in *Holland (Exor of Holland Deceased) v IRC* [2003] STC (SCD) 43, the Special Commissioner decided that a couple who had lived as husband and wife for 31 years did not qualify for the spouse exemption.

In the more recent case of *Burden v United Kingdom* [2008] STC 1305, it was decided that the spouse/civil partner exemption does not extend to co-habiting siblings.

Finance Act 2008 introduced provisions which enable the survivor of a married couple or civil partnership to inherit the unused proportion of the nil rate band of the first to die (*IHTA 1984, s 8A*). See **Chapter 3**.

Finance Act 2013 introduced provisions which increased the spouse exemption for non-UK domiciled spouses or civil partners to the nil rate band in force at the time (£325,000 for 2018/19).

Therefore for transfers until 5 April 2013:

- if immediately before the transfer, the transferor but not the transferor's spouse or civil partner, is domiciled in the UK the spouse or civil partner exemption is limited to a cumulative total of £55,000, without grossing-up for tax (*IHTA 1984, s 18(2)*);
- if a lifetime transfer to a non-domiciled spouse or civil partner exceeds £55,000, the excess will be treated as a PET and may become chargeable if the transferor dies within seven years;
- this restriction does not apply if both spouses or civil partners are non-UK domiciled individuals.

Finance Act 2013, s 177 inserted *IHTA 1984, ss 267A* and *268A* which amend these provisions for transfers from 6 April 2013 as follows:

- the non-UK domiciled spouse or civil partner can elect to be treated as UK domiciled, if one of two conditions is met:
  - condition A ('the lifetime exemption'): the person's spouse or civil partner must be UK domiciled at the time of the election and the person must not be UK domiciled; or
  - condition B ('the death exemption'): the person's spouse or civil partner died UK domiciled on or after 6 April 2013 and the person was not UK domiciled at that time and the election is made within two years of the UK domiciled spouse's date of death:
- if these conditions are met the restricted spouse or civil partner exemption is removed and it puts the non-domiciled spouse into the same position as a UK-domiciled spouse;
- the election can be backdated for a period up to seven years but not a date before 6 April 2013.

The election is irrevocable and brings the person's worldwide assets into the IHT net. Although the election cannot be revoked, if the person making the election is not UK resident for the purposes of income tax for the whole of any 'period specified', the election ceases to take effect. The 'period specified' is any period of four successive tax years beginning:

- in the case of a lifetime election, at any time after it takes effect; or
- in the case of the death exemption, at any time after the election is treated as having effect.

Finance (No 2) Act 2017 included amendments to *IHTA 1984, s 267* in that from 6 April 2017 the qualifying period for a person resident in the UK to become deemed will be reduced from 17 out of 20 years to 15 out of 20 years. This will extend the 'period specified' mentioned above from four years to five years. The practical effect of this is that a person who elected to be treated as domiciled in the UK remains domiciled for a five-year period on ceasing to be UK resident. It was also announced that individuals who were born in the UK and who have a UK domicile of origin will revert back to their UK-domiciled status for tax purposes while resident in the UK. For a more detailed discussion on deemed domicile see **Chapter 2**.

Care needs to be taken on lifetime gifts, as the election must state the date from which it is supposed to take effect to ensure that any gift benefits from the full spouse exemption.

Example 11.5—Spouse exemption and domicile

Scenario 1: death prior to April 2013

Mr Jones, who is UK domiciled, dies on 30 April 2012. In 2006, he married Maria Hofer, who is Austrian and moved to the UK following the marriage. Maria finds the English climate challenging and both she and her husband spend considerable time in Austria. She therefore remains domiciled in Austria, although she is resident in the UK. Mr Jones' estate was valued at £1 million and his will left his whole estate to his spouse:

IHT position on Mr Jones' death

	£
Estate	1,000,000
Less: nil rate band	325,000
Less: limited spouse exemption	55,000
Net estate	620,000
IHT @ 40%	248,000

Scenario 2: death after 5 April 2013

Mr Jones dies on 30 April 2018. As the death was after 5 April 2013, the spouse exemption will be £325,000, which will be in addition to the nil rate band with the result that £650,000 can pass to Maria free of IHT. Further, Maria can elect to be treated as UK domiciled and the estate can benefit from an unrestricted spouse exemption, which would save £140,000 of IHT.

However, as this will bring Maria's worldwide estate into the UK IHT net, it has to be considered carefully, especially as there is no IHT equivalent in Austria.

If Maria decides to make the election, but then moves back to Austria in November 2018, she will retain her UK-domicile status by election, despite being non-resident, until 6 April 2024.

Gifts to charities

11.18 Gifts to charity are exempt from IHT (*IHTA 1984, s 23*). This exemption was limited to gifts to UK-based charities – see below. Following *Finance Act 2002*, the definition of 'charity' has been extended and now includes community amateur sports clubs, if they are registered and open to the whole community, are organised on an amateur basis and have as their main purpose the provision of facilities for, and the promotion of participation in, one or more eligible sports.

By *IHTA 1984, s 23(6)*, the property that is the subject matter of the transfer must actually become the property of the charity, or must be held for charitable purposes. Where the value transferred (ie the loss to the transferor's estate as a result of the disposition), exceeds the value of the gift in the hands of the charity, the exemption extends to the whole value transferred (see Statement of Practice E13).

11.19 *Section 23(2)* of *IHTA 1984,* includes various restrictions to this exemption to prevent the abuse of charitable relief. The relief is not given, if the testamentary or other disposition by which it is given:

- takes place after any other transfer of value has had effect for any interest or period; or
- is conditional on something that does happen for 12 months after the transfer; or
- is defeasible, ie can be taken away from the charity after the gift for any reason.

Another restriction has been imposed in *IHTA 1984, s 23(4)* where the donor of the property wishes to continue living in the property after he has given it to the charity. The general rule is that the exemption does not apply if the donor, his or her spouse or a person connected to the donor has the right to possession of the property or to occupy the whole or part of the land rent free or at a rent that is below the market value.

A transfer that has not been defeated 12 months after it is to have taken effect and that, after that time, is indefeasible, is treated as charitable and secures the exemption.

Finance Act 2010 extended UK charity relief to certain EU organisations and community amateur sports clubs in the EU and the European Economic Area countries of Norway and Iceland, following a judgment in the European Court of Justice in January 2009. The extended definition of 'charity' applies for IHT purposes. HMRC (in their guidance to completing the IHT400 account) helpfully summarise the position as follows: 'All lifetime gifts and bequests on death to qualifying charities are exempt provided the gift was made to the charity outright'. They add: 'A qualifying charity is one that meets the following conditions:

- it is a charity established in the European Union or other specified country;
- it meets the definition of a charity under the law of England and Wales;
- it is regulated in the country of establishment, if that is a requirement in that country;
- its managers are fit and proper persons to be managers of the charity.'

The appeal case of *Routier v HMRC* [2017] EWCA Civ 1584 confirms that charity relief under *IHTA 1984, s 23* is not available to gifts to non-UK charitable trusts.

Gifts to political parties

11.20 All gifts made to qualifying political parties are exempt from IHT (*IHTA 1984, s 24*). A political party qualifies for the exemption if, at the last general election preceding the transfer of value:

- two members of that party were elected to the House of Commons; or
- one member of that party was elected to the House of Commons and not less than 150,000 votes were given to candidates who were members of that party.

Restrictions are the same as applied to charitable gifts.

Finance Act 2017 extends *IHTA 1984, s 24* in that the relief will be extended to parties with representatives in the devolved legislatures in Scotland, Wales and Northern Ireland and parties that have acquired representatives through by-elections.

Gifts to housing associations

11.21 Under *IHTA 1984, s 24A*, transfers of value to registered social landlords, as defined by the *Housing Associations Act 1985* or *Housing Act 1996* or *Housing (Northern Ireland) Order 1981, SI 1981/156 (NI 3)* are exempt to the extent that the value transferred is attributable to land in the UK.

Again, the restrictions are the same as applied to charitable gifts.

Gifts for national purposes

11.22 Gifts to certain national bodies are exempt from IHT (*IHTA 1984, s 25*). The list of national bodies can be found in *IHTA 1984, Sch 3* and includes, among others, the National Gallery, the British Museum and any university.

Again, the restrictions are the same as applied to charitable gifts.

Transfers to maintenance funds for historic buildings

11.23 Transfers into settlements for the maintenance, repair or preservation of historic buildings and assets of outstanding scenic, historic or scientific interest are, subject to certain conditions, exempt (*IHTA 1984, ss 30–35A, Sch 3*). There is a two-year time limit from transfer to bring the claim, which can be extended by HMRC concession.

Transfers of shares or securities by an individual to an employee trust

11.24 Following *IHTA 1984, s 28*, subject to certain conditions, transfers to trusts for the benefit of employees of a company without interests in possession are exempt from IHT and will escape ten-yearly IHT charges (*IHTA 1984, s 58(1)*). Such transfers can be made by individuals, close companies and settlements.

The trusts of the settlement must fit the requirements of *IHTA 1984, s 86(1)*. The conditions are that the settled property is held on trusts, which, either indefinitely, or until the end of a period, do not permit that property to be applied otherwise than for the benefit of:

- people of a class that is defined by reference to employment in a particular trade or profession; or
- people of a class defined by employment by, or holding an office with a particular body carrying on a trade, profession or undertaking; or
- people of a class by reference to marriage to, or a relationship to, or dependence on people of a class defined above; or

- other charitable purposes.

In addition, *IHTA 1984, s 28(1)(b)* determines that the exemption only applies if all or most of the people working for that body can benefit, or if the trusts fit a profit-sharing scheme that has already been approved by HMRC under *ICTA 1988, Sch 9*, or for trusts which are approved share incentive plans within *ITEPA 2003, Sch 2* (*s 86(3)*).

11.25 *Section 28(2)* of *IHTA 1984* imposes a number of additional restrictions, which are as follows:

- the trustees must hold at least half the shares in the company; and
- the trustees must have a majority of votes in the company; and
- there must be no provisions that effect the company or its management or its shares or securities under which this power of ownership or of voting can be brought to an end without the consent of the trustees.

Finally, no participator (ie someone who owns at least 5% of any class of the shares comprised in its issued share capital and on winding-up of the company is entitled to 5% or more of its assets) may benefit from the trust.

HMRC in their Revenue & Customs Brief 18/11 summarised their approach in relation to close companies. IHT charges therefore may arise if the disposition is intended to confer a gratuitous benefit under *s 10*. There is both a subjective and an objective test, both of which must be met. The subjective test is not met if there is the slightest possibility of a gratuitous intent when the contribution is made. The objective test must satisfy the conditions that the transaction must have been made at arm's length between persons not connected with each other, or was such as might be expected to be made in a transaction at arm's length between persons not connected with each other. This means that for close companies these conditions are rarely met in HMRC's view.

Section 28(A) of *IHTA 1984* was introduced by *FA 2014* and creates a new exemption for employee-ownership trusts (EOTs). It provides that a transfer of shares by an individual is an exempt transfer to the extent that the value transferred is attributable to shares in or securities of a trading company if the settlement meets all-employee benefit requirements and the shares transferred give the EOT control of the company at the end of the tax year in which the transfer is made.

DEATH EXEMPTION

Death on active service, emergency personnel and constables

11.26 Following *IHTA 1984, s 154*, no IHT is payable on the death of a person whilst on active service against an enemy or other service of a warlike nature. The Defence Council or the Secretary of State must certify that the person concerned:

- died from a wound that was inflicted when that person was on active service; or
- died from an accident that occurred during such service; or
- died from a disease contracted when the person was on that service.

Where a disease was contracted at some previous time, but it was aggravated during active military service and therefore death was brought on more quickly, the exemption also applies.

This exemption was invoked in the case of *Executors of 4th Duke of Westminster (otherwise Barty-King) v Ministry of Defence* QB [1978] STC 218 where the 4th Duke of Westminster died of cancer many years after his war wound. Although there was no direct causal connection between the war wound and the cause of his death, the exemption was successfully invoked.

All that is required is to find a 'reasonable link' which may have caused the death. For example a limp following a war injury may have caused a fall which resulted in death.

The following amendments are included in *FA 2014* to take effect for deaths on or after 19 March 2014:

- *IHTA 1984, s 153A* was introduced which covers the death of emergency and humanitarian aid workers responding to emergency circumstances.
- *IHTA 1984, s 155A* extends the IHT exemption to constables and armed service personnel targeted because of their status.
- *IHTA 1984, s 154A* extends the relief for armed forces personnel to injuries sustained when responding to emergencies.
- *Finance Act 2015, s 75* extends the death in service exemption to IHT payable on lifetime gifts that arises as a result of the death.

Decorations for valour or gallant conduct

11.27 Formerly ESC F19, now enacted in *IHTA 1984, s 6(1B)* and *s 6(1BA)*, a decoration or other award if awarded for valour or gallant conduct and it has never been subject of a disposition for a consideration in money or money's worth is 'excluded property' for IHT.

Legislation is included in *FA 2015* to treat all medals and decorations awarded by the Crown or a country or territory outside the UK to armed forces personnel, emergency service personnel and individuals for achievements and services in public life as excluded property. The changes will take effect for all transfers of values made on or after 3 December 2014.

Wartime compensation payments

11.28 This relief was originally only available to recipients of the £10,000 payment for Japanese prisoners of war, but has now been extended to a range of payments to victims of wrongs suffered during World War II. A list of qualifying payments can be found in *IHTA 1984, s 153ZA* (formerly Extra Statutory Concession F20.)

The amount of compensation received is assumed to be included in the deceased's assets. In effect, for any recipient of relevant compensation payments, the nil rate band for IHT is increased by the amount of compensation received.

New *IHTA 1984, s 153ZA* includes detailed provisions to enact this concession, which are backdated to 1 January 2015.

EXCLUDED PROPERTY

11.29 No transfer of 'excluded property' is chargeable to IHT following *IHTA 1984, ss 3(2)* and *5(1)*. The main categories of 'excluded property' are listed in *IHTA 1984, s 6* and are mentioned below.

Property situated outside the UK

11.30 Following *IHTA 1984, s 6* property situated outside the UK is excluded property if the person entitled to it is an individual who is domiciled outside the UK for the purposes of IHT. For the definition of domicile, see **Chapter 2**.

Settled property that is situated outside the UK is 'excluded property' if the settlor was domiciled outside the UK when the settlement was made (*IHTA 1984, s 48(3)*). The recent case of *Barclays Wealth Trustees (Jersey) Ltd and another v HMRC* [2015] EWHC 2872 confirms that the domicile status of the settlor needs to be re-examined if further funds are introduced into an excluded property settlement.

Following *IHTA 1984, s 82*, if the settlor retains an interest in possession either for himself or his spouse, and a discretionary trust arises on the termination of that interest, an additional test is imposed on the determination of the interest in possession. It will be necessary to ascertain where the settlor and his spouse are domiciled when their interests end and the discretionary trust arises.

Example 11.6—Settlement of excluded property

Hans, a German national, settles shares in a German company on a life interest trust for his wife Gemma in 1993. Both Hans and Gemma are domiciled in Germany. At the date of settlement, the shares are excluded property, being property situated outside the UK and settled by a non-UK domiciliary. However, the trust document determines that on the ending of Gemma's life interest, the trust assets should be resettled on discretionary trusts for Hans' grandchildren. It will therefore be necessary to revisit the settlement, when Gemma's interest ends (it ends in 2013).

Hans and Gemma decided that they prefer the English climate and moved to Suffolk in 1995. When Gemma's life interest ends in 2013, both Hans and Gemma are deemed UK domiciled for IHT. The German shares therefore will not qualify as 'excluded property' when Gemma's interest ends and a charge to IHT will occur, if the shares are valued above the nil rate band at that time.

If the trustees had used their power of appointment to resettle those same shares on discretionary trust prior to Hans and Gemma becoming deemed domiciled, the shares would have remained 'excluded property' and the settlement would have escaped the relevant property regime.

Property that is excluded or exempt despite being situated in the UK

Government securities

11.31 Following *IHTA 1984, s 6(2)* exempt government securities are excluded property if they are in the beneficial ownership of a person who satisfies the conditions for exemption attached to the stock. The exemption depends on the qualifying person having beneficial ownership and not the mere legal title.

Settled exempt government securities are excluded property if a person who satisfies the conditions for exemption is entitled to a qualifying interest in possession in the settlement (*IHTA 1984, s 48(4)*). 'Qualifying interest in possession' means an interest in possession to which an individual is beneficially entitled, or an interest in possession to which a company is beneficially entitled as a result of the commercial purchase of the interest in certain circumstances. If an annuitant (or other person entitled to part only of the income of the settled property) domiciled and resident abroad dies, or if his interest terminates at a time when the settled property is exempt government securities, the relevant 'slice' of the property is excluded property.

Settled exempt government securities not subject to a qualifying interest in possession will only be excluded property if the trustees can demonstrate that all known persons for whose benefit the settled property, or income from it, has been or might be applied, or who are or might become beneficially entitled to an interest in possession in it, are persons who satisfied or satisfy the exemption conditions for the beneficial owner of the securities.

These conditions previously included the requirement that the beneficial owner must be domiciled and ordinarily resident outside the UK. However, for deaths and other chargeable events on or after 6 April 1998, all government securities (with the exception of 3½% War Loan stock) are excluded property for IHT purposes by reference only to the ordinary residence of the beneficial owner, ie domicile is no longer relevant (see IHTM04291 and IHTM27241).

Holdings in an authorised unit trust and shares in an open-ended investment company

11.32 A holding in an authorised unit trust and a share in an open-ended investment company are excluded property if, in either case the person beneficially entitled to it is an individual who, for the purposes of IHT, is domiciled outside the UK, in relation to transfers of value or other events occurring after 15 October 2002 (see *IHTA 1984, s 6(1A)*).

An authorised unit trust is a scheme authorised as such under the *Financial Services and Markets Act 2000, s 243*.

An open-ended investment company is such a company within the meaning of the *Financial Services and Markets Act 2000, s 236* and which is incorporated in the UK.

Certain property owned by persons domiciled in the Channel Islands or Isle of Man

11.33 Some types of national savings contracts are excluded property if the beneficial owner is domiciled in the Channel Islands or Isle of Man. 'Domicile', for this purpose, has its ordinary meaning, and not the extended meaning given to it for certain IHT purposes. The consequence will be that no IHT is payable on the death of the owner, or on any lifetime transfer of the savings. The savings contracts in question are (see *IHTA 1984, s 6(3)*):

- war savings certificates;
- national savings certificates (including Ulster savings certificates but not national savings income bonds);
- premium savings bonds;
- deposits with the National Savings Bank or with a trustee savings bank;
- certified contractual savings schemes within the meaning of *ITTOIA 2005, s 703(1)* (ie SAYE schemes).

Visiting forces

11.34 *Section 6(4)* of *IHTA 1984* allows limited reliefs from IHT for visiting forces and the staff of allied headquarters. The reliefs fall into two categories. First, certain items of property belonging to visiting forces and staff are excluded property. Secondly, certain periods of residence in the UK are disregarded for IHT purposes. Details can be found in *IHTA 1984, s 155(1)* and are beyond the scope of this book.

Overseas pensions

11.35 Following *IHTA 1984, s 153*, some categories of foreign pensions relating to service in certain foreign colonial territories or relating to service for the government of an overseas territory are excluded property. The rule applies on death only and has the effect that the pension is left out of account in determining the value of a person's estate immediately before his death. The effect is that no IHT will be payable on the death of the pensioner, wherever he is domiciled and whatever the nature of his entitlement (eg a repayment of contributions due to the deceased's estate).

Non-sterling bank accounts

11.36 *FA 1982, s 96* introduced a statutory exemption from capital transfer tax in relation to qualifying foreign currency bank accounts held by individuals who are non-UK residents and non-UK domiciled. The exemption is now provided by *IHTA 1984, s 157* and is only available on death.

A 'foreign currency account' is any account other than one denominated in sterling.

A 'qualifying' foreign currency account is a foreign currency account with the Post Office, the Bank of England, an institution authorised under the *Banking Act 1987*, a relevant European institution, or an international organisation of which the UK is a member which is designated as a bank by Treasury order.

Foreign currency accounts were used to sidestep restrictions for the deductibility of liabilities introduced by *FA 2013,* which disallow a deduction of liabilities used for acquiring 'excluded property'. Anti-avoidance measures therefore were introduced in *FA 2014*, in that for deaths occurring on or after 17 July 2014 (the date of Royal Assent to *FA 2014*) no deduction will be allowed for liabilities incurred to fund foreign currency bank accounts.

Foreign works of art

11.37 ESC F7, as modified by Ministerial Statement dated 25 February 2003, previously provided that there would be no liability to IHT on a work of art normally kept overseas and beneficially owned by a foreign domiciliary, if it is situated in the UK at the date of death and was brought to the UK solely for the purposes of public exhibition, cleaning or restoration, or if it would otherwise have left the UK to be kept overseas but is retained in the UK solely for these purposes. The concession also applied to waive the periodic charge to tax if the work of art is comprised in settled property in which there is no interest in possession.

This concession was withdrawn (by *The Enactment of Extra-Statutory Concessions Order 2009, SI 2009/730, art 13*) with effect from 6 April 2009, but legislative effect is given to it in *IHTA 1984, ss 5(1)(b)* and *64(2)* respectively.

Property owned by diplomatic agents

11.38 The *Diplomatic Privileges Act 1964, s 2(1)* gives the force of law to Articles of the *Vienna Convention on Diplomatic Relations. Article 34* of the *Convention* provides that a diplomatic agent is exempt from all taxes with certain exceptions. These exceptions include dues and taxes on private immovable property situated in the territory of the receiving state, dues and taxes on private income having its source in the receiving state and capital taxes on investments made in commercial undertakings in the receiving state.

It would seem therefore that tax will not be chargeable on any transfer *inter vivos* by a diplomatic agent of property situated in the UK, but that it will in strictness be leviable on his death on his immovable property situated here, and on any movable property unless its presence in this country can be attributed solely to the deceased's presence as a member of a mission. Thus, his personal chattels would be exempt, and (presumably) his personal current bank account, but (probably) not any investment capital assets.

Reversionary interests

11.39 Following *IHTA 1984, s 48(1)* a reversionary interest is excluded property unless:

- it has at any time been acquired, either by the person entitled to it or by a person previously entitled to it, for a consideration in money or money's worth; or
- it is one to which the settlor or his spouse is or has been beneficially entitled; or
- it is an interest expectant on the determination of a lease of property which is for life or lives, or for a period ascertainable only by reference to a death and not granted for a full consideration in money or money's worth.

Provided that the above conditions are satisfied, the situs of the trust property, and the domicile of the settlor and reversioner, are irrelevant. The legislation was tested in the recent case of *M L Salinger and J L Kirby v HMRC* [2016] UKFTT 677 and the FTT found in favour of the taxpayer.

In addition, even if those conditions are not satisfied, a reversionary interest is excluded property if the interest, as distinct from the fund in which it subsists, is situated outside the UK and the person who owns the reversion, whether or not it has been acquired by purchase, is domiciled outside the UK.

11.40 *Section 48* of *IHTA 1984* was amended by *Finance Act 2006*, which inserted *IHTA 1984, s 48(3B)*. This provides that where property situated outside the UK is excluded property, such property will not continue to be excluded if a UK-domiciled individual purchases an interest in possession in the excluded property for consideration in money or money's worth after 5 December 2005. This in effect is an anti-avoidance measure against 'deathbed' arrangements to prevent UK-domiciled individuals with a limited life expectancy (eg elderly or infirmed individuals) purchasing excluded property shortly before death.

Example 11.7—Reversionary interest (I)

A fund consisting entirely of non-UK situs property is held on trust for Arthur for life, remainder to Bertie. Bertie dies.

There is no charge to IHT on Bertie's death. The domicile of the settlor and Bertie's domicile are irrelevant.

Example 11.8—Reversionary interest (II)

A fund consisting entirely of non-UK situs assets is held on trust for Arthur for life, remainder to Bertie. Bertie has sold his interest to Charlie. Charlie dies.

IHT is payable on the value of the reversion as part of Charlie's estate, as the condition in *IHTA 1984, s 48(1)(a)* has been breached.

The fund will escape a charge to IHT if, following *IHTA 1984, s 48(3)* the settlor was a non-UK domiciliary, Charlie was domiciled abroad at the date of his death and the reversion can be regarded as excluded property under *IHTA 1984, s 6(1)* (ie the trust is non-UK resident).

Example 11.9—Reversionary interest (III)

A fund is held on trust for Arthur for life, remainder to Bertie. The fund contains (*inter alia*) reversions purchased by the trustees as investments. Arthur dies.

There is a charge to IHT on Arthur's death except in so far as it consists of excluded property. If the settlor was domiciled outside the UK when the settlement was made, the reversion should be excluded property if (but only if) it is situated abroad.

Anti-avoidance provisions have been introduced in *IHTA 1984, s 81A*. Where a reversionary interest in relevant property, which was acquired for consideration by an individual, or his spouse or civil partner, comes to an end, and the individual, his spouse or civil partner become entitled to an interest in possession in the relevant property, this will be treated as a disposition of the reversionary interest at that time.

Chapter 12

Reliefs – General

SIGNPOSTS

- **Taper relief** – Available on lifetime transfers which exceed the nil rate band for inheritance tax and are made more than three years before death (see **12.2–12.3**).
- **Quick succession relief** – Provides relief against two charges to IHT where there was more than one chargeable transfer within a five-year period (**12.4–12.5**).
- **Related property relief** – If property was valued on death as 'related property' and is sold within three years at less than that valuation a claim can be made (see **12.6–12.7**).
- **Fall in value relief** – If the value of a PET or lifetime chargeable transfer has fallen since date of gift and date of death within seven years, relief can be claimed (see **12.8–12.12**).
- **Post-death reliefs on the sale of shares** – If there is a fall in value since date of death and date of sale within 12 months, PRs can claim relief (see **12.14–12.16**).
- **Post-death relief on the sale of land** – Relief can be claimed (subject to certain conditions) to substitute the sale value with the probate value (see **12.17–12.18**).
- **Woodlands relief and heritage property relief** – Subject to a number of conditions these reliefs may be useful albeit rare (see **12.24–12.30**).

INTRODUCTION

12.1 In addition to the reliefs listed in **Chapter 11** and business property relief and agricultural property relief detailed in **Chapter 13** there are a number of other reliefs which can reduce a charge to IHT (see also **1.21 ff**) (all statutory references in this chapter are to *IHTA 1984*, unless otherwise stated):

- Taper relief is available on both chargeable lifetime transfers and potentially exempt transfers made more than three years before death (*IHTA 1984, s 7*) (see **1.21**).
- Quick succession relief provides relief against two charges to IHT where there was more than one chargeable transfer within a five-year period (*IHTA 1984, s 141*) (see outline in **1.23**).
- Property valued on death as 'related property' (see **6.6**) may qualify for relief if it is sold within three years of death at less than that valuation (*IHTA 1984, s 161*).
- Relief is available when the market value of property transferred within seven years before death is lower at the date of death than at the time of the chargeable transfer (*IHTA 1984, ss 131–140*).
- Relief is available if quoted securities are sold within 12 months of death for less than their probate value (*ss 178*ff), and if land is sold within four years of death for less than its probate value (*IHTA 1984, ss 190*ff).
- Where the transferor is liable to IHT charges on the same assets in two jurisdictions, double tax relief may be available in certain circumstances.
- *The Inheritance Tax (Double Charges Relief) Regulations 1987, SI 1987/1130* and the *Inheritance Tax (Double Charges Relief) Regulations 2005, SI 2005/3441* prevent a person being charged to IHT twice on the same property in certain circumstances.
- An election can be made which enables the IHT chargeable on death in respect of growing timber and underwood to be deferred until sale (*IHTA 1984, ss 125–130*).
- Heritage property relief is a 'conditional exemption' which may be available on transfers of national heritage property if certain conditions are met (*IHTA 1984, s 30*).

These reliefs are covered in detail below.

TAPER RELIEF

12.2 IHT on all lifetime transfers (PETs and chargeable lifetime transfers) made within seven years before death may be subject to taper relief if the lifetime transfer was made more than three years before death, thereby reducing a potential charge to IHT. The taper relief rates are as follows (*IHTA 1984, s 7(4)*):

Table 12.1—Taper relief rates

Transfer:	3–4 years before death: rate reduced to:	80%
	4–5 years before death:	60%
	5–6 years before death:	40%
	6–7 years before death:	20%

IHT at full death rates is calculated at the time of death on any PETs made within seven years prior to death, subject to the availability of taper relief. The value of the transfer stays the same for taper relief purposes, but the full rate(s) of IHT charged are reduced by taper relief.

12.3 Tax on chargeable lifetime transfers is calculated at lifetime rates. If the transferor dies within seven years, the tax is recomputed at full death rates, subject to taper relief where the death is more than three years after the gift, but using the rates in force at the date of death.

However, if IHT on a chargeable lifetime transfer is recalculated on death with taper relief and produces a lower tax figure than the tax originally calculated at lifetime rates, no IHT repayments will result from the application of taper relief (*IHTA 1984, s 7(5)*).

Example 12.1—Taper relief on PETs made within seven years of death

In September 2012 Alice made a gift of £110,000 to her son Alistair. In October 2012 she made a gift of £110,000 to her daughter Jennifer. Alice then decided to give her second son James £115,000 in November 2012 and in December 2014 she gave her youngest daughter Eleanor £110,000.

Alice died in June 2018, so all four PETs become chargeable transfers. No annual exemptions are available, as Alice used them each Christmas to make gifts to the grandchildren.

Alistair's and Jennifer's gifts escape a charge to IHT, as they are within the nil rate band of £325,000. The IHT payable by James and Eleanor will be calculated as follows:

	£
James's gift	115,000
Available nil rate band 2018/9 (£325,000 – £220,000)	105,000
Taxable gift	10,000

Tax charge @ 40%	4,000
Taper to 40%	1,600
James' IHT liability therefore will be £1,600	
Eleanor's gift	110,000
The nil rate band has been used up, therefore available NRB	0
Taxable gift	110,000
Tax charge @ 40%	44,000
Taper to 80%	35,200
Eleanor's IHT liability therefore will be £35,200	

Example 12.2—Taper relief on chargeable lifetime transfers made within seven years of death

In July 2013 Alice's husband Felix made a potentially exempt transfer of £200,000 to his daughter Jennifer. He made a transfer to a discretionary trust of £500,000 in September 2014 and IHT at the lifetime rate of 20% was paid on this chargeable transfer. Felix died in August 2018 having made no other lifetime transfers. No annual exemptions are available, as Felix used these to make annual gifts to his grandchildren.

The IHT on the transfer to the discretionary trust payable during Felix's life is calculated as follows:

	£
Gift to discretionary trust	500,000
Deduct:	
Nil rate band 2014/15	325,000
	175,000
IHT payable at the lifetime rate of 20%	35,000

Following Felix's death the PET to Jennifer in July 2013 will become chargeable. This will use up any available annual exemptions and part of the nil rate band. The additional IHT on the chargeable lifetime transfer to the discretionary trust is calculated as follows. The IHT on the trust at death rates is:

(£500,000 – (£325,000 – £200,000)) × 40% = £150,000.

This is now subject to taper relief at the rate of 80%.

£150,000 × 80% = £120,000

From this must be deducted the lifetime IHT payment of £35,000 to arrive at additional IHT of £85,000 payable as a result of Felix's death.

QUICK SUCCESSION RELIEF

12.4 Quick succession relief (QSR) provides relief against two charges to IHT where there was more than one chargeable transfer within a five-year period (*IHTA 1984, s 141*).

QSR is given on death, where the value of a person's estate was increased by a chargeable transfer made within the previous five years. The previous chargeable transfer may have been made *inter vivos*, or on death. The property subject to the first chargeable transfer does not have to be part of the deceased's estate for the relief to apply, ie it may have been given away by the deceased, but still form part of the deceased's estate for IHT as a chargeable PET.

12.5 In relation to settled property, the relief is only available where the later transfer is of settled property and the transferor had an interest in possession in the property under the pre-*Finance Act 2006* rules. In relation to settlements the relief can be granted on death and *inter vivos* transfers.

QSR reduces the tax payable on the later transfer and the formula to calculate the relief can be found in *s 141(3)*. In essence it is calculated as follows:

$$\text{Percentage} \times \frac{(\text{Gross chargeable FT} - \text{Tax on FT})}{\text{Gross chargeable FT}} \times \text{Tax on FT}$$

FT = First transfer

The percentages for the periods between transfers are as follows:

- 100% if the period beginning with the date of the first transfer and ending with the date of the later transfer does not exceed one year.
- 80% if it exceeds one year, but does not exceed two years.
- 60% if it exceeds two years, but does not exceed three years.
- 40% if it exceeds three years, but does not exceed four years.
- 20% if it exceeds four years.

Example 12.3—QSR in action

On 1 July 2015 Anna's father Fred gifted Anna £40,000 (his favourite son Freddie having received a gift of £400,000 earlier in the year). Anna's father died shortly afterwards and Anna paid IHT of £16,000 on the failed potentially exempt transfer received from her father.

Anna's mother died on 15 June 2016 and Anna was entitled to an interest in possession (also called 'immediate post-death interest') in her mother's estate. Her mother had a net estate of £450,000 on which IHT of £50,000 ((£450,000 – £325,000) ´ 40%) was paid.

On 1 June 2018 Anna dies leaving assets valued at £500,000, which pass to her nephews and nieces. Her life interest in her mother's estate passes to her brother James and is valued at £275,000.

IHT on Anna's estate (before QSR):	£
Free estate	500,000
Settled property	275,000
Anna's estate	775,000
Deduct	
Nil rate band (2018/19)	325,000
Taxable estate	450,000
IHT payable @ 40%	180,000

Quick succession relief

The PET from Fred was made more than two years but less than three years before Anna's death and therefore quick succession relief of 60% applies.

$$60\% \times \frac{(£40{,}000 - £16{,}000)}{£40{,}000} \times £16{,}000 = £5{,}760$$

Anna's mother died more than one year but less than two years before Anna's death and therefore quick succession relief of 80% applies.

$$80\% \times \frac{(£450{,}000 - £50{,}000)}{£450{,}000} \times £50{,}000 = £35{,}556$$

Tax payable on Anna's death

		£
IHT on Anna's estate		180,000
Deduct		
	Quick succession relief on PET from Fred	5,760
	Quick succession relief on life interest	35,556
Total IHT payable		138,684

RELATED PROPERTY RELIEF

12.6 If property was valued on death as 'related property' under *IHTA 1984, s 161* (see **6.6** as to the valuation of 'related property') and is sold within three years at less than that valuation, a claim can be made to substitute that valuation with the value it would have been had it not been determined together with the related property or the other property in the estate (*IHTA 1984, s 176*). The following conditions must be complied with for the relief to apply (*IHTA 1984, s 176(3)*):

- the vendors are the persons in whom the property vested immediately after the death, or are the personal representatives of the deceased;
- the sale is at arm's length, for a price freely negotiated, and is separate from any sale of related property;
- no vendor (or any person having an interest in the sale proceeds) is, or is connected with, any purchaser (or any person having an interest in the purchase); and
- neither the vendors nor anyone having an interest in the sale proceeds obtain, in connection with the sale, a right to acquire the property sold or any interest in or created out of it.

12.7 Where the relevant property consists of shares in or securities of a close company, the relief is not available if, at any time between the death and the qualifying sale, the value of the shares or securities is reduced by more than 5% as a result of an alteration in the company's share or loan capital or in any rights attaching to shares in or securities of the company (*IHTA 1984, s 176(5)*). This provision was introduced as an anti-avoidance measure.

The relief is given only if claimed, and the claim must be made within four years after the date on which the IHT was paid, with effect from 1 April 2011 (*IHTA 1984, s 241*). Prior to that date, the time limit was six years.

The two examples below illustrate related property relief.

Example 12.4—Related property relief (I)

Husband owns land worth £15,000 and his wife owns adjoining land worth £25,000.

The combined value is £80,000.

The related property value of the husband's land is calculated as follows:

$$\frac{15{,}000}{15{,}000 + 25{,}000} \times £80{,}000 = £30{,}000$$

The above calculation was made to ascertain the value of the husband's land following his death. The husband's property is sold for £20,000 within three years of his death, so a claim can be made to substitute the value of £30,000 with £15,000.

Example 12.5—Related property relief (II)

On the husband's death on 31 October 2018, the share capital of a private property investment company was held as follows:

Issued share capital – 10,000 shares		
Husband	4,000	40%
Wife	4,000	40%
Others (employees)	2,000	20%
	10,000	100%

The value of an 80% holding is £80,000, while the value of a 40% holding is £24,000. In his will, the husband left his 4,000 shares to his daughter.

The related property rules apply to aggregate the shares of:

Husband	4,000
Wife	4,000
Related property	8,000

Chargeable transfer on legacy to daughter

IHT value of 8,000 shares (80%)	£80,000
IHT value attributed to legacy of husband's shares	$\frac{4{,}000}{8{,}000} \times £80{,}000 = £40{,}000$

> **Focus**
>
> - In **Example 12.5** above if the 4,000 shares are sold within three years of the husband's death for less than £40,000, a claim can be made to substitute the value of £40,000 with £24,000 to reclaim some of the IHT paid.
> - A detailed calculation will assist when deciding which action to take.
> - Advice from a share valuation specialist or suitably qualified accountant may be required.

TRANSFERS WITHIN SEVEN YEARS BEFORE DEATH

The relief

12.8 Where market conditions have changed following a PET or a chargeable transfer and the value of the property transferred is less at the time of the transferor's death (or on a prior sale by the transferee or his spouse) than at the time of his gift, relief is available in certain circumstances when computing the IHT or additional IHT, so that the tax or additional tax is charged on the reduced value (*IHTA 1984, s 131*).

The relief is available in the following circumstances:

- tax or additional tax is chargeable on the value transferred by a chargeable transfer or a potentially exempt transfer because of the transferor's death within seven years of the transfer; and
- all or part of the value transferred is attributable to the value of property which, at the date of the death, remains the property of the transferee or of his spouse, or has before the date of the death been sold by the transferee or his spouse by a qualifying sale.

12.9 For the purposes of the relief, it is important that:

- any transaction was an arm's length transaction for a price freely negotiable at the time of the sale; and
- the vendor (or any person having an interest in the proceeds of the sale) is not the same as or connected with the purchaser (or any person having an interest in the purchase); and
- no provision is made, in or in connection with the agreement for the sale, that the vendor (or any person having an interest in the proceeds of sale) is to have any right to acquire some or all of the property sold or some interest in or created out of it.

In order to avoid giving too much relief, there is a special rule for calculating the relief where the property also qualifies for business or agricultural relief. In this case the market values of the transferred property on the two dates that are compared to establish the reduction in value must be taken as reduced by the percentage appropriate to any available business or agricultural relief.

12.10 When valuing property transferred in order to ascertain whether relief should become available, no account should be taken of the related property under *IHTA, s 161* or property passing under another title with which it was originally valued (IHTM14626).

In the case of a transfer that was immediately chargeable at lifetime rates, the relief does not give rise to a repayment or remission of the tax that has already become payable during the transferor's life.

The relief also does not apply where the property has before the death been given away by the transferee or his spouse.

Wasting assets

12.11 The relief is not available if the transferred property is tangible movable property which is a wasting asset, such as a motor car (*IHTA 1984, s 132*). An asset is a wasting asset if immediately before the chargeable transfer it had a predictable useful life not exceeding 50 years having regard to the purpose for which it was used by the transferor.

Plant and machinery is always regarded as a wasting asset unless it is incorporated in the structure of the building, in which case it is immovable property.

'Fall in value' relief

12.12 Relief will only be given in respect of a fall in the value of shares or securities because of adverse market conditions. Therefore, if the value of the shares fell subsequent to capital payments, calls and corporate reorganisations, the relief will not be available. This prevents the relief being available if the value of the shares has been reduced deliberately by making capital payments by the company to its shareholders.

Example 12.6—Fall in value of property and shares

Mr Jones died on 8 June 2018. He made two PETs which are now chargeable to IHT. On 1 July 2014 he gifted a property, valued at £500,000, to his daughter Alice. On 1 July 2015 he passed his shares in ABC plc (BPR is not available) to his son Thomas. The shares were valued at £250,000.

Unfortunately, both investments have fallen in value since the PETs were made. When the assets were revalued on Mr Jones's death, it transpires that the property is only worth £450,000 and the shares are worth £125,000.

IHT payable on the PETs that are now chargeable is calculated as follows:

		£
PET of property to Alice		500,000
Deduct		
Annual exemptions (2013/14 and 2014/15)		6,000
Fall in value		50,000
		444,000
Deduct: Nil rate band (2018/19)		325,000
Chargeable to IHT		119,000
PET of shares to Thomas		250,000
Deduct		
Annual exemption (2015/16)		3,000
Fall in value		125,000
Chargeable to IHT		122,000
Total value of PETs		241,000
IHT payable	(£241,000 @ 40%)	96,400

Apportionment of tax:

PET of property to Alice $96{,}400 \times \frac{119{,}000}{241{,}000}$ =£47,600

PET of shares to Thomas $96{,}400 \times \frac{122{,}000}{241{,}000}$ = 48,800

The overall IHT saving in this example is £70,000. The relief can be extremely valuable in times when house prices and/or share prices fall.

Setting aside PETs and chargeable transfers

12.13 In exceptional circumstances PETs may be set aside, as was the case in *Griffiths (Deceased): Ogden and another v Trustees of the RHS Griffiths 2003 Settlement and others* [2008] STC 2008. Mr Griffiths made gifts in April 2003 and February 2004. However later in 2004 he was diagnosed with terminal cancer and died in April 2005 as a result of which both PETs failed. The High Court decided that the later gift was to be set aside on the grounds of mistake. Lewison J said that 'The operative mistake must, in my judgment, be a mistake which existed at the time when the transaction was entered into.'

Strangely, HMRC did not contest this case, especially as the tax at stake was in excess of £1 million. In cases where the deceased died unexpectedly after having made substantial PETs it may be worthwhile considering whether they can be set aside, but it is uncertain whether the lenient approach in *Griffiths* will be repeated.

In *Pitt and another v Holt and another* [2010] EWHC 45 (Ch) the second defendant was HMRC, taking an interest in opposing the reliance of the receiver under the Mental Health Act 1983 on the *Hastings-Bass* principle. Mrs Pitt made a settlement on behalf of her husband but in so doing failed to take IHT into account and later regretted her action. The second claimant was the husband's executor. At first instance the judge held that the *Hastings-Bass* principle need not apply only to trustees: a receiver was in a similar position to a trustee, and exercised a fiduciary power. The critical point here was that it was for Mrs Pitt to decide whether or not it was in the interest of her late husband for her to pass his property to the trustees. The case fell squarely within the tests imposed in *Mettoy Pension Trustee v Evans* [1990] 1 WLR 1587 and in *Sieff v Fox* [2005] 1 WLR 3811. The transfer was set aside, but HMRC appealed.

On 9 March 2011 the Court of Appeal allowed the appeal in the combined appeal of *Pitt v Holt and Futter v Futter* [2011] EWCA Civ 197 in which the Court re-examined the scope and application of the rule in *Hastings-Bass*. It was held that in *Pitt v Holt* the resulting tax liability was not a mistake to the legal effect of the disposition but as to the consequences and therefore it was not a mistake that could invoke the equitable jurisdiction to set aside a voluntary disposition for mistake.

The taxpayers in *Pitt* appealed to the Supreme Court which allowed the appeal on the grounds of mistake and set aside the trust stating that she was intending to create 'precisely the sort of trust to which parliament intended to grant relief by s 89 IHTA 1984' (see *Pitt v HMRC* and *Futter v HMRC* [2013] UKSC 26). For a more detailed discussion see **14.10**.

In contrast the Supreme Court unanimously dismissed the appeal in *Futter* stating that a Court should only intervene when trustees acted in such a way as to amount to a breach of their fiduciary duty. In this case the trustees' exercise of the power of advancement had been valid, but they relied on apparently competent professional advice which turned out to be wrong.

The ratio in *Pitt v Holt* was successfully relied upon in the recent case of *Freedman v Freedman others* [2015] EWHC 1457 (Ch). The settlement was set aside on the ground of equitable mistake as the solicitor had advised to transfer properties into an interest in possession trust in the mistaken belief that such transfer was a potentially exempt transfer and therefore escaped an immediate lifetime charge to IHT.

Rectification of a deed of variation which did not include the election that *IHTA 1984,s 142(1)* shall apply was ordered in the case of *Vaughan-Jones and another v Vaughan-Jones and others* [2015] EWHC 1086 (Ch).

Two recent cases where the High Court considered rectification are *RBC Trustees & Ors v Stubbs & Ors* [2017] EWHC 180 and *Bullard v Bullard and another* [2017] EWHC 3. The relaxed approach in these two cases suggests that relief may now be available in cases where unintended and disadvantageous tax consequences ensued as a result of trustees executing inept legal documents.

The HMRC Trusts and Estates newsletter in December 2016 includes guidance for agents who wish to contact HMRC prior to issuing proceedings for a trust law remedy in a court of equity for a claim of rectification, mistake or *Hastings-Bass*. The guidance states as follows:

> **'Rectification**
>
> Where it is claimed a deed contains an error or omission that means it doesn't properly reflect the parties' intentions, the parties may seek to have the deed rectified by a court.
>
> **Mistake**
>
> Individuals or trustees may claim that they have made a voluntary disposition under a mistake and seek an equitable remedy through a court.
>
> **Hastings-Bass**
>
> Where trustees act in error, with the result that they incur more tax than anticipated, the trustees may seek to overturn their actions through a court by invoking the principle in *Hastings-Bass*.
>
> In all these cases, the trustees may ask whether HMRC wants to be joined as a party to the proceedings.
>
> Any letters regarding rectification should be sent to:
>
> Trustsand Estates Technical
> HM Revenue and Customs
> Meldrum House
> 15 Drumsheugh Gardens
> Edinburgh
> EH3 7UL
>
> Any letters regarding mistakes should be sent to:
>
> Trusts and Estates Technical
> HM Revenue and Customs
> Fitzroy House
> Castle Meadow Road
> Nottingham
> NG2 1BD

Any letters regarding Hastings-Bass should be sent to:

Trusts and Estates Technical
HM Revenue and Customs
St John's House
Merton Road
Liverpool
L75 1BB

These addresses are to be used for contacting HMRC only before court proceedings are issued.'

Focus

Advisers need to be aware that the Court of Appeal's decision may put strict limits on the rule in *Hastings-Bass* and its future application.

However, a number of recent cases successfully relied on the grounds of equitable mistake rectifying deeds or setting aside transactions which resulted in avoidable tax charges.

POST-DEATH RELIEFS

Post-death relief: shares (IHTA 1984, ss 178–189)

12.14 When 'qualifying investments' (quoted shares and securities, holdings in an authorised unit trust and shares in a common investment fund (ie funds managed by the Public Trustee)) are sold within 12 months after death for less than their probate valuation on death, the personal representative, or anyone else who is liable to pay the IHT on the shares, may claim a repayment for IHT. The shares or securities must be listed on the Stock Exchange, so the relief does not apply to private company shares. Incidental costs of sale cannot be deducted.

All the investments sold within 12 months after death have to be taken into account, when the relief is claimed. Therefore, where investments have fallen in value since date of death, and where the relief would affect the amount of IHT payable, a personal representative should review the estate portfolio in good time before the 12-month period expires and:

- consider selling within 12 months of the death all holdings of quoted shares and holdings in authorised unit trusts and shares in any common investment fund ('qualifying investments') which have dropped in value since the death;
- keep qualifying investments which have risen in value since the death.

12.15 The relief is also available for shares, which are cancelled without replacement within 12 months of death, when the deemed sale value will be a nominal consideration of £1 at the date of cancellation. If shares are suspended within 12 months of death and remain suspended on the first anniversary of death, relief can be claimed on a deemed sale of the suspended investment at the value immediately before the first anniversary.

If during the 12-month period, the personal representative purchases qualifying investments, the original loss on sale relief is reduced proportionately. The reduction on the original relief is calculated as follows (*IHTA 1984, s 180(1)*):

$$\frac{\text{Value of reinvestment}}{\text{Sales proceeds}} \times \text{Original reduction in value}$$

12.16 The probate value of each of the investments sold will have to be adjusted both for inheritance tax and capital gains tax to the gross sale proceeds, plus the relevant proportion in the fall in value.

Example 12.7—Sale of shares by PRs

Anna Williams died on 31 January 2017 leaving a share portfolio to her nephews and nieces. A number of shares have fallen in value and the PRs decided to sell those shares and to claim the relief.

The probate value of the shares sold was £100,000, while the sale proceeds were only £25,000.

The executors purchased a new holding in A plc for £15,000 on 31 March 2017.

The estate included shares in B plc, which had a probate value of £1,000, but they were cancelled on 1 April 2017.

The shares in C plc, which had a probate value of £2,500, were suspended on 1 December 2016. On 31 January 2018 these shares were still suspended with an estimated value of £99.

		£
Value of investments at probate value:		
	Shares which have fallen in value	100,000
	B plc	1,000
	C plc	2,500
	Probate value	103,500
Sales proceeds		

	Shares which have fallen in value	25,000
	B plc (deemed value of £1)	1
	C plc (estimated value of £99)	99
	Sales proceeds	25,100
Reduction in estate's value		78,400

Therefore, the executors would initially be able to claim a reduction of £78,400.

However, following the purchase of the shares in A plc, the 'reduction in the estate's value' will be restricted as follows:

$$\frac{15,000}{25,000} \times £78,400 = £46,853$$

The total relief claimed is therefore £31,547 (£78,400 – £46,853).

Post-death relief: land (ss 190–198)

12.17 Similar to the relief on quoted securities, where an 'interest in land' is sold within three years of death, a claim can be made by the personal representatives to substitute the sale value with the probate value using Form IHT38. *IHTA 1984, s 197A* introduced a restriction for sale in that the election is not available for sales in the fourth year, if the sale value would exceed the probate value.

Following *Jones (Ball's Administrators) v IRC* [1997] STC 358, exchange of contracts does not qualify as a sale for this relief.

No claim can be made if:

- the sale value differs from the value on death by less than the lower of £1,000 and 5% of the value on death (*IHTA 1984, s 191(2)*);
- the sale is by a personal representative or trustee to the following:
  - a person, who, at any time between death and sale, has been beneficially entitled to, or has an interest in possession in, property comprising the interest sold, or
  - the spouse, child or remoter descendant of such a person, or
  - a trustee of a settlement under which such a person has an interest in possession in property comprising the interest sold;

- the vendor obtains a right in connection with the sale to acquire the interest sold or any other interest in the same land (*IHTA 1984, s 191(3)*).

12.18 If an estate comprises a number of interests in land, the loss relief claim cannot be made until four months have elapsed from the date of sale of the last interest in land, as there is the possibility of further purchases of land. If an estate only has one interest in land, the relief is available and HMRC Inheritance Tax will make a provisional payment of tax, but HMRC will not issue a certificate of discharge until the expiry of the statutory four-month time limit.

Expenses of sale, ie estate agent fees or legal fees cannot be deducted.

Example 12.8—Sale of land interests by PRs

Peter's estate (he died on 31 January 2015) includes four parcels of land.

The probate value of the land is as follows:

	£
Blackacre	100,000
Whiteacre	150,000
Greenacre	300,000
Peter's home	500,000
	1,050,000

In the four years since Peter's death, his executors sell all his interests in the above land. On 5 May 2017 a compulsory purchase order was made to purchase Peter's home to build a by-pass. The acquisition of Peter's home is finalised on 15 February 2019 and the executors receive £400,000. (Expenses of sale cannot be deducted):

	£
Blackacre sold 1 July 2015	99,100
Whiteacre sold 15 December 2017	125,000
Greenacre sold 1 February 2018	300,100
Peter's home sold 15 February 2019	400,000
	924,200

The claim

The sale of Blackacre is disregarded in the claim, as the loss on sale (£900) is less than 5% of £100,000 (£5,000) and is lower than £1,000.

Greenacre will be disregarded because it is sold in the fourth year since Peter's death and the sale proceeds are larger than the probate value.

The loss on Peter's home following the compulsory purchase order however can be included in the claim, as the compulsory purchase order was made within three years of Peter's death, although it was finalised more than four years after his death.

The overall allowable reduction therefore is £125,000 (£25,000 for Whiteacre and £100,000 for Peter's home).

If the executors purchase further interests in land within a period beginning with the death and ending four months after the date of the last sale, the available relief has to be reduced. Unlike for the relief on quoted securities, one has to revisit each interest to recalculate the relief, which is complex and beyond the scope of this book.

If the land sold was held in joint ownership and a discount of between 10 and 15% was allowed on this joint interest, care needs to be taken when making a loss relief claim, as the discount does not apply post-sale.

Example 12.9—Loss of relief claim and discount on joint ownership

Suzy and Fiona are sisters, both widowed. They decide to purchase a property which they both occupy and own jointly. On Suzy's death the property is valued at £500,000, before any discounts, and it passes to Fiona. Suzy's half share is valued at £250,000 and after the 10% discount, the value for IHT purposes is £225,000. Fiona, who cannot look after herself any longer, sells the property for £470,000. Suzy's estate's half share of the sale proceeds is £235,000. If a loss relief claim is submitted, the discount is disapplied and there will be IHT due of the additional £10,000 above the discounted value of £225,000.

DOUBLE TAXATION RELIEF

Introduction

12.19 Double taxation of gifts and inheritances can arise in a number of ways, and knowledge of the relevant provisions will become more relevant given the increase in the ownership of foreign property and the number of UK-domiciled persons moving abroad.

Below are a few examples where double charges to IHT may arise:

- A UK-domiciled person who makes a gift of a foreign asset may be liable to a foreign gift tax on the disposal and may also be liable to IHT in the UK either immediately if it is a chargeable transfer or, if the gift is a potentially exempt transfer, on his death within seven years.
- A person not domiciled in the UK may be liable to IHT in the UK, as well as gift tax or inheritance tax in his own country, if he dies while owning assets situated in the UK.
- A UK-domiciled person moving abroad with the intention of living there permanently remains UK domiciled for at least three years (*IHTA 1984, s 267(1)*), and therefore remains subject to IHT on his estate wherever it is situated. This is likely to increase to five years from 6 April 2017. Should he die during that period he may be liable both to IHT in the UK and to foreign estate tax in his country of residence.
- Similarly, a non-UK domiciled individual who has been resident in the UK for at least 17 of the last 20 tax years (the Government proposes to reduce these rules to 15 of the last 20 years from 6 April 2017) and who goes to live abroad permanently may be deemed to be domiciled in the UK for up to three years (increasing to five years from 6 April 2017) following his departure. Should he die during this period, his estate may be liable both to IHT in the UK and IHT in his country of residence.

12.20 Where IHT is chargeable in the UK and a similar tax is charged by another country on the same property, relief may be available in two ways:

- under the specific terms of a double tax agreement between UK and that country, following *IHTA 1984, s 158*; or
- under the unilateral double tax relief provisions in the UK legislation under *IHTA 1984, s 159*.

Double taxation agreements

12.21 The following countries have entered into double taxation agreements with the UK:

- France (*SI 1963/1319*);
- India (*SI 1956/998*);
- Italy (*SI 1968/304*);
- Ireland (*SI 1978/1107*);
- the Netherlands (*SI 1980/706* and *SI 1996/730*);
- Pakistan (*SI 1957/1522*);
- South Africa (*SI 1979/576*);

- Sweden (*SI 1981/840* and *SI 1989/986*);
- Switzerland (*SI 1957/426* and *SI 1994/3214*); and
- USA (*SI 1979/1454*).

Under these treaties, the country in which the transferor was domiciled is generally entitled to tax his whole estate. The other country is usually restricted to tax the property situated in that country, for example, land and buildings. Relief is then available on the double taxation of the same property.

Care ought to be taken, as some double tax agreements override the deemed domicile rules in *IHTA 1984, s 267* (see **2.9**).

Unilateral relief by UK

12.22 In the absence of double tax agreements, relief may be obtained by means of a credit for the foreign tax charged against the UK inheritance tax. This relief may also be important in cases where it is greater than the relief obtained under a double taxation agreement (*IHTA 1984, s 159*).

Unfortunately, in cases where the overseas tax suffered exceeded the UK liability before relief, no IHT will be payable in the UK, but the excess would not be repayable.

DOUBLE CHARGES RELIEF

12.23 The *Inheritance Tax (Double Charges Relief) Regulations, SI 1987/1130* prevent a person being charged IHT twice on the same property in various circumstances, where the event or transfer occurred after 17 March 1986.

Double charges relief applies in the following circumstances:

- where someone has made a lifetime transfer which following his death is a chargeable transfer and he has subsequently been given back the property comprised in the transfer (eg under the will of the donee) and he still owns the property on his death; or
- where someone has made a gift with reservation where the original gift was or turns out to be a chargeable transfer and the property comprised in the gift is also charged to IHT as property subject to a reservation; or
- where someone has died owing a debt which is wholly or partly non-deductible under *FA 1986, s 103* and has made a lifetime transfer to the person to whom the debt was owed which was or turns out to be chargeable.

The *Inheritance Tax (Double Charges Relief) Regulations* are complicated, partly because of the extensive use of cross-references. The *Schedule* to the

Regulations therefore includes helpful examples of how they are supposed to operate.

WOODLANDS RELIEF

The relief

12.24 An election can be made which enables the IHT chargeable on death in respect of growing timber and underwood to be deferred until sale. The relief is only available on death and does not extend to the IHT in respect of the land upon which the trees are growing.

Following *IHTA 1984, s 125(1)* certain conditions need to apply for woodlands relief to be available:

- the woodland must be based in the UK or, following *FA 2009*, elsewhere in the EEA; and
- the woodland does not qualify for agricultural property relief under *IHTA 1984, s 115(2)*. The District Valuer will be able to advise on this point; and
- the deceased must have owned the land throughout the five years up to his death or have acquired the land otherwise than for consideration in money or money's worth, ie through inheritance or gift; and
- an election for relief must be made in writing to HMRC within two years of the death or such longer time as they may allow.

The relief is given by leaving the value of the timber out of account in determining the value transferred on death. The value of the timber is then not taxed until the timber, or any interest in it, is disposed of.

Calculation of IHT on disposals of trees or underwood

12.25 Where woodlands relief has been given on death, if the whole or any part of the trees or underwood is disposed of, IHT is charged on the following amounts:

- if the disposal is a sale for full consideration in money or money's worth, on the net proceeds of the sale; and
- in any other case, on the net value, at the time of the disposal, of the trees or underwood.

The IHT is chargeable at the rate or rates at which it would have been chargeable on the death if that amount, and any amount on which IHT was previously chargeable in relation to the death, had been included in the value transferred on the death, and the amount on which the IHT is chargeable had formed the highest part of that value.

References to the net proceeds of sale or the net value of any trees or underwood are references to the proceeds of sale or value after deduction of any expenses allowable in *IHTA 1984, s 130(2).*

Example 12.10—Sale of timber following woodlands relief claim

Alice died in June 2017 leaving a net estate of £1,000,000, which included woodlands worth £500,000, of which £200,000 related to the land on which they stood (the value of the timber is £300,000). Her nil rate band was not available. Alice left her estate to her son Benedict, who elected for woodlands relief. In August 2019, Benedict sold timber from the woodlands for £500,000, incurring costs for felling of £100,000, sales commission of £10,000, and replanting expenses of £75,000.

The IHT chargeable on the death of Alice was £280,000 (Alice's taxable estate was £700,000 (ie £1,000,000 less value of the timber £300,000)). On the sale of the timber by Benedict, further IHT becomes payable as follows:

Gross proceeds of sale	£500,000
Deduct: Expenses incurred in disposal:	
Felling	£100,000
Sales commission	£10,000
Expenses incurred in replanting	£75,000
	£185,000
Net proceeds of sale (£500,000 – £185,000)	£315,000
The IHT chargeable on the disposal is calculated:	
IHT on £315,000 @ 40%	£126,000

Planning

12.26 Woodlands relief is generally less attractive than BPR, as it only postpones an IHT liability. Therefore, if the woodlands are managed on a commercial basis and if the other conditions for BPR are satisfied (see **Chapter 13**), one should apply for BPR rather than woodlands relief.

If BPR is not available it may, in certain circumstances, still be a difficult choice whether to make an election for woodlands relief or not:

- Where the woodland passes under the will to a spouse or to a charity, an election will not be appropriate, as the woodland will be exempt for IHT purposes in any event.
- If someone dies leaving a life interest in woodland to an elderly relative, whose estate (excluding the woodland) is just below the nil rate band, and there is little chance of a disposal during the elderly relative's lifetime, it may be better to defer the payment of IHT to avoid a charge to IHT.
- On the other hand, if someone dies leaving newly planted woodlands with a low value to a minor beneficiary, and the IHT rate is low (or nil) it would be better to pay a small amount of tax (or no tax), rather than elect and chance a much larger charge especially if the woodland is expected to increase in value.

In most cases, therefore, it is necessary to weigh the cash-flow advantages of an election and the possibility of avoiding the payment of tax altogether, against the possibility of having to pay a much larger amount of tax at the deceased's top tax rate on a greatly enhanced value at some future date.

HERITAGE PROPERTY

12.27 On certain conditions transfers of national heritage property (eg works of art, print or scientific objects) can be exempted from IHT (*IHTA 1984, s 30*). This conditional exemption applies to transfers of value made in lifetime and on death as well as to settled property. The conditional exemption cannot be claimed in relation to a potentially exempt transfer, unless and until the transferor dies within seven years of the transfer and it becomes a chargeable transfer.

The relief works as follows:

- An application for conditional exemption is made to HMRC within two years of the transfer, or within two years of death of the transferor.
- HMRC designate the property as 'heritage property' under *IHTA 1984, s 31*.
- An undertaking has to be given by a person HMRC consider appropriate, usually the transferor or personal representative.
- Death, disposal or a breach of the undertaking can be a chargeable event giving rise to a claim for IHT (*IHTA 1984, s 32*) (IHTM04115).

12.28 The following objects can be 'designated' as 'heritage property' within the conditional exemption:

(a) any relevant object which appears to HMRC to be pre-eminent for its national, scientific, historic or artistic interest;

(b) any collection or group of relevant objects which, taken as a whole, appears to HMRC to be pre-eminent for its national, scientific, historic or artistic interest;

(c) any land which in the opinion of HMRC is of outstanding scenic or historic or scientific interest;

(d) any building for the preservation of which special steps should in the opinion of HMRC be taken by reason of its outstanding historic or architectural interest;

(e) any area of land which in the opinion of HMRC is essential for the protection of the character and amenities of such a building;

(f) any object which in the opinion of HMRC is historically associated with such a building as is mentioned in (d) above.

12.29 In addition to the designation by HMRC, it is necessary for an undertaking to be given by the transferee – that is, the intended beneficial owner. Where the property will be subject to a trust, the trustee is also required to give the undertaking. With regard to pictures, prints, books, manuscripts, works of art, scientific collections and other things not producing income, the requisite undertaking is that, until the person beneficially entitled to the property dies or the property is disposed of, whether by sale or gift or otherwise:

- the property will be kept permanently in the UK and will not leave it temporarily except for a purpose and a period approved by HMRC; and
- steps will be taken for the preservation of the property and for securing reasonable access to the public, as agreed between HMRC and the person giving the undertaking.

12.30 The requirement of access to the public can give rise to considerable expense and difficulty where the objects are kept in a private house or flat. Where an undertaking is given after 30 July 1998, the steps agreed for securing reasonable access to the public must ensure that the access that is secured is not confined to an appointment-only basis. Although this only applies to post-*FA 1998* undertakings, it should be noted that *FA 1998* also introduces provision for pre-*FA 1998* undertakings to be varied so that there is public access without prior appointment.

The provisions *of IHTA 1984 Sch 6, para 4(2)* have been amended so that where the conditional exemption under *IHTA 1984, s 30* is granted on death, this will no longer make absolute an earlier exemption under the old estate duty regime. From 16 March 2016 HMRC will have the choice of raising either estate duty or IHT where the chargeable event happened on death. An amendment was also made to *FA 1930, s 40(2)* to bring in a charge on objects which have been exempted from Estate Duty but which have been lost. This is subject to HMRC's discretion not to levy a charge, where the loss is not due to the negligence of the owner. In essence the same approach will apply as is currently in place in the case for conditional exemption from IHT.

This is a specialised topic and the general practitioner is referred to specialist books on the subject and in particular to the decision of the Special Commissioner in the case of *Re an application to vary the undertakings of A; Re an application to vary the undertakings of B* [2004] SpC 439; [2005] STC (SCD) 103. There is also some useful information on tax-exempt heritage assets on HMRC's website.

Chapter 13

Business property relief and agricultural property relief

SIGNPOSTS

- **Scope** – An understanding of the broad scope of these headline reliefs and in particular when they apply, when they overlap, and when they fall into breach, is critical to any tax planning routine (see **13.1; 13.24**).
- **BPR and the business** – The differing treatment applied to a business structure must be appreciated to determine the applicable rate and preserve continuing access to BPR (see **13.3–13.4; 13.6; 13.21**).
- **Qualification** – The basic rules of ownership, usage, classification, sale and replacement must be continually monitored to ensure compliance (see **13.9–13.16; 13.36–13.39; 13.49**).
- **APR and the farmhouse** – The rules in this area are complex and confusing with interpretation subject to change – an awareness of case law is crucial (see **13.27–13.28; 13.31–13.34**).

SCOPE OF BUSINESS PROPERTY RELIEF

Unincorporated businesses

13.1 In the past it had always been considered that *IHTA 1984, s 105(1)(a)* confined relief to a 'business or an interest in a business' and in October 2012 HMRC published draft legislation to extend business property relief to businesses carrying on the business of a market maker, as defined within the Markets in Financial Instruments Directive (2004/39/EC). Notwithstanding this, a further reading of *IHTA 1984, s 105* suggested that this should be interpreted as referring to an unincorporated business with that focus centred on the business itself rather than the underlying assets. The position was unequivocally clarified by the case of *HMRC v Trustees of the Nelson Dance Family Settlement*: [2009] EWHC 71 (Ch) see **13.7** below.

Section 105(3) of *IHTA 1984* excludes investment-type businesses. In this respect property management itself may be a business, but only where the business is the supply of the service of management rather than the more passive management of assets belonging to that business – the distinction is fine but critical: see *Clark and Southern (Clark's executors) v HMRC* [2005] SpC 502; [2005] SSCD 823, *Trustees of the Zetland Settlement v HMRC* [2013] UKFTT 284 (TC), and more recently *Best v HMRC* [2014] UKFTT 77 (TC). Equally farming is a business, but it must be appreciated that where such activity is confined to passively managing land so as to produce a crop of grass, then that too is an investment-type business: see *McCall and Keenan v Revenue and Customs Commissioners* [2009] NICA 12 examined in greater detail at **13.14**.

The businesses of authors, painters, sculptors, musicians, and similar merit special attention because it is arguable that the income from copyright is not the business itself, but income from an investment asset. IHTM25152 requires Inspectors to refer such cases to Technical Group for guidance. Where the ongoing business is the exploitation of existing work it may be possible to show that it outlives the originator, for example where executors go to great lengths to ensure that a musician's catalogue or an author's works are regularly performed in order to encourage the fresh flow of royalties to the estate, ie the novels of Agatha Christie to include the Poirot and Miss Marple 'adventures'.

Difficulties commonly arise because an enterprise may well be a business for the purposes of income tax, or CGT, but yet not qualify for BPR under the more narrow IHT code – an obvious example is lettings of holiday cottages where the activities supporting the income source are subject to critical review (see also **13.15** for discussion on the *Pawson* case and the more recent cases of *ACC Green v HMRC* [2015] UKFTT 0236 (TC)) and *Marjorie Ross (dec'd) v HMRC* [2017] UKFTT 507). Owning one holiday cottage, which is used by the family for the most popular weeks of the year and is otherwise occupied by friends on a 'break-even' basis, is not regarded as a business for the purposes of BPR. However, owning and managing a seasonal holiday park, providing for short lets and offering catering, entertainment and other ancillary services ie on site shop, may meet the criteria for relief.

Section 103(3) of *IHTA 1984,* demands that the business must be carried on for gain (although the profit motive is not a requisite for APR as demonstrated in the *Golding* case discussed at **13.35**) – and this is a pre-eminent qualification. Accordingly, the passive management of a collection of classic cars which are only occasionally exhibited or used for films etc. and produce an income stream which barely covers the costs of storage and insurance, is unlikely to qualify for BPR through lack of profit motive.

Note: All statutory references in this chapter are to *IHTA 1984* unless otherwise stated.

13.2

> **Focus**
>
> The transfer of 'mere' assets can qualify for BPR to the extent such assets are used in the business and that business continues post transfer.

Until the decision in the *Nelson Dance* case it was widely thought and indeed generally accepted within professional circles that an interest in a business did not include a 'mere asset': see **13.7** below. A business may still exist even where a trade, even the principal trade, has been sold: see *Brown's Executors v IRC* [1996] STC (SCD) 277. The interest of a partner is an interest in the business unless and until the partner retires (see *Beckman v IRC* [2000] SSCD 59), whereupon the value of that partnership interest becomes a mere loan to the business that attracts no relief.

The position in relation to Lloyd's underwriters is complicated but may be summarised by the general principle that the assets that are actually at risk will qualify for BPR, whereas assets that secure a guarantee but far exceed in value the amount needed to support that guarantee will not so qualify. See, for example, *IRC v Mallender (Drury-Lowe's Executors)* [2001] STC 514 and in relation to the treatment of losses see *Hardcastle (Vernede's Executors) v IRC* [2000] STC (SCD) 532.

13.3 *Section 267A* of *IHTA 1984* governs the treatment of limited liability partnerships (LLPs) introduced by the *Limited Liability Partnerships Act 2000* with affect from 6 April 2001. Thus:

- Property belonging to the partnership is treated as the property of its members.
- Property occupied or used by the limited liability partnership is treated as occupied or used by the members.
- Business carried on by the limited liability partnership is treated as carried on in partnership by the members.
- An incorporation of the limited liability partnership is treated in the same way as formation of partnership, and changes are treated as they would be for a partnership.
- A transfer of value made by a limited liability partnership is treated as a transfer by its members.
- A transfer of value to a limited liability partnership is treated as a transfer to the members of the partnership.

HMRC guidance on LLPs states the following in relation to BPR (see IHTM25094):

> '…an interest in a LLP is deemed to be an interest in each and every asset of the partnership, while an interest in a traditional partnership is a "chose in action", valued by reference to the net underlying assets of the business. This may require you to consider issues of situs of property. In cases of doubt refer to Technical Group (TG) for advice. However, in considering if an LLP is an investment business … you should look at the nature of the business underpinned by those assets, rather than the nature of the assets themselves, to see whether IHTA84/S105(3) is in point.
>
> There has been an increase in the use of LLPs in commercial structures, and sometimes there can be a different outcome for Business Relief purposes than that available from a conventional corporate structure. In the case of an LLP simply taking the place of a holding company, *S 267A* has the effect of preventing the LLP from benefitting from *s 105(4)(b)*. In cases where the LLP itself also carries on a qualifying business, the business may be regarded as a hybrid, and if the shares in the subsidiary companies are used in the business (rather than being held as investments), then it is possible that the interest in the LLP may qualify for relief if it does not fail the "wholly or mainly" test (IHTM25264). The question of whether an asset is used in the business or held as an investment will be highly fact specific…'

A Jersey LLP may be a partnership or a company (see *R v IRC ex p Bishop* [1999] STC 531). However, HMRC seem inclined to treat such LLPs as 'opaque' (see *Tax Bulletin* Issue 83 (June 2006)), which is more in the nature of a body corporate than a partnership but this view has yet to be tested.

In the past, if a family wanted HMRC clarification on the availability of BPR before entering into planning transactions, this was simply not available – HMRC were not resourced for that purpose. For example, if an estate was wholly covered by the spousal exemption such that no IHT was payable regardless of the nature of the assets, HMRC would not be drawn into considering if BPR was potentially in point as no IHT was at stake: see IHT Newsletter 25 August 2006. This uncertainty over BPR qualification or not put taxpayers and their advisers on the spot.

Example 13.1—Frustrated appropriation or variation

On her death in May 2018, Samantha's estate was left as to cash equal to the unused available nil rate band to her children with residue to her husband, Peregrine – Samantha had made no lifetime gifts. The estate included (unquoted) shares in a business which had originally specialised in the provision of sunbeds, reflexology and other lifestyle services. Over the years, the profits were reinvested in premises and latterly there has been some repositioning of the business with the result that part became franchised with many of the outlets occupied on short leases. The bulk of the profits now come in the form of rents and franchise fees with very little derived from hands-on work and it is with this backdrop that the satisfaction of the 'wholly or mainly' test is worrying the family: see **13.10** below.

If BPR is available, Peregrine would be happy to see the company shares, now worth approximately £700,000, allocated to the children instead of the lower cash sum; but if not he will take the shares and make lifetime gifts of those shares over time in the hope of meeting the seven year survival test. Well within the two year period required by *s 142*, half the shares (value of approximately £350,000) are redirected to the children pursuant to a valid deed of variation, which is lodged on the basis that if BPR is denied, IHT will be due: in effect asking for a ruling in circumstances where if there is no BPR the IHT in point will at worst be only £10,000 ((£350,000 – £325,000) @ 40%).

HMRC will probably not be drawn into considering the relief not least since the tax in issue, after the exercise of valuation, is marginal. Rather HMRC may seek to read the variation back into the will: take the view that what is given is initially the nil rate band with the excess representing a gift (PET) from Peregrine; and that they will examine the issue of relief on his death. It is not an ideal situation but the family must nail their colours to the mast and decide whether or not to transfer the rest of the company's shares to the children.

A limited but valuable form of help by way of clearance is now available in situations of genuine difficulty. The procedure is described by HMRC on their website (www.gov.uk/guidance/non-statutory-clearance-service-guidance) and requires an application, preferably by e-mail, with supporting information. The following information must be supplied:

- particulars of the applicant;
- IHT reference, if any;
- details of the business, including UTR or company registration number;
- details of interest in the business held;
- contact details;
- what the application is about;
- why the transaction arises;
- description of the proposed transaction;
- what HMRC are being asked to clear;
- likely date of the transaction;
- contingencies involved;

- how important tax is to the transaction;
- the reason for doing the deal this way;
- other related clearances;
- the commercial importance of the issue to the business;
- two years' business accounts;
- the legislation in point;
- the doubt as to the application of the legislation, with reference to published guidance and case law;
- legal advice obtained that the taxpayer is willing to disclose;
- details of previous HMRC advice.

The broad description of the service suggests that the process has limited application and is aimed predominantly at those cases of genuine difficulty – in essence it is no substitute for a thorough study of the law and of guidance as to its application. However, it is the experience of the author that applications, properly made and fully supported with appropriate documentation, are dealt with promptly and can give much valued certainty. Some practitioners may simply find the completion of the application for clearance a useful tool for considering the matter in more detail and that, having thought the issues through, it may not then be necessary to proceed with clearance.

On 13 June 2017 HMRC updated their general online guidance but also the Business Property Relief checklist (Annex C). The section 'When HMRC will not provide advice under this service' has been amended to state that HMRC will confirm the reason why advice requested has not been provided and listed examples include:

- where all necessary information has not been provided;
- HMRC do not consider there are genuine points of uncertainty;
- the advice requested amounts to tax planning advice or approval of tax planning products or arrangements;
- the application is about the treatment of transactions that HMRC considers are for the purpose of avoiding tax;
- HMRC is already checking the tax position for the period in question;
- any return for the period in question has become final;
- there is a statutory clearance procedure; and
- the advice sought relates to the application of the settlements legislation in *ITTOIA 2005, Pt 5, Ch 5* or the tax consequences of executing non-charitable trust deeds or settlements.

Annex C (BPR checklist) has been updated to make clear that it may not be used for gifts to individuals, ten-year anniversary charges, conditional dispositions of property under a will, deeds of variation, the tax consequences of executing a trust deed, the application of *ITTOIA 2005, Pt 5, Ch 5*, valuations, or general confirmations of the status of businesses for business property relief: see www.gov.uk/government/uploads/system/uploads/attachment_data/file/377648/annex-c.pdf).

Interests in companies

> **Focus**
>
> 'All that glitters is not gold'. The definition of 'unquoted' for BPR purposes is not as wide as may be first thought – whilst it includes shares quoted *solely* on the alternative investment market (AIM) it excludes those quoted on 'any recognised stock exchange'. It is therefore perfectly possible for such shares to 'drift in and out' of qualification with potentially costly IHT consequences.

13.4 The chief and most accessible category of property qualifying for BPR, see *IHTA 1984, s 105(1)(bb),* is 'any unquoted shares in a company' (but see **13.10** for a more detailed discussion on excluded activities). Other categories are mentioned below. For this purpose, 'shares' means any kind of share – this can include a preference share, but tax practitioners should take great care to draft the company documents in such a way as to ensure that the preference share has all the attributes of an ordinary share and is not really a loan to the company disguised as a share. There is no case directly in point but the drafting must be robust.

'Unquoted' for this purpose has a defined meaning, see *IHTA 1984, s 105(1ZA)* and whilst in relation to UK companies this will usually mean not quoted on the full list of the London Stock Exchange it will also require a non-listing on *any* recognised exchange. This has given rise to considerable investor interest in small companies in light of the trust reforms contained in *FA 2006* which now bring more trusts within the relevant property regime.

Income Tax Act 2007, s 1005 was amended with effect from 19 July 2007 so as to allow HMRC to regard as a 'recognised stock exchange' any investment exchange that the Financial Services Authority designates as a 'recognised investment exchange'. This power was exercised, for example, in relation to part, but not all, of the market formerly known as OFEX, now ISDX. The result is confusing: some shares on ISDX qualify for BPR, while others do not and as a consequence great care should be taken in this area.

Since 2013, HMRC designated the following as recognised stock exchanges for IHT purposes:

- The Channel Islands Securities Exchange Authority (20 December 2013);
- GXG Main Quote (23 September 2013);
- Global Board of Trade (30 July 2013);
- GXG Official List (16 May 2013);
- ICAP Securities & Derivatives Exchange Ltd (25 April 2013);
- European Wholesale Securities Market (18 January 2013);
- National Stock Exchange of Australia (19 June 2014);
- Singapore Exchange Securities Trading Limited (7 October 2014);
- Singapore Exchange Derivatives Trading Limited (7 October 2014);
- Euronext London (4 February 2015); and
- GSX Ltd (16 August 2016).

Example 13.2—Diversified investments

Richard dabbled in stock market investments. On his death on 20 May 2018 his estate included holdings in the following fictional companies:

Microworks

IBC

Notel

Café Direct

Churchill Ware

Abraham

Of these, the first three holdings are of shares listed on a 'recognised stock exchange'. Unless in each case the holding is sufficiently large to give control, the shares will not qualify for BPR.

The other three holdings may all qualify for the relief. Café Direct is traded only on ETHEX, a matched bargain exchange. Churchill Ware is only on the Alternative Investment Market (AIM). Abraham is only on the part of ISDX that is not a recognised exchange.

Provided these last three companies are not simply investment companies, then subject to the point mentioned below, their shares may qualify for BPR because they are not deemed 'listed', even though prices for them are quoted regularly in the financial press. Note that where a company, say a mining enterprise, seems to qualify because its shares are traded on AIM, but it is also listed on another foreign stock exchange, BPR will nonetheless be denied if that other exchange is a 'recognised' one.

13.5 Shares or securities in a quoted company will qualify for BPR where they together comprise a controlling holding: see *IHTA 1984, s 105(1)(cc).* Unquoted securities of a company which, either by themselves or with other securities give the transferor control of that company, will qualify for BPR under *IHTA 1984, s 105(1)(b).*

In every case, *IHTA 1984, s 106* requires that the securities must have been held by the transferor for a minimum period of two years or must qualify for a holding period by virtue of the replacement provisions of *IHTA 1984, s 107,* the succession provisions of *IHTA 1984, s 108* or the provisions as to successive transfers in *IHTA 1984, s 109.*

Trading assets

13.6 BPR is also available under *IHTA 1984, s 105(1)(d)* and *s 105 (1)(e)* on business assets that are not in themselves an interest in the business but are so used in the business. The asset categories which include land or buildings, machinery or plant, will qualify for relief according to the basis of ownership. BPR is available on:

- assets used for the business of a company controlled by the transferor;
- assets used by a partnership of which the transferor is a member;
- assets used for a business carried on by the transferor but owned by a trust in which he has a qualifying interest in possession.

The last of these categories, as exemplified by *Fetherstonaugh v IRC* [1984] STC 261, may be of less importance in the future as a consequence of the *FA 2006* trust reforms.

The distinction between BPR on an *interest* in a company or partnership and BPR on the *assets* used in that company or partnership but now owned by that company or partnership is important in two ways. First, BPR on the externally (personally) owned trading assets used in the company or partnership is given at a lower 50% rate. Second, BPR on trading assets is available only where the asset is still held at the time of transfer and is not at that date subject to any binding contract for sale. Where, however, the claim is made in respect of the business rather than its assets, it does not matter that a particular asset may be in the course of sale at the time of transfer because that does not necessarily bring the business itself to an end: the principle is illustrated in the case of *Brown's Executors v IRC* [1996] STC (SCD) 277 mentioned above.

13.7 As mentioned at **13.1,** the long-held view that BPR under *IHTA 1984, s 106(1)(a)* was confined to an interest in a business, rather than an asset of that business was overturned in *Trustees of Nelson Dance Family Settlement v Revenue and Customs Commissioners* [2009] EWHC 71 (Ch). Mr Dance, a farmer, transferred land to a settlement. Agricultural relief (APR) was not in issue here rather the taxpayer wanted BPR because the land had development value. HMRC denied relief on the basis that the subject matter of the transfer was not an interest in his farming business but a 'mere asset'.

The taxpayer successfully argued that it was necessary to look not at the actual asset transferred, but at its transfer of value based on the 'loss to the estate' principle. The estate of Mr Dance was reduced by the transfer: what was reduced was the value of his farming business; he had been in farming for many years; so the transfer of value fell to be reduced by BPR.

At first instance the Special Commissioner could see a distinction between those cases involving spousal relief where the recipient is important, and the present situation where the basis of relief is determined by the transfer, not the underlying asset, commenting (at para 16):

> '… All these form part of an overall scheme. Everything turns on the loss in value to the donor's estate, rather than what is given or how the loss to the estate arises, except where the identity of the recipient is crucial to a particular exemption ….'

As expected, HMRC appealed to the High Court contending that the reference in the legislation to the value of business property implied that the transfer must be of business property, not merely business assets. Sales J dismissed the appeal.

It was sufficient that a possible and proper characterisation of the value transferred was that such value was attributable to the value of a business. The source of that value did not require an exclusive type of characterisation and thus it did not matter that the attribution could be to the value of the land transferred, as long as it could be said that the attribution could also be to the value of a business. That interpretation was simple and certain and sat well with *IHTA 1984, s 110* and with the 'loss to donor 'principle in *IHTA 1984, s 103*.

Does this mean that any transfer of a mere asset now attracts BPR? No: for example, such an asset owned jointly by sisters, one of whom does not trade, may not attract BPR. To rely on the rule now established, taxpayers must study the case report and bring themselves precisely within its facts.

It has to be said that a sole trader is in an advantageous position; in effect, he 'is' the business and he need make no distinction between those assets he trades with and others: he may not actually show all assets in his balance sheet and yet be using them for his business. To determine whether a particular asset is a business or a 'mere asset' it may still be necessary to refer to those old cases that were so relevant to the former CGT retirement relief but which may now enjoy a revival of interest in applying CGT entrepreneurs' relief, for example

McGregor (Inspector of Taxes) v Adcock [1977] STC 206; *Mannion (Inspector of Taxes) v Johnston* [1988] STC 758; *Atkinson v Dancer* [1988] STC 758 and *Pepper (Inspector of Taxes) v Daffurn* [1993] STC 466. In addition, for a more recent case directly concerning entrepreneurs' relief, see *Gilbert (t/a United Foods) v Revenue & Customs Commissioners* [2011] UKFTT 705 (TC).

Timing is important if not critical in relation to gifts of shares and assets in family businesses.

Example 13.3—Order of gifts: getting it wrong

Jason owned 60% of Fleece Ltd (the family business) his sons Artemis and Theseus each owning 20%. Fleece Ltd traded from an industrial estate which Jason also owned. Jason wished to keep the parts of the trading estate that were let to third parties but was tiring of the risks of business itself and wanted to hand over the company with its factory premises to his two sons.

He had intended all this as a celebration of his retirement on reaching the age of 80, but in the event the lawyers were slow to deal with the transfer of the land and this took place some weeks after the actual handover celebrations concerning the company itself.

The transfer of the shares qualified for BPR, but the later transfer of the factory premises did not, because at that later time Jason was no longer a (majority) shareholder in the company. Artemis and Theseus were therefore at risk of a liability to IHT until Jason had survived the gift by seven years. Understandably, they required the lawyers to pay them compensation equal to the cost of insuring Jason's life for that period for a sum sufficient to pay the IHT at risk.

Rate of relief

13.8 BPR at the rate of 100% applies to the following categories of property:

- business;
- interest in a business;
- unquoted securities of a company giving control;
- unquoted shares.

BPR at the reduced rate of 50% applies to the following categories of property:

- controlling holding of quoted company;

- land, building, machinery or plant used in the business of a company controlled by the transferor or a partnership of which the transferor is a member;
- similar trading assets used for a business carried on by the transferor but owned by a trust in which he has a qualifying life interest.

CONDITIONS

Period of ownership

> **Focus**
>
> Qualifying replacement property can 'piggyback' on the time qualification of the original asset in order to meet the two-year holding requirement and this can provide a platform for a useful planning strategy.

13.9 As previously stated, property will not qualify for BPR unless owned throughout the two years immediately preceding the transfer; see *IHTA 1984, s 106*. It may however be treated as satisfying that condition (see *IHTA 1984, s 107* where it replaces other property that would have otherwise qualified for BPR.

There is scope for a gap in ownership. *Section 107(1)(a)* of *IHTA 1984* requires the property held at the time of transfer and the property which it replaces to have been owned by the transferor for at least two years out of the five years immediately prior to the transfer. The replacement property concerned must qualify for BPR in all respects other than the period of ownership. It is important to note that there is generally no scope for 'trading up' within this rule. Capital reconstruction can be disregarded so as to 'look through' a period of ownership.

> **Example 13.4—Replacement property: business angel**
>
> Returning to the example of Richard (see **Example 13.2**), it appears that Richard had held the shares in Café Direct for only 18 months prior to his death. However, the money that he used to buy the shares came from the sale, only two months before, of shares in Coffee Ltd which, at the relevant time, was quoted on the Alternative Investment Market (AIM), and from Beans Ltd, an ISDX company. The records of those companies show that they were unquoted trading companies throughout the relevant time. As a result, BPR is available on the shares in Café Direct (the replacement property), even though those shares had not yet been owned for two years.

This does illustrate that investors who hope to secure the benefit of BPR by investing in unquoted shares must be vigilant and alert to change: companies migrate from smaller exchanges to larger as they develop, and it is only rarely (ie Young and Company Brewery plc which moved from the main exchange to an AIM listing) that they move the other way. Small companies by their very nature will always be vulnerable to takeovers thereby forcing the investor to seek new BPR opportunities.

Example 13.5—Period of ownership: capital changes

Jason, in **Example 13.3** above, had formed Fleece Ltd from a family partnership comprising himself and his sons. The partnership had been trading for a number of years before the incorporation but at the time of the share transfer, Jason had only held the shares for one year. However, his period of ownership of an interest in the partnership also counts when considering the time ownership test in *IHTA 1984, s 106*.

The period of ownership was the main issue in *The Executors of Mrs Mary Dugan-Chapman and another v Revenue and Customs Commissioners* [2008] SpC 666. The taxpayer had hoped that the use of a rights issue to capitalise a loan might effectively sidestep the two-year ownership rule by deeming the shares acquired under that rights issue to be treated as part of an existing shareholding which had been owned for the requisite period by relying on the reorganisation provisions of *Taxation of Chargeable Gains Act 1992, s 126* when read with *IHTA 1984, s 107(4)*. The case turned on its own very special facts, the description of which occupies 31 paragraphs of the report but it is nonetheless worth reading. Actions taken under extreme time pressures did not, it was held, achieve the effect that had been hoped for.

The general principles that practitioners may draw from the case are self-evident namely:

- The paperwork must be correct.
- Keep only one (correct) record of the transaction, not two conflicting notes.
- Do not delay.

In this case the parties had considered tax planning in light of the health concerns of the elderly shareholder but the latter then seemed to recover her health and at the instigation of her family there was delay. As a consequence precious weeks were lost, leaving everything to be done in a rush just before Christmas as her health deteriorated. In the end, the transactions were construed, not as a rights issue as intended, but as a cash subscription for shares, with the result that on the shareholder's death days later she had not satisfied the requirements of *IHTA 1984, s 106*.

The aftermath of that decision returned to the High Court as *Vinton and others v Fladgate Fielder* [2010] EWHC 904 (Ch) where the daughters of Mrs Dugan-Chapman sued the solicitors for damages to recover both the IHT now payable and the costs of the unsuccessful tax appeal. The solicitors applied to have the claim struck out as 'fanciful' but the court, in considering the evidence, refused to do so.

It is important to be aware that even if a rights issue is properly undertaken, there should still be a commercial need for cash, since otherwise the money subscribed for the new shares will be treated as an excepted asset within *IHTA 1984, s 112* (see **13.22** below). The directors should record the need for funds for the purposes of the business of the company.

Not investment business

Background

> **Focus**
>
> There can be a real threat to preservation of BPR where a business has multiple interests which combine active trading and passive investment. The extent of the latter could cause the business to fail the 'wholly or mainly' test such that BPR is lost in totality rather than simply restricted (see **13.22**).

13.10 It cannot be stressed too strongly that this is an area of great practical difficulty for advisers. A young business may comprise trading assets, intangible assets and may be burdened with substantial debt. A mature business may hold the undistributed profits earned over many years which have been reinvested in 'safe' assets such as property, perhaps because the personal tax burden on dividend distribution was unacceptably high. The problem thus comes in two forms: at its most extreme, BPR is denied on the entire company because it is no longer mainly trading but has moved into a predominantly investment vehicle. In a more moderate form, BPR is restricted under the rules as to excepted assets considered below.

BPR is denied by *IHTA 1984, s 105(3)* where the business of the trading entity, whether incorporated or not, '… consists wholly or mainly of one or more of the following, that is to say, dealing in securities, stocks or shares, land or buildings, or making or holding investments …'. Relatively few cases arise on simple land dealing whereas the directors of pure investment companies recognise that a claim to BPR would be hopeless. The main disputes arise where the accounts of the company show some trading activity and the receipt of some passive income, ie rental income.

Cases concerning lettings

13.11 For background reading, see the following cases and specialist works on the subject:

- *Martin (Moore's Executors) v IRC* [1995] STC (SCD) 5; *Burkinyoung (Burkinyoung's Executors) v IRC* [1995] STC (SCD) 29 and *Trustees of David Zetland Settlement v HMRC* [2013] UKFTT 284 (TC) all concerned businesses that were primarily making an income from lettings.
- See also the caravan park cases *of Hall (Hall's Executors) v IRC* [1997] STC (SCD) 126; *Powell v IRC* [1997] STC (SCD) 181; *Furness v IRC* [1999] STC (SCD) 232; *Weston (Weston's Executors) v IRC* [2000] STC 1064 and *IRC v George* [2003] EWCA Civ 1763, [2004] STC 147.

Two cases are worthy of mention. In the *Trustees of David Zetland Settlement v HMRC* [2013] UKFTT 284 (TC) the taxpayer claimed that the diversity and level of services carried out to the tenants of Zetland House meant that it ought to be classified as a business for the purposes of BPR. Access to the relief was very relevant since the Settlement was approaching its ten-year anniversary charge. Zetland House was originally a multi-storey factory occupied by a number of printing firms but the property had outlived its original purpose. There were a number of long-term leases and by 1997 one-quarter of the building was unoccupied – gross rents were £510,000 per annum.

The taxpayer acquired the premises and transformed them by offering flexible space for computer, media and high-technology businesses, all of which required major changes to both the physical appearance and the usage/occupation of the tenant. He made office space more available, offered attractive short-term leases and made the individual offices smaller. The gross rents and service charges in the year ended 5 April 2007 were approximately £2.4 million. The taxpayer hired more staff to provide a wider range of services and facilities to the tenants. The building had a restaurant, gym, cycle arch, wi-fi, portage, 24-hour access, meeting rooms, media events, outdoor television screens and an art gallery – it was run on the basis of a community with regular barbeques and social gatherings.

HMRC argued that the purpose of the additional services was to increase occupancy and hence increase the rental receipts – the services were no more than incidental to the core business of collecting rent and service charges. The tribunal looked closely at the income and profit of the various activities which clearly indicated that the bulk of income, well in excess of 50%, derived from the rent and service charge. It was held that the activities were predominantly investment activities or related to investment. The services provided were mainly of a standard nature aimed at maximising income through short-term tenancies. The non-investment side was incidental to the core business and the services were insufficient to make the business one that was mainly non-investment. The purpose of the activities was largely to improve the building and its fabric, to secure the tenancy and to keep the occupancy rates high.

In *Best v HMRC* [2014] UKFTT 77 (TC), Bullick Developments Ltd owned a business centre in County Antrim (Northern Ireland) which development was financed in part by the Local Enterprise Development Unit – the latter, it was argued, did not finance mere investments. The centre included offices, showrooms, industrial and warehouse space, from very small to quite large units. It was agreed that one self-contained area, bringing in 15% of the income, was an investment, 10% was office space, the rest comprised light industrial or warehousing. In total 400 people worked there.

The standard form licence agreements did not give exclusive possession of the land. Services were listed in two schedules but it was agreed that most of those in the first schedule were of a type commonly provided by a landlord. Further services were listed in the second schedule and much emphasis was placed on the availability of a forklift driver.

It was an identifiable weakness of the case that no copy invoices were provided. The company employed:

- a full-time site maintenance person, receptionist and a forklift driver;
- two part-time people; and
- three full-time security guards.

Most of the units had no separate landline, so calls were put through by the receptionist and many units were accessible only to small vehicles, making the forklift useful, though the extent of that use was not proved.

Income of £611,472 was broken down into:

Licence fees	£447,068
Service charges	£53,335
Sundry	£4,517
Equipment hire	£4,452
Heat and light	£31,284
Telephone	£45,568
Postage	£20,056
Parking	£5,192

Applying the tests in *George, McCall* and *Pawson*, the Tribunal considered that the provision of office-like facilities and of the forklift was not significant enough to save the business from its investment nature. Those services did not predominate when considering the business as a whole and it was considered that the business was 'well towards the investment end of the spectrum'. BPR was denied.

Landed estates

13.12 The leading case is and remains *Farmer (Farmer's Executors) v IRC* [1999] STC (SCD) 321, which considered an estate run as one business where the majority of income came from lettings or licence fees but the main capital value was held in the farmland, farmhouse and farm buildings. After a very detailed consideration BPR was granted on the basis there was a composite business of running a landed estate. The landed estate concerned comprised a substantial acreage and thus the case does not provide a steer on how small an estate conducted along similar lines but on a smaller scale may be able to qualify for BPR. There are doubtless many landholdings in the range of say 10 to 50 acres where a Tax Tribunal decision would be welcome clarification of the law.

The decision in the *Farmer* case was reinforced by the Scottish case of *Brander (Representative of Earl of Balfour deceased) v HMRC* [2010] UKUT 300 TCC albeit it is considered by this author that the position was not so robust as *Farmer* and did contain some areas of weakness that could be later exploited by HMRC. In *Brander* two issues arose: whether the requirements of *IHTA 1984, s 107* as to replacement property were satisfied (they were); and whether the business failed the 'wholly or mainly' test of *IHTA 1984, s 105(3)*. It was held that the lowland landed estate in question fully satisfied the tests for BPR: in particular the late Earl, in managing the tenancies of estate cottages, had selected tenants who could be of service to the estate rather than always going for the highest available rent, so the running of residential property was integrated into the overall business purpose of managing the estate. The case is very interesting given the diversity of the business components and it is strongly recommended that the full case be reviewed for its content and commentary.

Inter-company loans

13.13 A case of specialist interest is *Phillips & others (Phillips' executors) v HMRC* [2006] SpC 555; [2006] SSCD 639 where an unquoted company lent money to related family businesses. HMRC denied BPR under *IHTA 1984, s 105(3)* but an appeal to the Special Commissioner succeeded, on the basis that the company was the 'banking arm' for in-house transactions. Few would treat money-lending as a mere investment activity but in this instance the company was making loans, not investing in them, so BPR was allowed.

The case serves as a reference point for advisers. Commonly an elderly entrepreneur may be happy to give up the active cut and thrust of daily commerce to his children but might still be happy to support their activities by providing finance, even though that may involve him in significant commercial risk. Access to BPR will, of course, depend on the facts of each case.

The business of providing a crop of grass and livery

13.14 The released report of key BPR cases which come before the courts or tribunals regularly demonstrate that the particular tax issue has been considered with great care leading to a decision that is particularly helpful in establishing general principles, even if that decision is not always the result the taxpayers might hope for. Several such cases have been argued by William Massey QC (the successful advocate in the *Nelson Dance* case mentioned above); in particular he represented the taxpayers in *McCall and Keenan v Revenue and Customs Commissioners* [2009] NICA 12, where a parcel of land had an agricultural value, at the date of death, of £165,000 but a market value of £5.8 million. It was therefore important for the executors to show that at the date of death there was a business qualifying for BPR to soak up the development value rather than a mere agricultural interest with its lower APR coverage.

The evidence showed (just) that the son-in-law of the deceased had spent time looking after the land, which lay on the edge of a town. The work involved walking the land, repairing the fencing, cleaning drinking troughs, clearing the drainage systems of mud and leaves, cutting and spraying weeds. For these purposes, the son-in-law had a tractor and reaper and a knapsack sprayer. He probably worked no more than 100 hours per year but some work was contracted out but critically the grazier fertilised the fields.

At first instance the Commissioner reviewed the authorities, including several mentioned above and in particular the *indicia* noted by Gibson J in *Customs and Excise Commissioners v Lord Fisher* [1981] STC 238. He concluded that the son-in-law's activity of tending the land:

> '… was, just, enough to constitute a business …. but was it a trade? The letting of the land was earnestly pursued, the work of tending the land was modest but serious, the letting and tending were pursued with some continuity, the income was not insubstantial, the letting was conducted in a regular manner although the use of [the son-in-law's] time was something which is not a feature of an ordinary business, and the letting of land for profit is a common business. To my mind the Lord Fisher indicia point towards a business…'

However, it was held that the business consisted wholly or mainly of holding investments, within *IHTA 1984, s 105(3)*. After a detailed consideration of the nature of farming arrangements under the law of Northern Ireland (and which may not be of general application) the Commissioner held that:

> '… The test to be applied is that of an intelligent businessman, not a land lawyer. Such a person would be concerned with the use to which the asset was put. The deceased was making the land available, not to make a living on it but from it; the management activities related to letting the land; it was unlike "hotel accommodation for cattle" as suggested by Mr Massey; nor was it like a "pick your own" fruit farm after months of weeding, fertilising spraying and pruning, customers are licensed to enter to take the produce and pay by the pound for what they take away; in the business of letting the fields there was less preparatory work, the fields were let for the accommodation of the cattle as well as for the grazing, and the rent was paid by the acre rather than by the ton of grass eaten ….'

The Court of Appeal in Northern Ireland agreed – the Commissioner had properly understood the law. The test was that of the intelligent businessman (which phrase also surfaced in the recent *Pawson* case discussed at **13.15** below), who would look at the use to which the land was put – a landowner who derives income from land or a building will be treated as having a business of holding an investment even though he may carry out incidental work to obtain the income. Here, the activities of the son-in-law were in the nature of maintenance work to achieve a successful letting. The use of the land by graziers was exclusive, so the owner could not use the land for any purpose that interfered with the grazing. The appeal was dismissed.

The more recent case of *Maureen Vigne (dec'd) v HMRC* [2017] UKFTT 632 provide a useful insight into the livery business which traditional operation sits on the very margins of *s 105(3)*.

The late Mrs Vigne owned 30 acres of land from which she provided access to livery services to the horse owners. The horse had the right to reside in a field and was provided with a stable but the day-to-day care was wholly provided by the horse's owner. However, ancillary services were provided as part of the livery business which included:

- The provision of worming products and where an owner was unable and/or unwilling so to do, the administering of such products on a quarterly basis.
- A hay crop was grown on a part of the land referred to as the hayfield and this was used to provide feed during the winter months at a time when the grass in the field might not provide a sufficient food source.
- Collecting and removing horse manure from the fields in which the horses spent most of their time.
- Undertaking a daily check of the general health of each horse.

On Mrs Vigne's death, the executors claimed BPR on the livery business which HMRC refused on the grounds that the business was wholly or mainly one of making investments – namely, holding land from which an income was generated from licence fees. The executors appealed.

The tribunal looked carefully at the factual evidence (which was not significantly disputed), considered the case law and in particular paid close attention to the arguments considered in *IRC v George* [2003] EWCA Civ 1763, [2004] STC (see **9.11**)and *McCall and Keenan v Revenue and Customs Commissioners [2009] NICA 12 (*see **5.6***)*. HMRC placed heavy reliance on the 'minimal' time spent per horse on services over and above those of providing the land and stabling but the tribunal rejected this approach: picking up manure, for example, was not carried out on a 'per horse' basis but to clear the whole field. In total, the yard manager worked around 20 hours per week.

The tribunal appeared to indicate that a typical 'DIY' livery would likely be a business of holding investments, but described what was being offered in this case as 'enhanced livery'. The tribunal considered the livery business was 'providing a level of valuable services to the various horse owners, which prevents it being properly asserted that the business was mainly one of holding investments'. The taxpayer's appeal was allowed.

Holiday lettings

13.15 Great care is needed when dealing with holiday lettings but there is no doubt that the ability to secure BPR against that activity has been severely reduced following several high-profile cases all found in HMRC's favour. Original HMRC guidance indicated that BPR would generally be allowed if the lettings were short term (ie weekly or fortnightly) *and* there was substantial involvement with the holidaymakers both on and off the premises. This applied even if the lettings were for only part of the year.

HMRC guidance (IHTM25278) was amended in late 2008, and at time of writing states:

> '…HMRC's view is that furnished holiday lets will in general not qualify for business property relief. The income derived from such businesses will largely consist of rent in return for the occupation of property. *There may however be cases where the level of additional services provided is so high that the activity can be considered as non-investment, and each case needs to be treated on its own facts*' [emphasis added]

The guidance goes on to indicate that cases involving claims for business property relief on holiday lettings should be referred to HMRC's Technical Team (litigation) – it is clear that there is a great deal of unease within HMRC.

Although following a period of consultation, *FA 2010* has restored in part the favourable income tax treatment of furnished holiday lettings this does not impact on the IHT position which has always been dealt with quite separately under the IHT code. Nonetheless, it must be appreciated that any claim to BPR in respect of furnished holiday lets will always be carefully scrutinised by

HMRC and it must be said, with more than a jaundiced if not wholly negative approach. It is clear that HMRC do take a strong stance and thus the practitioner must be prepared to mount a robust defence.

The narrowness of the HMRC position was challenged in *Pawson (deceased) v Revenue and Customs Commissioners* [2012] UKFTT 51(TC). In this case the deceased had 25% interest (with the remaining ownership held by other family members) in a picturesque large seaside holiday letting cottage in respect of which the executors claimed BPR. The income from the property in recent years had steadily increased producing a small taxable profit in all but one year due to expenditure on necessary repairs etc. The property was fully furnished with heating and hot water turned on before the arrival of visitors, the well-equipped kitchen was kept in good working order, the cleaner attended the property between each letting and the gardener was hired to ensure that the grounds were kept in good order at all times during the letting season – the family owners dealt with the letting arrangements personally and attended the property on a regular basis. In a surprising decision at the First-tier Tribunal it was held that the activities amounted to a business and the claim to BPR was allowed. However, as expected, HMRC appealed to the Upper Tribunal and were successful in their bid to overturn the earlier decision.

This outcome effectively restores the position to that determined under *Stedman's Executors v IRC*; *CIR v George and another* namely that the rental exploitation of land with a view to profit is still fundamentally a business of holding the property as an investment. It is generally accepted that the *Pawson* case was rather weak such that the appeal decision was probably the correct one on the facts as they stood. However, the concern is that the Upper Tribunal commentary is sufficiently damming as to be likely to prevent a BPR claim in any furnished letting case. Leave to appeal was refused by the Court of Appeal in October 2013 on the fairly damning grounds that there would be no realistic prospect of any such appeal succeeding.

The decision was underpinned by the more recent case of *ACC Green v HMRC* [2015] UKFTT 0236 (TC) which considered the availability of BPR on transfer of 85% of the appellant's interest in an established self-contained holiday business. The appellant's team argued that a wide spectrum of businesses involved the use of property which at one end involved the granting of a tenancy and at the other end the running of a hotel and a shop but the tribunal were not swayed that the business in question fell on the hotel side. The tribunal placed heavy reliance on the authorities set out in the cases of *Pawson v HMRC* [2012] UKFTT (TC), *McCall v HMRC* [2009] NICA 12 STC 990 and *Best v HMRC* [2014] UKFTT 077 (TC) and concluded that 'the extra services provided are insufficient to demonstrate that the business is other than mainly one of holding the property as an investment'.

What must be considered as the final death knell was sounded in the case of *Marjorie Ross (dec'd) v HMRC* [2017] UKFTT 507 which considered a business of holiday cottage lettings. At the time of her death, Mrs Ross owned a share in the Green Doors Cottages Partnership, which owned a portfolio of properties comprising eight cottages and two flats. The cottages were all holiday lets, one flat was on a long-term let to a local hotel which used it for staff accommodation, and the other was rented out to the handyman, and sole employee, of the partnership. The executors claimed BPR which HMRC denied on grounds that the business was wholly or mainly one of holding investments and the executors appealed.

The tribunal quoted extensively from uncontested witness statements which gave a rounded view of the services provided by the partnership. These services included:

- regular cleaning;
- the ability to take meals at the hotel (which was originally owned by the deceased);
- local tourist advice;
- an onsite handyman to fix any problems;
- a laundry room;
- provision of dog bowls and creation of a pet friendly environment; and
- personal guest services provided at the hotel such as a left luggage facility and newspaper delivery.

One guest concluded by saying that: 'A stay at one of Green Door Cottages provided the complete holiday experience as it was similar to checking into a hotel but with the ability to self-cater'. However, that was not enough to convince the tribunal that BPR was due – self-catering cottages were fundamentally different from a hotel business, no matter how much their visitors made the comparison:

> 'However high the standard of services which were provided, and whatever the level of expenditure incurred on those services, what guests at Green Door Cottages really wanted was access to a property to call their own in a beautiful part of Cornwall to enjoy for a specific period. The essence of that is the right to rent land in the form of one of the Green Door Cottages for a specific period. That is an activity which consists mainly of the investment in property.'

The appeal was refused.

Other types of lettings involving land may also fall foul of *IHTA 1984, s 105(3)* in HMRC's view. Its guidance states (at IHTM25280): 'Consider whether investment holding is in point where exploitation of land ownership in other ways is involved, eg moorings or beach huts, and seek the views of Technical Group (TG).'

Small company group

13.16 A strict examination of *IHTA 1984, s 105(4)(b)*, with its emphasis on holding 'companies' rather than 'assets' suggests that where a holding company has no trade of its own but holds only:

- shares in a trading subsidiary; and
- the premises from which that company trades,

the shares in the holding company would appear to fail the test for BPR. What is the holding company 'wholly or mainly' doing? The problem would not arise if there were a trade within the holding company, but here there is none. Suppose that the trade is of little value relative to the value of the premises: does that make a difference? Would it be wise to set up a second subsidiary, just to hold the premises? It might be but what is clear is that it is necessary to look at the situation in the round: if the group as a whole is regarded as trading, and the land is held only to facilitate the trade, there should be no problem. HMRC appear to agree with that view, though of course each case will turn on its own facts.

VALUATION, EXCEPTED ASSETS

13.17 If the property is of the type identified at **13.22** as qualifying for 100% BPR, it might seem that valuation is not an important issue and sometimes that will be the case. However, where there are excepted assets it is still necessary to undertake the full valuation exercise to establish the quantum of that relief.

Shares

13.18 The vast majority of claims to BPR on shares will be on unquoted shares and related securities. The general principles of valuation of assets that are subject to restrictions will apply, as seen for example in *IRC v Crossman* [1936] 1 All ER 762. In practice there may be a conflict between arguments that were raised in valuing company shares for CGT purposes, especially as at March 1982 where the taxpayer may want to value high, and the value that may apply for probate, particularly where there is some restriction on relief and the taxpayer is valuing low.

Difficulties arise where 'clever' or bespoke structures are used as demonstrated in *I C McArthur's Executors v HMRC* [2008] SpC 700. In that case the main shareholder lent money to companies on terms that linked the loans to options to purchase other shares. On his death, HMRC required the valuation of the loans to reflect the value of the options. Although the executors argued that the options had little or no value, the Special Commissioner disagreed. There was evidence, in the form of 'writs' of the debtor, that there were loans and conversion rights. The unit of valuation was the loan plus the relevant conversion rights.

13.19 The level of information that would be available to a purchase of shares and many of the other general principles of valuation were considered in *Caton's Administrators v Couch* [1995] STC (SCD) 34. There the Special Commissioner had to decide: how much unpublished information would be available to a purchaser; the value of the shares on the date of Mr Caton's death; and whether professional costs including the appeal itself might be allowable in computing the chargeable gain. The Commissioner concluded that the purchaser of a small block of shares would not normally expect to receive as much information as a larger investor. He would get no more than the published data and be restricted to what he could find out without questioning the directors.

13.20 Family companies can involve competing factions and that competition can affect the value of the shares. These principles were examined in detail in *Hawkings-Byass v Sassen (Inspector of Taxes)* [1996] STC (SCD) 319 and in *Denekamp v Pearce (Inspector of Taxes)* [1998] STC 1120. A dispute in *CVC/Opportunity Equity Partners Ltd v Almeida* [2002] UKPC 16, forced the Privy Council to consider the valuation basis where a company in the nature of a limited partnership had expelled one of the partners. The court decided that in such a case the majority may exclude the minority only if they buy them out at a fair price. The continuing shareholders had to pay the expelled partner a value on a going concern basis without discount. For a contrary view, see *Phoenix Office Supplies v Larvin* [2002] EWCA Civ 1740, [2003] 1 BCLC 76, where a discount did apply.

The determining factor seems to be that there actually must be someone in the market who has a special reason for buying the shares. The valuer should consider whether there is, in the circumstances of the company, another shareholder who is prepared to offer full market value without discount. Arguably some discount will always be appropriate: see the decision in *Re Courthorpe* KB 1928 7 ATC 538. Although there has from time to time been comment to establish a rule of thumb, there is no hard and fast rule and the value must be negotiated each time.

Net value

13.21 One clear rule is established by *IHTA 1984, s 110* although it seems to apply only to unincorporated businesses (see the reference to 'a business or an interest in a business'). The value of the business is the net value and as a result, all liabilities incurred 'for the purpose of business' are set against the value of the company assets, whether or not secured on them and this same rule also applies to unincorporated businesses. There is, however, a distinction between debts incurred 'for the purposes of the business' and liabilities that are incurred in acquiring the business itself.

Example 13.6—Net value of business

(i) Charles sets up in business as a solicitor but having no real capital resources, the premises and equipment are rented. At the end of his second year of trade, Charles correctly recognises the value of some of his work in progress that has not been billed out because it related to work done partly by him and partly by assistants. However, there is no money to pay the tax, so the firm goes into overdraft. On a valuation of the business at that date the overdraft would be netted off against the value of the work in progress.

(ii) David gives up his job as a solicitor and buys a will-writing business. Having no capital, he negotiates a loan from his bank, secured on his house, to buy a franchise interest, comprising a fireproof safe, a collection of 500 wills and a software package of precedents. On a later valuation of the business for BPR, the loan secured against the house is not deducted from the value of the business, because it was a loan incurred to buy the business rather than for running the business.

(iii) Charles wants to retire and agrees to sell his business to David, who takes out a further loan. On a valuation of David's business some time later, the second loan probably would be deducted from the value because the purchase of Charles's business could be seen as a mere extension of the existing business so that the cost of finance was for the purposes of the business that David already owned.

Subject to the rule illustrated above, and prior to the *Finance Act 2013*, there was a general principle that a debt lies against the asset on which it is secured and thus repositioning a debt could affect relief. This was especially true for APR where the rule in *IHTA 1984, s 110* had no parallel and since this was a 'snapshot' test and not time based, repositioning the debt to gain unrestricted APR/BPR on the underlying asset only days before death could save significant tax. This device has now been curtailed by *FA 2013* which legislation operates to automatically offset the liability used to acquire the BPR/APR relievable asset before application of the BPR/APR relief. The *FA 2013* realignment applies to transfers of value made on and after 17 July 2013 but to new liabilities (to include any refinancing after that date: see IHTM28011) incurred with effect from 6 April 2013.

Excepted assets

Focus

BPR cannot be secured by simply placing non-business assets in a business wrapper – the nature of the asset must be reviewed and tested on its merits.

13.22 *Section 112* of *IHTA 1984* requires a double valuation exercise. First, the value of the business is calculated under general principles and secondly, it is recalculated excluding the value of 'excepted assets', namely those assets that are neither:

- used wholly or mainly for the purposes of the business

nor

- required at the time of transfer for future use

However, the rules are applied differently dependent on whether the business is incorporated or unincorporated. For companies it has been robustly and successfully argued that *IHTA 1984, s 112* will seldom apply because the business of a company is indivisible and therefore, if the asset contributes to the overall business success of the company, its value ought not to be excluded when calculating BPR unless the asset falls to be treated as a 'luxury' asset falling within the specific exception at *IHTA 1984, s 112(6)*. If the business is not incorporated, this argument does not apply and it becomes easier for HMRC to exclude an asset from relief.

13.23 In any event, there are specific exceptions to the 'robust' corporate argument:

The first exception is cash. In *Barclays Bank Trust Co v IRC* [1998] STC (SCD) 125 it was held that surplus retained cash did not qualify for BPR. In that case a substantial cash balance remained unused many years after the valuation date. The court held that, in the circumstances, cash was not 'required' for future use for business purposes within *IHTA 1984, s 112(2)(b)*. Despite government encouragement, the continued reluctance of high street banks to lend will have persuaded some owners of small businesses to retain and stockpile cash to see them through the recession. However, such greater levels of prudence are not embraced by HMRC and as a consequence this may have a detrimental impact when considering the tests for *IHTA 1984, s 112*.

The second exception applies where an asset is clearly not used for business purposes at all, such as a holiday flat used exclusively by the family of the majority shareholder – this falls squarely within *IHTA 1984, s 112(6)*.

A third and more borderline issue is whether certain 'passive' assets are excluded. It is considered that, for example, surplus funds for the company invested in quoted securities will probably not be excluded assets if they are moderate in value compared with the capital of the company as a whole. However, it is perhaps more difficult where over a number of years surplus profits have been invested in building up a portfolio of freehold investment properties. After a time, the existence of such substantial or non-trading assets can threaten the whole claim to BPR under the rule already noted relating to 'wholly or mainly holding investments' in *s 105(3)* – this is indeed a potential danger.

From initial review of the facts in *Executors of Marquess of Hertford v IRC* [2004] SpC 00444, it might have seemed that the rules as to excepted assets might be in point. In this case, HMRC sought to disallow BPR on the value of that part of Ragley Hall which was not open to the public, thus reducing a claim to BPR on the value of the business of opening the house to the public which itself had been the subject of a lifetime gift. However, it was successfully argued that the entirety of the house was an asset of the business – visitors saw the whole of the outside and most of the interior and the entire building was thus an integral part of the business. *Section 112(4)* of *IHTA 1984* was not in point because that concerned a building that would, but for relief, qualify for no BPR at all.

The placing of assets within a company group can be significant when claiming BPR. The interaction of *IHTA 1984, s 105(4)* and *IHTA 1984, s 111* has the effect that it may be best, in appropriate circumstances, for the 'working' freeholds of a group to sit with the top company and for ownership of any properties that are more in the nature of investments to be spread across the group.

In summary then, great care must be taken in this area to ensure that the balance is correct – assumption and complacency have no place. Whilst tax cases provide a valuable insight into the broader parameters, the outcome will inevitably turn upon the facts present in each individual case.

SCOPE OF AGRICULTURAL PROPERTY RELIEF

Agricultural property

13.24 One basic but important distinction between BPR and APR is that the exclusion from BPR of a 'mere asset' in the context of a business (subject to the *Nelson Dance* case) has no parallel in APR. Essentially, APR is only granted on 'mere assets' and of particular categories detailed as follows:

- agricultural land;
- pasture;
- woodland occupied with agricultural land or pasture where occupation ancillary;
- buildings used for intensive stock or fish rearing where occupied with agricultural land or pasture and occupation ancillary;
- farm cottages and their land of a character appropriate;
- farm buildings and their land of a character appropriate;
- farmhouses and their land of a character appropriate;
- stud farms;

- land in habitat schemes;
- a 'look through' provision to the assets of farming companies.

13.25 In practice, problems often arise through lack of scale of the farming enterprise. Land may have been sold off and the operation scaled down as the farmer grows older and becomes less agile. Interestingly and despite HMRC contention, from an APR viewpoint there is nothing in the legislation which requires the farming operation to be profitable (and this view was supported in the *Golding* case – see **13.35**). Many will argue that the mere growing of crops is now not enough to support a farming enterprise and that viability can be achieved only with a combination of growing of crops, and/or of stock, the use of various rural initiatives and the exploitation of grant schemes. The principal difficulties arise where the main, if not the only, source of income is the entitlement under the Basic Payment Scheme and where, in reliance on that scheme, the farmer has sold all his farm machinery and other equipment. In such a situation, farm buildings may well have become redundant and as such will lose APR, being no longer 'occupied for the purposes of agriculture' within *IHTA 1984, s 117.*

The distinction between whether a taxpayer is a farmer or landowner for general tax purposes was examined in the First-tier Tribunal case of *John Carlisle Allen* (TC5100). Similar to the *McCall* case (*McCall and Keenan v Revenue and Customs Commissioners* [2009] NICA 12) this also involved a conacre arrangement where the debate centered on the 'occupation' of land for the purposes of agriculture.

The taxpayer (and his brother) grew the grass which was eaten by the tenant's stock as permitted under the conacre agreement under which the taxpayer received £1,000 per annum described as 'a licence fee'. The taxpayer maintained the right to temporarily house animals on that land, supplied fertiliser when required, maintained fences and drainage, supplied water and undertook the weeding of the hedges. In addition to grazing access, the tenant was also permitted to remove silage at certain times and claim part of the farming subsidy. However, crucially the tenant was not able to spread artificial fertiliser but could only use farmyard manure or that supplied at no cost by the taxpayer when the grass became under nourished.

It was held that the land was occupied by the taxpayer for the purpose of husbandry and a key point in that decision was recognition that the taxpayer managed the land in such a manner as to maximise and maintain the quality of the grass crop.

13.26 Furthermore, property may be of the appropriate type, but may nevertheless fail to qualify for APR because of the specific requirements of *IHTA 1984, s 115* which when read together with the ownership conditions of *IHTA 1984, s 117* require that the land be occupied for the purposes of agriculture. For example, woodland may qualify under the agricultural purpose test if it adjoins meadow land and provides shade for 'meat' animals grazing nearby, but an isolated coppice which is effectively used only for shooting will not qualify because its occupation is not ancillary to that of agricultural land. Equally, as demonstrated in *Williams (Williams Personal Representative) v HMRC* [2005] SSCD 782; [2005] SpC 500, a building used for the intensive rearing of poultry does not qualify for APR where it stands on and dominates a small landholding because its use is not 'ancillary' to the land on which it stands.

The occupation test frequently gives rise to other problems, particularly in connection with cottages and houses.

Example 13.7—Loss of APR on farmhouse

Geoffrey farmed for many years and his house was the hub of that business. It adjoined a traditional range of farm buildings, some of which over the years had been adapted to allow the storage of modern farming equipment. It had been a small mixed farm, but over the years Geoffrey sold his stock and let some of the buildings as stabling and two of the fields as paddocks. Eventually, he scrapped the redundant farm machinery and sold the rest. He entered into an informal letting agreement with his farmer neighbour for the rest of the land.

On Geoffrey's death APR can be secured on the land let to the neighbour for farming (subject to the ownership requirement) but not on the paddocks because they are not occupied for the purposes of agriculture. The horses are not 'meat' animals, but family pets and thus APR is denied on the stable buildings. Finally, APR is denied on the farmhouse because it is no longer the hub of a farming business – it had become no more than the house where a retired farmer lived until the date of his death.

Farmhouses

13.27 Tax case *dicta* coupled with HMRC approach have made this a difficult but fluid area of law. With the limited exception of a period property of cultural importance which satisfies the onerous public access requirements to secure conditional exemption for heritage property (for more discussion on this point, see *Agricultural, Business and Heritage Property Relief (7th edn) (Bloomsbury Professional))*, there is virtually no other form of residence that can escape a charge to IHT (albeit sideway limited relief is now afforded from 6 April 2017 in the form of the residence nil rate band: see **Chapter 3**) and this in itself makes it very popular for taxpayers to claim that their personal residence should be treated as a farmhouse – it is and remains a contentious area which sparks keen HMRC interest. Farmhouses are often well situated, having slightly more seclusion than normal residential properties, so they can command a 'charm' premium. That seems certainly to have been true in the *McKenna* case, considered at **13.34** below. There are fewer working farms than in the past, so the likelihood that the occupier of a farmhouse makes his living from the adjoining land is much less now than it was even 50 years ago. Much greater use is now made of farming contractors than in bygone years and a farmer may now live some distance from the land where his business is carried on.

13.28 The combination of all these factors can result in a situation where arguably the basis for the APR has perhaps long since been lost. If income from farming activities consists predominantly or even solely of the Basic Farm Payment (BFP) there is now really no particular link between the farmhouse where the farmer lives and the land in respect of which the payment is earned. Some of these tensions are well reflected in the observations, admittedly *obiter*, of the Lands Tribunal in *Antrobus (No 2)* [2006] RVR 138, as was recognised in the *McKenna* case. Certainly practitioners are continuing to encounter regular challenge by HMRC to APR claims on farmhouses on grounds that there is really no viable business to be run from the house in question; and for this purpose HMRC also rely heavily on the *McCall* case to disregard a 'farming' business that consists only of owning land that is subject to grazing licences.

Section 115(2) of *IHTA 1984* allows APR on 'such cottages, farm buildings and farmhouses, together with the land occupied with them, as are of a character appropriate to the property'. This implies that the relief can apply not only to the farmhouse, but also to its garden but that for the relief to be available there must be 'the property' (the farm land) and crucially there must be some link between the farmhouse and 'the property'.

Consider the important decision in *Hanson v Revenue & Customs Commissioners* [2012] UKFTT 95 (TC), which was soundly upheld before the Upper Tribunal on 15 April 2013. After a detailed examination of the facts and careful analysis of the legislation the Upper Tribunal held that when determining whether a farmhouse qualifies for APR, both it and the land (to which the farmhouse is of 'character appropriate') must be in the same occupation but not necessarily, as HMRC argued, in the same ownership.

The facts of the case were straightforward. Immediately before his death in December 2002 Joseph Charles Hanson was the life tenant of a trust created by his father in 1957. The trust held a property which HMRC agreed was a 'farmhouse' for APR purposes with an agreed market value in December 2002 of £450,000. Mr Hanson's son lived in the farmhouse which he had occupied since 1978 under a rent-free licence and from there he farmed 215 acres of land of which 128 acres was owned by him personally and a mere 25 acres was part owned by Mr Hanson. The remainder of the 215 acres comprised 20 acres rented by the son from a third party and a further 42 acres whose ownership was unspecified. The only land in common ownership and common occupation with the farmhouse was the 25 acres part owned by Mr Hanson and farmed by the son.

Following Mr Hanson's death his executors claimed APR on the value of his interest in the farmhouse. HMRC denied the relief on the basis that there was insufficient agricultural land (25 acres) in both common ownership and common occupation with the farmhouse for the farmhouse to pass the 'character appropriate' test. The son appealed the decision in his capacity as sole trustee of the trust arguing that common occupation (the son in his capacity as farmer of the land) was the only connecting factor required between the farmhouse and the agricultural land to which it was of a character appropriate (namely the combined 25 acres owned by the deceased and the 215 acres owned by the son/A N Other). The tribunal agreed with the son.

This was a landmark defeat for HMRC but it is a welcome decision for the taxpayer and restores faith in good judgment based on a practical understanding of the farming operation. It will be of significance in situations where a downsizing farmer has moved out of the farmhouse and gives away much of the agricultural land.

Farming business? What farming business?

13.29 As previously commented and in stark contrast to BPR there is nothing within the legislation which actually demands that there must be a viable (profitable) farming business in order to gain access to APR. An unpublished decision of the Special Commissioners in 1994 stated that '... whether or not one can make a living from a given acreage of land cannot be determinative of the question whether a building is a farmhouse ...'. However, no relief is given on any agricultural property in the absence of its occupation for the purposes of agriculture as required by *IHTA 1984, s 116*.

A claim to APR on a home, irrespective of its title and location, can never be in point unless there is at least some recognisable farming activity. See, for example, *Dixon v IRC* SpC 297 [2002] SSCD 53 concerning a cottage, its garden and orchard of which the total area was 0.6 acres and the gross cash turnover (ignoring bartering arrangements) was £70 per year. It was held that the activities were consistent with the use of the property as a residence and garden, not for agriculture. The property was primarily a cottage with garden and orchard. APR was refused.

For a long time, it was HMRC practice to enquire closely into claims for APR on houses worth £250,000 or more where the land holding was 100 acres or less, but this value limit has now been eroded. The current HMRC approach now routinely met in practice is to deny relief on any farmhouse where the farm land does not seem extensive enough to support a viable business; and of course where values are moderate such cases may not reach the courts. Such cases must always be considered on their merits.

13.30 There may in the past have been a farming business, but it may no longer relate to the dwelling – that historical but now lost connection will deny access to APR. Thus, in *Rosser v IRC* SpC 368, [2003] SSCD 311, the relevant dwelling had for many years been a farmhouse for 41 acres comprising agricultural land, the house itself and a barn. Fatally, as it turned out, the deceased and her husband gave 39 acres of land to their daughter, who was married to a farmer and who then farmed that land with other land. That effectively 'demoted' the retained residence from its status of a farmhouse to that of a retirement home.

There is a restricted argument resulting from the decision of the Court of Appeal in *Starke (Brown's Executors) v IRC* [1996] 1 All ER 622. There the farmhouse had become separated in ownership from the adjoining farmland which was owned through the medium of a company. In that case the argument turned on a technicality, so the decision in *Starke* will not always decide the matter. In summary, a claim to APR on a dwelling will always be dependent upon first proving that there is a farming business and, as will be seen below, secondly, that the house is the place from which that business is run – past usage and current title have no impact if these two key requirements are not in place.

Unoccupied farmhouses cause problems: see the review at **13.38** below of *Harrold v IRC* [1996] STC (SCD) 195 and of *Atkinson v HMRC* [2010] UKFTT 108 (TC) TC00420. The latter case is of particular interest not least for its initial unexpected decision in favour of the taxpayer, a member of a farming partnership until his death but prevented from continued occupation of the farmhouse through ill health necessitating offsite residential care. Not surprisingly HMRC appealed the case to the Upper Tribunal but the executors of Mr Atkinson, concerned over costs, chose not to attend. HMRC's appeal was allowed thus soundly overturning the decision of the First-tier Tribunal (*HMRC v Atkinson and another* [2011] UKUT B26 (TCC)).

'Character appropriate'

13.31 There are many houses that look like farmhouses, but fail the test as to 'character appropriate' because they are disproportionate in size or quality to the farming business that purports to support them. The legislation originally included a category of dwelling that qualified for relief – mansion houses – but the removal of that category has strengthened the HMRC argument that grand houses should not qualify for APR. The test is whether the property is in substance a fine house surrounded by land, in which case APR will be hard to justify, or is a land holding that happens to contain a house, where the chances of APR will be better (for a more detailed discussion on the farmhouse, see *Agricultural, Business and Heritage Property Relief (7th edn) (Bloomsbury Professional)).*

13.32 In *Higginson's Executors v IRC* [2002] STC (SCD) 483 found in HMRC's favour, a property was set in a landed estate of 134 acres, of which only 63 were agricultural land. The gardens extended to three acres and there were 68 acres of woodland and wetland. This was a special property and, although it had for many years been occupied as a farmhouse for some time before the death of the owner, the farmland had been let and the woodland and wetland were made areas of nature conservation. The estate was not economically viable and was sold for £1.15 million a price described from a farming perspective as being 'an appalling investment in terms of yield', being well beyond farmers' means.

Antrobus

13.33 In *Lloyds TSB (Personal representative of Antrobus) v IRC* [2002] STC (SCD) 468 (*Antrobus (No 1)*) Cookhill Priory, which was within 126 acres of freehold land plus 6.5 acres of tenanted land, had been occupied by the Antrobus family since 1907. The original nunnery had been founded in 1260. The six-bedroom house dated to the mid-sixteenth century with an extension added in 1765 and alterations carried out in the Georgian period and in 1910. Father farmed the land until 1942, his widow died in 1959, Miss Antrobus occupied 124 acres and acquired the property from relatives in 1959, then farming it until her death. It was held that she was definitely a farmer. It was agreed that the land and buildings were agricultural property but the claim in respect of two let houses and Cookhill Priory was fiercely disputed by HMRC. Doctor Brice summarised the relevant questions to be answered in relation to any claim for APR on a farmhouse and that checklist was updated in the *McKenna* case, considered below.

McKenna

13.34 *Arnander (Executors of McKenna Deceased) v HMRC* [2006] SpC 00565 provides a valuable and very thorough examination of the issues outlined above, to which this summary cannot do justice and for that reason the author recommends that the full case transcript is read.

Rosteague House, Cornwall, overlooked the sea. It was in poor condition but nevertheless listed Grade II and '… at the very top end of the size of a farmhouse …', even in the context of the many fine examples in the district. It stood in 187 acres which included 52 acres of coastal slope and over a mile of sea frontage. It dated back in part to 1597, according to contemporary maps. It was a very substantial building with impressive gardens and there were farm buildings.

The farming history could be traced back to 1365, though in more modern times it had been conducted by agents and through contract-farming arrangements. The woodland area was extended with the help of a planting grant. The farm buildings were little used as such, but did house garden implements.

The owner spent perhaps an hour a day on farm work until illness prevented him and eventually the estate was sold – but not as a farm – for £3.05 million. Later evidence showed that urgent repairs would cost the purchaser nearly £200,000.

Against that background, Dr Brice found as follows:

- It was not a farmhouse. She quoted with approval the decision in *Rosser v IRC*. She approached the views of the Lands Tribunal in *Antrobus No 2* 'with some caution' as *obiter*, but held that the principle that '… the farmer of the land is the person who farms it on a day-to-day basis rather than the person who is in overall control of the agricultural business conducted on the land is a helpful principle…'. After a review of all the cases she set down the following principles:
    - A farmhouse is a dwelling for the farmer from which the farm is managed.
    - The farmer is the person who farms on a day-to-day basis, not the manager.
    - The purpose, not the status, of occupation is what matters.
    - If the premises are extravagantly large, then even though occupied for the purpose of agriculture they may have become something more grand.
    - Each case turns on its own facts, judged by ordinary ideas of what is appropriate in size, content and layout, taken in context with the buildings and the land.

  Based on this, Dr Brice found that the actual farming was not done from the house, which was too grand for the much-reduced farming operations carried on.
- It was not of a 'character appropriate' anyway. After referring to the *Antrobus* principles and to *Higginson* Dr Brice reviewed the elements as follows:
    - There were many fine farmhouses in Cornwall, some quite large and with very pleasant gardens.
    - Rosteague House was large and despite its condition had 'an interior of grace and charm'.
    - The farm buildings were not really used as such.
    - There was not enough land.
    - A layman would think of it as a large country house; it was in effect marketed as such.
    - On sale, 65% of the price realised was for the house, part for tenanted properties and only 12% for the agricultural land. It

would not attract commercial farmers needing to make a living from the land.

- It was not occupied for the purposes of agriculture. Neither Mr McKenna, nor Lady McKenna had been able to farm actively during the relevant two-year period.
- Most of the farm buildings were not occupied for the purposes of agriculture. One was a dung stead, latterly used in connection with livery, but livery of horses is not an agricultural purpose. On the facts, however, some were used for agriculture.

The tax practitioner would be well advised to consider the full impact of this decision when considering the availability of APR on similar 'fine' houses in future. Undeniably it makes a claim for a 'lifestyle' farmer in respect of a charming country house that much harder to pursue.

13.35 In *Executors of D Golding Deceased v Revenue & Customs Commissioners* [2011] UKFTT 352 (TC) the reverse scenario was considered. In this case, the deceased had for many years until his death at age 81, farmed a smallholding of just 16.29 acres – the diverse farming trade comprised some 600 chickens, seven to ten cattle, harvesting of fruit from trees and growing vegetables. The farm produced milk and crops of wheat and barley were produced for sale. It was accepted that old age and infirmity led to scaling back of activities confined to selling of eggs, fruit and vegetables which produced a net profit of approximately £1,500 pa on average over the last five years – equal to less than 25% of the deceased sustainable income. Even so, in the early years the farm had been sufficient to sustain a family albeit not to any great state of luxury. The farmhouse was small in size, without electricity in parts and in a very poor state of repair. HMRC had implied acceptance that the house in which the deceased lived and from which he carried out his farming activities, was a farmhouse for agricultural purposes but disputed that the property was of 'character appropriate' – the argument rested to a great extent on the profitability of the farm. In a refreshingly simple and clear analysis of the facts as presented, the tribunal in finding for the taxpayer stated '… we do not accept that the lack of substantial profit is detrimental to the decision that the farmhouse was of character appropriate …'.

Rather belatedly and in response to the outcome of the *Golding* case HMRC updated the guidance to their IHT manual (see IHTM24036 et seq and HMRC Guidance reported at STEP UK News Digest 13 May 2013) which considers the APR application to the farmhouse under the character appropriate test.

Farm buildings

13.36 It was noted earlier that farm buildings do not automatically qualify for APR by virtue of their use alone but rather such buildings must also be ancillary to the main land holding. This was confirmed in *Williams (Williams Personal Representative) v HMRC* [2005] SSCD 782; [2005] SpC 500.

CONDITIONS FOR APR

Period of ownership or occupation

13.37 Unlike its stronger BPR sibling where a single period of ownership test is required, APR is denied unless the property complies with one of two conditions which pivot on ownership and occupation (*IHTA 1984, s 117)*. The first condition applies to occupation by the transferor (owner) for the purposes of agriculture throughout the period of two years ending with the date of transfer. This can lead to slightly surprising results.

Example 13.8—Period of occupation: deathbed purchase

James and Phillip were brought up on their father's farm and eventually inherited it from him. James lived on in the family house whilst his brother moved into the bungalow which had been his father's home in retirement. For a time both brothers tried to run the farm between them, but there were differences of temperament and in reality the land holding was not big enough to support them both; thus they agreed to partition ownership of the land between them. James thereafter owned the main farmhouse plus half the land which he farmed in hand and he rented the remainder of the farm land from Phillip who no longer took any active involvement in the farming operation.

Some years later James was forced to sell part of his land to the Highways Authority, generating a substantial cash compensation receipt. Though no longer in good health he continued to farm the remaining land, to include the land originally rented from his brother but later purchased funded by the compensation. James died only days after the purchase of the land from Phillip was completed.

On James's death, APR will be allowed in respect of the whole acreage, including land that was purchased from his brother and which had only been in James's estate for a matter of days before his death. The two-year occupation test has been met by reason of James's farming of the land throughout ie first as tenant then as owner.

13.38

Focus

Unlike its stronger BPR sibling where direct involvement is required, the landowner can secure APR by 'piggy-backing' on the qualification of the underlying tenant.

The second and alternative qualification for APR under *IHTA 1984, s 117* is that the property was owned by the transferor (owner) throughout the seven years ending with the date of transfer and throughout that period it was occupied for the purposes of agriculture. For this second alternate test, it does not matter whether the land was occupied by the owner or by some other person rather it is the underlying use which is of importance. APR qualification under this route is most likely to be in relation to bare land rather than a farmhouse because of the arguments already noted in relation to farmhouses but certainly if the farmhouse is occupied by the tenant farmer then relief will be secured and also by virtue of the decision in *Hanson* (see **13.26** above), such relief is now secured even if the farmhouse and the land farmed by the occupier of the farmhouse are in different ownership.

Example 13.9—Period of occupation: small let farm

Alwen's family have always been farmers. The holdings were small hillside properties and the main occupation was sheep farming. Alwen's uncle eventually moved out of his 90 acre property, letting it (house, land and farm buildings) on a commercial basis to a neighbour. By his will the uncle left the property to Alwen who thereafter drew the rents continuing to own the property until her own death more than seven years later.

APR will be allowed on the land and on the house (at its tenanted value) since the entire holding has been occupied for the purposes of agriculture throughout the qualifying period of seven years.

Contrast the above outcome with **Example 13.7** which illustrated the circumstances in which APR was denied on the farmhouse since it was not occupied by the tenant farmer to whom the land was tenanted.

The need for actual occupation has been tested in two 'farmhouse' cases. The first, *Harrold v IRC* [1996] STC (SCD) 195, was a 'clawback' case triggered by death within seven years of a gift. A building that in all respects satisfied the farmhouse tests was in the process of being renovated before occupation by the donee commenced. Nevertheless it failed because it had not, at the relevant time, been occupied for agriculture because it was not occupied at all.

In *HMRC v Atkinson and another* [2011] UKUT B26 (TCC), referred to at **13.30**, the bungalow had been occupied, as part of a larger unit, by a farming partnership but at the date of death the farmer, Mr Atkinson a partner in the business, was in a nursing home. Evidence showed that he still took an interest in farm business. However, it was held that the occupation was not merely by the farmer but by the partnership, and the partnership had ceased to occupy the bungalow when Mr Atkinson moved into the care home. It was necessary to identify a strong connection between the use of the bungalow and the agricultural activities being carried out on the farm – the mere housing of personal possessions and occasional attendance by the partners to oversee the property could not be said to amount to occupation in the true sense.

Successions

13.39 When farming property passes on death, the person inheriting it is treated as owning it from the date of death and, if they later occupy the property, as having occupied it from the date of death whether they actually did or not; *IHTA 1984, s 120(1)(a)*. Importantly, where the inheritance in point is between spouses/civil partners the person inheriting the farming property is also credited with the period of occupation of the previous owner (but note that this does not apply to lifetime gifts between spouses/civil partners).

Example 13.10—Successions: keeping it in the family

Sarah ran a small stud farm and equestrian centre with arable land and pasture. Her lifelong companion Margaret helped with the horses and as soon as they were able to do so Sarah and Margaret formalised their relationship by registration as a civil partnership. Sarah left the property to Margaret on her death and Margaret herself died some 18 months later leaving the property to her niece.

APR, if allowable on the farming enterprise at all, is allowable just as much on the death of Margaret as it had been on that of Sarah since the combined period of two years' occupation has been met.

Replacements

13.40 There is not much turnover in farm property since as a general observation, when people sell farmland they tend to move away from farming altogether. Nevertheless, *IHTA 1984, s 118* operates to preserve entitlement to APR in circumstances where a person who previously owned agricultural property replaces it (directly or indirectly) for other agricultural property and occupies one property (or the other) for the purposes of agriculture for periods which together comprise at least two years within the five years ending with the date of transfer. This is in substitution for the two-year owner occupation condition in *IHTA 1984, s 117(A)*.

13.41 There is a corresponding provision by which replacement property may also qualify for the purposes of the seven-year owner landlord condition in *IHTA 1984, s 117(B)*. Where agricultural property is replaced, the test is satisfied if the new property and the old were held for periods together comprising at least seven years in the last ten prior to transfer and were occupied (by them or another) for the purposes of agriculture.

Importantly, it should be noted that *IHTA 1984, s 118* does not allow for 'trading up' in value. The relief is restricted to the extent that the net proceeds of the old property are reinvested in the new property.

Example 13.11—Replacements: trading up

Quentin's farm was small and inconvenient but he put up with it for many years until he came into some money from an inheritance. He then sold the farm for £400,000 net, purchasing a slightly larger and much more convenient property for £600,000.

There was then a general downturn in the value of all farms and on Quentin's death shortly after purchase, the new farm was worth only £550,000. APR was allowed only on £366,630, being the proportion of the value of the new farm that was referable to the earlier holding (£400,000/600,000 × 100 = 66.66%); see *IHTA 1984, s 118(3).*

The valuation of the transfer

13.42 All agricultural property must be valued twice for IHT – first to establish market value, and secondly to establish agricultural value.

Under the general rule in *s 160* the taxpayer must show the price the property might reasonably be expected to fetch on the open market at the time of transfer. That means the gross open market value and importantly not an off-the-cuff discounted 'probate' value. It also means that where several parcels of land are concerned (as is often the case) the appropriate value is that which would be achieved by offering the land in lots likely to yield the best value overall.

This issue of lotting is examined in detail in *Ellesmere (Earl) v IRC* [1918] 2 KB 735 and *Buccleuch (Duke) v IRC* [1967] 1 AC 506 and more recently, when considering two interests in the same parcel of land, the case of *Gray (surviving executor of Lady Fox) v IRC* [1994] STC 360. In this latter case, discussed in greater detail at **13.44** below, the Lands Tribunal considered that the 'natural unit' for sale would be to offer both the land itself and a partnership interest in it as the same item – this was on the basis that the hypothetical vendor must be regarded as having done whatever was reasonably necessary to get the best price including taking separate properties, or separate interests in property, and selling them together.

13.43 The open market value will however take account of the existence of any tenancy and that tenancy, even though not marketable or capable of assignment, will likely have a value. In *Baird's Executors v IRC* [1991] 1 EGLR 201 George Baird had given up the tenancy of an agricultural holding in favour of his daughter-in-law and his grandson. The tenancy had first been granted in 1921 and the transfer, to which the landlord consented, was made in December 1977. Mr Baird died in 1985. The gift of the tenancy was a chargeable transfer under the rules in *Finance Act 1975* and the Lands Tribunal had to decide whether the 'rump' of the lease retained had any value.

It was held that the lease could have and in fact did carry a value. The District Valuer's figure was 25% of vacant possession value, having regard to what the landlord might pay to get the land back, what a tenant might pay in a sale and leaseback, the sort of figure paid to a tenant on compulsory purchase of land and on prevailing rents of other similar land. The case, being brought in Scotland, was particularly concerned with *s 177*, which provides that in certain circumstances value of a lease may be left out of account.

13.44 In the *Lady Fox* case discussed above, the Court of Appeal reviewed the decision of the Lands Tribunal. Lady Fox owned an agricultural estate farmed by a partnership which had an agricultural tenancy. She was entitled to 92.5% of the partnership profits and on her death HMRC assessed capital transfer tax (CTT) on the basis that her personal interest in the land and her partnership share should be valued together. The vacant possession of the land could be discounted in a number of ways and the result of that argument was to produce a much higher valuation figure than would apply to the land if the partnership share had been disregarded.

The Lands Tribunal had originally decided that the assets should be valued separately but had also considered what the value would be if the assets were taken together, in accordance with the method that was approved by the Court of Appeal. Taking open market vacant possession value, the District Valuer deducted the amount that the partners other than Lady Fox would accept to sell their share of the tenancy. He took a percentage of the difference between a vacant possession of value and tenancy value and discounted it to compensate for risk and delay in obtaining vacant possession.

The Tribunal, applying the rules as required by the Court of Appeal, felt that there was no guarantee that the minority partners would accept the particular sum suggested by the District Valuer and would have been willing to accept a slightly larger discount for the uncertainty, but there was no evidence from the taxpayer on that point.

13.45 Every valuation of agricultural land will turn on its own facts. Where there is in existence an 'old' tenancy (one established before 1 September 1995) APR will be restricted to the lower 50% rate unless Extra-statutory Concession F17 is in point. The latter will permit access to the higher 100%

APR rate where possession of the land can be obtained within 24 months or where, notwithstanding the terms of any tenancy, the land is valued at an amount broadly equivalent to its vacant possession value. This situation can arise where the tenant is a company and where the transferor controls the company.

Example 13.12—ESC F17 in action

David owned 52% of the shares in Hanley Farms Ltd, having given a 24% shareholding to each of his sons Eric and Fred many years ago. The company held the tenancy of Old Hanley Farm, which was owned by David. Late in life David remarried – his new wife, Geraldine, was much younger and showed little interest in farming. David transferred a 50% share of Old Hanley Farm into her name but subject to the pre September 1995 lease in favour of the company.

By his will David left his 52% shareholding in Hanley Farms Ltd on trust (Immediate Post Death Interest – IPDI) to Geraldine for life with remainder to Eric and Fred. Geraldine who was the sole proving executor and trustee of the will and under ESC F17 she claimed that the farm should be valued at open market value with APR relief available at the 100% rate. ESC F17 conveniently ignores the fact that a surrender of the lease by the company, which lies in Geraldine's power by virtue of her controlling shareholding, would be action oppressive of the minority because it would take away value from the holdings of Eric and Fred.

As stated above, APR at 100% will be in point where vacant possession can be obtained within 12 months (or within 24 months under ESCF17) notwithstanding that the tenancy was granted before the 1 September 1995 watershed. However, in the case of farming partnerships, it is now increasingly common practice for HMRC to challenge the 100% relief where the partnership occupies land and that occupation is not otherwise supported by formal documentation which defines the precise terms of occupation and/or there is no formal partnership agreement.

The value for relief

Focus

APR is not applied to market value but restricted to the usually lower agricultural value, as determined. If BPR is in point, it can be used to soak up the shortfall.

13.46 The second valuation of agricultural land is required by *IHTA 1984, s 115(3)* and is '… the value which would be the value of the property if the property were subject to a perpetual covenant prohibiting its use otherwise than as agricultural property …'. In short, for the farmhouse this could mean an adjusted lower value of perhaps 70% of open market value unless particular circumstances dictate otherwise, as will be seen from the discussion below of the leading case, referred to many times in this chapter, of *Lloyds TSB Private Banking Plc (personal representative of Rosemary Antrobus deceased) v Twiddy* (IRCT) [2005] DET/47/2004 ('*Antrobus No 2*').

Example 13.13—Agricultural value: farmhouse in East Norfolk

Lower Bylaugh Farm comprises a four-bedroomed detached house with single garage standing in a 0.25 acres adjoining a range of modern farm buildings – the farm itself comprises 175 acres of arable land. The journey time from the farm to (London) Liverpool Street station is slightly over three hours, allowing for the distressed state of certain country roads, it is five miles to the nearest petrol station and seven miles to the nearest regular public transport network. Although the land is very productive the scenery is featureless and the existence or absence of an agricultural restriction would make little difference to the value of the property. It has no particular aesthetic charm and is so far from any centre of employment or of education that it would be of little interest to any purchaser who still had to earn a living or had teenage children. In the circumstances, the agricultural value of the property must be almost the same as the open market value.

Example 13.14—Agricultural value: farmhouse in Dedham Vale

Valley Farm is set in picturesque landscape – although not listed, the property retains many original features and is set in small but well-managed gardens as part of a holding of 50 acres all of which are managed by a farm contractor. The journey time from the farm to (London) Liverpool Street Station is just under one hour and the station itself is only 12 minutes away. There are excellent shopping and restaurant facilities, schools (and nightclubs) all within 15 miles.

The land is not enough to support a farming family, but that is irrelevant – the house and its setting is magnificent. The property will likely command a market value premium by virtue of its situation, the ease with which it can be managed and what was described in *Higginson's Executors v IRC* [2002] STC (SCD) 483 as 'a case where the property has a value greater than ordinary, not because of development potential but rather because of its "amenity value"'. In such a case the agricultural value of the farmhouse could be perhaps as low as 55% of its full market value.

13.47 In the past HMRC had operated a general rule of thumb that a grand 'manor' house did not qualify as a functional farmhouse and that the agricultural value of a farmhouse must always be set at 70% of its open market value, and indeed many IHT liabilities were settled on this basis. The matter of the 'grand' farmhouse was tested in the Lands Tribunal case known as '*Antrobus No 1*' which is discussed in full at **13.33** above where it was accepted that the house in question, Cookhill Priory, was indeed a farmhouse, albeit that that decision must be read carefully and taken in context. The matter of this standard 30% discount was fully examined in the follow up case (*Lloyds TSB Private Banking Plc (personal representatives of Antrobus (deceased) v Twiddy [2006] 1 EGLR 157*) known as '*Antrobus No 2*'. The open market value of the farmhouse and gardens was eventually set at £608,475 but HMRC, adopting the 70% approach, argued that APR should be available on only £425,932 and the tribunal fixed the agricultural value relevant for APR purposes at that figure. However, what the case demonstrates is that the 30% discount against market value is not a given.

13.48 The case was very fully and forcefully argued. The taxpayer had sought APR on the full market value arguing that some purchasers actually welcomed a restriction on the agricultural use of property because it kept other people away. However, these were perhaps not 'true' farmers but 'lifestyle' farmers who having perhaps made money in some other occupation could afford to pay a market premium for the seclusion of an agricultural property. There was evidence that offers had been made for Cookhill Priory of £935,000 and eventually £1,035,000. The Valuation Office argued for a discount of 30% because the terms of *IHTA 1984, s 115(3)* were even more restrictive than a 'planning tie' – the latter can eventually be lifted, whereas the effect of *IHTA 1984, s 115(3)* is permanent. No true agricultural purchaser would deliberately 'overpay' for a house because as a farmer he would have to buy land to go with it. The argument ran that the over bid by non-farming residential purchasers for the farmhouse with a small area of land adjoining it, should be excluded since that over bid or excess would depend on matters such as location, setting, views etc which did not impact on the viability of a farming operation.

13.49 To arrive at their decision, the Lands Tribunal considered what a farmhouse actually was and its link to the farm. They decided that '… a farmhouse is the chief dwelling house attached to a farm, the house in which the farmer of the land lived …', but went further to define the farmer as '… the person who lives in the farmhouse in order to farm the land comprised in the farm and who farms the land on a day-to-day basis …'. Based on that, the tribunal was able to ignore the premium price that might be paid by a 'lifestyle' farmer. It had already been established that lifestyle farmers were a substantial part of the market for this type of property, so if they were excluded the value of the property fell to only 70% of the open market value.

Here, as in many other aspects of APR, practitioners should consider HMRC's current guidance on APR (see IHTM 24150). However, it is important to note that as with all such HMRC guidance, it represents HMRC's view, and by that token it is not actually law. Nevertheless, to take a line that is inconsistent with HMRC's approach must put the adviser on a collision course which may end before the First-tier Tribunal and perhaps not even there.

LOSS OF BPR AND APR

Focus

A binding contract of sale will deny access to APR/BPR irrespective of the qualities of the business.

13.50 It is critical to the planning process to appreciate that BPR and APR is denied where the subject matter of the transfer is itself already subject to a binding contract for sale at the very time of the chargeable/potentially chargeable event: see *IHTA 1984, s 113* (for BPR) and *IHTA 1984, s 124* (for APR). In that sense there is a loss of relief, in that the owner of the property can no longer claim APR/BPR on a transfer made after the contract has been entered into. This point was keenly illustrated in the negligence case of *Swain Mason v Mills & Reeve* [2012] EWCA Civ 498 and operates as a salutary warning.

The provisions cause difficulty, especially in partnership situations where it may be suggested that there is, by virtue of the terms of a partnership deed, a binding contract under which surviving partners can and must buy in the share of the deceased partner. If all else fails, it will be necessary to look carefully to see if there has been a partnership change effected, not by deed, but by conduct. If there has, an argument that it is now a partnership at will only, should suffice to drive a coach and horses through the old partnership deed. Alternatively, consider the Statement of Practice SP12/80 and/or IHTM25292 for the HMRC view.

Another important occasion of unintended loss of relief is where there is some change in the nature of the asset during its period of ownership prior to transfer, ie where an unquoted trading company is listed on a recognised stock exchange or where a controlling shareholder who owns property used by an unquoted trading company reduces his shareholding to a less than controlling interest with the result that the conditions for BPR on that property is lost. As has been noted, there can be loss of APR on a farmhouse where it ceases to be the hub of a true farming business or where its occupation is separate from the end user of the land.

However, all these are instances of not so much of loss of relief previously granted but more where relief which might have been available is no longer in point. This section is concerned with clawback of relief under *IHTA 1984, ss 113A* and *124A* and although there is a separate code for BPR and APR, their wording is so similar that they are taken together with commentary.

BPR or APR may be lost where, following a transfer which would otherwise qualify for relief, certain conditions are not satisfied at point of later test – the APR/BPR that would have otherwise sheltered the transfer from IHT is in effect clawed back. Clawback applies in two circumstances:

(i) where a PET fails by reason of the donor's death within seven years; or

(ii) where there is a chargeable lifetime transfer (usually by transfer into a relevant property trust) and the donor dies within seven years thereof.

Clawback operates by applying the BPR/APR rules to the concept of a 'notional transfer' made by the donee of the property immediately before the death of the donor or, if earlier, of the death of the donee. The notional transfer tests the continued availability of APR/BPR that was originally in point – if the conditions for relief are not satisfied at that point of test it will be clawed back (cease to apply).

The conditions to be satisfied are:

- that the original property was owned by the donee throughout the period beginning with the date of the chargeable transfer and ending with the death of the donor (or donee if earlier); and
- that, subject to one exception specific to shares, in relation to a notional transfer of value made by the *donee* immediately before the death, the property would qualify for relief but for satisfaction of the requirement as to ownership or occupation by reference to that *donee*.

Example 13.15—Clawback of BPR

(i) Olive gave her friend Renee a 30% holding of unquoted shares which would have qualified for BPR by reference to Olive at time of gift. Olive died within seven years, so the PET failed and access to BPR must be re-examined. If Renee still held the shares and they still met the BPR qualification by reference to Renee at the date of Olive's death all is well and BPR will be in point to shelter the gift. However, if Renee had sold the shares no BPR (assuming the replacement provisions are not in point) will be available – there is no asset to test.

(ii) Albert gave his daughter Denise a 15% holding in an unquoted trading company which later listed on the London Stock Exchange. The shares qualified for BPR at the date of the gift but, even though Denise still owned them at the time of Albert's death within seven years, BPR is not available because on the notional transfer, deemed made by Denise as donee, on Albert's death the conditions for BPR are no longer satisfied (*IHTA 1984, s 113A(3A)(b)*).

There are rules for substitution/replacement of property of BPR and APR property in the IHT codes: the application of the rules are considered by HMRC in RI95, to which reference should be made and also discussed at **13.9** and **13.40**.

Computation of the tax in clawback

13.51 Where a gift of business property becomes a failed PET by reason of the donor's death within seven years, its testing for APR/BPR qualification is always by reference to the position of the donee (and not the donor) except in the case of shares or securities. Where clawback applies, this will affect the history of chargeable transfers by the donor – the cumulative clock.

Where the transfer was an immediate chargeable lifetime transfer that originally benefited from APR or BPR but no longer qualifies at point of later test, clawback operates to charge extra tax on the original gift on the basis that no APR (or BPR) is available. In this circumstance there is no change to the history of chargeable transfers by the donor, because the value of the property before relief has not changed – the cumulative clock remains unchanged.

Special rules apply to a gift of shares or securities which qualified for BPR at the time of gift and are now retested at the time of the donor's death under the clawback rules. It does not matter that the shares may qualify for relief by reference to a different subsection of *IHTA 1984, s 105* provided that the qualification is determined by reference to the donee.

Example 13.16—BPR: gift of minority shareholding

Sidney controls a quoted company and on 30 November 2016 he gifted a minority shareholding therein to his son Alfred. In Sidney's hands those shares, as a controlled quoted holding, qualified for BPR at 50% under *IHTA 1984, s 105(1)(cc)*.

Alfred kept the shares and still owned them when Sidney died only two years later on 30 November 2018. In Alfred's hands no BPR would normally be available – this is a minority holding in a quoted company. However, the gift of quoted shares falls within *IHTA 1984, s 113A(3A)(a)*, rather than within *IHTA 1984, s 113A(3A)(b)*, so that brings into play *IHTA 1984, s 113A(3)(b)*; thus in relation to the notional transfer that Alfred is deemed to make, it is not necessary to satisfy the earlier test.

Alfred, in effect, manages to keep the original claim to BPR at 50% on shares in a quoted company and suffers no clawback. The distinction between different classes of interest in a company used to be more important where the rate of relief was not always 100%.

13.52 One major area of difficulty used to concern gifts into trust. For the purposes of the clawback rules, it is important to note that the donee of the property in that instance are the trustees, not the underlying trust beneficiary. Under the rules in force prior to *FA 2006*, a transfer to a lifetime trust other than a relevant property trust would have been a PET and would therefore have come within *IHTA 1984, s 113A(1)* or *IHTA 1984, s 124A(1)*, so clawback could apply.

If the trustee appointed the property to a beneficiary within seven years of its entry into trust the donor could die within seven years of that transfer into trust thus there was a risk of clawback which the trustee could have avoided simply by not making the appointment. That option was not available where, for example, the trust was an A&M settlement prior to 22 March 2006, as will be seen in the example below.

Example 13.17—A&M trust: partial BPR clawback

On 31 March 2005, Dawn set up an A&M settlement for her four grandchildren and transferred to it shares in her trading company, Roller Doors Ltd. At the time of the gift the eldest beneficiary was aged 17 and the provisions of the *Trustee Act 1925, s 31* were not excluded. The powers of the trustees to accumulate were limited with the result that less than one year later (and before the 22 March 2006 watershed) the eldest beneficiary on attaining age 18, became entitled to an interest in possession in 25% of the fund. The other three beneficiaries were much younger and therefore had no qualifying interest in the remaining 75% of the Trust fund as at 22 March 2006.

On Dawn's death in February 2012 within seven years of the transfer into the settlement, the notional transfer by the trustees is re-examined. At that point the trustees still hold all of the gifted shares but, in relation to the eldest beneficiary, 25% of the trust fund (and hence 25% of the gifted shareholding) is now treated by virtue of *IHTA 1984, s 49* as being part of the estate of that beneficiary. To that extent the trustee no longer holds those shares and relief in respect of that part of the fund is clawed back. There is no clawback of the relief of the remaining 75% of the fund because that is still treated as held by the trustees.

13.53 Over the years there have been difficulties with clawback because of changes in the definition of 'quoted' affecting shares on the old Unlisted Securities Market. Such shares so listed are now treated as unquoted for the purposes of BPR clawback throughout the period from the date of transfer to the date of the notional transfer. The effect of a change in 1996 is to avoid clawback where it might otherwise have applied. However, as previously mentioned, if a company listed on the AIM exchange acquired a second listing, perhaps on a major foreign and 'recognised' stock exchange, it would lose its favoured BPR status and clawback could apply.

Comparison of PETs and chargeable transfers and the treatment for clawback

13.54 The following checklist may help to assess the effect on the transfer of business or agricultural property (CLT = chargeable lifetime transfer).

	PET Treatment	CLT Treatment
On lifetime gift: immediate charge to IHT?	No	Only on value as reduced by BPR/APR as appropriate
Death within seven years of transfer: assets retained by donee and continue to qualify for reliefs	No IHT: full relief secured	No IHT: full relief secured
Death within seven years of transfer where clawback applies: effect on the transfer itself	IHT charge, subject to availability of nil rate band. Charge is on the full amount of the original transfer.	IHT charge, subject to availability of nil rate band. Charge is on the full amount of the original transfer.
Death within seven years of transfer where clawback applies: effect on aggregation with later transfers	Full value is aggregated – cumulation principle	The value is nil and there is no cumulation with later gifts
Transferor lives seven years from gift and no benefit has been reserved	No IHT: transfer has become exempt	No IHT: transfer falls out of cumulation

Chapter 14

Lifetime planning

SIGNPOSTS

- **Reliefs** – Careful planning and a structured approach using all available lifetime reliefs will minimise a future IHT liability (see **14.1**).
- **Child Trust Funds, Junior ISAs and New ISAs (NISAs)** – A generous gesture by the government which is often overlooked, but can build up a sizeable fund which can grow outside the parents' or grandparents' estate (see **14.2**).
- **Potentially exempt transfers** – One of the most tax-efficient ways of reducing a large estate for as long as the donor survives seven years. PETs are sometimes used in more aggressive schemes, which ought to be approached with care (see **14.3–14.11**).
- **Disabled persons' trusts** – An IHT-efficient way of planning for persons with disabilities (see **14.12–14.19**).
- **Protected gifts without trusts** – As *FA 2006* severely restricted the use of trusts without triggering IHT charges, pensions and family limited partnerships may be worth investigating (see **14.20–14.25**).
- **Traditional protected gifts** – In addition to making lifetime gifts into trust, insurance policy trusts, discounted gift schemes and flexible insurance trusts are an alternative for estate planning purposes (see **14.26-14.34**).

USE ALL THE RELIEFS

Lifetime reliefs

14.1 The taxation of lifetime transfers is discussed in **Chapter 4**. The main exemptions and exclusions are described in **Chapter 11** and the reliefs of general application in **Chapter 12**. There is, naturally, some overlap between this chapter and **Chapter 3**, relating to the nil rate band. The cardinal rule for

IHT planning, if not of all tax planning, is first to use all of the reliefs that the legislation provides.

Finance Act 2006 restricted the scope for lifetime giving, making it more difficult for taxpayers with substantial estates to mitigate a future IHT liability. Several factors tend to restrict the use of lifetime gifts, all of which contribute to difficulties for taxpayers later in life. They can be seen from the following extended example (all statutory references are to *IHTA 1984*, unless otherwise stated).

Example 14.1—Case study (1): background

Ian worked for many years in local government and is now in his early sixties. He took early retirement, which has provided him with a generous pension. He now works from home, providing consultancy services to his former employer and to other local authorities. He was first married to Sarah. They had a daughter, Samantha, now a chartered accountant, and a son, Jonathan, who is employed by the NHS. Ian and Sarah were divorced many years ago. Ian eventually achieved a clean break settlement. He now lives with Prudence, but they are not married. Their only son, Ben, is a student.

Prudence came out of her own divorce with some savings, now worth £100,000. Ian has no worthwhile savings apart from his pension, but he does own the house in which they live, worth £1,000,000.

Ian gets on fairly well with Sam and Jon. Sam and her husband would like to start a family but their present mortgage is such that they both need to work to fund it. Jon is in rented accommodation and finding it difficult to get onto the property ladder. Prudence does not really object to the idea that Ian might make some provision for the children of his first marriage provided, of course, that Ben's interests are protected.

Example 14.2—Case study (II): existing wills etc

Prudence's will leaves her estate to Ben. Ian's will leaves the house to Prudence for life with remainder to Sam, Jon and Ben in equal shares. Ian has nominated Prudence as the main beneficiary of his pension if he dies before drawing it. His will leaves the residue of his estate, which would include the value, if any, of his consultancy, to Prudence.

If Prudence died first, there would be no IHT on her estate, which would pass to Ben free of tax. It is, however, assumed that Ian dies first. His pension provision was nominated to Prudence many years ago and falls outside his estate. The consultancy is worth £20,000, comprising the benefit of work in progress and some other realisable assets: these are all genuine trading assets and 100% BPR is available in respect of them. By then, the house is assumed to be worth £1,100,000. No gifts have been made, the nil rate band of £325,000 is set against the value of the house. Assume Ian dies during 2018/19 leaving in charge £775,000 and giving rise to a tax charge at 40% of £310,000.

As Ian's will leaves the property to Prudence and not a direct descendant, the residence nil rate band is not available. The family may want to consider entering into a Deed of Variation to take advantage of the residence nil rate band.

Although Prudence would have the benefit of a reduced pension, and could use her own savings to pay part of the IHT, she might decide that the house must be sold and ask the trustees to buy something more modest. If she were to die shortly thereafter, the estate to be considered would be her own capital of £100,000, the money realised from the consultancy plus the net value of the remaining trust fund, say £790,000 ignoring expenses. The IHT bill, if she died within a year of Ian's death, would reflect the benefit of quick succession relief.

Example 14.3—Case study (III): marriage and downsizing

If Ian and Pru had taken tax advice, things might have been rather different. Although they were living together they were not married. If he and Pru married, spouse relief could be available on the first death of either of them.

Second, following Ian's retirement there is no real need for them to continue to live in the London commuter belt. Ian's consultancy is not worth a significant amount. It therefore makes sense for Ian to sell the house and to buy something that is quite big enough for him and Prudence (and for Ben when he comes home from university). They find a suburban property in East Anglia, which they purchase in their joint names as tenants in common for £500,000.

Example 14.4—Case study (IV): gifts and wills

That leaves Ian with cash of £600,000 and increases Pru's estate to £350,000. Ian gives £100,000 each to Samantha and Jon. Ben has found a property in the university town where he is studying that could be bought for £250,000. Ian therefore gives Ben £100,000 as a deposit on the house.

Ben establishes that, even in the present market, with a substantial deposit a 'student/buy to let' mortgage is on offer at quite favourable terms. Having obtained confirmation of the rates available in the open market, he then borrows £150,000 from Ian on terms that are quite good for Ian but actually give Ben a significantly better interest rate than he could have secured elsewhere, so there is no reservation of benefit in the transaction.

Ben has student friends who will rent two-thirds of the property. The rent is enough to pay the interest to Ian.

That leaves Ian with £150,000. He invests £100,000 on the advice of a stockbroker friend in blue-chip securities. The last £50,000 is invested in a small AIM company providing services to local authorities in a commercial field that Ian happens to know about and which he thinks is reasonably safe.

Pru changes her will. She now leaves £100,000 to Ben outright, then leaves the balance on an immediate post-death interest trust for Ian, and on Ian's death absolutely to Jon, Sam and Ben in equal shares. Ian makes a will leaving the AIM shares to his children. He gives his executors power not to call in the mortgage on Ben's property. He leaves the residue of his estate to Pru for life with power to advance capital for her with remainder to his children. This ensures that not only the transferable nil rate band is available, but also the residence nil rate band.

Example 14.5—Case study (V): the tax effect of lifetime planning

Broadly, the effect of these arrangements is to make full use of the transferable and residence nil rate bands, as was the case under the previous part of the illustration, but this time there is no crippling IHT charge on Ian's death. If Pru were to die first the gift to Ben would be tax-free. The saving is substantial.

On the assumption that Ian dies first during 2018/19, his estate is as follows:

	£	£
Half share in house		250,000
Quoted shares		100,000
Unquoted shares		50,000
Consultancy		20,000
Loan		150,000
Sub total		570,000

Recent gifts (£300,000 less £6,000 exempt)		294,000
Estate before reliefs		864,000
Deduct		
BPR on shares	50,000	
BPR on consultancy	20,000	70,000
Estate after reliefs		794,000

The estate suffers no IHT, being exempt or relieved. Distribution is as follows:

Gross estate for distribution as above	864,000
Deduct balance of nil rate band (see below)	31,000
Residuary fund (below)	833,000
Spouse relief	833,000

The nil rate band is £325,000. From it are deducted the three gifts to the children totalling £300,000, less two annual exemptions of £6,000.

The specific gift of the AIM shares avoids the difficulties of *IHTA 1984, s 39A*: for more detail see **5.40**, **Example 5.3** and **15.25**.

Example 14.6—Case study (VI): incidental benefits for the family

The result of this arrangement is that Sam can reduce her mortgage and think about starting a family. Jon can put a deposit down on a property. Ben has secure accommodation whilst he is a student and, if he sells at a profit after he graduates, main residence relief will be available on the whole of the gain. In the meantime he can claim rent-a-room relief.

The family as a whole will benefit from BPR on the eventual disposal of the consultancy and on the investment in the AIM company. If the AIM company does no more than hold its value the saving after two years will be tax of £20,000 (though that saving only lasts if shares are still owned by Ian at the date of his death and if at that date the company is still an unquoted company).

Pru's position is more secure. She now owns half of the house she lives in and has a life interest in the other half. If she wanted to move, main residence relief should be available both to her and to the trustees. She has the income from the quoted securities and from Ben's mortgage. If Ben sells his house well when he graduates, he will have a substantial deposit and should find it easy to borrow in the open market, releasing £150,000 to the trustees.

If Pru finds that she does not need all of the income from the trust fund, she has one or two choices available to her. She may simply authorise the trustees to pay away to the family any income in so far as it exceeds a certain sum that she needs to live on. That would be entirely within the rule in *Bennett v IRC* [1995] STC 54 and the payments would quickly gain relief under *IHTA 1984, s 21*. Alternatively, she may release part of her life interest, allowing the children to become absolutely entitled. That would be a PET against which, if she gave notice to the trustees, she could set her annual exemption under *IHTA 1984, s 57*.

The estate will benefit from the transferable nil rate band (although small if Ian dies within seven years of the gift to his children) and potentially the residence nil rate band.

The Child Trust Fund, Junior ISAs and NISAs

14.2 The Child Trust Fund (CTF) was a casualty of the coalition government following its election in 2010, when government contributions were reduced and then stopped altogether in January 2011. Existing CTFs will carry on building up, largely tax-free, to age 18, and friends and family will continue to be able to pay in up to £4,128 a year. It offers substantial scope for saving income tax, capital gains tax and IHT. Although the amounts may seem modest the effects of full use of the allowance and of accumulation of income may be greater than is generally realised. On 26 October 2010 the government announced that it would introduce a new tax-advantaged account for saving for children, to be known as a Junior ISA. Junior ISAs were launched on 1 November 2011. They were available for any UK-resident child. From 1 July 2014, ISAs were reformed into a simpler product, the NISA, and all existing ISAs will become NISAs.

The CTF or Junior ISAs are essentially UK-based gross roll-up funds. Normally, a parent achieves no advantage from a settlement on his unmarried minor child, as any income of such a settlement is assessable on him if it exceeds £100 per parent (*ITTOIA 2005, s 629*). The CTF or Junior ISA avoids this difficulty. For CTFs the parent, or indeed any family member, was able to add £100 per month to the fund without the tax penalties that would otherwise apply. The limit of £1,200 per year was calculated by reference to the child's birthday, not the tax year. The limit for Junior ISAs was £3,840 per annum until 30 June 2014, increasing to £4,000 per annum from 1 July 2014. The allowance for 2017/18 was £4,128, increasing to £4,260 from 6 April 2018.

The government allows savings kept in a Child Trust Fund (CTF) to be transferred to a junior ISA from April 2015. The CTF scheme was closed to new deposits in 2010.

Example 14.7—Child trust funds, junior ISAs and NISAs: generous but forgetful grandfather

Robert's children had blessed him with several grandchildren, some born after 31 August 2002. On 1 May 2008, to celebrate his eightieth birthday he gave each of his grandchildren £500. For each of the younger children this was promptly added to the CTF that the parent had taken out. In late March 2009, having read about the CTF, Robert quickly sent £1,000 to the parent of each younger grandchild, to catch the end of the tax year. As Robert has a generous pension, he also adds £500 annually to Junior ISAs, or now NISAs.

In each case, if the pattern continues, it may be possible to argue that the gifts form part of Robert's normal expenditure and are within *IHTA 1984, s 21,* rather than PETs.

14.3 There is no way of deferring the enjoyment of the CTF or Junior ISA beyond the age of 18, but that is really the only drawback of the scheme.

In the past, secondary school education has often been funded by grandparents through A&M trusts. The facility of doing that is cut down significantly by *FA 2006*. If, therefore, the burden, for those who choose it, of funding secondary education falls more heavily on parents than on grandparents, the grandparents could use the CTF or Junior ISA to help with the cost of further education.

Focus

- Most banks and building societies are actively marketing ISAs.
- A wealth of information explaining the details and rates can be found on the internet.

INDIVIDUAL SAVINGS ACCOUNTS (ISAS), INHERITED ISAS, LIFETIME ISAS, FLEXIBLE ISAS AND INNOVATIVE FINANCE ISAS

14.4 Individual Savings Accounts (ISAs) have become more flexible and ISAs are seen by many as a simple tax-efficient way to save for retirement. The annual investment limit was £15,000 in 2013/14 and increased to £15,240 in 2015/16. *Finance Act 2016* contained provisions which kept the subscription limit for ISAs at £15,240 for 2016/17. *Finance Act 2017* included provisions which increased the subscription limit for ISAs to £20,000 from 6 April 2017.

The Individual Savings Account (Amendment No 2) Regulations, SI 2015/869 took effect on 6 April 2015, which provides that the spouse or civil partner of a saver who died on or after 3 December 2014 can benefit from an additional ISA allowance equal to the value of the ISA at the holder's date of death, also called an 'additional permitted subscription' (APS). This is in addition to the surviving spouse's or civil partner's own ISA allowance and the APS can be used within three years from the date of death or (if later) 180 days after the administration period has ended. One of the conditions is that the surviving spouse lived with the deceased at the time of his death. If so, the deceased's ISA can be transferred to the surviving spouse/civil partner.

Legislation is included in *Finance Act 2016* to amend *ITTOIA 2005, s 694A* in that it extends the income tax and CGT free exemption to estates during the administration period.

The government has issued draft regulations for changes to cash ISAs from 6 April 2016. This allows savers to withdraw from an ISA and then replace the amount withdrawn in the same year. *Finance Act 2016* also introduced a new pension savings account, called the Lifetime ISA (LISA). The LISA will be available from April 2017 for individuals under the age of 40, who will be able to contribute £4,000 per year with a 25% bonus received from the government.

Individuals will be able to make LISA contributions and receive the 25% bonus from the Government from the age of 18 up to the age of 50. This means that over their lifetime individuals can save up to £128,000 with a £32,000 bonus. Funds can be withdrawn to:

- purchase a first home worth up to £450,000 at any time after 12 months from opening the account;
- draw on the fund from the age of 60; or
- draw on the fund if terminally ill with less than 12 months to live.

On the face of it this sounds quite attractive but early withdrawals which are not used to purchase a first home will suffer a 5% charge and the bonus will need to be repaid.

The *Individual Savings Account (Amendment No 2) Regulations 2016* includes a list of qualifying investments for the new Innovative Finance ISA (IF ISA). This will be extended to debt securities issued by companies and offered via crowdfunding and possibly equity crowd funding. The IF ISA is high risk, as unlike other ISAs it is not protected, but it does offer returns up to 6%, which might make it attractive to some.

BPR and APR

14.5 The rate of BPR and APR has not always been as much as 100%. Future governments may consider reducing the rate if increased tax revenues are required.

14.6 The difficulty for families will be that the assets that qualify for BPR are those that involve some element of risk. Sometimes such assets are held more for the possibility of capital growth than for income. As a result, an elderly estate owner may wish to keep the assets that are safe and that yield a good income, whilst disposing of other assets. If IHT mitigation is the only consideration, the estate owner should probably do the opposite. If at his death his estate comprises entirely assets that qualify for APR or BPR there will be no IHT to pay except in so far as lifetime gifts, originally PETs, become chargeable. The exceptions are those gifts that by their very nature prejudice subsequent claims to relief. See the example 'Getting it wrong' at **Example 13.3** and of loss of relief on farmhouse at **Example 13.7**.

Another factor that will often influence the subject matter of gifts is the availability, or lack of it, of hold-over relief for CGT purposes. *TCGA 1992, s 165* offers fairly wide scope for holdover relief of business assets and is extended.

Example 14.8—BPR: recycling business property into investments

Alan invested in unquoted trading company shares, gradually building up a portfolio worth £800,000 in which all the holdings had been held for at least two years. He then transferred them all to his son, such that the transfer was a PET that might be subject to clawback of BPR if he died within seven years. None of the companies had a secondary listing on any recognised stock exchange, so the transfer attracted 100% relief, but subject for the next seven years to the clawback rule in *IHTA 1984, s 113A*.

The son was wary of such investments, fearing lack of liquidity and risk generally. He realised that a clawback charge could apply in the event of Alan's death, if they no longer held assets that qualified for 100% BPR, so he took out term insurance. Having done that, he sold all the shares and bought gilts and investment properties to stabilise the portfolio.

SHARES LISTED ON THE ALTERNATIVE INVESTMENT MARKET (AIM) AND OTHER TAX EFFICIENT INVESTMENTS

14.7 Shares traded on the Alternative Investment Market (AIM) qualify for BPR once the investor has owned the shares for two years. A number of providers offer AIM portfolio IHT plans which spread the risk. However, AIM shares are a higher risk, long-term investment, as AIM has less stringent rules and AIM company shares may be less liquid than those listed on the London Stock Exchange.

Another option is to invest in companies which benefit from the Enterprise Investment Scheme (EIS), the seed enterprise investment scheme (SEIS) and venture capital trusts (VCT). These investments also qualify for BPR after the investor has held the shares for two years, but again the risk associated with such investment has to be weighed up carefully.

The Enterprise Investment Scheme (EIS) is designed to help smaller higher risk trading companies to raise finance by offering a range of tax reliefs, including IHT, to investors.

Guidance can be found on www.gov.uk/government/publications/the-enterprise-investment-scheme-introduction. If certain conditions are complied with, such shares will benefit from BPR, once held for two years.

Shares listed on the Alternative Investment Market (AIM) and shareholdings in OFEX companies also qualify for BPR after the transferor held them for two years.

For more information, please see *Tax Planning 2018/19* (Bloomsbury Professional).

> **Focus**
>
> Both EIS shares and AIM listed shares potentially may be more volatile; and they may be more difficult to liquidate.

OUTRIGHT GIFTS

True outright gifts

14.8 Many people of moderate wealth will accept the present regime and will suffer the tax on discretionary trusts as the price to be paid for preserving family property from dissipation as a result of vesting at age 18.

The advantages of outright gifts are:

- simplicity;
- cheapness, in terms of legal fees saved;
- the transfer is a PET;
- holdover relief from CGT may be available under *TCGA 1992, s 165,* avoiding the complexities of *TCGA 1992, s 169B* that arise on gifts to settlor interested settlements.

The trouble with simplicity is its transparency. Many a potential donor seems to want something more complicated, as if that confers tax advantages. No formal deed is necessary to make a gift of cash: let the donor just write out a cheque and, mindful of the rule in *Curnock (Curnock's Personal Representative) v IRC* [2003] STC (SCD) 283, do it soon enough that it can be encashed before death. A gift of shares in a plc held in certificated form requires no more than a stock transfer, again delivered timeously to avoid the rule in *Rose, Re, Rose v IRC* [1952] 1 All ER 1217. For a gift of land to an adult, a transfer is enough; if in Scotland, the date of the disposition is the effective date, not the later date of registration (*Marquess of Linlithgow and Earl of Hopetoun v HMRC* [2010] CSIH 19). A car or a valuable chattel may be given by simple delivery, but it might be safer to execute a deed of gift.

Many of these transactions generate little in professional fees but are effective none the less. If reliance is to be placed on the *IHTA 1984, s 21* exemption, what is needed is not so much a formal deed as a record of the intention to make regular gifts and its execution over a period of years. Good record keeping showing that these gifts are made out of excess income is essential (see **11.9**).

Unwise gifts

14.9 A gift is perceived as being unwise where family assets as a result can be at risk of claim in matrimonial proceedings or at the suit of creditors. Apart from that, gifts may be unwise where they prejudice APR or BPR. This was illustrated in the **Example 13.3** of Jason where the transferor no longer had control of the company at the time of a gift of an asset used by that company.

This is illustrated in the case of *Rosser v IRC* SpC 368, [2003] SSCD 311, discussed at **13.30.** It is also illustrated by the considerations that have just been described above in relation to the choice of asset to give away.

14.10 There are other circumstances where a gift may prove to have been unwise. The example of Willie in **Example 10.17** how gifts may be taxable in the context of a discretionary trust. Certainly, if an outright gift has been made nearly seven years ago and the transferor is considering establishing a trust now, which will be treated as a discretionary one under the rules in *FA 2006*, it makes sense to allow the seven years from the earlier gift to run off so that it does not affect the calculation of the hypothetical transfer, see the example of Celia at **Example 10.3** where a failed PET came to light.

Care needs to be taken when money is gifted into a joint bank account for the donor and donee. Even if there is an intention to make the gift, but if the account is operated so that the donor potentially can withdraw the full amount, there might be a reservation of benefit and the whole account may remain within the donor's estate for IHT purposes (see *Sillars v IRC* (2004) STC (STD) 180 and *Matthews v Revenue and Customs Commissioners* [2012] UKFTT 658 (TC)).

Example 14.9—Failed PET: a gift that should not have been made

Henry, whose late wife had used her nil rate band in full, settled £400,000 on discretionary trusts on 18 June 2010. On 22 July 2015, he gave his daughter Jennifer a cheque for £160,000. When he died on 30 June 2018 his estate was £500,000 and had the benefit neither of APR nor BPR. The chargeable transfer to the discretionary trust was more than seven years before the death and therefore itself fell out of aggregation with the estate at death. However, as there was a chargeable transfer followed by a PET, there is a potential trap for the unwary advisor.

The PET in 2015 was less than three years before the death and outside the scope of taper relief. IHT on the PET is calculated by reference to the situation on the day that it was made. On that date the cumulative total of transfers was £400,000, so IHT on the failed PET is based on £560,000. The nil rate band is that on death, £325,000, leaving all of the £160,000 in charge at 40%, tax therefore £64,000.

The estate for probate purposes is £500,000. The failed PET of £160,000 must be taken into account. After allowing for the nil rate band in force at the date of death of £325,000 and two RNRBs of £125,000, the tax is £34,000 (ie £500,000 – (£325,000 + £250,000 – £160,000) × 40%). This liability is in addition to the IHT on the failed PET.

The situation could have been avoided if the gift had not been made and instead there had been equivalent provision by will. Assuming that the £160,000 had not been spent and that none of the income from it was saved, the estate at death might then have been £660,000. The tax would still be £34,000, but there would have been no failed PET and therefore no tax charge on it.

The moral of the story is that someone who has made a substantial lifetime chargeable transfer must weigh up quite carefully the advantages of early giving and the risk that a charge on his estate may apply by virtue of *IHTA 1984, s 7(1)*.

For a time, it seemed that if a taxpayer (or if we are honest, his adviser) made a mistaken gift, there was some scope for 'putting the toothpaste back in the tube' by relying on the principle in *Hastings-Bass Deceased, Hastings v CIR* [1974] 2 All ER 193. If, say, trustees had mistakenly appointed out funds on the wrong day, they could apply to have the deed set aside on the ground that they had not appreciated the full effect of the document when entering into it. Thus, Abacus Trust Co were twice before the courts, once with NSPCC and again with Barr, to seek help.

In *Sieff v Fox* [2005] WLR 3811 Lloyd LJ reformulated the *Hastings-Bass* principle as it relates to exercise by trustees of their discretion. The court will interfere '… if it is clear that [the trustees] would not have acted as they did had they not failed to take into account considerations which they ought to have … or taken into account considerations which they ought not …' He also observed that it might help the court if HMRC did not always decline the invitation to take part when such matters were litigated.

In *Tax Bulletin* 83 (June 2006), HMRC indicated that they would in future consider joining in litigation if much tax is in issue. They feel that where, as in *Abacus Trust Co (Isle of Man) Ltd v NSPCC* [2001] STC 1344, the trustee takes tax advice but fails correctly to implement it, there should be no relief. That would (though of course the *Bulletin* does not use such language) effectively blow many such cases out of the water. A mistake as to the intended tax effect of a document is unlikely to be the subject of rectification by the court (see *Allnutt and another v Wilding and others* [2007] EWCA Civ 412).

Litigation was joined in *Pitt v Holt* [2010] EWHC 45 (Ch) and *Futter and Futter* [2011] EWCA Civ 197, see the recent Supreme Court decision in *Pitt v HMRC; Futter v HMRC* [2013] UKSC 26.

In *Futter* the trustees of the two discretionary trusts exercised their power of advancement with the intention of transferring assets out of the settlement in such a way as to avoid a charge to CGT. The trustees' decision was made following professional advice which overlooked the provision in *IHTA 1984, s 2(4)* which provides that allowable losses within a settlement cannot be set off against gains attributed to beneficiaries, thereby resulting in unexpected CGT charges.

The Supreme Court unanimously dismissed the trustees' appeal and held that the trustees exercise of the power of advancement had been valid and that it would be contrary to principle and authority to set aside the decision by trustees who acted on wrong professional advice.

In *Pitt* the issue was whether a transfer of assets into a settlement can be set aside. Mrs Pitt, whose husband suffered serious head injuries in an accident in 1990, on advice of solicitors, transferred the damages received, into a settlement. However the form of settlement suffered substantial IHT liabilities. Mrs Pitt applied to the Court to set aside the settlement and a related settlement.

The Supreme Court unanimously upheld the appeal, holding that a voluntary disposition can be set aside on the grounds of equity. Based on the facts of the case the settlement could have been drafted so as to fall under the definitions of 'disabled trusts' under *IHTA 1984, s 89*. This approach was confirmed in the recent case of *Kennedy v Kennedy* [2014] EWHC 4129 Ch.

Two recent first-instance cases demonstrate the courts' willingness to rectify defective deeds. In *Bullard v Bullard and another* [2017] EWHC 3 (Ch), the claimant settlor/trustee sought rectification to remove *Trustee Act 1925, s 31* from the deed, which prevented the trust from being an interest in possession trust. In this case the court rectified the trust deed to exclude *s 31*. The second case concerns the creation of successive life interests – see *RBC Trustees (CI) Ltd and others v Stubbs* [2017] EWHC 180 (Ch). The trustees failed to appreciate that the creation of a successive life interest in 2008 and 2014 created an immediate IHT charge. Again the Court allowed rectification.

More subtle schemes

14.11 The steady rise in house prices has forced planners to explore ways of sheltering the home from IHT. At its least aggressive, this may involve the gift of a share in the home to a child who continues to live there and is likely to remain permanently.

If the sale is to an unconnected third party, pre-owned asset tax (POAT) will not be a problem, though it will otherwise be, unless the transaction took place before 7 March 2005, or (which is rather contrived) the consideration is not for money or readily convertible into money (*SI 2005/724, reg 5*).

More adventurous is the creation of a lease, followed by the sale of the freehold reversion and a gift of the proceeds of that sale. This level of planning must carry a health warning and must be carefully executed.

A variant of this idea is the sale of a share in the house followed by gift of the proceeds, but again it will have to be to a stranger, or not for cash, to avoid POAT.

Boldest of all is:

- the sale of the house (or perhaps an investment property) to a spouse;
- the price is satisfied by a debt; and
- the debt is given away (eg to adult children).

It has been argued that there was no gift with reservation, because:

- a sale is not a gift;
- the deduction should be allowable, unless *FA 1986, s 103* happens to be an issue; there will potentially be SDLT to pay, but no POAT, because it is an excluded transaction.

FA 2013 included new IHT provisions which amend *IHTA 1984, s 162(4)* and *(5)* and disallow a deduction from the value of an estate for liabilities owed by the deceased on death in the following circumstances:

- excluded property – no deduction will be allowed for a liability to the extent that it has been incurred directly or indirectly to acquire property which is excluded from the charge to IHT. However, where the acquired property has been disposed of or where the liability is greater than the value of the excluded property, the deduction may be allowed providing certain conditions are met – see new *IHTA 1984, s162A*; or

- where the liability has been incurred to acquire assets on which a relief suchas BPR, APR or woodlands relief is due, the liability will be taken to reduce the value of those assets that can qualify for relief. The deduction for the loan will be matched against the assets acquired and relief will be restricted to the net value of the assets. Any excess liability will be allowable as adeduction against the estate in general subject to the new rule about unpaiddebts – see new *IHTA 1984, s 162B*; or
- a deduction for a liability will be allowed only to the extent that it is repaid to the creditor, unless it is shown that there is a commercial reason for not repaying the liability and it is not left unpaid as part of arrangements to geta tax advantage – see new *IHTA 1984, s 175A*.

The measure will have effect for transfers of value, including transfers arising on death, made on or before 17 July 2013, the date on which *FA 2013* received Royal Assent. The provisions in *IHTA 1984, s 162B* dealing with liabilities in relation to relievable property only applies to liabilities incurred on or after 6 April 2013.

DISABLED PERSONS TRUSTS

14.12 Disabled persons interests (DPI) escaped some of the changes in *FA 2006*. The tax code for DPIs is complex and confusing following a series of changes in *FA 2006, FA 2013* and *FA 2014*.

There has long been a code for disabled trusts, which has been little used because it was inflexible and many of the advantages could be achieved through normal discretionary trusts.

Original s 89 disabled person's interest

14.13 The original DPI is defined in *IHTA 1984, s 89*:

'(1) This section applies to settled property transferred into settlement after 9th March 1981 and held on trusts—

(a) under which, during the life of a disabled person, no interest in possession in the settled property subsists, and

(b) which secure that not less than half of the settled property which is applied during his lifetime is applied for his benefit.

(2) For the purposes of this Act the person mentioned in subsection (1) above shall be treated as beneficially entitled to an interest in possession in the settled property.

(3) The trusts on which settled property is held shall not be treated as falling outside subsection (1) above by reason only of the powers conferred

on the trustees by section 32 of the Trustee Act 1925 or section 33 of the Trustee Act (Northern Ireland) 1958 (powers of advancement).

(4) The reference in subsection (1) above to a disabled person is, in relation to any settled property, a reference to a person who, when the property was transferred into settlement, was—

(a) incapable, by reason of mental disorder within the meaning of the Mental Health Act 1983, of administering his property or managing his affairs, or

(b) in receipt of an attendance allowance, or

(c) in receipt of a disability living allowance …'.

Therefore, until 22 March 2006 only discretionary trusts qualified as DPIs under *IHTA 1984, s 89.*

Finance Act 2006 changes

14.14 *Finance Act 2006* introduced three further types of DPIs:

- *IHTA 1984, s 89A* – self-settlement on discretionary trust on or after 22 March 2006 by person with a condition expected to lead to a disability;
- *IHTA 1984, s 89B(1)(c)* – DPI on interest in possession created by anyone during the lifetime of a settlor on or after 22 March 2006 for the benefit of a disabled person; and
- *IHTA 1984, s 89(B)(1)(d)* – self-settlement on interest in possession trust on or after 22 March 2006 by person with a condition expected to lead to a disability.

Therefore, after *FA 2006* there were four different DPIs. A transfer into these types of trust, therefore, is treated as a potentially exempt transfer for IHT rather than a chargeable transfer. In addition these types of trust do not suffer ten-yearly charges or exit charges for IHT.

IHTA 1984, s 49(1) provides that the disabled person will be deemed to be the beneficial owner of the trust fund with the result that the trust fund will be aggregated with the disabled person's other assets on death.

Following changes introduced by *FA 2014,* capital gains tax free uplift on death under *TCGA 1992, s 72* applies to DPIs with underlying interests in possessions for deaths on or after 5 December 2013.

Focus

- A major disincentive for creating *IHTA 1984, s 89* trusts was that half the income had to be paid to the disabled person, thereby making it less flexible than discretionary trusts. Following *FA 2013* this is now even more restrictive, as, for DPIs created on or after 8 April 2014, all the capital needs to be applied for the disabled beneficiary subject to an 'annual limit' of the lesser of £3,000 or 3% of the settled property.

- The potential double charge to IHT and CGT on the death of the disabled person with an interest in possession in the settled fund was another disadvantage. The CGT disadvantage has been addressed in draft *FA 2014*.

Section 89A – self-settlement under FA 2006

14.15 This type of trust was introduced to permit persons to provide for themselves in the anticipation of a future disability. This type of trust is useful when someone suffers from a degenerative illness.

The legislation defines this type of DPI as follows:

'(1) This section applies to property transferred by a person ("A") into settlement on or after 22nd March 2006 if—

(a) A was beneficially entitled to the property immediately before transferring it into settlement,

(b) A satisfies the Commissioners for Her Majesty's Revenue and Customs that, when the property was transferred into settlement, A had a condition that it was at that time reasonable to expect would have such effects on A as to lead to A becoming—

(i) a person falling within section 89(4)(a) above,

(ii) in receipt of an attendance allowance mentioned in section 89(4)(b) above, or

(iii) in receipt of a disability living allowance mentioned in section 89(4)(c) above by virtue of entitlement to the care component at the highest or middle rate, and

(c) the property is held on trusts—

(i) under which, during the life of A, no interest in possession in the settled property subsists, and

(ii) which secure that Conditions 1 and 2 are met.

(2) Condition 1 is that if any of the settled property is applied during A's life for the benefit of a beneficiary, it is applied for the benefit of A.

(3) Condition 2 is that any power to bring the trusts mentioned in subsection (1)(c) above to an end during A's life is such that, in the event of the power being exercised during A's life, either—

(a) A or another person will, on the trusts being brought to an end, be absolutely entitled to the settled property, or

(b) on the trusts being brought to an end, a disabled person's interest within section 89B(1)(a) or (c) below will subsist in the settled property.

(4) If this section applies to settled property transferred into settlement by a person, the person shall be treated as beneficially entitled to an interest in possession in the settled property.'

This type of DPI has to be a discretionary trust settled during someone's lifetime in expectation of a disability for his own benefit provided:

- if any capital is distributed during the settlor's lifetime, it will be distributed for the settlor's benefit; or
- if the trust is brought to an end during the settlor's lifetime, the settlor is entitled to the trust fund, or someone else is entitled to the trust fund, so that it will form their estate for IHT purposes.

Alternatively the settlement can be brought to an end in favour of another DPI's interest.

Section 89B as introduced by Finance Act 2006

14.16

Section 89B of *IHTA 1984* extends *IHTA 1984, ss 89* and *89A* to include interest in possessions to qualify as DPIs:

'(1) In this Act "disabled person's interest" means—

(a) an interest in possession to which a person is under section 89(2) above treated as beneficially entitled,

(b) an interest in possession to which a person is under section 89A(4) above treated as beneficially entitled,

(c) an interest in possession in settled property (other than an interest within paragraph (a) or (b) above) to which a disabled person becomes beneficially entitled on or after 22nd March 2006, or

(d) an interest in possession in settled property (other than an interest within paragraph (a) or (b) above) to which a person ("A") is beneficially entitled if—

(i) A is the settlor,

(ii) A was beneficially entitled to the property immediately before transferring it into settlement,

(iii) A satisfies Her Majesty's Commissioners for Revenue and Customs as mentioned in section 89A(1)(b) above,

(iv) the settled property was transferred into settlement on or after 22nd March 2006, and

(v) the trusts on which the settled property is held secure that, if any of the settled property is applied during A's life for the benefit of a beneficiary, it is applied for the benefit of A.'

IHTA 1984, s 89B(1)(c) applies to interest in possession trusts created by anyone during the settlor's lifetime for the benefit of a disabled person. This type of trust cannot be created on death, as the provisions in *IHTA 1984, s 49A,* which create immediate post-death interests, take priority.

IHTA 1984, s 89(1)(d) is similar to *IHTA 1984, s 89A* in that it allows for self-settlement in expectation of a disability, but on interest in possession trusts rather than discretionary trusts. Again this type of trust will be outside the relevant property regime for IHT.

New DPIs created or additions to existing DPIs on or after 8 April 2013

14.17

Section 216 and *Sch 44 of FA 2013* made the following main amendments to the existing regime:

- alignment of income and capital requirements imposed by the income tax, capital gains tax and IHT treatment for vulnerable beneficiaries (see **14.19**);
- inclusion in the definition of a DPI of persons who are in receipt of the new Personal Independence Payment.

A statutory meaning of 'disabled person' was amended by *FA 2013* with effect from 6 April 2013 (*FA 2005, Sch 1A*). A disabled person, therefore, is someone who falls into one or more of the following categories:

(a) incapable of administering his property or managing his affairs by reason of mental disorder within the meaning of the *Mental Health Act 1983*; or

(b) receiving attendance allowance; or

(c) receiving a disability living allowance by virtue of entitlement to the care component at the highest or middle rate; or

(d) receiving personal independence payment by virtue of entitlement to the daily living component; or

(e) receiving an increased disablement pension; or

(f) receiving constant attendance allowance; or

(g) receiving armed forces independence payment.

The requirements as to the allowances and payments, etc in (b) to (g) above are set out in the legislation (*Sch 1A, paras 2–7*).

The legislation is confusing, as the 'new definition' of disabled person applies from 6 April 2013 and not 8 April 2013 when the *Welfare Reform Act 2013* was enacted. The new rules relating to income and capital requirements only came into force on 17 July 2013. This means that DPIs created between 6 April 2013 and 17 July 2013 will have the new definition of disabled person but the old rules as to income and capital conditions.

Income and capital requirements for DPIs

14.18 For lifetime DPIs created prior to 8 April 2013, only 50% of capital had to be given to the disabled person. This meant that prior to *FA 2013* DPIs could be set up for a disabled person but with a wide class of beneficiaries, for example to include siblings, spouses, widows/widowers and children with the benefit that the trust did not qualify as a relevant property trust. As distributions now are limited to the 'annual limit' (see below), families will have to think carefully whether to opt for DPIs.

For DPIs created between 22 March 2006 and 7 April 2013, distributions to beneficiaries other than the disabled beneficiary which exceed the 50% rule and were made during the lifetime of the disabled person will be deemed to be potentially exempt transfers by the disabled beneficiary.

Finance Act 2013 amended the income and 50% capital rules in that for trusts created from 8 April 2013 all the capital needs to be applied for the disabled person subject to the exception of the 'annual limit' which is the lesser of £3,000 or 3% of the settled property applied for the benefit of another person during each tax year.

Distributions to beneficiaries other than the disabled beneficiary in excess of the 'annual limit' on or after 8 April 2013 will be subject to IHT exit charges on the excess above the annual limit.

Special income tax and capital gains tax treatment

14.19 The special income and capital gains tax regime for vulnerable beneficiaries introduced in *FA 2005, ss 23–45* applies to all four types of DPIs (see **14.13** and **14.14** above). Care needs to be taken that the capital and income requirements post-8 April 2013 are not breached, as otherwise the special treatment does not apply.

DPIs qualify for special treatment for income tax and capital gains tax purposes, if a vulnerable person election has been made and is effective for the tax year in question (*FA 2005, s 34(2)*). The election has to be made on Form VPE1 and signed jointly by the trustees and the beneficiary. The election is irrevocable and will continue until one of the following events occur:

- the vulnerable beneficiary ceases to be a vulnerable person;
- the trusts in relation to which the election is made cease to qualify; or
- the trusts are terminated.

On the occurrence of any of the above events the trustees are required to give notice to HMRC within 90 days of the event.

Where a claim for special treatment has been made, the regime provides that no more tax is paid in respect of the relevant income and gains of the trust for the tax year in question than would be paid had the income and gains accrued directly to the beneficiary.

The income tax liability of the trust is reduced to the actual income tax liability the beneficiary would pay if the income had been received directly in his own right. However, the liability remains the liability of the relevant trust; it is merely the calculation of the liability that is affected.

For the special capital gains tax treatment to apply, the following conditions must be satisfied:

- Chargeable gains arise in the tax year to the trustees on the disposal of trust property held on qualifying trusts for the benefit of a vulnerable person.
- The trustees would be chargeable to CGT in respect of those gains were it not for the application of *FA 2005, Ch 4*.
- The trustees are resident in the UK during any part of the tax year.
- The trustees make a claim for special treatment in the tax year.

If these conditions are fulfilled, the trustees and beneficiary are treated as if the chargeable gains had arisen to the latter, and he self-assesses accordingly. Thus, assuming the beneficiary had no other capital gains, the trustees would get the benefit of the full capital gains tax exemption (for 2014/15, £11,000) rather than the maximum reduced allowance for trusts (for 2014/15, £5,500); if a beneficiary has capital gains tax losses these would also be taken into account to reduce the tax charge on the trust. The beneficiary can then reclaim the tax back from the trustees (see HMRC Trusts, Settlements and Estates Manual TSEM3415).

The special treatment does not apply in the tax year the beneficiary dies.

PROTECTED GIFTS WITHOUT TRUSTS

Pensions for grandchildren

14.20 Notwithstanding the rules for age 18-to-25 trusts, many taxpayers who wish to provide for young members of the family will insist on a late vesting age and will not wish the fund to be subject to the complications that are set out in **Chapter 10**.

One possibility is opened up by the liberalisation of the pensions regime. Quite simply, assuming that no other pension provision has been made for the grandchild, the grandparent can set aside limited contributions to a pension policy for a grandchild, knowing that the fund cannot be touched for very many years. The paperwork with many of the recognised investment houses and investment trusts is simple and the fees moderate. Pensions (of moderate size) are favoured by the government and, although there is no recovery of tax on dividend income within the fund, freedom from repayable income tax and from capital gains tax will combine to help the fund to grow. If the premiums are, as would be likely, paid on a regular basis it may be possible for the grandparents (or their executors) to claim relief for all of the gifts under *IHTA 1984, s 21*.

Pensions for young children

14.21 Generally, apart from the Child Trust Fund or Junior ISAs described above, there is little scope for parents, rather than grandparents, to make tax-efficient provision for their children under the age of 18. The normal rules in the *Income Tax (Trading and Other Income) Act 2005, s 624* and following, especially *ITTOIA 2005, s 629*, prevent the arrangement from achieving any saving of income tax. For many years gains of trustees for children enjoyed the same low rate as individuals. The redefinition of 'settlor interested' for the purposes of CGT briefly had the effect of substituting the settlor's top tax rate. However *TCGA 1992, s 77* which imposed that rule, was no longer needed following the 18% rate of CGT and was repealed. The introduction of the 28% rate for all trusts has removed some of the attraction of trusts for young people.

However, parents, like grandparents, may within overall limits contribute to pension policies for children, which fall outside the trust regime and achieve useful long-term savings. Care should be taken not to try to take this too far, by using 'family pension pots' to try to slide assets down the generations free of IHT: that possibility has been foreseen by the legislation.

Options

14.22 This is a contentious area and one that a general practitioner should not enter without specialist advice. The clear intent of the government, when introducing *FA 2006*, was to deprive the benefit of gift relief as a PET to anything other than an outright gift. However, many taxpayers find it very difficult to bring themselves to make outright gifts, for a variety of reasons. Where the donor wishes to retain some benefit from the gift, such as the income, the result is clear. It is a gift with reservation within *FA 1986, s 102* and following. It is thus ineffective as a means of saving IHT.

14.23 More subtly, a donor may not wish actually to receive any benefit himself from the thing given away, but may wish to restrict the dispositive powers of the donee. This could apply either to shares in a family company of which the donor was still an active working director or to land, part of the family farm and still farmed by the donor. Many taxpayers who have worked hard to assemble capital are reluctant to risk its dissipation by their children, whether through the financial inexperience or waywardness, financial or marital, of the donees.

14.24 One structure that may be imagined is that of a gift which, sooner or later, is followed by the grant by the donee of an option to the donor that would allow the donor to repurchase the asset either at its market value or at some predetermined value if certain circumstances were to arise. There is probably little abuse where the option can be exercised only at full market value, because the donee exchanges the original subject matter of the gift for full value and no economic benefit passes back to the donor. The situation is more difficult where the option price is determined at the outset or where it becomes clear from a course of dealing between the parties that the donor would never have made the original gift unless the donee had already agreed in principle to enter into the option.

Given the very wide interpretation of the expression 'to the entire exclusion of the donor and of any benefit to him by contract or otherwise' as set out in RI55, it is likely that a 'gift plus option' arrangement might be challenged under *FA 1986, s 102*. Planners should also bear in mind the decision in the *Smith* case, noted in **Chapter 9**, on the issue of associated operations.

Family limited companies and partnerships

14.25 For a time practitioners explored the idea of a partnership within the family in which younger members could enjoy a share but subject to carefully drawn limitations to ensure that they never actually got to enjoy the money unless and until their elders approved. It is fair to say that this structure is not for everyone. Chief among the problems has been investment, where the received wisdom is that the partner who manages the family money will need help from managers who are FSA-registered. The cost of a dedicated adviser will put the arrangement out of the reach of most families and in any case reasonably wealthy families are often headed by an entrepreneur who would like to control the entity anyway. However, over time it may become possible to devise a form of partnership that does actually work and can be created and run at moderate cost.

Problems can arise in relation to IHT. Partnerships are regarded as opaque rather than transparent, with the partners holding a 'chose in action' in the partnership share. Shares in a holding company will not qualify for BPR when held in a partnership even though they would if held personally.

A further problem may arise on the death of a partner, as the underlying partnership share will not qualify for the CGT uplift on death (*TCGA 1992, s 62*).

Some of these drawbacks can be avoided by family limited companies. Again this is a complex area and specialist advice needs to be sought.

TRADITIONAL PROTECTED GIFTS

Existing interest in possession trusts and the TSI facility

14.26 Following the enactment of *FA 2006*, trustees should have reviewed the interests of beneficiaries, identifying those interests that were interests in possession on 21 March 2006 and retaining the old IHT treatment where that was beneficial. Trustees should also have considered the possibility of replacing existing interests in possession with Transitional Serial Interests as described at **9.27** and in the example of Marian and her surrender of the life interest.

The facility expired on 5 October 2008, although a limited TSI facility still exists in respect of spouses and civil partners, and in respect of life insurance contracts (*IHTA 1984, ss 49D, 49E*).

A&M settlements as part of the relevant property regime

14.27 For many trustees, the main issue will now be extraction of value from the trust with the benefit of holdover relief from CGT. Care needs to be taken, especially if the trustees hold property.

Policy trusts

14.28 These were examined in **Chapter 9**. *Section 46A* of *IHTA 1984* deals only with life interest policy trusts that already existed on 22 March 2006, by and large preserving their status. Trustees of policies, perhaps more than those holding any other property, often tend to take a relaxed view of their duties. They may not even know that they are appointed or that the policy is a trust with requirements as to compliance like any other. It is therefore possible that such trustees may have taken no action at all following the enactment of *FA 2006* and in particular will not have tried to vary the existing rights under the policies. In many cases, the best advice may have been to 'leave well alone'. As was noted at **9.41**,where the existing trusts are on an A&M basis it will have been important, as for any other 'ex-A&M trust', to see who the beneficiaries were and whether the trust should have been varied so as to accelerate vesting age. In one sense, it is still not too late to take action; such trusts have only recently entered the relevant property regime and the IHT charge on exit will not yet be significant, though the incidental costs of release may be.

There is one major conceptual difficulty for clients taking out policies and writing them in trust. Where the premiums are paid on a regular basis the donor may seek exemption under *IHTA 1984, s 19* or *IHTA 1984, s 21* (but not under *IHTA 1984, s 20* which refers to outright gifts only). An exempt transfer is not a chargeable one. It follows that the gift of a policy written in trust will often be outside the complications of **Chapter 10**. Previously, it was important to take care not to breach the limits described at **8.4** for reporting lifetime transfers, but the higher limits under the Regulations described in **Chapter 8** largely remove this worry.

Focus

- If the life insurance is intended to fund a potential IHT liability, you need to be aware of new restrictions introduced by *Finance Act 2013*.
- There has been no limit on the amount of premiums that may be paid into such 'qualifying policies'.
- A premium cap of £3,600 per year will apply from April 2013, although policies in force on this day will be excluded.

Discounted gift schemes

14.29 These arrangements became more popular after *FA 2006*. A capital redemption bond is put in trust. It leaves the estate of the settlor. There is an immediate discount, calculated by reference to the liability to make repayments, according to the sex, age and health, etc of the settlor. Withdrawals of 5% may be taken. The balance of the investment is a chargeable transfer for IHT. There are two separate interests, thus avoiding reservation of benefit; the settlor has no access to the balance of the investment. The key issue is the value of what is given away.

HMRC have considered discounted gift schemes; see the technical note posted to their website dated 1 May 2007. For a clear insight into the way that HMRC view such schemes, see IHTM20401 to IHTM20635, which contain not only a description of the schemes but also a 'checklist' of schemes in common use. It is considered that the taking out of the plan and the making of the gift are linked, as was found by the Special Commissioner in the similar, but slightly different scheme employed in *Smith v Revenue and Customs Commissioners* [2008] STC 1649.

The issue was fully explored in *HMRC v Bower and another (Executors of Bower Deceased)* [2009] STC 510. The deceased took out a life annuity in 2002, being then 90. She paid £73,000. The policy was issued to trustees of a settlement that she had created. She reserved rights to an annuity of 5%. She died within five months. That being within three years of the gift of the balance of the rights under the policy, there was a chargeable transfer of the amount of the gift. It was agreed that the gift was £73,000 less the value of the retained rights; but HMRC considered the value of the rights was negligible: £250, so the gift was of £72,750.

This contrasted with the insurance certificate, valuing the rights at £7,800, so the executors appealed to the Special Commissioner, who valued them at £4,200. That figure was arrived at by discounting the figure of £7,800 by one-third and by a further £1,000 for legal costs. HMRC appealed successfully to the High Court, which held that the Commissioner, in the absence of evidence, had gone too far in deciding the value.

Thus where the settlor is, by age or for any other reason uninsurable at the date of gift, the value of the retained rights will be nominal and virtually all the bond will be the gift. That will be true, see below, whenever the settlor is 90 or over. The May 2007 note explains the HMRC attitude to joint settlements and the apportionment of any discount. In the past, valuation was seldom necessary but that has changed now that the settlement is a chargeable transfer. The old procedure of lumping both discounts together is no longer appropriate. Instead, the discount must be calculated for each settlor in turn. In HMRC Brief 65/08, dated 31 December 2008, it was announced that the valuation rate of interest for discounted gift schemes, ie the discount rate (which the Commissioner had not felt able to use in *Bower*) would be reduced from 6.75% to 5.25% pa with effect from 1 February 2009. In HMRC Brief 21/09, issued after the High Court ruling in *Bower*, HMRC understandably reaffirmed their view of the valuation basis where the settlor is uninsurable or is (actually or for underwriting purposes) 90 or over at the transaction date. Only a nominal value will be attributed to the retained rights. Nothing in the legislation allows any withdrawals actually taken between the date of the gift and the death to be taken into account and set against the sum invested in the scheme.

The *Bower* case was confirmed in the recent First-tier Tribunal case of *Watkins and Harvey v HMRC* [2011] UKFTT 745 (TC).

Flexible reversion trusts

14.30 There is a constant desire among donors, which the life assurance industry tries to satisfy, to eat one's cake and still have it; to make an effective gift but to retain some 'comeback' if circumstances change. One such structure is the 'flexible reversion trust'. It is actually a settlement of a string of single premium endowment policies, but for clarity imagine a consignment of several cases of wine the contents of which will mature individually in successive years. The settlement of them, say for grandchildren, is a chargeable transfer, so best limited to the available nil rate band. The settlor retains the right, at maturity, to the proceeds (if he is still alive) but this is not treated by HMRC as the reservation of a benefit; nor is any payment to the settlor of those proceeds subject to an exit charge.

The trustees have wide powers, including the power to give one of the policies *before* maturity to beneficiaries or the power to defer maturity. As (it is hoped) the policy increases in value with time, that increase belongs to the trust, not the settlor. Although this is an insurance scheme, it is not limited to investment in life policies, so could admit some flexibility, though doubtless not actually into wine. It appears to have achieved a successful 'shearing' of the right to receive the maturity proceeds, not given away, from all the other rights under the policies: something possible with an insurance product but much harder to achieve with any other asset.

Lifetime gifts into trusts since FA 2006

14.31 Trusts, except disabled trusts, set up by life transfers after 22 March 2006 are relevant property trusts and their creation is a chargeable transfer, unless exempt. This will probably have two effects. The taxpayer of substantial means may in the past have been willing to delay making gifts on the basis that a large gift made into an interest in possession trust or an A&M trust would have been potentially exempt and, if he survived it by seven years, substantial value could be transferred whilst retaining safeguards over the capital.

14.32 *FA 2006* has curtailed that facility. Transferors will probably not wish to pay IHT on the establishing of lifetime trusts and will not want the complications of grossing up. Many will therefore limit their generosity to settlements that are within the nil rate band. This will lend urgency to the situation because seven years must elapse after the making of a nil rate band discretionary trust before another one can be made that will not be 'tainted' by the existence of the prior trust, leading to the complications that are described in **Chapter 10**. The message to wealthy estate owners is therefore: 'get on with it'.

14.33 The second effect of the rule that virtually all new lifetime trusts are chargeable will be that, below a certain level, many taxpayers will decide that the complexities of a discretionary trust are simply not worthwhile even though the burden of IHT on a nil rate band trust for the first ten years is nil and, as has been seen in **Chapter 10**, the burden of tax on quite a substantial trust is only moderate. It is therefore likely that fewer small trusts will be set up because their administrative costs will be unacceptable.

Disclosure of Tax Avoidance Schemes – DOTAS

14.34 When advising on any IHT planning, an advisor needs to consider, whether:

(i) any lifetime planning from 6 April 2011 is notifiable under the DOTAS regime;

(ii) whether any arrangement might amount to 'abusive' tax planning under the General Anti-Abuse Rules (GAAR); or

(iii) the arrangement might be caught as a GWR or be subject to POAT (see **Chapter 17**).

The *Inheritance Tax Avoidance Schemes (Prescribed Descriptions of Arrangements) Regulations 2017 (SI 2017/1172)* will come into force on 1 April 2018. These regulations will replace any previous regulations and will describe IHT avoidance schemes and arrangements which will have to be disclosed to HMRC, Arrangements are notifiable if one of their main purpose is to reduce the value of a person's estate, without giving rise to a chargeable transfer, or potentially chargeable transfer, and that the arrangement involves one or more 'contrived or abnormal' steps.

Chapter 15

Wills and estate planning

SIGNPOSTS

- **EU Succession Regulation (SR)** – Increased mobility means that many testators will have assets in other EU states. Although the UK has not opted into the SR, it may still affect the devolution of the testator's estate (**15.1–15.2).**
- **Nil rate band discretionary trusts** – For many years it was common to include such trusts for IHT saving. Following the introduction of the transferable nil rate band and more recently of the residential nil rate band, the emphasis has shifted and asset protection often is the main objective of setting up such trusts (see **15.3–15.12**).
- **The residence nil rate band** – An additional nil rate band, the residence nil rate band (RNRB), will be available from 6 April 2017, when a residence is 'closely inherited' (see **3.42–3.48**). This will have a major impact on will drafting (see**15.13**)
- **Wills leaving estate to surviving spouse** – This can be done either by an outright absolute gift or by passing the estate into an IPDI for the surviving spouse (see **15.14–15.19**).
- **Trusts for bereaved minors** – These trusts escape ongoing IHT charges for as long as the interests vest absolutely at age 18 (see **15.20**).
- **18-to-25 trusts** – The maximum IHT costs of such arrangements are 4.2% of the value of the fund (see **15.21**).
- **BPR, APR and woodland relief** – Careful will drafting avoids wasting these reliefs, especially where they overlap with the spouse exemption (see **15.23–15.29**).
- **Exempt gifts on death** – These include gifts to charity and gifts of heritage property (see **15.30–15.38**).
- **Post-death variations and disclaimers** – *IHTA 1984, s 142* permits families and advisors to 're-structure' the beneficial interests under a will or in the event of intestacy put provisions akin to a will in place (see **15.40–15.53**).

EU SUCCESSION REGULATION NO 650/2012

Background

15.1 The Succession Regulation (SR) is important in relation to testators who have assets in other EU countries. The UK opted out of the SR, but it applies to all other states in the EU, except Ireland, who also opted out, and Denmark, who did not participate. The SR was adopted on 4 July 2012 and most of the underlying rules take effect from 17 August 2015. The SR is also known as 'Brussels IV'. Despite the fact that the UK opted out, practitioners need to understand the underlying rules, as it will affect the devolution of someone's estate with assets in another EU country.

The governing law

15.2 The general rule is that if a testator is domiciled in England and Wales, his moveable property will be governed by English law, while his immoveable property is governed by the law of the country where the property is situated. In contrast the SR provides that the law of the country where the testator has his 'habitual residence' shall apply. Article 22 of the SR states that alternatively a testator can choose the law of their nationality – this will replace 'habitual residence'. As the UK has not signed up to the Regulation, the SR provides that member states will still accept renvoi from testators who are habitually resident in England, Wales or Scotland, unless such testators have made a choice of law to apply to their estate.

Example 15.1—UK national with holiday home in France

Simon is a UK national and is habitually resident in England, but he has a holiday home in France.

If no choice of law has been made in his will, English law will apply to his moveable and immovable property in the UK, while France will accept renvoi and French law will apply to his French property. If, on the other hand, his will states that the law of England and Wales shall apply to his entire estate, the French property will pass according to English law.

If Simon is habitually resident in France, and assuming he kept his UK nationality, he can also make a declaration for English law to apply.

Focus

- The SR does not determine which tax law applies and it therefore is important to ascertain the tax consequences of the chosen jurisdiction.

For example in Germany each beneficiary has the equivalent of a nil rate band, which depends on whether they are related to the testator, and if so how closely they are related.

- It is important to take tax advice in the country where the asset is situated or which the testator elects to apply.

THE NIL RATE BAND

Nil rate band discretionary trusts

15.3 It was for many years common for the public to avoid straightforward mirror wills by which spouses (or civil partners) left everything to each other with remainder to children. Before the introduction of the right to transfer the nil rate band, such simple wills were tax-inefficient because they failed to use the nil rate band of the first of the spouses or partners to die. Instead a more complicated structure was used, seldom fully understood by those implementing it. This was inefficient in a different way, imposing significant extra work on taxpayers, on the one hand; and on HMRC, because of the multiplicity of forms to be processed that yielded little or no tax (unless the taxpayer committed some procedural error, which it was the tiresome duty of HMRC to spot and to penalise). All this became largely unnecessary by virtue of *FA 2008, s 10* and *Sch 4*, which are fully discussed in the next chapter.

While the introduction of the transferable nil rate band might have been the end of nil rate band discretionary trusts, they are still useful in certain circumstances. For example if you are advising a widow or widower who has remarried, a nil rate band discretionary trust can be used to protect the transferable nil rate band of a predeceased spouse, which would otherwise be wasted.

The old 'debt' or 'charge' schemes

15.4 The solution commonly devised before the transferable nil rate band was a gift of the nil rate band to trustees coupled with a provision that that gift need not be satisfied by immediate payment, but might be satisfied either (and there were significant differences of approach here):

- by taking a charge over other assets in the estate; or
- by accepting a promise of payment from the surviving spouse or civil partner.

The difficulty was that few families really understood the structure. For example see *Wolff v Wolff and Wolff* [2004] STC 1633, in which the claimants were forced to apply to the court to set aside a reversionary lease scheme on the grounds that they had made a mistake as to the legal effect of the arrangement.

See also *Bhatt v Bhatt and others* [2009] EWHC 734 (Ch), as to the difficulties for 'ordinary' people in engaging in tax planning). To work well, the scheme needed the executors to take certain action at certain times: many cases are now coming to light where this was not done, or was skimped.

The effect of *Finance Act 1986, s 103* ('Treatment of certain debts and incumbrances') on the scheme was even less well understood. It was litigated in *Phizackerley v IRC* [2007] SpC 00591, where the Special Commissioner had to decide whether deduction of the liability under the scheme was prevented by *FA 1986, s 103*. He noted that *FA 1986, s 103* prevents the deduction of the debt where, and to the extent that, the consideration given for the debt or incumbrance consists of 'property derived from the Deceased' and held that:

- On the face of it, the half share in the house in issue was indeed derived from the deceased. It was the subject matter of a disposition made by the deceased.
- The debt incurred by the deceased in favour of the trustees of the nil rate band was not deductible.

The Special Commissioner dismissed the taxpayer's appeal.

Is the debt or charge scheme any use, now?

15.5 The decision in *Phizackerley* did not totally invalidate the debt or charge scheme. The structure should not be entered into where the family would benefit more from the provisions of a transferable nil rate band, as will usually be the case. It will fail if the parties behave as if the nil rate band fund was always, and would remain, at the disposal of the surviving spouse. The surviving spouse must understand that the value comprised in the discretionary trust *is not his/her money*. There must always be the risk, from the point of view of the surviving spouse, that the trustees could at any time call in the loan.

Where, in relation to an existing scheme, the surviving spouse later decides to 'trade down' in property terms, the trustees must consider calling in their debt, and should encourage the surviving spouse to use his or her own resources to purchase and refurnish the replacement property. They may give assurances that the fund will not be dissipated, but should not compromise their discretion. This may also help to shield the family fund from the burden of nursing home fees. The surviving spouse should come to the trustees for help only when those resources are used up.

Note that if *FA 1986, s 103* had originally been a problem that was obviated by the imposition of a charge before assent to the surviving spouse, the sale of that property and the purchase of a new one with some help from the trustees throws the surviving spouse back into the *Phizackerley* situation: another reason to favour the use of an IPDI instead. Alternatively, the discretionary trustees could, instead of making a loan, join in as purchasers. Provided that two years had elapsed from the death, to prevent any relating back to the death, the trustees could then give the surviving spouse a formal right to occupy the share of the house that they had bought. It would not be aggregable with the free estate on the second death, but main residence relief would be secured.

It is prudent to review existing wills in light of the case of *Loring v Woodland Trust* [2013] EWHC 4400 Ch, which is a useful decision on the interpretation of a nil rate band sum following the introduction of the transferable nil rate band. Here the testatrix made a will in 2001 leaving a nil rate band legacy with the residue passing to charity. The issue was whether the value of the nil rate band legacy was enhanced by the testator's husband's transferable nil rate band by a predeceased spouse, ie a total of £650,000 rather than £325,000. As this depends on the wording of the will, practitioners are advised to review any nil rate band legacy clauses and compare them with HMRC's guidance at IHTM43065 to ascertain the value of a nil rate band legacy, as this may have unintended consequences on the value of the residue.

Avoiding Phizackerley: proof of contribution to the house by the spouse

15.6 Where it is for any reason appropriate to retain a pre-*FA 2008* form of will, and *Phizackerley* issues arise, it must be increasingly common that, at some time during a marriage, particularly in the early years, both husband and wife will earn and pool those earnings. Most wives will be able to claim, that they have made a contribution to the cost of the house and that the purchase of the house in joint names does not lead to the automatic conclusion that '*the funds must have been provided by the Deceased*'. The facts of *Phizackerley* can be distinguished where families can show that:

- both husband and wife worked at various times during the marriage;
- both directly or indirectly contributed to the cost of one home after another; and
- the family home that is in their joint ownership at the time of the death of the first of them to die is truly owned by them equally.

A serious issue to address is that *Finance Act 1986, s 103* contains no time limit. The debt which the executors seek to deduct from the estate of the second spouse to die is (see *s 103(1)*):

> 'subject to abatement to an extent proportionate to the value of any of the consideration for the debt or encumbrance which consisted of
>
> (a) property derived from the deceased; or
>
> (b) consideration (not being property derived from the deceased) given by any person who was at any time entitled to, or amongst whose resources there was at any time included, any property derived from the deceased.'

It matters not how long ago the gift was made. It could still be caught.

How will all this be proved? Some executors will be reluctant to carry out an expensive enquiry into transactions long ago. Beware of breaching the duty of care in delivering accounts under *IHTA 1984, s 216*. If there is any clear link between the debt which is to be deducted from the estate of the surviving spouse and a gift made, however long ago, by that spouse to the first spouse to die, *Phizackerley* can apply. This case increases the burden on executors and their advisers, and the risk of a penalty for failure to make proper enquiries.

The effect of Phizackerley on existing wills

15.7 The enactment of *FA 2008* no doubt triggered the rewriting of many wills. Those left untouched can be 'mended' by prompt exercise of the power of appointment to create an IPDI, so as to nullify the structure and achieve a transferable nil rate band. Subject to that, where there has been no gift of an interest in the house (which will usually be the relevant asset), it may not be necessary to change anything purely in the light of the decision in *Phizackerley*. If there has ever been a substantial gift, existing structures should be reviewed. The problem arises only where the donor spouse is the second to die: so in the common case of value transferred in lifetime by husband to wife, where she survives him, there is no problem.

Focus

- NRB discretionary trusts are still useful in cases where asset protection is important, or where a widow/widower has remarried and the transferable nil rate band of the predeceased spouse would otherwise be wasted. Following the introduction of the RNRB, great care needs to be taken to ensure that this additional nil rate band is not wasted, as passing property into NRB trusts precludes the application of the RNRB.
- Such trusts enable trustees to benefit a number of beneficiaries if and when they need funds. They offer greater flexibility than IPDIs.
- However, the disadvantage of the 45% tax rate (2018/19) applicable to discretionary trusts and the administrative burden need to be considered carefully.

Procedural difficulties with existing structures

15.8 For the pre-*FA 2008* structures that remain, there may be difficulties of execution. Where, for example, the will has not been properly drawn and infant beneficiaries have interests in residue there can be difficulty in correcting the errors. Where there is a gift of the nil rate band, but no corresponding provision that that gift may be satisfied by an IOU, it is not possible, by simple deed of variation, to put matters right. Any deed of variation, to be effective, must alter the *dispositions* of the estate of the testator, so the inclusion of the desired clauses must effectively ride on the back of another variation.

Even supposing the paperwork all to be correct, further difficulties arise both as to the intention of the parties and execution of the structure. The problem with intention is that, if the surviving spouse from the outset refuses to acknowledge that the debt is inevitably repayable and if the trustees go along with that, there is effectively a 'sham' because the parties have rejected the thinking behind the scheme. However, if the family are 'stuck' with an old will, there might almost be an advantage in suggesting that 'we never really meant/understood it' to get out of an old debt/charge scheme and into a transferable nil rate band situation.

At a less acute level, there may be simply inaccuracies or lapses which cause the scheme to fail. On the eventual death of the second spouse or civil partner it may be impossible to prove that appropriate formalities were put in place to recognise the debt. There may be no evidence that the trustees ever at any time considered calling it in. The trustees must recognise the realities of what is happening. They are lending an amount equal to the value, in many parts of England, of a three- or four-bedroom detached house. Trustees would not normally lend that amount of money without taking security. Trustees must therefore consider whether or not to take security. If they fail to do so they should have a reason for their failure.

There is certainly a risk that people will fall between two stools: the old structure fails for want of proper execution but it has been partly effective to use the nil rate band so that it is not transferable. The difficulty for advisers is that the ongoing trust may be administered by the family who may not remember all the advice given when it was set up; or it may not be possible to show that such advice was given; and yet if the scheme fails at the second death people may be quick to claim that the original adviser was at fault.

Practical issues arising out of existing debt or charge scheme structures

Choice of trustees

15.9 The choice of trustees is important. They should not be subject to the control of the surviving spouse. It is therefore helpful, but by no means essential, for one of the trustees to be independent. The trustees should have due regard for the requirements of the arrangement and should meet at reasonable intervals to consider whether or not to call in the debt. If left indefinitely, it can become statute barred. As far as the surviving spouse is concerned, there must always be a *frisson* of uncertainty that the trustees could call in the debt. Certainly, if the surviving spouse decides to move house the original loan should be repaid in full and the surviving spouse should then approach the trustees to ask for a fresh loan of such amount as is needed to finance the new purchase.

Liquidity

15.10 The next issue is the extent to which liquidity in the estate of the first to die should have been applied towards satisfying the gift of the nil rate band. Although there is no case precisely in point, it lends reality to the whole structure if the executors apply available securities and other savings in part satisfaction of the nil rate band so that the debt or charge is only for such sum as cannot be satisfied from the available liquid assets. That may be unpopular with the surviving spouse.

Interest and index linking

15.11 Interest may, but need not, be charged on the debt. In many instances the charging of interest will be tax neutral. Receipt of interest by the trustees of the nil rate band will attract income tax at 45%, whilst reducing the estate of the surviving spouse and thus saving IHT at 40%. At that point, therefore, the exercise seems not to be worthwhile. If, however, there are many beneficiaries of the nil rate band who, perhaps because they are young, do not pay income tax, there will be a saving because after expenses the trustees can make distributions of income to the non-taxpaying beneficiaries who will recover some or all of the tax thus paid.

Occasionally, the nil rate band is index linked. On final resolution of matters it is certainly arguable that the extra money so received is essentially payment, by reference to time, for the use of money and is therefore interest receivable at the time of repayment of the loan, even though it is calculated by reference to inflation or a house price index. Others argue to the contrary: there is no decided case directly in point. HMRC have litigated, arguing that the extra money received represents interest which is subject to income tax. The case settled.

HMRC have stated in their HMRC *Trusts and Estates Newsletter* April 2017 that the uplift in value above the principal sum constitutes interest under *ITTOIA 2005, s 369 (1)* and that income tax is payable. Well-drawn wills allow the trustees to waive their rights as to index-linking or the charging of interest.

15.12 *Section 175A* of *IHTA 1984* (discharge of liabilities after death) will apply to old debt and charge schemes where the second spouse dies on or after 17 July 2013. The effect of this provision is that liabilities are only deductible in determining the value of an estate if they are actually repaid out of an estate on or after death unless there is a real commercial reason for the liability to remain outstanding.

Therefore, if the debt together with any interest is discharged on the second death, the full sum can be deducted as a liability from the estate. HMRC state that the interest received will have to be taxed by the trustees as income at the rate of 45%.

If the interest is waived, there is no income tax liability on the waived sum. However, HMRC state that there is unlikely to be any commercial purpose to the interest not being repaid as, had the creditor been at arm's length, they would have wanted the interest repaid as well. If the interest is waived, it cannot be taken into account as a liability on the estate. See HMRC's guidance at IHTM28029.

THE RESIDENCE NIL RATE BAND

Background

15.13 The residence nil rate band (RNRB) introduced by *F(No2)A 2015* with further legislation in *Finance Act 2016* inserted nine provisions (*ss 8D–8M*) into *IHTA 1984*. The RNRB has a major impact on will drafting and many wills which include a NRB discretionary trust may need to be reviewed. While the legislation comes into effect for deaths after 6 April 2017, it applies in respect of disposals on or after 8 July 2015 where either the taxpayer downsizes, or where the property is sold or given away because the taxpayer moves into residential care.

Families are advised to review existing wills to ensure that maximum use of the NRB and RNRB can be made on second death. For a more detailed analysis of the RNRB see **3.42–3.48**.

The importance for will drafting is that the RNRB is only available to a transfer of a residential property interest to a direct descendant and it is not available if the residential property or a share in the residential property is left on a discretionary trust. In general the transfer to a direct descendant must be outright, but some transfers into trusts for direct descendants qualify. They include:

- transfers into immediate post-death interest trusts;
- transfers into disabled trusts; or
- transfers into 18–25 trusts and trusts for bereaved minors.

Discretionary trusts over the residue on the death of the surviving spouse are a very flexible approach to plan for succession and asset protection. The main advantage of such flexible will trusts is that tax planning and succession planning can be deferred until death and any planning can be done based on the fiscal and family circumstances at the time. *IHTA 1984, s 144* will assist (see **15.49** below) to ensure that maximum use of the RNRB can be made on second death.

Alternatively it may be advisable to include provisions in the will to bank the RNRB by making an absolute gift of residence to lineal descendants, or passing the residence into an IPDI, bereaved minor's trust or 18-25 trust. This approach may be appropriate in second marriages where one or both parties have previously been widowed and where there therefore are more than two RNRBs available.

In valuable estates it may be advisable to use NRB discretionary trusts to reduce the value of the survivor's estate to avoid taper of the RNRB on second death.

Focus

- A transfer into a discretionary does not qualify as the property must be held directly for 'lineal descendants'. If such a trust is encountered when dealing with someone's estate, *IHTA 1984, s 144* can be used to appoint to lineal descendants and thereby attract the RNRB.
- It is common for parents to leave their estates to their children in equal shares with substitution for grandchildren in the event that a child predeceased their parent. If this includes an age contingency, for example 'for such of my daughter's children that reach the age of 25', and the daughter predeceases, and the grandchildren have not reached the age of 25 when the grandparent dies, the trust for the grandchildren will not qualify for the purposes of the RNRB. Again, *IHTA 1984, s 144* can come to the rescue.

DEFERRAL OF TAX USING SPOUSE RELIEF

Background

15.14 In its most simple form, this planning is acceptable and allowed for by the legislation.

Example 15.2—Spouse relief: post-war nuclear family

John was born in 1922, Susan in 1925. They married in 1950 and had two sons, born in 1951 and 1955. Returning to civilian life he became an engineer. She was a teacher. By 1985 they were both enjoying a retirement and spending time with their grandchildren when it became clear that

John would not live much longer. His will provided for legacies for his grandchildren but left the bulk of his estate to Susan.

Susan was widowed in 1992, then aged only 67 and in good health. On John's death she inherited from him free of IHT, sold the family home, traded down and made substantial gifts to her sons, hoping to live seven years so that the gifts would be free of tax. In the event Susan did survive until 2017. The gifts made soon after John's death fell out of account and her nil rate band, together with John's, was available to Susan's executors. So was the RNRB and the transferable RNRB from John.

15.15 The scheme of deferral of tax in the above example has worked substantially in the way that legislation intended, saving the family from an immediate IHT charge on the death of John. However, many circumstances arose prior to *FA 2006* where the relief was claimed in circumstances less acceptable to the government.

Example 15.3—Life interest for spouse: William's life

William was born in 1932. His first wife, Mary was born in 1935. They married in 1960 and had two children, one born later that year and another born in 1963. Mary died in 1975, leaving William to bring up the boys, then aged 15 and 12, just when his building business was reaching a very busy stage of its development. A family friend, Rachel, helped bring up the boys and William and Rachel had a daughter born in 1965. By 1985 the stresses of running a family business had taken their toll on the marriage and they divorced.

Whilst on holiday he met and married Anja who was Norwegian. By now, the construction business had developed substantially into a property investment business and was run by the younger of William's sons with some help from his daughter. In fairness to his children William wanted to provide substantially for them rather than Anja, so he made a will leaving the nil rate sum equally between his children and giving the residue of his estate to Anja on life interest trusts but with a power for the trustees to revoke those trusts at any time, with remainder to his children.

William died in 2000. There was no IHT on his death, because by then Anja had acquired a UK domicile of choice, so the residue of the estate qualified for unrestricted spouse relief. Anja then however indicated that she would like to return home. That suited the trustees well, because they had never intended that she should enjoy an interest in possession in the whole of the substantial estate for very long. Shortly after Anja left the UK, the trustees terminated the life interest. It was anticipated that Anja would live at least seven years. The cost of insuring against the possibility of her death within that period was moderate and was paid by the trustees.

Counteraction of perceived abuse

15.16 The device described in the example of William above was specifically counteracted by *FA 1986, s 102ZA*. The success of the device, as noted in the example, rested on the fact that the continued enjoyment of trust property after termination of an interest in possession in it was not reservation out of a gift because the gift had not been made by the former tenant for life. The government considered that the abuse was sufficiently serious that it should be brought to an end in two ways. As part of a general attack on trusts there was initially provision that denied spouse relief wherever there was an ongoing trust (except for minors) following the death of the spouse.

15.17 As was noted in **Chapter 9**, those proposals were in part withdrawn but the more specific provisions of *FA 1986, s 102ZA* remain. The operative section is *FA 1986, s 102ZA(2)*, which provides that, on the ending of an interest in possession, an individual is treated as if he had disposed by way of gift of property in which the interest in possession previously subsisted. That may be enough to bring the GWR code into play. The provision applies where:

- an individual enjoys an interest in possession in settled property; and
- that individual became entitled to the interest before 22 March 2006 or became entitled to the interest in possession after that date but the interest is an IPDI, a disabled persons interest or a TSI.

In other words it is one of the remaining categories of interest in possession that still falls to be taxed under the 'old' rules and is not treated as a relevant property trust.

15.18 The property that is deemed by the section to be given is described as 'the no-longer-possessed property'. This is any property in which there was an interest in possession, except such part of the fund as the life tenant actually retains and in which he or she does still have an interest in possession. Thus, if the fund is £100,000 and the trustees terminate the interest in three-quarters of it, the no-longer-possessed property is £75,000 because the remainder is still subject to the interest in possession.

Consequential amendments to *FA 1986, s 102* apply where there has been a termination of a life interest, now treated as being by way of gift under *FA 1986, s 102ZA*, but the property remains in the settlement. The new provision treats the property that is the subject of the deemed gift as consisting of the property that remains in the settlement except insofar as the trust fund does not consist of any asset in which there was an interest in possession that has been terminated by the gift.

There is an anti-avoidance provision to provide that the property in the deemed gift includes derived property, even including property derived from a loan made by the former tenant for life to the trustees. Accumulations of income are also treated as being derived from property. All of this operates to increase the size of the gift in respect of which an interest in possession may apply.

Example 15.4—Termination of interest: failure to revise a will

Alec, a widower aged 80, had two sons Brian, aged 45 and Charles aged 40 when he married Denise. He wanted to provide adequately for Denise, but substantially for Brian and Charles. He made a will leaving the nil rate band to Brian and Charles between them and residue on terminable interests in possession for Denise with remainder to Brian and Charles. His estate comprised a substantial house and investments not qualifying for reliefs. The plan had been to use Denise as a 'peg life' to get substantial value down to Brian and Charles free of inheritance tax.

Alec died on 1 February 2006 when the house in his name was worth £1.5 million and the residue of his estate after debts amounted to £3,275,000. The trust fund was therefore £4.5 million (ie the total net estate, less the nil rate band of £275,000). The trustees, then of course unaware of the impending terms of the Finance Bill 2006, terminated the interest in possession of Denise in the house but allowed her to go on living there. They also advanced £1 million of residue each to Brian and Charles.

FA 1986, s 102ZA treats the termination of the interest in possession in the house as a gift by Denise. The house is still in the trust. The interest in possession for Denise came into existence before 22 March 2006. The GWR code therefore applies so that, in the event of the death of Denise, the value of the house will be taxed as part of her estate. There is however no reservation of benefit out of the £2 million released to Brian and Charles. Those transfers are treated as PETs by Denise in the normal way. As she has survived the PET by more than seven years those gifts will fall out of account.

The tax planning has therefore partially succeeded. The PETs to the sons have now fallen out of account. It had however been hoped that the structure would effectively take the house out of the IHT net by way of gift whilst allowing Denise to go on living there. That part of the tax planning was frustrated.

Later IHT charge on a 'wait and see' basis

15.19 The prevalence of second marriages and second families resulted in a proliferation of wills that attempt to do justice to the reasonable expectations of the constituent parts of the family members. Each party to a second marriage may bring family and assets and may wish to benefit existing family alongside the issue of the union.

As originally drafted, the amendments in the Finance Bill 2006 were very strict. Any ongoing trust interests were taxed in such a way that spouse relief could very easily be lost. As revised, *IHTA 1984, s 49A* allows greater flexibility. Thus, parties to a second marriage may wish to give each other an interest in possession in the residue of estate with discretionary trusts thereafter so that the fund can be used according to the needs of the various beneficiaries at the time.

As noted in **Chapter 9**, an IPDI exists where a will trust provides for the tenant for life; and not for bereaved minors or for a disabled person; and the interest in possession exists continuously from the death. The termination of that interest in possession on the occasion where discretionary trusts arise is a chargeable transfer. The ongoing trusts are then taxed under the regime described in **Chapter 10**. If full flexibility is what the family want, they can have it, but at a price. All of this must also be considered in the light of the provisions as to transferability of the nil rate band and the residence nil band rate.

Focus

- 'Mirror' wills leaving the estate to the surviving spouse are much more common since the introduction of the transferable nil rate band.
- Such wills are suitable in 'straightforward' cases where the combined estate does not exceed £1m (ie two NRBs of £325,000 and two RNRBs of £175,000 by 2020/21).

Trusts for bereaved minors

15.20 Having reviewed the ongoing tax charges that would otherwise apply, many taxpayers may decide to 'grumble and give in'. If they provide that shares that pass to children or grandchildren vest absolutely at 18, including accumulations of income, they will achieve the simplest tax treatment that is now available and there will be no ongoing IHT trust charges.

Following the enactment of the *Inheritance and Trustees Powers Act 2014, Trustee Act 1925, ss 31* and *32* were amended. Trustees now have the power to apply income and to accumulate surplus income during the minority of a beneficiary 'as the trustees may think fit'. *Trustee Act 1925, s 32* has been amended to remove the limit on advancements of one half of vested or presumptive entitlement for trusts created on or after 15 May 2014.

18-to-25 trusts

15.21 Many families will want the slightly greater flexibility of a vesting age of 25. The maximum IHT cost of that arrangement, over and above the IHT charge on death, will be 4.2% as described in **Chapter 10**. In fact, as noted in that section, the actual ongoing IHT charge may be less than that.

Unfortunately the recent Government consultation into the simplification of periodic inheritance tax charges proved to be inconclusive. It intends to hold a further consultation but has rejected calls to exclude 18-to-25 trusts, accumulation and maintenance trusts and interest-in-possession trusts from the relevant property regime in *FA 2006*, because tax revenues would be lost.

Early life interest trusts

15.22 One possibility that in appropriate circumstances may give testators what they want is the creation by will of an immediate life interest in favour of a young beneficiary. An IPDI is now less restricted than formerly following the changes to the draft of *IHTA 1984, s 49A*. There is therefore scope for a long life interest (all subsequent statutory references are to *IHTA 1984,* unless otherwise stated).

Example 15.5—Life interest for grandchildren: by-passing the next generation

Fred's three sons George, Henry and Ian are all married and doing financially quite well. The grandchildren are respectively John, 9, Ken, 7, Lucy, 8, Mary, 6, Nancy, 5 and Olive, 3 (and it seems that there will be no more). It is hoped that they will attend good schools and go on to further education. Fred is widowed and does not need to provide for his sons. His will therefore divides the residue of his estate into six shares, held respectively for each of his grandchildren for life with wide powers of advancement of capital to each tenant for life (but not to any of the others) and with remainder to great-grandchildren with gifts over.

None of the grandchildren is disabled. The provisions of *IHTA 1984, s 71A* do not apply because those rules apply to children as opposed to grandchildren, and in any event the grandchildren will not automatically become entitled to capital at age 18. 'Condition 3' of *IHTA 1984, s 49A* is therefore satisfied and each of the interests in possession is an IPDI. If the trustees advance capital to any of the grandchildren to help fund secondary or tertiary education that is neutral for IHT because each already has an interest in possession so there is no change in the estate of any of them. Care needs to be taken to amend *TA 1925, s 31*.

If any of the grandchildren marries, spouse relief may become available to exempt a transfer that would otherwise become taxable on the termination of an interest in possession by an advance to the spouse or to the life tenant for the benefit of the spouse. The structure gives Fred's family considerable flexibility for years to come.

BPR, APR AND WOODLANDS RELIEF

Placing the relievable property

15.23 Gifts by will to spouses and civil partners are still exempt in 'uncomplicated' structures notwithstanding *FA 2006*. There is therefore overlap of reliefs and exemptions. This is wasteful but may be unavoidable.

Example 15.6—APR and spouse exemption (I): simple farming situation

Cedric inherited the family farm years ago and on his death its 75 acres were worth £450,000 and the house itself £400,000. Savings built up, when farming was better, have been eroded but still stand at £200,000. His wife Mary owns some adjoining land worth £100,000 which has always been occupied with the farm and savings of £300,000. They have two daughters. Cedric's will leaves the house and land to Mary and the cash to the daughters.

On his death in November 2017 there is no IHT because the gifts to the daughters are within the nil rate band (then £325,000), and the gift to Mary is exempt.

On Mary's death in May 2018, her estate comprises the house, land totalling £550,000 and savings, now reduced to £285,000. The nil rate band available is approximately 138.46% of the current figure of £325,000 ie £450,000, because 38.46% of the band was unused on Cedric's death and is thus still available (it is actually the same amount as was unused because the nil rate band is frozen but the calculation is set out to illustrate the principle).

Although Mary's death occurs only shortly after that of Cedric, APR is allowed on the farming assets under the succession provisions of *IHTA 1984, s 120*. Applying the valuation principles of *Antrobus (No 2)* [2002] STC (SCD) 468, APR on the farmhouse is restricted (ie to 70% of £400,000), so £120,000 of the value is chargeable, but even when added to her cash savings of £285,000, the resulting inheritance for Mary's daughters is within the RNRB and the nil rate band. The result is that the daughters inherit entirely tax free.

Example 15.7—APR and spouse exemption (II): wastage of exemption and the scope for 'double dipping'

The facts are the same as in the previous example, only some of the figures are larger. The house is worth £600,000, Cedric's savings are £400,000 (note the value of Cedric's farm remains at £450,000), and Mary has her own farmland worth £100,000 as before but her savings amount to £400,000. If the will provisions are the same, there is an IHT charge (in 2017/18) on Cedric's death on the amount by which his cash gift to his daughters exceeds the nil rate band (£400,000 – £325,000) ie 75,000 × 40% = £30,000. Mary's estate, on death soon after that of Cedric, is £1,550,000.

There are other problems. Farmland worth £450,000 belonging to Cedric has been enjoyed with a house valued at £600,000. Questions arise as to whether such a valuable property is indeed a farmhouse and whether, to a working farmer, the purchase of the landholding as a whole for £1,050,000 might represent 'an appalling investment in terms of yield' within the rule in *Higginson v CIR*. APR may be denied on the house on the basis that the entity as a whole is really 'a house with land' rather than a farm. Matters will be eased if Mary's own land is included, though it is of relatively little value and there may be little connection between it and the farmhouse, which could present a problem.

Assuming that that problem can be overcome, APR on the house will be restricted to £420,000 (70% of £600,000), leaving £180,000 in charge. The daughters therefore inherit the house, the land which should qualify entirely for APR and a further £400,000 of cash: a chargeable estate of £580,000. (The gift to them from their father's estate exhausted the nil rate band, so there is no transferable nil rate band.) The daughters will have the benefit of two RNRBs, but they are restricted to the chargeable value of the farmhouse of £180,000 after APR. Value of £75,000 after Mary's nil rate band (£325,000 in 2018/19) and the restricted RNRB of £180,000 is taxable at 40%, attracting IHT of £30,000.

Alternative structures to save tax by 'double dipping'

15.24 There may have been some wastage of relief in the above example. Nothing much could be done if Mary died within two years of Cedric but, if she had been in good health at the time of his death and had survived by two years or so, tax could have been saved by reordering his will. Cedric could have given his daughters the farmland, which it may be remembered was worth £900,000, and the nil rate band. That would have allowed them, on the rates in force when he died, to inherit value amounting to £1,225,000 tax free. Mary's estate would then comprise the farmhouse, her own land and cash of £475,000, being the £400,000 that she already had plus cash from Cedric's estate of (£400,000 less the nil rate band, leaving) £75,000.

Mary could have used her cash to buy some of the farmland from her daughters. Only if she lived two years from Cedric's death would APR again be available to her (because she would not be within *IHTA 1984, s 120*). On her death, assuming that she lived two years, her estate would comprise the farmhouse and the land. There would still be the argument as to whether the house was a farmhouse, but assuming that the executors were successful most of its value would be relieved, leaving (on the assumptions already made) £180,000 in charge, which is within Mary's NRB and RNRB.

The nil rate band (where there is no augmentation by transfer) is £325,000 for the time being. The daughters should have no tax to pay. However, as noted above, this arrangement works only where Mary lives long enough after the purchase of the relievable assets to qualify for APR in her own right under *IHTA 1984, s 117*. Depending on ages and other factors, many will hope that we may return to index-linking of the nil rate band, which would increase the eventual nil rate band available and preserve the freedom for the surviving spouse to control assets in the meantime.

Woodlands relief

15.25 Woodlands relief is available on death only. Calculation of the relief can be complicated and, where it is possible to show that there is commercial occupation of the woodlands, it may be simpler and more effective to claim BPR. There is, for example, provision for 50% reduction in value under *IHTA 1984, s 127*, but this is rare and the practitioner is referred to specialist books on the subject. One situation in which will planning can exploit woodlands relief is illustrated below.

Example 15.8—Woodlands relief: ownership of wood

Ralph owns very valuable woods. The trees are of a quality and age that are very attractive to the market. Ralph is not in good health but has an impecunious sister, Freda, who might well outlive him. Ralph leaves the woodland to Freda, who does not have a substantial chargeable estate and who, having no family of her own, is likely by her will to leave all of her estate to Ralph's children.

On Ralph's death an election is made to leave the value of the timber out of account on the basis that it will be chargeable on any later disposal by Freda. If Freda does dispose of the timber that will trigger an IHT charge against which can be set her nil rate band, but if she retains the woodland until her own death the charge (at 0%) on that death will frank the IHT charge on Ralph's death. Death is not an 'associated operation'. Alternatively, if the woodland is managed, claiming BPR on Freda's death might be more beneficial for IHT purposes.

15.26

Example 15.9—Woodlands relief: no deferral of taxable event

Steve owned woodlands similar to those of Ralph and recently had the land clear-felled and replanted. He leaves the woodland by will to his grandson. On his death woodlands relief is not claimed. The value of the timber at that time is negligible because the trees are still young and the cost of looking after them is greater than any economic benefit from the landholding.

There is no point in making an election for woodlands relief because when the deferred tax comes to be payable, it is hoped not until many years later, the woodlands may have increased considerably in value.

Although there might be some merit in electing for woodlands relief so as to relieve the value on the transfer to the grandson, on balance it will be better if residue can carry the moderate tax cost. Alternatively, BPR may be available, if the woodland is managed.

The problems of s 39A

15.27 The interaction of exempt transfers with business and agricultural property relief is examined at **5.30**. An inexpertly drawn will can easily lead to the complications of tax that are described at **5.31** and **5.32**. There is a single transfer on death to both chargeable and exempt beneficiaries. BPR and APR will be wasted on an exempt beneficiary such as spouse, civil partner or charity. BPR or APR should have been reserved for the children or other chargeable beneficiaries.

The computations required under *IHTA 1984, s 39A* are complicated and the reader is referred to specialist books on the topic. For the general practitioner the answer is simply to take care to avoid gifts of chargeable property that will trigger the rules as to grossing-up. If a chargeable specific gift is made of an asset that qualifies for relief, that will fix the availability of the relief.

Example 15.10—BPR and *s 39A*: a will that should be varied

Kenneth has made no chargeable transfers or PETs in the last seven years. His estate comprises:

Business property with 100% BPR	£1,000,000
Business property with 50% BPR	£650,000
Quoted shares	£370,000
House	£425,000

His existing will leaves the house and the business assets to his widow Linda and the investments to his daughter Melanie. The gifts to Melanie slightly exceed the current nil rate band, triggering a modest charge to IHT.

On present tax rates, his will should be varied in his lifetime or by deed after his death. Quite apart from considerations of the transferable nil rate band and RNRB, Melanie should receive the business assets and the remainder of the estate should go to Linda. After BPR the chargeable transfer is just slightly less than it was before, giving a small IHT saving; but more to the point the actual value that has passed to Melanie is now nearly double what it would have been.

The nil rate band and RNRB is still available on Linda's death and there will be an overall saving on the second death. As with the example of Mary above, the transfer of the business property direct to Melanie leaves open the possibility that Linda might use some of the liquidity to buy business property back from Melanie in the hope that Linda will live two years from the purchase. That will effectively use the BPR twice, if Linda lives two years from the purchase.

15.28 Some consideration must be given to the possibility of remarriage. That will affect IHT planning and may encourage the first spouse to die at least to use the nil rate band to protect any existing children from disinheritance. It is in such situations that the debt/charge scheme may still be attractive, or that a gift of the nil rate band to or in trust for the children will be wholly appropriate. After all, if the spouse does remarry there can be only one transferable nil rate band on eventual death, so perhaps best to use the elder spouse's nil rate band now.

Further complications

15.29 In family situations and in the drafting of wills it is easy for the practitioner to be distracted by the various considerations, as can be seen in the following extended example.

Example 15.11—Case study: will-drafting traps

Melissa and Wendy lived together but did not consider entering into a civil partnership. Melissa owned the house worth £300,000. Melissa also held stocks and shares worth £400,000 including £100,000 worth as a minority holding in her cousin's unquoted trading company.

Melissa instructed her solicitor that in the event of her death she would want Wendy to be able to continue to live in the house for as long as she wanted and to have a 'cushion' of money to tide her over. That provision ought to be tax free. Apart from that, Melissa wanted her estate as far as possible to go in equal shares to three charities and two cousins.

The first consideration for the draftsman will be to avoid the problems of *Re Benham*. This is explained at **5.40**. However, there is a second issue, *IHTA 1984, s 39A*, to be addressed by the will. It would also be unwise simply to give Wendy the right to continue to live in the house for life and a legacy tax free of such sum (not exceeding a stated maximum) as the executors might think necessary for her care. The reasons are as follows:

- The first is the rule in *Judge (personal representatives of Walden deceased) v Revenue and Customs Comrs* [2005] SSCD 863 (SpC 506), referred to at **9.3** and **16.34** et seq. Practitioners may consider that the decision in that case could have gone either way, in the light of the general rule of HMRC as expressed in Statement of Practice 10/79. The fact that one ill-drawn will did not create an interest in possession in a residence does not mean that SP 10/79 will never be invoked in future. There is therefore a risk that provision tax free of Melissa's house for Wendy to occupy for the rest of her life creates an interest in possession and, depending on the value, that gift alone could exhaust the nil rate band, particularly if the wide frontage of the property concerned constitutes access to back land and has considerable value. Supposing therefore that provision of the home for Melissa exceeds the nil rate band, grossing-up will be necessary.
- The second problem follows from the first. The further provision of the 'cushion' tax free will also require grossing-up and, applying the principles of *s 39A*, that gift will be seen as coming from the rest of the estate, including the part represented by the value of the unquoted shares which qualify for 100% BPR.
- Finally, the lack of a specific gift of the shares causes some of the BPR on them to be wasted on the charitable beneficiaries of residue.

A better drawn will would make a specific gift of the shares to the chargeable beneficiaries, perhaps especially the cousin who actually runs the company. That would secure BPR in full.

Great care should be taken in drafting the clause relating to the house so as to show that the right of Wendy to live there can be terminated at any time by the trustees so that she does not have an interest in possession.

An alternative would have been a lifetime gift by Melissa of a share in the house to Wendy, effectively giving Wendy a right of occupation by virtue of her share in the house. The retained share in the house could then have been given to the charities outright. They would not have been able to sell the share of the house until Wendy moved out; but they would not have received any benefit from the house until Wendy's death anyway. That arrangement would have given charitable exemption on the value of the retained share in the house.

The shares, now representing the residue can be split between the charity and IPDI for Wendy with remainder to the cousins.

EXEMPT GIFTS ON DEATH

Charities

15.30 Practitioners are regularly lobbied by charities to encourage clients to give in their wills. In the light of *RSPCA v Sharp* [2011] STC 553 some will writers may be discouraged from leaving residue, or a share of it, to charities, for fear that the charity may in some way 'make trouble' for the family, as (in the view of the High Court judge ([2010] STC 975) happened there. That is an issue to discuss carefully with the testator.

The issue in *Cancer Research Campaign v Ernest Brown & Co (a firm)* [1997] STC 1425 concerned the failure of a lawyer to take advantage of the relief. The facts are important enough to quote in detail.

Mr Berry died on 11 December 1986 leaving the residue of his estate to his sister Phoebe. They owned a house jointly which passed to Phoebe by survivorship. The rest of his estate amounted to some £170,000 from which were paid legacies of £30,000. About five months after her brother's death Phoebe visited Mr Palfreyman, a legal executive and executor of her brother's will, to make her own will. By then no application had been made for a grant of probate of the brother's will, but it was assumed that Mr Palfreyman knew how much Phoebe would inherit.

15.31 She left virtually all her estate to seven charities. Details of the interview are scant because Mr Palfreyman himself died before the case came to trial. There was no record of any discussion between Phoebe and Mr Palfreyman of the possibility of a deed of variation. It was therefore not possible to say whether Phoebe lived so modestly that she did not need the cash inheritance from her brother. Phoebe then died, having included Mr Palfreyman as an executor. Phoebe's will was not proved until June 1989; that of her brother not until October 1992. Phoebe's estate was thus swollen by the 'unnecessary' inheritance from her brother, which could have been diverted to the charities.

The charities were concerned that Phoebe, had she been so advised, could have varied her brother's will to provide direct benefit to the charities, taking advantage of *s 142*, with the result that IHT could have been saved. The last date on which an effective variation could have taken place was 10 December 1988, but at that time the charities did not even know of their entitlement. They only learned of it from the probate agents, Smee and Ford, on 23 June 1989, by which time it was too late. IHT on the brother's estate was about £203,000, but was not paid until 7 October 1992. The figure included substantial interest and penalties.

15.32 Held, the solicitors had no duty to advise Phoebe on the possibilities of saving IHT in relation to her estate; nor any duty to advise on tax mitigation when administering the estate of her brother. Further, there was no duty to communicate the tax-mitigation possibilities of a deed of variation to the residuary legatees. The solicitors were obliged to administer the estate properly, but were under no obligation to advise the charitable legatees of the potential legacy.

Practitioners may think, given the whole circumstances, including the long time that it took to administer the estates of Phoebe and of her brother, that the solicitors did well to escape liability. Certainly, in drafting wills and in administering estates the practitioner should always be aware of the interests of the charities and the possibilities of exemption.

15.33 Note the limitation on charitable relief in *IHTA 1984, s 23(2)*. There is no relief where the charitable disposition takes effect only on the termination of an interest or period after the transfer of value, or where it depends on a condition which is not satisfied within 12 months, or where it is defeasible.

Example 15.12—Gifts to charity: non-exempt charitable gifts

Samantha's will leaves £100,000 on trust for her brother Robert for life with remainder to the Children's Society. The gift is not exempt on the death of Samantha, but the fund will be exempt on Robert's death.

Finance Act 2012 introduced a reduced rate of IHT where 10% or more of a deceased's estate (after deducting IHT exemptions, reliefs and the nil rate band) is left to charity. HMRC published their guidance notes in April 2012 (IHTM45000). The legislation provides that the IHT rate of 40% will be reduced to 36% where death occurs on or after 6 April 2012 and more than 10% of the net estate is left to charity. It is clear that only large estates will be able to benefit from this reduced rate.

The legislation determines that a person's estate is made up of a number of components. As a first step it is necessary to identify the components of the estate, which are:

- The *survivorship component*, which includes all property comprised in the estate that pass by survivorship or under a special destination (in Scotland), or under anything corresponding to survivorship under the law of a country or territory outside the UK.
- The *settled property component* which includes all property comprised in the estate in which an interest in possession subsists and in which the deceased was beneficially entitled immediately before death.
- The *general component* which is made up of all other property comprised in the estate.

As a next step it is necessary to calculate the *donated amount* (which is the property attracting the charity exemption under *IHTA 1984*, *s 23(1)*, and the *baseline amount* which is gross value of assets in the components mentioned above after deducting liabilities, reliefs, exemptions and the available nil rate band (after taking into account any lifetime gifts).

Finally, it will be necessary to compare the *baseline amount* with the amount left to charity to see if the estate qualifies for the lower IHT rate.

An on-line calculator is provided by HMRC on their website to work out whether the estate qualifies for the reduced rate – see www.gov.uk/inheritance-tax-reduced-rate-calculator.

Example 15.13—Gifts to charity: calculation of reduced rate

Fred's estate (before legacies) is worth £1,200,000.

He lived with his spinster sister Frieda and they owned a property, which was valued at £500,000, as joint tenants – *survivorship component*. Fred was a life tenant under a pre-2006 family settlement which on his death passes to his two nephews in equal shares – the value of the settlement at the date of death was £450,000 – *settled property component*. The *general component* is valued at £250,000. His will, which was drafted more than 10 years ago, left a legacy of £100,000 to a cancer charity with the residue passing to Frieda absolutely.

Prior to the introduction of reduced IHT for estates in respect of charitable gifts, the IHT charged on Fred's death would have been £310,000 (ie £1,200,000 less the charitable legacy of £100,000, less Fred's nil rate band of £325,000 @ 40%).

Assuming Fred died after 6 April 2015, the executors now need to check whether the 36% IHT rate applies. The *donated amount* is £100,000. The *baseline amount* is £875,000. As the gift to charity exceeds the 10% threshold, the reduced rate of IHT of 36% will apply to Fred's estate. The executors will pay IHT of £279,000 ((£1,200,000 less the charitable legacy of £100,000, less Fred's nil rate band of £325,000) @ 36%). This represents a tax saving of £31,000.

Heritage relief

15.34 The relief is valuable but rare. For detailed analysis the reader is referred to specialist works on the subject. The gift of heritage property by will is unlikely of itself to take account of heritage relief except to the extent that property is transferred to a maintenance fund under *IHTA 1984, s 27*. Mainly, therefore, the way in which a will takes account of the existence of heritage relief will be in avoiding dispositions that force or encourage the sale of property in respect of which an undertaking has already been given, because such a forced sale would breach any undertaking that had already been given under *IHTA 1984, s 31* or earlier legislation in force.

It is a particular feature of heritage relief that property may have benefited many years ago from the relief at a time when capital taxation was much higher. Care must be taken not to trigger the clawback of relief that had been given on an earlier occasion. The difficulty for the owner of conditional exempt property is in knowing who is actually the 'relevant person' for the purposes of undertaking it at any time. This is because the rules work in such a way that the identity of the relevant person changes according to a retrospective test. There are three rules set out in *IHTA 1984, s 33(5)*, as follows:

Rule 1: Simple cases

15.35 Where there has been only one conditionally exempt transfer of the heritage property before the chargeable event, the relevant person is the one who made the transfer.

Rule 2: Two or more conditional transfers, one going back 30 years

15.36 In these cases it is necessary to consider the ownership of the property for the period of 30 years leading up to the chargeable event. Where the most recent transfer of that property was more than 30 years ago, the person who made that transfer is the relevant person. Where there have been several transfers, and one of them took place in the last 30 years, that transferor is the relevant person.

Rule 3: Two or more recent conditional transfers

15.37 Suppose that there have been two or more transfers in the last 30 years. HMRC may choose whichever of the transferors they please as the relevant person. The reason for this is to prevent avoidance of tax by channelling heritage property through those members of the family who have few other assets in the hope of ensuring that, where there is a chargeable event, the tax charged will be as low as possible.

These rules make life very difficult for executors and trustees. They may have to keep sums back in the administration of an estate against the possibility of clawback of tax on breach of undertaking. They will not necessarily know how much will be involved. Two cases on the subject may offer some guidance: *Bedford (Duke), Re, Russell v Bedford* [1960] 3 All ER 756 and *Re Scott* [1916] 2 Ch 268.

15.38 Claims to heritage relief must be made within two years of the date of transfer (see *IHTA 1984, s 30(3BA)*), 'or … such longer period as the board may allow'. HMRC have discretion to allow a longer time than two years and will consider a late claim on its merits. The difficulty for the practitioner is that the property that might be the subject of a claim might also by its very nature qualify for, say, APR, a protective claim should be made.

Provisions were introduced in *Finance Act 2016* to cover situations where the conditional exemption was granted prior to 1975 under the estate duty regime. HMRC now has the choice to charge either IHT or the higher estate duty rate when the charge crystallises. This will bring the legislation into line with lifetime transfers of heritage objects.

Legislation will be introduced to amend *Finance Act 1930, s 40(2)* to cover situations where the heritage object has been lost. IHT or estate duty will become chargeable unless the owner can convince HMRC that the loss was outside his control.

POLICY TRUSTS

15.39 These were discussed in **Chapter 9**. Apart from bare trusts, which give no flexibility as to choice of beneficiary or vesting age, trusts entered into after 22 March 2006 will generally be treated as discretionary. Their creation will be a chargeable transfer, though the value of a new policy under which regular premiums are paid is likely to be not merely within the nil rate band, but also within the annual exemption. The payment of further premiums on the policy is likely to be exempt under *IHTA 1984, s 21*. If the policy is a single premium bond, the transfer will usually be of its value at the time of gift. If substantial, that triggers the compliance issues discussed in **Chapter 8**.

The tax charge on such trusts therefore arises principally when, at the occasion of a ten-year anniversary, the policy value exceeds the nil rate band; or on an exit charge when the value of the fund exceeds that band. There is a valuation rule, see *IHTA 1984, s 167*, which can apply to a policy, but it is limited in scope. Usually, the value will be the market value rather than the total of premiums paid.

It is commonplace for a financial adviser quite correctly not only to sell a policy but to arrange for it to be written in trust.

POST-DEATH VARIATIONS

15.40 *IHTA 1984, s 142* permits families and their advisers to be 'wise after the event'. Subject to various safeguards it is possible to rewrite a will or to put in place provisions akin to a will where a person has died intestate. The document need not be a deed, only 'an instrument in writing'. It must be signed by anyone who would have benefited but for the changes brought about by the deed. A difficulty therefore arises if the beneficiaries of the will to be changed or under intestacy are minors.

The Chancellor announced a review of the use of deed of variations as part of the government's clampdown on tax avoidance in the 2015 Budget speech. Following representations from professional bodies, it was announced in the 2015 Autumn Statement that the government has decided not to restrict the use of deeds of variations for the time being, but that they will closely monitor it.

Variations where there are minor beneficiaries

15.41 Two courses are open. The first is to apply to the court for an order permitting the variation to take place on the ground that it is in the interests of the infant beneficiaries. The simpler course, which is not objected to by HMRC, is to frame any variation in such a way that it does clearly benefit younger members of the family.

Example 15.14—Minor beneficiaries: no need for an application to the court

Ian, a widower, left his estate in four equal shares, one for each of his three sons and the last for his grandchildren equally per capita. One of the sons does not need his inheritance and wishes his share to pass immediately to his children. There is no need for any of the children to sign the resulting deed of variation. None of them gives anything up. There is no need for any application to the court.

Example 15.15—Minor beneficiaries: avoiding an application to the court

Michael, who was widowed and who remarried late in life, made a will that banks the RNRB and TNRB from his predeceased spouse with residue to his widow for life with remainder in four shares, one to each of his sons and the fourth to his grandchildren equally per capita.

As was noted in **Chapter 5**, it is not possible simply to incorporate the requisite clauses by deed of variation. The parties therefore wish to enter into a deed that will comply with *s 142*. They agree to vary the terms of the will. The gift of residue is changed so that each son receives 20% only and the grandchildren receive 40% between them.

Although there will be no benefit to the grandchildren during the lifetime of their 'step-grandmother', it is nevertheless clear from the face of the deed that the grandchildren, who are themselves too young to sign the deed, are better off by virtue of the deed than they would have been under the will. It is therefore not necessary to seek the approval of the court to the variation.

Posthumous severance

15.42 *IHTA 1984, s 142* permits a variation of the dispositions of the property comprised in the estate of the deceased 'whether affected by will, under the law relating to intestacy or otherwise'. The words 'or otherwise' have been taken to include dispositions that take effect by operation of law, such as survivorship to joint property. Accordingly, it is possible by deed of variation posthumously to sever the joint tenancy in any property (for IHT purposes, at least) so that the share belonging to the deceased can pass under the will as varied rather than direct to the other joint owner. This is often essential where it is proposed to put in place the debt or charge scheme by deed of variation.

'Only one bite at the cherry'

15.43 A disposition that has been varied by deed of variation may not be further varied: see *Russell v IRC* [1988] STC195. The issue was discussed in *Law Society's Gazette* 22 May 1985, noting that the Revenue had taken further advice on the interpretation of *IHTA 1984, s 142* and had indicated that:

- an election which is validly made is irrevocable;
- an instrument will not fall within *IHTA 1984, s 142* if it further redirects any item or any part of an item that has already been redirected under an earlier instrument; and
- to avoid any uncertainty, variations covering a number of items should ideally be made in one instrument.

There must be no consideration for entering into a deed of variation, see *IHTA 1984, s 142(3)*, other than consideration consisting of the making in respect of another of the dispositions of a variation or disclaimer to which that subsection applies.

Abuse

15.44 Deeds of variation, like so many other documents, are open to abuse.

Example 15.16—Deed of variation: trying it on

By his will Henry left his estate to his son Ian absolutely. By deed of variation Ian changed the will so that it provided for Joan, the wife of Henry and the mother of Ian.

Careful reading of the deed showed that Joan's address was different from Henry's. Enquiries revealed that they had been separated for many years and that Joan was amply provided for. Further enquiries and the threat of the exercise of a power to call for documents under *IHTA 1984, s 219A* elicited from Ian the admission, fully documented in the solicitor's papers, that it was understood from the outset that Joan would release anything that she inherited from her husband's estate to Ian by way of gift.

Whilst a transfer from Henry to Joan would have been sheltered by spouse relief, since nothing in *IHTA 1984, s 18* requires spouses or civil partners to be living together, relief under *IHTA 1984, s 142* is likely to be denied on the basis that Joan gave Ian consideration within *IHTA 1984, s 142(3)*.

Finance Act 2012 changed the rules where there is a gift to charity by an instrument of variation. Unless the charity is informed of their benefit under the variation, *IHTA 1984, s 142* will not apply to the variation. A letter from the charity acknowledging the gift will be sufficient.

Disclaimers

15.45 A disclaimer has been described as a 'blunt instrument'. By *IHTA 1984, s 142(1)(b)* it has the effect of redirecting inheritance to another party though, apart from entering into the disclaimer in the first place, the original beneficiary has no control over the destination of the property disclaimed. Relief is not available under *IHTA 1984, s 142* in respect of a disclaimer if consideration has been given for it.

A disclaimer failed to achieve its purpose in *Lau (executor of Lau Deceased) v HMRC* [2009] SpC 740. The husband had left his son £665,000 free of IHT. There were other legacies to other children. Residue was left to his (second) wife. The son disclaimed his legacy; £3,800,000 was transferred to the widow; she transferred £1,000,000 to the son; correspondence showed that this was part of a plan to save IHT. HMRC refused to allow *s 142* to apply because of the direct link between the disclaimer and the later payment. It was held on appeal that the evidence showed a direct link. The evidence of the widow was 'utterly unpersuasive'. The appeal was dismissed.

Formalities of post-death variations

15.46 Since 31 July 2002, notice of any deed of variation need not now be given to HMRC, except where IHT is thereby increased, but relief will not be given by *IHTA 1984, s 142* unless the variation contains a statement, made by all the relevant persons, that they intend the relief to apply.

Statement of variation

15.47 The following will be enough:

> 'The parties to this variation intend that the provisions of section 142(2) [and where appropriate and section 62(6) Taxation of Chargeable Gains Act 1992] shall apply.'

The relevant persons are those making the instrument and, where extra taxes are payable by virtue of the variation, the personal representatives.

Footnote: the Glowacki case

15.48 A case which is special to its own facts is *Wells (Personal representatives of Glowacki deceased) v HMRC* [2008] STC (SCD) 188. A deed of variation was entered into which purported to deem a gift of a house to have been made immediately before death; but if the deed did not have the intended effect, the variation was to have no effect, giving the family a second chance of a variation by avoiding the *Russell* rule noted above.

HMRC determined that the effect of the deed was to set the benefit of the nil rate band against the value of the house in priority to the gift in the will of the nil rate band. The personal representatives appealed, arguing that *IHTA 1984, s 17(a)*, which provides that a qualifying deed of variation is not a transfer of value, had the effect of taking the house out of the estate before death, so £230,000 could pass under the gift of the nil rate band.

Held, *IHTA 1984, ss 4* and *17* did not work that way. *IHTA 1984, s 142* could not remove property from the estate to take it outside *IHTA 1984, s 4*. Any variation under *IHTA 1984, s 17* was of the dispositions on death only. The variation therefore failed. HMRC had decided the effect of the deed and had taxed accordingly. That was wrong: they should have decided whether *IHTA 1984, s 142* could be used in the way attempted; and should then have decided whether the deed remained in force as a result; which it did not, so part of the determination was quashed.

Alternative post-death relief: ss 143 and 144

15.49 There are two alternatives to the relief under *IHTA 1984, s 142*. By *IHTA 1984, s 143*, there is limited relief where the will sets out a wish that property be transferred by a legatee to other persons and the legatee does, within two years, carry out those wishes.

An attempt to push this rule to the limit was illustrated in the case of *Harding (executors of Loveday) v IRC* [1997] STC (SCD) 321. The will contained a discretionary trust for the widow and children. The executors appointed a fund to the widow. The Revenue argued that this was not an exempt transfer, being outside the terms of *IHTA 1984, s 144*. The executors appealed, wishing the appointment to be treated as a transfer under *IHTA 1984, s 143*. The Special Commissioner decided against the executors for three reasons: a legatee could include a trustee, but here the trustees were not legatees within *IHTA 1984, s 143*; an appointment of property was different from a transfer of it, so outside what *IHTA 1984, s 143* contemplated; and there was no evidence that the appointment was what the deceased had wanted, thus failing the requirement expressed in *IHTA 1984, s 143*.

In practice, a gift to a spouse that is quickly followed by an ongoing gift to a non-exempt beneficiary may well be challenged by HMRC.

A further form of relief applies under *IHTA 1984, s 144* to discretionary trusts established by a will. If trustees of a discretionary will trust exercise their discretion within two years of the death *IHTA 1984, s 144* applies so as to treat the release of funds or other transactions by the trustees as if they had been made by the testator.

15.50 However, the position is slightly more complicated than this summary might suggest, as the advisers found to their cost in *Frankland v IRC* [1997] STC 1450. Commonly, a will may establish a discretionary trust for the close family of the testator, including the surviving spouse. The idea is that, following the death and perhaps following establishment of reliefs such as APR and BPR, the executors will be able to decide on the relative needs of various members of the family and will be able to make appropriate provision. It was common in such situations, particularly where the surviving spouse was young and likely to live many years, to appoint funds to the surviving spouse in the hope that he or she could be used as a 'peg life'.

However, the mechanics of *IHTA 1984, s 144(1)(a)* refer to an event which, but for the relief, would trigger an IHT charge, being either the ten-year anniversary charge under *IHTA 1984, s 64* or the fixed rate under *IHTA 1984, s 79*; or which would be subject to an exit charge except for certain special reliefs. The effect was therefore that an appointment by the trustees which would not under any circumstances have triggered an exit or periodic charge did not fall within *IHTA 1984, s 144(1)*.

The proportionate charge, which is described in **Chapter 10**, does not apply during the first period of three months from the creation of settlement. As a result, an appointment made within the first three months of death does not benefit from relief under *IHTA 1984, s 144*. That, most unfortunately, had the result, in *Frankland v IRC* [1997] STC 1450, that an appointment that could otherwise have saved significant tax triggered a very substantial tax charge.

Legislation was included in *F(No2)A 2015* which in effect overrides *Frankland* in that, where an appointment is made within three months of date of death in favour of the deceased's surviving spouse or civil partner, it can be read into the will and spouse exemption under *IHTA 1984, s 18* will be given.

Other forms of post-death restructuring

15.51 Apart from deeds of variation the parties may feel that they want to reorganise beneficial interests under a will, as happened in *Executors of Patch deceased* [2007] SpC 600, where the deceased had left his estate to his wife for life with remainder to his children. The fund was mainly shares, and it was agreed that the widow should have one-third (represented by the house) and the children two-thirds. Under a deed of partition, not a deed of variation, the widow assigned her interest in the fund, other than the house, to the children. They in return assigned their interest in the house to her. She agreed to pay them £25,000 each within 30 days and to pay more later.

Only five months later, the widow died, not in fact having made the payments. Her executors sent HMRC details of the deed and of the widow's estate. Tax was levied on the value of the house; but later HMRC sought to tax also the value of the trust fund that had passed to the children because the arrangement had effectively achieved a transfer of value, taxable under *IHTA 1984, s 52(1)*, which was within seven years of death. The executors appealed, on two grounds: there was no transfer of value, because the money had never been paid over, and they had made full disclosure anyway.

Not so, held the Special Commissioner. The assignments were not conditional on the payment. There was a division of the fund, which was a transfer. The value that was deemed to have left the estate of the widow under the partition should have been included in the account of the estate. Further, there had not been full disclosure: although the deed itself was disclosed, the executors had not included in the account the value of the lifetime transfer, so HMRC were entirely right to claim the tax.

'Mending' discretionary trusts after FA 2006

15.52 The effect of *FA 2006* is to treat certain will trusts as discretionary that would not previously have been so treated. Amendments have been made to *s 144* so that estates caught by *FA 2006* may escape the full IHT charging regime if distributions are made of trust funds into one of the asset holding vehicles that is still acceptable under the 'new' regime.

Where *IHTA 1984, s 144(2)* now applies, tax is not to be charged on the basis of the original discretionary trust. In each case in which *IHTA 1984, s 144(2)* is in point tax is charged as if the will had provided that the fund should be held, not on the terms of the will but on the terms of the varied disposition. Whereas *IHTA 1984, s 144(1)* previously could apply only to a discretionary trust it can now, by virtue of *IHTA 1984, s 144(1A)*, apply to a conventional discretionary trust and to an interest in possession that is neither an IPDI nor a disabled person's interest.

15.53 Where the necessary conditions are satisfied *IHTA 1984, s 144(4)* provides that tax is to be charged as if the will had provided for the property to be held as it will be held by virtue of the actions of the trustees described below. Where that happens, the fund escapes the discretionary trust charging regime.

The conditions for this are as follows:

- Death on or after 22 March 2006.
- Property in the estate of the deceased settled by will.
- Within two years of death (but before there has subsisted, in relation to the property, either an IPDI or a disabled persons interest), there is a trust event. The event concerned is one by which the property in the estate comes to be held on favoured trusts ie:
  - an IPDI; or
  - a BMT; or
  - an 18-to-25 trust.

Effectively, by this amendment to *IHTA 1984, s 144*, trustees will be able to bring will trusts into line with the regime now favoured by the government.

Chapter 16

The family home and residence nil rate band

SIGNPOSTS

- **The family home** – This is the most significant and valuable asset in the estates of many individuals. Various non-IHT measures affecting residential property have been introduced in recent years. Those measures have had the general effect of discouraging IHT planning involving the family home. Furthermore, provisions were introduced in *Finance (No 2) Act 2017* broadly to restrict excluded property status and extend the scope of IHT to residential properties situated in the UK where they are held through offshore structures (see **16.1–16.5**).
- **Planning arrangements involving the family home** – A number of IHT schemes and arrangements have evolved over the years. Some of these were subsequently blocked by IHT anti-avoidance legislation, while others are affected by the 'pre-owned assets' income tax regime (see **16.6–16.11**).
- **Ownership** – The family home is sometimes owned by one spouse (or civil partner), or more commonly by both as 'joint tenants' or 'tenants in common' (other rules apply in Scotland). Different IHT considerations apply to each. The spouses or civil partners may sever a joint tenancy by written notice (see **16.12–16.13**).
- **Lifetime planning** – IHT planning arrangements involving the family home which are sometimes used include equity release arrangements or borrowing against the property to release funds to make gifts. Gifting the family home (or a share of it) can cause potential difficulties, such as under the 'gifts with reservation' anti-avoidance provisions (see **16.14–16.26**).
- **Will planning** – Spouses (or civil partners) who own the family home as tenants in common should make provision for their share of the property in their will. A non-exempt legacy of such a share (eg to adult children, or a discretionary trust) was a popular means of utilising the nil rate band of the first spouse to die. However, this

approach has been less common since the transferable nil rate band facility was introduced (see **16.27–16.54**).

- **Residence nil rate band** – Extra (or 'residence') nil rate band is available for deaths from 6 April 2017 if a qualifying residential interest is passed on death to lineal descendants (eg a child or grandchild). The maximum allowance is £100,000 in 2017/18, increasing in stages to £175,000 in 2020/21. However, the maximum nil rate band is subject to tapered withdrawal if the value of the deceased's estate exceeds £2 million. The residence nil rate band is in addition to the standard nil rate band of £325,000 mentioned above. As with the standard nil rate band, unused residence nil rate band is transferable to a surviving spouse or civil partner, subject to a successful claim being made. The benefit of the residence nil rate band was extended (in *FA 2016*) in certain circumstances involving 'downsizing' on or after 8 July 2015, in relation to deaths from 6 April 2017 (see **16.55–16.77**).

THE FAMILY HOME

Introduction

16.1 The family home (a term used in this chapter to include a property owned and occupied by husband and wife, or civil partners) is probably the most significant asset in the estates of most individuals, and often the most valuable in monetary terms. Escalating property prices over a number of years resulted in the value of an increasing number of family homes exceeding the IHT nil rate band, which did not rise in step with property prices and was frozen at £325,000 from 6 April 2009.

This chapter outlines some IHT planning considerations involving the family home. It must be remembered that transactions undertaken to save IHT must be considered 'in the round' taking into account any legal implications, as well as the possible implications for other taxes and/or possibly means-tested state benefits.

Care will be needed if a valuation of the property is necessary. As to valuation issues generally, see **Chapter 6**.

IHT planning involving the family home has been considered unnecessary or less desirable for individuals in many cases following the introduction of extra (or 'residence') nil rate band (*IHTA 1984, ss 8D–8M*) where a home is inherited on death by lineal descendants of the deceased on or after 6 April 2017 (see **16.55–16.77**). However, IHT planning in this area may still need to be considered in some cases, particularly in relation to high-value estates and/or if there are no lineal descendants.

16.2 A number of tax measures affecting residential property have been introduced in recent years.

Stamp duty land tax

The rate of stamp duty land tax (SDLT) on residential properties sold for chargeable consideration of more than £2 million was initially increased from 5% to 7%, with effect from 22 March 2012. However, a major reform of the SDLT structure, rates and thresholds for UK residential property costing more than £125,000 was introduced from 4 December 2014. The regime broadly charges SDLT at increasing rates for each property value band, with a top rate of 12% (NB: SDLT was replaced in Scotland by land and buildings transaction tax from 1 April 2015, and in Wales by land transaction tax from 1 April 2018).

Furthermore, legislation introduced in *FA 2016* provides for a higher SDLT charge (ie such that the rates are 3% higher than the equivalent normal residential rates for each of the SDLT bands) on the purchase of additional dwellings (eg second homes) costing more than £40,000, with effect from 1 April 2016.

A 15% SDLT charge was also introduced from 21 March 2012 for the purchase of an interest in a single dwelling where the chargeable consideration is more than £2 million and the purchaser is a company, a partnership one of whose members is a company, or a collective investment scheme (*FA 2003, Sch 4A*). However, legislation in *FA 2014* reduced the threshold for the 15% SDLT rate to £500,000 for land transactions with an effective date on or after 20 March 2014, subject to transitional rules.

It was announced in Autumn Budget 2017 that first-time buyers paying £300,000 or less for their residence would pay no SDLT and first-time buyers paying between £300,000 and £500,000 will pay SDLT at 5% on the amount of the purchase price over £300,000, for transactions with an effective date on or after 22 November 2017. The relevant legislation (*FA 2003, Sch 6ZA*) was subsequently introduced in *Finance Act 2018*.

Annual tax on enveloped dwellings

Finance Act 2013 introduced an annual tax on enveloped dwellings (ATED), ie an annual charge on residential properties worth more than £2 million that are owned by 'non-natural persons' (NNPs) (ie certain companies, partnerships with company members and collective investment schemes), subject to a limited range of reliefs (eg for property rental businesses, property developers, etc) (*FA 2013, Pt 3, Schs 33–35*). The ATED takes effect in relation to properties under the ownership of an NNP on or after 1 April 2013. The threshold of £2 million was progressively reduced to £500,000 in *FA 2014*.

From 1 April 2015, an annual charge of £7,000 applies for properties within a new band with a value greater than £1 million but not more than £2 million. From 1 April 2016, an annual charge of £3,500 applies to properties within an additional band with a value greater than £500,000 but not more than £1 million (*FA 2013, s 99(4)*, as amended by *FA 2014, s 110*).

In addition, *FA 2015* increased the annual ATED charges for properties valued at more than £2 million, over and above the normal consumer prices index (CPI) increase. The ATED charges are generally expected to increase annually to keep pace with inflation, in line with rises in the CPI. For example, the ATED charge in relation to properties valued at more than £2 million but not more than £5 million increased to £24,250 (from £23,550) for the period 1 April 2018 to 31 March 2019 (*Annual Tax on Enveloped Dwellings (Indexation of Annual Chargeable Amounts) Order 2017, SI 2017/1246*).

Capital gains

Legislation introduced in *FA 2013* extended the capital gains tax (CGT) regime to gains on disposals by NNPs of UK residential property or interests in such property from 6 April 2013, where the consideration exceeds £2 million (reduced proportionately if the NNP owns or disposes of only part of the property). The charge applies to both resident and non-resident NNPs, and affects those companies or collective schemes within the scope of the ATED (*TCGA 1992, ss 2B–2F, Sch 4ZZA*). A CGT charge of 28% is imposed (*TCGA 1992, s 4(3A)*). However, gains accruing before 6 April 2013 remain outside the scope of the CGT charge.

Provisions in *FA 2015* extended the ATED-related CGT charge to properties worth more than £1 million in relation to disposals occurring in the tax year 2015/16, and further extended the charge to properties worth more than £500,000 for disposals from 6 April 2016 (*TCGA 1992, s 2D*, as amended by *FA 2015, Sch 8*).

A change introduced in *FA 2014* reduced (subject to certain limited exceptions) the private residence relief final ownership period exemption for CGT purposes (in *TCGA 1992, s 223(1)*) from 36 months to 18 months, in relation to disposals from 6 April 2014.

Further provisions (introduced in *FA 2015*) extended the scope of CGT to include gains on the disposal of UK residential property interests by non-UK resident persons (or by individuals in the overseas part of a split year) from 6 April 2015, and also introduced 'non-resident CGT returns' (see *TMA 1970, ss 12ZA–12ZN*).

A restriction in private residence relief was also introduced in *FA 2015* for properties located in a territory in which the individual is not tax resident, broadly where the person does not meet a 90-day test for time spent in the property over the year (*TCGA 1992, s 222C*).

The rates of CGT were generally reduced by changes introduced in *FA 2016* with effect from 6 April 2016. The basic rate of CGT was reduced to 10% (from 18%), and the higher rate was reduced to 20% (from 28%), on most gains made by individuals, trustees and personal representatives. However, gains on the disposal of interests in residential properties that do not qualify for private residence relief (and also gains arising in respect of carried interest), remain subject to the 18% and 28% rates (including for 2018/19). ATED-related gains also remain subject to the 28% rate.

Following an announcement in Autumn Budget 2017 that all gains on non-resident disposals of UK immovable property accrued on or after April 2019 would be brought within the scope of UK tax, a consultation document was published on 22 November 2017. The changes under consideration also include: extending the tax charge to certain disposals by non-UK residents of interests in entities that derive their value from UK land; expanding the existing non-resident CGT rules to bring 'widely-held companies' and indirect disposals into scope; and harmonising the existing regime for ATED-related gains with the wider regime for taxing non-residents' gains on UK immovable property. The outcome of the consultation was awaited at the time of writing.

16.3 The above measures have had the general effect of discouraging IHT planning involving the family home.

If a non-UK domiciled individual holds a UK property, it will generally be chargeable to IHT on his death (unless, for example, the property passed to his spouse). Prior to changes introduced in *Finance (No 2) Act 2017*, an IHT planning consideration for such individuals therefore typically involved an offshore company holding the UK property, where the company's shares were held by the non-UK domiciled individual, perhaps via an offshore trust (such that the shares were excluded property, and outside the scope of IHT). Despite the potential implications for other taxes in relation to residential properties, the benefit of UK residential property being excluded from IHT might have seemed worthwhile for some non-UK domiciled individuals.

However, the government introduced provisions (in *Finance (No 2) Act 2017*) aimed at non-UK domiciled individuals holding UK residential property interests through a close company (ie a company which is, or would be if resident in the UK, a close company), partnership or trust, with a view to ensuring that the value attributable to such property is subject to IHT (*IHTA 1984, Sch A1*; see **1.15–1.19**).

Duty of care in connection with tax

16.4 The disposal of a property interest involves issues of both tax and non-tax law. Professional advisers must consider their duty of care to clients (and other people affected by the transactions).

A warning for tax advisers on this note was provided in *Hurlingham Estates Ltd v Wilde & Partners* [1997] STC 627. In that case, it was held that a professional (a reasonably competent conveyancer and commercial lawyer) owed a duty to his client to advise on the tax implications of the transaction unless his retainer was limited, or unless it was apparent that advice was not needed by the client.

16.5 A problem for an adviser is the level of expertise that he holds himself out as having and the extent to which, in his agreement with his client, he is able to limit his liability. It begins to look as if any family member who is disadvantaged by bad tax advice, even if not given to him direct but to a third party, may have a claim against the adviser.

The terms and scope of an engagement letter can be an important protection for professional advisers, provided that its terms are not exceeded.

In *Mehjoo v Harben Barker (a firm) and another* [2014] EWCA Civ 358, the Court of Appeal held that an accountancy firm had not been in breach of duty by not pointing out that a client might be non-UK domiciled and by not recommending that the client should seek tax advice from a 'non-dom specialist' in respect of a disposal of shares. However, firms lacking the necessary knowledge or expertise in a particular area to undertake appropriate planning on the client's behalf should limit the scope of their work in engagement letters, and as indicated above should be careful not to stray beyond the scope of their engagement.

In the context of advice on tax planning arrangements, professional advisers should consider giving adequate and timely warnings to clients about the risks of the arrangements being successfully challenged by HMRC (*Halsall & Ors v Champion Consulting Ltd & Ors* (Rev 1) [2017] EWHC 1079 (QB)).

Planning arrangements involving the family home

16.6 The consideration of other taxes when undertaking IHT planning involving the family home (and generally) was emphasised by the introduction of the 'pre-owned asset' (POA) income tax charge from 6 April 2005 (see **Chapter 17**), which is primarily aimed at what the government apparently regarded as unacceptable IHT avoidance.

A detailed consideration of those IHT avoidance schemes which apparently provoked the POA regime is outside the scope of this chapter. However, the main types of scheme used in the past involving the family home are briefly summarised below.

A section of guidance on the POA income tax charge is included in HMRC's Inheritance Tax Manual (IHTM44000–IHTM44128), replacing and expanding upon the guidance which had previously featured on HMRC's website.

Reversionary lease schemes

16.7 The intention of 'reversionary lease schemes' is broadly to allow the home owner to make a gift of an interest in the property to reduce his IHT estate, whilst continuing to occupy and without being subject to the 'gifts with reservation' (GWR) anti-avoidance rules (see **Chapter 7**).

This once popular planning arrangement typically involved the donor retaining the property freehold, but granting a deferred long lease as a gift, under which the right of the lessee to occupy is deferred (eg for 20 years).

The scheme was generally considered to be effective before 9 March 1999, although the position became less certain following legislative changes from that date. HMRC's guidance (at IHTM14360) indicates that reversionary lease schemes effected from 9 March 1999 are not caught by the GWR provisions in *FA 1986, s 102A* if the freehold interest was acquired more than seven years before the gift, as long as the lease contains no covenants of benefit.

In addition, HMRC guidance on reversionary lease schemes in the context of the POA income tax charge (at IHTM44102) confirms that where the freehold interest was acquired more than seven years before the gift, the continued occupation by the donor is not a 'significant' right (in view of *FA 1986, s 102A(5)*), so the GWR rules cannot apply and a POA charge arises instead.

HMRC's guidance at IHTM44102 also states that reversionary lease schemes established before 9 March 1999 succeed in avoiding the GWR provisions, so long as the lease does not contain any terms that are currently beneficial to the donor (eg covenants by the lessee to (say) maintain the property), and that the donor will consequently be subject to the POA charge (under *FA 2004, Sch 15, para 3(2)*). The HMRC guidance adds that the GWR provisions may apply if the lease contains terms currently beneficial to the donor, irrespective of when the freehold interest was acquired.

However, in *Buzzoni and others v Revenue & Customs* [2013] EWCA Civ 1684 (see **7.5**), the Court allowed an appeal against decisions by the First-tier Tribunal and Upper Tribunal that the deceased taxpayer had reserved a benefit (within *FA 1986, s 102(1)(b)*) in granting an underlease of her London flat to a trust in 1997. The underlease was subject to covenants. The covenants in the underlease mirrored the covenants in the headlease. On appeal, the Court held that the donor's benefit from the covenants made no difference to the lessees' enjoyment of the underlease. The imposition of duplicate obligations on the property did not add to the obligations already borne.

By contrast, in *Hood v Revenue & Customs* [2017] UKUT 0276 (TCC), the lifetime grant by the deceased of a reversionary sub-lease of property in London to her sons out of a head lease interest was held to be a gift with reservation of benefit (by virtue of *FA 1986, s 102(1)(b)*). The facts were similar to the *Buzzoni* case, though not identical. The First-tier Tribunal ([2016] UKFTT 59 (TC) noted in particular that, in contrast to the position in *Buzzoni*, the sub-lessees gave no direct covenants to the head lessor (ie the only positive covenants from the sub-lessees were those given in the sub-lease in favour of the deceased as sub-lessor). Furthermore, unlike the position in *Buzzoni*, the sub-lessees were under no obligation to the head lessor with respect to those covenants. The appellant's subsequent appeal to the Upper Tribunal was dismissed (see **7.5**).

Those reversionary lease schemes which are considered to be effective for IHT purposes are nevertheless subject to a potential income tax liability (from 2005/06) under the POA regime (*FA 2004, Sch 15, paras 3(2), (4)*), unless the donor elects out of the income tax charge and into the GWR rules for IHT purposes.

Lease 'carve-out' schemes

16.8 Lease carve-out arrangements were highlighted in *Ingram (Executors of Lady Ingram's Estate) v IRC* [1997] STC 1234 (see **7.11**), in which a carve-out scheme in relation to the late Lady Ingram's main residence and its transfer subject to leases was upheld by the House of Lords.

'*Ingram* schemes' involving lease carve outs were generally blocked from 9 March 1999 by changes to the GWR rules (*FA 1986, s 102A*), but as with reversionary leases (see **16.7**), carve-out schemes before that date appear to be effective for IHT purposes. However, like reversionary lease schemes, pre-9 March 1999 Ingram schemes are subject to an income tax charge under the POA rules (see IHTM44100), unless an election is made to the contrary.

Ingram schemes could still operate over 14 years. The GWR rules concerning interests in land (see **7.12**) state that a right or interest over land is not 'significant' for GWR purposes if it was granted or acquired before the seven-year period ending with the date of the gift (*FA 1986, s 102A(5)*). This exception could therefore apply if there was a gap of at least seven years between the creation of the lease and the gift of the freehold reversion. The gift to another individual would still be a PET, which would require the donor to survive a further seven years after making it. However, HMRC consider that *Ingram* schemes effected from 9 March 1999 are still caught by the GWR rules if the lease is not at a full rent (IHTM14360).

Ingram schemes caught by the GWR rules are not subject to a POA income tax charge (*FA 2004, Sch 15, para 11(5)(a)*). However, those schemes not subject to the GWR rules (eg effective schemes entered into before 9 March 1999) are not excluded from a POA charge, and therefore such arrangements are subject to those income tax rules.

'Eversden schemes'

16.9 In *IRC v Eversden (exors of Greenstock, decd)* [2003] EWCA Civ 668, [2003] STC 822, the Court of Appeal upheld the effectiveness against the GWR rules of an arrangement whereby property was initially placed into an interest in possession trust for the spouse, followed by a discretionary trust in which the beneficiaries included the settlor and spouse. Accordingly, changes to the GWR rules were introduced in 2003 to block '*Eversden* schemes' (*FA 1986, 102(5A)*), affecting settlements created from 20 June 2003 (see **7.9**).

For schemes involving the family home, a POA income tax charge is excluded for so long as the spouse or civil partner continues to have a beneficial entitlement to an interest in possession in the trust (*FA 2004, Sch 15, para 10(1)(c)*). However, this exclusion is unlikely to apply in practice, because the initial interest in possession of the property is normally terminated during the life of the spouse or civil partner.

Eversden schemes of the family home effected before 20 June 2003 are considered to be potentially subject to income tax under the POA rules if the spouse's life interest comes to an end during their lifetime and the settlor occupies the property, whereas if the spouse's life interest continues until their death, the transaction is excluded from POA under *FA 2004, Sch 15, para 10(1)(c)* (IHTM44101). For a spouse whose life interest ends on or after 18 March 2006, an IHT charge may arise on death if he or she had still benefited from the property, as the termination is treated as a gift (*FA 1986, s 102ZA*).

Schemes effected from 20 June 2003 are subject to the GWR rules in respect of the property, and therefore fall outside a POA charge. Furthermore, as mentioned the spouse may be subject to a separate GWR charge if the interest in possession terminates during their lifetime.

'Lifetime debt' or 'double trust' arrangements ('IOU schemes')

16.10

Example 16.1—'IOU scheme'

There are different names and variants of debt and trust arrangements ('IOU' or 'double trust' schemes), which were more popular prior to the introduction of stamp duty land tax (SDLT) from 1 December 2003.

However, an example of a typical scheme would be one in which an individual (Jake) sold his house for £1 million in February 2006, to a trust in which he has a life interest (Trust 1). Note that the transaction would be liable to SDLT.

The trustees gave Jake an IOU for the purchase price, which Jake gifted to a second trust for the benefit of his adult children (Trust 2). He remains in occupation of the property. The outstanding debt owed to Trust 2 reduces the value of the house in Trust 1 in Jake's estate for IHT purposes.

HMRC seem to have taken particular exception to IOU schemes, and have adopted an increasingly harder line with them. HMRC had not previously accepted that all types of double trust arrangements achieved their desired IHT objective. In particular, if the loan to Trust 2 is repayable on demand, HMRC's view is that there is a GWR until the trustees call in the loan. (*Note*: the GWR is considered to be in the loan, as opposed to the house.)

If the terms of the loan provide that the debt is only repayable after the death of the life tenant (ie Jake), HMRC initially appeared to accept that such schemes were not caught by the GWR rules in respect of the loan. However, HMRC's guidance was amended in October 2010 to the effect that loans repayable after the life tenant's death are caught under the GWR provisions (in addition to loans repayable on demand, which were previously considered to be caught). HMRC subsequently confirmed (in their Trusts & Estates Newsletter, December 2011) that their POA guidance had been updated to explain that HMRC's view is now that none of the home loan or double trust schemes succeed in mitigating IHT in the way intended.

HMRC's guidance on their website was updated in November 2011, but was subsequently replaced in March 2012 as part of a new POA section of its Inheritance Tax Manual. This confirms the view that where the terms of the loan are that the debt is only repayable after the death of the life tenant, the settlor still obtains a benefit that is referable to the gift. HMRC state that a GWR charge applies to the loan, and that a POA charge arises in respect of the house, on the basis that it is the asset previously owned by the individual (IHTM44105).

In addition to the above approach to the GWR provisions, HMRC's guidance advances the following arguments to negate the intended consequences of IOU schemes (IHTM44106):

> 'The first is that the provisions of FA86/S103 apply to disallow the deduction of the loan against the trust in which the individual retained a life interest. The sale of the property to the first trust is a disposition and since, in the majority of cases, the trustees had no means with which to pay for the property, the steps they took to fund their purchase created the debt which (through the trustees equitable lien) is an incumbrance against the property. The consideration for the debt was property derived from the deceased and FA86/S103 applies to abate the loan.'
>
> 'Secondly, having regard to the purpose and effect of home loan schemes, the steps taken are a pre-ordained series of transactions, and following the line of authority that is founded on *W T Ramsay v IRC* [1981] 1 AER 865, the individual steps should be treated as a single transaction comprising a number of elements which when taken together have the effect that the vendor has made a "gift" of the property concerned for the purposes of FA86/S102 and has continued to live there. So reservation of benefit arises in the property.'

The effectiveness (or otherwise) of home loan or double trust schemes is likely to be determined through litigation, although no cases have been reported at the time of writing. If there is a GWR in the property, a POA charge will not arise in respect of it. In that case, HMRC have previously stated that any POA income tax paid (ie on the basis that no such GWR applied) will be repaid with interest upon a claim being made, irrespective of the time limits for repayment that might otherwise apply (tinyurl.com/POAguidance6).

To assist executors and trustees in the administration of estates, HMRC stated that they would provide estimates of the tax that might be payable if HMRC succeed in future litigation. This would allow executors and trustees to make payments on account to HMRC to mitigate potential interest charges or to make an appropriate provision out of funds held (HMRC Trusts & Estates Newsletter, August 2012).

HMRC subsequently published guidance (at IHTM44128) stating that when a home loan or double trust scheme has been unwound, a repayment of all the POA income tax paid to date can be claimed (without time limit) by writing to: Pay As You Earn and Self-Assessment. HM Revenue and Customs, BX9 1AS. The taxpayer should enclose signed copies of the documents used to unwind the scheme in evidence.

16.11 In the above example, the value of Jake's life interest forms part of his estate for IHT purposes (note that this IHT treatment does not generally apply to interests in possession created from 22 March 2006: see **Chapter 9**), less the outstanding debt owed to the trustees of the children's trust. If the scheme is effective for IHT purposes and the GWR rules do not apply in respect of the property, a POA income tax liability potentially arises on the basis that the debt is an 'excluded liability' (*FA 2004, Sch 15, paras 11(6),(7)*), unless Jake elects out of POA and into IHT.

HMRC's guidance includes an example of a POA charge in the context of a home loan scheme, where the debt (plus accrued interest) is treated as an excluded liability (IHTM44051).

The *Charge to Income Tax by Reference to Enjoyment of Property Previously Owned Regulations 2005, SI 2005/724* provide relief from a double IHT charge for taxpayers who elect into the GWR regime after making lifetime double trust home loan arrangements, where the individual dies after 5 April 2005 and within seven years of gifting the loan (*reg 6*).

Some taxpayers may decide to unravel their double trust home loan arrangements, and possibly consider other forms of IHT planning instead. The *Inheritance Tax (Double Charges Relief) Regulations 2005, SI 2005/3441* provide relief from the double IHT charge that may arise for taxpayers in such circumstances, ie where the loan is written off, waived or released (so that the value of the house forms part of their estate again) and the individual dies after 5 April 2005 and within seven years of gifting the loan (*reg 3*).

For home loan or double trust schemes which have not been unwound but where taxpayers wish to do so, HMRC subsequently stated that it will be prepared to settle cases prior to a judicial decision on the basis set out in its guidance at IHTM44120-IHTM44128, which applies for IHT purposes only. HMRC reserves the right to alter its view, but states that 'any schemes unwound whilst this agreement is in place will not be revisited' (IHTM44120). However, HMRC's Trusts and Estates Newsletter (September 2017) warned that in some cases it will be necessary to consider the CGT or income tax consequences of unwinding the scheme in relation to the loan.

OWNERSHIP

16.12

> **Focus**
>
> The property may be owned in an individual's sole name (eg husband, wife or civil partner), or as joint tenants, or as tenants in common (different rules apply in Scotland; see **6.20**).
>
> - *Joint tenants* – On the death of a 'joint tenant', the survivor takes the entire interest absolutely by operation of law. Therefore, it is not possible (subject to severance, which HMRC currently accept can be effected for IHT purposes through a deed of variation) to leave an interest in jointly tenanted property to a third party, because this interest accrues automatically to the surviving joint tenant.
> - *Tenants in common* – By contrast, ownership as 'tenants in common' gives each spouse a separate (typically equal) share of the property, which can be left by will or disposed of during lifetime. This is frequently found to be the most satisfactory form of ownership from both an IHT planning and a practical point of view.

If the property is held by husband and wife (or civil partners) as joint tenants and the parties wish to sever the joint tenancy so that they become tenants in common instead, a simple form of severance notice should suffice. This notice should be given during lifetime because a joint tenancy cannot be severed by will (although a deed of variation can result in the tenancy being treated as such for IHT purposes). It is preferable for a severance to be agreed and signed by both parties.

A sample notice of severance is provided below.

Example 16.2—Joint tenancy: notice of severance

NOTICE OF SEVERANCE

TO: [Name of joint tenant (1)] of [full address]

FROM: [Name of joint tenant (2)] of [full address]

I HEREBY GIVE YOU NOTICE severing our joint tenancy in equity of and in [full address of property] ('the property') now held by yourself and myself as joint tenants at law and in equity. The property shall henceforth be held by yourself and myself as tenants in common in equity in ['equal' or relevant percentage] shares.

THIS NOTICE REQUIRES that you acknowledge and indicate your acceptance to this Notice by signing the Notice where indicated below.

SIGNED BY ....

DATED ....

I HEREBY ACKNOWLEDGE AND ACCEPT this Notice of Severance in respect of the aforementioned property

SIGNED BY ....

DATED ....

16.13 The notice itself is valid as soon as it has been signed by one joint owner and acknowledged by the other. However, this is a transaction between two people, one of whom will probably have died by the time it becomes necessary to look at the issue. Husband and wife (or civil partners) might sign the notice at the time of signing wills and might not realise that it is important to keep the notice of severance in a safe place so that it can be produced later on to show how the property is held.

If the notice of severance is mislaid, it may be difficult to substantiate that the joint tenancy has been severed, though not impossible. In *Chadda and others v Revenue & Customs* [2014] UKFTT 1061 (TC), the joint tenancy of a married couple's house was held on the evidence of the case, and on the balance of probabilities, to have been severed (ie such that the husband's interest in the house passed in accordance with his will, rather than by survivorship), despite the absence of a written notice of severance (NB: a notice had been prepared, but the signed notice could not be found).

The First-tier Tribunal in *Chadda and others* helpfully pointed out that a written notice of severance (under *LPA 1925, s 36(2)*) was only one of four possible bases of severance, the other three being: an act of any one of the persons interested acting on their own share (following *Williams v Hensman*

[1861] 70 ER 862); by mutual agreement; and any course of dealing sufficient to intimate that the interests of all the joint tenants were mutually treated as constituting a tenancy in common (ie 'mutual conduct').

If the title to the property is unregistered (very rare these days), the notice of severance should be placed with the original deeds. These will often be held by the bank or building society that financed the purchase.

Normally, the title will be registered: if so, the notice of severance should be lodged with HM Land Registry to bring the register of title up to date. This should provide clear evidence later on when it is needed.

General guidance on joint property ownership, including changing from joint tenants to tenants in common (or vice versa), can be found on the government's website (www.gov.uk/joint-property-ownership).

LIFETIME PLANNING

Equity release

16.14 A straightforward form of lifetime IHT planning involves releasing equity in the property, as opposed to making a direct gift of an interest in the property. The following possibilities could be considered.

Mortgage or loan

16.15 A loan or mortgage secured on the property will generally reduce its net value for IHT purposes, subject to certain restrictions (see below). The funds borrowed could be gifted to non-exempt beneficiaries such as adult children (ie a PET) or into trust from which the settlor is excluded as a beneficiary (the latter normally being a chargeable lifetime transfer since 22 March 2006).

Such an arrangement should be best suited to individuals whose life expectancy is restricted by old age or infirmity, as a commercial loan or mortgage will bear interest. However, the donor would normally need to survive at least seven years for the gifted proceeds to escape IHT consequences on death. Decreasing term assurance could be considered to cover any IHT liability (with the donees paying the premiums).

Prior to provisions introduced in *FA 2013*, if life expectancy was more than two years but less than seven years, consideration was commonly given to investing the loan proceeds in (for example) shares eligible for 100% business property relief (see **Chapter 13**), such as in the property owner's unquoted trading company, or in trading companies listed on the Alternative Investment Market (AIM) (albeit that commercially by their nature such investments are often high risk).

However, *FA 2013* introduced legislation which broadly provides that a liability used to acquire, maintain or enhance certain 'relievable property' (ie business property, agricultural property or woodlands relief property) reduces the value of that property, before business property relief (or agricultural property relief, or woodlands relief) is applied (*IHTA 1984, s 162B*). To that extent, the benefit of those reliefs is effectively lost.

Similarly, legislation introduced in *FA 2013* potentially restricts a deduction for a liability such as a loan or mortgage secured on a property, to the extent that the proceeds are used to acquire, maintain or enhance 'excluded property' (see **Chapter 11**). This general rule is subject to certain limited exceptions, such as where the excluded property has been sold and replaced by non-excluded property, or to the extent that the liability exceeds the value of the excluded property, and certain conditions are satisfied (*IHTA 1984, s 162A*).

A foreign currency bank account balance (within *IHTA 1984, s 157*) is left out of account on the death of a person who is not domiciled and not resident in the UK. Those funds are not excluded property as such. However, provisions introduced in *FA 2014* treat foreign currency accounts in UK banks in a similar way as excluded property for the purposes of restricting the deduction of liabilities (*IHTA 1984, s 162AA*).

Furthermore, a deduction from the value of a person's estate for liabilities unpaid on death is subject to certain conditions and possible restrictions in *IHTA 1984, s 175A* (see **5.13**), as introduced in *FA 2013*. This anti-avoidance provision could affect (for example) non-commercial loans, such as from friends or family members, which are unpaid following death.

'Downsizing'

16.16 Selling the family home and moving to a smaller, less expensive house represents an alternative form of equity release.

The surplus funds generated could be dealt with as outlined at **16.15** above. Note that the proceeds from trading down could be invested in business property (or other relievable property) without the restriction applying in respect of liabilities to finance such property (in *s 162B*) as mentioned in the previous paragraph, where any loan or mortgage had already been repaid.

Similarly, the restriction in respect of excluded property (in *IHTA 1984, s 162A*) does not apply if there was no mortgage or loan, and the surplus proceeds are used to acquire excluded property.

Although often unpopular with clients, the equity release arrangement has side benefits:

- It may reduce imbalance in asset allocation: far too many families have too much capital tied up in the family home, so its sale can release liquidity that enhances the lifestyle of the elderly.

- A smaller property may be cheaper to run, increasing disposable income and providing an opportunity to save tax, such as by making gifts out of income under *IHTA 1984, s 21*.
- Tax is payable in hard cash, albeit by instalments where property is concerned. The reallocation of resources to increase liquidity can make the estate much easier to administer after the death.

Provisions allowing residence nil rate band (see **16.55**) that would otherwise be lost as a result of downsizing to remain available in certain circumstances were introduced in *FA 2016* (see **16.70**).

Commercial sale

16.17 The house owner may wish to sell the whole of the property or an interest in it, so as to enhance his standard of living. A commercial sale is not a transfer of value for IHT purposes if it can be shown that there was no intention to confer a gratuitous benefit on any person, and *either* that it was an arm's-length transaction between unconnected persons, or that the transaction was on arm's-length terms (*IHTA 1984, s 10*).

Particularly in the case of sales between family members, independent property valuations should be obtained by both parties, to rebut any presumption by HMRC that gratuitous benefit has been conferred.

Similarly, for POA income tax purposes, the disposal of land (or chattels) is an 'excluded transaction' if it is a disposal by an individual of his whole interest in the property 'except for any right expressly reserved by him over the property', either by an arm's-length transaction or by a transaction such as might be expected to be made at arm's length between unconnected persons (*FA 2004, Sch 15, para 10(1)(a)*).

POA regulations also allow for *partial* arm's-length type equity releases in certain circumstances (the *Charge to Income Tax by Reference to Enjoyment of Property Previously Owned Regulations 2005, SI 2005/724, reg 5*). However, the scope of this exemption is restricted. It applies to transactions between unconnected persons. It also applies to any disposals between connected persons on arm's-length terms before 7 March 2005, or to disposals from that date if the consideration was *not* in money or readily convertible assets.

The latter exemption may assist in cases where an elderly or infirm parent gives an interest in their home to adult offspring in return for the provision of care in the property on an ongoing basis.

16.18 An alternative exclusion from the POA charge of possible relevance applies if the disposal was a disposition falling within *IHTA 1984, s 11* ('dispositions for maintenance of family'), such as a disposition in favour of a dependent relative for the reasonable provision of his care or maintenance.

This is acknowledged in HMRC's guidance, albeit that it casts some doubt over the availability of the exclusion in such circumstances (IHTM44037):

> 'For the purposes of the contribution conditions relating to land and chattels, the contribution by a person to the acquisition of any property is an excluded transaction in relation to the chargeable person if it was a disposition that meets the conditions of IHTA84/S11, dispositions for maintenance of family [...] FA04/Sch15/Para 10(2)(d).
>
> This provision is likely to be of limited application given that it is not easy to see how the contribution to the acquisition of a capital asset, such as land or chattels can be for the maintenance of the donee. However, the decision in *McKelvey v HMRC* [...] was that exemption under IHTA84/S11 could apply, and any case where this exclusion is claimed should be referred to Technical.'

In *McKelvey (Personal Representative of McKelvey Deceased) v Revenue and Customs Commissioners)* [2008] SpC 694, the deceased (D) was a spinster who lived with her widowed mother (M), who was 85 years old, blind and in poor health. D was diagnosed with terminal cancer, and in 2003 gave away two houses that she owned to M. D died in 2005, and M died in 2007. HMRC sought to charge IHT on the value of D's gift of the houses to M of £169,000. D's executor appealed, on the grounds that the gifts were exempt transfers within *IHTA 1984, s 11(3)* as a disposition being a reasonable provision for the care and maintenance of a dependent relative. The executor contended that D gave the houses to M so that they could be sold to pay for nursing care.

The executor's appeal was allowed in part. The Special Commissioner held that it was reasonable for D to assume that M would need residential nursing care. The difficulty in this case was in determining what was 'reasonably required' for this purpose. The Commissioner concluded that 'reasonable provision at the time the transfers were made amounted in all to £140,500'. This amount qualified for exemption under *IHTA 1984, s 11*, with the balance of £28,500 being a chargeable transfer (*IHTA 1984, s 3A(4)*).

Gifting the family home

16.19 Lifetime planning involving the family home often includes gifting an interest in the property, or sometimes the property as a whole. Of course, such a gift is a disposal for CGT purposes at market value, although private residence relief will normally be available (*TCGA 1992, s 222*).

It is possible that the donor(s) may wish to move out of the family home (eg into a residential nursing home or, for example, purchase a smaller property if they can afford to do so). For commentary on private residence relief, see the latest edition of *Capital Gains Tax* (Bloomsbury Professional).

Where the family home (or an interest in it) is being gifted, the 'gifts with reservation' (GWR) anti-avoidance rules (see **Chapter 7**) must be safely navigated for IHT purposes.

The GWR provisions can apply (*inter alia*) if an individual makes a gift of property (from 18 March 1986) which is not enjoyed to the entire exclusion, or virtually the entire exclusion, of the donor (*FA 1986, s 102(1)(b)*).

As there is no definition of 'virtually the entire exclusion' in the IHT legislation, HMRC published guidance on their view of the expression in *Revenue Interpretation 55* (see **7.28**), which interprets it to include visits to stay at the house for certain limited periods, normal social visits, certain short-term stays (eg due to convalescence following medical treatment) and domestic visits (eg babysitting the donee's children).

Care should be taken to ensure that stays at, or visits to, the house do not escalate beyond the *de minimis* limits and into a GWR charge. Examples given in *Revenue Interpretation 55* of situations in which those limits are exceeded include:

- a house in which the donor then stays most weekends, or for a month or more each year; and
- a house with a library in which the donor continues to keep his own books, or which the donor uses on a regular basis, for example because it is necessary for his work.

However, a GWR charge is avoided if the donor pays a market rent for any periods of occupation (eg a gift of the property to the children, followed by a leaseback at a full commercial rent throughout the period of occupation). An exception to the GWR rules applies if full consideration is paid in money or money's worth for occupying the land (*FA 1986, Sch 20, para 6(1)(a)*). Independent advice should be obtained, together with separate professional valuations to establish a full market rent.

HMRC guidance interprets the term 'occupies' widely (albeit in the context of the POA provisions), and states that occupation is not necessarily to be equated with residence, as the latter 'implies a greater level of permanence so a lower threshold is required to satisfy the occupation condition' (IHTM44003).

Other tax issues may also need to be considered. For example, the payment of rent and/or a lease premium in respect of a residential property in London has potential income tax implications for the recipient; in addition, the SDLT position of the lease must be considered. A subsequent sale of the property will also have CGT implications in respect of any increase in value of the property.

Gifting a share of the home

Joint occupation

16.20 The gift of an 'undivided share of an interest in land' (from 9 March 1999) can give rise to a GWR charge (*FA 1986, s 102B(1)*; see **7.14**), subject to certain 'let-outs' considered below.

Example 16.3—Joint occupation: gift to family member

Freda, who is an elderly widowed parent, gifts a share in the house (say 50%) to her adult unmarried daughter, Gertrude. Both live together in the house until Freda's death.

What is the GWR position?

16.21 The basic principle is that the GWR rules apply to the gift of an undivided share in land, except in three cases:

- The donor does not occupy the land (*FA 1986, s 102B(3)(a)*). This would appear to allow a non-occupying donor to receive a share of rent and profit from the property without constituting a GWR; but it does not assist Freda in **Example 16.3**.
- The donor occupies the land for full consideration in money or money's worth (*FA 1986, s 102B(3)(b)*). Whilst the parent's payment of rent to the daughter could reduce the eventual IHT liability on the parent's estate, it is often difficult to establish a market rent in these circumstances, and to ensure that the amount paid continues to reflect a market rent. In any event, the income tax implications for the daughter of receiving rental income are likely to make this option seem unattractive.
- Both donor and donee occupy the land, and the donor receives no benefit (other than a negligible one) provided by or at the expense of the donee in connection with the gift (*FA 1986, s 102B(4)*).

The third exception above appears to be based on a statement made by the Minister of State for the Treasury in 1986 (see below), although the above legislation did not take effect until 9 March 1999.

Hansard Statement

> 'It may be that my Hon. Friend's intention concerns the common case where someone gives away an individual share in land, typically a house, which is then occupied by all the joint owners including the donor. For example, elderly parents may make unconditional gifts of undivided shares in their house to their children and the parents and children occupy the property as their family home, each owner bearing his or her share of the running costs. In those circumstances, the parents' occupation or enjoyment of the part of the house that they have given away is in return for similar enjoyment of the children of the other part of the property. Thus the donors' occupation is for a full consideration.
>
> Accordingly, I assure my Hon. Friend that the gift with reservation rules will not be applied to an unconditional gift of an undivided share in land

merely because the property is occupied by all the joint owners or tenants in common, including the donor.'

16.22 The scope of the 'shared occupation' rule in *FA 1986, s 102B(4)* is potentially wider than the example given in the Hansard statement indicates. For instance, the legislation deals with land in general, not necessarily the family home. In addition, the requirement that the donor must not receive any connected benefit (other than a negligible one) does not necessarily mean that household running costs must be shared proportionately. The donor may wish to continue paying all the running costs, or the 'lion's share' of them. Otherwise, the difficulty arises in establishing how much the donee can safely pay, without the donor falling foul of the GWR rules.

In **Example 16.3**, Freda gifted a 50% share of the house to her daughter. *FA 1986, s 102B* does not contain an express requirement to gift an equal share. The donor may therefore wish to consider giving away more than a 50% interest. However, HMRC could contend that if two individuals occupy a property jointly, the most that can be given away is 50%; the Inheritance Tax Manual at IHTM14332 (which provides a number of examples involving joint property) includes a note with the following health warning:

> 'The joint property examples are on the basis that the joint owners take the property in equal shares. Refer any case in which the transferor takes less than an equal share to Technical.'

In cases where the interest given away is more than 50% (say 75%), it does not follow that the donee should pay 75% of the household running costs. To prevent the donor from receiving a possible benefit, any sharing of running costs should reflect their respective usage (eg water, gas and electricity), which may not be the same as their beneficial property ownership percentages. However, in practice it will often be difficult to measure such usage: it would probably be safer for the donor to continue paying all of the household running expenses.

The value of Freda's share of the house may be subject to a discount on her death of between 10–15%, subject to the Land Tribunal's agreement. The higher percentage potentially applies if the other co-owner continues to occupy the property (see **6.23**).

16.23 It should be noted that the above GWR exception applies while the property is occupied jointly. What would happen if, for example, the daughter left home to get married? A GWR could be avoided by the mother paying a full market rent for her continued occupation in respect of her daughter's share.

It is also important to note that the above exception applies to the gift of an interest in land, not the whole.

For income tax purposes, there is an exemption from a POA charge in joint occupation circumstances in which *FA 1986, s 102B(4)* would apply (*FA 2004, Sch 15, para 11(5)(c)*).

Changes in circumstances

16.24 Consider the following example:

Example 16.4—Gift of house and change in circumstances: infirmity of donor

George gifted his house ('Blackacre') to his adult son Harold in April 2013, which Harold occupied as his home.

In May 2018, George (who did not previously have any major health problems) suffered a serious heart attack, which left him needing constant care.

After George's discharge from hospital, he had to move back to Blackacre where Harold looked after him. George sadly died shortly afterwards.

16.25 There is a specific relieving provision to prevent an unfortunate GWR charge arising following such an unexpected and sad change in circumstances. The donor's occupation of the gifted land is disregarded if (as in the above example) the donee is a relative of the donor or his spouse (or civil partner), and certain other conditions are satisfied (*FA 1986, s 102C(3)*; *Sch 20, para 6(1)(b)*); see **7.31**), ie:

- the occupation results from an unforeseen change in the donor's circumstances (ie the GWR exception would not apply in the above example if George had a long history of ill health, and he made the gift when it was likely that he would need looking after); and
- the donor has become unable to maintain himself through old age, infirmity or otherwise; and
- the occupation represents reasonable provision by the donee for the donor's care and maintenance.

It should be noted that the above conditions are cumulative, and in practice this relieving provision may therefore be difficult to attain.

In the case of serious illness where the donor cannot maintain himself, HMRC accept that occupation represents reasonable provision for his care and maintenance (see the example at IHTM14342), although this exception would only be available until the donor sufficiently recovered.

For POA income tax purposes, there is also an exemption from charge if the above conditions are satisfied (*FA 2004, Sch 15, para 11(5)(d)*).

Statutory settlements

16.26 In some cases, a lifetime gift can result in a statutory settlement for IHT purposes, eg a leasehold interest for life for less than full consideration (*IHTA 1984, s 43(3)*). The same applies if property is 'held in trust for persons in succession or for any persons subject to a contingency' (*IHTA 1984, s 43(2)(a)*).

For example, the lifetime gift of a share in the family home between spouses or civil partners subject to provisions in their wills that the property may not be sold without the survivor's consent could result in HMRC arguing that there is an interest in possession of the deceased's interest if left to the children on the first death. See also **16.42** below, and *IRC v Lloyds Private Banking Ltd* [1998] STC 559 (at **16.45**) in particular.

In the *Trusts & Estates Newsletter* (April 2013), HMRC confirmed their view that the creation of a 'usufruct' (ie the right to the use and enjoyment of another's property) generally gives rise to a settlement under *s 43(2)*. The usufruct is treated as giving rise to an interest in possession in the property concerned.

WILL PLANNING

Will or intestacy?

16.27

Focus

- Spouses or civil partners who occupy the family home as 'tenants in common' (see **16.12**) should make provision in their wills concerning their shares in the property. The rules of intestacy (see **5.1**) do not give a surviving spouse or civil partner an automatic right to the deceased's interest in the family home.
- Property owned as joint tenants passes by survivorship. Therefore, if the owners wish to leave their interests on death other than to each other, the joint tenancy should be severed during their lifetimes, and suitable provision made in their wills.

It may be possible for an instrument of variation to redirect joint property to give effect to the survivor's continued occupation (assuming that those who would otherwise benefit agree), and also effectively to sever the joint tenancy for IHT purposes, if appropriate. The IHT provisions (*IHTA 1984, s 142*, 'Alteration of dispositions taking effect on death') apply to dispositions which are '… effected by will, under the law relating to intestacy, *or otherwise*' (emphasis added). The latter disposition would seem to cover property passing by survivorship, if the notice of variation so provides. This is a point that HMRC appear to accept (IHTM35092).

In any event, it would surely be easier, and would provide greater certainty, to deal with this issue in the wills of both spouses (or civil partners) during their lifetimes. The wills should be reviewed at regular intervals to ensure that they reflect current wishes, and to protect against unforeseen changes in circumstances.

Using the nil rate band

16.28 Prior to the transferable nil rate band legislation introduced in *FA 2008* (see **16.29**), it was generally important for married couples or civil partnerships to ensure that optimum use was made of the available IHT threshold (or 'nil rate band') on the first death (see **Chapter 3**).

If a deceased spouse (or civil partner) leaves their entire estate to the surviving spouse, then (unless the recipient spouse is non-UK domiciled) the legacy will normally be wholly exempt from IHT (*IHTA 1984, s 18*). However, the estate of the survivor increases accordingly. This could result in a potentially higher IHT liability on the second death, and a higher IHT liability overall. If each spouse (or civil partner) owned sufficient assets to constitute their nil rate bands, a non-exempt legacy on the first death could have saved IHT of an amount up to the nil rate band multiplied by the 40% 'death rate'.

A common IHT planning technique before the *FA 2008* changes was therefore to ensure that an amount up to the available nil rate band was left to (say) adult children directly, or possibly by way of a 'nil rate band discretionary trust' in which the surviving spouse could be included among the class of beneficiaries. This planning was relatively straightforward and simple to implement if each spouse (or civil partner) owned sufficient 'liquid' assets to constitute their nil rate bands, such as cash, shares and securities.

However, very often the only asset of any substantial value would be an interest in the family home.

Transferable nil rate bands

16.29 Estate planning for married couples and civil partnerships was simplified in many cases by the introduction of the transferable nil rate band facility from 9 October 2007 (*IHTA 1984, ss 8A–8C*).

The provisions broadly allow claims for the transfer of a spouse's or civil partner's unused nil rate band to surviving spouses or civil partners (who die on or after 9 October 2007). The amount that can be transferred is based on the unused percentage of the deceased's nil rate band. That percentage is applied to the nil rate band in operation on the death of the survivor. See **Chapter 3** for further commentary.

From an IHT planning perspective, it is therefore generally no longer necessary for spouses and civil partners to utilise the nil rate band on the first death, such as by providing for the transfer of an interest in the family home to non-exempt beneficiaries (although if both spouses or civil partners died before 9 October 2007, it is not possible to take advantage of the transferable nil rate band).

The availability of an increased ('residence') nil rate band where a home is passed on death to lineal descendants of the deceased from 6 April 2017 (see **16.55**) potentially enhances the attractiveness of such legacies. Alternatively, unused residence nil rate band may be transferred to the surviving spouse (or civil partner) in some cases. For example, if the family home (or an interest in it) passes to a surviving spouse a claim may be possible for unused residence nil rate band brought forward from the earlier spouse to die, where the survivor leaves the family home to lineal descendants.

Whilst nil rate band legacies of interests in the family home to discretionary trusts or other chargeable beneficiaries on the first spouse or civil partner to die have probably been less prevalent since the introduction of the transferable nil rate band provisions, there may be circumstances in which such legacies are necessary or preferred, such as where the property occupants are unmarried or are siblings (see *Burden v United Kingdom* [2008] All ER (D) 391 (Apr)), or to make provision for offspring.

In addition, aside from IHT considerations there may be other reasons why an interest in the home may be left on trust (eg due to concerns about asset protection).

Ownership by first spouse (or civil partner) to die

16.30 The commentary below deals with situations in which it is not possible, or not preferred, to leave an outright legacy of the family home to the surviving spouse or civil partner on the first death for the purpose of claiming the deceased's unused nil rate band or residence nil rate band on the death of the surviving spouse or civil partner.

If one spouse or civil partner owns the entire family home and dies first, an interest in it could be left to a chargeable party (eg a daughter), whilst enabling the surviving spouse or civil partner to occupy by leaving another interest. Their respective shares may depend upon factors including the value of the family home, and the proportionate interest necessary to constitute the nil rate band (assuming that the deceased owned insufficient assets to do so otherwise).

For example, the surviving spouse or civil partner may receive (say) a 25% tenant in common share, with 75% to the daughter (the latter interest perhaps being worth up to the available nil rate band, including, from 6 April 2017, extra (or 'residence') nil rate band if appropriate). The survivor would then be able to occupy the whole by virtue of their 25% interest as a tenant in common.

See **16.29** above, **16.55–16.77** below and **Chapter 3** regarding the transferable nil rate band for spouses and civil partners, and the residence nil rate band.

There must be no restriction on the daughter occupying the house as co-owner, as this would give the survivor an interest in possession in the whole, with the result that the same overall IHT liability would arise as if the house had been given to them outright, unless the interest terminates and occupation ceases more than seven years before the individual's death (ie the termination being a deemed PET). The survivor's occupation could be made informal (eg by way of a non-enforceable licence).

However, legal issues arise, such as 'security of tenure'. Can the daughter (assuming that she lives elsewhere) be trusted not to sell her interest? Even if she can be trusted, her interest is not secure from creditors and others.

Alternatively, the will of the deceased spouse or civil partner may create a trust of the family home (see below).

Life interest trust

16.31 For life interests created before 22 March 2006, a beneficiary with an interest in possession in settled property is treated as owning the underlying trust assets. This treatment continues to apply to certain life interests created from that date, such as those created by will.

Subject to this and certain other exceptions (see **Chapter 9**), interests in possession created on or after 22 March 2006 are subject to the same IHT treatment as discretionary trusts (see **Chapter 10**).

If (for example) the first spouse or civil partner to die already used the nil rate band (eg by making chargeable lifetime gifts) the deceased's will could establish a life interest trust of the whole home in favour of the survivor. From 22 March 2006, such an interest is an immediate post-death interest (*IHTA 1984, s 49A*), which qualifies for the spouse (or civil partner) exemption (*IHTA 1984, s 18*) and is 'inherited' for the purposes of the residence nil rate band (*IHTA 1984, s 8J(4)(a)*).

Alternatively, the deceased's will could establish a life interest in an appropriate share of the house to the surviving spouse, with the remaining interest to non-exempt beneficiaries (eg the children), in order to utilise the nil rate band, if available (including residence nil rate band from 6 April 2017, if appropriate).

16.32 Where the survivor was beneficially entitled to an interest in possession on their death (from 6 April 2017), the property (or the relevant proportion of it) is 'inherited' for the purpose of the residence nil rate band if another person becomes beneficially entitled to it on the survivor's death. The residence nil rate band may therefore be available if lineal descendants become beneficially entitled to the property on the survivor's death (*IHTA 1984, s 8J(5)*).

Prior to 22 March 2006, the lifetime termination of a life interest is not a disposal by way of gift for GWR purposes (*FA 1986, s 102(1)*). However, from that date, the lifetime termination of an interest in possession falls to be treated as a gift (*FA 1986, s 102ZA*). An IHT charge could therefore arise if an individual continues to derive a benefit from the property after their life interest has been terminated. See **Chapter 15**.

What if the surviving spouse or civil partner is a trustee? HMRC generally accept that the appointment of a donor, spouse or civil partner as a trustee is not of itself a GWR. The spouse or civil partner holds the property in a fiduciary capacity only, and is required to deal with it in accordance with their fiduciary duties as a trustee. The same applies if the donor, spouse or civil partner is entitled to payment for their services as trustee, if the trust deed allows and provided the remuneration is not excessive (IHTM14394). Nevertheless, it may be considered safer if the survivor is not a trustee.

For capital gains tax purposes, private residence exemption should be available (eg if the residence is sold during the survivor's lifetime) if he is 'entitled to occupy it under the terms of the settlement' (*TCGA 1992, s 225*).

It is important that the trust is properly administered and that the decisions of the trustees are made independently and in the best interests of the beneficiary, such as to reduce the possibility of a challenge by HMRC that the trust is a 'sham'. This point is discussed further at **16.54**. The same comment applies to trusts in general.

Discretionary trust

16.33 A discretionary trust is one in which the beneficiaries normally have no interest in possession of the settled property, because the discretionary nature of the trust means that they have no absolute entitlement to trust income or assets.

However, the trustees of a discretionary trust could possibly exercise their powers under the trust deed in favour of a beneficiary in such a way that an interest in possession is created. The IHT treatment of such an interest in possession broadly depends on whether it is deemed to arise before 22 March 2006 or since that date, subject to certain exceptions (see **16.31** above).

Statement of Practice 10/79 and the Judge case

16.34 HMRC Statement of Practice 10/79 ('Power of trustees to allow a beneficiary to occupy a dwelling house') states that if the trust deed allows

'… an exclusive or joint residence … for a definite or indefinite period … with the intention of providing a particular beneficiary with a permanent home, HMRC will normally regard the exercise of the power as creating an interest in possession'. In addition, a lease for life for less than full consideration is treated as an interest in possession (*IHTA 1984, s 43(3)*).

The correctness of SP 10/79 was called into question in *Judge (Personal representatives of Walden deceased) v Revenue and Customs Commissioners* [2005] SSCD 863, in which it was held that the beneficiary under a will trust had no right to occupy the property, but that the trustees had absolute discretion (not a duty) to allow her to occupy.

In the *Judge* case, Mr and Mrs Walden lived at 30 Perrymead Street in London. Mr Walden owned the property. He made a will. Clause 3 of that will, which dealt with the matrimonial home, included the following provision:

> 'AND I DECLARE my Trustees during the lifetime of my Wife to permit her to have the use and enjoyment of the said property for such period or periods as they shall in their absolute discretion think fit pending postponement of sale she paying the rates taxes and other outgoings and keeping the same in good repair and insured against fire to the full value thereof … '

16.35 Mr Walden subsequently died. His personal representatives concluded that the effect of Clause 3 of Mr Walden's will was to give Mrs Walden an interest in possession in the property. The IHT account submitted to Capital Taxes (as it then was) for Mr Walden's estate was completed on that basis. A claim for the IHT spouse exemption was made on the value of Perrymead Street, which was shown as £625,000. This resulted in no IHT being paid on Mr Walden's estate, because his other estate assets were covered by the nil rate band.

Mrs Walden died a few years later. Her personal representatives submitted an IHT account to the Revenue's Capital Taxes Office, but the account did not mention the Perrymead Street property. This was presumably on the footing that Mr Walden's will established a discretionary trust, so that the property was not part of Mrs Walden's estate. The Revenue issued a determination on the basis that Mrs Walden had an interest in possession in the property, and the personal representatives appealed to the Special Commissioner.

The Special Commissioner said that a right of occupation can be an interest in possession. However, a proper construction of the will was crucial to the decision whether an interest in possession had been created. The Commissioner had to interpret Mr Walden's will. Where Clause 3 referred to 'for such period or periods as they shall in their absolute discretion think fit' the Commissioner considered that those words were clear and unambiguous. They gave Mrs Walden no right to occupy Perrymead Street, but gave the trustees an absolute discretion to allow Mrs Walden to occupy it. There was no duty to allow her to occupy the property. Therefore, Mrs Walden did not have an interest in possession. The personal representatives' appeal was allowed.

Points to note

16.36 It should be remembered that gifts to discretionary trusts are immediately chargeable transfers (and also that special treatment can apply to discretionary trusts created by will (*IHTA 1984, s 144*; see **Chapter 15**)).

In the *Judge* case, Mr Walden's will created a discretionary trust with an asset worth £625,000 at the time of his death, ie well in excess of the nil rate band at the time. However, no IHT was paid because the personal representatives assumed (incorrectly as it turned out) that Mrs Walden had an interest in possession in the house. The Special Commissioner's decision effectively meant that no IHT was payable on the property from Mrs Walden's estate, but was payable on Mr Walden's earlier death.

16.37 If an interest in the property is left outright to the surviving spouse (or civil partner) and the other interest is owned by a discretionary trust, there is an argument that the survivor should not be treated as having an interest in possession in it, on the basis that (s)he is entitled to occupy by reason of the interest they own, ie as a tenant in common has a right to occupy the entire house (*Bull v Bull* [1955] 1 QB 234).

However, HMRC may challenge this analysis, particularly if the discretionary trust gives the survivor exclusive rights of occupation.

16.38 The *Trusts of Land and Appointment of Trustees Act 1996* provides for a trust of land, giving a statutory right of occupation of the family home to the surviving spouse or civil partner. The provisions confer on any 'beneficiary who is beneficially entitled to an interest in possession in land subject to a trust of land' a right of occupation if certain conditions are satisfied (*TLATA 1996, s 12*).

That right is not absolute – note the term 'interest in possession' does not necessarily confer the same meaning as for IHT purposes (although HMRC may contend that it does), and is subject to restriction (*TLATA 1996, s 13*). However, the trustees cannot exercise their powers to exclude or restrict occupation by a person who is in occupation of land from continuing to do so, unless consent is given or the approval of the court is obtained (*TLATA 1996, s 13(7)*).

Note that *TLATA 1996* does not extend to Scotland (*TLATA 1996, s 27(3)*).

16.39 In the case of a surviving tenant in common, some doubt has been expressed whether (s)he obtains an interest in possession in the whole property on the other's death. This is because *TLATA 1996, s 12* only gives rights of occupation to trust beneficiaries if the property (as opposed to a share in it) is held in trust (*TLATA 1996, s 22(1)*). Does *TLATA 1996, s 13(7)* effectively give the survivor a right to possess the whole property? Or is any right to occupy non-exclusive, so that the trustees may require a proportionate rent to be paid (indicating that there is not an interest in possession in the whole)?

If a half-share in the property was settled under the deceased's will, it is arguably possible to interpret *TLATA 1996, s 22(1)* as meaning that the trust beneficiaries have no right under *TLATA 1996, s 12*, so that *TLATA 1996, s 13* does not need to be considered. This would therefore seem to give the surviving spouse or partner the immediate right to possession. However, the position is not free from doubt, and ideally requires litigation to clarify the matter, or at least some detailed guidance on HMRC's view.

The application of *TLATA 1996* (*ss 12, 22*) also raises questions over the availability of only or main residence relief for the trustees under *TCGA 1992, s 225* on a disposal of their interest in the family home, on the basis that the surviving spouse has no right of occupation as a beneficiary, and in addition occupied the property by reason of their rights as joint beneficial owner, rather than under the terms of the settlement as required for CGT relief purposes.

However, in Appendix 5 of *Drafting Trusts and Will Trusts: A Modern Approach* (13th Edition, Sweet & Maxwell) by James Kessler QC and Charlotte Ford, the authors express the view that if the testator's interest in the property is appropriated to a nil rate band discretionary trust two years or more after the testator's death (ie to avoid the surviving spouse acquiring an 'immediate post-death interest', which would form part of the individual's estate) and the surviving spouse (who is not a disabled person for IHT purposes on the testator's death) is subsequently given an interest in possession in the trust's share, only or main residence relief should be available to the trustees when the property is eventually sold. The beneficiary would have an interest in possession in the trust's share of land (as required by *TLATA 1996, s 12*), and the relief in *TCGA 1992, s 225* does not require that the beneficiary is *only* entitled to occupy it by virtue of an entitlement under the settlement. The latter point is accepted in HMRC's guidance on co-owned property (at CG65407).

The arrangement described above is a simpler and potentially more convenient alternative way of dealing with a nil rate band trust than the 'debt' or 'charge' arrangements described at **16.48** below.

16.40 Consideration needs to be given to Statement of Practice 10/79 (see **16.34** above), which indicates that if the trustees have powers to allow the creation of an exclusive occupation and that power is exercised with the intention of providing a particular beneficiary with a permanent home, HMRC will normally regard the exercise of that power as creating an interest in possession.

However, notwithstanding SP 10/79 and depending on the circumstances, it would seem (following the *Judge* case) that trustees of a discretionary trust could claim private residence relief for CGT purposes, without the beneficiary who occupies the property being considered to have an interest in possession for IHT purposes (see also **16.41** below).

HMRC provided guidance ('Schedule 20 – SP 10/79 and Transitional Serial Interests') on interests in possession and SP 10/79 in November 2007, in response to queries raised by STEP and CIOT. HMRC's response included the following salient points:

- The circumstances in which HMRC would *not* regard the trustees as having exercised their power to give a beneficiary an exclusive right of occupation (ie so as not to create an interest in possession) are 'rare', but might include instances where there was no evidence of (or significant doubt as to) the intentions of the trustees.
- An SP 10/79 interest in possession generally arises if there is evidence that the trustees have knowingly exercised their powers so as to give a beneficiary exclusive occupation of the property.
- If the trustees have intended to grant a beneficiary the right to occupy a specific, named property owned by the trust, the beneficiary's interest in possession would end when the property was sold.

16.41 A CGT advantage of leaving a share in the family home to trustees (as opposed to a direct legacy to a family member who does not live there) is the potential availability of private residence relief on a subsequent disposal of the property. The relief applies if, during the trustees' period of ownership, a beneficiary is 'a person entitled under the terms of the settlement' to occupy the property as their only or main residence, and does so occupy it (*TCGA 1992, s 225*).

The relief is available to trustees of both interest in possession and discretionary trusts (*Sansom v Peay* [1976] STC 494; see also CG65407).

Appointing an interest in possession

16.42 Prior to *FA 2006*, a potential pitfall in HMRC successfully contending that the surviving spouse or civil partner had an interest in possession within Statement of Practice 10/79 in respect of the property interest held by the trustees of the discretionary trust was that the survivor fell to be treated as beneficially entitled to that property interest, which would therefore form part of their estate for IHT purposes.

However, following *FA 2006*, it does not normally matter if HMRC successfully argue that SP 10/79 applies, or if the trustees appoint an actual interest in possession to the surviving spouse or civil partner, provided that the interest does not arise within two years of death (or the survivor is not a disabled person, as defined for IHT purposes).

The relevance of this two-year period is that the provisions dealing with discretionary will trusts (*IHTA 1984, s 144*; see **Chapter 15**) broadly allow appointments of trust assets within two years following death to be effectively read back into the will. An interest in possession to the surviving spouse or civil partner on death would therefore fall to be treated as an 'immediate post-death interest' (see **Chapter 9**), subject to the spouse or civil partner exemption, resulting in the potential wastage of the deceased's nil rate band (although the transferable nil rate band facility could possibly assist in that case).

To avoid this treatment, the safest course of action for the trustees to consider would therefore be to wait until at least two years have expired following the first death if practical, before appointing an interest in possession in the family home to the survivor.

Joint ownership (tenants in common)

16.43 If the family home is jointly owned as tenants in common, the deceased spouse or civil partner may, for example, leave their share to adult children, to make use of the available nil rate band, including (from 6 April 2017) the residence nil rate band. The surviving spouse or civil partner may continue to occupy by reason of their own beneficial share in the home.

Interest in possession for survivor

16.44 An interest in possession created by will in favour of the surviving spouse or civil partner is generally subject to the spouse IHT exemption (*IHTA 1984, s 18*).

If, for example, the nil rate band has already been used elsewhere (and/or the residence nil rate band is not in point, such as where there are no lineal descendants), it may be that the deceased's estate is left on a 'flexible life interest trust' in which the trustees are given wide, overriding powers of appointment. Those powers may enable the trustees to appoint property in whole or part to the survivor absolutely, and/or to terminate the life interest in whole or part and appoint the property to other beneficiaries under the will (eg siblings). As to the IHT treatment of interest in possession trusts generally, see **Chapter 9**.

However, following *FA 2006* the lifetime termination of an interest in possession, after which the former interest holder continues to occupy 'the no-longer possessed property', can constitute a gift for GWR purposes (see **7.19**).

Even without a formal interest in possession trust, as indicated the terms of the will can create an effective interest in possession for the deceased. Such an interest in possession could be caused inadvertently.

16.45 In *IRC v Lloyds Private Banking Ltd* [1998] STC 559, an interest in possession was held to exist where a wife left her share in the matrimonial home, by her will, upon the following terms:

> '(1) While my husband remains alive and desires to reside in the property and keeps the same in good repair and insured comprehensively to its full value with Insurers approved by my Trustees and pays and indemnifies my Trustees against all rates, taxes and other outgoings in respect of the property my Trustee shall not make any objection to such residence and shall not disturb or restrict it in any way and shall not take any steps to enforce the trust for sale on which the property is held or to realise my share therein or to obtain any rent or profit from the property.
>
> (2) On the death of my said Husband … I devise and bequeath the said property … to my Daughter … absolutely.'

The High Court considered that the above clause in the wife's will was a dispositive provision, which conferred on the husband a determinable life interest in the half-share in the property. This created a settlement (within the meaning of *IHTA 1984, s 43(2)*) by which an interest in possession had been conferred on the husband. Accordingly, on his death IHT was charged on the basis that his estate included an interest in the entire property. This decision has been applied in other cases (*Woodhall v IRC* [2000] STC (SCD) 558, and *Faulkner (Adams' Trustee) v IRC* [2001] SSCD 112 (SpC 278)).

However, contrast those cases with the decision in the *Judge* case (see **16.34** above), in which the Special Commissioner held that the surviving spouse did not have an interest in possession of a residence because the deceased spouse's trustees had absolute discretion as to whether to permit her to occupy the property for any period, notwithstanding that a sale of the property required the consent of the surviving spouse.

'Nil rate band' discretionary trusts

16.46 An alternative to such a legacy of the first spouse or civil partner to die (eg the husband) is to gift the nil rate band in his will for chargeable beneficiaries through the use of a 'nil rate band discretionary trust'. The residue of his estate (ie in particular the home) is left to the widow. Such trusts are discussed in greater detail in **Chapter 15**.

The main asset in many estates is the family home. There may be insufficient other assets of value in the estate to constitute the nil rate band in some cases. This may result in an interest in the family home being used instead. Alternatively, arrangements commonly known as 'debt and charge' schemes may be considered (see **16.48** below). A detailed comparison of the features, potential merits and disadvantages of each route are beyond the scope of this book.

As indicated elsewhere in this chapter, the planned use of nil rate band discretionary trusts should be reviewed where appropriate, particularly following the introduction of the residence nil rate band from 6 April 2017, in view of the potential loss of the extra nil rate band if the interest in the family home is left to such a trust.

16.47 It must be remembered that nil rate band discretionary trusts of an interest in the family home involve both tax law and property law considerations. The latter is outside the scope of this book.

However, property law and tax law principles may diverge. For example, although HMRC will presently accept the purported severance of a joint tenancy in a deed of variation for IHT purposes under *IHTA 1984, s 142* (see **16.27**), it has no effect for general property law purposes. The joint tenant will normally obtain absolute ownership of the whole property on the death of the other owner.

The Land Registry's Practice Guide 70 'Nil rate band discretionary trusts' (tinyurl.com/LRPG70), which is aimed at solicitors, licensed conveyancers and other advisers, outlines some of the property law and land registration issues surrounding the creation of such trusts. However, general guidance of this nature cannot be a substitute for specific legal advice, as appropriate.

'Debt' or 'charge' schemes

16.48 As indicated at **16.29** above, following the introduction of the facility to transfer unused nil rate bands between spouses and civil partners from 9 October 2007, and the subsequent introduction of the facility to transfer unused residence nil rate band from 6 April 2017, in most cases it will not be necessary (or desirable) for married couples or civil partners to utilise the nil rate band on the first death (eg by leaving an interest in the family home to non-exempt beneficiaries, such as the trustees of a nil rate band discretionary trust).

Previously, if the home was the main asset in the estate, a relatively well-known IHT planning arrangement was for a nil rate band gift to be satisfied either by a *debt* or *charge* on the property in favour of the trustees of the nil rate band discretionary trust (see **Chapter 15**).

Such arrangements may still be a feature of many wills drafted before 9 October 2007 in particular, in which the will of the deceased spouse or civil partner may give the trustees the power to make loans or to charge over the house, and on favourable terms (say) for the widow (eg an interest-free loan, capital payments deferred). However, the debt should preferably be repayable on demand to the trustees, to reduce the possibility of an argument by HMRC that the survivor has an interest in possession.

The charge should generally be a deduction from the widow's estate on her death, with her ownership allowing for continued occupation of the house during lifetime. However, in the case of a debt arrangement, a deduction may be restricted or denied in the above scenario if the widow made lifetime gifts to the husband. A loan is not deductible from an estate to the extent that the loan was property derived from the deceased, ie in this case the widow (*FA 1986, s 103(1)(a)*).

16.49 For example, suppose that a widower, who had previously owned the family home in London, made a lifetime gift of a half share to his wife. The wife subsequently died, and her will created a nil rate band discretionary trust. The husband receives his wife's interest in the family home, and incurs a debt to the trust. HMRC are likely to contend that the widower's debt is disallowable for IHT purposes under *FA 1986, s 103*.

These were broadly the facts in *Phizackerley (Personal representative of Phizackerley, deceased) v Revenue and Customs Commissioners* [2007] SpC 591, where HMRC's disallowance of an 'IOU' as a liability of the surviving spouse's estate was upheld by the Special Commissioner (see **15.4**).

Such a challenge could be avoided by using charge arrangements instead, where the charge is made by the personal representatives. The home should be part of the residuary estate. This would allow the personal representatives to appropriate the home to the widow, subject to a charge. The identity of the personal representatives and the trustees of the discretionary will trust should not be identical (particularly as to the first named), and the surviving spouse or civil partner should preferably not be a personal representative.

16.50 The charge method may also avoid stamp duty land tax (SDLT) in the example at **16.49**. HMRC originally published guidance on stamp duty land tax and nil rate band discretionary trusts on their website. This information is now contained in their Stamp Duty Land Tax Manual (at SDLTM04045), which contrasts debt and charge arrangements and their SDLT consequences (see below).

> *HMRC guidance: Charge scheme – SDLT liability*
>
> 'Land is transferred to the surviving spouse or civil partner and the spouse or civil partner charges the property with payment of the amount of the pecuniary legacy. The nil rate band discretionary trustees accept this charge in satisfaction of the pecuniary legacy.
>
> The charge is money's worth and so is chargeable consideration for SDLT purposes.'
>
> *HMRC guidance: Charge scheme – no SDLT liability*
>
> 'The personal representatives charge land with the payment of the pecuniary legacy. The personal representatives and nil-rate band discretionary trustees also agree that the trustees have no right to enforce payment of the amount of the legacy personally against the owner of the land for the time being.

The nil-rate band discretionary trustees accept this charge in satisfaction of the legacy. The property is transferred to the surviving spouse or civil partner subject to the charge.

There is no chargeable consideration for SDLT purpose provided that there is no change in the rights or liabilities of any person in relation to the debt secured by the charge.'

16.51 By contrast, HMRC's view is that SDLT is payable if the surviving spouse or civil partner (or the personal representatives) creates the debt – as it is then arguable that the land is transferred for consideration, ie the 'promise' to pay (see below).

HMRC guidance: Debt scheme – SDLT liability

'The nil-rate band discretionary trustees accept the surviving spouse's or civil partner's promise to pay in satisfaction of the pecuniary legacy and in consideration of that promise land is transferred to the surviving spouse or civil partner.

The promise to pay is chargeable consideration for SDLT purposes.'

'The nil-rate band discretionary trustees accept the personal representatives' promise to pay in satisfaction of the pecuniary legacy and land is transferred to the surviving spouse or civil partner in consideration of the spouse accepting liability for the promise.

The acceptance of liability for the promise is chargeable consideration for SDLT purposes. The amount of chargeable consideration is the amount promised, not exceeding the market value of the land transferred.'

16.52 SDLT is a tax on 'land transactions', which is defined as 'any acquisition of a chargeable interest' (*FA 2003, s 43(1)*). A detailed discussion of SDLT is outside the scope of this book. However, in Appendix 3.3 of *Drafting Trusts and Will Trusts: a Modern Approach* (13th Edition, Sweet & Maxwell by James Kessler QC and Charlotte Ford), the authors advance the view that an SDLT liability should not normally arise on debt schemes. This is broadly on the footing that the execution of the survivor's undertaking to pay the debt does not involve the acquisition of a 'chargeable interest'.

Further, there is considered to be no SDLT on the assent of the land interest to the survivor, as an SDLT charge arises on 'chargeable consideration' (as defined in *FA 2003, Sch 4, para 1*), and the survivor's undertaking is not 'consideration' for acquiring the land. Whilst an SDLT charge arises in the above examples if the transfer is in fact in consideration of the spouse's promise to pay the nil rate band sum, the undertaking and assent do not need to be structured in this way.

Nevertheless, the charge route may be considered preferable to the debt route, on the basis that comfort is given in HMRC's confirmation that no SDLT charge arises if the documentation is in accordance with the wording of their statement above.

Some debt schemes are drafted on the basis that the spouse undertakes to pay the trustees an 'indexed-linked nil-rate sum', eg a nil rate sum increased by the retail price index. Charge schemes may be drafted on the basis that executors charge property with payment of the index-linked nil rate sum. The question arises whether the trustees are chargeable to tax on the indexation element when that amount is paid. It is understood that HMRC consider that such a tax charge arises. The authors of the above book (in Appendix 4) advance the view that the spouse undertaking should not (based on the drafts in the authors' book) give rise to tax on the payment of the indexed-linked sum, and that the benefit of a debt or charge is not a deeply discounted security for income tax purposes, or a debt on a security for CGT purposes.

However, a drafter unfamiliar with the tax rules could inadvertently create a debt on which interest accrues (liable to income tax if the interest is paid), or a deeply discounted security (liable to income tax on disposal), or a debt on a security (liable to CGT on disposal). Care and an understanding of the tax issues involved are therefore important.

As pointed out at **16.2**, SDLT was replaced in Scotland by land and buildings transaction tax (LBTT) from 1 April 2015 and in Wales by land transaction tax (LTT) from 1 April 2018. For detailed commentary on SDLT, LBTT and LTT, readers are referred to the latest edition of *Stamp Taxes* (Bloomsbury Professional).

16.53 For pre-owned assets income tax purposes, HMRC accept that no charge arises in respect of nil rate band discretionary trusts of a debt. HMRC's guidance on pre-owned assets in the context of debts and charge schemes includes the following example (IHTM44107):

> 'Jack and Jill own their home in equal shares as tenants in common. Under his Will, Jack leaves property not exceeding the nil-rate band for Inheritance Tax to a discretionary trust, of which Jill is one of the potential beneficiaries. The remainder of his estate passes to Jill absolutely. Following Jack's death, his executors transferred his half share of the property to Jill and, in return, she executed a loan agreement equivalent to the value of the half-share. No Inheritance Tax is payable on Jack's death and when Jill dies, her estate is reduced by the debt and she also has her nil rate band to set against the couple's assets.
>
> The POA charge does not apply here. As Jill did not own her husband's share at the relevant time and did not dispose of it, the disposal conditions (IHTM44004) in FA04/Sch15/Para3(2) are not met. If she did not provide Jack with any of the consideration given by him for the purchase of his half share the contribution condition (IHTM44005) in FA04/Sch15/Para3(3) will not apply either.

Even if she had provided him with some or all of the consideration the condition will still not apply as it would have been an excluded transaction (IHTM44032) under FA04/Sch15/Para10(2)(a). Had this been the case, however, the debt would not be allowable as a deduction on Jill's death by virtue of FA86/S103.'

Warning: 'sham' trusts

16.54

> **Focus**
>
> It is important that the trustees of nil rate band discretionary trusts (and trustees in general) act and properly perform their duties as such. Care should be taken to protect against accusations of a 'sham'.

It is not sufficient just to have a well-drafted trust deed. The trustees must be active rather than passive, and be seen to consider and (if appropriate) exercise their discretions and not just leave the survivor in indefinite, favourable occupation of the property. The trustees should meet regularly (eg twice a year) and carefully minute their decisions (eg whether to take a charge as opposed to a debt, as to the charging of interest, whether repayment of the loan should be requested, etc).

If the trustees merely 'sit on their hands' the whole arrangement can be challenged by HMRC, or it may be argued that the widow has an interest in possession in the trust property.

RESIDENCE NIL RATE BAND

Introduction

16.55 As indicated at **1.4**, chargeable transfers within the seven-year period ending with the date of the latest chargeable transfer are cumulated for the purposes of determining the IHT rate. Where chargeable lifetime transfers and the individual's death estate do not exceed the IHT threshold or 'nil rate band', there is no IHT liability.

In addition, the transferable nil rate band provisions (see **Chapter 3**) broadly allow claims for unused nil rate band of a deceased spouse or civil partner to be transferred to a surviving spouse or civil partner (who dies on or after 9 October 2007), thus potentially increasing the survivor's nil rate band by up to 100%, or one additional nil rate band.

16.56

> **Focus**
>
> Extra (or 'residence') nil rate band is also available in relation to deaths on or after 6 April 2017, where a qualifying residential interest is passed on death to a lineal descendant of the deceased (*IHTA 1984, ss 8D–8M*).
>
> It should be emphasised that the residence nil rate band applies for the purpose of calculating the IHT charge on a person's death. It does not apply to chargeable lifetime transfers of a residential interest (eg into trust), even if the beneficiary is a lineal descendant of the transferor, or if they have an interest in possession of the trust's assets.
>
> The residence nil rate band is in addition to the IHT threshold (or standard nil rate band), and any transferred nil rate band upon the earlier death of the deceased's spouse or civil partner.
>
> In calculating IHT on the deceased's estate, the residence nil rate band is not applied directly to the value of the qualifying residential interest but to the value of the person's estate on death, before applying the nil rate band (if available). The benefit of the residence nil rate band is therefore shared across the chargeable estate on death. The nil rate band (and transferable nil rate band, if appropriate) is applied to any remaining chargeable death estate after the residence nil rate band has been applied (IHTM46070).
>
> HMRC's Inheritance Tax Manual includes a section with technical guidance on the residence nil rate band at IHTM46000–IHTM46100.

Unused residence nil rate band is generally transferable to a spouse or civil partner upon a claim being made, subject to an overriding maximum amount (see **16.57**).

The residence nil rate band is subject to tapered withdrawal for estates valued at more than £2 million on death.

Residence nil rate band must be claimed. The claim is made on form IHT435, which can be downloaded from the gov.uk website (tinyurl.com/HMRC-IHT435). As to claims for the transfer of any unused residence nil rate band, see **16.68**.

16.57 The maximum amount of the residence nil rate band (or the 'residential enhancement', as the legislation describes it) for 2017/18 to 2020/21 is as follows (*IHTA 1984, s 8D(5)(a)*):

Table 16.1—The 'residence nil rate band'

Tax year	**Residential enhancement**
	£
2017/18	100,000
2018/19	125,000
2019/20	150,000
2020/21	175,000

The maximum amount of the residence nil rate band (and the taper threshold – see **16.59** below) is subject to indexation increases by reference to the CPI, unless Parliament determines otherwise, in a similar way to the IHT threshold. The relevant amounts for each year are to be specified in regulations. However, there is to be no such increase until 2021/22 at the earliest.

The value of an individual's estate generally takes into account liabilities (*IHTA 1984, s 5(5)*). A mortgage secured on the property will normally reduce the value of the property (see **16.61**), and therefore potentially the amount of the available residence nil rate band.

16.58 The residence nil rate band applies for the purposes of calculating the amount of IHT on a person's death (under *s 4*) on or after 6 April 2017. In the case of settled property, the residence nil rate band is only available in certain circumstances (see **16.65**).

The legislation sets out certain terms and abbreviations (in *IHTA 1984, s 8D(5)*) used for the purposes of determining the residence nil rate band available:

- TT is the 'taper threshold' (see **16.59**) at the person's death;
- E is the value of the person's estate immediately before the person's death; and
- VT is the value (if any) transferred by a *chargeable* transfer (under *IHTA 1984, s 4*) on the person's death.

The deceased's residence nil rate band (if greater than nil) broadly results in IHT being charged at a rate of 0% on the portion of VT falling within it; any remainder of VT is charged at the IHT rates on death (*s 8D(2), (3)*).

Tapered withdrawal

16.59

> **Focus**
>
> The residence nil rate band is subject to a taper threshold, which reduces the residence nil rate band available according to the value of the deceased's estate (ie assets less liabilities, before reliefs or exemptions, if applicable).

This 'taper threshold' is set at £2 million (for 2017/18 and subsequent tax years). It is subject to indexation increases (to be specified in regulations) by reference to the CPI unless Parliament determines otherwise, but is fixed at £2 million until 2021/22 at the earliest.

The person's residence nil rate band allowance is adjusted using a formula set out in the legislation (*IHTA 1984, s 8D(5)(g)*), which withdraws the 'default allowance' (see below) by £1 for every £2 that the value of the estate exceeds the taper threshold:

$$\text{Default allowance} - \left(\frac{E - TT}{2}\right)$$

where:

- 'default allowance' is the total of the residence nil rate band at the person's death, plus any 'brought forward allowance' (ie unused residence nil rate band transferred on an earlier death of a spouse or civil partner) (see **16.66** below);
- E (see **16.58**) is the value of the person's estate immediately before death (ie before any reliefs and exemptions); and
- TT is the taper threshold at the person's death.

The result of the formula is described in the legislation as the 'adjusted allowance'.

> **Example 16.5—Tapered residence nil rate band**
>
> Arthur and Belinda jointly own their matrimonial home equally as tenants in common.
>
> Arthur died on 1 June 2018. His estate is worth £2.1 million. In his will, Arthur left his interest in the home, which is valued at £450,000, to his son Colin. The rest of his estate was left to Belinda.

Arthur's residence nil rate band is £125,000 (for 2018/19). His 'adjusted allowance' is:

$$£125{,}000 - \left(\frac{£2{,}100{,}000 - £2{,}000{,}000}{2}\right) = \underline{£75{,}000}$$

In calculating the IHT on Arthur's estate, a residence nil rate band of £75,000 may be deducted from the value of his estate in respect of the property interest of £450,000, in addition to the standard nil rate band of £325,000 (for 2018/19), if available.

16.60 Thus for 2020/21, the residence nil rate band will be reduced to nil if the person's estate value is £2,350,000 or higher. This assumes that no residence nil rate band (£175,000 for 2020/21) has been brought forward (ie transferred) following the earlier death of a spouse or civil partner.

Where it appears that the taper threshold will be exceeded on death, consideration might be given to the making of lifetime gifts (eg a cash gift to a nil rate band discretionary trust for family members) to reduce the value of the estate accordingly, in appropriate circumstances.

Eligibility and amount

16.61 The residence nil rate band applies if a person's estate includes a 'qualifying residential interest' (see **16.63** below), and all or part of that interest is left to one or more lineal descendants (ie it is 'closely inherited' – see **16.65** below). The value attributable to the qualifying residential interest is after the deduction of liabilities (*IHTA 1984, s 162(2)*, eg a mortgage or loan secured on the property) and any agricultural property relief and business property relief.

For estates not exceeding the taper threshold, if the value of the residence that passes to direct descendants is less than the 'default allowance' (ie the person's residence nil rate band, plus any amount transferred on the earlier death of a spouse or civil partner), the residence nil rate band is limited to the value of the residence; any unused residence nil rate band is available for transfer to a spouse (or civil partner) (*IHTA 1984, s 8E(2)*).

Example 16.6—Interest in home passing to a direct descendant

John and Karen jointly own their matrimonial home as tenants in common.

John died on 31 August 2020. His interest in the property was worth £125,000, and the rest of his estate was worth £500,000. In his will, John leaves the property interest to his adult daughter, Lisa.

The percentage of John's property interest that is 'closely inherited' (see **16.65**) is 100%.

The maximum residence nil rate band for 2020/21 is £175,000. However, John's residence nil rate band is restricted to his interest in the residence (ie £125,000).

The unused element is available to transfer to Karen, expressed as the unused proportion of the residence nil rate band of 28.5714% (ie £50,000/£175,000) × 100).

If the value of the residence passing to direct descendants is greater than or equal to the person's default allowance, the residence nil rate band available is the default allowance, so none of the residence nil rate band is transferable to the spouse (*IHTA 1984, s 8E(3)*).

For estates above the taper threshold, if the value of the residence passing to direct descendants is less than the 'adjusted allowance' after taper relief has been applied (see **16.59** above), the residence nil rate band is limited to the value of that residence; any unused residence nil rate band is available for transfer to the spouse (*IHTA 1984, s 8E(4)*). If the value of the residence passing to direct descendants is greater than or equal to the person's adjusted allowance, the residence nil rate band available is the adjusted allowance, so none of the residence nil rate band is transferable to the spouse (*IHTA 1984, s 8E(5)*).

However, the above provisions in *IHTA 1984, s 8E(2)–(5)* are subject to the downsizing rules in *s 8FC* (see **16.73**) and the conditional exemption rules in *IHTA 1984, s 8M(2B)–(2E)* (see **16.69**). In addition, it is provided that if the value of the residence exceeds the value of the estate (ie after deducting liabilities), the residence nil rate band is instead restricted to the value of the chargeable estate, and any unused excess is available for transfer to a spouse (*IHTA 1984, s 8E(6), (7)*).

16.62 If the deceased's estate does not include a 'qualifying residential interest' (see **16.63** below), or if it does include such an interest but none of it is closely inherited, the person's residence nil rate band is nil. However, the residence nil rate band that has not been used is available for transfer to a spouse (*IHTA 1984, s 8F*).

Thus a surviving spouse who is the sole owner of the matrimonial home may still be able to claim the deceased spouse's unused residence nil rate band (see **16.66**).

Qualifying residences, etc

16.63 The legislation sets out the meaning of 'qualifying residential interest' and also 'qualifying former residential interest' and 'residential property interest', in the context of the residence nil rate band, including for downsizing purposes and cases involving conditional exemption (**IHTA 1984, s 8H,** as amended by **FA 2016**).

A residential property interest is broadly an interest in a dwelling house that was the deceased's residence when it was part of their estate. There is no requirement that the property was occupied as a residence throughout the entire period of ownership. For example, an individual may still own a property on death that he lived in previously, but which was rented out at the date of death (IHTM46011). Where the person's death estate includes only one residence, that residence will be the qualifying residential interest. If the person's estate includes more than one residence, the deceased's personal representatives may nominate one of them, and that residence will be treated as the qualifying residential interest.

A dwelling house for these purposes includes land that is occupied and used as its garden or grounds, but excludes any trees or underwood in relation to which a woodlands election is made (under *IHTA 1984, s 125*) in relation to the person's death (*IHTA 1984, s 8H(5)*).

If a person lives in 'job-related' accommodation (ie within *TCGA 1992, s 222(8A)–(8D)*) and owns a house that they intend occupying as a residence in due course, that house is treated as if the person occupied it as such (*IHTA 1984, s 8H(6)*).

The deceased may have had more than one interest in a former residence (eg outright ownership in 50% of the residence, and a life interest in the other 50%). If the person made a lifetime disposal of one or more interests in a nominated former residence on the same day (on or after 8 July 2015), that interest (or those interests) will be a qualifying former residential interest(s) for the purposes of any downsizing addition (*IHTA 1984, s 8H(4B)*). If the person disposed of an interest (or interests) in a nominated former residence on different days, the personal representatives can nominate only one of those days, and the interest (or interests) disposed of on that day will be qualifying one(s) for the purposes of any downsizing addition (*IHTA 1984, s 8H(4C)*).

If an interest in a residence has been gifted but the donor continues to benefit from it within the gifts with reservation provisions (*FA 1986, s 102*), the gift does not count as a disposal for the purposes of determining the qualifying residential interest and downsizing addition. However, if the reservation subsequently ceases (eg upon moving out of the property) such that there is a deemed PET (under *FA 1986, s 102(4)*), the donor is treated as making a disposal of the residential property interest (*IHTA 1984, s 8H(4D)*).

The above provisions in respect of former residential property interests were introduced (in *FA 2016*) with the downsizing legislation for residence nil rate band purposes (see **16.70–16.77**).

16.64 Further legislation (*IHTA 1984, s 8HA*, also introduced in *FA 2016*) deals with former residences held in interest in possession trusts, for the purposes of determining whether a person's residence held in such a trust may be considered as a qualifying former residential interest for downsizing purposes (in *IHTA 1984, s 8H(4A)–(4C)*: see above). It applies broadly where the person is beneficially entitled to an interest in possession in settled property (see below) which holds an interest in a residence.

If the trustees dispose of the residence (other than to the beneficiary) but the beneficiary has an interest in possession in the trust property, the disposal is treated as being made by the beneficiary (under *IHTA 1984, s 49(1)*) for downsizing purposes, if that interest in possession is one to which the beneficiary became beneficially entitled before 22 March 2006 (and *IHTA 1984, s 71A* does not apply to the settled property), or if the beneficiary became beneficially entitled to the interest in possession on or after that date and the interest is an immediate post-death interest, disabled person's interest, or transitional serial interest, and in either case the interest in possession has subsisted from the time he became beneficially entitled to it up to the time of disposal; or alternatively if the beneficiary became beneficially entitled to it from 22 March 2006 and the interest in possession falls within *IHTA 1984, s 5(1B)*.

Similarly, if the beneficiary disposes of the interest in possession, or the beneficiary's interest in possession ends during their lifetime, and the trust property includes a residence, the beneficiary is treated as having made a disposal of the residence, if that interest in possession falls within one of the above categories (*IHTA 1984, s 8HA(3)–(8)*).

For commentary on the downsizing provisions for residence nil rate band purposes, see **16.70-16.77**.

'Inherited' and 'closely inherited'

16.65 The legislation also defines when property in a deceased person's estate ('D') is 'inherited' by another person ('B') for the purposes of the residence nil rate band (*IHTA 1984, s 8J*).

B inherits a property if it is transferred to B under D's will, or under the intestacy rules or otherwise as a result of D's death. The term 'or otherwise' in the legislation seemingly has a deliberately wide meaning, to potentially include a disposition by survivorship, or under an instrument of variation (*IHTA 1984, s 142*) or a distribution of the property out of a discretionary will trust to a lineal descendant beneficiary within two years of death (within *IHTA 1984, s 144*).

However, the meaning of 'inherits' is such that it does not generally apply to property becoming settled on D's death, unless B becomes entitled to an immediate post-death interest or disabled persons interest, or unless the property becomes on D's death settled on trusts to which *IHTA 1984, s 71A* (ie trusts for bereaved minors) or *IHTA 1984, s 71D* applies (ie age 18 to 25 trusts) and is for B's benefit (*IHTA 1984, s 8J(4)*).

If the property was settled property in which D was beneficially entitled to an interest in possession immediately before death, B inherits the property if he becomes beneficially entitled to it on D's death (*IHTA 1984, s 8J(5)*).

Where the property is treated as forming part of D's estate immediately before death as a result of the gifts with reservation provisions (*FA 1986, s 102(3)*) applying to the gift, B inherits the property if he or she was the recipient of D's gift (*IHTA 1984, s 8J(6)*).

Something is 'closely inherited' for the above purposes if it is inherited by the person's child, grandchild or other lineal descendant. The definition extends to the spouse or civil partner of the deceased's lineal descendant. It also includes such a spouse (or civil partner) where the lineal descendant died (no later than the deceased), if they did not re-marry in the subsequent period ending with the deceased's death.

The meaning of closely inherited is extended to include stepchildren. Furthermore, an adopted person may be treated as a child of a natural parent or an adoptive parent. A person who was fostered at any time is treated (at that and all subsequent times) as the foster parent's child. Where a guardian or special guardian (both as defined) has been appointed for a person under 18 years old, that person is subsequently treated as a child of the guardian or special guardian. The lineal descendants of someone treated as a child of another person for these purposes are also to be treated as lineal descendants of that other person (*IHTA 1984, s 8K*).

Transferable allowance

16.66 As indicated at **16.59** above, a person's 'default allowance' is the total of the residence nil rate band (ie 'residential enhancement') in force at the person's death, plus any brought forward allowance.

'Brought forward allowance' (or transferable residence nil rate band) is available from what the legislation describes as a 'related person' (*IHTA 1984, s 8G(2)*). This is broadly the earlier spouse (or civil partner) to die. The parties must have been spouses immediately before the earlier death, so the nil rate band will not be transferable if the spouses were divorced (unless they subsequently remarried each other).

Focus

There are detailed rules for calculating the amount of residence nil rate band available for transfer (*IHTA 1984, s 8G(3)*).

In broad terms, the calculation involves identifying unused residence nil rate band available from a deceased spouse, expressed as a percentage (ie of the residence nil rate band at the spouse's death). The percentage is aggregated if appropriate (eg if the surviving spouse was married twice, and both of the deceased spouses had unused residence nil rate band), subject to an overriding maximum of 100%, or one additional residence nil rate band.

However, no amount can be transferred unless a claim is made; the brought forward allowance is treated as nil in the absence of the claim (*IHTA 1984, s 8G(3)*; see **16.68** below).

16.67 The much-publicised announcement by the government upon the introduction of the residence nil rate band was that this meant an effective IHT threshold of £1 million per married couple (or civil partnership). However, it should be noted that this threshold cannot be achieved until 2020/21.

As the residence nil rate band is worth more in 2020/21 than in (say) 2017/18 (see **16.57**), it might seem attractive not to use it on the first death. For example, spouses may wish to consider leaving their estates (including their interest in the family home) to the survivor, so that a higher residence nil rate band is potentially available on the second death (see below). However, this would enlarge the survivor's estate, and could result in tapering (see **16.59**) of the residence nil rate band on the survivor's death. In addition, the risk of future abolition of the residence nil rate band before the survivor's death should be taken into account.

The above £1 million threshold assumes that the spouses (or civil partners) each have a full standard nil rate band of £325,000 and residence nil rate band of £175,000 available.

Example 16.7—Effective IHT threshold of £1 million

David and his wife Eve jointly own their matrimonial home equally as tenants in common.

David died on 31 March 2018. He made no lifetime gifts in the previous seven years. David's death estate comprised an interest in the home worth £275,000, bank and building society account balances of £100,000 and investment properties worth £300,000. David leaves his entire estate to Eve in his will.

Eve dies on 30 November 2020. She had made no lifetime gifts in the previous seven years. Eve's death estate is worth £1.6 million. It comprises the home (now worth £700,000), bank and building society balances of £250,000 and investment properties worth £650,000. Eve's entire estate passes to her adult daughter, Frances.

Eve's personal representatives claim David's transferable nil rate band and residence nil rate band. The unused percentage of both nil rate bands was 100%. A claim is therefore made to add 100% of £325,000 (ie the nil rate band maximum for 2020/21) and 100% of £175,000 (ie the residence nil rate band maximum for 2020/21) to Eve's own nil rate bands. The combined nil rate bands therefore amount to (£650,000 + £350,000 =) £1 million.

The IHT payable in respect of Eve's estate is as follows:

		£	£
	Family home		700,000
	Other assets		900,000
			1,600,000
Less:	Residence nil rate band		(350,000)
			1,250,000
Less:	Nil rate band		(650,000)
			£600,000
	IHT £600,000 × 40%		£240,000

Focus

If the death of the earlier spouse occurred before 6 April 2017, the survivor's residence nil rate band is increased without regard to whether the spouse qualified for the residence nil rate band when (s)he died. The standard amount available to transfer for the above purposes (and also the residence nil rate band) is treated as being £100,000.

HMRC guidance on the residence nil rate band points out that as no residence nil rate band was available for deaths before 6 April 2017, the brought forward amount will be 100% of the residential enhancement in force at the later death of a spouse or civil partner (IHTM46040).

However, if the net value of the earlier spouse's death estate exceeds the £2 million taper threshold (see **16.59** above), their residence nil rate band available for transfer is subject to a reduction by tapering, ie it is reduced by £1 for every £2 that the estate value exceeds the £2 million threshold (*IHTA 1984, s 8G(4), (5)*).

Claims for the transferable residence nil rate band

16.68

> **Focus**
>
> The transferable residence nil rate band (and downsizing addition, if applicable) must be claimed (*IHTA 1984, s 8L*).
>
> The claim may be made by the deceased's personal representatives within a permitted period. Alternatively, a claim may be made by any other person liable to IHT on the person's death within such later period as HMRC may allow.
>
> A claim to transfer unused residence nil rate band can be made on form IHT436, which can be downloaded from the gov.uk website (tinyurl.com/HMRC-IHT436).

The 'permitted period' is two years from the end of the month in which the deceased died, or if later three months from the date when the personal representatives start to act. HMRC may allow a longer period at its discretion. A claim made within the normal time limits may be withdrawn no later than one month after whichever of those time limits applies *(IHTA 1984, s 8L(1)–(3))*.

The claim provisions also deal with situations involving a series of deaths where a claim was not made on the earlier death of a person ('P' in the legislation) to transfer any unused residence nil rate band, which would have affected the IHT liability on the later death of another person ('A'), but not P or anyone else. A claim may be made by A's personal representatives for unused residence nil rate band in respect of P's estate within an allowed period. Alternatively, a claim may be made by any other person liable to IHT on A's death within such later period as HMRC may allow.

The 'allowed period' is two years from the end of the month in which A died, or if later three months from the date when the personal representatives start to act. A longer period may be allowed by HMRC at its discretion.

A claim made within the normal time limits may be withdrawn no later than one month after the end of the relevant time limit *(IHTA 1984, s 8L(4)–(7))*.

Conditional exemption

16.69 In some cases, a residence may form part of an estate, where some or all assets of the estate are conditionally exempt from IHT. The conditionally exempt assets could include a qualifying residential interest. The residence nil rate band provisions are adapted accordingly to deal with such cases

(*IHTA 1984, s 8M*). The provisions in *IHTA 1984, s 8M* were amended (in *FA 2016*) to take into account circumstances involving downsizing (see **16.70**).

For deaths from 6 April 2017, to the extent that a qualifying residential interest is conditionally exempt, it is not eligible for the residence nil rate band. The conditional exemption provisions for residence nil rate band purposes apply when at least some of the qualifying residential interest is closely inherited by direct descendants. The legislation applies a formula approach (see *IHTA 1984, s 8M(2A)*) to calculate the proportion of the conditionally exempt qualifying residential interest which is not eligible for the residence nil rate band.

If the whole of the qualifying residential interest is conditionally exempt (ie none of it qualifies for the residence nil rate band) and there is no entitlement to the downsizing addition (ie none of the assets in the estate are closely inherited), all of the unused residence nil rate band is available to be carried forward. If some or all of the assets are closely inherited, and there is entitlement to a downsizing addition, the residence nil rate band is equal to the downsizing addition, and any unused amount is available to carry forward (*IHTA 1984, s 8M(2B), (2C)*).

If only part of the qualifying residential interest is conditionally exempt, the residence nil rate band (and any downsizing addition) is restricted to the proportion which is closely inherited, and also to the percentage which is not conditionally exempt (*IHTA 1984, s 8M(2D), (2E)*).

Where assets other than the qualifying residential interest are conditionally exempt, and the deceased is entitled to a downsizing addition (ie assets are closely inherited), and the downsizing addition is more than the value of non-conditionally exempt other assets (ie 'Y' in the legislation), the downsizing addition applies to any non-conditionally exempt assets first, and it is not reduced (under *IHTA 1984, s 8M(2G)*) if it is equal to or less than Y (*IHTA 1984, s 8M(2F)*).

The downsizing addition is subject to a reduction for assets other than the qualifying residential interest which are conditionally exempt (see *IHTA 1984, s 8M(2G), (2H)*).

Where conditional exemption ceases to apply and IHT becomes chargeable (under *IHTA 1984, s 32* or *IHTA 1984, s 32A*) on a chargeable event related to the residence (and, following *FA 2016*, any other assets in the estate – see below) (ie if the conditional exemption undertakings are not kept, or if the beneficial owner dies, or on disposal), the relevant provisions (in *IHTA 1984, s 8M(3)*) allow the residence nil rate band and any downsizing addition to be taken into account in the calculation of the IHT charge (under *IHTA 1984, s 33*), broadly by reversing any reduction in the downsizing addition, and by enabling the residence nil rate band to be recalculated.

The provisions in *IHTA 1984, s 8M(3)*, which are in point when conditional exemption ceases to apply following a chargeable event and a tax charge arises, were extended in *FA 2016* to ensure that the residence nil rate band and any downsizing addition applies when conditional exemption ceases in respect of the qualifying residential interest and any other assets in the estate.

The deceased's (D's) surviving spouse or civil partner (P) may have died before the chargeable event resulting from conditional exemption ceasing to apply (see below). On the other hand, if the IHT charge arises after P's death and any residence nil rate band was previously transferred from D to P, the residence nil rate band available in the calculation of the IHT charge is reduced by the amount transferred to P (*IHTA 1984, s 8M(5)*).

If the IHT charge arises before P's death, the amount of residence nil rate band available for transfer to P is recalculated using a 'recapture percentage' by means of a formula (in *IHTA 1984, s 8M(6)*), to take account of any residence nil rate band used in the IHT charge when the conditional exemption ceased to apply. The calculation is adjusted accordingly if there has been more than one chargeable event (*IHTA 1984, s 8M(6)-(7)*).

DOWNSIZING AND THE RESIDENCE NIL RATE BAND

Introduction

16.70 Following the introduction of the residence nil rate band provisions (in *F(No 2)A 2015*), the benefit of the residence nil rate band was extended (in *FA 2016*) in certain circumstances involving 'downsizing' on or after 8 July 2015, in relation to deaths from 6 April 2017.

The broad effect of these provisions is that the residence nil rate band, including the part that would otherwise be lost on the deceased's death (from 6 April 2017) as a result of downsizing (on or after 8 July 2015) generally remains available, provided the less valuable qualifying residential interest held on death and assets worth up to the 'lost' residence nil rate band are closely inherited by direct descendants etc (see **16.65**).

The same applies if the deceased sold their only qualifying residential interest and the sale proceeds have been left to direct descendants; or if the deceased otherwise ceased to own the residence and other assets worth up to an equivalent value have been left to direct descendants.

Less valuable residence in death estate

16.71 The downsizing provisions dealing with 'low value' interests in the home apply broadly where a person has downsized from a more valuable residence and there is a less valuable residence left in the estate on death. The value of the residence in the estate must be less than the deceased's default or adjusted allowance (see **16.59**) for a downsizing addition to potentially be available.

Where certain conditions (A to F in the legislation) are all met, there is entitlement to a 'downsizing addition' (ie an increased amount of residence nil rate band). Those conditions are broadly as outlined below (see *IHTA 1984, s 8FA*):

- Condition A has two alternative requirements. The first is that there is a residence in the estate on death which qualifies for the residence nil rate band (ie a 'qualifying residential interest') but the full amount is not due because the value of the residence (or the proportion which is 'closely inherited' by direct descendants; see **16.65**) is below the maximum residence nil rate band available for that person.

  The alternative requirement is that there is a residence in the estate on death but none of it is closely inherited and the value of the residence is less than the maximum residence nil rate band available for that person.

  Condition A only tests whether there is scope for any downsizing addition (ie it does not give effect to it), so *s 8E(6), (7)* and any entitlement to the downsizing addition are ignored for these purposes.
- Condition B is that the value transferred by the chargeable transfer on death (VT) is more than the value of the residence (ie the person's 'qualifying residential interest'). In other words, there must be other chargeable property on the death apart from the residence.
- Condition C is that there is a 'qualifying former residential interest' (see *IHTA 1984, ss 8H(4A)–(4F), 8HA*), ie broadly the person previously had a residence (on or after 8 July 2015) which could have qualified for the residence nil rate band.
- Condition D is that the 'value of the qualifying former residential interest' (as defined in *IHTA 1984, s 8FE(2)*) is more than the chargeable value of the residence in the estate on death.
- Condition E is that at least some of the 'remainder' (ie other assets in the estate immediately before death, other than the qualifying residential interest) is closely inherited.
- Condition F is that a claim is made for the downsizing addition, in accordance with the provisions in *IHTA 1984, s 8L(1)–(3)* (see **16.68**).

If the conditions are satisfied, the downsizing addition equals the lost residence nil rate band (ie the 'lost relievable amount'; see *IHTA 1984, s 8FE*) resulting from the downsizing move. As to the calculation of the lost relievable amount, see **16.75**. However, the additional amount is limited to the value of other assets (or proportion of that value) which is closely inherited, if that amount is lower. Furthermore, there is a potential reduction in certain cases involving conditional exemption (see *IHTA 1984, s 8FA(8), (9)*).

No residence in death estate

16.72 The downsizing provisions also deal with circumstances where a person has ceased to own a residence, so that there is no residence in the estate on death. A downsizing addition is available if certain conditions (G to K in the legislation) are all satisfied. Those conditions are broadly as outlined below (see *IHTA 1984, s 8FB*):

- Condition G is that there is no residential property interest in the person's estate on death.
- Condition H is that the value transferred by the chargeable transfer on death (VT) is greater than nil.
- Condition I is that the person previously had a qualifying former residential interest (see **16.63**).
- Condition J is that at least some of the assets in the estate are closely inherited (see **16.65**).
- Condition K is that a claim is made for the downsizing addition (see **16.68**).

If the conditions are satisfied, the downsizing addition equals the lost residence nil rate band (ie the 'lost relievable amount'; see *IHTA 1984, s 8FE*) as a result of disposing of the residence. As to the calculation of the lost relievable amount, see **16.75**. However, the additional amount is limited to the value of the other assets (or proportion of that value) which are closely inherited, if that amount is lower. There is also a potential reduction in certain cases involving conditional exemption (see *IHTA 1984, s 8FB(7)–(8)*).

The 'downsizing addition'

16.73 The effect of the downsizing addition depends on whether or not an interest in the home is left to direct descendants.

If there is an entitlement to a downsizing addition because a person has downsized and the residence in their estate (or a part of it) is left to direct descendants, the downsizing addition is added to the residence nil rate band that would otherwise be due (see *IHTA 1984, s 8E*), to arrive at the total residence nil rate band for the estate (*IHTA 1984, s 8FC*).

16.74 If no residence is left to direct descendants (ie where entitlement arises because either a person has downsized but none of the residence has been inherited by direct descendants, or has disposed of a residence so that it cannot be inherited by direct descendants), the effect of the downsizing addition is given by *IHTA 1984, s 8FD*. *IHTA 1984, s 8F* ('Residence nil rate amount: no interest in home goes to descendants etc') does not apply, such that the downsizing addition is available even if no part of the residence is inherited by direct descendants.

The residence nil rate band in these circumstances is equal to the downsizing addition *IHTA 1984, s 8FD(3)*.

If the downsizing addition equals the residence nil rate band plus any transferred residence nil rate band (ie the 'default allowance' where the value of the estate is below the taper threshold, or 'adjusted allowance' if it is above the taper threshold), no amount is available to carry forward, as the downsizing addition is fully used and nothing is available to be transferred to a spouse or civil partner's estate.

If the value of the estate is equal to or below the taper threshold and the downsizing addition is less than the residence nil rate band plus any transferred residence nil rate band (ie the default allowance), the difference between the downsizing addition and the default allowance is available to be carried forward to a spouse's or civil partner's estate.

If the value of the estate is above the taper threshold and the downsizing addition is less than the residence nil rate band plus any transferred residence nil rate band (the adjusted allowance), the difference between the downsizing addition and the adjusted allowance is available to be carried forward to a spouse or civil partner's estate (*IHTA 1984, s 8FD(4)–(6)*).

The lost relievable amount

16.75 The calculation of the 'lost relievable amount' as a result of downsizing where a less valuable residence is left in the death estate (under *IHTA 1984, s 8FA(8)*; see **16.71**), or as a result of disposal where there is no residence in the estate on death (under *IHTA 1984, s 8FB(7)*; see **16.72**), is dealt with by applying steps in a calculation process (in accordance with *IHTA 1984, s 8FE*).

The value of a person's qualifying former residential interest for these purposes is the open market value of the residence (or interest in it) upon completion of the disposal.

A person's 'former allowance' comprises the following (*IHTA 1984, s 8FE(3)*):

(a) the available residence nil rate band at the time of completion of the disposal of the qualifying former residential interest;

(b) any brought forward allowance (ie transferred residence nil rate band) that would have been due if the person had died at that time; and

(c) the difference (if any) between the brought forward allowance which would have been due at the time of completion of the disposal and the actual brought forward allowance at the time of the person's death.

For the purposes of (b) above, there are provisions for calculating the brought forward allowance that would have been due had the person died at the time of completion of the disposal of the former residence (*IHTA 1984, s 8FE(4)*). In addition, for the purpose of (c) above, the calculation of the brought forward allowance where the allowance on death is the adjusted allowance (ie where the taper threshold has been exceeded) involves several steps (see *IHTA 1984, s 8FE(5)*). The calculation broadly reduces the brought forward allowance by reference to the taper reduction. Furthermore, if completion of the disposal of the residence occurs before 6 April 2017, for the purposes of (a) and (b) above the residence nil rate band is treated as £100,000, and the brought forward allowance is treated as being nil (*IHTA 1984, s 8FE(6)*).

The calculation of the lost residence nil rate band as a result of downsizing to a less valuable residence (ie the 'lost relievable amount' in *IHTA 1984, s 8FA*) is a multi-step process (see *IHTA 1984, s 8FE(9)*):

- Step one broadly involves calculating the percentage of the residence nil rate band that was 'lost' at the time of the disposal.
- Step two calculates the percentage of the residence nil rate band on death that is used up by the residence on death (up to a maximum of 100%).
- Step three calculates the difference between those two percentages.
- Step four multiplies the person's allowance on death by the percentage calculated in step three to determine the lost relievable amount.

HMRC guidance (at IHTM46060) features several worked examples applying the multi-step step process.

Example 16.8—Downsizing to a less expensive residence

George (who is divorced) downsized in September 2017 from a home worth £250,000 to a ground floor flat. He died in September 2020, when the flat was worth £140,000. The residence nil rate band is calculated as follows:

Step 1 – Percentage of 'lost' residence nil rate band at the time of downsizing:

$$\frac{£250{,}000}{£100{,}000} \times 100\% = 250\%$$

However, the above percentage is restricted to 100%.

Step 2 – Percentage of residence nil rate band on death used up by the residence on death:

$$\frac{£140{,}000}{£175{,}000} \times 100\% = 80\%$$

Step 3 – Subtract the percentage in *Step 2* from the percentage in *Step 1*:

100% – 80% = 20%

Step 4 – Lost relievable amount:

£175,000 × 20% = £35,000

George has potentially lost 20% of the full residence nil rate band of £175,000 (in 2020/21), which would otherwise have been available.

However, the full residence nil rate band may still be available on George's death in September 2020 if he left the home (worth £140,000) plus £35,000 of other estate assets to his adult daughter Henrietta. This residence nil rate band is in addition to George's standard nil rate band of £325,000 (for 2020/21), if available.

16.76 The calculation of the lost relievable amount resulting from the lifetime disposal of the residence where there is no residential property interest in the estate on death (in *IHTA 1984, s 8FB*) also involves a multi-step process (see *IHTA 1984*, s *8FE(10)*):

- Step one broadly calculates the percentage of the residence nil rate band that was 'lost' at the time of the disposal.
- Step two involves multiplying the person's allowance on death by that percentage, to determine the lost relievable amount.

The downsizing addition cannot exceed the value of the assets which are closely inherited.

HMRC guidance (at IHTM46062) features several worked examples applying the multi-step step process.

Example 16.9—No residential interest at death

Harriet (a widow) sold her home for £300,000 in May 2020 due to illness and moved into nursing care. She died in March 2021. Her estate on death was valued at less than £2 million.

The residence nil rate band is calculated as follows:

Step 1 – Value of qualifying former residential interest as a percentage of former allowance

Harriet's 'former allowance' is the residence nil rate band at the time of disposal of the qualifying former residential interest (£175,000), plus the transferred residence nil rate band that Harriet would have been due upon death at the time of disposal (£175,000), plus any difference between the brought forward allowance on Harriet's death (if that would be greater) and the brought forward allowance at the time of disposal (£nil), ie £350,000 (see *s 8FE(3)–(5)*).

$$\frac{£300{,}000}{£350{,}000} \times 100\% = 85.7142\%$$

Step 2 – Lost relievable amount £350,000 × 85.7142% = £300,000

In her will, Harriet left £500,000 to her only child, Irene. Harriet's personal representatives may therefore claim a residence nil rate band of £300,000.

Other points

16.77 The downsizing provisions can apply in some circumstances where an individual had more than one interest in a former residence, or if the former residence was held in certain types of interest in possession trust, or if an individual gave away a residential property interest but continued to live in it and subsequently moved out (see **16.63–16.64**).

As indicated above, a claim must be made for the downsizing addition, where applicable. The deceased's personal representatives can nominate only one disposal of a residence (or an interest in it) on or after 8 July 2015 (and before the person's death) to qualify for the downsizing addition. However, where more than one residential property interest (eg an absolute interest and a qualifying interest in possession) has been disposed of in the same residence on or after 8 July 2015 but the disposals were on the same day, all of the disposals taken together can be treated as a single qualifying former residential interest (IHTM46053).

There could be any number of downsizing moves between 8 July 2015 and the individual's death. A practical issue to address will therefore be the retention of adequate records to support a claim for the optimum enhanced element of the residence nil rate band following several such moves from the above date.

As to the application of the residence nil rate band provisions concerning conditional exemption in circumstances involving downsizing, see **16.69.**

Chapter 17

Pre-owned assets

SIGNPOSTS

- **POAT on land, chattels and intangible property** – The scope of the POAT legislation can be very wide as illustrated in various examples (see **17.3–17.11**).
- **POAT 'plugged' a loophole in the GWR legislation** (see **Chapter 7**) – The provisions can be traced through cash (see **17.13**).
- **Calculation of POAT on land, chattels and intangible property** – A complex formula is applied to calculate the charge (see **17.14–17.17**).
- **Excluded transactions** – A number of transactions in relation to land and chattels are excluded. Excluded transactions have no application to intangible property (see **17.18**).
- **Exemptions** – There are a number of exemptions from POAT arising on land, chattels and intangible property (see **17.19–17.26**).
- **Opting out of POAT** – Procedural issues (see **17.27–17.28**).
- **Remedial action in relation to existing arrangements** – A tax analysis of unscrambling an arrangement which is subject to POAT (see **17.29**).

INTRODUCTION

17.1 *Finance Act 2004* (*s 84* and *Sch 15*) introduced a charge to tax which draws on a combination of income tax and inheritance tax rules.

Ever since the introduction of the gift with reservation (GWR) rules in 1986 (see **Chapter 5**), tax advisers have been devising schemes by which individuals could make gifts of property without being caught by the reservation of benefit rules, while at the same time continuing to enjoy the property given away. The pre-owned assets (POAT) legislation has primarily targeted artificial inheritance tax avoidance schemes, as outlined below, but some more 'innocent' arrangements are also now caught. The schemes (see **5.10**ff for an illustration of the various schemes) initially targeted are as follows:

- Lease carve-out schemes (*Ingram* schemes) following the case *of Ingram (Executors of Lady Ingram's Estate) v IRC* [2000] 1 AC 293.
- Settlements on interest in possession trusts (*Eversden* schemes) following the case of *IRC v Eversden (executors of Greenstock, decd)* [2003] EWCA Civ 668, [2003] STC 822.
- Reversionary lease schemes.
- 'Double trust' or 'Lifetime debt' schemes.

Focus

- HMRC stated that they are challenging home loan and double trust schemes and now contend that none of the schemes work.
- HMRC now consider that any home loans scheme fails to mitigate IHT. However a test case was settled in favour of the taxpayer as HMRC accepted that the taxpayer had acted in reliance on the Guidance at the time.
- HMRC now state that 'Where there has been an enquiry into the POA charge and HMRC has accepted that the charge applies, either in the figures returned or after adjustment, HMRC may not revisit the position on death'.
- If there has been no such POAT enquiry, HMRC have indicated that the scheme was ineffective. However, no case has yet determined the likely failure of the scheme.
- HMRC advise PRs to contact them if an estate involves a home loan arrangement. HMRC will provide a figure for PRs to make payment on account for a potential IHT liability. Guidance has now been published as to how HMRC might settle the various schemes.

It is very rare indeed to see entries on personal tax returns relating to the tax, suggesting that:

- people have unscrambled offensive transactions; or
- the values involved are covered by the *de minimis* rules; or
- most likely people do not realise that the transactions that were entered into offend the rules; or
- the transactions entered into did not achieve their tax objective and were caught by the gift with reservation rules.

Perhaps it is too early to assess the impact of the POAT rules, which will be seen more clearly when taxpayers die who in their lifetimes have tried to circumvent the GWR rules.

However it seems to be clear that any arrangement which circumvents the GWR rules is likely to be challenged by HMRC.

17.2 The pre-owned asset tax is not a charge to inheritance tax. The regime imposes an income tax charge on the use of capital based on:

- the benefit an individual enjoys from the occupation of land or the possession or use of chattels which they once owned, or which they assisted other persons to acquire; and
- their deemed power to enjoy intangible property in certain settlor-interested settlements.

The pre-owned asset tax can be charged on the use of:

- land;
- chattels; and
- intangible assets.

The legislation provides that certain transactions are excluded (see **17.18** below) and there are a number of exemptions (see **17.19**ff below). It also gives the option to elect out of the pre-owned assets charge arising (as discussed in **17.27**ff below). All references in this chapter are to *FA 2004*, unless otherwise stated.

HMRC, on their website provide useful guidance on how the pre-owned asset charge is assessed.

THE PRE-OWNED ASSETS CHARGE ON LAND

17.3 A charge to income tax may arise when an individual:

- occupies any land, whether alone or together with other persons; and
- either the 'disposal condition' or the 'contribution condition' is met in respect of that land (*FA 2004, Sch 15, para 3(1)*).

Unfortunately, the term 'occupation' is not defined within the legislation. HMRC's Technical Guidance provides the following, rather vague, explanation (see IHTM44003):

> 'The meaning of the word "occupies" should be taken quite widely. It goes wider than the chargeable person being physically present at the property concerned. Case law suggests that the word "occupy" requires some element of control. So a visitor may not be in occupation (even someone who stays for an extended period of time due to illness) but someone who has a key and can freely enter and leave premises as they please is more likely to be in occupation; even if they are absent for significant periods. It does not mean

the place you reside which implies a greater level of permanence so a lower threshold is required to satisfy the occupation condition.'

Each case is likely to be decided on the facts and the particular circumstances relating to it. However, in line with HMRC's Interpretation of inheritance tax and gifts with reservation (RI 55 (November 1993)) – the list of examples which excludes the pre-owned assets charge on a *de minimis* basis can be found in **7.28**.

17.4 Examples of more significant use of the property which may bring the chargeable person within the scope of *FA 2004, Sch 15, para 3* are as follows:

- a house in which the chargeable person stays most weekends or for more than a month each year;
- a second home or holiday home which the chargeable person and the owner both then use on an occasional basis;
- a house with a library in which the chargeable person continues to keep their own books, or which they use on a regular basis, for example because it is necessary for their work.

An exemption from a pre-owned assets charge may apply if the property in question is treated for inheritance tax purposes as being subject to the gift with reservation rules (see **17.21**).

17.5 In addition to the 'occupation' condition, the 'disposal condition' or the 'contribution condition' has to be satisfied for the pre-owned asset charge to apply.

The 'disposal condition' (in *FA 2004, Sch 15, para 3(2)*) in relation to any land is that:

- at any time after 17 March 1986 the individual owned an interest in the relevant land; or
- in other property, the proceeds of the disposal of which were (directly or indirectly) applied by another person towards the acquisition of an interest in the relevant land; and
- the individual has disposed of all, or part of, his interest in the relevant land or the other property, otherwise than by an excluded transaction (see **17.18** below).

17.6 The 'contribution condition' (in *FA 2004, Sch 15, para 3(3)*) in relation to any land is that:

- at any time after 17 March 1986 the individual has directly or indirectly provided, otherwise than by an excluded transaction, any of the consideration given by another person for the acquisition of:
  - an interest in the relevant land; or

- an interest in any other property the proceeds of the disposal of which were (directly or indirectly) applied by another person towards the acquisition of an interest in the relevant land.

HMRC confirm in IHTM44005 that the contribution condition is not met where a lender resides in property purchased by another with money loaned to him by the lender (even if the loan was interest free), as the outstanding debt remains part of the lender's estate for IHT.

Whether the pre-owned asset charge applies can best be illustrated by a number of examples. Some of the examples below, while prima facie being caught by the charge, may escape a charge to income tax due to one of the exemptions listed at **17.19**ff below.

Example 17.1—No POAT charge: father moves in with donee son

Mr Jones gifts one of his three properties to his son. After later having been widowed, Mr Jones moves in to live with his son. While the disposal condition is met, Mr Jones is likely to escape a charge to income tax as (by virtue of *FA 2004, Sch 15, para 11(5)(a)*) the property will be subject to a gift of reservation for inheritance tax purposes. For exemptions, see **17.19**ff; see also **Example 17.15**.

Example 17.2—POAT and IHT: sale at an undervalue

Mrs Smith required funds to renovate her property. She considered a number of commercial options but then decided to sell a half-share in the property to her son for £100,000. The market value of the half-share is £300,000. Mrs Smith continues to live in the house.

The disposal condition is met and Mrs Smith may face an income tax charge on the £100,000 cash. However, as she will have reserved a benefit in two-thirds of the half share, she is likely to escape a charge to income tax on that share, as it will be subject to the gift with reservation rules.

Example 17.3—Link with property broken

Mrs Williams owned a number of investments which she gave to her daughter, who subsequently sold them and used the proceeds to extend her existing house, adding a 'granny flat' in which Mrs Williams now lives.

Neither the disposal condition nor the contribution condition is satisfied, because the proceeds of the sale of the shares were applied by the daughter in improving her existing property and not in acquiring an interest in land.

Example 17.4—Contribution condition: funding of residence

In 2010, Mr Smith gifts his son £300,000, which in 2015 he uses to buy a house where Mr Smith now lives with him.

The contribution condition is met and Mr Smith may face an income tax charge. The gifts with reservation rules do not apply, as they do not trace through gifts of cash (see **17.12**).

Example 17.5—Contribution condition: change of circumstances

Mr White decided to move to Spain and after he sold his property in England, he gave his daughter £200,000. She used this money to purchase a property. Mr White now finds that the heat in Spain in summer is too much for his health and he therefore stays with his daughter for three months of each year.

The contribution condition is met during each period of occupation and it will be a question of fact whether he will be seen to be in occupation during the remaining nine months. If, for example, he has a room set aside for him for the rest of the year, he will be seen as in occupation for the whole year and Mr White's occupation may be subject to income tax.

THE PRE-OWNED ASSETS CHARGE ON CHATTELS

17.7 The pre-owned assets charge on chattels (*FA 2004, Sch 15, para 6*) is similar to that on land. Therefore, a charge to income tax may arise on an individual where:

- the individual is in 'possession' of, or has the 'use' of, a chattel, whether alone or together with other persons; and
- either the 'disposal condition' or the 'contribution condition' is met in respect of the chattel.

17.8 The terms 'possession' and 'use' are not defined in *FA 2004* and HMRC's Technical Guidance is vague (see IHTM44006):

> 'Very limited or occasional use of the chattel in question will not incur an income tax charge under this schedule.'

In line with the GWR legislation the example of a car used to give occasional lifts (ie less than three times a month) to the chargeable person will not be liable to the charge. But if the chargeable person is taken to work every day in the car it is likely an income tax charge will be incurred.

17.9 The expression 'chattel' is defined for the purpose of *FA 2004, Sch 15* (at *para 1*) and includes any tangible movable property other than money.

The 'disposal condition' (in *FA 2004, Sch 15, para 6(2)*) in relation to any chattels is that:

- at any time after 17 March 1986 the individual owned the chattel; or
- any other property, the proceeds of the disposal of which were (directly or indirectly) applied by another person towards the acquisition of the chattel; and
- the individual has disposed of all, or part of, the chattel or the other property, otherwise than by an excluded transaction (see **17.18** below).

17.10 The 'contribution condition' (in *FA 2004, Sch 15, para 6(3)*) in relation to any chattel is that at any time after 17 March 1986 the individual has directly or indirectly provided, otherwise than by an excluded transaction, any of the consideration given by another person for the acquisition of:

- the chattel; or
- an interest in any other property the proceeds of the disposal of which were (directly or indirectly) applied by another person towards the acquisition of the chattel.

17.11 Some of the examples below, while prima facie being caught by the charge, may escape a charge to income tax due to one of the exemptions listed at **17.19**ff below.

Example 17.6—Exemption from charge: retained painting

Mr Smith gives a valuable painting to his daughter, but he keeps the painting hanging on display in his own house for safekeeping and to meet insurance requirements.

The disposal condition is met, but (by virtue of *FA 2004, Sch 15, para 11(5)(a)*) Mr Smith is likely to escape an income tax charge, as the gift is subject to the gift with reservation rules.

Example 17.7—Possession of chattels: costly storage arrangements

Mrs Jones gifted a flat to her son. He sold it in 2012 for £500,000. He purchased another flat for £350,000 and with the remaining £150,000 he purchased several pieces of art. The son is now working abroad and let his flat. All his possessions are in storage apart from the valuable paintings, which are temporarily displayed in his mother's house. As the mother is 'enjoying' the chattels, she may now face an income tax charge. The gift with reservation rules do not apply.

Example 17.8—Contribution condition: shared campervan

Mr Williams gave his daughter cash of £100,000, which, in 2013, she used towards the purchase price of a £50,000 motor home. Mr Williams borrows the motor home for long holidays.

The contribution condition is met during each period of its use and Mr Williams may face an income tax charge.

PRE-OWNED ASSETS CHARGE ON INTANGIBLE PROPERTY COMPRISED IN SETTLOR-INTERESTED SETTLEMENTS

17.12 The pre-owned assets charge on intangible property (*FA 2004, Sch 15, para* 8) is drafted in different terms from the charges on land and chattels.

The charge arises, when all the following elements exist:

- a person has settled any property (not necessarily intangible property); and
- the terms of the settlement, as they affect any property comprised in the settlement, are such that any income arising from the property would be treated by virtue of *ITTOIA 2005, s 624* as settlor-interested; and
- such income would be so treated even if *ITTOIA 2005, s 625(1)* ('Settlor's retained interest') did not include any reference to the spouse/civil partner of the settlor; and
- that property includes any intangible property which is or represents property which the chargeable person settled, or added to the settlement, after 17 March 1986.

For the pre-owned assets charge on intangible property to apply, it is only necessary that the above elements exist. There is no need for the individual to benefit from the intangible property in question, and no need for that intangible property to produce any actual income.

A charge under *para 8* is not triggered where *ITTOIA 2005, s 624* only applies because the settlor's spouse rather than the settlor has retained an interest within *ITTOIA 2005, s 625*. However if, for example, the settlor sets up a trust where his wife receives the income but he can benefit if she dies, an income tax charge may potentially apply subject to any relevant exemptions.

The expression 'intangible property' is defined for the purposes of *FA 2004, Sch 15* (at *para 1*) as meaning any property other than chattels or interests in land. Therefore most investments are caught, and it also includes money. The pre-owned assets charge on intangible property does not apply to any land or chattels included in a settlement.

The intangible charge does not apply to intangibles which are owned by a company which is in turn owned by a trust. However the shares of the underlying company are caught by the POAT charge.

None of the 'excluded transactions' provisions (see **17.18**) apply in relation to intangible property, but all of the exemptions (see **17.19**ff) potentially apply.

SCOPE OF THE PRE-OWNED ASSETS LEGISLATION

17.13 The pre-owned assets legislation is drafted in much wider terms than the gift with reservation (GWR) rules (see **Chapter 7**). For example, for inheritance tax purposes, an absolute gift of cash is not subject to the GWR rules. In contrast, for pre-owned assets purposes, tracing through cash is permissible when determining whether proceeds on disposal have been applied or consideration has been provided in respect of land or chattels, for a period of up to seven years (*FA 2004, Sch 15, para 10(2)(c)*).

The use of the expression 'directly or indirectly' in the contribution condition extends the scope of this provision to cover circumstances where an individual routes a gift indirectly through a third party. However, it is considered that a contribution can only be traced through a third party where that party is obliged, or expected to pass this gift on.

Example 17.9—Cash gift: no trace of the money

A grandfather gifts £300,000 to each of his two sons. One of the sons is well off and decides to pass his share to his daughter, who subsequently buys a property with these funds. The grandfather, who in the interim was widowed, moves into the property with his granddaughter.

Although the gift of £300,000 was used in purchasing the property, the grandfather is likely to escape a charge to income tax. However, if there was an agreement or understanding between the grandfather and his son, that he would pass the gift of money on to his daughter, the contribution condition is likely to be met and the grandfather may face a charge to tax.

CALCULATION OF TAX CHARGE IN RELATION TO LAND

17.14 In relation to land, income tax will be charged on the 'rental value' less the amount of certain allowable payments made by the taxpayer in respect of their occupation of the relevant land. The 'appropriate rental value' is based on a hypothetical letting from year to year where the tenant undertakes to pay all taxes, rates and charges usually paid by a tenant, and the landlord undertakes to pay for repairs, insurance and any other necessary maintenance. Where the taxpayer occupies the property for less than a year, the rental value is applied pro rata and the income tax charge is adjusted accordingly.

HMRC's Technical Guidance does not indicate whether (and, if so, how) the appropriate rental value may be reduced to reflect any limitations or restrictions on the taxpayer's occupation of the land. For example, where the relevant land is a holiday home that is available for occupation by the taxpayer and by other persons and occasional use is made of it by the taxpayer and by others, it is unclear what adjustments can be made to the appropriate rental value to reflect any periods of non-use or shared use by the taxpayer.

The 'appropriate rental value' is defined as such proportion of the rental value (R) as is found by the following formula (*FA 2004, Sch 15, para 4*):

$$R \times \frac{DV}{V}$$

R is the rental value of the relevant land for the taxable period;

V is the value of the relevant land at the valuation date; and

DV can assume a variety of different values, as follows:

- where the disposal condition is met and the taxpayer owned an interest in the relevant land, DV is the value at the valuation date of the interest in the relevant land disposed of by the taxpayer; or
- where the disposal condition is met and the taxpayer owned an interest in replaced property, DV is such part of the value of the relevant land at the valuation date as can reasonably be attributed to the property originally disposed of by the taxpayer;
- where the contribution condition is met, DV is such part of the value of the relevant land at the valuation date as can reasonably be attributed to the consideration provided by the taxpayer.

In calculating the chargeable amount, certain payments made in respect of the occupation of the land may be deducted. These are payments which, in pursuance of any legal obligation, are made by the taxpayer to the owner of the land in respect of the occupation by the chargeable person.

Example 17.10—Calculation of POAT on land: moving in with daughter

Mr Jones gifts his daughter £500,000 to purchase a property. He subsequently moves in and now lives there with his daughter. He has use of the whole house. He pays his daughter £50 per week to cover expenses. The contribution condition has been met and (subject to any exclusions or exemptions, which are discussed below) the question now arises how to assess the 'appropriate rental value'. The value of the house is £600,000. The rental value is £18,000. The payments made by Mr Jones do not qualify for deduction as they are not made in relation to rental payments and also are not made under a legal obligation.

If Mr Jones had paid the £50 each week as rental payments following a legal obligation, they would be deductible from the rental value.

Mr Jones will pay income tax on £18,000 at his marginal tax rate. Therefore, if he is a 40% taxpayer, the pre-owned asset charge will cost him £7,200 per annum.

In contrast, if the house had included a self-contained annexe and he only occasionally visited the main house, eg for Sunday lunch, the income tax charge would have been assessed on the 'appropriate rental value' of the annexe rather than the whole house.

CALCULATION OF TAX CHARGE IN RELATION TO CHATTELS

17.15 In relation to chattels, income tax will be charged on the 'appropriate amount' less the amount of certain allowable payments made by the taxpayer in respect of his possession or use of the chattel.

In contrast to the pre-owned assets charge on land, which is based on rental value, the charge on a chattel is based on the notional amount of interest that would be payable for the taxable period if interest were payable at the 'prescribed rate' on an amount equal to the value of the chattel at the valuation date. Therefore, the fact that the donor is paying a market rent for the use of the chattel, does not necessarily prevent a charge to income tax.

The 'prescribed rate' of interest is set by regulations and is equal to 'the official rate of interest' as defined for the purposes of taxable benefits on taxable cheap loans (see the *Charge to Income Tax by Reference to Enjoyment of Property Previously Owned Regulations, SI 2005/724, reg 3*). The official rate of interest is defined by *ITEPA 2003, s 181*. On 1 March 2009 it decreased from 6.25% to 4.75%, with a further decrease to 4% from 6 April 2010. For 2012/13 the rate remains at 4%, reduced to 3% from 6 April 2016 with a further reduction to 2.5% from 6 April 2017.

The 'appropriate amount' is found by multiplying the prescribed interest (N) for the taxable period by the fraction as follows (*FA 2004, Sch 15, para 7*):

$$N \times \frac{DV}{V}$$

N is the notional interest for the taxable period, at the prescribed rate, on the value of the chattel at the valuation date;

V is the value of the chattel at the valuation date; and

DV can assume a variety of different values, as follows:

- where the disposal condition is met and the taxpayer owned an interest in the chattel, DV is the value at the valuation date of the interest in the chattel disposed of by the taxpayer; or
- where the disposal condition is met and the taxpayer owned an interest in replaced property, DV is such part of the value of the chattel at the valuation date as can reasonably be attributed to the property originally disposed of by the taxpayer;
- where the contribution condition is met, DV is such part of the value of the chattel at the valuation date as can reasonably be attributed to the consideration provided by the taxpayer.

In calculating the chargeable amount, certain payments made in respect of the possession or use of the chattel may be deducted. These are payments which, in pursuance of any legal obligation, are made by the taxpayer to the owner of the chattel in respect of the possession or use of the chattel by the chargeable person (*FA 2004, Sch 15, para 7(1)*).

Example 17.11—Calculation of POAT on chattels: gift and leaseback

The following example is contained in HMRC's guidance notes IHTM44018.

Hermione gives away a sculpture subject to a lease over it in her favour. The POA charge first applies to Hermione on 6 April 2005 when the open market value of the sculpture is £600,000 and the value subject to the lease is £400,000. The official rate is 5%, so the value for N is £30,000. The appropriate amount is therefore:

30,000 × (400,000 ÷ 600,000) = £20,000.

This will be the amount subject to the POA charge for Hermione in tax year 2005/06. The values for the sculpture will remain the same in the next four tax years, although the amount subject to the POA charge will vary in line with changes to the official rate; so for tax year 2009/10, the POA charge will be £19,000 (official rate of 4.75%). The valuation process will need to be repeated again on 6 April 2010 and on 6 April 2015, etc to establish the capital values to use for the next five tax years.

If Hermione had been paying a rent of £5,000 for the use of the sculpture, the amount subject to the POA charge would be reduced for 2005/06 to £15,000.

CALCULATION OF TAX CHARGE IN RELATION TO INTANGIBLE PROPERTY

17.16 In relation to intangible property, the 'chargeable amount' is broadly as follows (*Sch 15, para 9*):

N minus T

where:

N Is the 'prescribed interest'

T Is the 'tax allowance'

The 'prescribed interest' is the amount of interest that would be payable for the taxable period if interest were payable at the prescribed rate on an amount equal to the value of the relevant property at the valuation date. The 'prescribed rate' is set by regulations and is equal to 'the official rate of interest' as defined for the purposes of taxable benefits on taxable cheap loans, and was reduced to 3% from 6 April 2015.

The 'tax allowance' is the amount of any income tax or capital gains tax payable by the taxpayer in respect of the taxable period by virtue of any of a number of specified provisions, so far as the tax is attributable to the relevant property. The provisions in question are *ITTOIA 2005, ss 461, 624*, *ITA 2007, ss 720–730*, and *TCGA 1992, ss 77* (although this section was repealed from 2008/09), *86*.

In contrast to the computation of the pre-owned assets charges relating to land and chattels, there is no provision for the deduction of any allowable payments made by the taxpayer in respect of his enjoyment or potential enjoyment of the intangible property.

Example 17.12—Calculation of POAT on intangibles

The following example is contained in HMRC's guidance notes IHTM44025, but amended to reflect current tax rates

Andrew is the UK resident and domiciled settlor of a non-resident settlor interested settlement. The settled property does not form part of his estate nor has he reserved a benefit in the settled property. The settlement comprises 'intangible' property of cash and shares with a value of £1,500,000 at the valuation date.

In the tax year 2017/18 the trustees receive income of £20,000 which is chargeable to income tax on the trustees, but Andrew also will need to report this income under *ITTOIA 2005, s 624*. A further £150,000 capital gains on the sale of shares are realised which are deemed to be Andrew's gains by virtue of *TCGA 1992, s 86*.

Income tax of £9,000 (£20,000 × 45%) and CGT of £30,000 (£150,000 × 20%) becomes payable by the trustees. As Andrew is a higher rate taxpayer, he can reclaim some of the tax paid by the trustees (5%) ie the difference between 40% and 45% tax rate – hence £1,000. This sum will have to be repaid to the trustees. The tax allowance (T) against the potential charge under *FA 2004, Sch 15, para 8* is therefore £38,000 (£30,000 + (£9,000 – £1,000)).

The chargeable amount (N) is 2.5% (the prescribed rate from 6 April 2017) × £1,500,000 = £37,500, so there will not be an additional tax charge under *FA 2004, Sch 15, para 8.*

VALUATION PROBLEMS

17.17 For the purposes of the pre-owned asset charge, the value of any property is broadly the price which the property might reasonably be expected to fetch if sold in the open market at that time (*FA 2004, Sch 15, para 15*); this reflects the 'market value' provision for inheritance tax purposes (*IHTA 1984, s 160*).

In relation to any land, chattel or intangible property, the 'valuation date' is prescribed by regulations (*Charge to Income Tax by Reference to Enjoyment of Property Previously Owned Regulations, SI 2005/724*) and is 6 April in the relevant year of assessment or, if later, the first day of the 'taxable period'. The regulations dispense with annual valuations but instead require a new valuation on the 'five-year anniversary' of the previous valuation.

A new valuation may be required when the value of the retained benefit is reduced, for example, because the taxpayer moved into a smaller property.

The second fifth anniversary of the implementation of POAT charge passed on 6 April 2015, therefore taxpayers who have been subject to POAT will need to obtain relevant capital or rental values as of 6 April 2015. If any adjustments to the payment of income tax need to be made, the deadline will be 31 January 2017.

EXCLUDED TRANSACTIONS

17.18 The concept of excluded transactions has no application to intangible property. The provisions only serve to exclude certain transactions in relation to land and chattels from the income tax charge.

FA 2004, Sch 15, para 10 includes different provisions for the 'disposal' condition and 'contribution' condition in relation to interest in possession trusts for the spouse/civil partner, as outlined below:

- Disposals of entire interests to unconnected third parties at arm's length are excluded transactions.
- Disposals of entire interests to connected parties at arm's length are excluded transactions, if the transaction is such as might be expected at arm's length between unconnected parties.
- An inter-spouse/civil partner disposal remains an excluded transaction in relation to the original donor, even if it is followed by an onward disposal to a third party.
- A disposal by virtue of which the property became settled property in which his spouse/civil partner or former spouse/civil partner is beneficially entitled to an interest in possession, and that interest in possession has not come to an end *except* on the death of the spouse/civil partner or former spouse/civil partner. In relation to the disposal condition, it is stipulated that the disposal has to be a gift, while under the contribution condition it is only required that the property become settled on acquisition.
- A disposition falling within the inheritance tax exemption available in respect of dispositions for the maintenance of family members (*IHTA 1984, s 11*).
- The provision by a person of consideration for another's acquisition of land or chattels is an excluded transaction if it constituted an outright gift of money by the individual to the other person and was made at least seven years before the earliest date on which either the individual occupies the land or, in the case of chattels, the individual is in possession of, or has the use of the chattel.
- It is an outright gift to an individual and is wholly exempt by virtue of either the inheritance tax annual exemption (*IHTA 1984, s 19*) or the inheritance tax small gifts exemption (*IHTA 1984, s 20*).

Note that there is no exclusion from the pre-owned assets regime for gifts that are exempt from inheritance tax under the provisions relating to normal expenditure gifts out of income, or gifts in consideration of marriage.

Example 17.13—Equity release: daughter moves in

In 2015 Mr Miller sold a half-share of his property to his daughter Alice at full market value. This is not a transfer of value for inheritance tax purposes. The transaction however is a disposal under *FA 2004, Sch 15, para 3(2)*, but does not qualify as an excluded transaction under *FA 2004, Sch 15, para 10*. According to HMRC guidance Mr Miller's occupation of the half-share would be subject to an income tax charge if the appropriate rental value exceeds the *de minimis* limit.

If he had sold all his interest, the transaction would have been excluded from the pre-owned asset charge. However, see below regarding the full consideration exemption in **17.23** and reference to the gift with reservation exemption following *Finance Act 1986, s 102B(4)* (see **17.22**).

As to the equity release exemption and its limitations, see **17.24**.

Example 17.14—Excluded transaction: gift of cash

In 2008, Mrs Smith gave her daughter £500,000, which the daughter uses to purchase a property. In 2017, the mother moves into the property.

As Mrs Smith's commencement of her occupation occurred more than seven years after the gift was made, this will be an excluded transaction (*FA 2004, Sch 15, para 10(2)(c)*).

EXEMPTIONS

17.19 There are a number of exemptions (in *FA 2004, Sch 15, paras 11, 12* and *13*) from the pre-owned assets charge otherwise arising on land, chattels or intangible property:

- exemption for property that is in the taxpayer's estate for inheritance tax purposes;
- exemption for property that is deemed to be in the taxpayer's estate under the gift with reservation of benefit (GWR) provisions;
- property that escapes the GWR provisions by virtue of certain specified inheritance tax exemptions or reliefs;

- property covered by certain equity release arrangements defined in regulations; and
- certain *de minimis* amounts.

Exemption for property in the taxpayer's estate

17.20 There is no pre-owned assets charge on land, chattels or intangible property where the taxpayer's estate for inheritance tax purposes includes the following (*FA 2004, Sch 15, para 11(1)*):

- the relevant property; or
- other property which derives its value from the relevant property and whose value, so far as attributable to the relevant property, is not substantially less than the relevant property.

This exemption recognises that the pre-owned assets charge should not penalise taxpayers in respect of their enjoyment of property that is still included in their estate for inheritance tax purposes.

Exemption where the gift with reservation rules apply

17.21 There is no pre-owned assets charge on land, chattels or intangible property where the 'gift with reservation' (GWR) provisions apply for IHT (see *FA 2004, Sch 15, para 11(5)*), or would apply but for certain specified provisions, to:

- the relevant property; or
- other property which derives its value from the relevant property and whose value, so far as attributable to the relevant property, is not substantially less than the relevant property.

This exemption for property that falls within the GWR provisions is fundamental to the concept of the pre-owned assets charge, and recognises that the charge should not penalise taxpayers in respect of their enjoyment of property that is still deemed to be included in their estate under the GWR provisions, or would be deemed to be so included but for certain specific inheritance tax exemptions.

17.22 See **Chapter 7** for discussion on when property is subject to the GWR rules. The GWR exemption from the pre-owned assets charge extends to property subject to the GWR rules, and property that would have been subject to the GWR rules but for certain specified provisions contained in *FA 2004, Sch 15, para 11(5)*:

- Any of the exemptions in *FA 1986, s 102(5)(d)–(i)*, which cover certain cases where disposal by way of gift is an exempt transfer for inheritance tax purposes. This includes gifts to charities, gifts to political parties, gifts to housing associations, gifts for national purposes, maintenance funds for historic buildings and employee trusts (see **Chapter 9**).

- *FA 1986, s 102B(4)*, which deals with gifts with reservation (share of interest in land). This relief from inheritance tax was introduced with effect from 9 March 1999; it applies where an individual disposes by way of gift of an undivided share of an interest in land, which is then occupied by donor and donee without the donor receiving any benefit, other than a negligible one, provided by or at the expense of the donee for some reason connected with the gift.
- *FA 1986, s 102C(3)* provides that in applying *FA 1986, ss 102A* and 102*B*, no account is to be taken of a donor's occupation of land in circumstances where that occupation would be disregarded in accordance with *FA 1986, Sch 20, para 6(1)(b)*. It allows occupation by the donor to be disregarded where:
  - it arises from an unforeseen change in circumstances; and
  - it arises when the donor has become unable to maintain himself through old age, infirmity or otherwise; and
  - it represents reasonable provision by the donee for the care and maintenance of the donor; and
  - the donee is a relative of the donor or his spouse/civil partner.

Example 17.15—POAT exemption: illness intervening (see Example 17.1)

Mr Jones gives his son £300,000 to purchase a property. After having been widowed, Mr Jones moves in to live with his son. The contribution condition is met and Mr Jones may face a charge to income tax.

Assuming Mr Jones moves in because he became unable to maintain himself through age or infirmity and the occupation represents reasonable provision by his son for his father's care and maintenance, Mr Jones will escape a charge to income tax, as well as an inheritance tax charge under the GWR rules. This is provided by *FA 2004, Sch 15, para 11(5)(d)* and *FA 1986, s 102C(3)*.

Exemption – Foreign element

17.23 The pre-owned asset charge does not apply in relation to any person for any year of assessment during which he or she is not resident in the UK for the purposes of income tax (*FA 2004, Sch 15, para 12*).

Where a person is resident but not domiciled in the UK the pre-owned asset charge does not apply to him unless the land, chattel or intangible property in respect of which the charge arises is situated in the UK.

The deemed domicile rules of *IHTA 1984, s 267* (see **Chapter 1**) have seemingly been imported for the purposes of the income tax charge on pre-owned assets. Whilst not specifically stated in the legislation, a person is regarded as domiciled in the UK if he or she would be treated as such under *IHTA 1984*.

Under *IHTA 1984, s 48*, settled property that is not situated in the UK is excluded from a charge to IHT if the settlor was non-UK domiciled when the settlement was made. Holdings in authorised unit trusts and open-ended investment companies (OEICs) are also excluded from IHT despite being situated in the UK.

However POAT still applies to holdings in authorised unit trusts and OEICs situated in the UK. The settlor, despite being non-UK domiciled and the settlement being an excluded settlement under *IHTA 1984, s 48*, therefore is subject to an income charge on the value of any such holdings unless he or she makes an election for IHT to opt into the gift with reservation rules.

Example 17.16—Not UK resident

See **Example 17.4** – Mr Smith has been paying POAT since moving into the property. However in March 2018 he decides to move to Spain and the property is let. As Mr Smith is not resident in the UK for tax purposes during 2018/19, he will not be liable to the POAT charge. He will be subject to POAT during 2017/18 though.

Example 17.17—Not UK domiciled

Boris, a wealthy Bulgarian is resident in the UK, but is non-UK domiciled. He owns a property in France, which he uses for extended periods during spring and summer. The property is owned by an offshore company.

As a non-UK domiciled person Boris will escape POAT on the property. The scenario will have to be revisited when Boris becomes deemed domiciled for IHT during 2017/18.

Focus

- An election treats the property as being subject to a gift with reservation (see **17.27**).

- However as the gift with reservation rules have no application to excluded property settlements, the settlor will escape any IHT liabilities.

Equity release exemption

17.24 Following concerns whether equity release schemes were affected by the pre-owned asset charge, the Treasury used its power to confer further exemptions by regulations (*Charge to Income Tax by Reference to Enjoyment of Property Previously Owned Regulations, SI 2005/724*).

Under this exemption, the pre-owned assets charging provisions on land and chattels do not apply to a person in relation to a disposal of *part* of an interest in any property if:

- the disposal was by a transaction made at arm's length with a person not connected with him; or
- the disposal was by a transaction such as might be expected to be made at arm's length between persons not connected with each other and the disposal was for a consideration not in money or in the form of readily convertible assets; or
- the disposal was made before 7 March 2005 (*SI 2005/724, reg 5*).

Note that this exemption applies to transactions between unconnected persons. It also applies to any disposals on arm's-length terms before 7 March 2005, or disposals from that date in the limited circumstances described above. Sadly, despite representations, the treatment for unconnected parties is not extended to similar transactions within the family, even if on full commercial terms.

De minimis exemption

17.25 An individual will not be chargeable to pre-owned assets in a year of assessment if the aggregate of the amounts specified below in respect of that year do not exceed £5,000 (*FA 2004, Sch 15, para 13*). Those amounts are:

- the appropriate rental value in relation to land (see **17.14** above);
- the appropriate amount in relation to chattels (see **17.15** above); and
- the chargeable amount in relation to intangible assets (see **17.16** above).

Focus

- Note that the amounts to be included in respect of land and chattels are not the chargeable amounts.

- Instead, they are the sums arrived at before deducting any eligible payments made in respect of occupation, possession or use. A person therefore cannot avoid the tax charge by paying an annual rent to bring himself below the £5,000 limit.

17.26 The *de minimis* exemption is available to each individual, and therefore applies independently to husband and wife. When the pre-owned assets provisions were introduced, the then Paymaster General, Dawn Primarolo, explained the effect of the exemption as follows:

> 'With regard to the £5,000 … I would call it a cliff edge effect: essentially, if the value is £5,001, taxation would be paid on the whole £5,001, not just on the £1 excess.'

Example 17.18—*De minimis* exemption: over the limit

Alice gave her daughter £500,000, which she used towards the purchase of a property and towards the purchase of a painting that is displayed in her property. Alice now lives in the property with her daughter, and pays her £50 per week as rent under a legal agreement. The contribution condition applies in respect of the relevant land and the chattel. The appropriate rental value of the land amounts to £5,000, and the appropriate amount in respect of the painting amounts to £1,000.

The aggregate of the amounts is £6,000 which exceeds the *de minimis* exemption of £5,000, therefore Alice must pay the pre-owned assets tax charge. The fact that she pays an annual rent of £2,600 will not help her to bring herself within the *de minimis* exception.

'OPTING OUT' OF THE PRE-OWNED ASSETS CHARGE

17.27 An individual taxpayer facing the pre-owned asset charge has a right to elect that *FA 2004, Sch 15* shall not apply to him during the 'initial year' and subsequent years of assessment by reference to that property or any other property for which it has been substituted (*FA 2004, Sch 15, paras 21–23*).

The opt-out election treats the property as though it were subject to a reservation under the gift with reservation rules, even though there had been no gift. The opt-out provisions dispense with the requirement for there to have been a gift; an election simply invokes the GWR rules as though there had been a gift.

An election to opt out of the pre-owned assets charge in respect of land, chattels, or intangible property, must be made in the prescribed manner. The election must be made on form IHT500. The relevant filing date for the 'opt-out' is 31 January in the year of assessment immediately following the 'initial year' when the pre-owned asset charge arises. The *Finance Act 2007* relaxed this deadline, so that (from 21 March 2007) elections can be accepted at HMRC's discretion that would otherwise be late (*FA 2004, Sch 15, para 23(3)*, as amended).

HMRC will accept a late election in certain circumstances. Examples of what they may accept as 'reasonable' excuses are:

- the election is lost or delayed in the post;
- loss of the chargeable person's financial records or relevant papers;
- serious illness;
- bereavement.

17.28 The pre-owned assets legislation, as originally enacted, created a possibility that, where a valid opt-out election is made and the taxpayer dies within the next seven years, there might be two inheritance tax charges on the same underlying asset value. The government recognised this as a particular risk for taxpayers using 'double trust' schemes, and the regulations introduced a new relief from inheritance tax in such circumstances. The relief ensures that tax is due on only one of these components, whichever gives the larger tax liability (the *Inheritance Tax (Double Charges) Regulations 2005, SI 2005/3441*): see HMRC's Technical Guidance at IHTM44061.

Whether or not to opt out of the pre-owned assets regime in respect of particular property will depend upon the facts in each case, in particular the financial position and life expectancy of the taxpayer. If the taxpayer is elderly with a relatively low life expectancy, he may decide to pay the pre-owned assets charge rather than elect for a full 40% inheritance tax charge on death.

REMEDIAL ACTION IN RELATION TO EXISTING ARRANGEMENTS

17.29 It is unlikely that clients, who have taken appropriate advice, will enter into new arrangements that fall foul of the POAT rules. Any who were caught by those rules in relation to existing structures should long since have taken advice and, if appropriate, remedial action to avoid payment of the pre-owned asset charge. The available options depend on the clients' circumstances and the type of scheme they entered into, but in essence they are as follows:

- Pay the pre-owned asset charge. This will depend upon a number of factors including the age and life expectancy of the chargeable person and any potential inheritance tax, capital gains tax and income tax charges which may become payable when opting for one of the alternatives.

- Pay rent in respect of the occupation of the land or the use of the chattel. As such rent payments have to be paid out of taxed income and are likely also to be taxed in the hands of the recipient, this option may not be very attractive.
- Opt into the gift of reservation legislation, which will make the previous arrangement ineffective for IHT planning, while at the same time, the property will continue to be subject to capital gains tax in the hands of the donee, as there will no uplift in the value of the asset on the donor's death.
- Unwind the arrangements and pass the property or chattel back to the donor. The taxation consequences (including IHT, CGT and in some cases stamp duty land tax) may be prohibitive and each case requires careful consideration. As the donee (whether this may be an individual or in many cases trustees) has to consent to the 'unravelling', this alternative may not be feasible.
- End the benefit, ie cease occupation of the property in question or enjoyment of the chattel. Especially in relation to property this often is not practical as the donor may not have sufficient funds to purchase alternative accommodation.

As litigation surrounding the various double trust/home loan schemes continues and a final decision on the correct IHT treatment of these schemes has not been reached, HMRC have published guidance on the correct tax treatment of unwinding any such arrangements. The guidance is found at IHTM44120 – see https://tinyurl.com/y8bs5osv.

HMRC confirmed that when a home loan or double trust scheme has been unwound a repayment of all the pre-owned assets tax without time limit paid can be claimed.

One feature that may work in favour of the taxpayer is stability in the value of property, both in terms of capital and rental value. Many schemes relating to the family home that were later caught by the POAT were sold to families of moderate wealth. The schemes were often short-term in nature, being entered into by elderly home owners, so might run their course before the quinquennial review of the value of occupation. The review was mentioned at **17.17** and is required by the *Charge to Income Tax by Reference to Enjoyment of PropertyPreviously Owned Regulations 2005, SI 2005/724, reg 4*. Often the value of occupation initially fell below £10,000 and was therefore potentially covered by the *de minimis* charge, if there were two estate owners.

Example 17.19—Property subject to the 'Ingram' scheme

Mr Moore entered into an *Ingram* scheme in January 1999. The value of the property was £500,000. Mr Moore retained the leasehold, valued at £200,000 in January 1999 and the freehold (valued at £275,000) was passed into an accumulation and maintenance trust for the benefit of his grandchildren.

House prices increased in the interim and, on 6 April 2015 (this is the second five-year anniversary since introduction of POAT – see **17.17**), the value of the freehold interest subject to the lease was £450,000; the leasehold interest also was valued at £450,000. The market value of the freehold interest in possession (ie assuming that it is not subject to the lease carve-out) is £1 million.

The market rent is £1,000 per week (£52,000 per annum).

Mr Moore has a number of options. Mr Moore's financial and personal circumstances have to be considered carefully. For example, if his life expectancy is low, it may be preferable to pay the pre-owned asset charge rather than choosing one of the alternatives. His options were as follows:

1. *Pay the income tax charge*

As Mr Moore retained the leasehold the appropriate rental value is calculated as follows:

$$\text{Market rent} \times \frac{\text{Value of freehold as of 6 April 2015}}{\text{Value of freehold (without leasehold)}}$$

$$£52{,}000 \times \frac{£450{,}000}{£1{,}000{,}000} = £23{,}400$$

As Mr Moore is a 40% taxpayer, he will suffer an annual income tax charge of £9,360.

The leasehold will remain in Mr Moore's estate for IHT and on his death his estate will face an IHT charge of £180,000 (£450,000 @ 40%), assuming that his nil rate band has been used elsewhere.

If the trustees, after Mr Moore's death, decide to sell the property, they will incur a substantial charge to CGT, as the base cost is only £275,000 and the freehold over time will increase in value with the diminishing term of the lease.

2. *Pay a market rent to the trustees of the A&M settlement*

The payment of the market rent has to be made subject to a legal obligation and will cost Mr Moore £52,000 per annum. At that level, from 6 April 2015 the trustees of the A&M settlement will have to pay tax of £23,400 (£52,000 @ 45%) (for earlier tax years, the tax charge would depend on the trust tax rate).

Alternatively, the rent could be paid to the trustees following a deed of covenant which would avoid a charge to income tax payable by the trustees under *ITTOIA 2005, s 727*.

The IHT and CGT considerations outlined in option 1 will also have to be considered.

This option has to be considered carefully, as Mr Moore may not have sufficient funds to continue paying rent until his death or until he moves out of the property.

3. *Elect for the property to be charged to IHT*

Mr Moore could opt into the reservation of benefit rules and elect to have the property charged to IHT as an asset of his estate. Assuming that the nil rate band has been exhausted, an IHT charge of £400,000 (£1,000,000 @ 40%) will arise on his death.

In addition to the IHT charge, the trustees of the A&M settlement will suffer a charge to CGT if they decide to sell the property after Mr Moore's death (see option 1 above).

Mr Moore is outside the time limit for an election. In practice, HMRC have discretion (from 21 March 2007) to consider any election that should have been made (by 31 January 2007) to see whether there may be a reasonable excuse for the delay (see **17.27** above).

4. *Unscramble the scheme*

If the trustees of the A&M settlement agree to unscramble the scheme, they will face a substantial charge to CGT when the freehold passes back to Mr Moore.

The property then will form part of his estate for IHT with a potential charge of £400,000 (£1,000,000 @ 40%).

5. *End the benefit*

Mr Moore could consider moving out of the property, but this will only be a viable option if he has sufficient funds to purchase or rent another property. Any rent received on the property will have to be taxed and, for CGT and IHT considerations, the problems outlined in option 1 remain.

Index

[*All references are to paragraph number*]

'3 year rule'
domicile, and 2.9
'14-year backward shadow'
calculating IHT, and 4.27
'15 out of 20 rule'
domicile, and 2.10–2.11
'17 out of 20 rule'
domicile, and 2.12
18-to-25 trusts
See also **Bereaved minors trusts**
See also **Relevant property trusts**
chargeable amount 10.11
conditions 10.8
deemed potentially exempt transfers, and 4.12
estate planning, and 15.21
generally 10.7
interest in possession trusts, and 9.31
introduction 10.5
notional transfer 10.14
post-death variations, and 15.52–15.53
problem areas 10.9
relevant fraction 10.12
settlement rate 10.13
spouse exemption, and 15.21
tax charge 10.10

A

Acceptance of property in lieu
payment of tax, and 8.36
Accounts and returns
See also **Returns**
death, on
estimates 8.15
generally 8.10
normal expenditure out of income 8.12–8.13
personal effects 8.14
reporting lifetime transfers after death 8.11
developments
compliance 8.3
Accounts and returns – *contd*
forms 8.2
estimates 8.15
excepted settlements 8.8
excepted terminations
generally 8.7
introduction 8.5
excepted transfers
generally 8.6
introduction 8.5
exempt transfers 8.7
fixed value funds 8.7
fixed-value transfers 8.6
introduction 8.2
lifetime transfers, on
excepted settlements 8.8
excepted terminations 8.7
excepted transfers 8.6
generally 8.4–8.5
reporting after death, and 8.11
trustees, and 8.9
nil rate band 8.7
normal expenditure out of income 8.12–8.13
personal effects 8.14
reporting lifetime transfers after death 8.11
small transfers 8.7
trustees, and 8.9
uncertain value transfers 8.6
variable value funds 8.7
Accumulation and maintenance trusts
See also **Age 18-to-25 trusts**
See also **Bereaved minors trusts**
See also **Relevant property trusts**
generally 10.5
legislative changes 10.5
migration to new regime 10.24–10.25
potentially exempt transfers, and 4.8
protected gifts, and 14.27
tax charge 10.10
Active service, death on
estate on death, and 5.5

Active service, death on – *contd*
  generally 11.5
  introduction 1.20
Additional permitted subscription (APS)
  ISAs, and 14.4
Administration expenses
  liabilities on death, and 5.17
Age 18-to-25 trusts
  See also **Bereaved minors trusts**
  See also **Relevant property trusts**
  chargeable amount 10.11
  conditions 10.8
  deemed potentially exempt transfers, and 4.12
  estate planning, and 15.21
  generally 10.7
  interest in possession trusts, and 9.31
  introduction 10.5
  notional transfer 10.14
  post-death variations, and 15.52–15.53
  problem areas 10.9
  relevant fraction 10.12
  settlement rate 10.13
  spouse exemption, and 15.21
  tax charge 10.10
Agricultural property
  transferable nil rate band, and 3.33
  valuing lifetime transfers, and 4.19
Agricultural property relief
  acquisition of relievable property, and 10.65
  'agricultural property' 13.24–13.26
  calculation of tax, and 13.51–13.53
  'character appropriate'
    Antrobus decision 13.33
    generally 13.31–13.32
    Golding decision 13.35
    McKenna decision 13.34
  comparison of PETs and chargeable transfers 13.54
  conditions
    occupation or ownership period 13.37–13.38
    replacements 13.40–13.41
    successions 13.39
    valuation of transfer 13.42–13.45
    value for relief 13.46–13.49
  double dipping, and 15.24
  estate on death, and 5.3
Agricultural property relief – *contd*
  estate planning, and 15.23–15.29
  exemptions and exceptions, and 11.13
  farm buildings 13.36
  farmhouses 13.27–13.28
  farming business 13.29–13.30
  gifts with reservation, and 7.23
  lifetime planning 14.5–14.6
  loss of 13.50
  'mere assets', and 13.24
  occupation period 13.37–13.38
  ownership period 13.37–13.38
  potentially-exempt transfers, and 13.54
  reduction
    rate of tax, in 10.63
    tax charge, in 10.62
  relevant property trusts, and
    acquisition of relievable property 10.65
    clawback 10.64
    control 10.61
    effect at commencement 10.60
    reduction in rate of tax 10.63
    reduction in tax charge 10.62
  replacements 13.40–13.41
  scope
    'agricultural property' 13.24–13.26
    'character appropriate' 13.31–13.35
    farm buildings 13.36
    farmhouses 13.27–13.28
    farming business 13.29–13.30
    types of asset 13.24
  settled gifts, and 7.23
  successions 13.39
  transfer on death, and 5.30
  types of asset 13.24
  valuation of transfer 13.42–13.45
  value for relief 13.46–13.49
Allied headquarters staff
  estate on death, and 5.5
Allocation of burden of tax
  transfer on death, and 5.38–5.39
Alterations of capital
  close companies, and 1.29
Alternative Investment Market (AIM)
  lifetime planning, and 14.7
Alternatively secured pensions (ASP)
  transferable nil rate band, and 3.14–3.15

Annual exemption
estate on death, and 5.4
exempt property, and 1.20
generally 11.7
lifetime transfers, and 4.3
Annual tax on enveloped dwellings (ATED)
'high-value' residential properties, and 16.2–16.3
Annuities
accounts and returns, and 8.23
exempt property, and 1.20
Anti-avoidance
estate on death, and
gaming debts 5.10
generally 5.5
general rule (GAAR) 17.1
interest in possession trusts, and
generally 9.10
termination 9.16
settled excluded property, and 7.37
Appeals
'basic' appeal 8.60
categories 8.58
'complex' appeal 8.62
costs 8.65
'default paper' model 8.59
generally 8.64
internal reviews, and 8.63
overview 8.66
'standard' appeal 8.61
Approved pension schemes
estate on death, and 5.5
Assessments
time limits 8.54
Asset valuations
'ascertained' 6.34
bank accounts 6.21
debts 6.32
development value 6.26–6.27
discounted gifts schemes 6.15
discounts 6.28
'estate concept' 6.5
gifts with reservation 6.31
guarantees, and 6.35
HMRC's approach 6.2–6.3
'hope value' 6.27
household goods 6.33
introduction 6.1
Asset valuations – *contd*
joint property
bank accounts 6.21
generally 6.20
land 6.22–6.28
money 6.21
land
development value 6.26–6.27
discounts 6.28
generally 6.22–6.25
liabilities, and 6.35
life policies
'back-to-back' arrangements 6.14
lifetime transfers 6.12
transfers on death 6.13
lifetime transfers, and
generally 4.19
PETS 4.20
transfers by close companies 4.21
'loss to estate' principle 6.4
money 6.21
open market value
'estate concept' 6.5
generally 6.1
HMRC's approach 6.2–6.3
'loss to estate' principle 6.4
personal effects 6.33
principles
'estate concept' 6.5
generally 6.1
HMRC's approach 6.2–6.3
'loss to estate' principle 6.4
quoted shares and securities 6.16
related property rule
application 6.7–6.9
'appropriate portion' 6.8
generally 6.6
relief 6.10
settled property 6.29
specific asset rules 6.11
transfers on death, and
generally 5.19
related property 5.20
unit trusts 6.17
unquoted shares and securities 6.18–6.19
Associated operations
lifetime transfers, and 4.23–4.24
Authorised unit trusts
generally 11.32

Authorised unit trusts – *contd*
introduction 1.13
valuation of assets, and 6.17

B

'Back-to-back' arrangements
life policies, and 6.14
Bank accounts
valuation of assets, and 6.21
Bare trusts
generally 8.16
Bereaved minors trusts
See also **Age 18-to-25 trusts**
See also **Relevant property trusts**
conditions 10.6
estate planning, and 15.20
generally 10.6
interest in possession trusts, and 9.31
introduction 10.5
post-death variations, and 15.52–15.53
problem areas 10.9
spouse exemption, and 15.20
Bereavement questionnaire
IHT compliance, and 5.43
Business property
transferable nil rate band, and 3.33
valuing lifetime transfers, and 4.19
Business property relief
calculation of tax, and 13.51–13.53
comparison of PETs and chargeable transfers 13.54
conditions
not an investment business 13.10–13.16
ownership period 13.9
crops of grass 13.14
double dipping, and 15.24
estate on death, and 5.3
estate planning, and 15.23–15.29
excepted assets 13.22–13.23
exemptions and exceptions, and 11.13
gifts with reservation, and 7.23
holiday lettings 13.15
inter-company loans 13.13
'interest in a business' 13.1–13.2
landed estates 13.12
lifetime planning 14.5–14.6
limited liability partnerships, and 13.3
loss of 13.50
'mere assets', and 13.2

Business property relief – *contd*
net value 13.21
'not an investment business'
background 13.10
cases concerning lettings 13.11
crops of grass 13.14
holiday lettings 13.15
inter-company loans 13.13
landed estates 13.12
small company group 13.16
ownership period 13.9
potentially-exempt transfers, and 13.54
quoted shares in a company 13.5
rate 13.8
relevant property trusts, and
acquisition of relievable property 10.65
clawback 10.64
control 10.61
effect at commencement 10.60
reduction in rate of tax 10.63
reduction in tax charge 10.62
scope
'interest in a business' 13.1–13.2
limited liability partnerships 13.3
'mere assets' 13.2
quoted shares in a company 13.5
rate of relief 13.8
shares in a company 13.4–13.5
trading assets 13.6–13.7
settled gifts, and 7.23
shares in a company
generally 13.4–13.5
valuation 13.18–13.20
small company group 13.16
trading assets 13.6–13.7
transfer on death, and 5.30
unincorporated business, and 13.1–13.3
unquoted shares in a company 13.4–13.5
valuation
net value 13.21
introduction 13.17
shares 13.18–13.20

C

Calculation of tax
lifetime transfers, and
'14-year backward shadow' 4.27

Calculation of tax – *contd*
generally 4.26
nil rate band 4.26
taper relief 4.28
transfer on death, and
death estate 5.23
double tax relief 5.27
general 5.21
lifetime transfers 5.22
quick succession relief 5.26
transferable nil rate band 5.24–5.25
Capital gains tax
relevant property trusts, and 10.4
Capital transfer tax
generally 1.1
Care fees
transferable nil rate band, and 3.34
Cash options
estate on death, and 5.5
'Character appropriate'
Antrobus decision 13.33
generally 13.31–13.32
Golding decision 13.35
McKenna decision 13.34
Chargeable transfers
death, on 1.12
generally 1.3
lifetime transfers, and
generally 4.16–4.18
introduction 1.11
reporting 4.29
relevant property trusts, and 10.2
Charitable gifts
accounts and returns, and 8.19
estate on death, and 5.5
estate planning, and 15.30–15.33
exempt property, and 1.20
generally 11.18–11.19
gifts with reservation, and 7.25
lifetime transfers, and 4.3
Chattel gifts
gifts with reservation, and 7.4
Child Trust Fund
generally 14.2–14.3
Civil partners, transfers between
accounts and returns, and 8.19
aged 18-to-25 trusts 15.21
bereaved minors trusts 15.20
estate on death, and 5.5
estate planning, and
Civil partners, transfers between – *contd*
aged 18-to-25 trusts 15.21
background 15.14–15.15
bereaved minors trusts 15.20
counteraction to perceived abuse 15.16–15.18
life interest trusts 15.22
'wait and see' charge 15.19
exempt property, and 1.20
generally 11.16–11.17
gifts with reservation, and
Eversden schemes 7.9
generally 7.25
life interest trusts 15.22
lifetime transfers, and 4.3
transferable nil rate band 8.20
Civil partnerships
exemption 11.16–11.17
Clawback of nil rate band
alternatively secured pension funds 3.14–3.15
clearance certificates 3.16
introduction 3.11
penalties 3.17–3.18
second death, after 3.13
surviving spouse still alive, whilst 3.12
valuations 3.19
Clearance certificates
transferable nil rate band, and 3.16
Close companies
alterations of capital, and 1.29
lifetime transfers, and
generally 4.16
valuation 4.21
transfers of value, and 1.27–1.28
Clubs
gifts as exempt property, and 1.20
Cohabiting couple
transferable nil rate band, and 3.32
Commorientes
transfer on death, and 5.7–5.8
Compliance
acceptance of property in lieu 8.36
accounts
introduction 8.2
lifetime transfers 8.4
annuities 8.23
appeals
'basic' appeal 8.60

Compliance – *contd*
categories 8.58
'complex' appeal 8.62
costs 8.65
'default paper' model 8.59
generally 8.64
internal reviews, and 8.63
overview 8.66
'standard' appeal 8.61
bare trusts 8.16
charitable gifts 8.19
costs 8.65
death, and 5.43
determinations
form of notice 8.57–8.58
procedure 8.56
development value of land 8.22
direct payment scheme 8.35
disclosure of tax avoidance schemes (DOTAS) 8.37
estimates 8.15
excepted estates and settlements
bare trusts 8.16
charitable gifts 8.19
small estates 8.18
small foreign estates 8.21
spouse exemption 8.19
transferable nil rate band 8.20
transfers on death 8.17–8.21
excepted settlements 8.8
excepted terminations 8.7
excepted transfers
generally 8.6
introduction 8.5
exempt transfers 8.7
fixed-value fund 8.7
gifts out of income 8.12–8.13
IHT on death, and 5.43
incidence of tax 8.1
Inland Revenue charge 8.33
instalment payments
generally 8.29
interest 8.31
loss of option 8.32
section 228 shares 8.30
interest
generally 8.49
instalment payments 8.31
internal reviews, and 8.63
joint property 8.24

Compliance – *contd*
liability for tax 8.1
lifetime transfers
accounts 8.3
due date 8.28
payment of tax 8.26–8.28
reporting after death 8.11
nil rate band 8.7
normal expenditure out of income 8.12–8.13
payment of tax
acceptance of property in lieu 8.36
death, on 8.34
direct payment scheme 8.35
Inland Revenue charge 8.33
instalments, by 8.29–8.32
introduction 8.25
lifetime transfers 8.26–8.28
penalties
blaming the adviser, and 8.51
degrees of culpability 8.39
disclosure, and 8.42
failure to file 8.46
incorrect returns 8.47–8.48
introduction 8.38
late filing 8.53
late payment 8.52
levels 8.40–8.41
mitigation of 30% penalties 8.43
mitigation of 70% penalties 8.44
mitigation of 100% penalties 8.45
new approach 8.38
reductions for disclosure 8.42
suspension 8.50
personal effects 8.14
potentially exempt transfers 8.4
record keeping 8.55
returns
estimates 8.15
gifts out of income 8.12–8.13
introduction 8.2
lifetime transfers 8.11
normal expenditure out of income 8.12–8.13
personal effects 8.14
potentially exempt transfers 8.4
transfers on death 8.4
small estates 8.18
small foreign estates 8.21
small transfers 8.7

Compliance – *contd*
spouse exemption 8.19
suspension of penalties 8.50
time limits for HMRC assessments 8.54
transferable nil rate band 8.20
transfers on death
charitable gifts 8.19
generally 8.17–8.21
payment of tax 8.34
returns 8.4
small estates 8.18
small foreign estates 8.21
spouse exemption 8.19
transferable nil rate band 8.20
variable value funds 8.7
Conditionally exempt transfers
lifetime transfers, and 4.3
Consideration of marriage, gifts in
estate on death, and 5.4
exempt property, and 1.20
gifts with reservation, and 7.25
lifetime transfers, and 4.3
Constables
estate on death, and 5.5
generally 11.26
introduction 11.5
Consumer Prices Index (CPI)
calculating IHT, and 4.26
Costs
determinations and appeals, and 8.65
Crops of grass
business property relief, and 13.14
Cumulation
generally 1.4–1.5

D

De minimis exceptions
gifts with reservation, and 7.28
pre-owned assets charge, and 17.25–17.26
Death, IHT on
accounts and returns, and
estimates 8.15
generally 8.10
normal expenditure out of income 8.12–8.13
personal effects 8.14
reporting lifetime transfers after death 8.11
Death, IHT on – *contd*
agricultural property relief, and
chargeable and exempt estate 5.30
estate planning 15.23–15.29
allocation of burden of tax 5.38–5.39
asset valuations
generally 5.19
related property 5.20
business property relief, and
chargeable and exempt estate 5.30
estate planning 15.23–15.29
calculation of tax
death estate 5.23
double tax relief 5.27
general 5.21
lifetime transfers 5.22
quick succession relief 5.26
transferable nil rate band 5.24–5.25
chargeable and exempt estate
agricultural property relief, and 5.30
allocation of burden of tax 5.38–5.39
business property relief, and 5.30
construing wills 5.42
division of residuary estate between exempt and chargeable gifts 5.40–5.41
grossing up 5.32–5.37
introduction 5.28
partly exempt gifts 5.31
terminology 5.29
chargeable transfers, and 1.12
charitable gifts 15.30–15.33
commorientes 5.7–5.8
compliance 5.43
constables
generally 11.26
introduction 11.5
construing wills 5.42
death on active service
generally 11.26
introduction 11.5
'debt or charge' scheme
background 15.4
choice of trustees 15.9
existing wills, and 15.7
future reform 15.5–15.6
index-linking 15.11–15.12
interest 15.11–15.12
liquidity 15.10

Death, IHT on – *contd*
procedural difficulties 15.8
transferable nil rate band, and 3.1–3.4
trustees 15.9
decorations for valour or gallant conduct
generally 11.27
introduction 11.5
deferral of tax 15.14–15.22
division of residuary estate between exempt and chargeable gifts 5.40–5.41
double tax relief 5.27
emergency personnel
generally 11.26
introduction 11.5
estate on death
calculation of tax, and 5.23
commorientes 5.7–5.8
exemptions and exclusions 5.4–5.5
general 5.2–5.3
survivorship 5.7–5.8
woodlands relief 5.6
estate planning
agricultural property relief 15.23–15.29
business property relief 15.23–15.29
charitable gifts 15.30–15.33
deferral of tax 15.14–15.22
EU Succession Regulation 650/2012, and 15.1–15.2
heritage relief 15.34–15.38
nil rate band 15.3–15.12
policy trusts 15.39
post-death variations 15.40–15.53
spouse exemption 15.14–15.22
woodlands relief 15.25–15.26
EU Succession Regulation 650/2012, and
generally 15.1
governing law 15.2
exemptions and exclusions
charitable gifts 15.30–15.33
death on active service 11.26
decorations for valour or gallant conduct 11.27
generally 5.4–5.5
heritage relief 15.34–15.38
summary 11.5

Death, IHT on – *contd*
war compensation 11.28
general 5.2–5.3
gifts out of income 8.12–8.13
grossing up
double 5.36–5.37
introduction 5.32
single 5.33–5.35
heritage relief 15.34–15.38
introduction 5.1
liabilities
amount 5.13–5.18
funeral expenses 5.16
general 5.9–5.11
guarantee debts 5.12
Schedule IHT419 5.18
valuation 5.13–5.18
nil rate band discretionary trust
debt or charge scheme 15.4–15.12
generally 15.3
partly exempt gifts 5.31
police constables
generally 11.26
introduction 11.5
policy trusts 15.39
post-death variations
abuse, and 15.44
alternative relief 15.49–15.51
child beneficiaries 15.41
disclaimers 15.45
formalities 15.46
further variations, and 15.43
Glowacki case 15.48
introduction 15.40
post-22 March 2006 discretionary trusts 15.52–15.53
posthumous severance 15.42
statement of variation 15.47
quick succession relief 5.26
rates of tax, and 1.6
residence nil rate band 15.13
spouse exemption 15.14–15.22
survivorship 5.7–5.8
transferable nil rate band 5.24–5.25
war compensation 11.28
woodlands relief
estate planning 15.25–15.26
generally 5.6
Death on active service
estate on death, and 5.5

Death on active service – *contd*
generally 11.26
introduction 11.5
'Debt or charge' scheme
background 15.4
choice of trustees 15.9
existing wills, and 15.7
family home, and 16.48–16.53
future reform 15.5–15.6
index-linking 15.11–15.12
interest 15.11–15.12
liquidity 15.10
practical issues
choice of trustees 15.9
index-linking 15.11–15.12
liquidity 15.10
trustees 15.9
procedural difficulties 15.8
transferable nil rate band, and 3.1–3.4
trustees 15.9
Debts
valuation of assets, and 6.32
Decorations for valour or gallant conduct
excluded property, and 1.13
generally 11.27
introduction 11.5
Deeds of partition
generally 15.51
Deeds of variation
see **Post-death variations**
Deemed domicile
generally 2.10–2.11
Deemed PETs
See also **Potentially exempt transfers**
age 18-to-25 trusts 4.12
from 22 March 2006 4.12–4.13
introduction 4.10
prior to 22 March 2006 4.11
transitional serial interest 4.12
Determinations
form of notice 8.57–8.58
procedure 8.56
Development value of land
accounts and returns, and 8.22
valuation of assets, and 6.26–6.27
Diplomatic agents, property owned by
excluded property, and 11.38
Direct payment scheme
payment of tax, and 8.35
Disabled person's interest
see also **Disabled persons' trusts**
definition 14.13
estate on death, and 5.2
introduction 14.12
Disabled persons' trusts
addition to existing DPI's on or after April 2013 14.17
capital requirements 14.18
capital gains tax treatment 14.19
deemed potentially exempt transfers, and 4.8
'disabled persons' interest' 14.13
discretionary trusts, and 14.13
FA 2006 changes 14.14
income requirements 14.18
income tax treatment 14.19
interest in possession 14.16
introduction 14.12
new DPI's on or after April 2013 14.17
relevant property trusts, and 10.5
self-settlement 14.15
tax treatment 14.19
Disclosure
penalties, and 8.42
Disclosure of tax avoidance schemes (DOTAS)
generally 8.37
lifetime planning 14.34
Discounted gift schemes
protected gifts, and 14.29
Discretionary trusts
accumulation and maintenance trusts
generally 10.5
legislative changes 10.5
migration to new regime 10.24–10.25
acquisition of relievable property 10.65
age 18-to-25 trusts
chargeable amount 10.11
conditions 10.8
generally 10.7
introduction 10.5
notional transfer 10.14
problem areas 10.9
relevant fraction 10.12
settlement rate 10.13
tax charge 10.10
background 10.1

Discretionary trusts – *contd*
bereaved minors trusts
conditions 10.6
generally 10.6
introduction 10.5
problem areas 10.9
capital gains tax, and 10.4
chargeable transfers, and 10.2
clawback 10.64
control 10.61
deemed potentially exempt transfers, and 4.16
disabled trusts 10.5
effluxion of time, and 10.3
entry charge
introduction 10.16
migration from old regime 10.23–10.25
simple cases 10.17–10.22
exit charge
'appropriate fraction' 10.37
'effective rate' 10.36
'Frankland' trap 10.26
general considerations 10.26–10.27
'hypothetical transfer' 10.28–10.35
introduction 10.16
tax charge 10.37
family home, and
generally 16.33
points to note 16.36–16.41
Statement of Practice 16.34–16.35
'Frankland' trap 10.26
identifying the taxable entity 10.2
IPDI trusts 10.5
legislative background 10.1
letter of wishes, and
generally 10.71
introduction 10.3
life interest trusts 10.15
operation 10.3
periodic charge
additions to fund 10.50
'effective rate' 10.56
distributions from trust 10.54–10.55
failed PETs 10.53
general considerations 10.38–10.39
'hypothetical transfer' 10.40–10.48
later anniversaries, and 10.59
other non-relevant property funds within trust 10.42

Discretionary trusts – *contd*
previous transfers 10.49–10.53
related settlements 10.43–10.48
tax charge 10.57–10.58
transfer of value 10.41
property reliefs, and
acquisition of relievable property 10.65
clawback 10.64
control 10.61
effect at commencement 10.60
reduction in rate of tax 10.63
reduction in tax charge 10.62
proportionate charge
'appropriate fraction' 10.37
'effective rate' 10.36
'Frankland' trap 10.26
general considerations 10.26–10.27
'hypothetical transfer' 10.28–10.35
tax charge 10.37
reduction in rate of tax 10.63
reduction in tax charge 10.62
special charge
application 10.70
background 10.66
rate 10.67–10.68
variations on rate 10.69
ten-year charge
additions to fund 10.50
'effective rate' 10.56
distributions from trust 10.54–10.55
failed PETs 10.53
general considerations 10.38–10.39
'hypothetical transfer' 10.40–10.48
later anniversaries, and 10.59
other non-relevant property funds within trust 10.42
previous transfers 10.49–10.53
related settlements 10.43–10.48
tax charge 10.57–10.58
transfer of value 10.41
termination 10.3
transfer into trust, and
migration from old regime 10.23–10.25
simple cases 10.17–10.22
types 10.1–10.15
Dispositions for maintenance of family
generally 11.12
introduction 11.3

Domicile
background 2.1
choice, of 2.4
deemed
exceptions 2.14
'formerly domiciled resident rule' 2.13
generally 2.10–2.11
'17 out of 20 rule' 2.12
dependence, of 2.5
elective 2.6–2.7
'15 out of 20 rule' 2.10–2.11
'formerly domiciled resident rule' 2.13
general law, under 2.2
introduction 2.1
long-term residence 2.10–2.11
origin, of 2.3
pre-owned assets charge, and 17.23
reform proposals
'15 out of 20 rule' 2.10–2.11
'formerly domiciled resident rule' 2.13
long-term residence 2.10–2.11
'17 out of 20 rule' 2.12
statutory residence text 2.2
'3 year rule' 2.9
DOTAS
generally 8.37
lifetime planning 14.34
Double charges relief
generally 12.23
Double dipping
generally 15.24
Double tax agreements
domicile, and 2.9
generally 12.21
Double taxation relief
double taxation agreements 12.21
generally 12.19–12.20
gifts with reservation, and 7.38–7.39
introduction 1.24
transfer on death, and 5.27
Treaty relief 1.25
unilateral relief 1.26, 12.22
'Double trust' arrangements
family home, and 16.10–16.11
pre-owned assets, and 17.1
Downsizing
nil-rate band, and
'downsizing addition' 16.73–16.74
Downsizing – *contd*
introduction 16.70
less valuable residence in death estate 16.71
lost relievable amount 16.75–16.76
no residence in death estate 16.72
other points 16.77
Duty of care
family home, and 16.4–16.5

E

Effluxion of time
relevant property trusts, and 10.3
18-to-25 trusts
See also **Bereaved minors trusts**
See also **Relevant property trusts**
chargeable amount 10.11
conditions 10.8
deemed potentially exempt transfers, and 4.12
estate planning, and 15.21
generally 10.7
interest in possession trusts, and 9.31
introduction 10.5
notional transfer 10.14
post-death variations, and 15.52–15.53
problem areas 10.9
relevant fraction 10.12
settlement rate 10.13
spouse exemption, and 15.21
tax charge 10.10
Elective domicile
generally 2.6–2.7
Emergency personnel
estate on death, and 5.5
generally 11.26
introduction 11.5
Employee trusts
exempt property, and 1.20
generally 11.24–11.25
gifts with reservation, and 7.25
lifetime transfers, and 4.3
Enterprise Investment Scheme (EIS)
lifetime planning, and 14.7
Entry charge
See also **Relevant property trusts**
introduction 10.16
migration from old regime 10.23–10.25
simple cases 10.17–10.22

Equity release
commercial sale 16.17–16.18
introduction 16.14
loan or mortgage 16.15
pre-owned assets charge, and 17.24
'trading down' 16.16
Estate agency fees
liabilities on death, and 5.17
'Estate concept'
valuation of assets, and 6.5
Estate duty
generally 1.1
Estate on death
calculation of tax, and 5.23
commorientes 5.7–5.8
exemptions and exclusions 5.4–5.5
general 5.2–5.3
survivorship 5.7–5.8
woodlands relief 5.6
Estate planning
aged 18-to-25 trusts 15.21
agricultural property relief 15.23–15.29
bereaved minors trusts 15.20
business property relief 15.23–15.29
charitable gifts 15.30–15.33
'debt or charge' scheme
background 15.4
choice of trustees 15.9
current use 15.5
existing wills, and 15.7
future reform 15.5–15.6
index-linking 15.11–15.12
interest 15.11–15.12
liquidity 15.10
procedural difficulties 15.8
use 15.5
deferral of tax
aged 18-to-25 trusts 15.21
background 15.14–15.15
bereaved minors trusts 15.20
counteraction to perceived abuse 15.16–15.18
life interest trusts 15.22
'wait and see' charge 15.19
EU Succession Regulation 650/2012, and
generally 15.1
governing law 15.2
family home, and
Estate planning – *contd*
introduction 16.27
joint ownership 16.43–16.53
nil rate band 16.28–16.29
ownership by first spouse to die 16.30–16.41
heritage relief 15.34–15.38
life interest trusts 15.22
nil rate band discretionary trust
debt or charge scheme 15.4–15.12
generally 15.3
policy trusts 15.39
post-death variations
abuse, and 15.44
alternative relief 15.49–15.51
child beneficiaries 15.41
disclaimers 15.45
formalities 15.46
further variations, and 15.43
Glowacki case 15.48
introduction 15.40
post-22 March 2006 discretionary trusts 15.52–15.53
posthumous severance 15.42
statement of variation 15.47
spouse exemption
aged 18-to-25 trusts 15.21
background 15.14–15.15
bereaved minors trusts 15.20
counteraction to perceived abuse 15.16–15.18
life interest trusts 15.22
'wait and see' charge 15.19
woodlands relief 15.25–15.26
Estimates
generally 8.15
EU Succession Regulation 650/2012
generally 15.1
governing law 15.2
'Eversden' schemes
family home, and 16.9
gifts with reservation, and 7.9
Excepted settlements
generally 8.8
Excepted terminations
generally 8.7
introduction 8.5
Excepted transfers
generally 8.6
introduction 8.5

Excluded property
authorised unit trust holdings 11.32
categories 11.29
decorations for valour 1.13
diplomatic agents, property owned by 11.38
foreign property 11.30
foreign works of art 11.37
generally 11.6
government securities 11.31
introduction 1.13
National Savings certificates and deposits 1.13
non-sterling bank accounts 11.36
OEIC holdings 11.32
overseas pensions 11.35
Premium bonds 1.13
property owned by persons domiciled in Channel Islands or Isle of Man 11.33
reversionary interests 11.39–11.40
settled property
generally 1.14
introduction 1.13
visiting forces 11.34
war savings certificates 1.13
Exempt transfers
generally 8.7
fixed value funds 8.7
fixed-value transfers 8.6
introduction 8.2
Exemptions and exceptions
See also Excluded property
accounts and returns, and
charitable gifts 8.19
small estates 8.18
small foreign estates 8.21
spouse exemption 8.19
transferable nil rate band 8.20
transfers on death 8.17–8.21
active service death
generally 11.26
introduction 11.5
agricultural property relief, and 11.13
allocation 11.13
annual exemption 11.7
business property relief, and 11.13
categories
death exemptions 11.5
Exemptions and exceptions – *contd*
dispositions which are not transfers of value 11.3
excluded property, and 11.6
'general' exemptions 11.4
introduction 11.1
lifetime exemptions 11.2
charitable gifts 11.18–11.19
civil partnership exemption 11.16–11.17
death exemptions
death on active service 11.26
decorations for valour or gallant conduct 11.27
generally 5.4–5.5
introduction 11.5
war compensation payments 11.28
decorations for valour or gallant conduct
generally 11.27
introduction 11.5
dispositions for maintenance of family
generally 11.12
introduction 11.3
dispositions which are not transfers of value
introduction 11.3
maintenance of family 11.12
employee trusts 11.24–11.25
excluded property, and 11.6
family maintenance 11.12
'general' exemptions
charitable gifts 11.18–11.19
civil partnership exemption 11.16–11.17
employee trusts 11.24–11.25
housing associations, gifts to 11.21
introduction 11.4
maintenance funds 11.23
national purposes, gifts for 11.22
political gifts 11.20
spouse exemption 11.16–11.17
summary 11.4
gifts with reservation, and
de minimis 7.28
full consideration 7.29–7.30
general 7.25–7.27
gifts made before 18 March 1986 7.24
infirmity provision 7.31

Exemptions and exceptions – *contd*
instruments of variation 7.32
non-UK assets of non-UK domiciliary 7.33–7.37
old age provision 7.31
historic buildings, maintenance funds for 11.23
housing associations, gifts to 11.21
infirmity provision 7.31
interaction with reliefs 11.13–11.15
introduction 11.1
lifetime transfers, and
allocation of exemptions 11.13–11.15
annual exemption 11.7
dispositions for maintenance of family 11.12
family maintenance 11.12
generally 4.2–4.4
interaction with reliefs 11.13–11.15
introduction 11.2
marriage gifts 11.11
normal expenditure out of income 11.9–11.10
small gifts 11.8
summary 11.2
wedding gifts 11.11
maintenance funds 11.23
marriage gifts 11.11
national heritage property 11.4
national purposes, gifts for 11.22
normal expenditure out of income 11.9–11.10
old age provision 7.31
political gifts 11.20
pre-owned assets charge, and
de minimis 17.25–17.26
equity release 17.24
foreign element 17.23
GWR rule apply 17.21–17.22
introduction 17.19
property in taxpayer's estate 17.20
reliefs, and 11.13–11.15
small gifts 11.8
spouse exemption 11.16–11.17
summary 1.20
transferable nil rate band 8.20
transfers of value, and 1.9
transfers on death, and
death on active service 11.26

Exemptions and exceptions – *contd*
decorations for valour or gallant conduct 11.27
generally 5.4–5.5
introduction 11.5
war compensation 11.28
wartime compensation payments
generally 11.28
introduction 11.5
wedding gifts 11.11
Exit charge
See also **Relevant property trusts**
'appropriate fraction' 10.37
'effective rate' 10.36
'Frankland' trap 10.26
general considerations 10.26–10.27
'hypothetical transfer' 10.28–10.35
tax charge 10.37
Extra statutory concessions
funeral expenses 5.16
wartime compensation payments 11.5

F

Failure to file
penalties, and 8.46
'Fall in value' relief
generally 12.12
Family home
advisers' duty of care 16.4–16.5
annual tax on enveloped dwellings 16.2–16.3
appointing an interest in possession 16.42
'debt or charge' schemes 16.48–16.53
discretionary trusts
generally 16.33
points to note 16.36–16.41
Statement of Practice 16.34–16.35
'double trust' arrangements 16.10–16.11
equity release
commercial sale 16.17–16.18
introduction 16.14
loan or mortgage 16.15
'trading down' 16.16
estate planning
introduction 16.27
joint ownership 16.43–16.53
nil rate band 16.28–16.29

Family home – *contd*
ownership by first spouse to die 16.30–16.41
'Eversden' schemes 16.9
gift of share of interest
change of circumstances 16.24–16.25
joint occupation 16.20–16.23
statutory settlements 16.26
gift of whole of interest 16.19
interest in possession
appointing 16.42
survivor, for 16.44–16.45
introduction 16.1–16.3
IOU schemes 16.10–16.11
joint ownership
'debt or charge' schemes 16.48–16.53
interest in possession for survivor 16.44–16.45
introduction 16.43
nil rate band discretionary trusts 16.46–16.47
notices of severance 16.12–16.13
'sham' trusts 16.54
lease carve-out schemes 16.8
life interest trust 16.31–16.32
'lifetime debt' arrangements 16.10–16.11
lifetime planning
equity release 16.14–16.18
gift of share 16.20–16.26
outright gift 16.19
nil rate band
discretionary trusts 16.46–16.47
downsizing, and 16.70–16.77
generally 16.28
residence 16.55–16.69
transferable 16.29
use 16.28–16.29
notices of severance 16.12–16.13
outright gift 16.19
ownership
first spouse to die, by 16.30–16.41
generally 16.12–16.13
ownership by first spouse to die
discretionary trust 16.33–16.41
generally 16.30
life interest trust 16.31–16.32
planning arrangements, and 16.6

Family home – *contd*
relevant property trusts
generally 16.33
points to note 16.36–16.41
Statement of Practice 16.34–16.35
residence nil rate band
allowance 16.66–16.67
amount 16.61
claims 16.68
conditional exemption 16.69
downsizing, and 16.70–16.77
eligibility 16.61
enhancement 16.57
generally 16.55–16.58
rates 16.57
tapered withdrawal 16.59–16.60
transferable allowance 16.66–16.67
reversionary lease schemes 16.7
'sham' trusts 16.54
tenancies in common
'debt or charge' schemes 16.48–16.53
interest in possession for survivor 16.44–16.45
introduction 16.43
nil rate band discretionary trusts 16.46–16.47
'sham' trusts 16.54
'trading down' 16.16
transferable nil rate bands 16.29
Family limited companies and partnerships
protected gifts without trusts, and 14.25
Family maintenance
exempt lifetime transfers, and 4.4
transfers of value, and 1.9
Farming
see **Agricultural property relief**
'15 out of 20 rule'
domicile, and 2.10–2.11
Fixed value funds
accounts and returns, and 8.7
Fixed-value transfers
accounts and returns, and 8.6
Flexible ISAs
generally 14.4
Flexible reversion trusts
protected gifts, and 14.30

Foreign currency bank accounts
estate on death, and 5.5
exempt property, and 11.36
Foreign property
excluded property, and
generally 11.30
introduction 1.13
interest in possession trusts, and 9.33–9.34
Foreign works of art
excluded property, and 11.37
'Formerly domiciled resident rule'
generally 2.13
'14-year backward shadow'
calculating IHT, and 4.27
Free estate
estate on death, and 5.2
Funds for historic buildings
exempt property, and 1.20
generally 11.23
gifts with reservation, and 7.25
lifetime transfers, and 4.3
Funeral expenses
liabilities at death, and 5.16

G

Gaming debts
estate on death, and 5.10
General anti-abuse rule (GAAR)
lifetime transfers, and 4.25
'General' exemptions
charitable gifts 11.18–11.19
civil partnership exemption 11.16–11.17
employee trusts 11.24–11.25
housing associations, gifts to 11.21
introduction 11.4
maintenance funds 11.23
national purposes, gifts for 11.22
political gifts 11.20
spouse exemption 11.16–11.17
summary 11.4
Gifts
exempt property, and 1.20
share of interest in family home, of
change of circumstances 16.24–16.25
joint occupation 16.20–16.23
statutory settlements 16.26
transfers of value, and 1.9
Gifts – *contd*
whole of interest in family home, of 16.19
Gifts out of income
accounts and returns, and 8.12–8.13
claims 8.12–8.13
estate on death, and 5.4
exempt property, and 1.20
generally 11.9–11.10
lifetime transfers, and 4.3
Gifts with reservation (GWR)
agricultural property relief 7.23
asset valuation, and 6.31
business property relief 7.23
chattel gifts 7.4
civil partner exemption, and
Eversden schemes 7.9
generally 7.25
de minimis exceptions 7.28
'delivery' 7.4
donors 7.4
double tax relief 7.38–7.39
effect of rules 7.7–7.8
entire exclusion condition 7.5
estate on death, and 5.3
Eversden schemes 7.9
exceptions and exclusions
de minimis 7.28
full consideration 7.29–7.30
general 7.25–7.27
gifts made before 18 March 1986 7.24
infirmity provision 7.31
instruments of variation 7.32
non-UK assets of non-UK domiciliary 7.33–7.37
old age provision 7.31
'gift' 7.6
gifts made before 18 March 1986 7.24
infirmity provision 7.31
Ingram schemes 7.11
insignificant benefit 7.5
instruments of variation 7.32
insurance policies 7.22
interest in possession trusts 7.19
interests in land rules
Ingram schemes 7.11
introduction 7.10
other issues 7.15

Gifts with reservation (GWR) – *contd*
reversionary lease schemes 7.13
share of interest in land 7.14
statutory rules 7.12
interest in possession trusts 7.19
introduction 7.1–7.2
lifetime transfers, and 4.22
non-UK assets of non-UK domiciliary 7.33–7.37
old age provision 7.31
pre-owned assets charge, and
generally 17.21–17.22
introduction 7.3
'property' 7.6
relevant period 7.5
reversionary lease schemes 7.13
scope of rules 7.4–7.6
settled gifts, and
agricultural property relief 7.23
business property relief 7.23
insurance policies 7.22
interest in possession trusts 7.19
introduction 7.18
settlor as trustee 7.21
tracing 7.20
share of interest in land 7.14
'shearing' arrangements 7.40
spouse exemption, and
Eversden schemes 7.9
generally 7.25
tracing rules
generally 7.16–7.17
settled gifts 7.20
valuation of assets, and 6.31
Governing law
EU Succession Regulation 650/2012, and 15.2
Government securities
generally 11.31
introduction 1.13
Grossing up
double 5.36–5.37
generally 1.8
introduction 5.32
single 5.33–5.35
Guarantees
liabilities at death, and 5.12
valuation of liabilities, and 6.35
GWR rules
See **Gifts with reservation**

H

Help-to-buy ISAs
generally 14.4
Heritage property
estate planning, and 15.34–15.38
generally 12.27–12.30
transferable nil rate band, and 3.11
Historic buildings, funds for
exempt property, and 1.20
generally 11.23
gifts with reservation, and 7.25
lifetime transfers, and 4.3
HMRC toolkits
IHT compliance 5.43
Holiday lettings
business property relief, and 13.15
Home
advisers' duty of care 16.4–16.5
annual tax on enveloped dwellings 16.2–16.3
'debt or charge' schemes 16.48–16.53
discretionary trusts
generally 16.33
points to note 16.36–16.41
Statement of Practice 16.34–16.35
'double trust' arrangements 16.10–16.11
equity release
commercial sale 16.17–16.18
introduction 16.14
loan or mortgage 16.15
'trading down' 16.16
estate planning
introduction 16.27
joint ownership 16.43–16.53
nil rate band 16.28–16.29
ownership by first spouse to die 16.30–16.41
'Eversden' schemes 16.9
gift of share of interest
change of circumstances 16.24–16.25
joint occupation 16.20–16.23
statutory settlements 16.26
gift of whole of interest 16.19
interest in possession
appointing 16.42
survivor, for 16.44–16.45
introduction 16.1–16.3
IOU schemes 16.10–16.11

Home – *contd*
joint ownership
'debt or charge' schemes 16.48–16.53
interest in possession for survivor 16.44–16.45
introduction 16.43
nil rate band discretionary trusts 16.46–16.47
notices of severance 16.12–16.13
'sham' trusts 16.54
lease carve-out schemes 16.8
life interest trust 16.31–16.32
'lifetime debt' arrangements 16.10–16.11
lifetime planning
equity release 16.14–16.18
gift of share 16.20–16.26
outright gift 16.19
nil rate band
discretionary trusts 16.46–16.47
downsizing, and 16.70–16.77
generally 16.28
residence 16.55–16.69
transferable 16.29
use 16.28–16.29
notices of severance 16.12–16.13
outright gift 16.19
ownership
first spouse to die, by 16.30–16.41
generally 16.12–16.13
ownership by first spouse to die
discretionary trust 16.33–16.41
generally 16.30
life interest trust 16.31–16.32
planning arrangements, and 16.6
relevant property trusts
generally 16.33
points to note 16.36–16.41
Statement of Practice 16.34–16.35
residence nil rate band
allowance 16.66–16.67
amount 16.61
claims 16.68
conditional exemption 16.69
downsizing, and 16.70–16.77
eligibility 16.61
enhancement 16.57
generally 16.55–16.58
rates 16.57

Home – *contd*
tapered withdrawal 16.59–16.60
transferable allowance 16.66–16.67
reversionary lease schemes 16.7
'sham' trusts 16.54
tenancies in common
'debt or charge' schemes 16.48–16.53
interest in possession for survivor 16.44–16.45
introduction 16.43
nil rate band discretionary trusts 16.46–16.47
'sham' trusts 16.54
'trading down' 16.16
transferable nil rate band 16.29
'Hope' value
accounts and returns, and 8.22
valuation of assets, and 6.26–6.27
Household goods
valuation of assets, and 6.33
Housing associations, gifts to
exempt property, and 1.20
generally 11.21
gifts with reservation, and 7.25
lifetime transfers, and 4.3

I

IHT100
generally 8.2
IHT400
generally 8.2
Immediate post-death interest (IPDI)
care fees, and 3.34
estate on death, and 5.2
generally 9.9
relevant property trusts, and 10.5
termination 9.20
transferable nil rate band, and
care fees 3.34
generally 3.36
Incidence of tax
generally 8.1
Incorrect returns
penalties, and 8.47–8.48
Index-linking
'debt or charge' scheme, and 15.11–15.12
joint ownership of family home, and 16.52

Individual savings accounts (ISAs)
generally 14.4
Infirmity, provision for
gifts with reservation, and 7.31
Ingram schemes
interests in land rules, and 7.11
Inheritance Tax Toolkit
IHT compliance, and 5.43
Inherited ISAs
generally 14.4
Inland Revenue charge
generally 8.33
Instalment payments
generally 8.29
interest 8.31
loss of option 8.32
section 228 shares 8.30
Instruments of variation
gifts with reservation, and 7.32
Insurance policies
interest in possession trusts, and
existing trusts 9.36
life policies 9.41
new trusts 9.39
pensions 9.40
transitional provisions 9.37–9.38
transitionally protected interests 9.36
settled gifts, and 7.22
Intangible property comprised in settlor
calculation 17.16
generally 17.12
Inter-company loans
business property relief, and 13.13
Inter-spouse transfers
exempt property, and 1.20
gifts with reservation, and 7.25
Interest
'debt or charge' scheme, and 15.11–15.12
generally 8.49
instalment payments 8.31
Interest in a business
business property relief, and 13.1–13.2
Interest in possession trusts
age 18-to-25 trusts, and 9.31
anti-avoidance 9.10
bereaved minors trusts, and 9.31
burden of tax, and 9.42
Interest in possession trusts – *contd*
case law developments 9.3–9.5
definition 9.5
disposal
exceptions from charge 9.12
general rule 9.11
estate on death, and 5.2
excluded property trusts
foreign assets 9.33–9.34
loss of status 9.35
reversionary interests 9.32
family home, and
appointing 16.42
survivor, for 16.44–16.45
gifts with reservation, and 7.19
immediate post-death interests (IPDI)
generally 9.9
termination 9.20
incidence of tax 9.42
insurance policy trusts
existing trusts 9.36
life policies 9.41
new trusts 9.39
pensions 9.40
transitional provisions 9.37–9.38
transitionally protected interests 9.36
introduction
case law developments 9.3–9.5
old law 9.1–9.2
Statement of Practice 9.6
statutory changes 9.7–9.10
life policies 9.41
lifetime transfers, and 4.14
offshore trusts 9.26
old law 9.1–9.2
pensions 9.40
policy trusts 9.28–9.30
pre-owned assets, and 17.1
protected gifts, and 14.26
reversionary and purchased interests
changes to tax treatment of IIP 9.25
general rule 9.22
offshore trusts 9.26
purchase of interests in trusts 9.24
rule in *Melville v IRC* 9.23
s 5(1B), under 4.14
Statement of Practice (10/79) 9.6
statutory changes
background 9.7

Interest in possession trusts
outline 9.8–9.10
termination
anti-avoidance 9.16
exceptions from charge 9.21
immediate post death interests, of 9.20
law from 22 March 2006 9.19
maintenance funds 9.18
old law 9.13–9.14
revertor to settlor 9.15
use of annual exemption 9.17
transfers on death, and 5.2
transitional provisions 9.27–9.31
transitional serial interests 9.27
transitionally protected interests 9.36
Interests in land rules
Ingram schemes 7.11
introduction 7.10
other issues 7.15
reversionary lease schemes 7.13
share of interest in land 7.14
statutory rules 7.1
Intestate estates
order of distribution 5.1
IOU schemes
family home, and 16.10–16.11
IPDI trusts
estate on death, and 5.2
generally 9.9
relevant property trusts, and 10.5
termination 9.20

J

Joint ownership of family home
'debt or charge' schemes 16.48–16.53
index-linked nil rate sums 16.52
interest in possession for survivor 16.44–16.45
introduction 16.43
nil rate band discretionary trusts 16.46–16.47
'sham' trusts 16.54
Joint property
accounts and returns, and 8.24
land
development value 6.26–6.27
discounts 6.28
generally 6.22–6.25
money accounts 6.21
Joint property – *contd*
valuation of assets, and
generally 6.20
land 6.22–6.28
money accounts 6.21
Junior ISAs
generally 14.2–14.3

L

Land
post-death relief, and 12.17–12.18
pre-owned assets charge, and
calculation 17.14
generally 17.3–17.6
valuation of assets, and
development value 6.26–6.27
discounts 6.28
generally 6.22–6.25
Landed estates
business property relief, and 13.12
Late filing
penalties, and 8.53
Late payment
penalties, and 8.52
Lease carve-out schemes
family home, and 16.8
pre-owned assets, and 17.1
Letter of wishes
See also **Relevant property trusts**
generally 10.71
introduction 10.3
Liabilities on death
amount 5.13–5.18
funeral expenses 5.16
general 5.9–5.11
guarantee debts 5.12
Schedule IHT419 5.18
valuation 5.13–5.18
Liability for tax
generally 8.1
Liability of individuals
generally 1.2
Life insurance policies
deemed potentially exempt transfers, and 4.5
interest in possession trusts, and 9.41
protected gifts, and 14.28
settled gifts, and 7.22
valuation of assets, and

Life insurance policies – *contd*
'back-to-back' arrangements 6.14–6.15
lifetime transfers 6.12
transfers on death 6.13
Life interest trusts
See also **Relevant property trusts**
estate planning, and 15.22
family home, and 16.31–16.32
generally 10.15
'Lifetime debt' arrangements
family home, and 16.10–16.11
pre-owned assets, and 17.1
Lifetime exemptions
allocation 11.13–11.15
annual exemption 11.7
dispositions for maintenance of family 11.12
family maintenance 11.12
generally 4.2–4.4
interaction with reliefs 11.13–11.15
introduction 11.2
marriage gifts 11.11
normal expenditure out of income 11.9–11.10
small gifts 11.8
summary 11.2
wedding gifts 11.11
Lifetime ISAs (LISA)
generally 14.4
Lifetime planning
accumulation and maintenance trusts 14.27
agricultural property relief 14.5–14.6
business property relief 14.5–14.6
Child Trust Fund 14.2–14.3
disabled trusts
government policy 14.12
requirements 14.13–14.14
self-settlement 14.15–14.18
disclosure of tax avoidance schemes (DOTAS) 14.34
discounted gift schemes 14.29
discretionary trusts 14.31–14.33
family home, and
equity release 16.14–16.18
gift of share 16.20–16.26
outright gift 16.19
family limited partnerships 14.25
flexible reversion trusts 14.30
Lifetime planning – *contd*
individual savings accounts (ISAs) 14.4
interest in possession trusts 14.26
life policy trusts 14.28
lifetime gifts into trusts 14.31–14.33
options 14.22–14.24
outright gifts
generally 14.8
subtle schemes 14.11
unwise gifts 14.9–14.10
pensions
children, for 14.21
grandchildren, for 14.20
policy trusts 14.28
post-22 March 2006 trusts 14.31–14.33
protected gifts
accumulation and maintenance trusts 14.27
disclosure of tax avoidance schemes 14.34
discounted gift schemes 14.29
flexible reversion trusts 14.30
interest in possession trusts 14.26
life policy trusts 14.28
options 14.22–14.24
pensions for children 14.21
pensions for grandchildren 14.20
policy trusts 14.28
post-22 March 2006 trusts 14.31–14.33
relevant property trusts 14.31–14.33
transitional serial interests 14.26
relevant property trusts 14.31–14.33
unwise gifts 14.9–14.10
use of reliefs 14.1
Lifetime transfers
'14-year backward shadow' 4.27
accounts and returns, and
excepted settlements 8.8
excepted terminations 8.7
excepted transfers 8.6
generally 8.4–8.5
reporting after death, and 8.11
trustees, and 8.9
accumulation and maintenance trusts 4.8
age 18-to-25 trusts 4.12
allocation of exemptions 11.13–11.15

Lifetime transfers – *contd*
annual exemption 11.7
associated operations 4.23–4.24
calculation of tax
'14-year backward shadow' 4.27
generally 4.26
nil rate band 4.26
taper relief 4.28
chargeable transfers
generally 4.16–4.18
introduction 1.11
reporting 4.29
close companies, by
generally 4.16
valuation 4.21
deemed PETs
age 18-to-25 trusts 4.12
from 22 March 2006 4.12–4.13
introduction 4.10
prior to 22 March 2006 4.11
transitional serial interest 4.12
disabled trusts, gifts to 4.8
discretionary trusts 4.16
dispositions for maintenance of family 11.12
dispositions which are not transfers of value
introduction 11.3
maintenance of family 11.12
due date for payment 8.28
excepted settlements 8.8
excepted terminations 8.7
excepted transfers 8.6
exemptions
allocation 11.13–11.15
annual exemption 11.7
dispositions for maintenance of family 11.12
family maintenance 11.12
generally 4.2–4.4
interaction with reliefs 11.13–11.15
introduction 11.2
marriage gifts 11.11
normal expenditure out of income 11.9–11.10
small gifts 11.8
summary 11.2
wedding gifts 11.11
family maintenance 11.12
gifts with reservation 4.22

Lifetime transfers – *contd*
interests in possession under s 5(1B) 4.14
introduction 4.1
life insurance polices, and 4.5
maintenance of family 11.12
marriage gifts 11.11
nil rate band 4.26
normal expenditure out of income 11.9–11.10
payment of tax 8.26–8.28
planning
agricultural property relief 14.5–14.6
business property relief 14.5–14.6
Child Trust Fund 14.2–14.3
disabled trusts 14.12–14.19
individual savings accounts (ISAs) 14.4
outright gifts 14.8–14.11
protected gifts 14.20–14.34
unwise gifts 14.9–14.10
use of reliefs 14.1
potentially exempt transfers
accumulation and maintenance trusts 4.8
deemed PETs 4.10–4.13
definition 4.5–4.8
disabled trusts, gifts to 4.8
from 22 March 2006 4.7
implications 4.15
interests in possession under s 5(1B) 4.14
introduction 4.1
life insurance polices, and 4.5
prior to 22 March 2006 4.6
purchased reversionary interests 4.9
scope 4.5–4.8
valuation 4.20
purchased reversionary interests 4.9
rates of tax
generally 4.26
introduction 1.6
relevant property trusts 4.16
reporting requirements
after death 8.11
generally 4.29
small gifts 11.8
taper relief 4.28
valuation

Lifetime transfers – *contd*
generally 4.19
PETS 4.20
transfers by close companies 4.21
wedding gifts 11.11
Limited liability partnerships
business property relief, and 13.3
Long-term residence
generally 2.10–2.11
'Loss to estate' principle
valuation of assets, and 6.4

M

Maintenance funds for historic buildings
exempt property, and 1.20
generally 11.23
gifts with reservation, and 7.25
lifetime transfers, and 4.3
Marriage gifts
estate on death, and 5.4
exempt property, and 1.20
generally 11.11
gifts with reservation, and 7.25
lifetime transfers, and 4.3
Medals for valour or gallant conduct
excluded property, and 1.14
Mitigation of penalties
30% 8.43
70% 8.44
100% 8.45
Multiple trusts
lifetime transfers, and 4.25

N

National heritage transfers
generally 11.4
introduction 4.3
National purposes, gifts for
exempt property, and 1.20
generally 11.22
gifts with reservation, and 7.25
lifetime transfers, and 4.3
National Savings Bank deposits
excluded property, and 1.13
National Savings Certificates
excluded property, and 1.13
Net value
business property relief, and 13.21
Nil rate band
see also **Transferable nil rate band**
accounts and returns, and 8.7
cumulation, and 1.4–1.5
debt or charge scheme
background 15.4
choice of trustees 15.9
current use 15.5
existing wills, and 15.7
future reform 15.5–15.6
index-linking 15.11–15.12
interest 15.11–15.12
liquidity 15.10
procedural difficulties 15.8
use 15.5
downsizing, and
'downsizing addition' 16.73–16.74
introduction 16.70
less valuable residence in death estate 16.71
lost relievable amount 16.75–16.76
no residence in death estate 16.72
other points 16.77
family home, and
discretionary trusts 16.46–16.47
downsizing, and 16.70–16.77
generally 16.28
residence 16.55–16.69
transferable 16.29
use 16.28–16.29
generally 15.3
residence
allowance 16.66–16.67
amount 16.61
claims 16.68
conditional exemption 16.69
downsizing, and 16.70–16.77
eligibility 16.61
enhancement 16.57
generally 16.55–16.58
rates 16.57
tapered withdrawal 16.59–16.60
transferable allowance 16.66–16.67
Non-domiciled individuals
gifts with reservation, and 7.33–7.37
liability 1.2
Non-natural persons (NNP)
annual tax on enveloped dwellings 16.2

Non-sterling bank accounts
generally 11.36
introduction 1.13
Non-UK assets of non-UK domiciliary
gifts with reservation, and 7.33–7.37
Non-UK domiciled individuals
UK residential property, and
generally 1.15–1.17
IHT charge 1.18–1.19
Normal expenditure out of income
accounts and returns, and 8.12–8.13
claims 8.12–8.13
estate on death, and 5.4
exempt property, and 1.20
generally 11.9–11.10
lifetime transfers, and 4.3
Notices of severance
family home, and 16.12–16.13

O

Offshore trusts
interest in possession trusts, and 9.26
Old age, provision for
gifts with reservation, and 7.31
Online bereavement questionnaire
IHT compliance, and 5.43
Open-ended investment company investments
generally 11.32
introduction 1.13
Open market value
'estate concept' 6.5
generally 6.1
HMRC's approach 6.2–6.3
'loss to estate' principle 6.4
Options
protected gifts, and 14.22–14.24
Outright gifts
family home, and 16.19
generally 14.8
subtle schemes 14.11
unwise gifts 14.9–14.10
Overseas pensions
estate on death, and 5.5
excluded property, and 11.35
Ownership of family home
first spouse to die, by 16.30–16.41
discretionary trust 16.33–16.41
generally 16.30
Ownership of family home – *contd*
life interest trust 16.31–16.32
generally 16.12–16.13

P

Partly exempt gifts
transfer on death, and 5.31
Payment of tax
acceptance of property in lieu 8.36
death, on 8.34
direct payment scheme 8.35
Inland Revenue charge 8.33
instalments, by
generally 8.29
interest 8.31
loss of option 8.32
section 228 shares 8.30
introduction 8.25
lifetime transfers 8.26–8.28
Penalties
blaming the adviser, and 8.51
degrees of culpability 8.39
disclosure, and 8.42
failure to file 8.46
incorrect returns 8.47–8.48
introduction 8.38
late filing 8.53
late payment 8.52
level
generally 8.40
strengthening deterrents for offshore avoidance 8.41
mitigation of 30% penalties 8.43
mitigation of 70% penalties 8.44
mitigation of 100% penalties 8.45
new approach 8.38
reductions for disclosure 8.42
suspension 8.50
transferable nil rate band, and 3.17–3.18
Pension schemes
children, for 14.21
estate on death, and 5.5
grandchildren, for 14.20
interest in possession trusts, and 9.40
Periodic charge
See also **Relevant property trusts**
additions to fund 10.50
'effective rate' 10.56
distributions from trust 10.54–10.55

Periodic charge – *contd*
failed PETs 10.53
general considerations 10.38–10.39
'hypothetical transfer' 10.40–10.48
later anniversaries, and 10.59
other non-relevant property funds within trust 10.42
previous transfers 10.49–10.53
related settlements 10.43–10.48
tax charge 10.57–10.58
transfer of value 10.41
Personal effects
accounts and returns, and 8.14
valuation of assets, and 6.33
Personal pension schemes
estate on death, and 5.5
exempt property, and 1.20
'Pilot' trusts
lifetime transfers, and 4.25
Planning
see also **Estate planning**
transferable nil rate band, and
agricultural property 3.33
business property 3.33
care fees 3.34
cohabiting couple 3.32
earlier marriages or civil partnerships 3.31
use of nil rate band on first death 3.24–3.30
Police constables
estate on death, and 5.5
generally 11.26
introduction 11.5
Policy trusts
estate planning, and 15.39
interest in possession trusts, and 9.28–9.30
protected gifts, and 14.28
Political gifts
exempt property, and 1.20
generally 11.20
gifts with reservation, and 7.25
lifetime transfers, and 4.3
Post-death reliefs
land 12.17–12.18
shares 12.14–12.16
Post-death variations
abuse, and 15.44
alternative relief 15.49–15.51
Post-death variations – *contd*
child beneficiaries 15.41
deed of partition 15.51
disclaimers 15.45
formalities 15.46
further variations, and 15.43
Glowacki case 15.48
introduction 15.40
post-22 March 2006 discretionary trusts 15.52–15.53
posthumous severance 15.42
statement of variation 15.47
Potentially exempt transfers (PETs)
accounts and returns 8.4
accumulation and maintenance trusts 4.8
age 18-to-25 trusts, and 4.12
agricultural property relief, and 13.54
business property relief, and 13.54
deemed PETs
age 18-to-25 trusts 4.12
from 22 March 2006 4.12–4.13
introduction 4.10
prior to 22 March 2006 4.11
transitional serial interest 4.12
definition 4.5–4.8
disabled trusts, gifts to 4.8
failed PETs
bringing into account 10.53
from 22 March 2006
generally 4.12–4.13
introduction 4.7
generally 1.10
implications 4.15
introduction 4.1
life insurance polices, and 4.5
periodic charge, and
bringing failed PETs into account 10.53
prior to 22 March 2006
generally 4.11
introduction 4.6
purchased reversionary interests 4.9
returns 8.4
scope 4.5–4.8
setting aside 12.13
transitional serial interest, and 4.12
valuation 4.20

Pre-owned assets charge
chattels, on
calculation 17.15
generally 17.7–17.11
de minimis exemption 17.25–17.26
domicile of taxpayer 17.23
equity release exemption 17.24
excluded transactions 17.18
exemptions
de minimis 17.25–17.26
equity release 17.24
foreign element 17.23
GWR rule apply 17.21–17.22
introduction 17.19
property in taxpayer's estate 17.20
family home, and 16.5
foreign element exemption 17.23
gifts with reservation, and
exemptions 17.21–17.22
generally 7.3
intangible property comprised in settlor, on
calculation 17.16
generally 17.12
introduction 17.1–17.2
land, on
calculation 17.14
generally 17.3–17.6
opting out 17.27–17.28
property in taxpayer's estate 17.20
remedial action to existing arrangements 17.29
residence of taxpayer 17.23
scope of legislation 17.13
valuation 17.17
Premium savings bonds
generally 1.13
introduction 1.13
Probate fees
liabilities on death, and 5.17
Professional fees
liabilities on death, and 5.17
Professional negligence
family home, and 16.4–16.5
Proportionate charge
See also **Relevant property trusts**
'appropriate fraction' 10.37
'effective rate' 10.36
'Frankland' trap 10.26
general considerations 10.26–10.27
Proportionate charge – *contd*
'hypothetical transfer' 10.28–10.35
tax charge 10.37
Protected gifts
accumulation and maintenance trusts 14.27
disclosure of tax avoidance schemes (DOTAS) 14.34
discounted gift schemes 14.29
interest in possession trusts 14.26
life policy trusts 14.28
options 14.22–14.24
pensions for children 14.21
pensions for grandchildren 14.20
policy trusts 14.28
post-22 March 2006 trusts 14.31–14.33
relevant property trusts 14.31–14.33
transitional serial interests 14.26
Public benefit, gifts for
exempt property, and 1.20
gifts with reservation, and 7.25
Purchased reversionary interests
generally 4.9

Q

Quick succession relief
generally 12.4–12.5
introduction 1.23
overview 12.1
transfer on death, and 5.26
Quoted shares and securities
business property relief, and 13.5
valuation of assets, and 6.16

R

Rates of tax
death 1.7
grossing-up 1.8
lifetime transfers 1.6
lifetime transfers, and
generally 4.26
introduction 1.6
transfer on death, and 1.6
Record keeping
generally 8.55
transferable nil rate band, and 3.21
Registered clubs
gifts as exempt property, and 1.20

Related property relief
generally 12.6–12.7
introduction 6.10
overview 12.1
Related property rule
application 6.7–6.9
'appropriate portion' 6.8
generally 6.6
introduction 5.20
relief 6.10
Relevant property trusts
accumulation and maintenance trusts
generally 10.5
legislative changes 10.5
migration to new regime 10.24–10.25
age 18-to-25 trusts
chargeable amount 10.11
conditions 10.8
generally 10.7
introduction 10.5
notional transfer 10.14
problem areas 10.9
relevant fraction 10.12
settlement rate 10.13
tax charge 10.10
background 10.1
bereaved minors trusts
conditions 10.6
generally 10.6
introduction 10.5
problem areas 10.9
capital gains tax, and 10.4
chargeable transfers, and 10.2
deemed potentially exempt transfers, and 4.16
disabled trusts 10.5
effluxion of time, and 10.3
entry charge
introduction 10.16
migration from old regime 10.23–10.25
simple cases 10.17–10.22
exit charge
'appropriate fraction' 10.37
'effective rate' 10.36
'Frankland' trap 10.26
general considerations 10.26–10.27
'hypothetical transfer' 10.28–10.35
introduction 10.16

Relevant property trusts – *contd*
tax charge 10.37
family home, and
generally 16.33
points to note 16.36–16.41
Statement of Practice 16.34–16.35
'Frankland' trap 10.26
identifying the taxable entity 10.2
IPDI trusts 10.5
legislative background 10.1
letter of wishes, and
generally 10.71
introduction 10.3
life interest trusts 10.15
operation 10.3
periodic charge
additions to fund 10.50
'effective rate' 10.56
distributions from trust 10.54–10.55
failed PETs 10.53
general considerations 10.38–10.39
'hypothetical transfer' 10.40–10.48
later anniversaries, and 10.59
other non-relevant property funds within trust 10.42
previous transfers 10.49–10.53
related settlements 10.43–10.48
tax charge 10.57–10.58
transfer of value 10.41
property reliefs, and
acquisition of relievable property 10.65
clawback 10.64
control 10.61
effect at commencement 10.60
reduction in rate of tax 10.63
reduction in tax charge 10.62
proportionate charge
'appropriate fraction' 10.37
'effective rate' 10.36
'Frankland' trap 10.26
general considerations 10.26–10.27
'hypothetical transfer' 10.28–10.35
tax charge 10.37
special charge
application 10.70
background 10.66
rate 10.67–10.68
variations on rate 10.69
ten-year charge

Relevant property trusts – *contd*
additions to fund 10.50
'effective rate' 10.56
distributions from trust 10.54–10.55
failed PETs 10.53
general considerations 10.38–10.39
'hypothetical transfer' 10.40–10.48
later anniversaries, and 10.59
other non-relevant property funds within trust 10.42
previous transfers 10.49–10.53
related settlements 10.43–10.48
tax charge 10.57–10.58
transfer of value 10.41
termination 10.3
transfer into trust, and
migration from old regime 10.23–10.25
simple cases 10.17–10.22
transferable nil rate band, and 3.38
types 10.1–10.15
Reliefs
agricultural property relief
and see **Agricultural property relief**
conditions 13.37–13.49
lifetime planning 14.5–14.6
loss of 13.50–13.53
scope 13.24–13.36
business property relief
and see **Business property relief**
conditions 13.9–13.16
excepted assets 13.22–13.23
lifetime planning 14.5–14.6
loss of 13.50–13.53
scope 13.1–13.8
valuation 13.17–13.21
Child Trust Fund 14.2–14.3
disabled persons' trusts
addition to existing DPI's on or after April 2013 14.17
capital requirements 14.18
capital gains tax treatment 14.19
'disabled persons' interest' 14.13
discretionary trusts, and 14.13
FA 2006 changes 14.14
income requirements 14.18
income tax treatment 14.19
interest in possession 14.16
introduction 14.12

Reliefs – *contd*
new DPI's on or after April 2013 14.17
self-settlement 14.15
tax treatment 14.19
double charges relief 12.23
double taxation relief
double taxation agreements 12.21
generally 12.19–12.20
introduction 1.24
Treaty relief 1.25
unilateral relief 1.26, 12.22
'fall in value' relief 12.12
gifts
outright gifts 14.8
protected gifts 14.20–14.35
unwise gifts 14.9–14.10
heritage property 12.27–12.30
individual savings accounts (ISAs) 14.4
introduction 12.1
land 12.17–12.18
lifetime planning
agricultural property relief 14.5–14.6
business property relief 14.5–14.6
Child Trust Fund 14.2–14.3
disabled trusts 14.12–14.19
individual savings accounts (ISAs) 14.4
outright gifts 14.8–14.11
protected gifts 14.20–14.35
unwise gifts 14.9–14.10
use of reliefs 14.1
outright gifts
generally 14.8
subtle schemes 14.11
unwise gifts 14.9–14.10
post-death reliefs
land 12.17–12.18
shares 12.14–12.16
protected gifts
accumulation and maintenance trusts 14.27
disclosure of tax avoidance schemes (DOTAS) 14.34
discounted gift schemes 14.29
interest in possession trusts 14.26
life policy trusts 14.28
options 14.22–14.24

Reliefs – *contd*
pensions for children 14.21
pensions for grandchildren 14.20
policy trusts 14.28
post-22 March 2006 trusts 14.31–14.33
relevant property trusts 14.31–14.33
transitional serial interests 14.26
quick succession relief
generally 12.4–12.5
introduction 1.23
overview 12.1
related property relief
generally 12.6–12.7
introduction 6.10
overview 12.1
setting aside PETs 12.13
shares 12.14–12.16
taper relief
generally 12.2–12.3
introduction 1.21–1.22
overview 12.1
transfers within seven years before death
'fall in value' relief 12.12
generally 12.8–12.10
setting aside PETs 12.13
wasting assets 12.11
wasting assets, and 12.11
woodlands relief
disposal of trees or underwood 12.25
generally 12.24
planning 12.26
Reporting requirements
lifetime transfers, and 4.29
Residence
See also **Domicile**
pre-owned assets charge, and 17.23
statutory test 2.2
Residence nil rate band
allowance 16.66–16.67
amount 16.61
background 3.42–3.43
claims 16.68
'closely inherited' 16.65
conditional exemption 16.69
death, and 15.13
downsizing, and
'downsizing addition' 16.73–16.74
Residence nil rate band – *contd*
introduction 16.70
less valuable residence in death estate 16.71
lost relievable amount 16.75–16.76
no residence in death estate 16.72
other points 16.77
eligibility 16.61
enhancement 16.57
generally 16.55–16.58
'inherited' 16.65
introduction
background 3.42–3.43
transferability 3.44–3.48
overview 15.13
qualifying residences 16.63–16.64
rates 16.57
tapered withdrawal 16.59–16.60
transferable allowance 3.44–3.48, 16.66–16.67
Retirement annuity contracts
estate on death, and 5.5
exempt property, and 1.20
Returns
death, on
estimates 8.15
generally 8.10
normal expenditure out of income 8.12–8.13
personal effects 8.14
reporting lifetime transfers after death 8.11
developments
compliance 8.3
forms 8.2
estimates 8.15
excepted settlements 8.8
excepted terminations
generally 8.7
introduction 8.5
excepted transfers
generally 8.6
introduction 8.5
exempt transfers 8.7
fixed value funds 8.7
fixed-value transfers 8.6
introduction 8.2
lifetime transfers, on
excepted settlements 8.8
excepted terminations 8.7

Returns – *contd*
excepted transfers 8.6
generally 8.4–8.5
reporting after death, and 8.11
trustees, and 8.9
nil rate band 8.7
normal expenditure out of income 8.12–8.13
personal effects 8.14
small transfers 8.7
trustees, and 8.9
uncertain value transfers 8.6
variable value funds 8.7
Reversionary interests
changes to tax treatment of IIP 9.25
excluded property, and
generally 11.39–11.40
introduction 1.13
general rule 9.22
offshore trusts 9.26
purchase of interests in trusts 9.24
rule in *Melville v IRC* 9.23
Reversionary lease schemes
family home, and 16.7
interests in land rules, and 7.13
pre-owned assets, and 17.1

S

Seed Enterprise Investment Scheme (EIS)
lifetime planning, and 14.7
Settled life policies
generally 10.17
Settled property
estate on death, and 5.2
excluded property, and
generally 1.14
introduction 1.13
gifts with reservation, and
agricultural property relief 7.23
business property relief 7.23
insurance policies 7.22
interest in possession trusts 7.19
introduction 7.18
settlor as trustee 7.21
tracing 7.20
interest in possession
and see **Interest in possession**
case law developments 9.3–9.5
disposal 9.11–9.12
Settled property – *contd*
excluded property trusts 9.32–9.35
insurance policy trusts 9.36–9.41
old law 9.1–9.2
purchased interests 9.22–9.26
reversionary interests 9.22–9.26
Statement of Practice 9.6
statutory changes 9.7–9.10
termination 9.13–9.21
transitional provisions 9.27–9.31
no interest in possession
exit charge 10.26–10.37
periodic charge 10.38–10.59
property reliefs, and 10.60–10.65
proportionate charge 10.26–10.37
special charge 10.66–10.70
ten-year charge 10.38–10.59
transfer into trust 10.17–10.25
types of relevant property trusts 10.1–10.15
trusts
interest in possession 9.1–9.42
non-interest in possession 10.1–10.71
valuation of assets, and 6.29
Settlors
settled gifts, and 7.21
Seven years before death, transfer within
'fall in value' relief 12.12
generally 12.8–12.10
setting aside PETs 12.13
wasting assets 12.11
'17 out of 20 rule'
domicile, and 2.12
'Sham' trusts
family home, and 16.54
Share transfers to employee trusts
exempt property, and 1.20
generally 11.24–11.25
gifts with reservation, and 7.25
lifetime transfers, and 4.3
Shares
post-death relief, and 12.14–12.16
Shares and Assets Valuations (SAV)
HMRC guidance 6.3
'Shearing' arrangements
gifts with reservation, and 7.40
Small company group
business property relief, and 13.16

Small estates
accounts and returns, and 8.18
Small foreign estates
accounts and returns, and 8.21
Small gifts
estate on death, and 5.4
exempt property, and 1.20
generally 11.8
gifts with reservation, and 7.25
lifetime transfers, and 4.3
Small transfers
accounts and returns, and 8.7
Special (s 70) charge
See also **Relevant property trusts**
application 10.70
background 10.66
rate 10.67–10.68
variations on rate 10.69
Spouse exemption
accounts and returns, and 8.19
estate on death, and 5.5
estate planning, and
aged 18-to-25 trusts 15.21
background 15.14–15.15
bereaved minors trusts 15.20
counteraction to perceived abuse 15.16–15.18
life interest trusts 15.22
'wait and see' charge 15.19
exempt property, and 1.20
generally 11.16–11.17
gifts with reservation, and
Eversden schemes 7.9
generally 7.25
lifetime transfers, and 4.3
transferable nil rate band 8.20, 3.35
Stamp duty land tax
residential properties, and 16.2
Statements of Practice
interest in possession trusts, and 9.6
Statutory residence test (SRT)
domicile, and 2.2
Succession Regulation 650/2012
generally 15.1
governing law 15.2
Superannuation funds
estate on death, and 5.5
Survivorship
commorientes, and 5.7–5.8

T

Taper relief
generally 12.2–12.3
introduction 1.21–1.22
lifetime transfers, and 4.28
overview 12.1
Tax agents
IHT compliance 5.43
Ten-year charge
See also **Relevant property trusts**
additions to fund 10.50
'effective rate' 10.56
distributions from trust 10.54–10.55
failed PETs 10.53
general considerations 10.38–10.39
'hypothetical transfer' 10.40–10.48
later anniversaries, and 10.59
other non-relevant property funds within trust 10.42
previous transfers 10.49–10.53
related settlements 10.43–10.48
tax charge 10.57–10.58
transfer of value 10.41
Tenancies in common
'debt or charge' schemes 16.48–16.53
interest in possession for survivor 16.44–16.45
introduction 16.43
nil rate band discretionary trusts 16.46–16.47
'sham' trusts 16.54
'3 year rule'
domicile, and 2.9
and see **Nil rate band**
cumulation, and 1.4–1.5
Toolkit
IHT compliance, and 5.43
Time limits
HMRC assessments, and 8.54
Tracing rules
generally 7.16–7.17
settled gifts 7.20
Trading assets
business property relief, and 13.6–13.7
'Trading down'
family home, and 16.16
Transferable nil rate bands
accidental use 3.37
agricultural property 3.33

Transferable nil rate bands – *contd*
alternative pension funds, and 3.14–3.15
background 3.1–3.4
business property 3.33
calculation of tax on transfer on death, and 5.24–5.25
calculation of unused nil rate band 3.6
care fees 3.34
clawback of nil rate band
alternative pension funds 3.14–3.15
clearance certificates 3.16
introduction 3.11
penalties 3.17–3.18
second death, after 3.13
surviving spouse still alive, whilst 3.12
valuations 3.19
clearance certificates 3.16
cohabiting couple 3.32
deaths before 25 July 1986, and 3.116
'debt or charge' schemes, and 3.1–3.4
documentation in support 3.22–3.23
earlier marriages or civil partnerships 3.31
excepted estates, and 8.20
family home, and 16.29
heritage assets 3.11
immediate post-death interest, and
care fees 3.34
generally 3.36
outline of rules 3.5
penalties 3.17–3.18
planning issues
agricultural property 3.33
business property 3.33
care fees 3.34
cohabiting couple 3.32
earlier marriages or civil partnerships 3.31
use of nil rate band on first death 3.24–3.30
record keeping 3.21
relevant property trusts, and 3.38
supporting documentation 3.22–3.23
surviving spouse exemption, and 3.35
trading down by surviving spouse 3.37
transfer claims 3.8–3.10
transfers on death, and 8.20
unexhausted ASP funds 3.14

Transferable nil rate bands – *contd*
use of nil rate band on first death 3.24–3.30
valuations 3.19
woodlands 3.11

Transfers of value
chargeable lifetime transfers 1.11
close companies, by 1.27–1.28
death, on 1.12
excluded property 1.13
generally 1.9
non-UK domicile and UK residential property
generally 1.15–1.17
IHT charge 1.18–1.19
potentially exempt transfers 1.10
settled property 1.14

Transfers on death
accounts and returns, and
charitable gifts 8.19
generally 8.17
small estates 8.18
small foreign estates 8.21
spouse exemption 8.19
agricultural property relief, and
chargeable and exempt estate 5.30
estate planning 15.23–15.29
allocation of burden of tax 5.38–5.39
asset valuations
generally 5.19
related property 5.20
business property relief, and
chargeable and exempt estate 5.30
estate planning 15.23–15.29
calculation of tax
death estate 5.23
double tax relief 5.27
general 5.21
lifetime transfers 5.22
quick succession relief 5.26
transferable nil rate band 5.24–5.25
chargeable and exempt estate
agricultural property relief, and 5.30
allocation of burden of tax 5.38–5.39
business property relief, and 5.30
construing wills 5.42
division of residuary estate between exempt and chargeable gifts 5.40–5.41

Transfers on death – *contd*
grossing up 5.32–5.37
introduction 5.28
partly exempt gifts 5.31
terminology 5.29
chargeable transfers, and 1.12
charitable gifts 15.30–15.33
commorientes 5.7–5.8
compliance 5.43
construing wills 5.42
death on active service
generally 11.26
introduction 11.5
'debt or charge' scheme
background 15.4
choice of trustees 15.9
current use 15.5
existing wills, and 15.7
future reform 15.5–15.6
index-linking 15.11–15.12
interest 15.11–15.12
liquidity 15.10
procedural difficulties 15.8
use 15.5
decorations for valour or gallant conduct
generally 11.27
introduction 11.5
deferral of tax 15.14–15.22
division of residuary estate between exempt and chargeable gifts 5.40–5.41
double tax relief 5.27
estate on death
calculation of tax, and 5.23
commorientes 5.7–5.8
exemptions and exclusions 5.4–5.5
general 5.2–5.3
survivorship 5.7–5.8
woodlands relief 5.6
estate planning
agricultural property relief 15.23–15.29
business property relief 15.23–15.29
charitable gifts 15.30–15.33
deferral of tax 15.14–15.22
EU Succession Regulation 650/2012, and 15.1–15.2
heritage relief 15.34–15.38
nil rate band 15.3–15.12

Transfers on death – *contd*
policy trusts 15.39
post-death variations 15.40–15.53
spouse exemption 15.14–15.22
woodlands relief 15.25–15.26
EU Succession Regulation 650/2012, and
generally 15.1
governing law 15.2
exemptions and exclusions
charitable gifts 15.30–15.33
death on active service 11.26
decorations for valour or gallant conduct 11.27
generally 5.4–5.5
heritage relief 15.34–15.38
summary 11.5
war compensation 11.28
general 5.2–5.3
grossing up
double 5.36–5.37
introduction 5.32
single 5.33–5.35
heritage relief 15.34–15.38
introduction 5.1
liabilities
amount 5.13–5.18
funeral expenses 5.16
general 5.9–5.11
guarantee debts 5.12
Schedule IHT419 5.18
valuation 5.13–5.18
nil rate band discretionary trust
debt or charge scheme 15.4–15.12
generally 15.3
partly exempt gifts 5.31
payment of tax 8.34
policy trusts 15.39
post-death variations
abuse, and 15.44
alternative relief 15.49–15.51
child beneficiaries 15.41
disclaimers 15.45
formalities 15.46
further variations, and 15.43
Glowacki case 15.48
introduction 15.40
post-22 March 2006 discretionary trusts 15.52–15.53
posthumous severance 15.42

Transfers on death – *contd*
statement of variation 15.47
quick succession relief 5.26
rates of tax, and 1.6
spouse exemption 15.14–15.22
survivorship 5.7–5.8
transferable nil rate band 5.24–5.25
war compensation 11.28
woodlands relief
estate planning 15.25–15.26
generally 5.6
Transfers within seven years before death
'fall in value' relief 12.12
generally 12.8–12.10
setting aside PETs 12.13
wasting assets 12.11
Transitional serial interests
deemed PETs, and 4.12
estate on death, and 5.2
generally 9.27
protected gifts, and 14.26
Transitionally protected interests
generally 9.36
Trustees
accounts and returns, and 8.9
Trusts
and see **Relevant property trusts**
accumulation and maintenance trusts
generally 10.5
legislative changes 10.5
migration to new regime 10.24–10.25
age 18-to-25 trusts
chargeable amount 10.11
conditions 10.8
generally 10.7
introduction 10.5
notional transfer 10.14
problem areas 10.9
relevant fraction 10.12
settlement rate 10.13
tax charge 10.10
bereaved minors trusts
conditions 10.6
generally 10.6
introduction 10.5
problem areas 10.9
general anti-abuse rule (GAAR), and 4.25
Trusts – *contd*
interest in possession
and see **Interest in possession**
case law developments 9.3–9.5
disposal 9.11–9.12
excluded property trusts 9.32–9.35
insurance policy trusts 9.36–9.41
old law 9.1–9.2
purchased interests 9.22–9.26
reversionary interests 9.22–9.26
Statement of Practice 9.6
statutory changes 9.7–9.10
termination 9.13–9.21
transitional provisions 9.27–9.31
no interest in possession
exit charge 10.26–10.37
periodic charge 10.38–10.59
property reliefs, and 10.60–10.65
proportionate charge 10.26–10.37
special charge 10.66–10.70
ten-year charge 10.38–10.59
transfer into trust 10.17–10.25
types of relevant property trusts 10.1–10.15

U

UK-domiciled individuals
liability 1.2
Uncertain value transfer
accounts and returns, and 8.6
Unit trusts
generally 11.32
introduction 1.13
valuation of assets, and 6.17
Unincorporated business
business property relief, and 13.1–13.3
Unquoted shares and securities
business property relief, and 13.4–13.5
valuation of assets, and 6.18–6.19

V

Valuation
and see **Valuation of assets**
agricultural property relief, and
transfer 13.42–13.45
value for relief 13.46–13.49
business property relief, and
net value 13.21
introduction 13.17
shares 13.18–13.20

Valuation – *contd*
liabilities at death, and 5.13–5.18
pre-owned assets charge, and 17.17
transferable nil rate band, and 3.19
Valuation of assets
'ascertained' 6.34
bank accounts 6.21
debts 6.32
development value 6.26–6.27
discounted gifts schemes 6.15
discounts 6.28
'estate concept' 6.5
gifts with reservation 6.31
guarantees, and 6.35
HMRC's approach 6.2–6.3
'hope value' 6.27
household goods 6.33
introduction 6.1
joint property
generally 6.20
land 6.22–6.28
money accounts 6.21
land
development value 6.26–6.27
discounts 6.28
generally 6.22–6.25
liabilities, and 6.35
life policies
'back-to-back' arrangements 6.14
lifetime transfers 6.12
transfers on death 6.13
lifetime transfers, and
generally 4.19
PETS 4.20
transfers by close companies 4.21
'loss to estate' principle 6.4
open market value
'estate concept' 6.5
generally 6.1
HMRC's approach 6.2–6.3
'loss to estate' principle 6.4
personal effects 6.33
principles
'estate concept' 6.5
generally 6.1
HMRC's approach 6.2–6.3
'loss to estate' principle 6.4
quoted shares and securities 6.16
related property rule
application 6.7–6.9

Valuation of assets – *contd*
'appropriate portion' 6.8
generally 6.6
relief 6.10
settled property 6.29
specific asset rules 6.11
transfers on death, and
generally 5.19
related property 5.20
unit trusts 6.17
unquoted shares and securities 6.18–6.19
Valuation of liabilities
guarantees 6.35
Valuation Office Agency (VOA)
IHT manual 6.3
Variable value funds
accounts and returns, and 8.7
Venture capital trusts (VCT)
lifetime planning, and 14.7
Visiting forces
estate on death, and 5.5
excluded property, and 11.34

W

Waivers of remuneration
transfers of value, and 1.9
War compensation claims
generally 11.28
introduction 1.13
summary 11.5
War savings certificates
excluded property, and 1.13
Wasting assets
reliefs, and 12.11
Wedding gifts
estate on death, and 5.4
exempt property, and 1.20
generally 11.11
gifts with reservation, and 7.25
lifetime transfers, and 4.3
Will planning
aged 18-to-25 trusts 15.21
agricultural property relief 15.23–15.29
bereaved minors trusts 15.20
business property relief 15.23–15.29
charitable gifts 15.30–15.33
'debt or charge' scheme
background 15.4

Will planning – *contd*
choice of trustees 15.9
current use 15.5
existing wills, and 15.7
future reform 15.5–15.6
index-linking 15.11–15.12
interest 15.11–15.12
liquidity 15.10
procedural difficulties 15.8
use 15.5
deferral of tax
aged 18-to-25 trusts 15.21
background 15.14–15.15
bereaved minors trusts 15.20
counteraction to perceived abuse 15.16–15.18
life interest trusts 15.22
'wait and see' charge 15.19
EU Succession Regulation 650/2012, and
generally 15.1
governing law 15.2
family home, and
introduction 16.27
joint ownership 16.43–16.53
nil rate band 16.28–16.29
ownership by first spouse to die 16.30–16.41
heritage relief 15.34–15.38
life interest trusts 15.22
nil rate band discretionary trust
debt or charge scheme 15.4–15.12
generally 15.3
policy trusts 15.39

Will planning – *contd*
post-death variations
abuse, and 15.44
alternative relief 15.49–15.51
child beneficiaries 15.41
disclaimers 15.45
formalities 15.46
further variations, and 15.43
Glowacki case 15.48
introduction 15.40
post-22 March 2006 discretionary trusts 15.52–15.53
posthumous severance 15.42
statement of variation 15.47
spouse exemption
aged 18-to-25 trusts 15.21
background 15.14–15.15
bereaved minors trusts 15.20
counteraction to perceived abuse 15.16–15.18
life interest trusts 15.22
'wait and see' charge 15.19
woodlands relief 15.25–15.26

Woodlands
transferable nil rate band, and 3.11
valuing lifetime transfers, and 4.19

Woodlands relief
disposal of trees or underwood 12.25
double dipping, and 15.24
estate planning, and 15.25–15.26
generally 12.24
introduction 5.6
planning 12.26